212

LOTUS NOTES AND DOMINO 4.5

Professional Reference

JAY FORLINI

BILL MAXWELL

RANDY DAVISON

BILL DRAKE

CHUCK GRIFFIN

MARK LAWRENCE

DAVID SANDERS

WAYNE WHITAKER

New Riders Publishing, Indianapolis, Indiana

Lotus Notes and Domino 4.5 Professional Reference

By Jay Forlini, Bill Maxwell, Randy Davison, Bill Drake, Chuck Griffin, Mark Lawrence, David Sanders, Wayne Whitaker

Published by:
New Riders Publishing
201 West 103rd Street
Indianapolis, IN 46290 USA

Printed in the United States of America 1 2 3 4 5 6 7 8 9 0

CIP data available upon request

Warning and Disclaimer

This book is designed to provide information about Lotus Notes and Domino 4.5. Every effort has been made to make this book as complete and as accurate as possible, but no warranty or fitness is implied.

The information is provided on an "as is" basis. The authors and New Riders Publishing shall have neither liability nor responsibility to any person or entity with respect to any loss or damages arising from the information contained in this book or from the use of the disks or programs that may accompany it.

Publisher	*Don Fowley*
Associate Publisher	*David Dwyer*
Publishing Manager	*Julie Fairweather*
Marketing Manager	*Mary Foote*
Managing Editor	*Carla Hall*
Director of Development	*Kezia Endsley*

Acquisitions Editor
Ami Frank

Senior Editors
Sarah Kearns
Suzanne Snyder

Development Editor
Stacia Mellinger

Project Editor
John Sleeva

Copy Editors
Amy Bezek
Margo Catts
Keith Cline
Sharon Wilkey

Technical Editor
Randy Davison

Software Specialist
Steve Flatt

Assistant Marketing Manager
Gretchen Schlesinger

Acquisitions Coordinator
Amy Lewis

Administrative Coordinator
Karen Opal

Manufacturing Coordinator
Brook Farling

Cover Designer
Karen Ruggles

Cover Illustrator
Nikolai Punin/SIS

Cover Production
Aren Howell

Book Designer
Sandra Schroeder

Director of Production
Larry Klein

Production Team Supervisors
Laurie Casey
Joe Millay

Graphics Image Specialists
Kevin Cliburn

Production Analyst
Erich J. Richter

Production Team
Tricia Flodder, Janelle Herber, Linda Knose, Susan Van Ness, Daniela Raderstorf, Maureen West

Indexer
Kevin Fulcher

About the Authors

Jay Forlini has been involved with Lotus Notes in some fashion for more than three years. Starting primarily as a Level 1 instructor, he often assisted with administration and development whenever he was not in class. He has been certified as a developer and adminstrator for the past two years. In many of the classes he has taught, he assisted adminstrators and developers who learned things the hard way. He is hoping by doing this book that some of the pitfalls mentioned in class will be avoided. For the last year, he has taken on a new position with XLSource and XLConnect as the Corporate Lotus Notes Director. In this position, he has focused his attention on migrating servers in these companies to Windows NT, a new domain, hierarchical IDs, and Lotus Notes version 4.x.

William Maxwell, an award-winning Lotus Notes Instructor, has been working in the computer field for 12 years. Bill started his computer career while in college working towards a B.S. in computer science, by repairing computers at the chip level (he has the solder burns to prove it). After college, in 1986, Bill went to work as a service technician in Memphis, TN, repairing and installing personal computer systems. Within a year, Bill became a Novell certified technician, installing and maintaining Novell and other network operating systems. Over the next couple of years, Bill became one of the first Certified Novell Engineers, a Banyan Certified Engineer, a TCP/IP-certified professional (Wollongong), an Oracle-certified developer, and an IBM-certified technician focusing on Token Ring. During this same time period, Bill was working with several different computer languages including dBASE III/IV, ABASIC, IBM, COBOL, and so forth.

In 1992, Bill started working with a little known product from Lotus (a company known for a spreadsheet called 1-2-3) called Notes 2.0. Notes was a neat groupware product that included the standard e-mail with some form management in a document-based database format. Everything was relatively calm for Bill, who continued his work on networks and setting up small Notes systems. Finally, after numerous delays, Notes 3.0 was released and the Notes market explosion began. Bill upgraded his Notes 2.0 Certified Engineer status to a Notes 3.0 Certified Notes Specialist and worked for the next couple of years installing Notes 3.x systems and writing Notes applications. In 1995, Bill switched gears by becoming a Level II Certified Notes Instructor and started teaching full-time. Since then, Bill has become a member of the Lotus Instructor Honor Roll and been nominated to the Professional Who's Who. Bill is currently a Lotus Notes System Administrator and Developer (including LotusScript and Internet development using Domino). Bill is Director of the Advanced Education Group of XLConnect Incorporated (of Atlanta), an award-winning Lotus Authorized Education Center.

Chuck Griffin has been working with computers for 17 years as a designer, programmer, trainer, and, of course, user, including work as a crime analyst for the Indianapolis Police Department, an administrative assistant at the Court of Appeals of Indiana, a gun-for-hire (everyone should try self-employment at least once), and now a Certified Lotus Professional with XLConnect in Indianapolis. He also has experience working with NotesSQL, Domino, InterNotes, LotusScript, Access, Visual Basic, and macro writing in Lotus 1-2-3.

On days when he gets away from the office at a reasonable hour and does not have a book to write, Chuck pursues his interests in music composing, arranging, and performance as a member of the Indianapolis Guitar Quartet. His other interests include documentaries, James Taylor, basketball stat league, Pepe Romero, computer games, his nephew Luke and niece Rachel, Dave Brubeck, and his little brother in the Big Brothers program, Chris. Chuck received his degree in Music Theory and Composition from Butler University where he studied with composer Dr. Michael Schelle.

Randy Davison is an Enterprise Systems Consultant for XLConnect, in Atlanta, Georgia. Randy began using Notes in 1989 when he implemented version 1.0 for Management Science America (now known as Dun & Bradstreet Software). Randy spent over two years growing that implementation before joining Lotus in 1992. After spending two years with Lotus as a field marketing engineer, Randy joined XLConnect (then known as The Future Now) as one of three Notes engineers. Randy has been a key component in the development of XLConnect's Lotus Notes consulting practice as it has grown from three people in 1994 to more than forty full-time consultants and instructors today.

After spending the last three and a half years assisting clients such as The Coca Cola Company, First Union National Bank, Blue Cross Blue Shield of Alabama, and Ciba Vision with their enterprise design of Lotus Notes, Randy is now acting as the Marketing Manager for XLConnect's UltraNets.Product Suite. The Suite is a modular, integrated, Web-enabled suite of business applications built in Lotus Notes and powered by the Lotus Domino server. Randy is responsible for certifying XLConnect's twenty-five branches to sell the UltraNets.Product Suite as well as major presence in marketing activities.

Bill Drake is Vice-President of Aphelion Informatics Inc., a Lotus Premium Business Partner based in Ottawa, Ontario, Canada. Bill has worked as both a Lotus Notes trainer and consultant for sites all across North America. Over the past thirteen years, Bill has worked through a number of major technologies including dBASE, Clipper, NetWare, Groupwise, cc:Mail, Notes, SQL Server and MQSeries. Bill is certified as a Principal Lotus Notes Application Developer, Principal Lotus Notes System Administrator, Microsoft SQL Server Product Specialist, and MQSeries Systems Engineer. Bill uses these complimentary skills on major systems integration projects. Bill holds a B.S. in Physics from Carleton University. He can be reached at bdrake@aphelion.com.

With over 10 years of experience in the design, deployment, and operation of local- and wide-area networks, **Mark Lawrence** works for XLConnect in Atlanta as a Principal Consultant. He has worked previously for the federal government (Air Force and F.A.A.), G.E. Medical Systems, and as a private consultant. He has developed both single-user and multi-user applications in LAN and WAN environments, and for the past 2 and a half years has worked exclusively with Notes in both application development and system administration. In addition to Notes, he has formal training in project management, various network protocols, Total Quality Management, Unix system administration, and SQL.

David Sanders began his formal career in the computer industry in 1994 as a technical support representative for Lotus Development Corporation. Over a two year period, Mr. Sanders provided telephone support services for various Lotus products, including Ami Pro, 1-2-3 for Windows, Word Pro, and Lotus Notes Premium.

Mr. Sanders is a Lotus CLP and is currently employed as a Product Development Manager for XLConnect Solutions, Inc. of Exton, PA.

Wayne Whitaker discovered he liked to push buttons early in life. Many times a set of magic markers transformed an empty box into a spaceship or command center with panels of buttons and flashing lights, all powered by imagination. Needless to say, he was overjoyed when he was able to get his hands on a "real" computer—a Commodore Business Machine—when he was 11. Who would ever be able to fill up 64k of RAM?

Since then, Wayne continued pushing buttons through college where he got degrees in Computer Science and Math, and now spends most of his time teaching others to create and push virtual buttons as the Senior Instructor for Notes Application Development at the Atlanta office of XLConnect Solutions, Inc. He often finds himself discussing many of the same topics covered in the application development and LotusScript portions of this book in an academic setting, and eagerly awaits the future of computing with itching index fingers.

Trademark Acknowledgments

Contents at a Glance

Part VII: Domino and the Web Up Close   759

Part VIII: Appendixes   877

Table of Contents

Part V: Notes Application Architecture   387

Introduction

As the popularity of Lotus' amazing groupware product Notes grows to unanticipated heights, Lotus released another phenomenal upgrade for the product line, Notes 4.5. Notes 4.5 is much more then a simple upgrade. The Notes and Domino 4.5 release introduces dramatic new improvements with the addition of Calendaring and Scheduling, and many, many new enhancements. 4.5 is also a firming of the direction of the Notes product set. The Notes server product is now called Domino after the http add-on available with Notes 4.1. The Internet is obviously the future of all Notes products.

This book focuses on the newer features of Notes 4.5 with a special focus on the responsibilities of the Notes administrator. The Notes administrator has always had a lot of responsibilities to add and maintain users, servers, and workstations. Domino 4.5 adds new features that add to an administrator's responsibilities, and new tools to help manage a server or a group of servers. This book attempts to demystify the administrator's job with the steps to success, tips and tricks, and tons of reference material.

Who This Book Is Written For (and Who It Is Written By)

This book is specifically intended to fill the gap in the market for advanced Lotus Notes books. This book is not for Notes users or those who have never set up or managed Notes networks before. The target audience for this book is purposefully multi-fold, and includes the following:

◆ Existing Notes administrators who need to jump-start an upgrade to Notes 4.5 from Notes 4.x or 3.x

◆ Network administrators who have suddenly found themselves inheriting or installing a Notes 4.5 infrastructure

◆ Application developers who need advanced information about Notes 4.5 development technologies, such as LotusScript libraries, without the typical basic form and view design

In general, if you need an advanced reference for Domino 4.5 for administration, development topics, or both, and you are a seasoned computer professional, this book is for you.

Because the authors step outside the realm of the standard regurgitated-manual guides, some of what you will read will be the subjective opinions of a particular author. This is probably the most valuable part of this book because of the vast knowledge of both Notes and networking technologies that the authors hold. The authors' specialties include Notes administration, Notes development, and general network technology. Certifications held by the authors include Certified Lotus Professional R3 and R4, Certified Lotus Instructors, Certified Novell Engineers, and dozens of others.

How This Book Is Organized

Lotus Notes and Domino 4.5 Professional Reference is written with several goals in mind. This book is a reference; you should be able to turn to a specific section and find how-to steps to guide you through difficult or obscure Notes procedures. In addition to the idea of a standard reference book, however, this book is a kind of Notes "cookbook," leading you through the recipes for success. This book can also be read cover to cover for an overview of Notes 4.5 features and technologies. It is broken up into eight parts, and even further into 24 chapters (and three appendixes).

Part I: Overview

Part I, "Overview," eases you into Notes and Domino technology and touches briefly on the new features of version 4.5, the most recent version.

Chapter 1, "Introducing Lotus Notes and Domino 4.5," explains the phenomenon of Lotus Notes in both the computer technology world and the corporate world. This chapter answers basic questions: What is groupware? Where does Notes fit in my network? And how does Notes impact productivity?

Chapter 2, "Introducing the New Features of Notes and Domino 4.5," summarizes the new features incorporated in Lotus Notes 4.5, including the Domino server, Calendaring and Scheduling, end-user enhancements, and so on. After reading this chapter, you should have a feel for the rich groupware environment that will change the way your company works.

Part II: Calendaring and Scheduling

Calendaring and Scheduling is one of the biggest (if not the biggest) advanced addition to version 4.5. Part II, "Calendaring and Scheduling," focuses on this new and exciting technology.

Chapter 3, "Introducing Calendaring and Scheduling," introduces the technology and usage of the new Calendaring and Scheduling features of Notes 4.5. This chapter examines setup and security considerations, and the look and feel of the Calendaring and Scheduling process.

Chapter 4, "Incorporating Calendaring and Scheduling into Your Applications," takes an in-depth look at database issues surrounding using Calendaring and Scheduling, specifically view design and limitations.

Part III: Notes 4.5 Basic Administration

Part III gets your feet wet with some administration information.

Chapter 5, "Selecting an Operating System," is a primer of network operating systems and offers a comparison of the NOSs from a Notes perspective.

Chapter 6, "Installing Domino 4.5 Server Software," reviews server installation issues, including terminology, naming conventions, and server security.

Chapter 7, "Installing Lotus Notes 4.5 Client Software," covers specific workstation installation topics for Notes 4.5.

Chapter 8, "Examining Notes 4.5 Administration Features," covers administration tools, including the Admin Panel, user maintenance, gateways, and much more.

Chapter 9, "Statistic Tracking and Event Notification for Domino 4.5 Servers," covers various Notes monitoring tools, including the Statistics Reporter, Event Notifier, and Notes View.

Part IV: Advanced Administration

Chapter 10, "Migrating to Lotus Notes and Domino 4.5," covers migration strategies and techniques for moving to Notes 4.5, including administrator and developer issues.

Chapter 11, "Securing Your Notes and Domino 4.5 System," covers security issues including server access security, database security, Domino specific issues, and firewall security.

Chapter 12, "Troubleshooting Notes and Domino 4.5," is sort of a question-and-answer session covering the most common Notes problems and their solutions for Lotus Notes 4.5.

Part V: Notes Application Architecture

Part V gets into more development-type information for Notes experts.

Chapter 13, "Constructing Notes Databases," covers Notes database construction issues, including each of the elements surrounding database construction. It also walks you through the actual construction of a database.

Chapter 14, "Advanced Application Design Issues," covers Notes design issues such as Physical Architecture (monolithic versus distributed) and Logical Architecture (replication, routing considerations, and security).

Chapter 15, "Domino-Specific Application Development Considerations," covers Domino application issues including, Notes-centric applications, Web-centric applications, and hybrid applications.

Chapter 16, "Building a Sample Web-Centric Application," focuses on a sample Web application using Lotus Notes 4.5 with recommended techniques and Web-centric enhancements.

Part VI: Notes Advanced Development

Part VI takes the discussion of development to an even more advanced level.

Chapter 17, "Notes Advanced Development," provides a specific and in-depth discussion about data integration and data security.

Chapter 18, "LotusScript Fundamentals," focuses on LotusScript in Notes 4.5, from a basic introduction to the new Notes Object Model.

Chapter 19, "Advanced LotusScript," has a two-fold purpose: first, the LotusScript weapons issued to you in the last chapter will be further sharpened; and second, these newly honed weapons are turned specifically toward Lotus Notes.

Chapter 20, "Java: A New Way to Interact with Notes," looks at the growing popularity of Java and its availability in Notes 4.5, and the future Java programming interface for Notes.

Part VII: Domino and the Web Up Close

Part VII focuses on Domino and how Notes can be used in conjunction with the Internet.

Chapter 21, "Installing and Setting Up Domino," fully prepares you for use of Domino with the Web.

Chapter 22, "Using Domino to Publish on the Web," addresses techniques for making Notes databases generally known to the public via Domino.

Chapter 23, "Building Web Applications with Domino.Action," takes a close look at the Domino. (pronounced "domino dot") family of applications, most specifically Domino.Action.

Chapter 24, "Security and Reporting," explores security options for Domino and reporting features.

Part VIII: Appendixes

Appendix A, "Comparing Domino to Other Intranet Technologies," is a comparison of Domino technology to other leading intranet suppliers, including Netscape and Microsoft.

Appendix B, "Domino HTTP Web Server Console Options," touches on the available options related to the HTTP Web server process.

Appendix C, "SMTP MTA Gateway," includes valuable information on how to install, configure, and maintain the gateway.

Special Text Used in This Book

Throughout this book, you will find examples of special text. These passages have been given special treatment so that you can instantly recognize their significance and easily find them for future reference.

Authors Notes, Tips, Warnings, and Sidebars

Lotus Notes and Domino 4.5 Professional Reference features many special "asides" set apart from the normal text. Three distinct types of "asides" are set apart by icons: Author Notes, Tips, Warnings, and Sidebars.

Author Note An Author Note includes "extra" information that you should find useful, but which complements the discussion at hand instead of being a direct part of it. An Author Note is the author's direct line to you the reader. Author Notes may describe special situations that can arise when you use Notes/Domino under certain circumstances, and tells you what steps to take when such situations arise.

Tip A Tip provides quick instructions for getting the most from your Notes/Domino system as you follow the steps outlined in the general discussion. A Tip might show how to conserve memory in some setups, how to speed up a procedure, or how to perform one of many time-saving and system-enhancing techniques.

Warning A Warning tells you when a procedure may be dangerous—that is, when you run the risk of losing data, locking your system, or even damaging your hardware. Warnings generally tell you how to avoid such losses, or describe steps that you can take to remedy them.

Sidebars Offer Additional Information

A Sidebar, conceptually, is much like an Author Note—the exception being its length. A Sidebar is by nature much longer than an Author Note, but offers the same extra, complementary information. Sidebars offer in-depth insight into the topic under discussion.

New Riders Publishing

The staff of New Riders Publishing is committed to bringing you the very best in computer reference material. Each New Riders book is the result of months of work by authors and staff who research and refine the information contained within its covers.

As part of this commitment to you, New Riders invites your input. Please let us know if you enjoy this book, if you have trouble with the information and examples presented, or if you have a suggestion for the next edition.

Please note, though: New Riders staff cannot serve as a technical resource for Domino- or Lotus Notes-related questions. Please refer to the documentation that accompanies the Lotus software or Lotus support for Notes questions.

If you have any questions or comments about any New Riders book, there are several ways to contact New Riders Publishing. We will respond to as many readers as we can. Your name, address, or phone number will never become part of a mailing list or be used for any purpose other than to help us continue to bring you the best books possible. You can write us at the following address:

New Riders Publishing
Attn: Publisher's Assistant
201 W. 103rd Street
Indianapolis, IN 46290

You can send electronic mail to New Riders at the following Internet address:

jfairweather@newriders.mcp.com

Thank you for selecting *Lotus Notes and Domino 4.5 Professional Reference*!

PART I

Overview

CHAPTER 1

Introducing Lotus Notes and Domino 4.5

Lotus Notes is the premier groupware product on the computer market today. The Notes set of products includes both client software (Lotus Notes) and a network-based server platform (Domino server). This book covers concepts and features that are part of the 4.5 release of Lotus Notes. The features include built-in Internet access, and Calendaring and Scheduling. This chapter starts with a history of Notes to give the reader a feel for the concept of Notes, includes an overview of the concepts of Notes, including a brief definition of groupware, and finishes with a Return on Investment review.

A Brief Look Back

Before jumping headlong into Lotus Notes and Domino 4.5, this section takes a brief look back at the history of the development of Notes.

The Incarnation of Notes

In the early 1970s, a college student stared in wonder at a computer system called PLATO at the University of Illinois. PLATO, Programmed Logic for Automated Teaching Operations, allowed multiple users to interact in elementary games, electronic chatting and mail, and simplistic bulletin boards. The users of that system primarily were not programmers, they were students learning chemistry, physics, or business. That college student was Ray Ozzie, leader of Iris, the development team that created Notes.

In 1981, Ozzie was exposed to another computer environment that appealed to non-computer professionals involving these miniture computers that actually sat on users' desk for personal productivity. This was the beginning of the personal computer explosion. Personal computers were great, but they had one problem—all of the users had to share data using diskettes; there was no readily-available networking technology. Simple electronic messaging, which had been available in the main-frame/minicomputer market for years, was not available.

Ozzie and some of his computer associates decided it was time to come up with a way to integrate the glassy-eyed interaction of the PLATO users with the personal computer. They needed money, time, and someone with the same vision to invest in Ozzie's idea. They found all of this in Mitch Kapor of Lotus.

Kapor was truly a pioneer in the personal computer arena. (Kapor is still involved in a pioneering way with his work with EFF.) Lotus was responsible for the application that fueled the fires of the personal computer revolution, Lotus 1-2-3 (in fact, the name Lotus was synonymous with 1-2-3 for years). Ozzie and his crew, however, were working towards another evolution in the computer industry. Ozzie's basic idea was to develop a group-interaction system dealing with information, not simply data. In his words:

> "Data is just facts. You fill out a form, you press a key, the data is stored. Later, if you fill out a query, you get your answer or report. Plain and simple.
>
> Information, on the other hand, is recorded knowledge. It's a subjective opinion. It's a judgment call. It's a hot tip. It contains sarcasm or subtle innuendo. It's the stuff that makes up interpersonal communications! When dealing with

knowledge, the techniques for finding answers to questions are dealing with knowledge, the techniques for finding answers are better understood by librarians than by computer scientists. It requires a rich body of recorded information, good indexing techniques, a lot of reading, and the intuition gained by experience and exposure to information.

We began the project because we believed that the tools needed to manipulate data (forms packages, query tools, report writers) were not the same as the tools needed to deal with information. We wanted to create a compelling interpersonal communication system—a computer-assisted collaboration system that would enable companies to build customized information-sharing applications.

Circa 1989, history was made by the introduction of Lotus Notes into the marketplace. After years of idea and product development, finally a product existed that could be used for document management, collaborative learning, and electronic mail. Lotus Notes—access to information, not just data.

Lotus Notes Releases 2.x and 3.x—Finding a Market

In retrospect, Lotus Notes 2.0 was a relatively simplistic tool for group interaction and data sharing. It didn't have all the bells and whistles currently associated with Notes; 2.0 was simply a document-based system that replaced paper-based systems. At the time, though, an almost magical air surrounded this strange new product called Notes.

After a couple of years of Notes 2.x—and a year of hype and slipped release dates— Notes 3.0 was introduced. Notes 3.0 contained the basic document design of Notes 2.0 while representing a dramatic increase in functionality over Notes 2.x. All of the components that make up Notes were upgraded, including user interface improvements, a new set of programmer tools, and new Notes server environments and protocols.

Lotus Notes 4 Increases Programmability

Notes 4.0 introduced a new era of programmability to the Notes environment. In its own way, Notes 4.0 was an even more dramatic improvement than Notes 3.0. The marketplace was very different when Notes 4 was released due to the large base of more-sophisticated Notes users. Notes 3.x was pushed to the bleeding edge of functionality and beyond to make it work in almost any conceivable business situation. Notes 4's introduction enabled Notes to fill those business needs without painful programming involving multiple macros. The "look and feel" of Notes also went though a major face-lift, as shown in figure 1.1.

Figure 1.1

A sample Lotus Notes Revision 4.1 workspace.

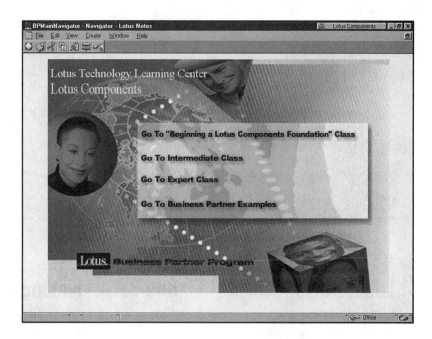

Many of the new Notes enhancements centered around making Notes easier to use. One of these features was a three-pane user interface, which includes a View pane, a new Views and Folders pane, and a Preview pane. A common request of Notes 3.x users was a menuing mechanism. This enhancement was introduced in Notes 4.0 as a graphical tool called *Navigators*. Navigators can contain graphic images or buttons that activate agents, create documents, change views, or any other activity needed by the end-user. Figure 1.2 shows a sample navigator. Other enhancements included a modified menu based on refined user interface methodologies, layout regions for the creation of dialog boxes, and new programming functions such as @Dialogbox (to display layout regions).

Another common complaint often heard about Notes 3.x is the lack of common mail features in Notes 3 e-mail. Notes 4 includes a dramatically evolved e-mail system, including common features such as an "Out of Office" notice.

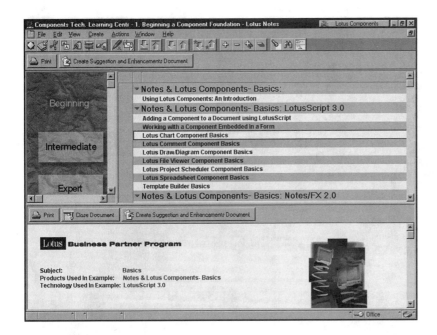

Figure 1.2

A sample Lotus Notes navigator as a common menuing interface.

Enter Lotus Notes 4.5 (and Domino)

Notes 4.5 introduces amazing new technology in the form of the Domino server (the newly named combination of Lotus Notes server and the Domino HTTP server), long-sought features such as Calendaring and Scheduling, and many enhancements in the areas of system administration and application development.

Notes 4.5 is the result of a planned paradigm shift that Lotus and Iris have been working on for years. The plan is to shift away from network-scope groupware products and toward new generation products that integrate groupware concepts and the power of the document model into the Internet technology arena. We now have the best of the maturing groupware and team-approach application servers managing the volatile and still immature information-sharing possibilities of the Internet.

For the developer, Notes 4.5 is a dream realized. With Notes 4.5, true object-oriented procedural programming was finally available as LotusScript (see fig. 1.3). LotusScript is an ANSI BASIC-compatible scripting language that includes the Notes object set. LotusScript is also available with other Lotus products such as WordPro, making it a cross-application scripting language. Lotus Notes also supports ODBC (Microsoft's Open Database Connectivity standard) and OLE 2.0 to access and use data from other applications.

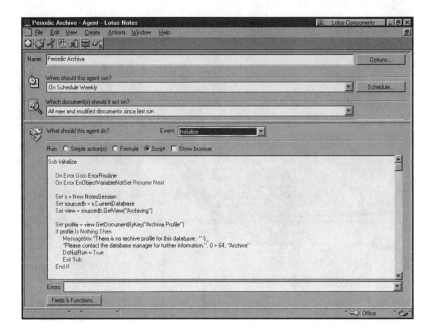

Figure 1.3

*LotusScript in
Lotus Notes 4.5.*

Notes 4.5 is a very powerful product, and one of the reasons is the strong under-girding groupware concepts. The following section introduces a brief theoretical review of those concepts.

Understanding Groupware

To understand the need for Lotus Notes and the amazing market response to Notes in the last couple of years, you first have to understand the business needs that are filled by Notes. The catch phrase that comes to mind when considering Lotus Notes is *groupware.*

Groupware is an elusive term. Not only are there different definitions in almost every article, but the concept is colored by our own experience with one or most aspects of group-interaction. A common definition of groupware is a product that allows a defined group of users to interact through data exchange, such as e-mail, and data sharing, such as informational databases, while providing a framework of flow control and security.

E-Mail

When most people think of groupware, e-mail comes to mind. In this environment, users are able to interact with other users by sending and receiving electronic documents. This type of transaction represents the simplest form of electronic communication. When the number or participants, locations, or both is increased, however, this environment becomes much more complex for the end-users and system administrators. To add to this complexity, many e-mail systems have pseudo-integrated group scheduling and other aspects of group interaction in an attempt to simulate "true" groupware.

Notes includes a complete, well-organized, and relatively easily managed e-mail system. As one of the few true graphical e-mail packages available today, Notes offers users a way to send and receive mail while viewing graphics "live" in the e-mail. The introduction of Notes 4.5 also improved the overall user interface as well as adding functionality available in other mail packages. Notes Mail uses the existing Notes servers as mail servers and gateway platforms to send mail to users on distant Notes servers or other mail systems such as on the Internet.

Form Routing

Form routing is a way to send information in a serial fashion from one user to another, usually based on pre-established routing rules and the underlying e-mail infrastructure. This type of environment supports more complex business processes such as purchase requests or expense reports.

Workflow

The inclusion of e-mail in Notes enables a developer to easily add workflow to applications. Workflow is not an add-on or another language to learn, it is an available part of any Notes application. The importance of workflow in Notes should not be underestimated. Workflow is the process that changes Notes from a simple document management tool to a full-blown process re-engineering system. For example, Notes can fully replace an existing paper-based system such as expense reporting. The workflow for expense reporting may involve multiple forms, routing rules based on dollar amounts, departments, and so forth, and potentially very complex security issues related to who can place an order or approve orders. With Notes, this type of workflow can be "coded" into a dynamic system that is based on the powerful Notes database structures and the existing e-mail system.

Data Sharing

Another common component of groupware is data sharing. This is an important part of groupware and is certainly one of those aspects missing from the e-mail concept, as described above. Data sharing includes a central repository of information that can be accessed by any users that have the necessary rights via that system's security. Data sharing is an important way to stimulate group discussions and to support collaborative learning. An example is a problem reporting and resolving Notes database. As problems occur in a given company, the information can be recorded about both the problem specifics and the resolution. This type of information is generally open for all users to keep users from "re-inventing the wheel" for recurring problems.

How Notes Fits In

Notes is about data sharing. Users work in Notes by adding information in the form of documents to the various databases in which they participate as part of a group. These documents are available immediately to other members of these virtual groups. This data-sharing technology is necessary to stimulate increased speed of responsiveness and a general understanding of both the processes involved and the corporate infrastructure. Documents can be freeform information, such as general discussions, or very specific information based on the database structure. Documents can also be containers for other application data, such as word processing documents, spreadsheets, presentations, and so forth.

True groupware products incorporate all of the preceding facets. Notes is a powerful, mature data sharing tool with document working and workflow capabilities built on the Notes electronic mail engine.

Lotus Notes is a product that incorporates a companies existing network or internet structure (or both). The following section investigates how Notes fits in.

Notes and the Network

Networks were introduced in the mid-80s to enable personal computers to use shared resources. Although additional resources have been added to benefit the end-user, the primary resources are still file and print sharing. The prevalent network operating system since the mid-80s has been Novell NetWare. In the last couple of years, however, Microsoft has taken over a sizable portion of the network market with Windows NT. Both network operating systems allow for native file and print services. Other network operating systems with followings include Banyan Vines, and OS/2 Warp.

The interaction and impact of Domino servers and Notes clients on an any company's network is an important concern for all network administrators implementing or considering Notes products. Notes was written with the network "in-mind" by the fine people of Iris. This means that they fully integrated concepts such as sending only the data needed into the client/server Notes infrastructure. For example, when the user opens a view over the network, only a portion of the view is sent (a couple of screens worth). When the user opens a document, that document is sent fully to the client system, however, as the user modifies the document, that work is done off-line on the user's workstation. Only when the document is saved is the network used again to transfer the data back to the database server.

Lotus Domino Server (called Lotus Notes Server before version 4.5) is a network-based application server. An *application server* is a server that shares application data only, as opposed to *a file server*, which shares files and printers. Usually, Notes is integrated into the network at the network/protocol level. In other words, Notes is available to the network users over the common protocol. In the NetWare environment, for example, the workstation and the Notes servers would run the protocol SPX. The user does not have to be logged in to access the Notes server (which is also not logged into NetWare), the user gains access over the protocol. This type of arrangement is true for most networking environments. The Notes server in this case is not necessarily a Novell/Notes server. The Notes server operating system could be OS/2, Windows NT, or any of the supported Unix flavors. The protocols include SPX, NetBIOS, NetBEUI, and TCP/IP. Notes also supports various dial-up or wide area network options, including X.25, SNA, and TCP/IP dial-up (PPP).

To help understand how Notes works with the wide array of supported protocols, it helps to look at a model of network interaction. The most commonly used model is OSI (Open Systems Interconnection), which has seven layers.

For this wide array of protocols that reside on different levels, Lotus needed to "fill the gap" between the Application layer (Notes) and the protocols.

One major security concern with Notes is the built-in dial capabilities of Notes servers. The protocol used by Notes for dial-in is called *XPC*. When a Notes client connects to a Notes server using XPC, the connection is strictly Notes-to-Notes. The client can only access databases on the Notes server; the client does not have any access to the file structure on that system or any other system resource. The only exception with an XPC dial-in is when accessing servers through a passthru server. With a passthru server set up at the client and the server, clients can access any other servers on the wide area network they are dialing into. Passthru servers are also accessed only at the Notes level and must be setup completely by the administrator. There is no default passthru setup.

Notes and Intranets

An intranet is a very simple concept. Basically, an *intranet* is the use of Internet technologies on a company's local area or wide area network. The technologies used include components such as TCP/IP, HTTP servers, HTML pages, Web browsers, and applications to share internal data. As the concept of intranets grew, the idea of groupware as a major part of intranets became self-evident.

It is uncertain at this point how many companies have implemented intranets, however it seems clear that most or all large organizations will have one in the next few years. One estimate from the International Data Corporation (IDC) is that there were 100,000 intranet Web servers in 1995, and by the year 2000, there will be an estimated 4.7 million!

Companies implement intranets for many reasons. Although intranets can be limited in scope or very broad in business process application, they will play an important role in the future of all applications. Some common uses for an intranet include:

◆ E-mail

◆ Online references

◆ Online training

◆ Collabrative learning

◆ Memos and bulletin boards (threaded discussions)

◆ Sales and process reporting

◆ Workflow

◆ Online graphics or other files

Two things are obvious about the preceding list. First, groupware has matured to the point that it can be used for most (or all) of the requirements of an in-house intranet. Second, Lotus not only anticipated growth in the Internet/intranet market several years ago, but carefully crafted an internet-intelligent groupware product far advanced beyond anything else currently available.

Notes and the Internet

The growth of the Internet has been phenomenal over the past several years. More and more business is done online through the Internet. The introduction of security measures—such as SSL (Secure Socket Layer) with data encryption—has enabled this growth to continue, ensuring that the Internet will be a central element of future computing. Any product that wants to survive in that future business market will have to be constructed to fit cleanly into Internet and intranet technologies.

Domino is the result of years of effort on the part of Iris and the Lotus development and implementation team. Domino is the synthesis of several Notes components, including a Web server (http) to share Notes databases with non-Notes users and all users of the Internet, a publisher such as the replaced Web Publisher to convert Notes databases into HTML format, and a Notes-based browser (which is part of the Notes 4.5 client). Some important improvements in Notes 4.5 include the elimination of the need for a third-party Web server, direct database to HTML conversion (on-the-fly as opposed to creating HTML files as in the Web Publisher), and a robust Web Navigator product that supports industry standards including JAVA applets. The renaming of the Notes server product to Domino (the beta was simply the http component of the server) indicates the importance Lotus places on the integration of groupware and the Internet. Companies that currently have Notes *will* need to quickly be a presence on the Web. Companies that are exploring the Web *will* need groupware to compete in their market. Notes is the intersection of the technologies needed to move into the next century.

Introducing the Notes Database Structure

The database structure of Notes is fairly unique. Although the last couple generations of Notes have had many changes, the basic database structure remained the same. In Notes, there is the common of a Notes application. An application fills some business need. To put together an application, Notes developers use Notes databases. An application can be a single database or multiple databases that interact. Databases are constructed by documents. Documents are free-form storage for data.

Documents can be special purpose or data documents. Special purpose documents include the Access Control List document and the design documents. The design documents are the pieces of the Notes puzzle that the developer puts into place.

The two primary design documents are form(s) and view(s). Forms contain fields, which are individual storage areas for data. Fields can contain a single value or an array of values of the same type. The designer adds field structure information to the form, such as the data type of the field. The form is then used to compose a data document (simply called a document). This document contains the actual data entered by the user. Documents (also called Notes) are built using the form used, fields are added if data is entered. Fields that haven't been entered don't exist in the document.

Notes also uses a series of internal fields to control and track documents within a database. To display a list of available documents, Notes includes views. Views are structured indexes that display documents, generally one per row. The columns displayed are chosen by the database designer. The documents displayed, the sorting pattern, and the general look and feel of the view are also set up and controlled by the database designer.

There can be multiple forms to enter and display the data, and multiple views to see the data indexed. Other available design elements include agents (a way to automate redundant or difficult tasks), subforms and shared fields (to ease the designer's headaches with maintenance on multiple forms), navigators, LotusScript libraries, and more (the database icon, help documents, and so on). All the designer elements and their interaction are covered in-depth in the development section of this book.

Lotus Notes and the Amazing Return on Investment

In an attempt to quantify the value of Notes in an organization, the IDC was commissioned to do a report on Lotus Notes and its return on investment (ROI). Sixty-five companies were included in this study with between 2 to 20,000 employees and the companies based in over a dozen different countries. The average ROI was 176 percent over a three-year span. The average investment in Notes software and hardware was $240,000.

The study uncovered the way Notes impacts a company at various levels, including not only the amount and ease of work but also the type of work. Notes causes a fundamental paradigm shift in the workers' and management's view of *what* work is and *how* it should get done. The following sections offer examples of the specific impact of Notes in the 65 companies.

Justifying the Technology Infrastructure

It is difficult for many companies to justify the expense of a computer network. Notes makes this justification much easier because Notes is usually implemented to fill a specific, measurable business-process need. Therefore, Notes can actually justify the network infrastructure at many companies, or upgrades for the network or workstations/systems.

Enhancing the Corporate Culture

Notes has an important side effect in many companies where it is implemented. Notes becomes the great equalizer of employee interaction. Not only do the more withdrawn or quiet employees get to equally voice their opinions or add their knowledge to the corporate mix, the amount of work being done often exposes both those who have silently done most of the work, and those who are lacking (by simply looking at who contributes to the databases). For example, in an order entry system, it is very easy to see who is preparing the majority of the orders.

Disintegrating Departmental Barriers

Interdepartmental work and team building has always been a challenge in any corporation or business. Different departments sometimes develop a walled-in attitude, which can increase misunderstandings and miscommunications. This type of environment can result in departments working towards their own internal goals, often to the disadvantage of corporate goals. Notes tends to break down these walls by pulling employees together in database-created teams that are often interdepartmental. A good example of this is a Quality Assurance application, which often includes members from several or possibly all departments within a company.

Developing a Corporate Memory

One of the immediate results of using Notes applications is the creation of corporate knowledge pools and a documented history. Business transactions can now be tracked online, providing an extended history without the need for paper in filing cabinets. Also, the knowledge base that is built can be used to find immediate solutions for recurring problems and to avoid mistakes of the past. This concept is becoming more and more recognized as an important component of a company's capability to compete. The current catch-phrase for this shared knowledge is "collaborative learning."

Creating Organizational Flexibility

Flexibility is fast becoming the key to keeping a customer base in the current market. If companies don't respond in a timely manner to customer requests, regardless of the difficulty involved or the new concepts needed, their business will be taken elsewhere. Notes helps a company build in three ways:

◆ Allowing teams to be free-form, based on the application or database

◆ Allowing employees to work in the office, at the customer's site, or out of their home

◆ Allowing users to work off-line through replication

Summary

The IDC study found that a thought-out, management-supported implementation of Notes should have an immediate impact on personal and group productivity. Notes' rapid-application-development environment enables speedy development and implementation of business-process improvements and automations. Steve McConnell says:

> Software developers are caught on the horns of a dilemma... One horn of the dilemma is that people don't have time to learn more about the rapid development; the other horn is that they won't get the time until they do learn more about rapid development.

Notes is a quick-start product with developers working quickly towards completed applications, learning as they go. You can read the entire IDC study at the Lotus Web site at http://www.lotus.com/ntsdoc96/roi.htm.

CHAPTER 2

Introducing the New Features of Notes 4.5 and Domino

Notes 4.5 is an important step in the evolution of the Notes product. In general terms, the upgrade offers the following:

◆ A new version of Notes with needed features

◆ A change in direction (or a straightening of an existing path)

◆ A standard bug-fix and minor improvement release

When 4.0 shipped, it had obvious bugs that resulted in a standard series of patch and minor-update releases, the most current of which is Notes 4.12. (It is interesting to note that Notes 4.12 shipped after Notes 4.5.) Notes 4.5 is not a cheap upgrade for customers, and Lotus recognizes that many Notes customers will slowly implement Domino and Notes 4.5. At the same time, many companies will recognize that the new features of Domino and 4.5 are needed immediately and will migrate to 4.5 as quickly as possible.

While Notes 4.5 introduces several new features, the one new feature users have begged for since the inception of Notes is Calendaring and Scheduling. Several years ago, Lotus bought a product called Organizer to fill this gap in their application suite of programs, but Organizer never had more than e-mail–related links to the Lotus flagship, Notes. The new Calendaring and Scheduling basically has two executable server tasks that run management for the process on every server. Once the system is up and running, Calendaring and Scheduling is available to all Notes e-mail users who convert their mail file to the Notes 4.5 mail template. Also, the features of Calendaring and Scheduling are available for developers to add to any Notes application.

The old idea of a Notes server is dead. The new Domino server is here with a new attitude. Calling the new Notes server Domino, Lotus has set the company's course fully into integrating the Notes groupware concept and strong back-end database engine with Internet technology. Now companies can make their Notes databases available to anyone with a browser on the Internet or on their intranet. The user with a browser can go through views, read documents, compose documents, kick-off background processes on the server, and even run included Lotus Notes Components objects (currently based on ActiveX with Web availability). The Domino server is a true HTTP server that can share Notes databases on the Internet by performing real-time translation of Notes document/view/design formats into HTML documents. The Domino server also handles interaction with Web clients, allowing for some very important features, including Notes mail. Domino also supports SSL encryption security and User Name/Password security maintained by a Notes administrator. Also, as part of the Internet-focused direction of Lotus, the new Notes Web browser is available to any user currently running Notes 4.5. This browser is similar to all the other popular browsers on the market, such as Microsoft's Internet Explorer, and includes features such as Java support.

Finally, Notes 4.5 incorporates the bug fixes built into the release of Notes 4.1x, as well as many additional minor (but very nice) enhancements. These enhancements include changes to the Server Administration screen, a live remote-server console (finally!), color-coded LotusScript, Windows NT integration for passwords and event monitoring, and many others (as reviewed in the rest of this chapter).

Although the Domino upgrade affects the life of all Notes users, including developers, the majority of the new features enhance the administrator's capabilities in Notes. This chapter is an introduction to the these new features in Domino/Notes 4.5. It is not intended to be a thorough treatment of the features, merely a summary. The rest of the book covers these topics in explicit detail, with a focus on Notes administration.

Calendaring and Scheduling

When users upgraded their mail files from Notes 3.x to Notes 4.0 format, they were in for a shock. The Notes 4.0 e-mail files included cleaner ways for users to manage their inboxes (a new concept introduced with Notes 4 for Notes mail), To-Do and Task items, and standard e-mail tools including an Out of Office agent. Notes 4.5 expands this structure with the inclusion of Calendaring and Scheduling tools, which developers can add as needed to any application. For example, an application such as customer tracking may include scheduling capabilities tied to customer meetings. Calendaring and Scheduling include documents and views in the new Mail template to allow the users to manage their schedule or to set up group meetings. The following sections touch on some of the features and capabilities of Lotus' new Calendaring and Scheduling.

Calendar Views

The Calendar views include daily, weekly and monthly Calendar views (see fig. 2.1). These views should seem very familiar to Lotus Organizer users because the structures are based on Organizer views. Entries in these views can be "dragged and dropped" onto other days or times to easily move appointments or events. If the option is enabled, overlapping appointments display a conflict flag in the view.

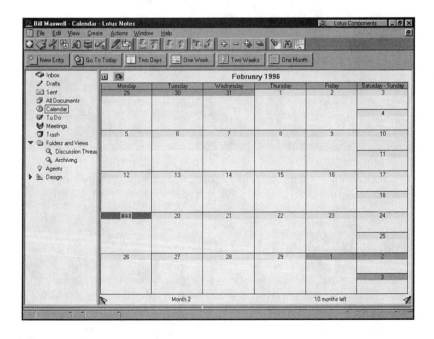

Figure 2.1

A sample Lotus Notes Calendaring and Scheduling Calendar view.

Meeting View

By clicking on the New Entry action in the Meeting view (or any of the Calendar views), any user can create an appointment, event, reminder, or anniversary, or schedule a meeting. The actual Calendar Entry document includes a description of the event, the time and date, a list of available scheduled resources (such as meeting rooms), and the list of invited attendees (see fig. 2.2). Action bar actions enable users to check their current calendars, set alarm requests, or set the entry as a repeating calendar event (using rules based on daily, weekly, or scheduled events). A button on the Calendar Entry document gives the user the ability to search for free time for invited meeting attendees.

Figure 2.2

A sample Calendar Entry document.

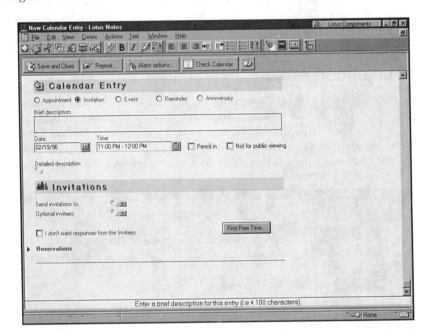

When a meeting is scheduled, each attendee is notified with the date, time, and place. The person being notified can choose to accept, delegate, or reject the appointment.

Checking Other People's Schedules

Some employees need to manage or access other users' schedules. A user can view any other user's calendar *if* he has permission to access that calendar. The default calendar setting enables users to see only their own schedules. The capability to view other schedules can be enabled using a delegation profile. This profile is added by the user who needs or desires to share his own calendar with others. The profile specifies whether an outside user can view the entire mail file or just the scheduled information. See a sample Delegation document in figure 2.3. Also, the Delegation document can be used to grant other users the ability to add appointments directly to another user's mail file. Many vice presidents and managers, for example, have Administrative Assistants (AA) who manage their schedules. A Delegation document can easily be added to enable an AA to both read and manage a manager's schedule and entire e-mail file (read, reply to, and delete e-mail messages).

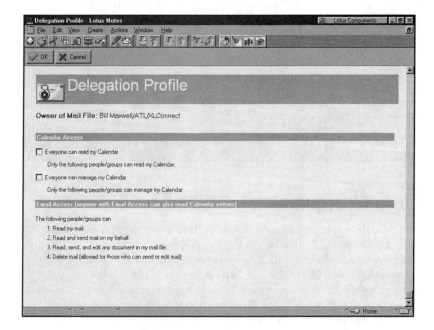

Figure 2.3

A sample Delegation profile.

Calendar Profile

Calendar preferences can be set up for each individual user using a Calendar profile (see fig. 2.4). This profile includes information such as when the user's work week starts and allowable free times.

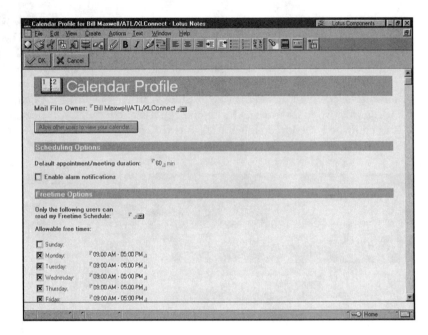

Figure 2.4

A sample Calendar profile.

Lotus Notes and Organizer

Calendaring and Scheduling supports an API system that allows other Calendaring and Scheduling systems to read and write data to the Notes Calendaring and Scheduling. Initially, the Notes Calendaring and Scheduling system ships with ties to both Organizer and the widely used IBM OfficeVision. Organizer is the Lotus Personal Information Management (PIM) system that has been used by many organizations for several years. For those sites that are using Organizer currently, it is an important addition to Notes 4.5 that the Lotus Calendaring and Scheduling tools tie to the Organizer scheduling databases. Additional product ties via the API will ship with future releases.

Notes Development Using the Calendaring and Scheduling System

Calendaring and Scheduling is an important and necessary addition to Notes because it allows users to use Notes as a tool for personal and group scheduling. Calendaring and Scheduling also is a tool developers can use for time-tracking and billing, as well as for other calendar, scheduling, or reservation-centric applications. The Calendaring and Scheduling features available to Notes developers include:

◆ **Calendar and Time controls.** Calendar and Time controls can be added to a TimeDate field in a Layout region.

◆ **Calendar views.** If you specify the Calendar style setting in the View Properties dialog box (see fig. 2.5), any view that has a TimeDate field in the first column will become a Calendar view.

Figure 2.5

The View Properties dialog box for a view with the Calendar style defined.

◆ **NotesName.** NotesName is a new LotusScript class used to simplify mail addressing in workflow applications.

◆ **NotesSession.** FREETIMESEARCH is a new LotusScript method that enables access to the free time system via LotusScript.

New Administration Functions, Tools, and Features in Domino and Notes 4.5

Many new features and improvements have been added to help administrators manage Notes users, servers, and security issues. One of the most important new features is the inclusion of the Domino HTTP server. The following section discusses this new Domino technology. Subsequent sections touch on additional new features and improvements, such as directory assistance, database management tools, automated administration, and many others.

Domino Server Technology

Thousands of companies have implemented Notes for literally hundreds of thousands of Notes clients. It makes sense, therefore, that an Internet/intranet server that takes full advantage of the existing Notes infrastructure and current Internet technology would be an instant leader in the Internet server field.

The Basic HTTP Server

The Domino server is a true HTTP server; it makes Notes information available to any client with a browser. The basic functionality of the Domino server includes:

◆ Security features (including Basic Web Authentication) that require a login name and password, and SSL, a mechanism supported by all major browsers for data encryption and authentication.

◆ The capability for clients to create, edit, and delete documents.

◆ Access to full-text indexes stored on the Domino server.

◆ Access to views, including standard Notes features such as expanding and collapsing documents.

◆ The ability to execute CGI scripts.

◆ The sharing of data from the standard Notes data storage (database structure), standard HTML files, or both.

What's New in the Domino Web Server in 4.5?

Domino was initially introduced as an add-on service for Notes 4.1. In Domino 4.5, the Web server has been both included in the standard server product and upgraded with many enhancements. These enhancements include:

◆ The capability to control the layout of views and the interaction of the standard view navigators and actual document views

◆ Increased flexibility in the rich text field area, including the capability to attach files to Notes documents from browser clients

◆ Calendaring and Scheduling capabilities for browser clients

◆ The capability to serve ActiveX components to Web browser clients

◆ Improved formatting of forms and documents

◆ Enhanced data-lookup capabilities, including the use of the @DB functions for keyword field generation

◆ Increased support for client SSL encryption

◆ Additional server platform support, including Sun Solaris, AIX, HP/UX and OS/2

Other Domino Tools and Enhancements

Lotus support for the Domino product includes enhancing and simplifying the basic Web server and continuing the development of additional tools and sample applications.

Domino.Action

Domino.Action is the first in a suite of Internet applications being introduced by Lotus. Domino.Action is a tool to simplify the creation and maintenance of Web sites for Internet or intranet applications.

Domino.Action offers a template of standard forms, views, and databases as a starting point for any Web site. The templates can be fully customized to enable developers at each company to implement Domino.Action and mold it to their own needs. Web sites created with Domino.Action, therefore, can be as simplistic as several intercon-nected Web pages or as complex as a series of inter-related databases with full Basic Web, and Access List security. For more information about Domino.Action, see Chapter 23, "Builiding Web Applications with Domino.Action."

Simplified Proxy Setup and Administration

Several new features are now available in the 4.5 version of Domino to simplify setting up and maintaining proxy servers. These new features include:

◆ Full HTTP proxy support for Domino servers and Web navigator clients.

◆ SOCKS version 4 support has been added to those Domino server and Web navigator clients running IP.

◆ RPC proxy support has been included so that Notes encryption can be used for Web clients using the SSL Tunneling Specification.

Web Navigator in Lotus Notes 4.5

Notes 4.0 included the capability to use the Notes client as an Internet browser to access and interact with Web sites and Web pages. A limitation of the Notes 4.0 release, however, was the requirement that a Web process must be running on an available Notes server to make the connection to the Internet. Clients *did not* directly browse the Web. Also, a special database had to be used to retrieve pages and work with data sharing. The new Notes 4.5 navigator expands the capability for all Notes users and works in a similar fashion to most Web navigators on the market. New features of the Web navigator include:

◆ The client can now directly retrieve Web pages, which can be cached locally instead of on the server. This means faster access to Web pages.

◆ A personal Web navigator database is available for local page caching. This database is also a way for clients to control how pages are retrieved and cached as well as other Web navigator settings.

◆ A new agent in the personal Web navigator database called "Page Minder" automatically manages pages cached in the database. Pages are updated (or not) according to settings in the Web navigator Setup document.

◆ A new agent in the personal Web navigator database called "Web Ahead" retrieves pages linked to any page specified to any number of levels specified.

◆ Java applets can now be executed from pages retrieved from the Internet or from Domino servers. Platforms that support Java applets with the initial release of Notes 4.5 include Windows 95, Windows NT, Sun Solaris, HP/UX, and AIX.

◆ Netscape Plug-In API support is included to enable the execution of plug-in files embedded in Web pages.

◆ The Web navigator now fully supports the HTML 3.2 specification, including background bitmaps and new table features.

◆ Web pages are now retrieved in a progressive manner, and elements of the page appear on the client's screen as they are retrieved.

◆ Notes now supports the capability to launch directly into a Notes document or a Web page.

◆ Clients can single-click URL linked text to launch that linked page.

◆ If the Web navigator is not the user's favorite browser, alternative browsers are now supported.

Directory Assistance

Directory Assistance is a tool that enables Notes users to look up information in other domains' address books. The Notes administrator sets up the guidelines for this process by defining the rules of Directory Assistance.

The Administration Process (AdminP)

The Administration Process (AdminP) was introduced in Notes 4.0 to rename users and servers, move users or servers to a different level in the existing naming hierarchy, and to handle routine server tasks. One of the problems with the original AdminP process was that it would change a user's ID and personal documents, modify other records in the Public Name & Address book, and potentially change the ACLs of all server-based databases. It could not, however, dig deeper into the databases to change security issues such as reader- or author-name fields. The Domino server's version of AdminP can modify reader and author fields, create and delete mail files, and create and move replicas of databases, in addition to the renaming capabilities introduced in Notes 4.0.

Database Management Tools

Several new management tools have been introduced in Domino 4.5. These tools can be used to analyze and manage databases on multiple servers from the Server Administration screen. The next several sections detail each of these new tools.

Administration Server Tool

The Administration Server tool simplifies the administrator's tasks in a menu-driven environment (see fig.2.6).

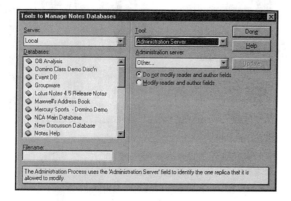

Figure 2.6

The Administration Server tool.

Analyze a Database Tool

The Analyze a Database tool is used to analyze changes to a Notes database within a defined period of time (see fig. 2.7).

Cluster Management Tool

The Cluster Management tool is used to simplify the various functions that are required by the administrator. Figure 2.8 shows the initial Cluster Management screen.

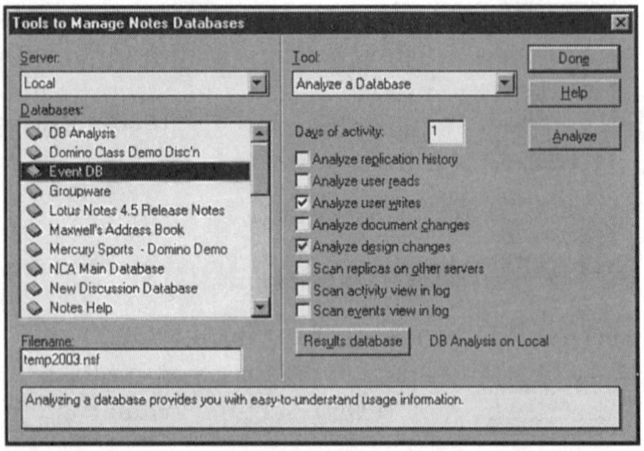

Figure 2.7

*The Analyze a
Database tool.*

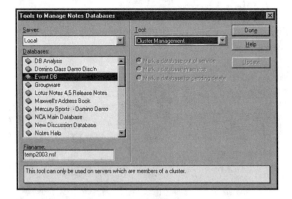

Figure 2.8

*The Cluster
Management tool.*

Compact Tool

Compacting a database removes white space (unused space in a database) that may be
eating up disk space. See figure 2.9 for the Compact tool.

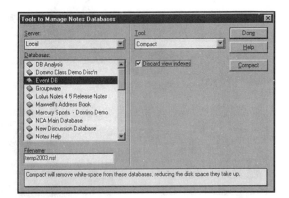

Figure 2.9

The Compact tool.

Consistent ACL Tool

Maintaining a consistent ACL for a database is important for true database security, especially on a local copy of a database. See figure 2.10 for the Consistent ACL tool.

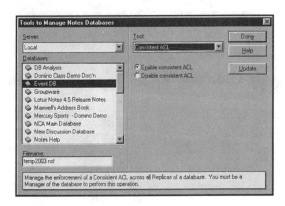

Figure 2.10

The Consistent ACL tool.

Create a Replica Tool

The Create a Replica tool is used to create replica copies of databases on different servers (see fig. 2.11).

Figure 2.11

*The Create a
Replica tool.*

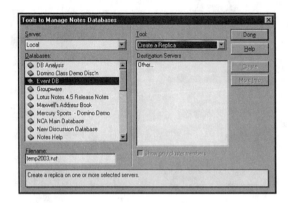

Full Text Index Tool

The Full Text Indexing tool is used to set up full text indexing for a database. See
figure 2.12 for a sample screen.

Figure 2.12

*The Full Text
Index tool.*

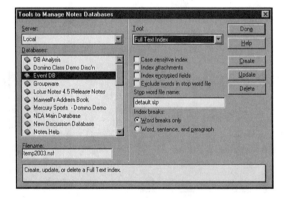

Move a Database Tool

The Move a Database tool is used to relocate a database onto a new server (see fig.
2.13).

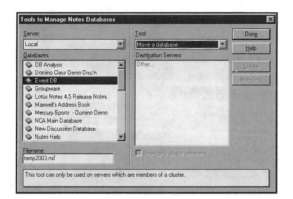

Figure 2.13

The Move a Database tool.

Multi Database Indexing Tool

The Multi Database Indexing tool is used to set up a full text index across databases. See a sample screen in figure 2.14.

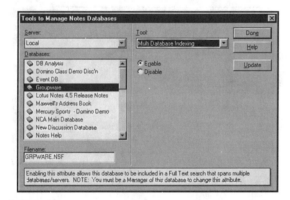

Figure 2.14

The Multi Database Indexing tool.

The NoteID Tool

The NoteID tool is used to display the hexadecimal ID for documents in a given database. See figure 2.15 for a sample screen.

Figure 2.15

The NoteID tool.

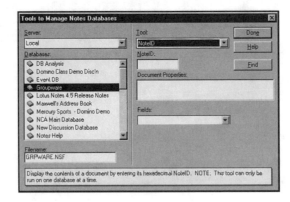

The Quotas Tool

The Quotas tool enables you to set quotas for multiple databases at the same time. See figure 2.16 for a sample screen.

Figure 2.16

The Quotas Tool.

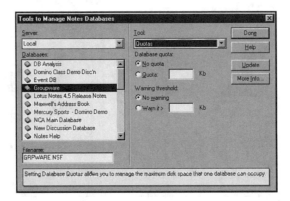

The Replication Tool

The Replication tool is used to enable or disable replication for a single or group of databases. See figure 2.17 for a sample screen.

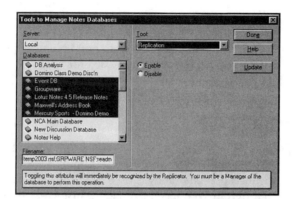

Figure 2.17

The Replication tool.

The following are additional tools and features of Notes 4.5.

Apple Remote Access (ARA)

Notes 4.5 introduces the capability for Macintosh users to connect to Domino servers via Apple Remote Access (ARA). Notes clients can also manage the actual dial-up, saving the user the step of manually initiating the dial to the server. For more information, see the documentation from Lotus on the Macintosh client.

Multiple Passthru Server Support

Administrators using Domino 4.5 can set up a single phone number for multiple passthru servers. These servers then act like a "hunt" group for dial-in users.

Automated Installations

Installation of Domino servers for Notes users can be automated through the use of scripts fed into the installation process. These scripts can change the way that servers are set up without administrator intervention.

Server Clusters

Server clustering groups up to six Domino servers together for load balancing and fail-over capabilities. A real-time replication scheme can be set up in a clustered environment to make sure the copies of the databases on all the clustered servers remain in sync. Load balancing is set up by the Notes administrator who specifies a threshold. If the threshold is crossed on a given server, that server passes new sessions to another server in the cluster. Fail-over is the process that automatically switches users with active sessions and a failing server to another server in the cluster.

Accounting and Billing

The accounting features of Notes 4.5 enable developers to build billing functionality into their Notes applications. The billing feature can be used for bill-back tracking within a company or when building applications for other companies.

Partitioned Domino Servers

Domino servers can be partitioned into several logical servers. This capability enables the server to support multiple IP addresses for Internet or intranet access. Those IP addresses can be tied to individual domain names. This capability is very useful for groups that maintain several different Web servers for clients inside or outside of the company.

Certified and De-Certified Operating Systems for Lotus Notes 4.5

Lotus Notes 4.5 supports the following collection of new server operating systems:

◆ Microsoft Windows NT 4.0

◆ IBM OS/2 Warp Server 4

◆ IBM AIX 4.2 for Unix

Lotus Notes 4.5 supports the following collection of new client operating systems:

◆ Microsoft Windows NT 4.0

◆ IBM OS/2 Warp 4

◆ IBM AIX 4.2 for Unix

The following client operating systems are no longer certified under Lotus Notes 4.5:

◆ AIX 4.1.3

◆ Sun Solaris 2.4

The following server operating systems are no longer certified under Louts Notes 4.5:

◆ AIX 4.1.3

◆ Solaris 2.4

◆ OS/2 2.11 SMP

New Messaging Features in Notes 4.5

Several new messaging features have been introduced with Notes 4.5. Messaging has always been an important part of the Notes product set. Messaging incorporates the idea of e-mail, mail gateways, and workflow applications using the Note mail model. Mail routing is an important part of daily administration, troubleshooting, and the maintenance cycle.

SMTP/MIME MTA

The SMTP/MIME MTA is included in Notes 4.5 to give any Domino server the capability to exchange e-mail with Internet users. SMTP (Simple Mail Transfer Protocol) is used for mail transfer on the Internet. SMTP does not allow for the transfer of attachments. MIME is the standard mail set of enhancements that allows for attachment encoding and decoding and other advanced mail functions. The SMTP Mail Transfer Agent is a gateway between Notes mail and Internet mail.

cc:Mail MTA

The cc:Mail MTA is included in Notes 4.5; it gives Notes mail networks full integration with cc:Mail systems. The cc:Mail Mail Transfer Agent is a gateway process that transfers mail between Notes and cc:Mail. The cc:Mail MTA also includes directory synchronization, if enabled.

POP3 Support

Domino mail messages can be downloaded by POP3 clients such as Eudora. The POP3 support includes password and SSL support.

Domino Server Security

Domino 4.5 introduces a handful of new security features. Security is always an important part of an administrator's life. The set of security features in Notes includes Web security via password or SSL, server-level security, database-level security, and Notes ID authentication. The following sections touch on these features.

Execution Control Lists (ECL)

The Execution Control List (ECL) is a security mechanism at the workstation level for protection from viruses, Trojan horses, mail bombs, and other problems related to running executables from the Internet and other sources. The ECL specifies what an executable can do on a specific user's system. See figure 2.18 for a list of options for this feature. The ECLs can be managed by an individual user or by an administrator in the Public Address Book.

Figure 2.18

A sample user's Execution Control List.

New Password Setting

One problem that has existed in Notes from the very beginning is the fact that users fully control their own passwords. Capabilities common in network operating systems, such as password expiration time frames, have not been available to Notes administrators. Notes 4.5 finally introduces this feature to Notes. The expiration is set by the Notes administrator either as a period of time or a set date. When the expiration period or date is reached, the user is prompted for a new password.

Java Applet Source Specification

Java source specification enables Notes administrators to determine the allowable sources for Java applets that will be executed in Notes. The options can include specific Internet hosts, only hosts within the firewall, or from all hosts except those specified. This is an important feature for Notes administrators because Java applets can potentially affect the user environment or read data from the user's workstation.

Windows NT Integration

Windows NT integration is an important new feature Lotus Domino 4.5. The features include passwords that can be used for both Notes and Windows NT. Notes events can be sent to the Windows NT event service, enabling Windows NT administrators to have a central interface for managing events from both Notes and Windows NT. Another very important new feature for Windows/Notes administrators is the capability to add and manage user accounts in Windows NT for users that have both Windows NT and Notes accounts.

SNMP and Domino Servers

Simple Network Management Protocol (SNMP) is a protocol used in TCP/IP environments to manage network resources such as Unix systems, network servers, network interface cards, network hubs, routers, and so on. Notes can tie into existing management systems using the SNMP standard. Lotus even markets a Notes-specific component for HP's OpenView product called NotesView. To use NotesView to monitor Notes servers, it is necessary to install the NotesView SNMP agents on any required Domino servers. The SNMP agents support the Notes MIB and can send Notes events to any SNMP management station. Current systems supported by the SNMP agents include Windows NT, OS/2, NetWare, HP/UX, Solaris, and AIX. The latest version of the NotesView SNMP agents can be downloaded from the Web from http://www.lotus.com/system.

New Features for the Notes Developer in Notes 4.5

The release of Notes 4.5 includes dozens of enhancements and new features for the Notes application development environment.

In the same way that shared fields and subforms enable reusable design components within a database, script libraries enable designers to add LotusScript "modules" that can be invoked as needed in multiple locations in the application. Figure 2.19 shows an example of the script library list.

Figure 2.19

An example of script libraries.

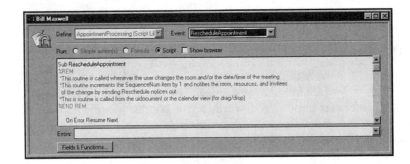

Notes 4.5 finally introduces OLE support for Macintosh users. This support has been available for Windows and OS/2 clients for years but has been lacking for Macintosh users. This ability is used to transfer data between various applications over the Macintosh operating system.

New LotusScript classes, methods, properties, and functionality introduced in Notes 4.5 include:

◆ Open database events for conditional script execution

◆ A function that enables one LotusScript agent to run another LotusScript agent

◆ An enhanced LotusScript Data Object that includes the capability to both read and write non-Notes data

The Future of Domino

Lotus has already begun work on what will probably be known as Domino 5.0. And while Domino 5.0 will certainly bring some amazing new features to the Notes arena, the direction for the Notes product set has been clearly defined by Domino 4.5. Eventually, clients will simply be used to organize data stored in any number of locations on the local system, the local area network, the wide area network, or the Internet. Domino is the product that is positioned to bring this data storage capability to the Internet and the world, using the existing Notes database infrastructure in conjunction with unquestionable market-leading groupware expertise.

Summary

This chapter introduced the new features of Domino 4.5. The new features enhance existing features or add new features for both developers and administrators. The administration features include messaging changes, security enhancements, and the Web issues of implementation, the navigator, and security. Starting with the next chapter, the new features of Notes 4.5, as well as some features for review from Notes 4, will be covered in detail.

PART II

Calendaring and Scheduling

CHAPTER 3

Introducing Calendaring and Scheduling

This chapter focuses on the Calendaring and Scheduling features included with Lotus Notes 4.5. With the use of these new tools, you can track meetings, set appointments, and keep yourself on track with your daily routines. In this chapter, you will find an in-depth discussion of Calendaring and Scheduling. You will discover how to schedule appointments and set up Calendaring and Scheduling on a workstation. You will also become familiar with the server commands and discover how your Domino server runs the Calendaring and Scheduling features.

Conceptual Background

Calendaring and Scheduling is a powerful enhancement that many Lotus Notes users have been asking for since early version 3.0. Many mail users enjoyed the calendar features present with the Profs (Office Vision) product first developed by Amoco and then purchased for reselling by IBM. The product was widely used by IBM and many other large corporations for a number of years. Profs has some impressive features; it is now considered by many to be a legacy system. The product is a mainframe-based mail system that requires knowing many function keys, and many of the processes are not intuitive. When Lotus Notes initially came out, IBM created a new product called Time & Place to replace the scheduling capability Profs offered. The market share for this product, however, was not very significant. A much more popular product, Lotus Organizer, was preferred by most Lotus Notes users. The largest drawback of Lotus Organizer was the inability to search for free time in calendars.

With Calendaring and Scheduling, Lotus has integrated some of the core features of Organizer into the standard Notes Mail template, enabling all users to have access to these features. The following are some of the key features:

- ◆ **Task scheduling.** Standard personal task scheduling can be accomplished using the new Calendaring and Scheduling functions. It is further enhanced by the capability to set alarms (visible and audible) for these tasks.

- ◆ **Meeting scheduling.** With this feature, you can fill in meeting details, select attendees, and then verify that the attendees are available by using the "Free Time" planning tool. This tool checks all of your invitees' calendars to see if they are available during your suggested time. If not, the tool suggests alternate times.

- ◆ **Calendar views.** You now can view the tasks in a Calendar format by day, week, 2 weeks, or a month. This Calendar looks just like Organizer's Calendar view.

All of the preceding features are now available to developers. Any of these features can be incorporated into a Notes application. All of these features have become part of the Notes core code, so developers can add them to any application.

A Quick Look at Calendaring and Scheduling Setup and Use

The Calendaring and Scheduling feature enables you to organize your daily events. With this addition, you can schedule rooms, meetings, appointments, and general events.

For Calendaring and Scheduling to function correctly, you must be using AdminP on your server. For more information about AdminP, see the "AdminP" section of Chapter 8, "Examining Notes 4.5 Administration Features."

All users' mail files that have been changed by the Mail45.ntf template include a new Calendar view and a new meeting view. To schedule an appointment, open the mail database and select the Calendar view. As you can see from figure 3.1, there are also buttons to change the perspective to two days, one week, two weeks, or one month. The Go To Today button takes you to the current day, but it does not change your perspective.

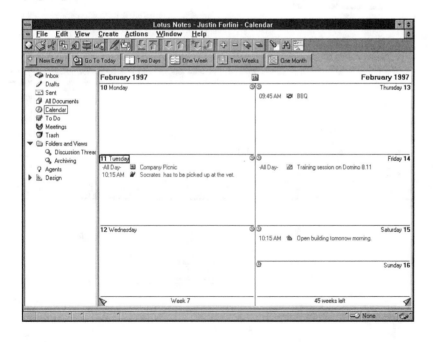

Figure 3.1

Calendar view by one week.

For Calendaring and Scheduling to function, both server and workstation must be using Domino 4.5 and Lotus Notes 4.5, respectively. In addition, the mail file must be upgraded to the design from the Mail45.NTF template. For information about conversion of mail files, see the section about upgrading mail files in Chapter 10, "Migrating to Lotus Notes and Domino 4.5."

As a Lotus Notes 4.5 user opens the new mail database for the first time, he is presented with a Profile record (see fig. 3.2). In the event that changes need to be made in the future, the user can reopen the Profile record by choosing Actions, Calendar Tools, Calendar Profile (see fig. 3.3).

Figure 3.2

A Profile record.

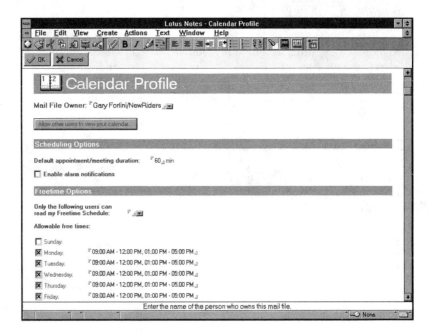

Figure 3.3

*The Actions
menu.*

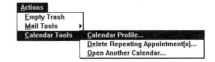

Users can fill out this profile so that their working hours are known by fellow workers. As you can see in figure 3.4, the profile displays Allowable free times check boxes, which are checked by default for weekdays from 9 a.m. to noon and from 1 p.m. to 5 p.m. A user can change the times, deselect available days, and add weekend days. As a worker schedules a meeting, birthday, or other event, the hours are checked by the server using the schedule task. If there is a conflict with the hours the recipient works or another appointment is scheduled, the server notifies the originator. For more information about the Profile record, see the Profile record section of this chapter.

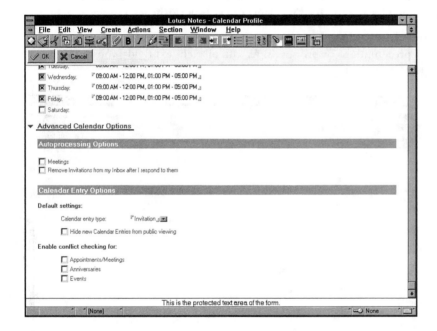

Figure 3.4

The bottom of the Profile form.

Once in the Calendar view, you can select the New Entry button. As you can see in figure 3.5, you are then presented with a form containing five different types of scheduling events: Appointment, Invitation, Event, Reminder, and Anniversary.

These selections present new fields and check boxes:

Each of these Calendar entries has different fields and options, but the following six are on each selection:

◆ **Brief description.** Enter approximately a one-sentence caption about the item.

◆ **Date.** You can type in a date or use the gray button to view a calendar and click on the date.

◆ **Time.** You can type in a time or use the gray button to view a timeline and choose the appropriate time. (Event does not have this field.)

◆ **Pencil in.** If this option is not selected, Notes places the item into the Calendar and Meetings views, and marks the specified time in your schedule as busy (not available with Reminder).

◆ **Not for public viewing.** The Not for public viewing option prevents others from seeing the individual item in your Calendar. However, the server can still see the time blocked when a Free Time query is performed.

◆ **Detailed description.** This rich-text field enables you to put such things as attached presentations or proposals. As with all rich-text fields, you can put as much as 1 GB of data.

Figure 3.5

An appointment entry.

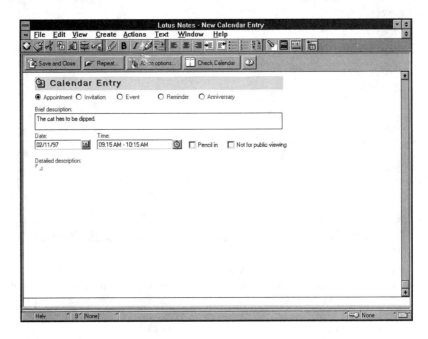

The following sections take a closer look at each of the scheduling selections available on the Calendar's new entry form.

The Appointment Selection

Looking more closely at the Appointment selection (see fig. 3.5), you can see that it is not possible to include others to join you. Therefore, the appointment is generally something you do on your own or with an outside customer or vendor.

The Invitation Selection

An Invitation is different from all other calendar selections because it is the only one in which you have the capability to reserve rooms and request the presence of others. Notice in figure 3.6 that when this option is selected, two sections appear—Invitations and Reservations.

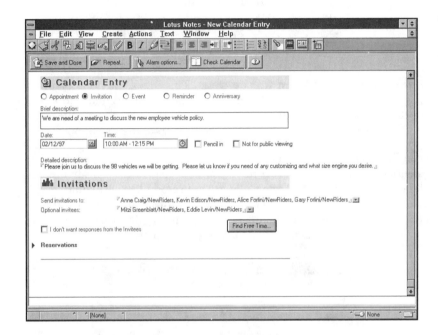

Figure 3.6

An Invitation calendar entry.

Invitations Section

In the Invitations section, the following fields and button are available:

◆ **Send invitations to.** You can either type the fully qualified name (such as Justin Forlini/Sales/NewRiders), or you can use the small gray arrow to bring up a list from the Public Name and Address Book. Much like general e-mail addressing, this field includes type ahead. Type ahead automatically looks at the Public Name and Address Book as you are typing and attempts to finish the name for you.

◆ **Optional invitees.** Just as in Send invitations, you can use the type ahead feature, or you can select from the Public Address Book. This field is reserved for people that are not crucial to the meeting (or people you actually hope will not attend, but you feel that you must include them for political reasons).

As you save your entry (or make changes to the entry), you are asked whether you want to inform the invitees of the invitation (see fig. 3.7). You also are presented with a confirmation prompt after the message has been sent.

Figure 3.7

The prompt asking if you want to notify invitees.

◆ **I don't want responses from the Invitees.** This check box is left blank by default, as you usually will want to be informed of the availability and interest of the invitees. If you turn on this check box, no request is made of the invitees to respond. (However, they still receive a mail notification of the invitation.)

◆ **Find Free Time button.** As you can see in figure 3.8, this option searches other calendars to make sure there is not a conflict. According to this figure, schedules for Alice Forlini and Anne Craig are not responding. Schedules are not available if a server cannot be reached or if the individual has not filled out a profile. For more information about a Free Time query, please see the section "Understanding the Free Time System" later in this chapter.

Figure 3.8

The Free Time dialog box.

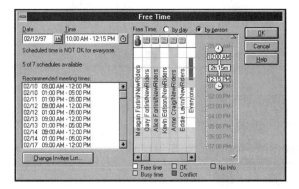

Reservations Section

In the Reservations section, the following buttons are available:

◆ **Reserve Specified Room.** This button (see fig. 3.9) reads from another database created for room use. For more information about the creation of the room database see Chapter 4, "Incorporating Calendaring and Scheduling into Your Applications."

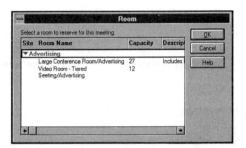

Figure 3.9

Reserving a specified room.

◆ **Find Available Room.** If a specific room is not available or it does not matter what room you use, this option searches the rooms database according to the size of your party (and whether you prefer smoking or non-smoking). As shown in figure 3.10, you simply select the appropriate site and then the rooms for that site will be listed.

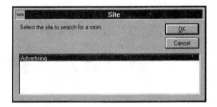

Figure 3.10

Finding an available room.

◆ **Reserve Resources.** This button enables you to request mobile devices like overhead projectors, projection systems, or white boards. For information about creating a resource database, see the section "Setting Up (and Deleting) Rooms and Resources" later in this chapter.

◆ **Display invitee responses.** This button only appears after the document has been saved and reopened. As you can see in figure 3.11, you can view acceptance or denial of invitations.

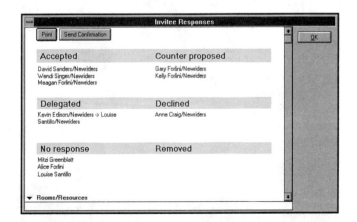

Figure 3.11

The Invitee Responses dialog box.

The Event Selection

The Event option does not have a time field; it instead has a duration of days field. An Event is generally designed to inform you about such things as seminars or a week of training (see fig. 3.12).

Figure 3.12

A sample Event calendar entry.

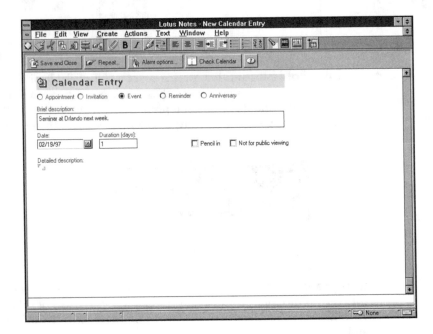

The Reminder Selection

A Reminder is used to inform you when you should remember an important date or time (see fig. 3.13). This option is terrific for remembering Secretary's Day or your pets' grooming day. Pencil in is not an option for this selection.

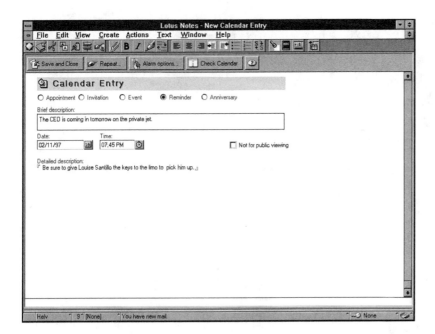

Figure 3.13

A sample Reminder entry.

The Anniversary Selection

The Anniversary feature helps you remember to get flowers for your special someone or to schedule the branch meeting to celebrate the company's founders' day. As you can see in figure 3.14, there is no time element with this feature so your special someone gets to celebrate all day, not just for an hour.

In addition to these five selections, a couple other options available with each scheduling form are worthy of discussion.

Figure 3.14

*A sample
Anniversary
entry.*

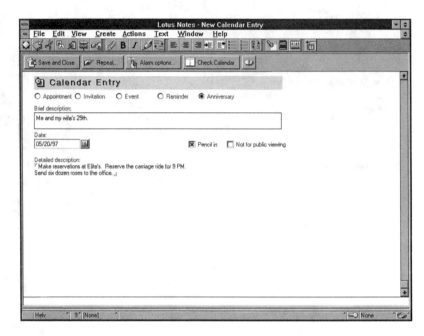

Setting Alarms

With any of the preceding options, you can set up an audible or visual alarm to notified you when scheduled items are due. If you have not first enabled the alarms option in your Profile record, you are prompted to turn them on the first time you use the feature (see fig. 3.15).

Figure 3.15

*The Enable
Alarms
verification.*

You can set alarms to notify you minutes, hours, or days prior to the scheduled occurrence. Click on the alarm button and select the desired time. As you can see in figure 3.16, a check box is also provided if you prefer to disable the notification.

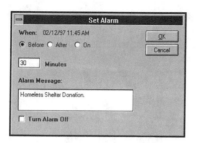

Figure 3.16

The Set Alarm dialog box.

Entries That Repeat

The Repeat... button is designed to copy any item to another week, month, or year (depending on the type of item you are scheduling). As you can see in figure 3.17, this makes it fairly effortless to plan years in advance.

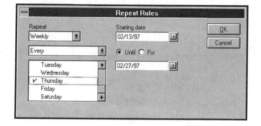

Figure 3.17

The Repeat Rules dialog box.

Security with Calendaring and Scheduling

Other people will need to view your calendar, which is located in your personal mail file. For this reason, a new security feature allows only limited rights in your mail file. This feature is accessed through your Calendar Profile. You can edit your Calendar Profile by selecting your mail file and then choosing Actions, Calendar Tools, Calendar Profile (see fig. 3.18). After making this choice, the screen shown in figure 3.19 appears.

Figure 3.18

The Actions menu.

Figure 3.19

A Profile record.

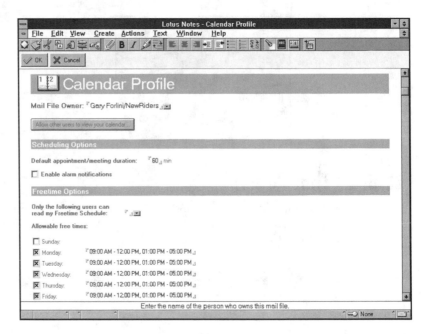

The Profile record includes a section called Freetime Options, which contains a field called "Only the following users can read my Freetime Schedule." Groups or individuals listed here can perform Free Time lookups on your schedule. You can type names directly into this field or select them from the Public Name & Address Book by using the small gray arrow found next to the field (see fig. 3.20). A blank field means all users can view your Free Time information when they schedule an appointment.

When your profile is changed, the Access Control List is altered with one of the following changes:

◆ **Read public documents.** People with this level of access will see only documents, folders, and views that have been designated as available for public access in the Form/Folder/View Properties Infobox. These properties are only on the Calendar view of the mail file. This feature is only alterable if the people or groups are assigned No Access (see fig. 3.21).

◆ **Write public documents.** This option enables you to give fellow workers create and edit access to specific documents without giving them author access. The attributes of the form must be designated as available for public access viewers.

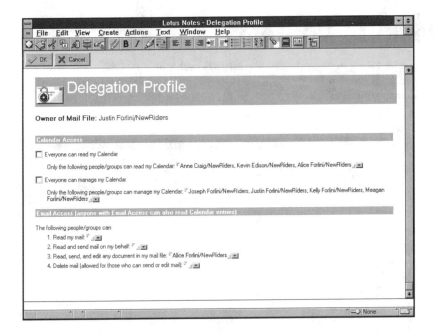

Figure 3.20

*A sample
Delegation Profile.*

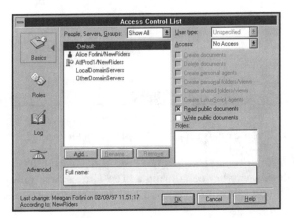

Figure 3.21

*The Access
Control List
dialog box.*

Note   For more information about assigning rights in the Access Control List, see Chapter 11, "Securing Your Notes and Domino 4.5 System."

Scheduling To Do Items

In addition to scheduling appointments, you can also schedule To Do items. As you can see in figure 3.22, the To Do view is used to remind you of items you (or fellow workers) need to accomplish. These items can be added and deleted from your Calendar as needed.

Figure 3.22

A sample task view.

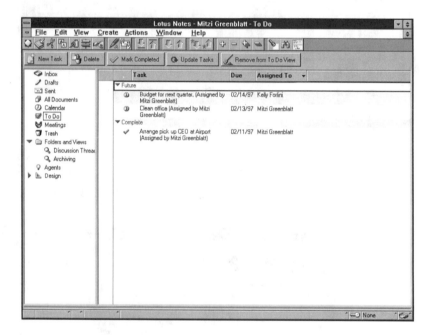

When you create a new task, you can also specify the priority (see fig. 3.23).

If you find you cannot (or do not want to) do a task, you can assign it to others (see fig. 3.24). No items in this view can be seen during a Free Time search unless you use the Display Task on My Calendar button.

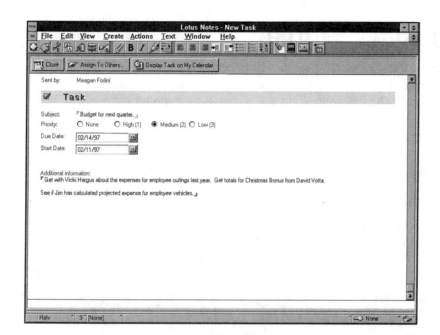

Figure 3.23

A sample task document.

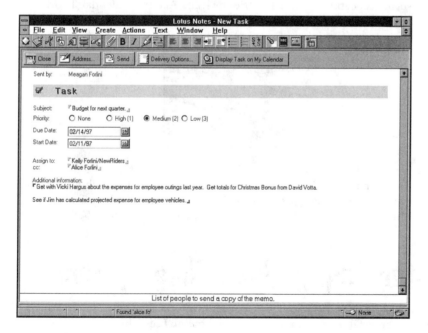

Figure 3.24

Task delegation.

The Calendar Profile

The Calendar Profile includes each user's work schedule and general defaults for calendar entries. The first field on the profile is automatically populated with the mail file owner's name. The following additional sections and buttons exist on the Calendar Profile record:

- ◆ Allow other users to view your calendar

- ◆ Scheduling Options

- ◆ Freetime Options

- ◆ Autoprocessing Options

- ◆ Calendar Entry Options

Removing Repeating Calendar Entries

You can remove any repeating Calendar entries by using Actions, Calendar Tools, Delete Repeating Appointment(s). You must first select the item that is repeating and then use the action to remove all duplicate entries in the future (see fig. 3.25).

Figure 3.25

The Change Repeating dialog box.

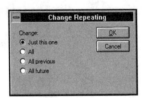

The following sections contain information about Calendaring and Scheduling from an administrator's perspective. You will be reading a much more in-depth discussion of server tasks and processes that make it possible for the user to do Free Time searches and you will see server tasks associated with Calendaring and Scheduling.

Understanding the Free Time System

When a user attempts to find available time for fellow workers, a Free Time search is performed. This Free Time search is accomplished by the Free Time system. The Free Time system consists of two server tasks: Schedule Manager (SCHED.EXE) and Calendar Connector (CALCONN.EXE). These files can be found in the Notes subdirectory (typically C:\Notes). When you install your Domino 4.5 server, these programs are automatically added to the server's Notes.ini file on the `ServerTasks=` line.

Schedule Manager

The first time the Schedule Manager task starts on a server, it creates a Free Time database (BUSYTIME.NSF) in the Data directory (typically C:\Notes\Data). This database does not show up in File, Database, Open and can only be opened at the server initially because the Access Control List only includes the server's name. In addition, for each mail user on the server (as specified in the person record of the Public Name & Address Book), an entry is created in the Free Time database. The Free Time database does not replicate between servers. Schedule Manager runs continually, and each time a person makes a change to his calendar, it enters the change in the Free Time database. If you delete the Free Time database (if the file becomes corrupt for instance), the next time you start the server, the Free Time system re-creates the database again.

When an individual invites people to a meeting and chooses to search for the invitees' free time, Schedule Manager searches the Public Name & Address Book for the location of each invitee's mail server and mail file. It then searches for schedule information in the Free Time database of each server as necessary (with the help of Calendar Connector). Schedule Manager returns a list of meeting dates, times, and the number of available invitees. The list is in descending order from the most feasible date and time to the least feasible time (fewest available invitees).

> **Note**　Only Schedule Manager has access to the Free Time database. You can open this file directly on the server and make changes just like any other Lotus Notes database. There should be no need to, however, because the validate command removes and adds any users that are deleted or added to the server. For more information about the validate command, see the "Using Console Commands" section of this chapter.

Calendar Connector

Calendar Connector essentially finds the most efficient path from one server to another when a request is made for Free Time information about a different server. These different servers can be in any Notes domain.

Figure 3.26 shows for an example of Calendar Connector in action. When Michelle Ashley requests Warren and Justin to join her in a meeting, a Free Time Search is requested. Because Warren and Justin are both on different servers, the Calendar

Connector queries the BusyTime database. In order for Justin's server to be reached, an Adjacent Domain Record is needed. For more information about Adjacent Domain Records, see the section "Multiple Domains" later in this chapter.

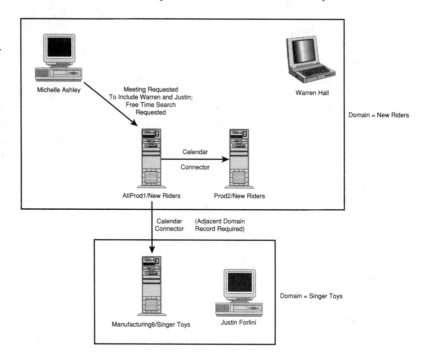

Figure 3.26

An example of Calendar Connector at work.

If you want to search for free time in third-party programs (such as Office Vision or Organizer), you must create a Foreign Domain Document. If you have separate domains, you must setup up an Adjacent Domain record. See the section "Multiple Domains" later in this chapter.

Now that you have discovered how the Calendar Connector is used during a Free Time search, the next section guides you through the other operations performed during a Free Time search. You will be reading about the databases and server tasks that are involved.

How the Free Time Query Process Works

The location of the invitee's mail server determines the action the Free Time system takes to direct the Free Time query to the correct Free Time database. The Free Time system tries to conduct Free Time queries directly because they must be performed in real time to avoid scheduling conflicts.

After a person requests the presence of others at a meeting, Notes sends the request for Free Time to the corresponding mail servers. The Free Time system collects and displays Free Time and busy time for all invitees and suggests the best times to schedule the meeting.

| **Note** | It is still possible for invitations to be sent to those that are not available. Conflicts occur in a calendar when an "unavailable" person double-books a time in his calendar. This conflict appears in the view with a red line next to both entries. |

The invitation is sent as if the person is available. The person can still accept the invitation and no warnings will be encounted if two things are booked. A red line appears next to the entries but only after they have left the document.

Using Console Commands

New console commands exist specifically for the Calendaring and Scheduling feature. Using these commands enables you to diagnose problems, collect statistics, or stop various Calendar tasks. These commands include the following:

◆ Tell Sched Show [*username*]

◆ Tell Sched Validate [*username*]

◆ Show Stat Calendar

◆ T Sched Q

Tell Sched Show [*UserName*]

The Tell Sched Show [*UserName*] command shows Calendar entries for the individual you specify. As you can see in figure 3.27, this command is very helpful in determining if a user's schedule is being read correctly. If you receive "user not found in schedule database," you may need to validate the user.

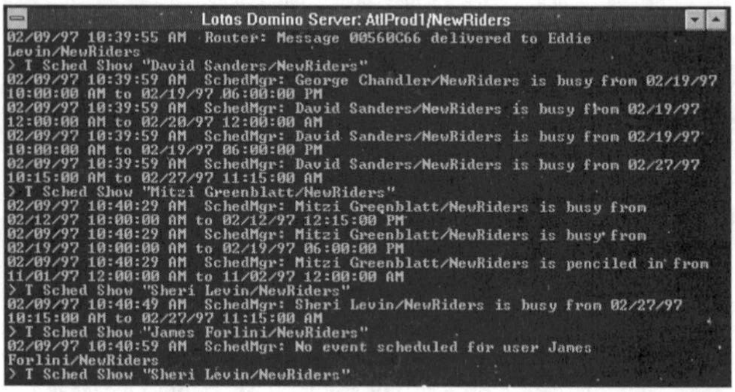

Figure 3.27

The Tell Sched Show command at work.

Tell Sched Validate [*UserName*]

If you just moved mail to a different server, you can issue the Tell Sched Validate [*UserName*] command to force the new user to be recognized by the server. By default, this process runs at 2 a.m. daily for all users. Notice in figure 3.28 that prior to issuing the validate command, Gary Forlini was not in the schedule database.

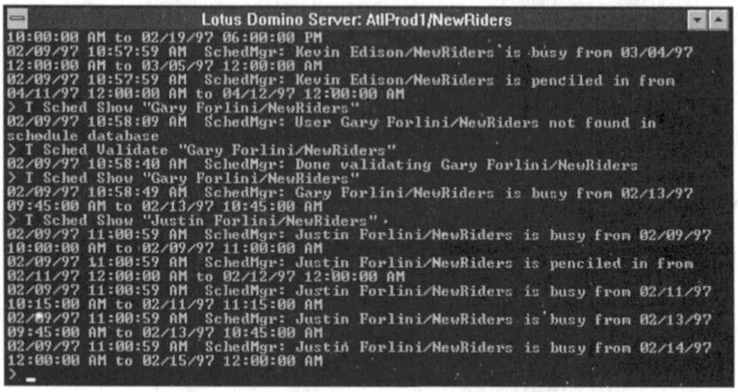

Figure 3.28

Using the Tell Sched Validate command.

Show Stat Calendar

The Show Stat Calendar command is shown in figure 3.29. Issuing this command shows information about activity for Calendar functions on a server.

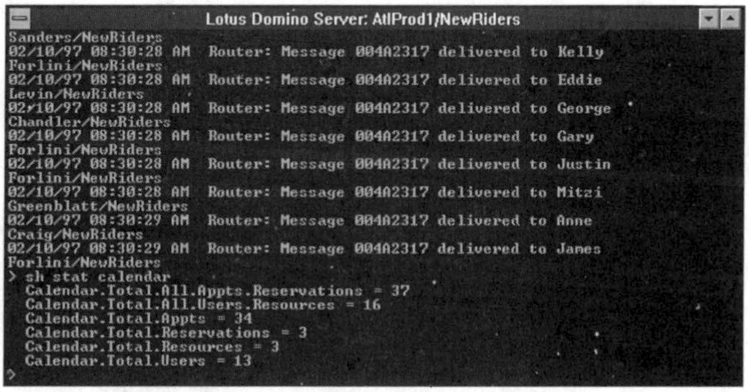

Figure 3.29

Showing statistics for Calendar.

T Sched Q

The T Sched Q (tell sched quit) command stops the schedule manager process (see fig. 3.30). You must restart the program with L Sched (load sched).

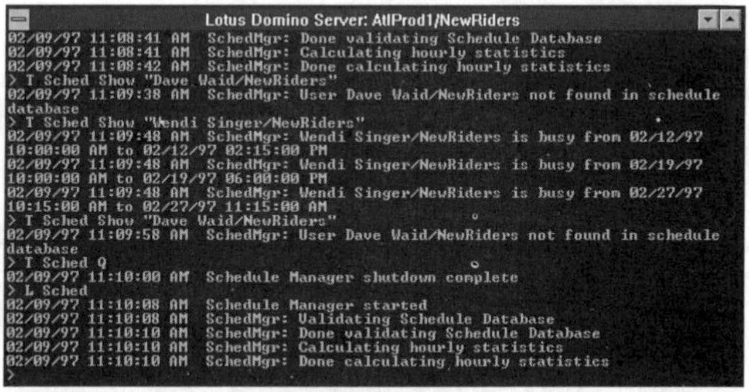

Figure 3.30

Stopping and restarting schedule manager.

For more information about server commands, see the "Remote Console" section of Chapter 8, "Examining Notes 4.5 Administration Features."

Setting Up (and Deleting) Rooms and Resources

You can have rooms and resources (such as conference rooms or visual equipments) available for meetings and appointments. To include these rooms and resources, you should make a new database using the Resource Reservations template. The following steps guide you in making the new database and creating rooms and resources:

1. To create this database, select File, Database New. You can call the database anything you like, and it can be placed anywhere on your server. You must be certain, however, to use the Resource Reservations Template (resrc45.ntf). The dialog menu for creating this database is shown in figure 3.31.

Figure 3.31

Rooms database creation using the New Database dialog box.

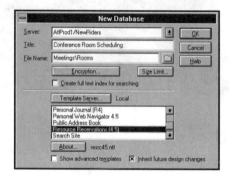

2. After you create the new database, you should then create a site document (see fig. 3.32). You should make a separate site document for each geographical location in your company that you intend to have available rooms and resources (additional sites can be made in separate databases if you prefer). You must be listed in the Create Resource role of the Access Control List to have the ability to create sites and rooms.

Figure 3.32

Creating a Site Profile.

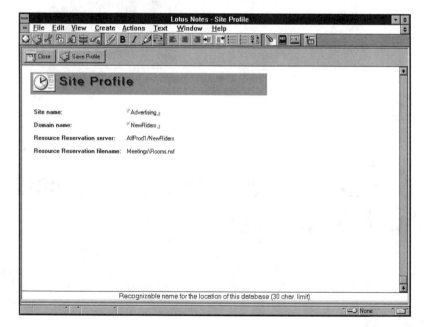

3. When you save the site profile, you also need to select a server so that various agents can run in the database (see fig. 3.33).

Figure 3.33

Choosing a server for agents to run on.

4. Once the site exists, you can create documents for the resources and rooms you want to include. Essentially, these items become hierarchical (they are not a true ID, however), as the site becomes the latter portion of the object's name. For example, Large Conference Room/Advertising. See figure 3.34 for an example.

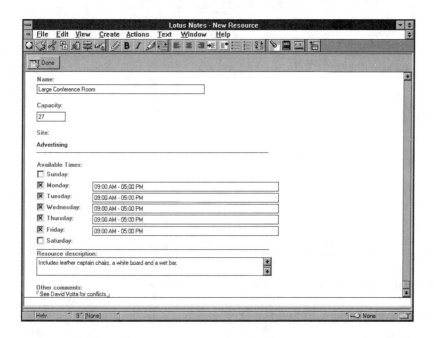

Figure 3.34

A Large Conference Room example document.

If a lunch room can be used as a conference room, be sure to block out lunch time in the profile for the room.

After a site, room, or resource is created, it cannot be changed. It must be deleted in the Administration Requests database (Admin4.nsf) and then re-created.

Rooms, sites, or resources must be deleted from the Administration Request Database. First select the item you want to delete from the room or resource database (see fig. 3.35).

Figure 3.35

*Deleting the
Projection system.*

After you initiate the deletion of the item, the request is sent to the server and then to the Administration Request Database (Admin4.nsf). Use the Pending Administration Approval view to find the requested deletion (see fig. 3.36).

Figure 3.36

*The Pending
Administration
Approval view.*

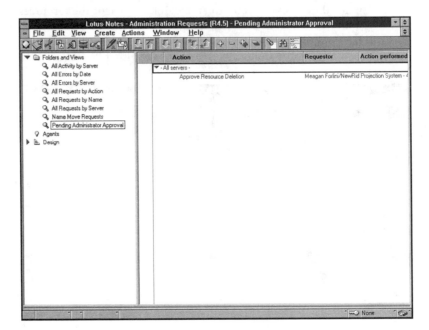

To complete the deletion, you must place the document in edit mode (click the Edit Button with the Red Pencil) and then click the Accept (thumb up) or Deny (thumb down) button at the top of your screen (see fig. 3.37).

You then are prompted to confirm the deletion of the room or resource (see fig. 3.38).

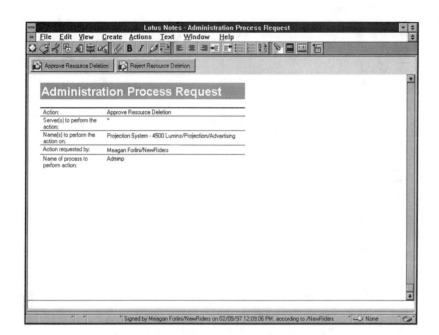

Figure 3.37

Using AdminP to delete a room.

Figure 3.38

Approving or denying a deletion.

Multiple Domains

In some instances, you may have more than one domain that will need to do Free Time searches. Separate domains exists in different companies or in very large companies. To search for Free Time in other domains, an Adjacent Domain record is needed. The Adjacent Domain record was originally intended to prevent unwanted mail from passing through your domain. As shown in figure 3.39, however, this record now has an additional field (Calendar server name) to include Free Time searching.

Figure 3.39

*An Adjacent
Domain record.*

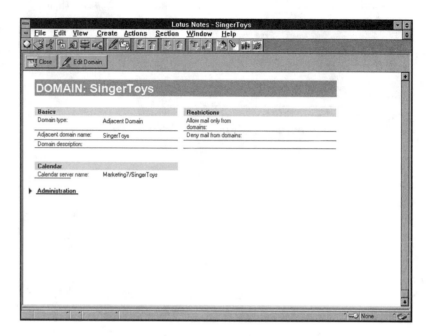

To make an Adjacent Domain record, you should open your Public Name & Address
Book and select Create, Domain. The default for the domain type is Foreign Domain.
Change this field to Adjacent Domain. In the past, only the Basics and Restrictions
section existed. If you wanted to limit who could send mail through your domain, you
would exclude or include domain names at your discretion. Now you have a new
section for Calendar Server Name. Enter the names of the Adjacent Domain and the
server name that you will be connecting to.

Using Plug-In Products with the Free Time Search

If your company has been using Lotus Organizer, and you now want to convert to
the new Calendaring and Scheduling in Lotus Notes, a conversion utility will be
available around the second quarter of 1997. An API can also be written so that the
Free Time search utility can be used with other third-party products (plug-ins). The
API would allow you to use both a plug-in product and Lotus Notes for Calendaring
and Scheduling.

To use other plug-in programs with a Free Time search, you must create a Foreign Domain record and alter the Calendar system and Calendar server name fields (see fig. 3.40). After this record is created, a Person record must be created for each person using the plug-in product. The Person record should include the name of the person (in the user name field) and the name of the Calendar domain (in the Domain field). You should use the same name you gave the Foreign Domain record.

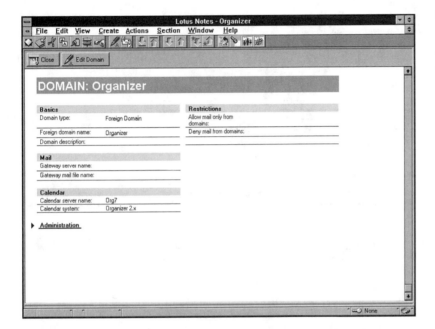

Figure 3.40

A Foreign Domain record.

The plug-in that links Notes to Organizer 2.x, for example, is called Organizer 2.x. You can create a Foreign Domain record called Organizer2x with a Calendar system field containing Organizer 2.x. This would then direct the Free Time system to send requests intended for the Organizer2x domain. You then would add a Person record for Mitzi Greenblatt and change the Calendar Domain field to Organizer2x. Figure 3.41 shows an example of a Person record.

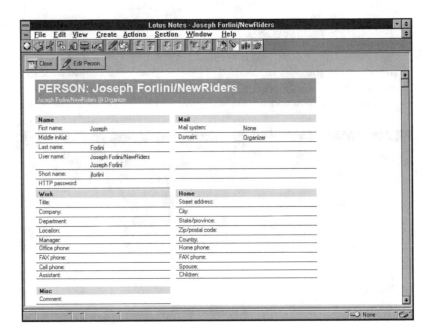

Figure 3.41

*An example of a
Person record.*

Laptop Owners

Laptop owners also need to schedule people on occasion. Therefore, it is possible to
replicate schedules to the machine locally. When the client is installed, a
BusyTime.nsf file is added automatically to the data directory. The icon for the file
appears on the workspace and on the last page (the Replicator page). As figure 3.42
shows, it is possible to capture the current schedule of selected fellow workers. When
you receive this data, it is actually not replication but a copy of the data.

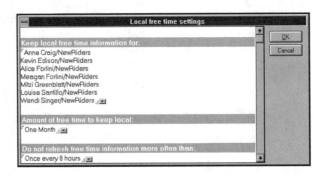

Figure 3.42

*Copying schedules
to a laptop.*

Restrictions

As with any Lotus Notes database, Calendaring and Scheduling should exclude any real-time entries and intense financial requests. Lotus Notes was not intended to do real-time updates of data without constant intervention from the end-user. In addition, any elaborate financial calculating should be done in other programs (such as spreadsheets), then Lotus Notes can be used to store the data.

Although there will be migration tools and Free Time searches in both Organizer and Profs (Office Vision), it is assumed you will quit using the plug-in products as soon as possible. Migration tools are intended to help during a transition, not to continuously be used regardless of version. It is unlikely that Lotus Notes will continue to include support for plug-in in future releases.

There are some instances in which using Calendaring and Scheduling is not appropriate. Initially (because the feature is new) there will be little support for external devices such as pocket calendars. If the CEO of your company insists on using such a device, you might want to wait to use Lotus Notes Calendaring and Scheduling until it is possible to send and receive data to and from the device.

The Calendaring and Scheduling features are not ideally suited for use with frequently changing schedules. The Free Time search task reads other calendars to determine availability of others. In industries that require frequently changing schedules (retail for instance), the Free Time task will yield incorrect results (you will appear available when in reality you are working).

The new 4.5 Mail Template is approximately 400 KB larger than the previous template. The size of mail files will likely grow as you introduce these new features. How much larger the mail files get will greatly depend on how much the features are used. Many found the shared mail task introduced with 4.0 to greatly reduce disk space. Much of a person's calendar is personal, and therefore there is no need for a share file when entering data into calendars. With the advent of Calendaring and Scheduling, you will likely notice disk space to be on the increase again. For information about limiting mail file sizes, see the "Database Tools Button" section of Chapter 8.

The 4.5 mail file is designed for use with the Domino 4.5 server and Lotus Notes 4.5 client and will not work with previous versions. Furthermore, an end-user will receive many errors if he attempts to use the new calendar feature with a previous version of Lotus Notes. The previous version of the Room Reservations database (Reserve4.ntf) does not work with the new Calendaring and Scheduling features. This database existed prior to 4.5 for Calendaring and Scheduling but does not function with the new features in 4.5 (such as Free Time searching). There is no harm in continuing to use the older style database, but it does not include the features of the new Calendaring and Scheduling add-on. Starting over with a new database with the new 4.5 Resource Reservations Template is the easiest (and likely the least time-consuming) method of taking advantage of the new Calendaring and Scheduling features.

Summary

In this chapter, you discovered the features of Calendaring and Scheduling. You learned about the strong desire for these tasks to be included with Lotus Notes. You also found out how to implement and use the various aspects of the tools, including how to setup the profile on the client, how to schedule and use the Calendar features, and how to use the server commands associated with the tasks. Finally, you discovered the various restrictions with these new tools.

CHAPTER 4

Incorporating Calendaring and Scheduling into Your Applications

Calendaring and Scheduling has been one of the most eagerly awaited additions to Lotus Notes. Calendaring and Scheduling capabilities enable you to track appointments, meetings, and other obligations in your Notes mail database in a familiar, comfortable calendar interface. This calendar makes the information available at a glance and provides access to more specific details as needed.

Even more impressive, however, is how relatively simple it is to include Calendar view capabilities in any database. By adjusting your view slightly and relying on some new view properties, you can display your view information via the new calendar interface, allowing you to create new entries by double-clicking the Calendar view, to reschedule documents to a new day via drag and drop, and to watch for time conflicts. In this chapter, you will learn the ins and outs of incorporating calendar capabilities into your applications.

View Considerations with Calendaring

Calendars within Notes 4.5 are actually specially formatted views that display with a calendar interface. Because a calendar is a specially formatted Notes view, it is important to be aware of what changes and considerations you need to keep in mind. This is the focus of this section.

As with any view, your Calendar view is initially created by selecting Create, View, and then selecting the view type and supplying a view name. If you are using the typical Notes navigator—known as Folders—Notes will add your new view name to the list of views already showing, and display a mangifying glass next to it.

 If you create your Calendar view as a shared view with the special reserved view name ($Calendar), Notes will display a clock icon in the Folders navigator for your view and give your view the name "Calendar," as displayed in figure 4.1.

After the view is created, you will need to close the database and re-open it for the clock icon to display. This forces the navigator display to refresh so that your change displays.

Figure 4.1

Clock icon displayed in the Folders navigator.

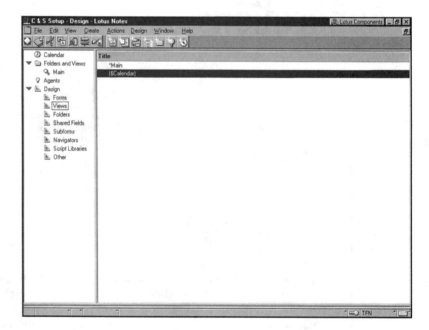

Now that you have created the view, you have several choices to make if you want to implement a calendar interface for that view. This view must be formatted in a specific fashion in order to use a calendar interface, the details of which are covered in the following section. The following sections detail the changes made to the View Properties box when using the calendar interface.

Layout of the Calendar View

After the view has been created and named, the result is an empty Notes view, using the Standard Outline style of view interface by default. To take advantage of the calendar style interface new to Notes 4.5, your view must be formatted as the next few paragraphs indicate.

> **Note**   While in design mode, every view appears to be a typical column-based, standard outline view. It is only when the view is displayed for actual use that the calendar interface appears.

The first column of any view using the calendar interface must be a sorted column displaying a date-time value for each entry in the view. It is the values within this column that Notes uses to determine which day of the calendar each entry appears on. This column is usually hidden.

The second column of the view needs to show the duration in minutes for each calendar entry. The value in this column is what Notes refers to for blocking out the appropriate amount of time for each item. This entry can be 0 for simple reminders or other items that do not span a range of time. However, a formula of

```
(EndDateTime-StartDateTime)/60
```

is more typical. This formula refers to two date-time fields within the document, StartDateTime and EndDateTime. If your date-time fields are named differently, make sure this formula reflects that. Date values residing in date-time fields are internally stored as the number of seconds that have passed since 12/31/1899. Subtracting two date-time values results in the number of seconds between those two dates. Dividing this number by 60 yields the appropriate number of minutes Notes is expecting for this view column. This column is also usually hidden.

Any additional columns are used to display information on the calendar itself and can take advantage of any available column properties to do so. Just as with a standard view, the hidden column property can be used to affect the sort order of the information. Furthermore, the "Display values as Icons" column property can be included to provide a quick, visual representation of what type of data that document contains. The Calendar view within your Notes mail uses both of these tactics.

The Right View Properties for Calendars

Once you have the first two columns of your Calendar view in the required format, it is then necessary to choose Calendar from the Style drop-down list in the View Properties box. This instructs Notes to display this view using the calendar interface. Figure 4.2 shows where this setting can be found.

Figure 4.2

Choosing the Calendar interface.

Selecting this option causes subtle changes throughout the tabs of the View properties box: specifically, the Style tab, the Text tab, and the Time-Date tab.

The Style Tab

The Style tab, denoted by a multicolor S, changes to reflect choices available for each specific type of view. In Calendar view, you can choose what color to use for the background, busy time slots, day separators, and today's date, as well as whether to show conflict marks. Figure 4.3 shows how this tab appears for a Calendar view.

Figure 4.3

The Style tab on the View Properties box as it appears for a Calendar view.

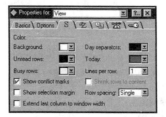

This dialog box also contains a Show selection margin checkbox. The *selection margin* is the column within a view that displays a checkmark for each selected document, a trash can for a document marked for deletion, and a star for an unread document. Placing checkmarks in this column next to multiple documents allows the user to perform an operation such as printing, copying, or running an agent on just those selected documents. Because space is limited in most Calendar views, you can gain additional room to display information by turning off the Show selection margin setting. Figures 4.4 and 4.5 illustrate the enabling and disabling of the Show selection margin, respectively.

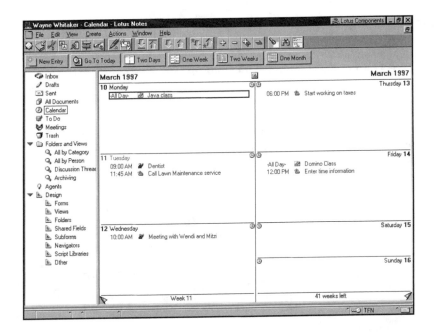

Figure 4.4

The effect of enabling Show selection margin.

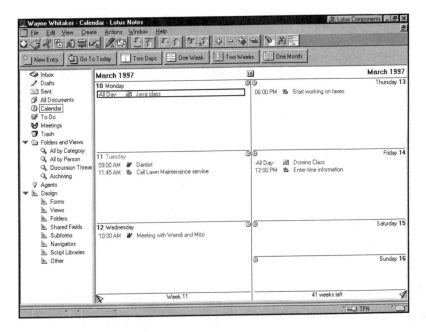

Figure 4.5

The effect of disabling Show selection margin.

Note that the selection margin displays in front of each entry, taking up space that could display information of your choosing.

Although turning off Show selection margin implies that you are no longer able to select multiple documents to work with, this is not the case. If you click any document with your mouse, you can display the selection margin by pressing your spacebar, enabling you once again to select multiple documents.

The Text Tab

In addition to the changes on the Style tab, you will also see a Text Style tab appear, indicated by the aZ symbol in the properties box. This tab enables the designer to format the text in Time Slots, Headers (typically the Month and Year), and Day & Date values. Figure 4.6 shows this tab of the View properties box.

Figure 4.6

The Text Style tab on the View properties box as it appears for a Calendar view.

The Time-Date Tab

The third tab that appears when you choose a view type is the Time/Date tab, indicated by the clock and calendar page (see fig. 4.7). The options on this tab enable the designer to change how individual dates appear. You can, for example, specify start and end times for a day and enable time slots of a specific length.

Figure 4.7

The Time-Date tab of the View properties box as it appears for a Calendar view.

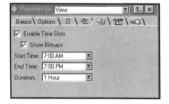

Because space is limited in a Calendar view, you probably will not want to display all the time slots all the time. You can either turn off the Enable Time Slots setting so that only filled times show or, in addition to enabling the time slots, also enable the Show Bitmaps option. This gives the user the capability to display all the time slots when needed; otherwise they remain hidden (except in the two-day calendar format, which has plenty of room to always display time slots).

Suggestions

This section gives suggestions to make life easier when using a Calendar view.

One suggestion when working in Calendar view is to experiment with smaller point sizes in order to maximize the amount of information displayed on-screen. The default typeface, Helvetica, does not scale below 8 points, so you might want to try other fonts. The Truetype font Arial is similar in appearance to Helvetica but will scale to very small sizes. In addition, make sure all columns within your view—including hidden and icon columns—are set to use this smaller typeface and point size. The typeface and point size designated for each column in design mode is what will be used to display that column's information on the calendar, just as in a standard outline view.

Second, your Calendar views do not print with the calendar interface. When you print a Calendar view, you get a printout of each date followed by the items assigned to that date. It is not, however, formatted in a calendar format like you are seeing on the screen. The suggestion here is to make the users of your Calendar view aware that if they try to print in Calendar views, they will be disappointed. Lotus hopes to include calendar printing capability in the next release of Notes.

Third, is a brief discussion about deleting calendar entries. In a standard view, a trash can graphic displays in the selection margin for the currently selected documents whenever you press the Delete key on your keyboard. With a Calendar view, however, you will not see the trash can when marking an entry for deletion. Instead, Notes draws a line through the entry to indicate it is marked for deletion (see fig. 4.8). As with any view, any document marked for deletion will not be erased until you refresh the view or close the database.

A final suggestion relates to a usability issue. Any time a Calendar view is displayed on-screen, the View menu contains a Calendar drop-down menu, as shown in figure 4.9.

Many users are not aware of this Calendar drop-down and, consequently, do not realize they can change the way their calendar displays. For this reason, it benefits the user if the designer includes action buttons at the top of the view that duplicate the functionality found under the Calendar drop-down. To accomplish this, you need to use a couple @Commands related exclusively to Calendars: [CalendarFormat] and [CalendarGoTo]. These @Commands are useful in changing the way your Calendar displays.

Figure 4.8

A Calendar entry marked for deletion.

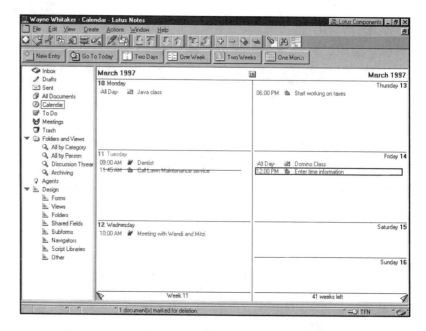

Figure 4.9

The Calendar drop-down menu.

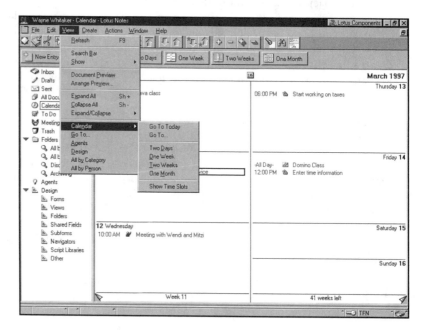

Calendar-Specific @Commands

To change the number of days that display on your Calendar view, use the @Command([CalendarFormat]; "*NumDays*"), in which "*NumDays*" is either "2," "7," "14," or "30." Note that these are text values, so the quotes should be included as part of the parameter. These values display the two-day, one-week, two-week, and one-month views, respectively.

To take the user to a specific day on the calendar, use the @Command ([CalendarGoto]; *datevalue*) function. If a time-date value is used for the optional second parameter, Notes takes the user to that date. For a Go To Today action button, the @Today function would serve well as the second parameter. If no second parameter is specified, Notes displays a dialog enabling the user to choose a date to go to, as figure 4.10 shows. This flexibility makes going to any specified date very easy.

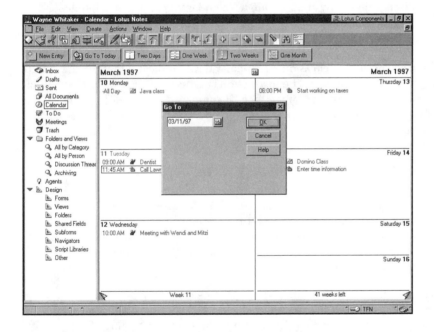

Figure 4.10

The @Command ([CalendarGoTo]) function.

Calendar-Specific Events

In addition to providing calendar-specific @Commands, Notes 4.5 also offers events relating exclusively to Calendar views. *Events* within Lotus Notes are special programs or formulas executed in response to a particular occurrence. You tap the real power of an event when you place executable code within an event, thereby causing your code to execute whenever the event occurs. Most events expect LotusScript instructions to indicate what they do, so more information about events and how to use them is available in Chapter 19, "Advanced LotusScript." Unlike most events, however, the three calendar-specific view events discussed in this chapter allow @Function formulas within them. The three calendar-specific view events discussed in this chapter are RegionDoubleClick, QueryDragDrop, and PostDragDrop. Additional view events are discussed in Chapter 19.

RegionDoubleClick

This event's name indicates that some region is being double-clicked. If you know that the region in question is a blank area within a Notes Calendar view, you might have an idea how this event can be used. With typical views, it does not make sense for a user to double-click an empty area. Within a Calendar view, however, double-clicking an empty area causes the RegionDoubleClick event—and any code you have included within it—to execute. This gives you the capability to make anything you want happen when a user double-clicks a blank area of a Calendar view. Typically, however, when a user double-clicks on a particular day, it indicates that the user wants to create a new entry for that day. The instructions in this event usually instruct Notes to create a new calendar entry by using either @Command([Compose]; "*formname*") in the @Function language, or the .ComposeDocument method of the NotesUIWorkspace class.

QueryDragDrop and PostDragDrop

As the similarity in name might imply, these two events are related—they execute before and after a drag-and-drop operation, respectively. More specifically, QueryDragDrop executes after the user has finished indicating where the dragged document should be dropped, but before Notes actually performs the drop. After Notes drops the document into its new location, the PostDragDrop event executes just before control is given back to the user.

QueryDragDrop is used to determine whether the selected document is allowed to be moved to the new location. If it is not allowed (and LotusScript is being used), the operation can be stopped by setting the Continue parameter to a value of False. The Continue parameter is built-in to the QueryDragDrop LotusScript event for just this purpose. Using @Functions in this event does not provide the same capability.

You could use QueryDragDrop to prevent a Meeting document displaying in a Calendar view from being dragged from a weekday and dropped on a weekend. This is assuming, of course, that the business meeting won't be taking place on the weekend. LotusScript can be used to look at the date of the target drop day and to set the Continue parameter to False if that target date falls on a Saturday or Sunday.

PostDragDrop is used for resetting fields—especially time-date fields—to reflect the values of their new location. If a meeting document is dragged from Monday 3/10/97 and dropped on Wednesday 3/12/97, the PostDragDrop event is used to change the MeetingDate field to the date of the new value.

Although these three events do allow @Function formulas, their true power and flexibility comes through when using LotusScript. See Chapters 18, "LotusScript Fundamentals," and 19, "Advanced LotusScript," for a more in-depth discussion about LotusScript.

Form-Related Considerations

So far, this chapter discusses viewing data via the calendar interface. In order to view information, however, you must have documents existing within the database. These documents have date and time values and, of course, have been created using a Notes form. The next few sections take these facts into consideration and offer some suggestions toward making those forms more date friendly.

Date and Time Selector

Instead of typing a date or time value into a blank, Notes can display a Date or Time Selector icon next to the field, enabling the user to select from a drop-down list. The user can decide whether to type in the date or pick it from a list. Figure 4.11 shows the Date Selector icon and the following steps tell how to make it appear.

Two conditions make this indicator display:

1. The time-date field must be in a layout region.

2. The Show drop-down list on the Basics tab must be set to display only the date (see fig. 4.12).

Figure 4.11

The Date Selector icon for a date field.

Date selector icon

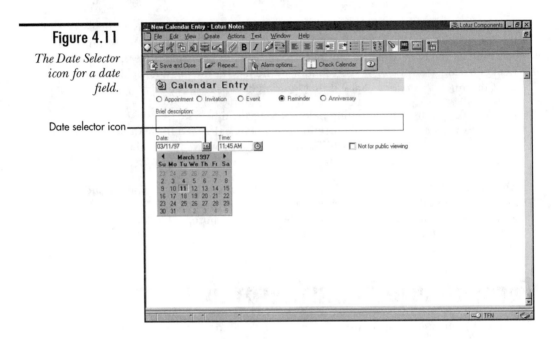

Figure 4.12

The Show drop-down list must be set to display only the Date.

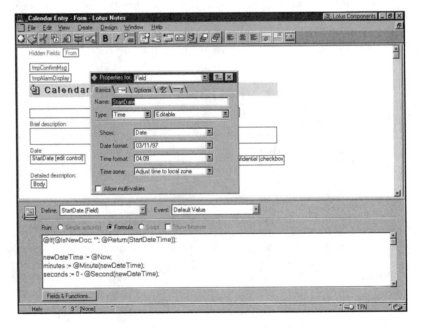

If a time-date field within a layout region is formatted to display time only, the Time Selector icon displays (see fig. 4.13).

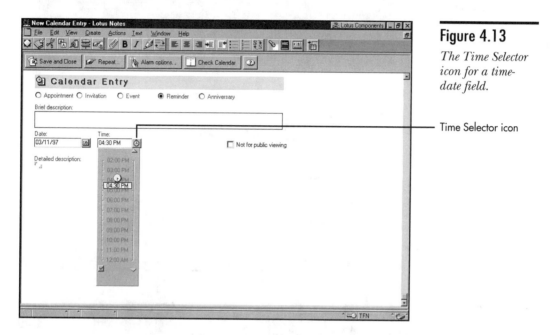

Figure 4.13

The Time Selector icon for a time-date field.

Time Selector icon

The time selector pop-up in figure 4.13 does not display a range of times, but rather a single time value. This setting is appropriate for a reminder but not for a meeting, which usually occupies a range of time. As figure 4.14 displays, it is possible to choose a range of time via the time selector pop-up.

If you would like to provide your users with the capability to select a range of time by using the time selector pop-up, make the following changes:

1. The time-date field must be in a layout region.

2. The Show drop-down list on the Basics tab must be set to display only Time.

3. The Allow multi-values setting on the Basics tab needs to be enabled (checked).

4. Both the Multi-value options listed on the Options tab need to be set to Blank Line. Figure 4.15 displays the Options tab as it should appear.

Figure 4.14

The time selector can be used to select a range of time.

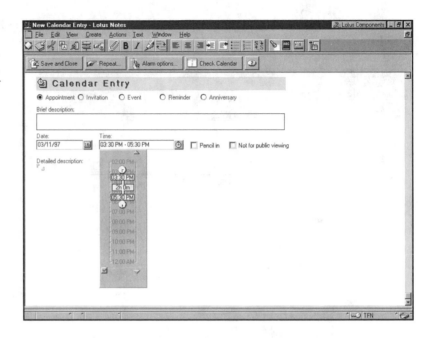

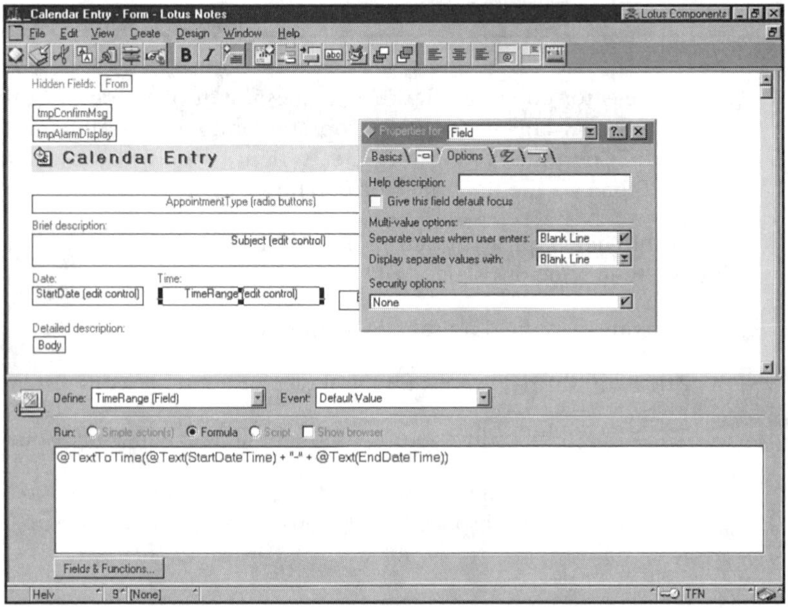

Figure 4.15

The Options tab as it should appear for a time-range selector to display in a layout region.

Following the preceding steps provides you with the time-range selector displayed in figure 4.14.

The start time and the end time can be moved independently of each other to increase or decrease the duration. If the user points to the middle of the time range, the entire range can be moved as a block.

Now you can give your users the capability to easily select a date or time value with the click of a mouse. The following section discusses a possible use for this capability: setting an alarm as a reminder.

Adding Alarm Capabilities

If you think your users might need digital string on their fingers to remind them of the document you've just created, adding an alarm capability can be the way to go. Be warned, however—adding alarms is not for the faint. Figure 4.16 shows a typical alarm within Notes 4.5.

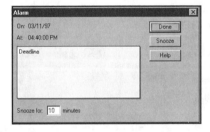

Figure 4.16

An alarm in Notes 4.5.

Where alarms are concerned, two reserved fields are of importance:

◆ **$AlarmTime** is a time-date field that indicates the date and time the alarm is supposed to ring.

◆ **$AlarmDescription** is a text field that contains the message that will display when the alarm goes off.

Specifying values for these two fields is the beginning of the alarm-setting process. This can be accomplished in one of two ways:

◆ If you make these fields editable, the user can simply fill-in the date, time, and text of the alarm.

◆ Otherwise, you as the designer need to provide code elements—@Functions or LotusScript—to fill these fields with the appropriate values.

Your Lotus Notes mail database adopts the second method of setting the values for these fields, asking you for the date, time, and message of your reminder by means of a dialog box, and then storing that information in hidden versions of the fields mentioned earlier. The following paragraphs discuss other considerations when using the alarm capabilites of Lotus Notes.

At the beginning of this chapter, you were told about the reserved view name ($Calendar) and how using it causes special things to happen in Notes. Similarly, Notes 4.5 mail files have a reserved folder named ($Alarms) that is used to gather all items for which an alarm has been set. A dedicated piece of software known as the *alarm daemon*, once awakened, watches the documents in this folder until the $AlarmTime field matches the system clock for one of them. The daemon then displays the Alarm dialog, using the contents of the $AlarmDescription field as its message. The daemon is relatively narrow-minded, however, as it looks only in this one folder, and only in your mail database. Consequently, it is only for documents in this folder within your mail file for which reminders display.

The narrow focus of the alarm daemon makes two very special implications:

◆ Any document you create in another database that you want to set an alarm for needs to end up in your mail file.

◆ The document also needs to show up in the ($Alarm) folder (which is hidden) within your mail file.

Needless to say, these can be involved tasks.

The easiest way to get the document into your mail file is to mail it there. You can accomplish this in a number of ways. In the scope of this chapter, however, try following these steps:

1. Add the reserved field *SendTo* to the document you want to be reminded of. Make it multi-value, if more than one recipient is possible. If Notes sees this field on a document, it knows to use the names contained there as the mail recipients for the document.

2. Turn on the "Store form in document" setting on the Defaults tab of the Form Properties box for this form.

3. Create a hidden computed field called *Mailer* (although the name is immaterial). Give it the following formula:

```
@IF(@IsDocBeingSaved; @MailSend; "")
```

This formula mails the current document to the recipients listed in *SendTo* whenever this document is saved. This means that additional saves result in additional mailings. If this is not desired, the "@IsDocBeingSaved" portion of the @IF statement can be replaced with "@IsDocBeingSaved & @IsNewDoc" to mail this document only the first time it is saved.

This takes care of getting the document into the mail database. Now you need to get it into the ($Alarms) folder.

One possible approach is an agent that runs on newly received mail, checks to see if the $AlarmTime field is in that document, and places any such document into the ($Alarms) folder. This approach, however, would involve the yet undiscussed topic of LotusScript, and consequently is not undertaken here.

There is an alternate approach. You may remember that earlier we enabled the Store form in document property for the form used to create your document. You can use this to your advantage: all programmable events from the form itself are available wherever this document goes. The PostOpen form event is the one to use in this situation. This event allows @Function formulas or LotusScript instructions, depending on the designer's preference. The idea is to create a formula or script that automatically puts this document into the ($Alarms) folder when a user opens the document to read it.

A relatively simple @Function formula can accomplish the task.

```
@IF(@Now > $AlarmTime | @IsNewDoc; @Return(""); "");
@Command([Folder]; "($Alarms)"; "0");
@CheckAlarms;
```

The purpose of the first line is to short-circuit the entire formula and exit early via the @Return function if either the alarm time has already passed or if this is a new document.

The second line places the current document into the ($Alarms) folder. Because folders do not inherently allow duplicates, it does not hurt if this function gets executed multiple times: once for each time the document is opened and read before the alarm occurs.

The final line is an @Function new to Notes 4.5, designed especially for alarm management. The @CheckAlarms function nudges the alarm daemon, forcing it to see if any alarm-related information has changed that it should take note of.

 Anytime information related to an alarm is added, deleted, or changed, it is good practice to call the @CheckAlarms function.

A companion to @CheckAlarms might also need to be used at least once to enable the whole concept of alarms within Notes in the first place. The command @EnableAlarms("1") sets the appropriate Notes.ini variable needed to awaken the alarm daemon and start the whole alarm-watching process. Executing this function once, probably early in the process, ensures that any ensuing alarms work successfully.

Because the previously listed code resides in the PostOpen event, it won't be executed until the document itself is opened. Because you are mailing this document into the mail file of the user, it displays as new mail; so the chances are good that it will be opened once anyway. If you deem necessary, additional measures can be taken. You might want to temporarily change whatever information is displaying within the calendar to a tantalizing "Double-click for this event" to encourage your users to open the document.

One last @Command should be mentioned in the form-related considerations context. The [FindFreeTimeDialog] causes the Free Time dialog box to display, allowing your users to search for a suitable time when all necessary parties, rooms, and resources are available. It has a long list of parameters, as follows:

```
@Command([FindFreeTimeDialog]; RequiredAttendees; OptionalAttendees;
➥RequiredRooms; OptionalRooms; RequiredResources; OptionalResources;
➥RemovedAttendees; StartDateTime; EndDateTime)
```

Summary

People tend to think of date and time values better in the context of a calendar, enabling each to view his commitments at a glance to see just how busy he is about to be. This chapter has introduced you to the Calendaring and Scheduling building blocks now available within Lotus Notes 4.5 and has offered some insight into using those in your database. The first section discussed what you need to know about calendars from the perspective of a Notes view, including new view properties, calendar-specific @Functions, and view events.

Then, the next section introduced you to several calendar-related considerations to keep in mind from the viewpoint of the Notes form you used to create your calendar entries.

At the end, there was a brief discussion about alarms, the alarm daemon, and some suggested @Functions to use if you are considering integrating alarm capabilities into your calendar entries.

The addition of the Calendar view interface along with the new time-related capabilities in Notes forms enables you to track information within Notes in a familiar and helpful calendar format.

PART III

Notes 4.5 Basic
Adminstration

CHAPTER 5

Selecting an Operating System

One of the great advantages of using Lotus Notes is that you can select from a number of different operating systems. Which platform you select, however, can be quite important to the success of Lotus Notes in your company. This chapter discusses hardware considerations and compares operating systems that the Domino server supports. You will also gain additional knowledge about other hardware and software considerations such as U.P.S. devices, virus protection utilities, and others.

Chances are you will select a platform your company is familiar with. If you have had years of experience with Novell, for example, you likely will want to use the NLM version of Lotus Notes (even if it is viewed as the most difficult). In the past, the Iris Group at Lotus developed Notes in OS/2 (although the first release was written in DOS). Today, 4.x versions are developed in NT initially and then developed in other operating systems.

If you are currently debating which operating system is ideal for your company, this chapter will get you thinking about your current or future Lotus Notes topology.

Selecting just one platform undoubtedly makes configuring and administering company servers much easier. When an administrator is not available at one site, another administrator may be able to step in (perhaps even over the phone) to assist with server problems. If you have expertise and cross training for multiple operating systems, however, Lotus Notes provides the capability to have many different operating systems. You also have the options of Unix machines, AS/400, Intel, or Alpha. As you select a platform, consider the following:

◆ Cost of the initial purchase and upgrades.

◆ Current platforms commonly used in your company today.

◆ Employee skill-level match for various operating systems. You might gather this through a survey that inquires workers about their experience with each platform.

◆ Current and future supported platforms of Lotus products that you intend to use, such as fax gateways, MTAs (message transfer agents), and others.

◆ Protocol(s) you intend to use.

◆ Third-party software (firewalls, network drivers, backup utilities, and so on) available for the platform you are considering. (This should include hardware as well as the operating system.)

◆ Remote manageability.

◆ Ease of installation and configuration of the various operating systems.

◆ Availability of outside sources to assist you with deployment and configuration of the operating system.

The following operating systems are not supported with Lotus Domino server 4.5:

◆ HP-UX 9.04 and 9.05

◆ IBM AIX 3.2.5 and earlier versions

◆ OS/2 2.1 and earlier versions

◆ Microsoft Windows 3.1 and earlier versions

◆ Microsoft Windows NT 3.5

Hardware Considerations

The type of hardware you purchase, in many ways, will be dictated by the type of operating system that is right for your company. It is important to think ahead, however, and to prepare for the growth of your Lotus Notes environment. You should try to select machines that allow for expansion of memory, processors, and disk space (or implementation of RAID drives). Also, don't forget about the footprint (size) of the machine. You should measure your server room to make sure that the machine will fit in the desired space allotted. If at all possible, you should also try to use the same manufacturer for your servers (and the workstations too). This makes understanding the system and upgrades a little easier. You only have to use one support number, and you likely will get a volume discount.

Many Lotus Notes administrators would agree that purchasing a system to support as many people as possible is not necessarily the right approach for the success of Lotus Notes. The disadvantage of housing as many users as possible on one system is that you are creating a central point of failure. Because of the powerful and efficient features of replication, many servers can be used throughout your organization. For more information about replication, see Chapter 6, "Installing Domino 4.5 Server Software."

As you make your shopping list, be sure to take into account the following valuable items. You want to be careful to purchase an operating system and hardware that will support these features, if you intend to use them:

◆ **Remote control.** Although Lotus Notes includes many features to help manage servers remotely, you might want to purchase additional software products that grant you more control. Some of these software programs include Distributed Console Access Facility (DCAF), PolyPM/2, and PC Anywhere. NetWare includes RConsole so that you can do many operating system commands from a remote location.

◆ **Mobile solutions.** You might want to consider additional products to support mobile professionals in your organization. You might consider using a Remote Access Service (RAS) or products such as PC Anywhere, Citrix, or LapLink.

◆ **Virus utilities.** With more than 100 viruses created every day, you need a virus-checking program. Ideally, you will want one that scans all incoming messages and replications (including attachments). McAffee is a very common virus-checking utility that scans attachments in Notes.

◆ **U.P.S.** To have a sound and reliable network, you have to be prepared for disaster recovery. This includes having a U.P.S. (uninterrupted power supply).

To date there are very few U.P.S. units that "gracefully" down the Domino server before the system is taken down. PowerChute, by American Power Conversion, is a widely used U.P.S. that executes the Quit command prior to downing the server.

◆ **Backup software.** Many vendors are attempting to design backup software that back up open Lotus Notes databases and do incremental database backups. Two leading companies in this area are Cheyenne and IBM. Cheyenne makes ArcServe and IBM makes ADASM.

◆ **Raid drives.** Raid technology keeps your data safe in the event of a drive failure. If you want to be sure that you will still have all data, even in the event of a disk failure, Raid can provide that for you.

You can find information and stay informed by subscribing to trade magazines. Computer magazines can be a great source of information, and most will compare the many products available and make suggestions specific to platforms you might select. You can gather information about hardware, operating systems, virus utilities, backup solutions, and much more.

Hardware Recommendations for All Platforms

With each operating system that support Lotus Domino servers, you will want to use a LAN adapter that is fully compatible with supported networks, an optional color display supported by the operating system, a mouse, optional modems, and optional printers.

As your use of Notes increases, you should prepare to add RAM and disk space as needed. You will likely use about 30 MB of disk space for each mail user. Additional disk space for applications can be tough to determine. The many variables include how many applications you intend to use, the nature of the application, the amount of database it takes to use the application, and the list goes on. You should add about 1 MB more RAM for each four concurrent attached users on your system. In other words, if you have a peak of 40 users attached to the server in a typical day, you should add 10 MB of RAM. You can check for number of users by using the server command Sh Stat (which turns on periodic statistics) or Sh Task. For more information on server commands, please see the "Remote Console" section of Chapter 8, "Examing Notes 4.5 Administration Features."

Microsoft Windows 95

Although Microsoft Windows 95 has a large customer base and is very user-friendly, it is not an ideal server. Microsoft Windows 95 only supports five connections, and therefore, only five clients can attach to the server. Unless you work for a small company or a small division in a large company, it not likely you will select this as a platform to run a Domino server. Windows 95 running on a powerful desktop or laptop, however, can be an excellent combined development and testing platform—running the Domino server, the Notes client, and a Web browser at the same time.

The recommended minimum hardware of the Lotus Domino server for Windows 95 includes an 80486 processor (or better), 24 MB RAM, and 300 MB free hard-drive space (plus supported monitor, keyboard, and mouse). The recommended disk swap is 16 MB, and a printer and modem are optional.

The supported networks and protocols for Windows 95 include the following:

◆ NetBIOS

◆ Novell NetWare SPX

◆ TCP/IP

◆ X.PC

The supported Lotus Notes workstations for Windows 95 include the following:

◆ AIX 4.1.4 or 4.2

◆ HP-UX 10.01

◆ Macintosh

◆ OS/2 Warp version 4 or OS/2 Warp Connect

◆ Sun Solaris Intel Edition 2.5, or Sun SPARC Solaris 2.5 or 2.5.1

◆ Windows 3.1 or Windows for Workgroups 3.11

◆ Windows 95, or Windows NT 3.51 or 4.0

Microsoft Windows NT

Windows NT is a very stable platform that works with up to eight processors, can have multiple drives, and can handle over a thousand connections. The best features of NT are its ease of use and its compatibility with peripheral devices. The largest drawback with selecting NT is the length of time it has been in the marketplace (three years). Because the product is not yet seasoned, you will not find as many powerful features in the product (Unix will work with 30 processors, for instance), and you might not find as many add-on products (such as firewall or backup programs). These concerns might be short-lived, however, because the operating system appears to be quickly gaining tremendous market share. Windows NT is a logical choice if you are not as concerned with power as with ease of use, ease of setup, and compatibility.

As previously mentioned, Notes 4.x versions were written in Microsoft Windows NT first. In addition, Lotus has added the following features for NT:

◆ **Unified logon.** The capability to have a single logon for users.

◆ **Directory synchronization.** You can register new people in either Notes or NT and the other will automatically be populated.

◆ **NT Event logger.** Only one log file for both Notes and NT.

The recommended minimum hardware of the Lotus Domino server for Windows NT 3.51 or 4.0 includes an 80486 processor or better, 64 MB RAM, and 500 MB free disk space (plus supported monitor, keyboard, and mouse). Partitioned servers need an additional 24 MB RAM and 100 MB for each additional server. The recommended disk swap size (for paging) is 64 MB. You also can have accessible printers and modems, if desired.

Supported networks and protocols for Windows NT include the following:

◆ AppleTalk

◆ Banyan VINES (not Windows NT/Alpha)

◆ NetBIOS

◆ Novell NetWare SPX

◆ TCP/IP

◆ Lotus Notes Connect for SNA version 3.0a on OS/2

◆ X.PC

◆ X.25

Supported Lotus Notes workstations with Windows NT include the following:

◆ AIX 4.1.4 or 4.2

◆ HP-UX 10.01

◆ Macintosh

◆ OS/2 Warp version 4 or OS/2 Warp Connect

◆ Sun Solaris Intel Edition 2.5, or Sun SPARC Solaris 2.5 or 2.5.1

◆ Windows 3.1 or Windows for Workgroups 3.11

◆ Windows 95, or Windows NT 3.51 or 4.0

OS/2

IBM OS/2 is obviously the preferred platform in IBM as well as many school systems. Many select OS/2 because it is a graphical environment and because of the old saying "Nobody ever got fired for buying IBM." One of the biggest drawbacks of OS/2 is its instability. Certainly in OS/2 2.1, the server would frequently crash (a HEX dump) on many occasions for no obvious reason. This was a guaranteed event if you launched the client software prior to launching the server task. Additionally, it can be tough to configure and difficult to find support for OS/2 drivers and additional peripherals.

The recommended minimum hardware of the Lotus Domino server for OS/2 includes an 80486 processor or better, 48 MB RAM, 500 MB unused disk space, 16 MB disk swap file space, a monitor, a keyboard, and a mouse. A modem and printer are optional.

The Domino server for OS/2 runs with the following network protocols:

◆ AppleTalk (not on OS/2 Warp Server SMP)

◆ Banyan VINES (not on OS/2 Warp Server SMP)

◆ NetBIOS

◆ NetWare SPX on OS/2 (not on OS/2 Warp Server SMP)

◆ TCP/IP

◆ Lotus Notes Connect for SNA version 3.0a on OS/2

◆ X.PC

◆ X.25

Workstations that can connect to the OS/2 server include the following:

- AIX 4.1.4 or 4.2

- HP-UX 10.01

- Macintosh

- OS/2 Warp version 4 or OS/2 Warp Connect

- Sun Solaris Intel Edition 2.5, or Sun SPARC Solaris 2.5 or 2.5.1

- Windows 3.1 or Windows for Workgroups 3.11

- Windows 95, or Windows NT 3.51 or 4.0

Unix, IBM AIX, HP-UX, and Sun Solaris

If you are searching for a powerful, reliable system and money is no object, Unix is an obvious choice. Unix has often proven to be the most sound and stable server environment (not just with Lotus Notes). Unix is widely used in many school systems today and is the primary backbone for the Internet. This operating system can work with up to 30 processors, support multiple hard drives, and provide clustering for fail-over (to another, available server).

If you are not already familiar with this operating system, however, there can be quite a learning curve to become familiar with the environment. Even with GUI versions of the operating system, many of the commands are still text-based. As a colleague once put it, "This is a seriously geeky OS." In addition, Unix machines typically have a very large footprint (size). You should be sure you have enough floor space to accommodate the machine.

One other point about the Unix system bears mentioning. The Iris Group at Lotus must rewrite code for all three flavors of Unix. Because of this, add-in products are rarely written exclusively (if at all) for Unix operating systems.

AIX

The recommended minimum hardware of the Lotus Domino server for AIX includes an IBM RISC System/6000, 128 MB RAM, 500 MB free disk space, a monitor, a keyboard, and a mouse. Partitioned servers require 64 MB RAM and 100 MB fixed disk for each additional server.

Supported network protocols with AIX include the following:

- ◆ IPX/SPX for AIX V2.1 or AIX Connections version 4.1 (SPX II)

- ◆ TCP/IP (native)

- ◆ X.PC protocol (supplied with the Domino software)

Supported Lotus Notes workstations with AIX include the following:

- ◆ AIX 4.1.4 or 4.2

- ◆ HP-UX 10.01

- ◆ Macintosh

- ◆ OS/2 Warp version 4 or OS/2 Warp Connect

- ◆ Solaris Intel 2.5, or Sun SPARC Solaris 2.5 or 2.5.1

- ◆ Windows 3.1 or Windows for Workgroups 3.11

- ◆ Windows 95, or Windows NT 3.51 or 4.0

HP-UX

The recommended minimum hardware of the Lotus Domino server for HP-UX includes a HP 9000 Series, 128 MB RAM, 500 MB fixed disk space, and 128 MB disk swap space (plus a supported monitor, keyboard, and mouse). Partitioned servers require an additional 64 MB RAM and 100 MB disk space for each server.

Supported network protocols with HP-UX include the following:

- ◆ NetWare 3.12 for the HP 9000 with SPX stack for 10.04 (SPX II)

- ◆ TCP/IP (native)

- ◆ X.PC protocol (supplied with the Domino software)

Supported Lotus Notes workstations HP-UX include the following:

- ◆ AIX 4.1.4 or 4.2

- ◆ HP-UX 10.01

- ◆ Macintosh

- ◆ OS/2 Warp version 4 or OS/2 Warp Connect

- ◆ Sun Solaris Intel Edition 2.5, or Sun SPARC Solaris 2.5 or 2.5.1

- ◆ Windows 3.1 or Windows for Workgroups 3.11

- ◆ Windows 95, or Windows NT 3.51 or 4.0

Sun Solaris

The recommended minimum hardware of the Lotus Domino server for Sun Solaris includes a Sun SPARC system, 128 MB RAM, 500 MB fixed disk space, and 128 MB disk swap space (plus a supported monitor, keyboard, and mouse). Partitioned servers require an additional 64 MB RAM and 100 MB disk space for each server.

The Lotus Domino server for Solaris runs with the following network protocols:

- ◆ Connect/NW 2.0

- ◆ TCP/IP (native)

- ◆ X.PC protocol (supplied with the Domino software)

The Domino server for Solaris can connect to Lotus Notes workstations running on the following platforms:

- ◆ AIX 4.1.4 or 4.2

- ◆ HP-UX 10.01

- ◆ Macintosh

- ◆ OS/2 Warp version 4 or OS/2 Warp Connect

- ◆ Sun Solaris Intel Edition 2.5, or Sun SPARC Solaris 2.5 or 2.5.1

- ◆ Windows 3.1 or Windows for Workgroups 3.11

- ◆ Windows 95, or Windows NT 3.51 or 4.0

NetWare NLM

Because of the large customer base and age of NetWare, many administrators select the NLM version of Lotus Domino. Novell has a large customer base and has been on the market for more than 13 years. One major drawback of this OS is that the work-station software is not present directly on the system. You must have an additional system to administer the server.

Recommended minimum hardware for the NetWare File Server includes an 80486 processor, 96 MB RAM, 500 MB free disk space (plus a supported monitor, keyboard, and mouse).

 Note It is not possible to load and use workstation software directly on a NetWare Domino server. To install the Domino server for NetWare, therefore, you need two separate machines. The Notes for NetWare Administration client must map a drive to the file server that hosts the Domino server and utilizes the Notes.ini file that is also used by the Domino server.

The Lotus Domino server for NetWare runs with the following network protocols:

◆ AppleTalk

◆ IPX/SPX

◆ TCP/IP

◆ X.PC

Supported workstations with NetWare include the following:

◆ Macintosh

◆ OS/2 Warp version 4 or OS/2 Warp Connect

◆ Windows 3.1 or Windows for Workgroups 3.11

◆ Windows 95, or Windows NT 3.51 or 4.0

Purchasing Lotus Domino

After you have finished purchasing all the items needed to support your Domino server, you are off to purchase the Domino server software. As you purchase the Lotus Domino server, you might consider purchasing an Advanced Services License for your systems. With a Lotus Domino Advanced Services License, you gain three primary server enhancements:

◆ Domino server clusters

◆ Partitioned servers

◆ Billing features

Note Domino partitioned servers are supported only on Windows NT Intel and Alpha, and Unix.

A *Domino cluster* is a group of up to six Domino servers in the same domain connected by a local area network. A Domino partitioned server shares the resources of a single computer with other Domino servers. The Domino billing feature enables a Domino server to track system usage. The Domino billing server task collects this information and records the data for billing processes. For more information about advanced servers, see the "Advanced Services" section of Chapter 8.

Domino Server.Planner

You now have a good understanding of the basic requirements to run Domino servers in various operating systems. But, you likely will also want to know what kind of equipment will be needed if you have a large volume of users. To help you plan your Lotus Notes server equipment purchasing, Lotus has a capacity planning tool. As shown in figure 5.1, this feature is available at the Lotus Web site (www.notes.net) and is called Domino Server.Planner.

From the www.notes.net site, select Downloads, Other Downloads. Then choose Domino Server.Planner.

Although this software is in the early stages of development, it should prove to be a very powerful decision-maker for many that make decisions on the purchase of equipment. The main elements of the tool are Bench.EXE and NotesNum.EXE. The data set is contained within NotesNum.EXE. A probe task, which opens and closes a database within one to five seconds, also is used in analyzing hardware. Bench.EXE compares the data set with the specifications you are currently considering. With this tool, you can compare what you think you might purchase against certified testing done by the hardware vendor. Lotus certifies the results, so you can be sure this tool is accurate. The tool is designed so you can enter the desired version of Domino, the operating system, and hardware specifications (memory, fixed disk, processor, and so on) and compare this to a database of testing on that machine. The results will aid you in making your decision for a platform.

After you have the software, you can query on data as shown in figure 5.2.

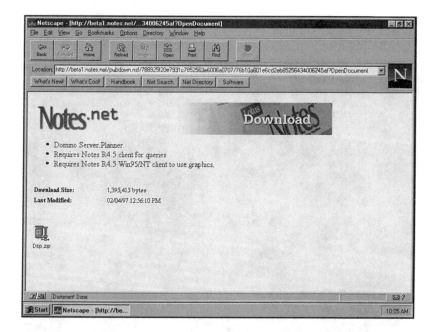

Figure 5.1

*Download
Domino
Server.Planner—
a hardware
analysis tool.*

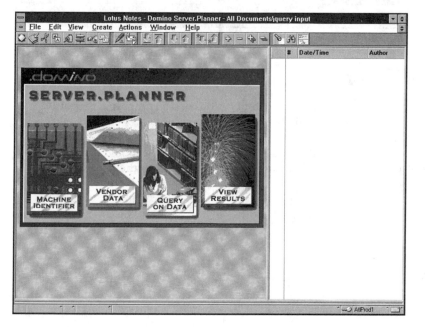

Figure 5.2

*Main navigator
for Domino
Server.Planner.*

An example of a query is shown in figure 5.3. Notice that you can select the type of server, the preferred response time, and the operating system you will be using.

Figure 5.3

Example document used to query in Domino Server.Planner.

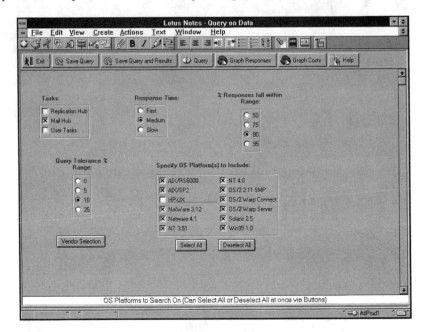

Summary

In this chapter, you have discovered the implications of using multiple platforms versus one. You have also been enlightened as to what purchases may be needed as you develop your Lotus Notes network. You discovered the recommended hardware configurations for all possible Domino operating systems. Finally, you learned about a planning tool and how to perform a query on analysis by hardware vendors.

CHAPTER 6

Installing Domino 4.5 Server Software

The primary focus of this chapter is to explore issues with installing a Domino 4.5 server. You will first see a fundamentals section on topics you may have been exposed to during training or general administration of a Notes server. This section acts a refresher for any administrator that does not have in-depth experience with administration tasks in previous versions of Lotus Notes. You will then see information about installing a Domino server. Last, you will see details on how to secure your server and grant or deny access to various features of a Domino server.

Fundamentals of Domino Server Administration

This section focuses on basic Domino server adminstration. The topics here should help you remember general topics you may have learned in a class but perhaps did not use right away. You will see information about mail routing, Noted Names Networks, replication, full text indexing, groups, and more. If you have been administrating a Lotus Notes server every day for more than a year, you likely do not need much of the information contained in this first section.

Replication

The transmission of data (replication) in Lotus Notes has been unmatched by any other groupware product. Replication is the process of synchronizing data between databases, and can take place between servers or workstations. As a database is replicated, each new or changed database element is sent to the same database on another workstation or server. These databases are defined as the same because they share a common replica ID. The ID can be found in either the catalog.nsf file on a server or by exploring the properties of the database. You can find a replica ID by using File, Database, Properties, i tab as shown in figure 6.1.

Figure 6.1

The Properties menu.

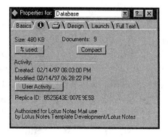

Replication in 4.x is done at the field level. Doing so reduces replication conflicts and the amount of time required (as much as four times what was seen in version 3.x).

Forcing Replication

You can force replication from the workspace or from a server with a server console command. From a workstation, you replicate in the background with the last server replicated with, or your can replicate with options (see fig. 6.2). The Replicate with options selection enables you to choose a different server and choose to send documents from the server, receive documents from the server, or both. For more information about workstation replication, see the "Laptop" section of Chapter 7, "Installing Lotus Notes 4.5 Client Software."

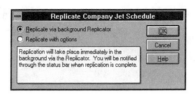

Figure 6.2

*Forcing
replication.*

You can force replication with a server by issuing the command Rep <*servername*> from the server console or the remote console. For more information about server commands, see the "Remote Console" section of Chapter 8, "Examining Notes 4.5 Administration Features."

Document Conflicts

Conflicts occur with documents in one of two ways:

◆ Save conflicts

◆ Replica conflicts

A *save conflict* occurs when two individuals edit the same document on the same server at the same time. The first person to save the document does not receive an error. The second person receives the message shown in figure 6.3.

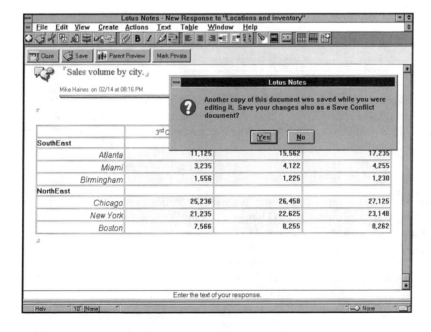

Figure 6.3

Save conflict.

If the person selects No, the changes are not saved and he or she must reopen the changed (by the other user) document to enter his or her changes again.

If the individual selects Yes, a document appears as a reply to the original. As seen in figure 6.4, the view contains the following message:

```
[Replication or Save Conflict]
```

Figure 6.4

Conflict in view.

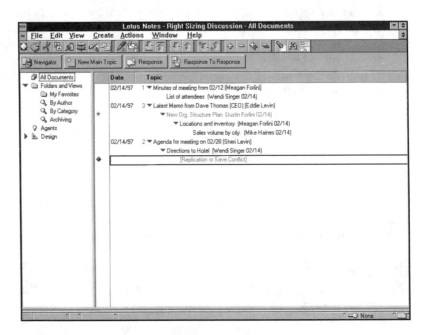

A *replication conflict* occurs when the same document is stored and edited on different servers, and then the databases are replicated. The document with the most changes does not get altered. Other versions of the document appear as replies to the original document with the following message in the view:

```
[Replication or Save Conflict]
```

Replication conflicts are a rare occurrence in most companies because an end user must have better than Author Access to change a document that he or she did not create. For more information about Access Control Lists, please see the section about Access Control Lists in Chapter 11, "Securing Your Notes and Domino 4.5 System." Additionally, it is rare that a document is changed by more than one person within a replication cycle. Finally, in Notes 4.x, replication conflicts can be reduced significantly.

As shown in figure 6.5, you can use the Merge Replication Conflicts feature on a Form Definition. This feature avoids replication conflicts by merging a document changed in two different locations (in different fields) so that it remains one document. For example, Mitzi Greenblatt and Sheri Levin are on different servers working with the New Riders profile document. Mitzi changes the address field and Sheri changes the phone number field. Because Merge Replication Conflicts is turned on, and because they both used different fields, the "two" documents merge to become one.

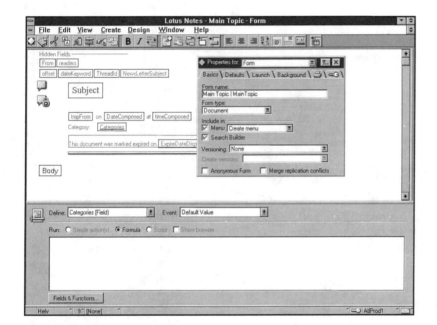

Figure 6.5

Merge Replication Conflicts feature.

Notes Named Networks

Notes Named Networks (NNN) are essentially groups of servers that share the same protocol and same physical location. Of all the essential elements in a Lotus Notes environment, this is the easiest to change. As you can see in figure 6.6, defining a Notes Named Network is done simply by changing a line on the server document in the Public Name & Address Book.

Figure 6.6

Server record.

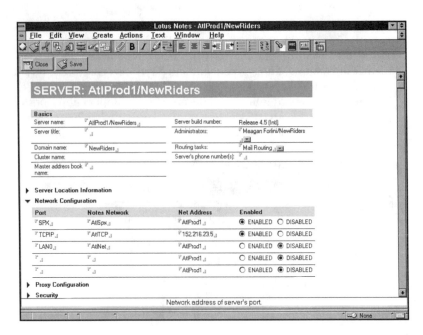

When servers are in the same NNN (and same domain), no mail Connection records are needed, which means that mail routes automatically. Additionally, when an end user chooses File, Database Open, only the server in the same Named Network appears in the menu. Other servers are accessible, but the user has to type the name of the server. Typically, an NNN specifies the location and protocol that is in use. For instance, SPXSF might be SPX in the San Francisco area (see fig. 6.7.)

Figure 6.7

Example of Notes Named Networks.

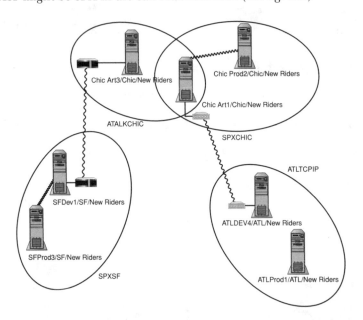

Mail Routing

Each server runs a process called Router. As a person composes and sends a message, the router looks in the address book to find which server the person uses as a Home Server. If the servers are in the same Notes Named Network and domain, the message is delivered to the destination server. If the servers are in different Notes Named Networks, the router then checks Connection records in the address book to find the cheapest route to the final destination. The cost of routing is determined by the number you assign to the Routing Cost field of the Connection record.

Messaging

Lotus Notes messaging consists of the following components:

- ◆ Mailer
- ◆ Router
- ◆ Mail.box
- ◆ Person records and Server records
- ◆ Connection records

Mailer

Mailer is the process of a Lotus Notes client sending a message to a Domino server. If the user is attached to the server, the type ahead feature of Mailer attempts to find the recipient from the Public Name & Address Book. A laptop owner can also use the Public Name & Address Book while not attached to the server (see the "Laptop" section in Chapter 7).

Router

The Router task loads by default on every server. The Notes.INI file launches the task from the line SERVERTASKS=Router, Replica, and so on. For more information on the Notes.INI file, please see the "Notes.ini" section of this chapter. The router works to find the recipient's mail file by looking in the Public Name & Address Book for the Mail Server field in the Person record.

Mail.Box

A mail.box file is found on every server that has the router process loaded. The mail.box file receives all new mail whether from another server or a workstation. It functions as a system similar to a post office. As the router determines how to locate the recipient, the mail message resides in the pending view of the mail.box file (see fig. 6.8).

Figure 6.8

Mail box view.

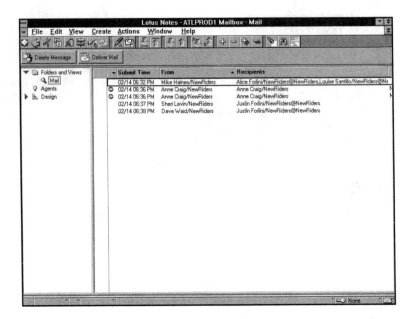

After the router determines a path to the recipient, the message is removed by the router. Because the mail file is constantly receiving documents and having them deleted, the file is in need of compacting from time to time. The server process compacts the mail file for you each day around 4:00 a.m., as shown in the following listing:

```
04:00:04 AM  Router: Shutdown is in progress
04:00:04 AM  Router: Beginning mailbox file compaction
04:00:05 AM  Router: Completed mailbox file compaction
```

Connection Records

A Connection record contains information that the router needs to send mail to other servers. The Connection record contains the fully distinguished server name, the port to be used during connection, and the times when the server can be reached. As you can see in figure 6.9, the Connection records can be used for mail routing and replication.

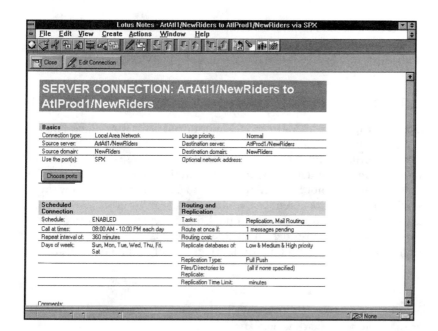

Figure 6.9

The Connection record.

Domain

A domain is defined as all Notes servers sharing a common Public Name & Address Book. The Public Name & Address Book is the single most important database in the Lotus Notes environment. This database determines mail routing, security, replication schedules, server configurations, and many other functions. Most companies have only one PNAB and it is created during the creation of the first server.

When launching a Lotus Domino server for the first time in any company, you are presented with an option for First Server or an additional server. A new Public Name & Address Book is created if you select First Server. If you select additional server, you are replicating the address book from another server in the domain.

Domains are mostly tied to mail routing. When a user sends a message from outside of your company, he or she addresses it using an @ Symbol. The name placed after the @ symbol is the domain for your company. The are generally only a couple of reasons to have multiple domains: you have a very large company (more than 100,000 users), you have a test server for development of databases, or you have a connection server to outside companies.

Having one domain in your company can simplify administration of servers as well as make mail routing more efficient and easier on your users.

The Public Name & Address Book is the most important database in your Lotus Notes environment. With this use of this database, you determine mail routing, replication, security, server changes, cross certification, and many other functions.

Full Text Indexing

The full text indexing capability in Notes creates an index of every word in every document in a single database. This index then provides a very fast method of searching for specific terms in the database. Full text indexing gives you the ability to search for keywords in a document using multiple criteria Boolean searches. If you search a database that is not full text indexed, you can search for words within a view or search through each document in the same way a word processor searches. You can create full text indexes for a database on a Domino server or you can create a full text index for a database that resides on a workstation or laptop. Typically, full text index searches are more efficient on a Domino server rather than on a local system.

 Note When a full text index is created, a new directory (with an .ft extension) is created in the same directory where the database exists.

To create a full text index, select a database and then choose File, Tools, Properties. From the Full Text tab, select Create Index. The Full Text Create Index dialog box appears (see fig. 6.10).

Figure 6.10

The Full Text Create Index dialog box.

The options of this menu are defined as follows:

◆ **Case sensitive index.** To search for case-sensitive data, enable this option. Plan on about 10 percent more disk space used.

◆ **Index attachments.** If the database contains attachments (spreadsheets, word processing documents, and so forth), enable this option to search within the supported document types. This can be a large increase in the size of the index, depending on how many attachments you are using in the database.

◆ **Index encrypted fields.** Encryption is a security feature that prevents individuals from seeing fields unless they possess a key distributed by the developer.

◆ **Exclude words in Stop Word file.** A Stop Word file contains items that you typically would not search for (such as articles or prepositions). Not using this feature would result in about a 30 percent increase in the size of the index and the disk space used on your server.

Groups

Groups define mailing lists as well as security. When mail is being addressed from a workstation, it can be addressed to an individual or a group. If a group name is typed, the mail is sent to all the people in that group. Groups can also be used to determine rights for server access, server privileges, Access Control Lists, and others. For more information about groups and security, please see the section on groups in Chapter 11. As shown in figure 6.11, groups can be four different types:

Figure 6.11

Group types.

◆ **Multi-purpose.** This group type can be used for both mail routing and access control.

◆ **Access Control List only.** A group of this type cannot be used for mail routing, it is used for security only.

◆ **Mail only.** This type of group is reserved as an electronic mail distribution list only.

◆ **Deny List only.** A group of this type is designed to deny access to your server. A separate view houses these groups (Server/Deny Access Only).

Note   Changing the group type to something other than Multi-purpose makes your server more efficient, particularly when mail routing. Doing so causes the views for security and mail to contain smaller indexes because fewer groups are contained within them.

Cross Certification

When IDs are created in different organizations, they do not possess the same certifier for authentication. For instance, the following IDs do not have the capability to authenticate each other when first created:

◆   Hub1/ATL/Oil

◆   Hub1/ATL/H2O

Through the process of cross certification, these IDs can have the capability to communicate. You can create cross certificates one of two ways. One, you can physically swap safe copies of server IDs or Certifiers between the companies. Or, you can have both servers "call" each other and create cross certificates remotely.

> **Note**   You can also cross certify IDs by reading the public keys, but we do not recommend the operation because one wrong number or letter in the Public ID string causes the process to fail.

After you receive a safe copy of an ID, you can cross certify it by using File, Tools, Server Administration. With the Administration Panel open, select Certifiers, Cross Certify ID File. You are then prompted for the certifier ID and then the ID to be certified (the safe copy). As shown in figure 6.12, you can change the expiration date of this certification.

Figure 6.12

The Cross Certify ID dialog box.

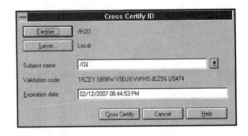

After the IDs are cross certified, a document exists in the Server, Certificates view of the Public Name & Address Book.

Companies that started with Lotus Notes version 1 or 2 may still have flat (non-hierarchical) naming. A flat name does not have any forward slashes (/). When two companies want to communicate, they must share a third certificate in common. To accomplish this, a third non-hierarchical certifier ID must be made. To do so, follow these steps:

1. Choose File, Tools, Server Administration.

2. Select Certifiers, Register Non-Hierarchical (see fig. 6.13).

Figure 6.13

Creating a non-hierarchical ID.

3. You can call the certifier anything using letters and numbers.

4. Using the new ID, select Certifiers, Certify ID File for both IDs. If you are using r3, you should select File, Administration, Certify ID.

Explanation of Document Deletions

When documents are deleted from a database, two things occur:

◆ White space exists where the documents are removed.

◆ Deletion stubs are created for each document that is deleted.

White Space

White space is used as new documents are added again to the database. These new documents are not likely to be in contiguous space. Therefore, if you do not add more documents to a database or you want to better utilize space in a database, you should compact the file. Compacting can be done with an individual file or many files at once. To compact an individual file, you can highlight any database and then select File, Database, Properties. Then use the i tab to select Compact.

With version 4.5, this task takes place in the background, even on a workstation. Compact requires enough disk space to copy the file to another location on the fixed disk temporarily.

To schedule Compact, you can use a Program document in your Public Name & Address Book. The Program document launches the Compact process at the time desired. You may also have Compact run automatically on the server by adding it to one of the ServerTasksAt# lines in the server's Notes.ini file.

I recommend that you do database compaction on Sundays or on your least busy day. Compaction can take time and resources on your server, and if you run the task at a peak time, end-users will notice the server running more slowly. Additionally, databases cannot be used while being compacted.

Deletion Stubs

Deletion stubs exist in a database to inform the next replica copy to delete the document as well (see fig. 6.14).

Figure 6.14

Illustration of document deletions.

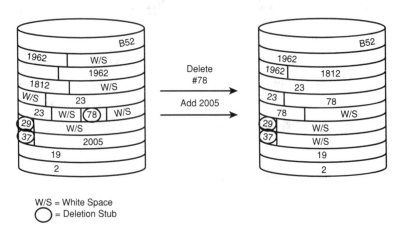

Deletion stubs take up a small amount of space in a database, and eventually you should remove these stubs. Stubs are removed based on the purge interval setting. The purge interval setting can be found by using File, Replication, Settings. As shown in figure 6.15, the first menu you see is for Space Savers.

Figure 6.15

Replication settings for right sizing discussion database.

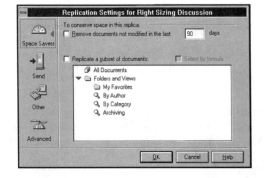

At the top of this menu is a line that reads "Remove documents not modified in the last." This line actually has two purposes. When the option is on, the server periodically removes documents. Whether this option is on or not, it is also the purge interval setting for the database. The number found in the box to the right of this message is three times the purge interval. The default number is 90 days and therefore the purge interval is 30 days. If the option is turned on, a new document would be deleted in 90 days (assuming the document is not modified). In another 30 days, the deletion stub for the same document would then be removed. All replicas of the database should replicate at least once during each purge interval so that all deletions will take place in every replica of the database.

Notes.ini

The Notes.ini file contains configuration information for servers and workstations. This file is typically found in the Notes subdirectory (c:\notes). Many options can be changed in this file. However, it is generally better to use menus for these options if they exist. For instance, you can set up modems in this file or by using the Ports menu in the workspace. There is far less room for error by using the menu. It is rare that there is not a menu or graphical option to change most settings in your Notes.ini. The following is an example of a Notes.ini file:

```
[Notes]
KitType=2
Directory=c:\notes\data
WinNTIconPath=c:\notes\data\W32
$$HasLANPort=1
Preferences=8916081
Passthru_LogLevel=0
Console_LogLevel=2
VIEWIMP1=Lotus 1-2-3 Worksheet,0,_IWKSV,,.WKS,.WK1,.WR1,.WRK,.WK3,.WK4,
VIEWIMP3=Structured Text,0,_ISTR,,.LTR,.CGN,.STR,
VIEWIMP4=Tabular Text,0,_ITAB,,.PRN,.RPT,.TXT,.TAB,
VIEWEXP1=Lotus 1-2-3 Worksheet,0,_XWKS,,.WKS,.WK1,.WR1,.WRK,
VIEWEXP3=Structured Text,0,_XSTR,,.LTR,.CGN,.STR,
VIEWEXP4=Tabular Text,1,_XTAB,,.LTR,.RPT,.CGN,.TAB,
EDITIMP1=ASCII Text,0,_ITEXT,,.TXT,.PRN,.C,.H,.RIP,
EDITIMP2=Microsoft Word RTF,0,_IRTF,,.DOC,.RTF,
EDITIMP3=Lotus 1-2-3 Worksheet,0,_IWKSE,,.WKS,.WK1,.WR1,.WRK,.WK3,.WK4,
EDITIMP4=Lotus PIC,0,_IPIC,,.PIC,
EDITIMP5=CGM Image,0,_IFL,,.GMF,.CGM,
EDITIMP6=TIFF 5.0 Image,0,_ITIFF,,.TIF,
EDITIMP7=BMP Image,0,_IBMP,,.BMP,
EDITIMP8=Ami Pro,0,_IW4W,W4W33F/V0,.SAM,
```

```
EDITIMP17=WordPerfect 5.x,0,_IW4W,W4W07F/V1,.DOC,
EDITIMP22=PCX Image,0,_IPCX,,.PCX,
EDITIMP28=Binary with Text,0,_ISTRNGS,,.*,
EDITIMP29=WordPerfect 6.0/6.1,0,_IW4W,W4W48F/V0,.WPD,.WPT,.DOC,
EDITIMP30=Excel 4.0/5.0,0,_IW4W,W4W21F/V4C,.XLS,
EDITIMP31=Word for Windows 6.0,0,_IW4W,W4W49F/V0,.DOC,
EDITIMP32=GIF Image,0,_IGIF,,.GIF,
EDITIMP33=JPEG Image,0,_IJPEG,,.JPG,
EDITEXP1=ASCII Text,2,_XTEXT,,.TXT,.PRN,.C,.H,.RIP,
EDITEXP2=Microsoft Word RTF,2,_XRTF,,.DOC,.RTF,
EDITEXP3=CGM Image,2,_XCGM,,.CGM,.GMF,
EDITEXP4=TIFF 5.0 Image,2,_XTIFF,,.TIF,
EDITEXP5=Ami Pro,2,_XW4W,W4W33T/V0,.SAM,
EDITEXP14=WordPerfect 5.1,2,_XW4W,W4W07T/V1,.DOC,
EDITEXP21=WordPerfect 6.0,2,_XW4W,W4W48T/V0,.DOC,
EDITEXP22=WordPerfect 6.1,2,_XW4W,W4W48T/V1,.WPD,.WPT,.DOC,
EDITEXP23=Word for Windows 6.0,2,_XW4W,W4W49T/V0,.DOC,
DDETimeout=10
NAMEDSTYLE0=020042617369630000000000000000000000000000000000000000000000000000
00000000101010010000A0000000000000100A0050000A005000000000000000000000000000000
00000000000000000000000000000000000000000000000000000000000000000000000000
NAMEDSTYLE1=020042756C6C6574000000000000000000000000000000000000000000000000000
00000001010100000A000000000000000008070000080700000000000000000000000000000000
00000000000000000000000000000000000000000000000040000000000000000000
NAMEDSTYLE2=0200486561646C696E65000000000000000000000000000000000000000000000000
00000000010101010B0C000000000000100A0050000A005000000000000000000000000000000
00000000000000000000000000000000000000000000000000000000000000000000000000
$$$OpenSpecial=NotesNIC, InterNotes
$$$NotesNIC=CN=Home/OU=Notes/O=NET, welcome.nsf, Notes NIC Welcome, Notes
Network Information Center on the Internet
ServerTasks=Replica,Router,Update,Stats,AMgr,Adminp,Sched,CalConn
ServerTasksAt1=Catalog,Design
ServerTasksAt2=UpdAll,Object Collect mailobj.nsf
ServerTasksAt5=Statlog
SPX=NWSPX, 0, 15, 0
TCPIP=TCP,0,15,0,,12288,
LAN0=NETBIOS, 0, 15, 0
VINES=VINES, 0, 15, 0
AppleTalk=ATALK, 0, 15, 0
COM1=XPC,1,15,0,
COM2=XPC,2,15,0,
COM3=XPC,3,15,0,
COM4=XPC,4,15,0,
COM5=XPC,5,15,0,
```

```
Ports=SPX,TCPIP
DisabledPorts=LAN0,VINES,AppleTalk,COM1,COM2,COM3,COM4,COM5
LOG_REPLICATION=0
LOG_SESSIONS=0
ExistingServerName=CN=ATLProd1/OU=ATL/O=XLConnect
KeyFilename=server.id
CertificateExpChecked=c:\notes\data\server.id 02/14/97
MailServer=CN=AtlProd1/OU=ATL/O=NewRiders
Domain=NewRiders
Admin=ATLAdmin
TemplateSetup=2
Setup=49
ServerSetup=7
ZONE_SET=1
Timezone=5
DST=1
CertifierIDFile=A:\atl.id
ADMINWINDOWSIZE=34 48 326 453
StackedIcons=1
DESKWINDOWSIZE=17 24 420 288
MAXIMIZED=1
WinNTIconCommonConfig=Universal
WinNTIconSize=2
WinNTIconPos=2
WinNTIconHidden=0
WinNTIconRect=-1 -1 641 25
Win32InfoboxPos=97 128
FileDlgDirectory=C:\NOTES\data
EmptyTrash=0
SDI_WINDOW=0
EnableJavaApplets=0
PhoneLog=2
Log=log.nsf, 1, 0, 7, 40000
BCASEWINDOWSIZE=17 24 420 288
CONSOLE_Lotus_Notes_Server=80 25 7 4 28 652 355
NetWareSpxSettings=0,0,0,0,0,1,24587
ECLSetup=3
NAMES=names.nsf
WeekStart=1
SPELL_DIR=c:\notes\data
CONSOLE_Lotus_Domino_Server=80 25 7 4 21 652 348
EnablePlugins=1
TCPIP_TcpConnectTimeout=0,5
AddInMenus=D:\SENTINEL\DIPROF32.DLL
```

Some key points about this file:

◆ KitType is used to notify Notes whether the system is a server or a workstation. KitType=1 is a workstation. KitType=2 is a server.

◆ Directory= is used to advise Notes of the locations of the working data directory.

◆ WinNTIconPath= is used to determine where the smart icons reside.

◆ The ServerTasks= line is used for all constantly running processes on the server that will start automatically when the server starts.

◆ With ServerTasksAtX=, you can set up tasks to run at certain times in the evening. By default, you have Design, Update, Object Collect, and Catalog assigned. For more information about these events, see Chapter 8, "Examining Notes 4.5 Administration Features."

◆ Notice that the preceding listing includes several lines for ports, but editing the Notes.ini file is not as handy as using the menus in the Notes Workspace.

◆ The Names= line can be used to designate Public Name & Address Books that the server should use. You can specify multiple address books here that can be used as cascading address lookups for mail routing.

This concludes information about basic Domino server administration. Now that you have been reminded of general administration techniques, you will better understand many of the chapters ahead.

Understanding Naming Conventions

Before building a Lotus Notes network in your company, many decisions need to be made. You should decide on your preferred platform, protocols, and more. Perhaps of most importance are naming conventions. You should select names of servers, a domain(s), an organization(s), and many others. These decisions should be made prior to installing and using your first server. If you do not, you may have to undo a great deal of work (re-create your servers and workstations).

The Importance of Hierarchical IDs

Prior to release 3 of Lotus Notes, the only way to distinguish like names was to use a middle initial or add a number to the name. If you had six people in your company named John Smith, you had to know what number he was or know his middle initial before you could be sure to whom you were sending mail.

Hierarchical IDs are now considered by many as a requirement. It is unlikely that flat naming will be supported in version 5.0. Lotus has given many new features to Notes IDs since version 3. Most of these features are only available if you have hierarchical IDs, because making the features available to non-hierarchical (or flat) IDs requires two to three times the effort. Some features that are only supported with hierarchical IDs include:

◆ Multiple passwords

◆ Expiring passwords

◆ Automated recertification or name changes

◆ Integration with Windows NT

Eventually, Lotus will likely no longer have support for flat (or non-hierarchical) IDs. As Lotus attempts to integrate more with third-party software manufacturers, using hierarchical IDs becomes paramount.

International or North American IDs

Before a discussion about server naming, it is also important to select your ID type. You can select one of two types: International or North American. If you are an international company (doing business outside of the U.S. or Canada), you should be prepared for traveling laptops. Because of the encryption technology reserved for use only by a North American license, it is a federal offense take a North American ID (as well as North American software) outside of the U.S. or Canada. Therefore, you should think ahead and determine which ID is most suitable. After you have determined which ID is appropriate, this also dictates the software version that you purchase.

 I have found this to be one of the most costly mistakes made by administrators. If North American IDs are created and then you change your mind, you have to reregister every laptop and change the software for all these systems as well.

Server Names

Server names should always be unique in your company. The first 16 characters of the common name for your servers must be unlike any other in your company. Using numbers in your server name is an excellent way to avoid having difficulty with duplicate server names. For instance, you may need two development servers at one branch. You might consider naming them:

- VADev1/VA/NewRiders

- VADev2/VA/NewRiders

Note Generally, names that you create should be limited to letters and numbers without spaces. The \ (backslash), , (comma), and @ (at sign) are not acceptable characters and can cause errors that are very difficult to define and correct. Although things such as the & (ampersand), - (dash), . (period), (space), _ (underscore), and ' (apostrophe) are acceptable characters, I do not recommend them. Each of these characters can make your life more unpleasant as you issue server commands, access servers or send mail.

When a first server is created in your company, two things are created: a new Public Name & Address Book and a cert.id. For an explanation of the Public Name & Address Book, see the "Domain" section of this chapter. The cert.id is crucial for an administrator. Without this ID, no other ID can be created.

Organizational Units

It is likely that you will want to take your new cert.id and create some new IDs from it. Depending on the size of your company, separating servers, departments, or regions may be paramount to the success of Lotus Notes in your company. Making these separations requires some forethought. You will want to select a division that will change the least (or you will have to reissue IDs more often). If you typically move people in your company on a regular basis, region is not a convenient choice. If you reorganize your company periodically, again location is not a good choice. After you have decided on a division, create an Organizational Unit (OU). Organizational Units further qualify server and user IDs. You can make up to four Organizational Units for use in an ID. For illustration of a typical ID hierarchy, see figure 6.16.

Figure 6.16

Example of ID hierarchy.

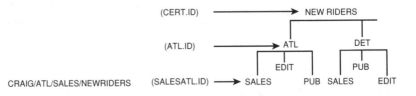

To create a sales certification ID (Sales.ID), place the diskette that contains the original certifier in drive a: (cert.id). Select File, Tools, System Administration, Certifiers, Register Organizational Unit. You are first asked to put in the password for the cert.id. Type in the name of your new Organizational Unit and a password (see fig. 6.17).

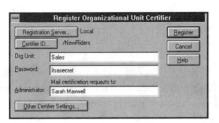

Figure 6.17

Register organizational unit.

After the cert.id is created, you can then register any new server or user ID.

Note   You would create a lot of work if a cert.id is lost. Without your cert.id, you can no longer register servers or workstations. Therefore, it is recommended that you place your cert.id on three diskettes and delete it from your server's fixed disk. The first diskette you use on a daily basis, the second diskette is kept under lock and key in your office in the event that the first diskette gets destroyed or lost. The third diskette is kept in your home (or a safe deposit box with your backup tapes) in the event that the first two diskettes are destroyed in a disaster.

Unique Organizational Units (UOU) can be made for an individual name. When you encounter the rare occurrence in which two or more people working in the same branch or department have the same name, you can use this feature to distinguish them. As shown in figure 6.18, you might consider adding an UOU called "Golfer" to John Smith's name. His ID then might be John Smith/Golfer/Sales/Chicago/NewRiders.

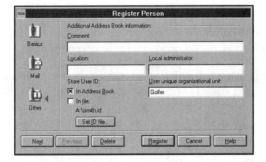

Figure 6.18

Unique Organizational Unit.

Installing the Server Software

This section addresses many aspects of a Domino server installation. You will first see pre-installation proceedures and then the installation steps. The instructions that follow are written for Microsoft Windows NT. For specific differences in operating system installations, please see the "Platform Install Differences" section of this chapter. The Domino server Install program accomplishes three primary tasks. It copies and decompresses the Domino server files and workstation files into specified directories, and updates the operating system configuration file (such as the config.sys or Notes.ini).

To use your Domino server with the Internet, the Domino server install program launches components for the InterNotes Web Navigator and the Domino Web server. However, you must complete additional configuration steps for these features. For the configuration steps and more information about Internet integration, please see Chapter 20, "Java: A New Way to Interact with Notes."

Pre-Installation

Before installing Lotus Notes on a server, take some preventive measures to make the installation process easier:

1. Determine your preferred platform (see Chapter 5, "Selecting an Operating System").

2. Determine your naming conventions and ID Types. You should decide which type of Lotus Notes licenses you are going to use and the structure of your hierarchical IDs. These decisions may have already been made elsewhere in your company. For more information, please see the "Naming Conventions" section of this chapter.

3. Make sure that the minimum required hardware, software, and network components are functional.

4. Test network cards and protocols. To test the network card of your system, see whether it is possible to log onto a file server or see your networks (such as through Network Neighborhood in Windows products or using ping with TCP/IP).

5. Make sure you close any currently running programs. Leaving applications running could prevent the Install program from copying files or updating shared files. Additionally, it is sometimes necessary to reboot during installation (depending on the platform and whether Notes has been on your system before) so you have to close the programs anyway.

6. Temporarily turn off screen savers, TSR (terminate and stay resident) programs, and virus-detection software.

7. If you are upgrading to a new release of Notes, be sure to back up any files that you may have customized (such as templates (.nft extension) or modem files (.mdm extension). Also, it is a good idea to back up your desktop.dsk, names.nsf and user.id (possibly called another name with the .id extension) files.

Main Tasks of the Install Program

The Notes Install program has three main tasks:

◆ Copying and decompressing the Notes program and data files into specified directories

◆ Updating the operating system configuration file (such as config.sys)

◆ Creating the default Notes configuration file (Notes.ini)

Distribution of Install Files

Lotus ships the Domino Release 4.5 files on CD-ROM. You can create additional CDs with a CD burner. However, you can set up installation alternatives for users without a CD-ROM. You can install from diskettes, a file server, or a shared drive.

You can create diskette images from your CD-ROM. A DISK_KIT directory is on your CD for each platform. You can copy each image directory to a corresponding diskette. You can make mirror images of your CD with a CD burner. You can then distribute the diskettes or the CD to your fellow workers. You may also want to create a software library to track your sets of diskettes and CDs.

To put the install files on a file server or shared drive, place the CD into the CD-ROM drive. If you are running NT 3.51, select File, Run from the Program Manager. If you are running Windows 95 or Windows NT 4.0, select Start, Run. You can use Browse to find:

```
drive:\win32intel\install
```

When you are prompted with the first install screen, select File server install. As shown in figure 6.19, you can use this menu to allow for node installs or complete installations.

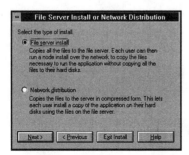

Figure 6.19

Installing on a file server.

A node install copies only needed data files to the end user's fixed disk. The executables and other program files are kept on the file server. Node installs can make it easier for you to upgrade stations in the future. This type of installation would not be logical for traveling laptops because Notes cannot be used without a file server.

 Use caution with the number of machines that you are installing at once because you can slow down your file server if you install many machines at the same time.

Installation Steps

After the files exist on the file server, you should follow these steps:

1. Be sure to read and complete the pre-installation section of this chapter before you begin the Install Program.

2. If you are using Windows 95 or Windows NT 4.0, choose Start, Run. If you are using diskettes, you can simply type **A:\INSTALL**. If you are using another method, you can use browse to locate the following file on your CD-ROM, file server, or shared drive:

   drive:\win32intel\install

3. As you can see from figure 6.20, you should enter your name and company name. You do not want to select the Install on a file server option. Click Next to continue with confirmation of the names you have typed.

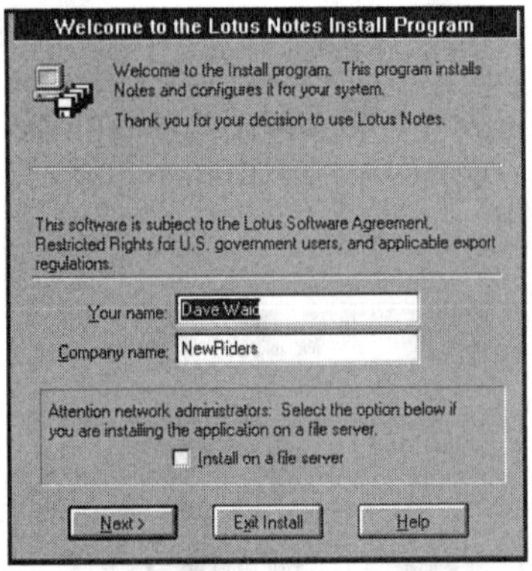

Figure 6.20

The initial install screen.

4. As shown in figure 6.21, you are then prompted to confirm your names, click Yes if they are correct or No to re-enter them.

Figure 6.21

Confirmation of names.

5. If Notes was installed previously on the current machine, a warning appears indicating that a copy of Notes is already installed on your hard disk (see fig. 6.22). Click Next to confirm the message.

Figure 6.22

Previous install.

6. Select either Server Install or Customize features - Manual Install. The Server Install option includes the workstation software for the server. The Standard Install option is intended only for workstations. For more information about different installation types please see the "Domino Install Types" section in this chapter.

7. Using eight or fewer characters (even if your operating system supports long file names), specify the drive and directory or folder for Notes program files and Notes data files. As you can see in figure 6.23, the default drive and directory or folder is C:\notes for program files and C:\notes\data for data files. If you intend to run more than one version of Notes, be sure to type in a different directory. After you have changed the desired settings, click Next.

8. As shown in figure 6.24, Notes creates a Lotus Applications group for you or you can choose a different folder. Select the desired program group or program folder for the Notes icon (or type a name to create a new one). Click Next.

9. As you can see in figure 6.25, you are prompted to begin copying files to your system. If you do not have enough fixed disk room, you are informed by the install program. Click Yes to begin copying files to the current system.

10. When installation is complete, click Done.

11. If this is the first time Notes has been installed, you must reboot your machine.

Figure 6.23

The Install Options menu.

Figure 6.24

Folder destination.

Figure 6.25

The Begin Copying Files dialog box.

Domino Install Types

You can use either Server Installation or Custom Installation to install your Domino server. Server Installation installs all the components needed to run the Domino server and workstation (if applicable). Standard Installation is intended for workstations only and cannot be used if you intend to install a server.

Custom Installation is a manual install that lets you select which components you want to put on your Domino server. You must select this option if you want to install full online Help (approximately 35 MB), the documentation databases, Notes as a Service in NT, or additional Notes templates on your workstation. You should install these additional databases on your Domino server, so you can save disk space by not installing them on your workstation.

When you select Custom Installation, the Notes Install program selects all possible features. If you do not want to install a feature, deselect it. At a minimum, you must select Notes Workstation (if applicable), Notes Server, and Personal Data Files to run a Domino server (see fig. 6.26).

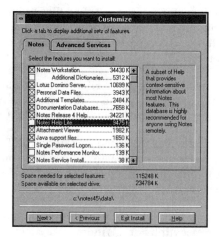

Figure 6.26

Custom installation.

In many cases, you do not install many of these components on a workstation and, therefore, they must be available on the server for your end-users. The components include:

◆ Notes Workstation contains the needed data files and program files to run Notes.

◆ Additional Dictionaries contains files for international dictionaries.

◆ Personal Data Files includes the files that identify the server and how Notes was installed on the server.

◆ Notes Server is also needed for a server installation. Be sure to select this option.

◆ Additional Templates contains database templates for building common Notes applications. These files are used by developers and administrators.

◆ Documentation Databases include guides to installation, Notes administration help databases, and migration information. These files are placed in a directory called doc (typically \notes\data\doc).

◆ Notes Release 4 Help is a large (about 35 MB) database that provides context-sensitive information about all Notes features. If you do not install help on workstations, the help database must be available on the server if the users are to get online help.

◆ Notes Help Lite (about 15 MB) is a subset of the large Notes Help database. Assuming that you install the larger help database on a server (and you should because the clients will use it), this database is not needed. To conserve disk space, you should deselect this option.

◆ Attachment Viewer offers filters for viewing attached files (such as spreadsheets and word processing documents). Documents are rarely opened directly at the server, but it would be better to be prepared in the event that you do need to open documents at the server.

◆ The Notes Web Navigator needs Java Support Files to run Java applets. It is very unlikely that you will use the server to run the workstation Web Navigator, but there is no harm in installing the feature if you think you might need it.

◆ Single Password Logon includes files that enable a Windows NT password to be cached for use by the Notes ID. You must be a Windows NT administrator to install this feature. For more information, please see the "Windows Integration Features" section of this chapter.

◆ Notes Performance Monitor creates files for use as a Performance Monitor that automatically pops up on a Dec Alpha or a Windows NT system.

◆ Notes Service Install installs files so the Domino server can run as a Windows NT service. You want this feature if you intend for the Domino server to restart after a power failure. This feature is available only on Windows NT.

◆ User Synchronization installs files so you can synchronize the Notes user and Windows NT account information.

◆ Domino Partitioned Server contains the program and data files necessary for partitioned servers on Windows NT. To install partitioned servers, at a minimum you must select the Domino Server, Notes Workstation, and Personal Data Files components on the Notes tab, and the Domino Partitioned Server and Advanced Services Data on the Advanced Services tab.

◆ Domino.Action Templates can help you establish libraries and links on an Internet/Intranet site. For more information, please see Chapter 20.

As seen in figure 6.27, the Advanced Services tab contains Domino Partition and Advanced services. These advanced features require the purchase of an advanced license from Lotus.

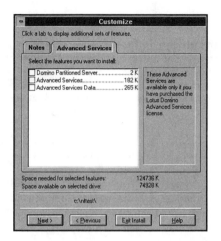

Figure 6.27

The Advanced Services tab.

The advanced features include the following:

◆ **Partitioned servers.** You can use one server to act as eight. You should select this option for only the first Domino server installed on the system. For more information, please see the "Windows Integration" section of this chapter.

◆ **Clusters.** Enables you to connect up to six Domino servers together for maximum availability.

◆ **Billing.** Used to track and record system usage.

Directories and Files Defined

Tables 6.1 and 6.2 describe various directories and files. These files or directories appear in the Notes directory on your server. It might be necessary for you to move, backup, delete, or modify these files from time to time. Learning about them here will give you an even better understanding of how your Domino server works and how you can better configure your server.

TABLE 6.1
Important Files in the Notes Directory

C:\NOTES	Purpose
NOTES.INI	Contains configuration paramenters. See the "notes.ini" section of this chapter.
DESKTOP.DSK	This file contains all the workspace settings, such as what icons have been added, private views, and so forth.
*.EXE	Many executable files for the server are contained in this directory.

TABLE 6.2
Important Files in the Data Directory

C:\NOTES\DATA	Purpose
MAIL.BOX	Temporary storage of all mail. Please see the "Mail.Box" section of this chapter.
*.NTF	All templates used by the server or end-users. These show when using File, Database, New.
BUSYTIME.NSF	This file captures schedules for Calendaring and Scheduling. For more information about Calendaring and Scheduling, please see Chapter 3, "Introducing Calendaring and Scheduling."
ADMIN4.NSF	This file is used by the AdminP process (changing user names, recertifying, and so on). For more information, see the "AdminP" section of Chapter 8.
CATALOG.NSF	The catalog file for notes. This file is rebuilt each evening. It contains all the notes databases and directories on the Domino server.
LOG.NSF	The log file for notes. All events (such as replication, mail routing, and so on) that occur on the server are stored in this file.
NAMES.NSF	This file contains a great deal of information about users, security, server configuration, replication, mail routing, and so forth.

You also have a modem directory and SmartIcon directory. The modem directory is typically notes\data\modem and the SmartIcons directory on Windows NT is notes\data\W32. If desired, you can use the operating system to hide these directories so they are not seen when people use the Domino server.

You also have a notes/doc directory that contains the documentation database for Lotus Notes. Things such as additional help files, migration databases, and others can be found in this directory.

NT Integration Features

Three features are specifically designed to work with Windows NT systems. These include:

◆ **Single User Logon.** Enables a Windows NT password to be cached for use by the Notes ID. The Lotus Notes Single Logon runs as a native NT service in the NT service control panel. After the end-user logs onto the NT system, the user does not get prompted for an additional Notes password. Instead, the request to unlock the user's Notes ID is sent to the Single Logon Service, which unlocks the Notes ID (assuming the password is the same for both). You must be a Windows NT administrator to install this feature.

◆ **Lotus Domino Directory Synchronization.** As you can see in figure 6.28, you can register both an NT account and a Notes ID for a user.

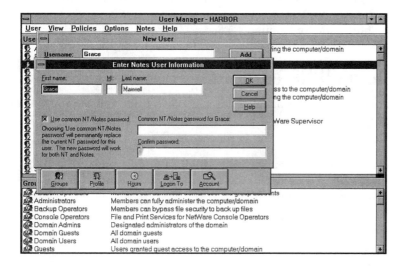

Figure 6.28

NT registration.

Lotus Domino directory synchronization is done by the Notes User Manager Extension. As you can see in figure 6.29, special menu options and dialogs are added to Windows NT User Manager during Notes installation.

These menus enable you to specify that changes made to NT user accounts are reflected in the Domino Address book. Additionally, if you are running Notes on Windows NT, you can "synchronize" Person documents in the Notes Public Address book with NT user accounts in the Windows NT User Manager. Therefore, you can manage user information in the Domino Name and Address book and NT User Manager through a single interface, either Notes or Windows NT. You must be a local Windows NT administrator to install this feature and this feature is available only on Windows NT.

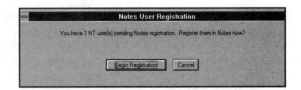

Figure 6.29

*Registration
in NT.*

◆ **Event Logging.** You have the option of recording Notes/Domino events in
the Windows NT Event Viewer. This enables you to record and view all Notes/
Domino and operating system events in a single location. This feature is
enabled in Notes by altering the event database to send messages to the NT
Event Viewer. For more information, please see Chapter 9, "Statistic Tracking
and Event Notification for Domino 4.5 Servers."

Platform Install Differences

There are various differences during installation of OS/2, Unix, and Novell NetWare.

OS/2

For OS/2, the config.sys statement adds a line for LibPath. This line is needed for
Notes to function. If you use an older config.sys statement, be sure to copy the
LibPath information between the two files.

When you launch the Installation Software, use the following file:

```
drive:\directory\instpm
```

You may find it useful to add the Domino server icon to the startup group. This will
make the Domino server software launch as soon as the operating system boots.

Unix

You can install the Domino server to a single host or multiple hosts. To install
Domino to a single host, you must specify a destination host hostname. The specified
destination host does not need to be the same host or operating system running the
Install program. To install Domino to multiple hosts, you must specify the name of
each destination host in a hostlist file. A hostlist file is an ASCII file listing the destination host names, one host on each line. You can create this list before you start the
Install program, or you can create or edit the list during the Install program. Use this
file from the CD-ROM drive to install the software:

For HP-UX, type:

```
./INSTALL\;1
```

For Sun Solaris and IBM AIX, type:

```
./install
```

When you install Domino on multiple hosts, Domino uses the same configuration settings for each destination host.

One of these configuration settings is the destination path of the Domino files. By default, Domino installs the software to the /opt/lotus/ destination. If you install to a different directory, the Install program creates a symbolic link from /opt/lotus/ to the install directory that you specify. The final directory name of the path must be "lotus"; if you do not include it in the path, the Install program adds "lotus" to the path.

Domino uses the user and group IDs that you specify during install for the user and group ownership of the Domino server files. By default, Domino uses *notes* as the user ID, and *notes* as the group ID. You should create these IDs and use the same IDs during the Install program and the server Setup program. Make sure the IDs you specify are not the same as any system IDs defined by any of the destination hosts.

For each system that runs the Domino server software, you need to create a Unix administrative account for running the Domino server processes. This account should be local to the system, for both security and performance reasons. Use a unique name, such as *notesadm*, to differentiate this account from the software account (*notes*).

Novell NetWare

The installation and configuration of the NLM version of the Domino server must be performed from a Windows workstation. This workstation must have a drive mapped to the root of the drive where you intend to install the software (drive N:, for example).

You must first edit the AUTOEXEC.NCF file. From a client machine, map a drive to the NetWare file server. Then type:

```
load install
```

For NetWare 4.1, choose NCF File Options. For NetWare 3.12, choose System Options. Then select Edit system AUTOEXEC.NCF File from the Available System Options. The following lines need to be added to the file:

```
load clib
load mathlib (only if your machine has a math coprocessor)
load tli
load ipxs
load spxs
load netdb
load notessrv (must be placed after the patchman statement)
```

The load notessrv command enables the Domino server for NetWare to start automatically when the NetWare file server starts.

 You might want to leave the load notessrv line out of the NCF file until you get everything running smoothly. If you have problems getting the server to run, having the server start up automatically can be frustrating. During configuration, you can load the server task manually from the Novell command line. After things are running smoothly, add the load notessrv line to the NCF file.

When you install the Domino on the NetWare file server, you are using a Windows client. To install the file on the server, you should launch:

```
drive:\NetWare\install\install
```

During installation, you simply need to specify the mapped drive of your Domino server.

Launching the WorkSpace

After you have installed the software, you are ready to begin with the configuration of your Domino server. Your first step is to launch the workstation software on the server machine (see fig. 6.30). You launch the server icon later after you have configured the software.

Figure 6.30

Workstation and server icons.

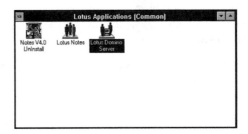

The first screen you see after double-clicking the Lotus Notes WorkSpace icon is the license agreement. Click I Agree if you agree to the terms of the software. Click I Do Not Agree if you have stolen the software. As you can see from figure 6.31, you are prompted with a radio button when initially launching Lotus Notes.

Figure 6.31

First server or additional.

The answer to this radio button has significant consequences. If you have not already done so, please see the discussion of a first server in the "First Server" (of the refresher section) of this chapter. If Lotus Notes exists elsewhere in your company, you should select an additional server (please see "Setting Up An Additional Server" section of this chapter). If Notes has never existed in your company before, select First Server. After selecting First Server, you must fill out the dialog box for the various fields as shown in figure 6.32.

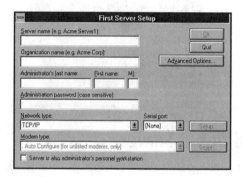

Figure 6.32

First server setup.

The example shown in figure 6.33 can be used as a guideline for filling in this menu. However, you should read the "Naming Conventions" section of this chapter before proceeding if you have not already done so.

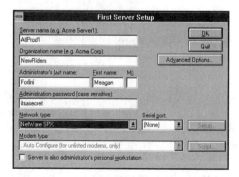

Figure 6.33

Completed first server setup.

The first item is the Server name. Server names should be selected carefully. Try to select a name that you expect to keep. For instance, do not use a name that includes location if you know that the server will be moved. The next item is the Organization name. This is what appears on all hierarchical IDs (such as Mike Haines/NewRiders). You should put in the administrator's first and last name and middle initial if desired. You should select the appropriate network type and the appropriate port. For more information about protocols, please see the "Protocols" section of this chapter.

As shown in figure 6.34, if you desire to change your Domain or Network name, you must select Advanced Options.

Figure 6.34

Advanced options.

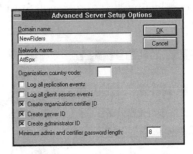

Setting Up an Additional Server

For a server to sign on as an additional server, a Server record must exist in the Public Name & Address Book and you must have an ID for the server. The Server record and ID are created during the registration of additional servers.

To register an additional server, select File, Tools, Server Administration, Servers, Register Server

Place either the original certifier ID or an OU certifier in your diskette drive. Type in a name for the server, a password, a domain name (if it is not the same), and the administrator's name.

Note Be sure to change the password length from 1 to 0. If you do not change the setting to 0, the server must have a password. Without a password on the server ID, you gain a large advantage because the server can restart after a power failure without the administrator's intervention.

After the server is registered, you can then set up the new server. You should first install and test the network card and then install the Lotus Domino software. After the software is installed, launch the WorkStation software (except on an NLM server). As you see in the initial dialog box shown in figure 6.35, you should select the An additional Lotus Notes server in your organization option.

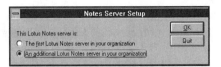

Figure 6.35

First or additional server.

You then must type in the fully distinguished name of the server (such as ArtAtl/ NewRiders). Figure 6.36 gives an example.

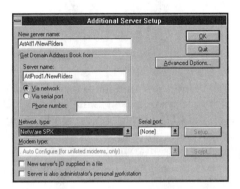

Figure 6.36

An additional server setup.

The address book for the domain is replicated during the installation. Therefore, you must connect in some manner (even if via modem) to some other Domino server in the same domain.

The Server is also administrator's personal workstation check box is used to make it possible to do remote console and other operations while being physically at the server. Unless you plan on using the server's client process as your Notes workstation, do not select this option.

Protocols

You can select from three primary protocols when you set up your Domino server: NetBIOS, SPX, and TCP/IP.

NetBIOS is fairly easy to install and use. However, it cannot be routed (although a bridge is acceptable). Typically, one loads NetBIOS because it is great for a small company or branch. It can be (in some ways) a security feature. If you load only NetBIOS for your users, they cannot access servers outside of that branch without loading additional protocols on their own.

For several reasons, many organizations select TCP/IP as the exclusive protocol for their systems. This protocol is typically more patient and performs better over wide area networks. However, it can be somewhat more difficult to configure and does have some potential security risks. Without a DNS server, you cannot configure a system with TCP/IP initially. This limitation causes frustration for many because this means setting up the system with a different protocol (or no connection at all) and then changing the configuration so that the system uses TCP/IP exclusively.

NetWare SPX is highly secure protocol. SPX is also fairly easy to load and use on most platforms. It can also be routed across wide area networks (although not as effectively as TCP/IP).

Security

Many security options are available with your Domino server. The following section describes the physical security of your server as well as the features included with the software. Many companies (even the CIA) purchase Notes and Domino because of the impressive security features available. This section will help you take the needed measures to properly implement security on your Domino server.

Physical

It is important to ensure limited physical access to your Lotus Domino server. This means passcode or badge reader access or limited distribution of a server room key. Although you can put your server in the open, you want to take some precautions. At the very least, you should enable a screen saver with password protection. Additionally, you might consider some other devices such as locked keyboard and drive doors.

Directory Level

Directory level security is a terrific way to limit rights to directories or files. All server-based Notes databases must be physically or logically in (or off of) the Notes data directory (typically C:\Notes\Data). A Domino server provides a facility called DIR files that enable the administrator to place Notes databases physically outside of the data directory (even on a separate drive) and create a logical pointer to the new location. The DIR file can be a simple pointer, making the Notes server believe that the databases are in the actual data directory, or they can include an additional level of security.

DIR files do not have to be a security mechanism. You might simply want to use another drive if you are running out of disk space. Simply put, you make an ASCII file with the drive and directory name, and groups or names for access rights. The following is an example of such a file:

```
{File Name = C:\NOTES\DATA\Mail.DIR}
E:\NOTES\MAIL
AtlantaOffice
```

This file can be placed in your Notes data directory (typically C:\Notes\Data). As your users do File, Database, Open, they are presented with a directory called Mail. If the person is listed in the Atlanta Office group, he or she can access the directory.

With Domino 4.5, directory security has become even easier. You can create directories and limit access with the Administration Panel. As you can see from figure 6.37, you can make the directory (or database) link and assign rights to the directory.

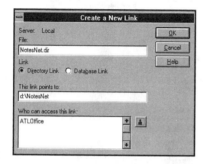

Figure 6.37

Directory and database links.

As you can see in figure 6.38, you can also delete links and create or delete directories.

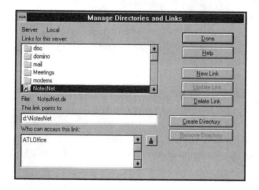

Figure 6.38

Creating links.

Server Level

Server level security can range from granting rights to access the server to granting rights to administer the server. You can limit who can add databases, use the administration panel, and many other privileges on your Domino server.

At the top of a Server record is a line called Administrators (see fig. 6.39). Each group or person listed in this field has the ability to do remote console. You can do everything remotely that you can at your server. The obvious advantage with this feature is that you do not have to sit in your cold server room. You can even stop your server (but you cannot restart it) from the comfort of your office. For more information on server console, see Chapter 8.

Figure 6.39

Server record.

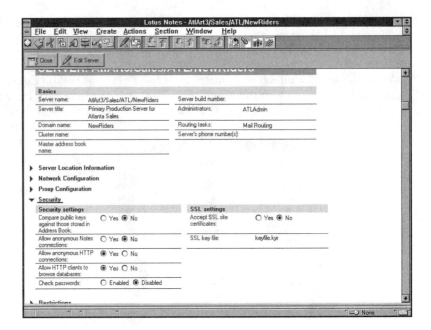

The Security, Agent Manager, and Restrictions sections of your Server record enable you to limit who can use your server and what rights they have after they arrive.

Security Section

The security section is illustrated in figure 6.39. The Compare public keys against those stored in the Address Book option would guarantee access by only those that are registered in your public address book. The default is No. Anonymous connections only allow an anonymous user to connect to the server. Databases open for anonymous access must have an Anonymous entry in the ACL with an appropriate access level specified.

> **Note** This feature can cause access to be slightly slowed. Additionally, you have no room for error. All public keys must agree with what is stored in your address book.

Allow anonymous Notes connections can be used on public servers that you are using with other companies that use Lotus Notes. If you develop Lotus Notes applications, this field prevents you from having to cross certify with other companies. The default is No.

Allow anonymous HTTP connections is used for public servers on the Internet/intranet. The default is Yes.

I highly recommend that you change this setting for all servers that are not intended for the Internet.

Allow HTTP clients to browse databases gives permission to Internet/intranet users to access any databases on your server. The Access Control List must be set to reader or higher for users to search these databases. The default is Yes.

Accept SSL site certificates—SSL stands for Secure Sockets Layer and is used with a POP3 Server. With a POP3 server, you can access a mail file from the Internet. For more information about POP3, see Chapter 20.

The SSL key file further configures Secure Sockets Layer. See Chapter 20 for more details.

Restrictions Section

The Restrictions section is illustrated in figure 6.40. Only allow server access to users listed in this Address Book limits use of the server generally to people in your organization (or if you have made Person records for people in other companies). However, this option means quite literally people and therefore, other servers are denied access. The default is No.

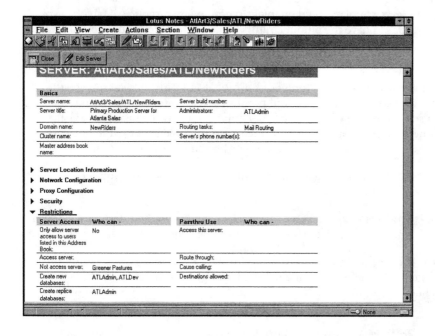

Figure 6.40

Restrictions section of Server record.

Access server enables only users or groups listed to access your server. This can be a very large list depending on the use of the server. It is commonly preferred to use the Not Access Server because it is typically a smaller list of people. A blank field means that no one is denied access.

Not access server is used to deny access to the server. A group called terminations is generally made in companies' address books so it can be used in this field. You can call this group anything you like (some prefer Greener Pastures). If you have many branches, it is ideal to have a separate group for every branch (this avoids many replication conflicts). However, all branches should still use the terminations group on each Server record so that you are sure to exclude all former workers regardless of branch. For more information about replication conflicts, please see the "Replication Conflicts" section of this chapter.

The Create new databases field permits users to put new databases on the server. A blank field enables anyone to put a new database on the server. Often, you do not want anyone to be able to create new databases on a server (or you find that you have a very disorganized directory structure, many unwanted and unused files, and you start to run out of disk space). Therefore, you should use a group that lists the developers in your company.

The Create replica databases field enables users to create new replica files on your Lotus Domino server. A blank field enables no one to add a replica database. Typically this field should have the administrators group (and perhaps the developers).

A passthru server can be useful when you need to access multiple servers with one phone call or if you need to access multiple servers running different protocols, as long as the passthru server is running both protocols. Essentially, one server with several modems can be used as a central point of origin so that you may go to many destination servers. At the very least, two documents must be changed for passthru access to function. The first document is the server document in the Public Name & Address Book. The second is the location record on the client machines.

Looking at the Passthru use column under the Restrictions section, you see a few fields that make passthru possible:

◆ **Access this server.** The Access this server field is used on destination servers. By listing groups or individual names, you can give permission to access a server.

◆ **Route through.** If you want to route through one server to get to another, you can change this field to include the names or groups that require this access. This field is typically used when the user does not have the same protocol as the server.

◆ **Cause calling.** You can use this field to access a server that is only reachable by modem on another server. All individuals or groups listed in this field can force the server to dial another via modem.

◆ **Destinations allowed.** All servers listed in this field are the only servers that can be reached after passing through a server. Listing servers that can be reached is a tighter security method than disabling servers with the Access Field (as previously explained).

Agent Manager Section

This area of the server document limits who can use various types of agents on the server. Agents (called macros in version 3) can do very powerful actions on a server, so care should be used in determining these rights. This section includes the following fields:

◆ **Run personal agents.** Depending on the rights a person has in a database, a personal agent can find and change documents.

◆ **Run restricted LotusScript agents.** Members of this field can use a subset of LotusScript agents. For more information about LotusScript, please see Chapter 14, "Advanced Application Design Issues."

◆ **Run unrestricted LotusScript agents.** This field can grant access to run DOS commands, change ACL's, delete files, send mail, and many other powerful commands.

 For more information on security (including database, view, and document level) see Chapter 11.

Summary

This chapter has described many fundamental server features and how to install a Domino server. In the event that you needed a reminder, you discovered the processes of replication, mail routing, document deletions, full text indexing, and more. You then gained information about how to install a Domino server, which included installing the software, launching the configuration menus, and setting up security. The following chapter assists you with setting up Lotus Notes client machines to attach to your Domino servers.

CHAPTER 7

Installing Lotus Notes 4.5 Client Software

In this chapter, you will discover how to set up and configure Notes clients. You will read information about how to install a Notes client on various operating systems. You will also see information about configuring many laptop machines and how to enable Web features on a client for your end users. After reading the information in this chapter, you should be able to efficiently install and set up your end users' Notes clients.

Selecting an Operating System

Choosing an adequate operating system (in preparation for installing Lotus Notes 4.5 client software) is obviously very important. You need to select an operating system for workstations that is compatible with your servers. The subject is worthy of mention here because it is a crucial step in the installation process. For more detailed coverage, however, see Chapter 5, "Selecting an Operating System."

Registering Users

For a Notes client to use a Lotus Domino server, they must first be registered. You must register the user before you will be able to finish installing a client. It is likely that registering users is the most frequent task you do as an administrator. The act of registering creates two items: an ID for the person and a person document in the Public Name & Address Book. Both of these items are created during a user's registration process. To register a user, select File, Tools, Server Administration. Then select People, Register Person, as shown in figure 7.1.

Figure 7.1

Register Person.

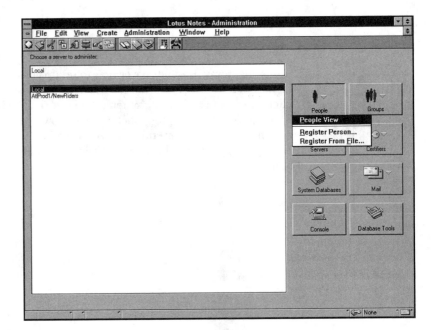

As shown in figure 7.2, you see a dialog box informing you that a license must be purchased for each new user. No returns you to the Administration Panel. Yes causes the registration process to search for the last used cert.id. A cert.id is created when a First Server is setup. For more information about cert.id's, see the sections "Server Names" and "Organizational Units" in Chapter 6.

Figure 7.2

License check.

You are then asked for the password if the ID is found (see fig. 7.3). If you do not know the password of the previously used cert.id, you can select Cancel and then select the cert.id you intend to use from the correct drive and directory.

Figure 7.3

Password screen.

After you have typed in the password for the cert.id, you are presented with the first of two Register Person dialog boxes.

The Register Person Dialog Box #1

The first Register Person dialog box is illustrated in figure 7.4. This first dialog box is general compared to the second and therefore you are addressing queries for all the users you intend to register. You will not see this menu again unless you exit registration.

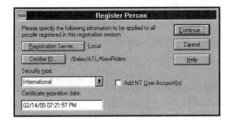

Figure 7.4

Register Person dialog box #1.

This dialog box contains the following selections:

◆ Registration Server

◆ Certifier ID

◆ Security Type

◆ Add NT User Account(s)

◆ Certifier Expiration Date

Registration Server

The registration server is simply server where you want the person record placed after you complete the registration of the user. You can (and should) use Local if you are working directly at the server. However, you should not use Local if you are working from your personal workstation. Doing so places the person record in your personal address book and not on any server.

Certifier ID

The Certifier ID button gives you the opportunity to select another certifier ID. If the current one that is selected is not correct, you can switch to another simply by clicking on the button and selecting the appropriate drive and directory.

Security Type

You can select North American or International for the clients you are registering. A North American license can only be used in the United States or Canada. For more information on security types, please see "International or North American IDs" in Chapter 6, "Installing Domino 4.5 Server Software."

Add NT Users

You can create NT User accounts while registering Lotus Notes clients. The feature is only available if you are using NT and the option was installed for the server. For more information about server installation and NT Integration, please see Installation and NT Integration in Chapter 6.

Certifier Expiration Date

By default, all new user IDs expire in two years. If you have a contract employee, you might consider setting a shorter time frame. However, be aware that the user receives notification about an expiring ID two months prior to its expiration. It might be a great annoyance to someone to receive a message about expiration the first day that he or she uses the ID.

Note It is not recommended to extend the date beyond two years. As unlikely as it may seem, people do leave companies. It is best to only be concerned with the ID for a few months after that employee has left the company.

Click on Continue to move on to the second of the two Register Person dialog boxes.

The Register Person Dialog Box #2

The second Register Person dialog box contains the following divisions:

◆ Basics

◆ Mail

◆ Other

Basics

As you can see in figure 7.5, the Basics view of the second Register Person dialog box includes the new person's name, the initial password, the license type, and profile. You can type in the first name, middle initial (if desired) and last name of the new person. Then type in a password that the new person uses initially to gain access to the ID. The default password length is eight alphanumeric characters or digits. You can change this to your preferred company standard. The license type menu determines what features the user will have when he or she uses Lotus Notes.

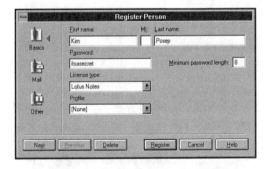

Figure 7.5

Registration Basics.

Lotus Notes currently offers four different license types. Each has different privileges and different costs associated with it. Working from lowest privileges to highest, the types are as follows:

◆ **Domino Mail.** An individual with this license type does not have a Notes Workstation. The user may only send and receive mail from the internet (just like a POP3 client).

◆ **Mail Access.** This license permits access to the workstation software and any database that was created with the basic Lotus Templates.

◆ **Notes Desktop.** This license gives the user all privileges with the exception of allowing him or her to be able to see any design elements or use administration features.

◆ **Lotus Notes.** This license grants full privileges to all menus. The end-user can use the workstation software and use all menus.

Profiles can be used to automatically configure dial-up servers, add databases to the workspace, and change many other default settings.

Mail

The Mail section of the registration menu includes information about the Home Server and the name of the mail file (see fig. 7.6).

Figure 7.6

The Mail tab of the registration dialog box.

The Home Server is primarily used to determine how the servers in your company route mail to a user. The first field for Mail type includes selections for Notes or None. The Mail file name field shows the directory and file name for the new user. The mail file name must be unique. If you use the same mail file name, Notes prompts you to decide whether you want to override the file. If you select no, you can then change the name, as shown in figure 7.7.

Figure 7.7

Rename mail file.

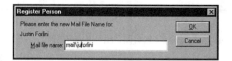

You can create mail files immediately or during the client installation. If you wait to create the file during client installation, the new person must have rights to add a database to the server (see "Server Security" in Chapter 6.

The Home Server field is placed on the person record for the individual. This field is checked by the router on a Domino server whenever mail is sent to the user. Also, as the client machine is created, the Home Server is needed to complete the setup.

Other

You can add comments, change storage defaults for the new ID, or make a Unique Organization Unit in the Other section of the registration menu. The comment and location fields are optional fields so that you can describe the new user in more detail (see fig. 7.8).

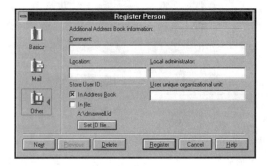

Figure 7.8

The Other tab of the registration dialog box.

The local administrator field is used when requesting new certificates. The User Unique Organizational Unit (UUOU) can create an additional qualifier to the person's hierarchical name.

Note   For more information about UUOU's, see the "Unique OU" section of Chapter 6.

You can store user IDs in the Public Name & Address Book or in a file. Leaving the ID in the Public Name & Address Book is a security risk. If a user can figure out the password, he or she can use the ID. For more information about storage of IDs, please see Chapter 11, "Securing Your Notes and Domino 4.5 System."

Understanding Registration Profiles

Setup profiles enable you to create standard user configurations. When you register new users, you can specify a profile. A setup profile can save you a lot of time because you automate many tasks rather than doing them manually. With setup profiles, you can do the following automatically when registering users:

◆ You can add databases to a workspace automatically, by using database links. To do this, select a database, choose Edit, Copy as a Link, Database Link. Then, in the Database links field in the setup profile (see fig. 7.9), choose Edit, Paste. When the new Notes client signs on, the database is added to the desktop.

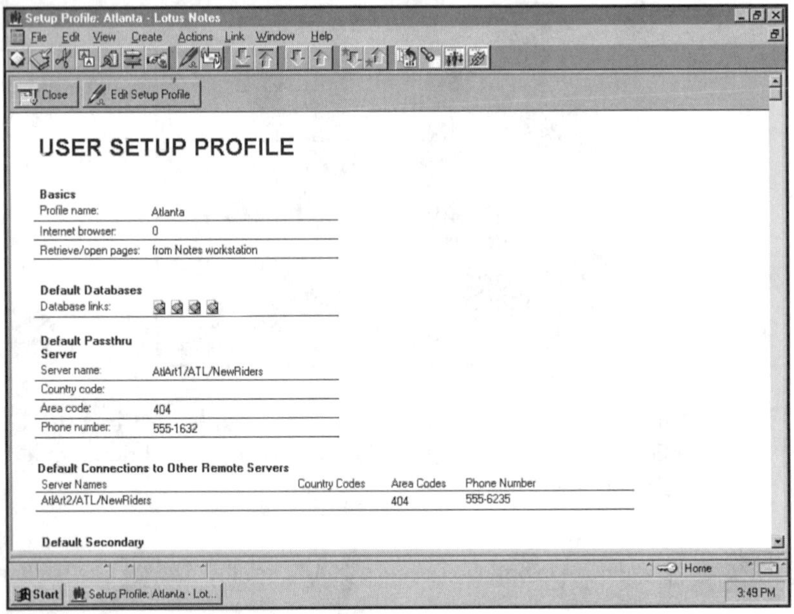

Figure 7.9

Upper Setup Profile document.

◆ You can enter the name and the phone number of a default passthru server to automatically set up a passthru server on the location record of the clients. For more information on a passthru server, see the "PassThru Server" section in Chapter 8.

◆ You can automatically create connection records for the client machines to reach your servers via modem. You can accomplish this by entering the names and phone numbers of the remote dial-up servers in the Default Passthru Server section of the Setup Profile record.

◆ If available, you can enter the names and addresses of secondary TCP/IP and NDS Notes name servers (see fig. 7.10).

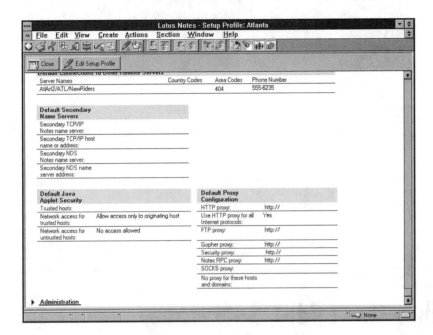

Figure 7.10

*Lower Setup
Profile document.*

◆ If desired, you can select default Java Applet security options and default Proxy configuration options.

To create setup profiles, you should open your Public Name & Address Book. You can then select the Setup Profiles view. From the Setup Profiles view, you can select the Add Setup Profile button (see fig. 7.11).

Now that you have explored how to register a user and how to make that process more efficient, the rest of this chapter will involve installing the Notes client.

Figure 7.11

Creating setup profiles.

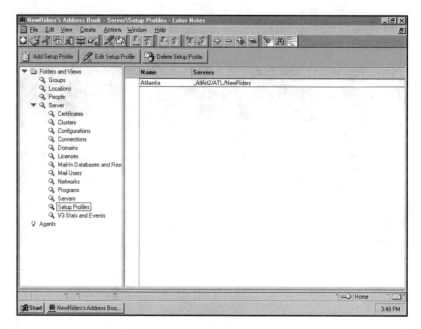

Installing the Client Software

The following sections give you information about installing a Notes client. You will first see information about things you should do prior to installing the software. You will then see details about copying and running the software for the first time.

Preinstallation

Before installing Lotus Notes on a workstation, take some preventive measures to make the installation process easier:

1. Make sure that the minimum required hardware, software, and network components are functional. For information about hardware and software recommendations, please see the Suggested Hardware section of this chapter. To test the network card of your system, see whether it is possible to log onto a file server or see your networks (such as through Network Neighborhood in Windows 95). If you are using TCP/IP, try to ping the server before installation. If you can't, you should get this problem solved before proceeding.

2. Make sure you close any currently running programs. Leaving applications running could prevent the Install program from copying files or updating shared files. Additionally, it is sometimes necessary to reboot during installation (depending on the platform and whether Notes has been on your system before) so you will likely have to close the programs at some point anyway.

3. Temporarily turn off screen savers, TSR programs, and virus-detection software.

4. If you are upgrading to a new release of Notes, be sure to back up any files that you may have customized, such as templates (.NTF extension) or modem files (.MDM extension). Also, it is a good idea to back up your desktop.dsk, names.nsf, and user.id (could be called another name with the .id extension) files.

Installation Steps

You can install from CD-ROM, disk, a file server, or a shared drive. For more information about granting access to Notes install files, please see "Distribution of Install Files" in Chapter 6.

The following instructions apply to Microsoft Windows. For information on other platforms, please see "Platform Install Differences" in this chapter. After you have the install files, perform the following tasks:

1. Be sure to read and complete the pre-installation section of this chapter before you begin the Install Program.

2. If you are using Windows 95 or Windows NT 4.0, choose Start, Run. If you are using diskettes, you can simply type A:\INSTALL. If you are using another method, you can use browse to locate the following file on your CD-ROM, file server, or shared drive:

   drive:\win32intel\install

   If you are using Windows 3.1, Windows for Workgroups 3.11, or Windows NT 3.51, choose File, Run from the Program Manager menu. If you are using diskettes, you can simply type A:\INSTALL. If you are using another method, you can use browse to locate the following file on your CD-ROM, file server, or shared drive:

   drive:\win16\install

   The screen shown in figure 7.12 appears.

Figure 7.12

Name menu.

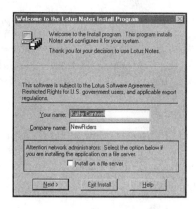

3. Enter your name and company name. You do not want to select "Install on a file server" because you are installing only one client at this time. Click Next to continue with confirmation of the names you have typed.

4. As you can see in figure 7.13, you are then prompted to confirm your names. Click yes if they are correct or No to re-enter them.

Figure 7.13

Name confirmation.

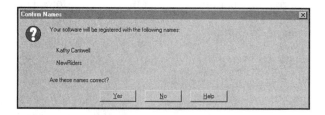

5. If Notes was installed previously on the current machine, a warning appears (see fig. 7.14) indicating that a copy of Notes is already installed on your hard disk. Click Next to confirm the message.

Figure 7.14

Warning message.

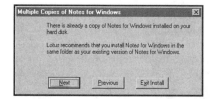

6. In the dialog box shown in figure 7.15, select either "Standard Install" or "Customize features - Manual Install." To conserve disk space, you should not select server install for a client machine. For more information about different installation types please see the Installation Type section of this chapter.

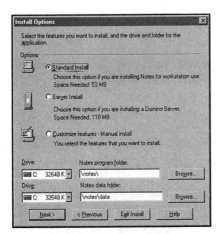

Figure 7.15

Install options.

7. Using eight or fewer characters, specify the drive and directory or folder for Notes program files and Notes data files. The default drive and directory (or folder) is C:\NOTES for program files and C:\NOTES\DATA for data files. If you intend to run more than one version of Notes, be sure to type in a different directory. After you have changed the desired settings, click Next. It is strongly recommended that you accept the default settings unless you have a compelling business reason for changing paths, directory names, and so on.

The screen shown in figure 7.16 appears.

Figure 7.16

Folder selection.

8. Select the desired program group or program folder for the Notes icon (or type a name to create a new one). Click Next.

9. As you can see in figure 7.17, you are prompted to begin copying files to the system. Click Yes to begin copying files to the current system.

Figure 7.17

Copy files.

10. As shown in figure 7.18, you are informed if you do not have more than adequate fixed disk space. When installation is complete, click Done.

Figure 7.18

Warning about low disk space.

11. If this is the first time Notes has been installed or if you installed Single Password Logon, you must reboot your machine. For more information on single password logon, please see the "NT Integration" section of Chapter 8.

Installation Types

The Install program offers the following workstation install methods:

◆ Standard Install

◆ Server Install

◆ Custom Install

Standard Install

Standard Install installs the minimum components needed to run a Notes workstation. It installs personal data files, Notes Help Lite, and database templates (approximately 60 MB). Many files that a workstation may need are available on a Domino Server. Therefore, the full Help Database, development templates, and documentation databases are not included. However, you can select the Custom Installation if you desire these files.

Server Install

Server install is not used for a client installation. This option uses up disk space unnecessarily. For information about Server Install, please see Chapter 6.

Custom Installation

This is a manual install that lets you select which components you want to install. You must select this option if you want to install full online Help (approximately 35 MB), the documentation databases, or additional Notes templates on your workstation. These additional databases are generally available on a Domino server so you can save disk space by not installing them on a client machine.

When you select Custom Installation, the Notes Install program selects all possible features. As you can see in figure 7.19, if you do not want to install a feature, deselect it.

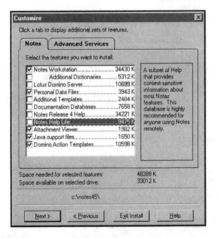

Figure 7.19

Custom installation.

At a minimum, you must select "Notes Workstation" and "Personal data files" to run a Notes workstation. The complete roster of components is represented in the following list:

◆ **Notes Workstation.** Contains the needed data files and program files to run Notes.

◆ **Additional Dictionaries.** Contains files for international dictionaries.

◆ **Lotus Domino Server.** This component is not needed for a Workstation install. Be sure to deselect this option.

◆ **Personal Data Files.** Includes the files that identify the workstation and how Notes was installed on the workstation.

◆ **Additional Templates.** Contains database templates for building common Notes applications. These files are often desired by developers and administrators but are normally installed on a Domino server. Install them only if you need them locally.

◆ **Documentation Databases.** Includes guides to installation, Notes administration help databases, and migration information. These files are generally also installed on a Domino Server in the \doc subdirectory.

◆ **Notes Release 4 Help.** A large (about 35 MB) database that provides context-sensitive information about all Notes features. If you do not install this database, the workstation can get help information from a Domino Server. If you install Notes Help, to conserve disk space you should not install "Notes Help Lite" and vice versa.

◆ **Notes Help Lite.** A subset (about 15 MB) of the large Notes Help Database. If you install Help Lite, you do not need to install the full Help Database.

◆ **Attachment Viewer.** Offers filters for viewing attached files (such as spreadsheets and word processing documents). This feature is often used when an application (word-processing spreadsheet or graphic program) is not available to the user.

◆ **Java Support Files.** Needed for the Notes Web Navigator to run Java applets.

◆ **Domino.Action Templates.** Installs two additional templates that you can use to design a Web site on your client. This takes an additional 12 MB, so you will probably only install these for developers.

◆ **Single Password Logon.** Includes files that enable a Windows NT password to be cached for use by the Notes ID. You must be a Windows NT administrator to install this feature.

◆ **Notes Performance Monitor.** Creates files for use as a Performance Monitor that automatically pops up on either a Dec Alpha and a Windows NT system. This option is available for Domino servers only.

You are in need of only one help file (if any). "Notes Help Lite" is intended for laptop owners (ideally for laptop owners who are not administrators or developers). Because Help Lite is a subset of Help, you should deselect either "Notes Release 4 Help" or "Notes Help Lite." Furthermore, if you are installing a desktop machine that is constantly connected to a Domino Server, you are really in need of neither. When help is requested, the desktop machine automatically reads the help file from the Domino server.

For a workstation installation, you should not install either of the two features found in the Advance Services tab. These features are intended for use with a server and use disk space unnecessarily.

Understanding the Workstation Setup Program

After you complete the workstation Install program, the first time you double-click the Notes icon the Notes workstation Setup program starts automatically. If you do not complete the Notes Setup (because of network problems or the like), the Setup program restarts the next time you start Notes.

If you can connect to your Domino server during the Setup program, Notes adds your mail file icon and the Public Address Book icon to your workspace. Notes also creates your Personal Address Book on the local hard drive and adds the icon for it to your workspace.

Completing Pre-Setup Tasks

Before you begin the Notes Setup program, it is important to know that end users need the following information to complete a client configuration:

◆ The exact spelling of the hierarchical name for their home server (where their mail file is stored).

◆ An ID stored in the Public Name & Address Book or contained on a diskette.

◆ The original password of the user.id (including case).

◆ How they intend to connect to their home server and the preferred protocol. This information determines how their workstation connects to Notes servers. For example, you can have a network connection, remote connection (via modem), network and modem connections, or no connection. If you are setting up a workstation to have a network connection to servers, you need to know which protocol your workstation uses to connect to your home server. If you are setting up your workstation to dial into a server from a remote location, you also need to know your modem type and the phone number for the user's home server.

Platform Install Differences

There are various differences during installation of OS/2, Unix, and Apple, as explained in the following sections.

OS/2

For OS/2, The Config.sys statement will add a line for LibPath. This line is needed for Notes to function. If you use an older Config.sys statement, be sure to copy the LibPath information between the two files.

When you launch the installation software, use the following file:

drive:\directory\instpm

Unix

To find out how much available disk space you have for /opt (the default installation directory), you can use the df command. For example, you could use the following syntax:

```
#cd <directory>
#df -k .
```

For each system receiving Notes, you should make sure that a Unix user account and a Unix group account are set up for ownership of Notes software. It is wise to set up a user ID account named *notes* and a group ID account named *notes*. For this purpose, make sure that these IDs are available on each target host by an appropriate method (NIS, per host, or otherwise) for your site.

Apple

You can either setup the AppleTalk protocol on your Domino server or use Apple's TCP/IP protocol to connect to a Domino server.

Setting Up Notes on a Workstation

Now that you have installed the software and reviewed the pre-setup tasks, you begin the final stages of setting up the Lotus Notes workstation:

1. Double-click the Notes icon on your desktop.

   Figure 7.20 illustrates the initial Notes Setup Dialog menu.

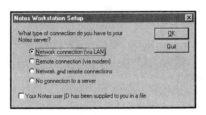

Figure 7.20

Workstation setup.

It is divided into the following parts:

◆ **Network connection (via LAN).** This connection is often used for desktop machines that do not have a modem installed. You must connect via some protocol (SPX, NetBios, etc.) to use this option. This option does not make a modem inoperable.

◆ **Remote connection (via modem).** This option is designed for laptop owners that do not have the capability to connect to the network with a protocol. This option does not make a network card inoperable.

◆ **Network and remote connection.** For most laptop owners, this is the ideal selection. Choosing either of the two above does not cause a network card or modem to be inoperable.

◆ **No Connection to a server.** If you intend to use a server at some time, the three options above are much easier and less time-consuming to use. Typically, this option is only used for home machines or demo situations.

◆ **Your Notes ID has been supplied to you in a file.** This check box should only be used if you have been handed the ID on a diskette (or other means). If the ID is stored in the Public Name & Address Book, you should not check this feature.

2. Select the type of connection you want your workstation to use to connect to the Domino server.

3. If you are prompted with a message asking whether you want your ID file copied to your data directory, you should click Yes.

4. When Notes asks for a password, type the password, and then click OK. Remember, passwords are case sensitive.

Note If you are using the Single Password Logon feature (with Windows NT), you can set a Notes password to match the corresponding Windows NT password. You are prompted to do this after you start Notes. Passwords must be no more than 14 characters (which is the maximum length of a Windows NT password).

5. If you chose "Network connection (via LAN)," you should do the following:

   ◆ Type in the full user name exactly as it appears in the Public Name & Address Book. Your name is automatically entered if your user ID was supplied to you in a file.

   ◆ Type the fully distinguished name of the home server (for instance AtlProd1/Sales/NewRiders). Figure 7.21 gives an example.

Figure 7.21

Network connection menu.

   ◆ Select the preferred type of network protocol the workstation uses to connect to a Domino server. To change the default settings for the network type, click Setup. Change the settings and click OK. Click OK when you are finished setting up the network connection.

 You must use File and Print Services to use SPX on a Windows Machine. TCP/IP cannot be used to set up a workstation unless you have a DNS (Directory Names Server).

   Continue with step 9 of this procedure.

6. If you chose "Remote connection (via modem)," do the following (see fig. 7.22):

   ◆ Type in the full user name exactly as it appears in the Public Name & Address Book. Your name is automatically entered if your user ID was supplied to you in a file.

   ◆ Type the fully distinguished name of the home server (for instance IndyProd1/Sales/NewRiders).

   ◆ Type the home server's phone number and a dialing prefix (if necessary). Do not enter any spaces or hyphens between the numbers.

   ◆ Select a modem type and modem port. Autoconfigure works for most modems that do not appear in the list.

   Continue with step 9 of this procedure.

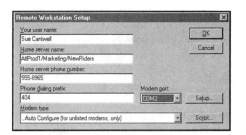

Figure 7.22

*Remote
connection menu.*

7. If you chose "Network and remote connections," do the following (see fig. 7.23):

    ◆ Type in the full user name exactly as it appears in the Public Name &
    Address Book. Your name is automatically entered if your user ID was
    supplied to you in a file.

    ◆ Type the fully distinguished name of the home server (for instance
    IndyProd1/Sales/NewRiders).

    ◆ Type the home server's phone number and a dialing prefix (if necessary).
    Do not enter any spaces or hyphens between the numbers.

    ◆ Select a modem type and modem port. Autoconfigure works for most
    modems that do not appear in the list.

    ◆ Select the correct type of network protocol your workstation uses to
    connect to Notes servers. To change the default settings for the network
    type, click Setup. Change the settings and click OK. Click OK when you
    are finished setting up the network connection.

    ◆ Select the preferred type of network protocol the workstation uses to
    connect to a Domino server. To change the default settings for the
    network type, click Setup. Change the settings and click OK. Click OK
    when you are finished setting up the network connection. Specify how you
    want to connect to the server after completing the Setup program (by
    network or by modem port) and click OK.

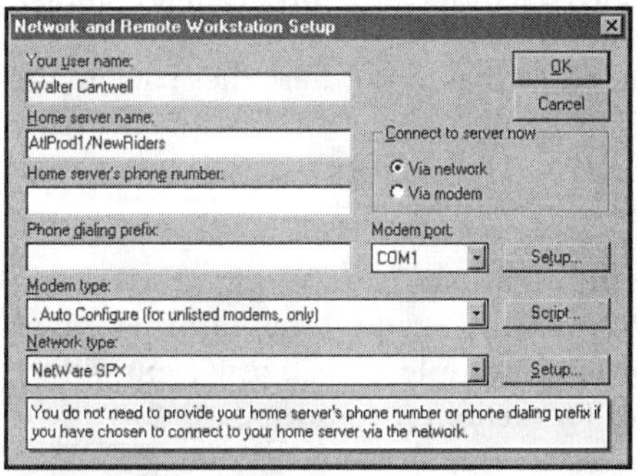

Figure 7.23

*The Network and
Remote
Workstation
Setup.*

You must use File and Print Services to use SPX on a Windows Machine. TCP/IP cannot be used to setup a workstation unless you have a DNS (Directory Names Server).

Continue with step 9 of this procedure.

8. If you chose "No connection to a server," type the full user name. If the user's ID was supplied in a file, Notes automatically enters the name. As shown in figure 7.24, you should then select the License type and click OK.

Figure 7.24

Unconnected Workstation setup.

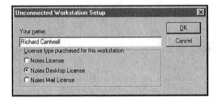

Note No connection to a server must be reconfigured if you intend to connect to a server at another time. When you connect to a server, you must change connection records and obtain the user ID (if you did not have it initially). Additionally, an ID is generated—but it is useless for connecting to other servers.

9. As shown in figure 7.25, you should select a time zone. Select "Observe Daylight Savings Time April-October" if appropriate. Click OK.

Figure 7.25

Time zone.

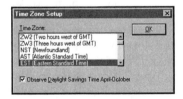

10. Click OK when the Notes workstation Setup program is complete.

11. If you backed up any Notes data files, copy these files back to the Notes data directory.

You are now ready to begin using Lotus Notes.

You have now gained valuable information about setting up client systems for Lotus Notes. In the following section, you will see additional information about setting up laptops and configuring systems for multiple users. Lastly, you will see information about setting up a Web browser for a client machine.

Laptop Owners

You can install a modem for a laptop if you did not install one when installing the Lotus Notes software. This task is accomplished by selecting File, Tools, User Preferences. Selecting the last option, Ports, enables you to reconfigure or add a modem. To reconfigure a modem, choose the port you want to change, and then click on COMX Options. As you can see in figure 7.26, you can then change the modem driver, speed, time out, and volume.

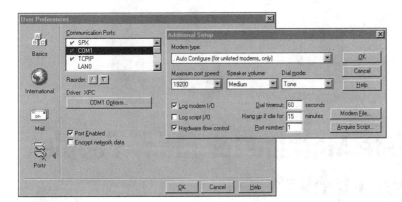

Figure 7.26

Additional setup.

Note If at all possible, you should use a modem driver that is written for your modem. Using autoconfigure works with most models but you get better performance from a driver designed for use with your modem.

The Help Lite database is about 12 MB and intended for use with laptops. However, if the owner is a developer or an administrator, you should strongly consider adding the larger version of Help (about 35 MB).

For mail addressing, it can be quite handy to have the Public Name & Address Book available. However, the file is often larger than 30 MB and includes many records that a client system does not need. You can replicate just the address field of the Public Name & Address Book and use far less disk space. This is accomplished by selecting the company Public Name & Address Book and choosing File, Replication, New Replica, Replication Settings. As shown in figure 7.27, you can replicate All Fields, Minimum Address Book, and other variations. Typically, laptop owners want just the minimum necessary to address mail.

Figure 7.27

Replication of Address Book.

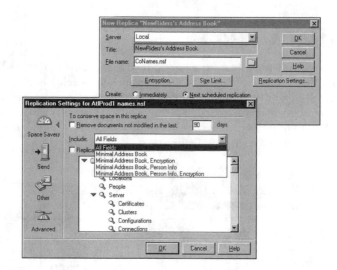

Using One Machine for Many People and Reusing Systems

You can have multiple people using one machine by making separate location records for each person. The easiest way to accomplish this is simply to copy and paste an existing location document and then change the name of the document to the user's name. As you can see from figure 7.28, the Advanced Section of the location record contains a field to make an ID active.

By adding these documents after installation, you can make it possible for one client machine to service many. This can significantly reduce the amount of machines you have to purchase. Use caution, however, so that you do not frustrate users by not having enough equipment available for those that need it.

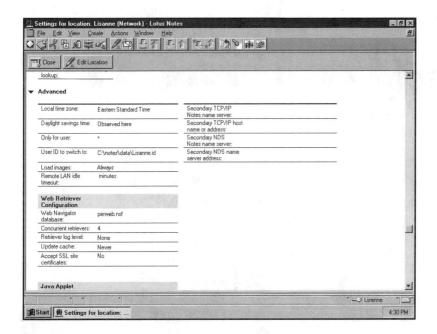

Figure 7.28

ID field.

Web Navigator

As shown in figure 7.29, Notes 4.5 has Web-browsing capabilities built in to it.

The Location document contains a section for the Web Browser you want to use. This field can be set for Notes, Netscape Navigator, Microsoft Internet Explorer and Other. As you can see in figure 7.30, after the Web Browser is set to Notes, retrieved Web pages can be cached in a typical Internotes Server database, or in a database on a local Notes workstation.

Figure 7.29

Web page.

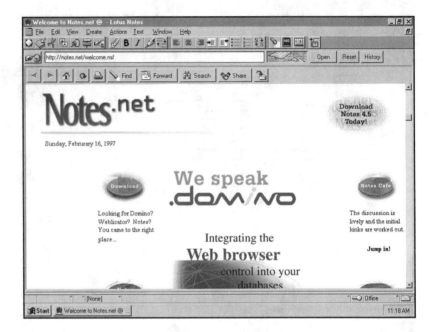

Figure 7.30

Location record.

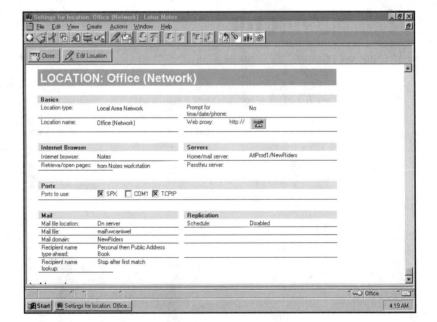

To use the Retrieve/open pages option, you must create a database on the client called PerWeb.nsf (must be this name) using the PerWeb45.nft template (see fig. 7.31).

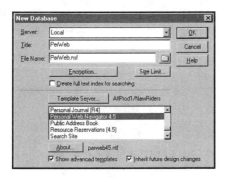

Figure 7.31

Creation of Web database.

If you desire to customize the database, you can select Actions, Internet Options. As you can see in figure 7.32, you can change things such as your perferred home page, Web Ahead, and Web Minder.

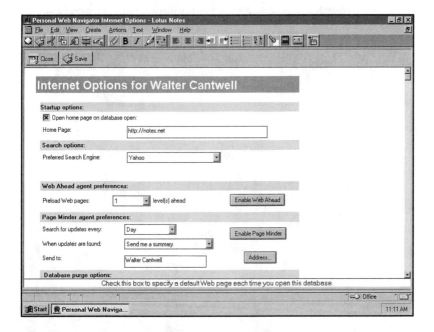

Figure 7.32

Internet options.

Web Database Agents

The WebAhead, PageMinder, and Housekeeping agents offer some additional capabilities. The additional capablties enable you to use your Notes client on the Internet. You may desire to set this up for your end-users so that they can take advantage of these powerful features.

 To use agents on a client machine, you must turn on the Enable Scheduled Local Agents setting under File, Tools, User Preferences.

WebAhead is useful for taking the next step for you in the background while you look at a Web page. It goes ahead and retrieves pages for you, and caches them in the database for quicker access when you want them.

PageMinder watches to make sure the cached pages are the most current. If it finds something more current during a scan of the Internet, it lets you know.

As shown in figure 7.33, you can also change many other preferences such as purge of old data, collaboration with fellow workers, and presentation choices. The Network Preferences has a button that brings up the current location record.

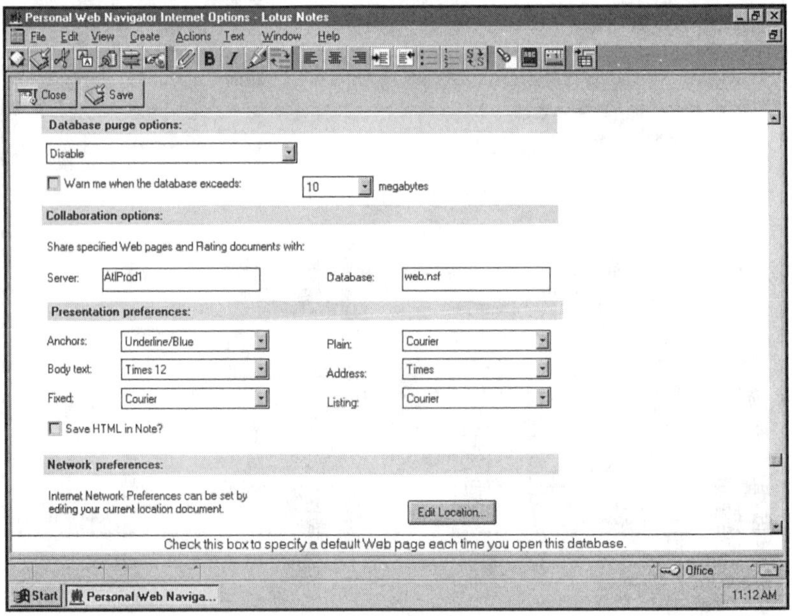

Figure 7.33

Bottom on Internet options.

Suggested Hardware Configurations for Notes Clients

The server platform you select usually dictates the client platform for your users. Whatever platform you select, you should be sure you have the minimum processor, RAM, and fixed disk space.

The following information guides you in making decisions for purchasing hardware for various platforms.

Recommended Hardware and Software for Windows Systems

The Notes workstation for Windows suggested minimum hardware includes a PC with an Intel 80486 or Pentium processor, 8 MB of RAM for Windows 3.1 and Windows for Workgroups 3.11, 12 MB of RAM for Windows 95, and Windows NT 3.51 or 4.0, 60 MB diskspace, a VGA Monitor, a mouse, and an optional printer and modem.

Supported Networks and Protocols for Windows Clients

The Notes workstation for Windows runs with the following network protocols:

- ◆ Banyan VINES
- ◆ Novell NetWare SPX
- ◆ NetBIOS, NetBEUI
- ◆ TCP/IP

Suggested Hardware for OS/2 Systems

For OS/2, it is recommended that you have a PC with an Intel 80486 or Pentium processor, 12 MB of RAM, and 50 MB of disk space.

Supported Networks and Protocols for OS/2

The Notes workstation for OS/2 runs on the following network protocols:

- ◆ Banyan VINES
- ◆ NetBIOS
- ◆ NetWare SPX
- ◆ TCP/IP

Recommended Hardware for Macintosh Workstations

Lotus Notes works with a Macintosh II-based, Performa, Macintosh Quadra, or PowerBook (except Model 100) model supporting a 68020, 68030, or 68040 processor; or a PowerMacintosh. You should also have 20 MB of RAM, and 45 MB of disk space (75 MB for a full custom install).

Supported Networks and Protocols for Macintosh

The Notes workstation for Macintosh runs on the following network protocols:

- ◆ AppleTalk
- ◆ TCP/IP

Recommended Hardware for Unix Systems

For IBM AIX, you should use an IBM RISC System/6000 running IBM AIX version 4.1.4 or 4.2. HP-UX requires an HP 9000 Series running HP-UX 10.01. Solaris requires a Sun SPARC system running Sun Solaris 2.5 or 2.5.1. You should also have 64 MB of RAM recommended memory and 150 MB recommended disk space.

The Notes workstation for AIX runs with the following network protocols:

- ◆ IPX/SPX for AIX V2.1 or AIX Connections version 4.1 (SPX II)
- ◆ TCP/IP (native)

The Lotus Notes workstation for HP-UX runs with the following network protocols:

- ◆ NetWare v3.12 for the HP 9000 with SPX stack for 10.04 (SPX II)
- ◆ TCP/IP (native)

The Lotus Notes workstation for Solaris runs with the following network protocols:

◆ Connect/NW 2.0

◆ TCP/IP (native)

Summary

This chapter has explored the installation and setup of the Lotus Notes client. You have gained information about steps to prepare for installation and how to install the files with different methods. You discovered how to set up laptops computers and some suggestions for machines that travel. You also explored the new Web navigation capabilities with Notes. Finally, you read about the hardware recommendations for various platforms.

CHAPTER 8

Examining Domino 4.5 Administration Features

This chapter explores many aspects of administration. The first section examines the many features of the adminstration panel. In this same section, you will find the most frequently used server console commands. The primary focus of the Admin Panel section is to guide you through the mechanics of the buttons and menus. You will then see additional sections that cover AdminP, Shared Mail, PassThru server, and more. After reading this chapter, you will understand the most commonly used Domino server tools.

Admin Panel

The Admin Panel (see fig. 8.1) can give you the ability to administer all the servers in your company. The Admin Panel contains many powerful features and is generally the starting point for all your adminstrative tasks.

Figure 8.1

The Admin Panel.

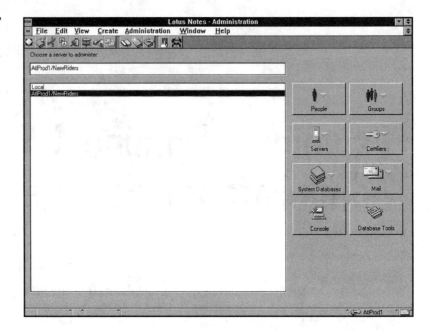

You can remotely maintain the Notes.ini file parameters, add or change directory and database links, issue console commands, troubleshoot problems, and perform many other tasks. Together with the Live Console feature, which shows Notes server console messages as they are generated, this panel almost entirely removes the need to physically access the Notes server. The Administration Panel can be used only if the following is true:

◆ The user is listed in the Administration field of the server document (either by group or explicitly).

◆ The ID is a full Lotus Notes License (not a Desktop, Domino Mail, or Mail version).

For more information on security or assigning rights for Lotus Domino servers, please see the "Server Security" section in Chapter 7, "Installing Lotus Notes 4.5 Client Software."

People Button

As you can see from figure 8.2, the People button is found at the top left of the administration panel. This button is used to see and register people so that they may use a Lotus Domino server. Specifically, the options for this button include People View, Register Person, and Register From File. The first option simply opens the address book in the people view so that you can either view or edit the documents. The second option allows you to register a person, which includes the creation of both the document and the ID for that user. For more information on registration of users, please see Chapter 7. Finally, the Register From File option allows you to register many users at once.

Figure 8.2

The People button.

 I find the Register From File option to be rather taxing to set up correctly. If you elect to use this option, be certain to back up your address book prior to attempting this process. One missing character could cause you to destroy your address book!

Groups Button

The Groups button allows you to create and edit various groups in the Public Name & Address Book (fig. 8.3).

Figure 8.3

The Groups button.

Groups are used for assigning security privileges and mail distribution lists. Groups can be used to give rights to the server, the administration process, directories, databases (via the ACL), views, documents (either to edit or read), and sections of a document. For information about groups and security, please see the "Access Control List" section in Chapter 11, "Securing Your Notes and Domino 4.5 System." Additionally, groups can be used as distribution lists for mail routing. When mail is addressed, the user types a group name in the to: cc: or bcc: fields.

By changing the group type from Multi-purpose, you can reduce the size of view indexes used by the server. Therefore, using group types other than Multi-purpose can make your server more efficient. If you change a group from Multi-purpose to Mail Only, it is placed only in the routing resolution view ($user). If you use Access Control Only, the group is placed only in the authentication view ($access).

Servers Button

The Servers button on the second row (see fig. 8.4) is used to register, analyze, view, and configure servers.

Figure 8.4

The Servers button.

The possible selections include:

◆ Servers View

◆ Configure Servers

◆ Directories and Links

◆ Register Server

◆ Log Analysis

◆ Cluster Analysis

Servers View

The Servers View option takes you into the address book so that you can view or change any server document in the Name & Address Book. For more information about server records, please see Chapter 6, "Installing Domino 4.5 Server Software."

Configure Servers

The Configure Servers option allows you to change a parameter on a server remotely. In a nutshell, it allows you to create a configuration document that is stored in the Public Name & Address Book. In Lotus Notes 3.x, the only way to change the Notes.ini file was to edit the file in a text editor and restart the server process. Today, you can change many options without rebooting the server. This change is also written to the Notes.ini file. As an example, you can change the number of replicators on your server or use shared mail. As shown in figure 8.5, you can choose from a list of possible Notes.ini parameters and then you are presented with help in the dialog menu so that you can have an idea of what value is most appropriate.

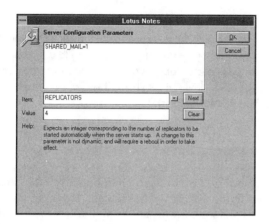

Figure 8.5

Server configuration parameters.

The Configuration records are read about every five minutes by the server. After the change is discovered by the server, the change is implemented and the Notes.ini is altered the next time the server task is downed. You should make only one configuration document for each server. If you want to change the configuration for many servers, you can use an asterisk (the default) in the server name field. However, if you are going to specify the server(s), be sure to remove the asterisk. The name of the server must be spelled correctly and must be fully distinguished (such as AtlProd1/ATL/NewRiders).

Directories and Links

The Directories and Links selection allows you to remotely create and give rights to directories on a server. This was not possible prior to Lotus Notes 4.5. See figure 8.6 for an example of a directory link.

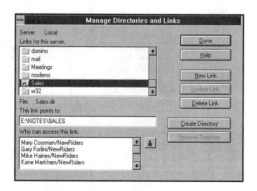

Figure 8.6

Directory link.

For more information on directory and database links, see Chapter 6.

Note Using directory and database links makes selecting files to back up your server more difficult. Until you examine the text contained in the link file, you do not know where the real database files are stored. If you are going to use these features, document which directories and databases are links and locate the databases that they refer to. If you use other drives, it also helps if you always use Notes before each directory (such as e:\Notes\sales).

Log Analysis

The Log Analysis feature allows you to search your Log.NSF file for certain key words (such as "failure" or "replication"). This saves you time so that you do not search for items manually when you are trying to diagnose a problem. However, you should check your log file on a daily basis so that you can be generally informed about the occurrences (replication, mail routing, and so on) of your server(s).

Cluster Analysis

Cluster Analysis was not present prior to Domino 4.5. Using this option, you can check the configuration of clusters. Clusters are new to 4.0 and above. Using Clusters enables your network to have higher fault tolerance of downed servers. When a server is not operating, the user fails over to another server in that cluster. For more information about clusters, please see Chapter 20, "Java: A New Way to Interact with Notes."

Certifiers Button

The Certifiers button found second on the second row (see fig. 8.7) is used to change or create IDs.

Figure 8.7

The Certifiers button.

The options include:

◆ Certify ID File

◆ Cross Certify ID File

◆ Cross Certify Key

◆ Edit Multiple Passwords

◆ Register Organizational Unit

◆ Register Organization

◆ Register Non-Hierarchical

Certify ID File

Certify ID File is used primarily to recertify a user. If a user's ID has expired (the default is two years), you may have to go to that user's station to recertify the user. Follow these steps to recertify a user at that user's station:

1. Take both the cert.id and your personal ID with you.

2. At the user's station, switch to your ID using File, Tools, Switch ID. If the user is not a full Lotus Notes License Type (Desktop or Mail Client), you must restart Lotus Notes.

3. Choose File, Tools, Server Administration, Certify ID File.

4. The first ID that is requested is the cert.id (on diskette). Be sure to use the cert.id when this screen is present.

5. The next screen requests the ID that you wish to certify. In this case, you are certifying the user's ID. It is likely called User.id and found in the c:\Notes or c:\Notes\data directory.

Additionally, the Certify ID File is used very often with flat or non-hierarchical IDs (say that three times fast!). In flat IDs the certificate is stored in the ID file rather than in a document in the address book. When you desire to have a flat ID to communicate with a hierarchical ID, the two files must carry a certificate in common. For more information about certifying, please see the refresher section of Chapter 6.

Cross Certify ID File

The Cross Certify ID File option is used with hierarchical IDs. When two IDs that do not have a certificate in common need to communicate, they must be cross certified. For example, the following two IDs do *not* have a certificate in common:

◆ Hub12/SingerToys

◆ Testing3/WHMInc

For more information about cross certification, please see the refresher section of Chapter 6.

Cross Certify Key

With the Cross Certify Key option, you can build a cross certify record in the Public Name & Address Book. You might use this to cross certify over the phone. You verbally read the public key to the other party and they do the same for you.

 Constructing a cross certificate record verbally can be a very taxing process (especially if it does not work the first time). If possible, have the public key code faxed or mailed to you so that you can at least read the information rather than relying on verbal communication.

Edit Multiple Passwords

As shown in figure 8.8, Edit Multiple Passwords can be used to give an ID two or more passwords.

Figure 8.8

Multiple passwords.

This feature can be used as a safety net in planning for a disaster. The cert.id is perhaps where you might use such an option. If, for example, your administrator is ill, a CEO with a separate password can still open the ID file for a replacement administrator. Multiple passwords can also be used for the problem of users forgetting passwords. An alternate password can be used to give access to the file.

 The multiple password option is not related to rights or privileges. In other words, one password does not give a person higher rights than another password. After the ID is usable, the same rights and privileges apply. Also, be aware that multiple passwords make the ID unusable in a 3.x environment (it is not backwards-compatible).

 We do not recommend that you make the alternate password something generic, such as "password" or first initial plus last name. Instead, make a simple database that contains the person's name and a unique password you selected when the ID was first made.

Register Organizational Unit

An organizational unit is any item between the common name and the organization. An ID will accept up to four organizational units. For more information on naming conventions, please see Chapter 6.

Register Organization

Register Organization is generally used to create a new organization for a separate company. This might be needed in the event that a division of a parent company is spun off to become a separate entity.

Register Non-Hierarchical

Register Non-Hierarchical primarily aids in certifying with a flat ID. In this case it is not actually cross certification but rather carrying a certificate in common. For more information about cross certification and flat IDs, see the "Fundamentals of Domino Administration" section in Chapter 6.

System Databases Button

Found on the third row, the System Databases button (fig. 8.9) assists with opening various databases that a system administrator uses on a periodic basis.

Figure 8.9

The System Databases button.

The system databases include:

◆ **Address Book (Names.nsf).** As you have already discovered, this file is the most crucial of all databases found in your Lotus Notes environment. After you have opened the file, you can go to any view (such as People, Groups, Servers, and so on) and read or change the documents.

◆ **Log (Log.nsf).** This file should be checked daily for errors they may have occurred on your server. You essentially find all events that have occurred on your server (primarily the console).

◆ **Catalog (Catalog.nsf).** This file is used to list all databases and directories of your Lotus Domino server. It is also important to note that this file builds a list of all databases for File, Database, Open. This file is created and updated by a process called *catalog*. If you place a new directory on your system, you have to load catalog (L Catalog) for the new directory to appear for your users.

◆ **Statistics (StatRep.nsf).** This database enables you to examine your servers and do threshold analysis.

◆ **Administration Requests (Admin4.nsf).** This file makes the administration process possible. All name changes are presented to this database. For more information about the administration process, please see the "AdminP Process" section in this chapter.

◆ **Outgoing Mail Box (Mail.box).** Notice that the extension is different for this file than a typical Lotus Notes database. Pending and dead mail reside in this file. You can also discover whether you have dead or pending mail by using the command SH Server. For more information about general mail features, see the "Fundamentals of Domino Administration" section in Chapter 6.

This last selection on the System Databases button is called Configure Statistics Reporting. This allows you to set up monitoring of your server. For more information about this process, see Chapter 9.

The Mail Button

As shown in figure 8.10, the Mail button has two options: Open Outgoing MailBox and Send Mail Trace.

Figure 8.10

The Mail button.

Notice that you can open the outgoing mailbox (Mail.BOX) with the System Databases button or the Mail button.

All mail is temporarily stored in the mail.box database before the router process determines the final destination of the message.

Additionally, if you are troubleshooting problems with mail, you can open the mail.box to see all pending and dead letters. The Mail Trace feature can be used to determine the path that is taken to send mail to another person (in the same or another domain). For more information on troubleshooting mail issues, see Chapter 12.

The Console Button

The Console button on the bottom is used to send commands to the Lotus Domino server remotely (see fig. 8.11).

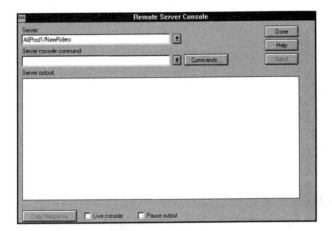

Figure 8.11

The Remote Server Console dialog box.

You can also double-click on any of the servers listed to the left of the buttons to bring up the remote console feature. After you are in the menu, you can issue commands to the server in much the same way as you do when you are physically at the server. In 4.5, you can now just choose commands from a Commands button and you can also connect live. For more information on the remote console option, please see the "Remote Console" section of this chapter.

The Database Tools Button

The final button, Database Tools, is used to bring up a separate menu for administering databases (see fig. 8.12).

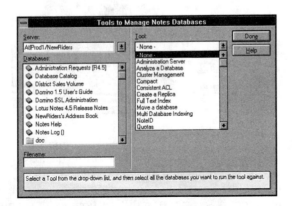

Figure 8.12

The Database tools menu.

As you can see in this figure, there are twelve options as follows (each of these is explained in more detail after this section):

◆ Administration Server

◆ Analyze a Database

◆ Cluster Management

◆ Compact

◆ Consistent ACL

◆ Create a Replica

◆ Full Text Index

◆ Move a database

◆ Multi Database Indexing

◆ NoteID

◆ Quotas

Administration Server

The first of twelve options is used to select an Administration Server. See figure 8.13 for an example of this feature.

Figure 8.13

*The
Administration
Server option.*

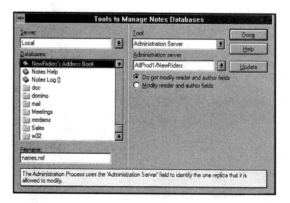

This setting is needed during the AdminP process. When an Administration Server is set, the AdminP process changes the Access Control List for the database on only the specified server. The change is then replicated to other servers. A radio button enables you to select changes to the Reader and Author Names field. For more information on the AdminP process, see the "AdminP" section of this chapter.

Analyze a Database

The Analyze a Database feature allows you to examine a database for such things as replication history, reads, writes, document changes, design changes, and activity in the log file. As shown in figure 8.14, the details of this query are sent to a results database (dba4.nsf).

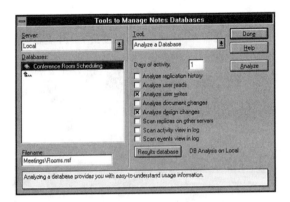

Figure 8.14

The Analyze a Database option.

Cluster Management

Cluster Management forces a user to use a database on another server during maintenance or moving of that file. See figure 8.15 for an example.

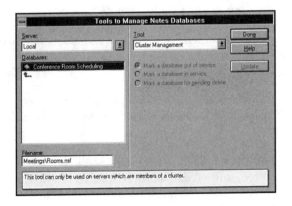

Figure 8.15

The Cluster Management option.

The available options include:

◆ Mark a database out of service

◆ Mark a database in service

◆ Mark a database for pending delete

Clusters require the purchase of an advanced server license. For more information about clusters, please see Chapter 20, "Java: A New Way to Interact with Notes."

Compact

The Compact option is used to clean up and reduce the size of a database. See figure 8.16 for an example.

Figure 8.16

The Compact option.

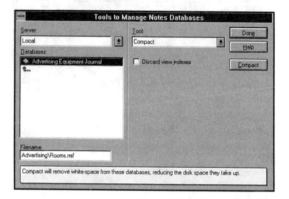

When documents are deleted from a Lotus Notes database, white space remains. This white space is used when new documents are added. However, the compact option organizes the documents so that they are not defragmented and removes any remaining white space. Another check box enables you to remove the database view indexes. This means that views no longer exist and therefore a great deal of disk space is freed up. However, the user may notice that it takes longer to use the database again because the views must be rebuilt.

 End users cannot use a database while it is being compacted. Additionally, any database that is in constant use by the server (such as log.nsf and mail.box) cannot be compacted.

While Compact is working, the file is copied to a temporary file in the same subdirectory. The file is then reorganized and all white space is removed. The file is then copied back in its original file name. Compact requires you to have the same amount of free disk space on the same drive as the database you are compacting. For more information about compacting, please see the "Document Deletions" section of Chapter 6.

Consistent ACL

The Consistent ACL setting changes the database and all replica copies so that the Access Control List is enforced in all circumstances. As shown in figure 8.17, you must be a manager of the database to change this option. You should use caution with this feature because you can lock yourself out of the file. Also, if you want different ACLs at different locations, you should not use this feature. Replication does not occur between servers if you attempt to turn this feature off while it is enabled on the sending or receiving server.

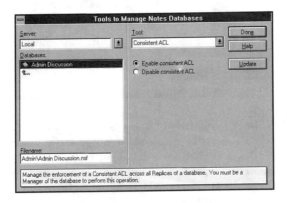

Figure 8.17

The Consistent ACL option.

Create a Replica

Using Create a Replica, you can make a new replica on one or more servers. Prior to Lotus Notes 4.5, you could only make one replica copy at a time. As shown in figure 8.18, this feature makes it possible to replicate a file to many servers at once.

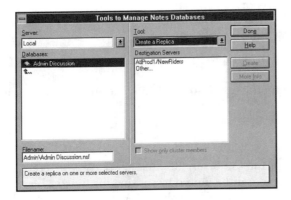

Figure 8.18

The Create a Replica option.

Full Text Index

Creating a Full Text Index on a database makes searching for data much easier for the end user. See figure 8.19 for an example of this option.

Figure 8.19

The Full Text Index option.

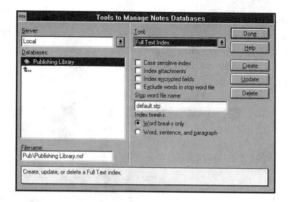

When you create a Full Text Index a new subdirectory is created with the extension .FT. Several files in this subdirectory make it possible to do powerful searches on a database. After a Full Text Index is created for a database, a new search bar appears in that database. With this search bar, more complex searches are possible (such as with Boolean characters). The following options exist with this feature:

◆ Case sensitive index

◆ Index attachments

◆ Index encrypted fields

◆ Exclude words in stop word file

◆ Word breaks only

◆ Word, sentence, and paragraph

For more information about full text search indexing, please see the refresher section of Chapter 6.

Move a Database

The Move a database command can be useful when new servers are created. In previous versions, a file could only be moved by copying the file to a file server or making a new replica and then deleting the old file. As shown in figure 8.20, this feature is only available on cluster servers.

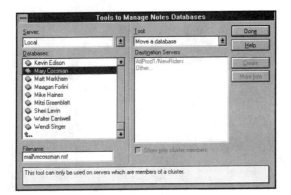

Figure 8.20

The Move a database option.

Multi Database Indexing

The Multi Database Indexing feature enables you to create many indices at once. After these indices exist, it is possible to search more than one database at a time for data (such as a client's name or company name). This feature can be extremely helpful when designing a Web page. As shown in figure 8.21, you must be a manager of the file to enable this option.

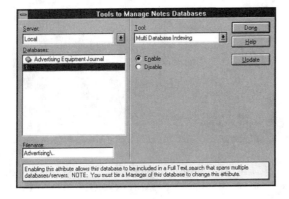

Figure 8.21

The Multi Database Indexing option.

NoteID

The NoteID feature enables you to view a document based on its hexadecimal number. On occasion, you may find references to hex numbers in your log file. If you desire to see the contents of the document, you can copy the hex number to your clipboard and then paste the number into this screen. The Edit, Paste menu cannot be reached while you have this menu open, so you must use Ctrl+V (or Shift+Insert for OS/2). An example is shown in figure 8.22.

Figure 8.22

The NoteID option.

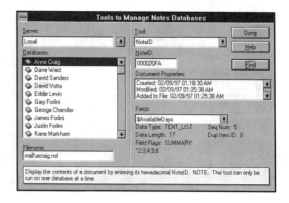

Quotas

The Quotas operation lets you dynamically change the maximum size of a database. As shown in figure 8.23, you can set both a quota and a warning.

Figure 8.23

The Quotas option.

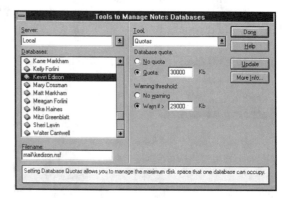

These options can be terrific for discouraging large mail files. As the size of the file reaches the warning threshold, messages appear whenever data is saved. Users can still create, receive, or save documents in a database with a warning. When the quota is exceeded, an end user cannot save documents in the database. However, mail can still be sent to the database from the server, and documents can still be created and sent from the file.

When a user attempts to put information into a database that is over its quota, the server gives the error message shown in figure 8.24.

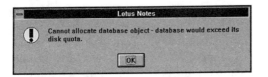

Figure 8.24

The error message for a database over its quota.

The Replication toggle gives you the option to temporarily disable replication in a database. Notice the message in figure 8.25 that points out that you must be a manager of the database to toggle replication.

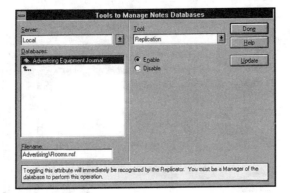

Figure 8.25

The Replication option.

The previous sections have focused attention on the features contained within the Database Tools button. The following section will help you explore the Remote Console button and the many facets of using Remote Console.

Remote Console

Remote Console allows you to do many commands just as if you were at the server. You can even call a server and issue commands from your home if needed. The flexibility you gain by being able to monitor and administer your server from afar can be very much to your advantage. You can gain access to Remote Console by either double-clicking on server names to the left of the Admin Panel buttons or selecting a server name and pressing the Console Button. As you use Remote Console, a temporary file is created and immediately deleted.

After the remote console is open, you can issue any server command to the server just as if you were at the server. Any valid command can be repeated by selecting it from the drop-down list box. The last ten commands are stored in memory until you close the remote console menu. A command can be up to 255 characters and any command argument that contains a space must be enclosed in quotation marks. If you are not sure how to type a desired command, you can simply use the Command button to the right of the text box (new in Notes 4.5). See the example shown in figure 8.26.

Figure 8.26

An example of Remote Console.

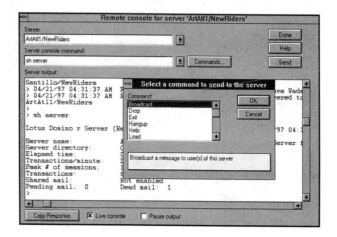

These commands include (letters in bold can be used as abbreviations):

◆ **B**roadcast

◆ **D**rop

◆ **E**xit (or **Q**uit)

◆ **Ha**ngup

◆ **Hel**p

◆ **L**oad

◆ **Pu**ll

◆ **Pu**sh

◆ **Rep**licate

◆ **Ro**ute

◆ **Set C**onfig

◆ **Set S**ecure

◆ **Show Cl**uster

◆ **Show C**onfig

◆ **Show Da**tabase

◆ **Show Dir**ectory

◆ **Show Dis**k

◆ **Show M**emory

◆ **Show Pe**rformance

◆ **Show P**ort

◆ **Show Sched**ule

◆ **Show Server**

◆ **Show T**asks

◆ **Show U**sers

◆ **Tell**

The next several sections focus on the most common server commands. You will see an example of each command and an explanation of why you would use the command. Although these sections emphasize Remote Console, all the commands can be issued at the console as well. Most of these commands are shown typed in their entirety. However, it is possible to issue abbreviated commands by using the bold characters shown in the above list.

Broadcast

Broadcast can be useful for informing users that your server is going down. The structure of the command is Broadcast "message" "users name." Two examples of this command follow:

◆ Broadcast "Server is going down in five minutes"

◆ Broadcast "Please come to the server room" "Dave Waid/NewRiders" (see fig. 8.27)

Figure 8.27

The Broadcast command.

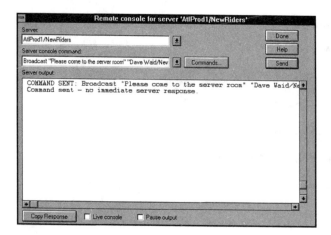

The first command is received by all users with an active session. The latter is sent specifically to Dave Waid. The message is seen in the message menu of the user's WorkSpace. Additionally, a low beep occurs as the message arrives.

 We find that a broadcast message can be so subtle (it shows up in the client message bar) that you may want to issue the command a few times to get a user's attention. You can reissue a command simply by selecting it from the list box of stored commands.

Drop

Drop can be used to release a port or user. Drop SPX disconnects all users currently using the SPX protocol on the Domino server. As shown in figure 8.28, Drop All disconnects all users currently using the Domino server. This command can be used when you notice the server is responding slowly. It will free up the server temporarily until users access databases again.

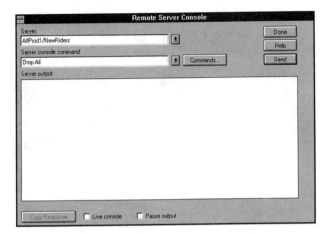

Figure 8.28

The Drop All command.

A dropped user is not prevented from reestablishing a connection. Except for a slight delay, the user is not likely to notice any change. This command is beneficial for releasing users that are connected but not actively reading or changing documents. If you have fifty users signed onto a Domino server and only ten of them are actually doing work at that moment, it is wise to drop the fifty users. The server can release all users, which frees up resources (memory, disk, processor, and so on). As the ten active continue to use the server, they use fewer resources.

Exit

The Exit command downs your Domino server, stopping all processes and ending the server task. As shown in figure 8.29, you get a warning message to be certain that you are not using the command by accident. You do not get this added safety net when you issue the command directly at the console.

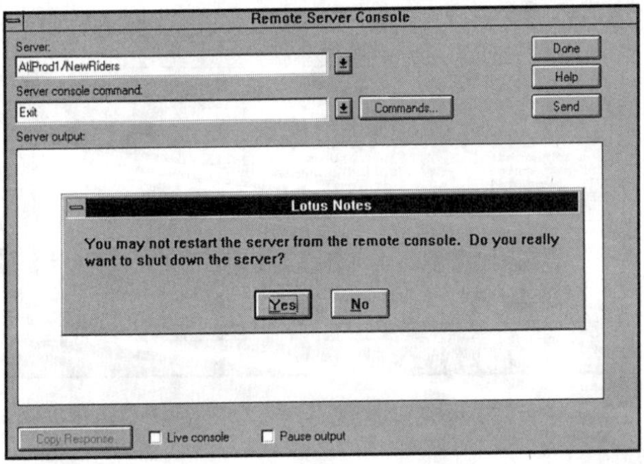

Figure 8.29

Confirming the Exit command.

Hangup

Hangup is used with modem ports (see fig. 8.30).

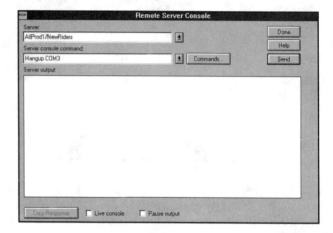

Figure 8.30

The Hangup command.

If you issue the command Hangup COM3, the modem disconnects any user or server that is currently using the modem. Use care with this feature because the user or server then needs to recall your server.

Help

Help lists all the server commands and the syntax for each. See figure 8.31 for an example of this command.

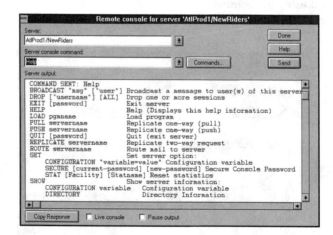

Figure 8.31

The Help command.

Load

Load is used to start processes on your server. For instance, L Router launches the router task on your server (see fig. 8.32). To end the task, use T Router Q (Tell Router Quit).

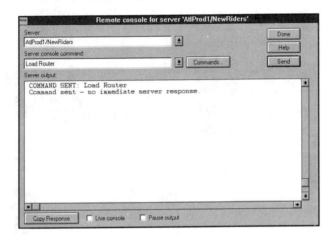

Figure 8.32

The Load Router command.

Pull

The Pull command is used to receive new or changed data from one server to another, which is essentially half of what the replication command does. You can either pull all data on a server or indicate a specific file. For instance, Pull AtlArt4 receives all new or changed replica copies from the AtlArt4/NewRiders (source) server to the server where the command was issued (destination) (see fig. 8.33).

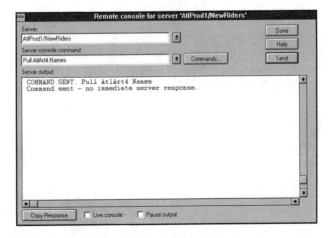

Figure 8.33

The Pull command.

For more information about replication, please see the refresher section of Chapter 6.

Push

The Push command is used to send new or changed data to another server (destination) from the current server (source), which is essentially half of what the replication command does. Push SalesProd1 sends any new or changed replica copies to the SalesProd1/Sales/NewRiders server (see fig. 8.34).

Figure 8.34

The Push command.

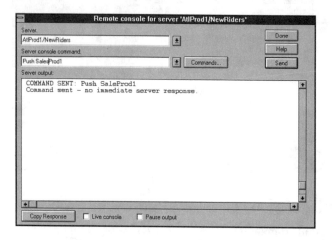

You can also indicate specific files if desired. For more information about replication, please see the refresher section of Chapter 6.

Replicate

Replicate is a two-way event during which two servers receive database changes. When the command Rep Publishing is issued, any new or changed data is pulled from each server. For more information about replication, please see the refresher section of Chapter 6. As shown in figure 8.35, you can also indicate a specific file.

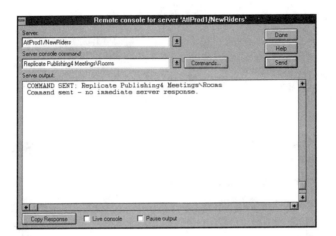

Figure 8.35

The Replicate command.

Route

The Route command is used to force mail delivery between two servers. If mail is pending in the mail.box, it can be sent immediately by using the Route command. For instance, RO DalDev3 forces all mail that is pending for the DalDev3/Dal/ NewRiders server to be sent from your server (source) to the DalDev3 server (destination). See figure 8.36 for an example.

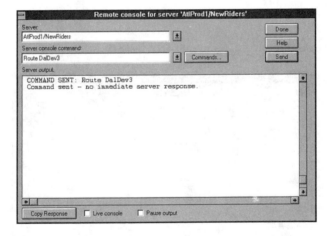

Figure 8.36

The Route command.

For more information about mail routing, see the refresher section in Chapter 6.

Set Config

The Set Config command can be used to change settings, including a change to the Notes.ini file. It is a good idea to use the Show Config command to discover the current settings of the Notes.ini file. This command works in much the same way as the configuration document works in the Public Name & Address Book. Notice the example shown in figure 8.37.

Figure 8.37

The Set Config command.

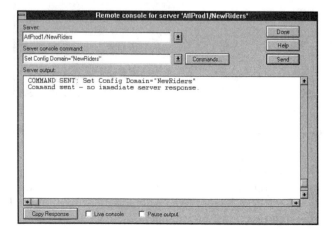

Set Secure

Set Secure adds a password to server commands (see fig. 8.38).

Figure 8.38

The Set Secure command.

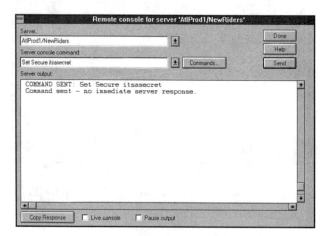

Adding a password is typically used in the event that you cannot put your server behind locked doors.

 We do not recommend this feature as a security measure. This command simply puts a line in your Notes.ini (SetSecurePassword=XXXX), which can be deleted.

Show Cluster

Show Cluster displays all servers in the same cluster as the server on which the command was issued. An example of this command is shown in figure 8.39.

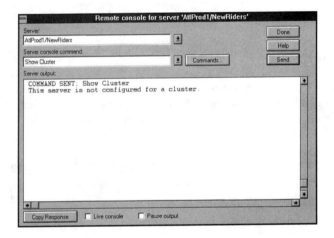

Figure 8.39

The Show Cluster command.

You must purchase an Advanced Server License to use clusters. For more information about clusters, please see Chapter 20.

Show Config

The Show Config command is very useful for checking the current settings of the Notes.ini file. If you want to change any setting in the Notes.ini file, you can use a variety of methods. See the "Changing the Notes.ini File" section of this chapter. Notice the example in figure 8.40.

Figure 8.40

The Show Config command.

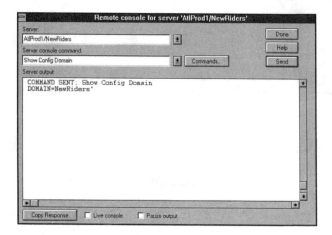

Show Database

The Show Database command lists additions, deletions, view names, and other information about a database. This command has two switches. The D switch is used to show information about a database and the V switch is used to receive information about views. See figure 8.41 for an example of the Show Database command.

Figure 8.41

The Show Database command.

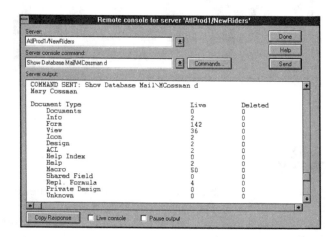

Show Directory

The Show Directory command lists all databases in a directory and the last time the file was modified. See figure 8.42 for an example of the mail directory with this command.

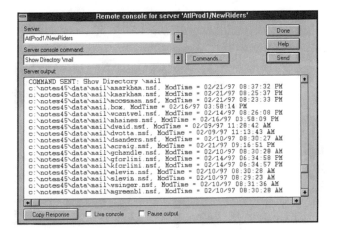

Figure 8.42

The Show Directory command.

Show Disk

The Show Disk command can be used to see the currently available space on a fixed disk. You can specify the drive letter just as in the example in figure 8.43.

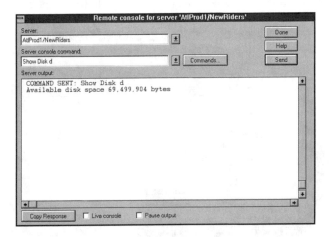

Figure 8.43

The Show Disk command.

Show Memory

The Show Memory command shows all memory that is currently available to the Lotus Domino server. The number returned also includes virtual memory (RAM plus usable fixed disk memory). See the example in figure 8.44.

Figure 8.44

The Show Memory command.

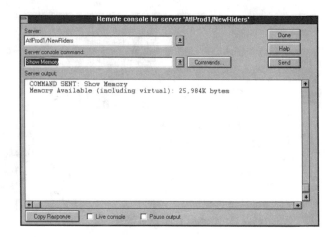

Figure 8.44

The Show Memory command.

Show Performance

Issuing the Show Performance command turns on frequent status reports about your server performance. As with all console messages, this information can be seen in the Log.NSF file or simply by watching the console. See figure 8.45 for an example.

Figure 8.45

The Show Performance command.

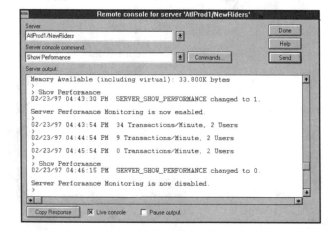

Show Port

The Show Port command enables you to see the traffic occurring on the specified port. It is often a good exercise to check your Com ports prior to shutting down a Domino server. This lets you know whether someone has recently connected so that you do not interrupt the person if you can avoid it. See figure 8.46 for an example of the Show Port command.

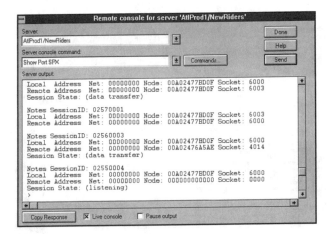

Figure 8.46

The Show Port command.

Show Schedule

The Show Schedule command displays the times of future events that will occur on the server. As shown in figure 8.47, items such as mail routing, replication, and compact are displayed by the server.

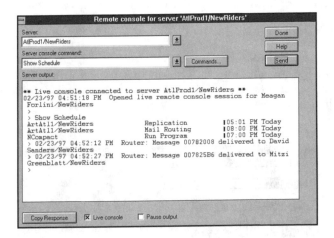

Figure 8.47

The Show Schedule command.

Show Server

Show Server is more or less a subset of Show Tasks. The Show Server command enables you to know the current version of Domino that is installed on the server and where dead or pending messages are (see fig. 8.48).

Figure 8.48

The Show Server command.

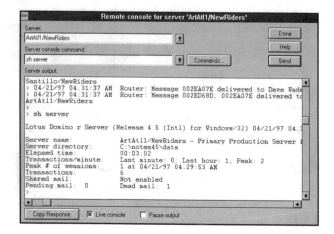

Show Tasks

The Show Tasks command displays all current processes that are occurring on the server plus the current version of Domino and whether there are any pending or dead letters. This command is extremely useful when determining whether your last command was carried out, or it can be used to investigate problems with the server.

Show Users

Show Users displays all the current Lotus Notes Users that are actively on the Lotus Domino server. If you are considering downing your server, it can be helpful to see how many and which users are actively using the Domino server. An example is shown in figure 8.49.

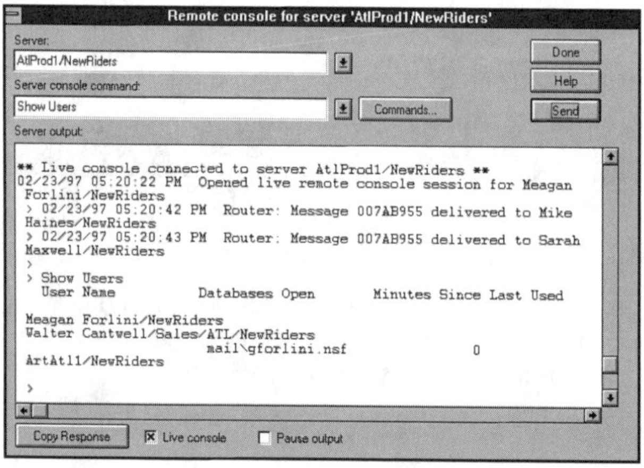

Figure 8.49

The Show Users command.

Tell

The Tell command is (with few exceptions) used to end a task. For instance, T Router Q stops the router process. This command ends any task that was loaded at server startup or by the Load command. Please see the next section on the Load and Tell commands.

L Process and T [Process] Q

Many processes must be initiated with the Load command. To stop these same processes, use Tell [Process] Quit. For example, if you are interested in starting the router on your server, use L Router. If you want to stop the router on your server, use T Router Q. The processes that are used with Load (and Tell) include:

◆ **Replica.** You can start and stop replication on your Domino server (see fig. 8.50).

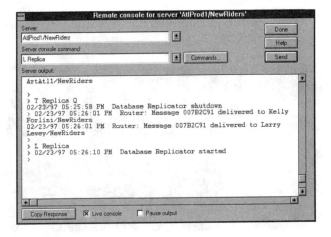

Figure 8.50

Replica.

◆ **Fixup.** Fixup finds and removes damaged documents. It leaves no deletion stub when it removes the documents, so you may be able to get the document back during the next replication of the database. Notice in figure 8.51, Fixup can be loaded remotely or at the console as is the case with any server command. For more information about document deletions, see the "Fundamentals of Domino Administration" section in Chapter 6.

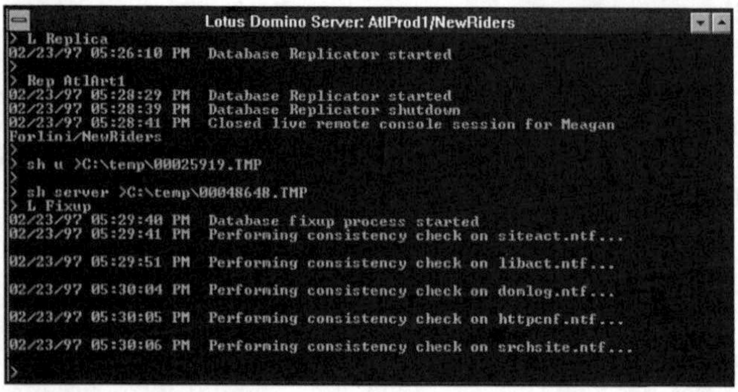

Figure 8.51

Fixup.

◆ **Report.** Report can be used to gather statistics on your server. For more information, see Chapter 9.

◆ **Event.** Event can be used to monitor changes to databases and other occurrences on your Domino server. For more information, see Chapter 9.

◆ **Router.** If you are experiencing difficulty with mail, you can start or stop the mail router with this command. See figure 8.52 for an example.

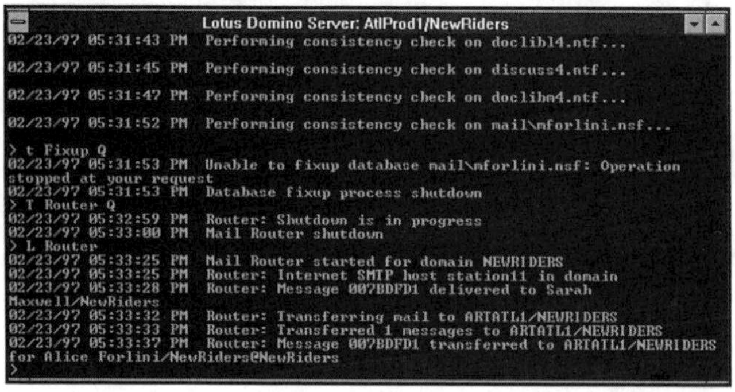

Figure 8.52

Router.

◆ **Amgr.** The Agent Manager process runs agents in databases. You can limit the use of agents on a Domino server with the restrictions section of the Server record. For more information, see the "Server Security" section in Chapter 6. As shown in figure 8.53, the Agent Manager can be started and stopped.

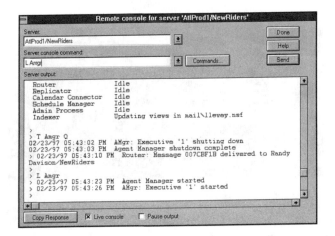

Figure 8.53

Agent Manager.

◆ **AdminP.** The AdminP process is used to change names and recertify or delete users and servers. For more information, please see the AdminP section of this chapter. As seen in figure 8.54, you can stop and start AdminP with the Load and Tell commands.

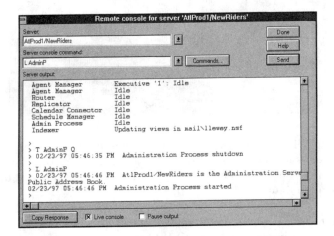

Figure 8.54

AdminP.

◆ **Catalog.** Each night, the Catalog process runs to update information about directories and all database files on your Domino server. As you can see in figure 8.55, you can use the Load command to begin the process immediately.

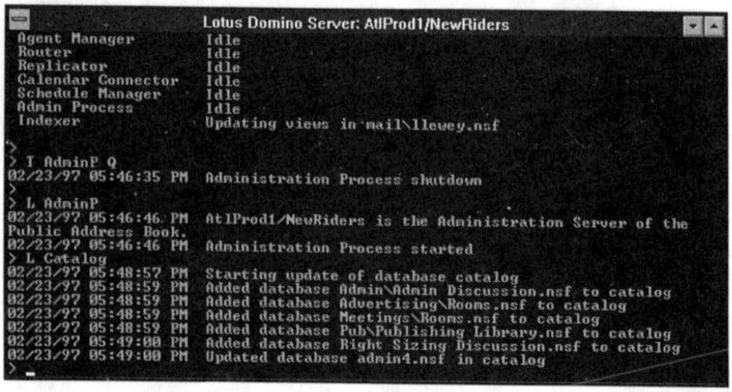

Figure 8.55

Catalog.

◆ **Design.** Design typically runs on every Domino server each night. As you can see in figure 8.56, this command forces databases to be redesigned based on the elements in the associated template.

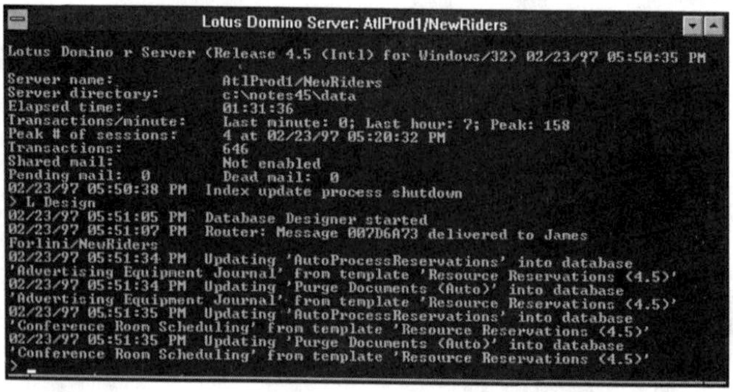

Figure 8.56

Design.

◆ **Updall.** The Updall command reindexes all views and full text indices. (Actually, Indexer is launched with Updall for full text indices.) By default, this task runs each night on your Domino server. You can see an example of the Updall command in figure 8.57.

This concludes all information about the Admin Panel and Remote Console. The next few sections will cover in detail more advanced administration features such as shared mail, AdminP, and PassThru server.

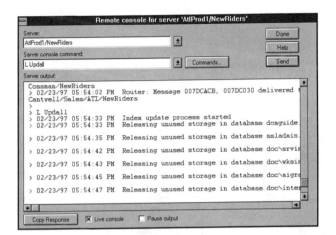

Figure 8.57

The Updall command.

Advanced Administration Features

The following section includes many select features introduced in version 4.x that enable you to automate many processes that in previous versions were manual and often time-consuming. These advanced features include Shared Mail, AdminP, Notes.INI changes, Expiring ID's, PassThru Server, and Advanced Server License.

Shared Mail

For anyone fond of reducing used disk space, shared mail is a great feature. In Lotus Notes v3, all mail messages were sent as individual documents to each mail file in all circumstances. Today with v4.x, shared mail uses a common Object Store to reduce used disk space.

Author Note By default, shared mail is not enabled when you install your Domino server.

By using shared mail, you can conserve disk space because the body of messages is stored in one central place and the top portion of the mail (the header) is the only part of the message stored in a mail file. There are two different types of shared mail and three ways to enable shared mail. The two different types of shared mail are shared mail = 1 and shared mail = 2. The following sections discuss how to configure shared mail.

An Example of Shared Mail

An example of shared mail is illustrated in figure 8.58.

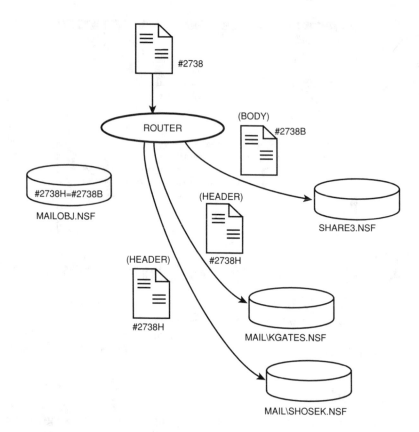

Figure 8.58

A shared mail illustration.

As a mail message is being sent to a server, it is received by the router process. The router breaks the message into two pieces. The first piece, called the header, contains the To:, cc:, bcc:, and the subject fields. The header of the message is placed in each individual mail file. The rest of the message (body) is stored in a shared mail file (in this case Share3.NSF). Only a single copy of the body is needed because the header will be matched with the body whenever the message is needed. The command SH Server enables you to know the name of the shared mail file that the router is currently using. A separate file called MailOBJ.NSF links the header with the body of the message. MailOBJ.NSF is a highly secure file and cannot be named anything else.

Shared Mail=1

When the Shared Mail=1 option is selected, the server uses a share file only when the message is intended for more than one recipient on the server. Setting Shared Mail=1 makes your server more efficient when messages are only intended for one user, but it also conserves disk space when a message is intended for many.

Shared Mail=2

When you enable the Shared Mail=2 option, shared mail is used in all circumstances. It does not matter whether the message is intended for one or many. It does not even matter whether a user has mail on that server. This option can make mail routing inefficient (particularly on a Hub server that does not have mail files).

Turning Shared Mail On

You can turn shared mail on in the following ways:

◆ Changing the Notes.ini manually

◆ Updating with a Configuration document

◆ Using the T Router command

Changing the Notes.ini Manually

Before changing the Notes.ini, you must shut down your Lotus Domino server. This is done by issuing either the Q (quit) or the E (exit) command. After your server has stopped running, you can use any text editor to change the file. You can find the Notes.ini in the Notes directory or the Windows directory (WinNT35 for instance) (see fig. 8.59). After the file is opened, scroll to the bottom of the file to add a new line with Shared Mail= and the number you desire.

Figure 8.59

Editing Notes.ini.

Updating with a Configuration Document

You can enter the Address Book Configurations view by either opening the Address Book directly and switching to the Configurations view, or using File, Tools, Server Administration, Servers, Configure Servers.

After you are presented with the Configurations view, find the Configuration Document for the server you are changing (shown in fig. 8.60).

Figure 8.60

Configurations view.

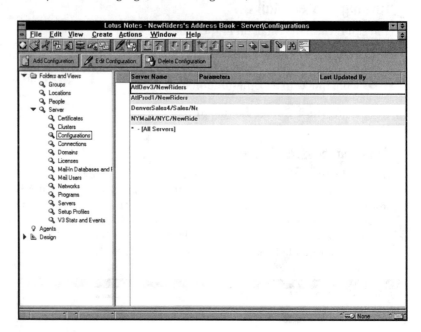

If one does not exist, you can make one by selecting the button Add Configuration. After you open the Document, make sure the server name is set to the specified server and is spelled correctly (be sure to remove the asterisk if needed). At the bottom of the Document, select Set/Modify Parameters. Select Shared_Mail from the list. As shown in figure 8.61, type the desired setting in the field below the selection.

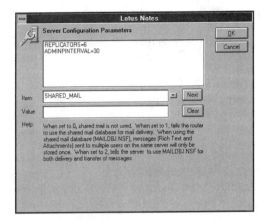

Figure 8.61

The configuration menu.

Ten or fewer minutes after saving the document, your server should create two new shared mail databases. The first is the MailOBJ1.NSF (for storage of rich text and attachments) and the second is MailOBJ.NSF (so that each header can be matched with the corresponding body).

Using T Router Command

When you use T Router Use Share1.NSF, shared mail is turned on. At the moment you issue the T Router command, two new files are created (Share1.NSF for the body of the messages and MailOBJ.NSF to match header and body). One advantage of using the T Router command is that you can specify the shared mail file name rather than using the default file name (MailObj1.NSF). This command can also be used to move to a new shared mail file. It is a good idea to use a new shared mail file on occasion (approximately every three months) so that you are better prepared in a disaster (loss of the current mail file). As you can see in figure 8.62, when using this command, Shared Mail is set to 2.

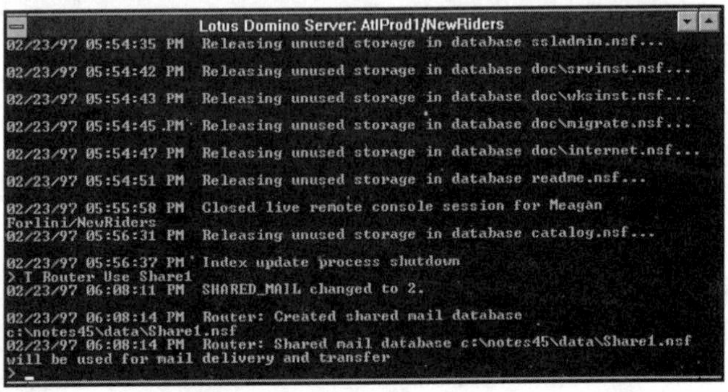

Figure 8.62

Shared mail.

Other Shared Mail Commands

There are some other shared mail commands that will allow you to further configure shared mail:

◆ **Load Object Unlink *SHARED.NSF*.** With this command, you can remove all objects stored in the shared file. This is necessary before deleting the file or if you want to stop using shared mail. When this process is used, Notes unlinks each document in the shared mail database and stores a copy of it in its entirety in the mail file of each user that shares the document.

◆ **Load Object Unlink *Mail\USERMAIL.NSF*.** If it is necessary to move a user to another server, you should first unlink the user's mail file from the shared mail database. When you use this command, all messages in their entirety are married into the user's mail file.

◆ **Load Object Collect *SHARED.NSF*.** After all header data has been removed from mail files, you should delete the unneeded body from the shared mail file. By default, this process runs each night against the *currently* used shared file at 2 AM. This command is particularly important for old shared mail files. You may want to run the Object Collect task manually on them from time to time (fig. 8.63).

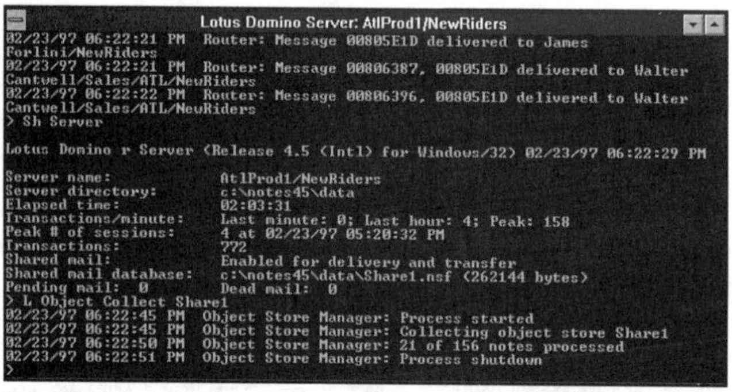

Figure 8.63

The Load Object Collect command.

◆ **Load Object Set -Never *Mail\USERMAIL.NSF*.** If you find it necessary to exclude some users from using the shared mail file, you can use this command on the mail file.

◆ **Load Object Reset -Never *Mail\USERMAIL.NSF*.** If you previously excluded a mail file from using Object Store, you can enable it again with this command.

◆ **Load Object Link *Mail\USERMAIL.NSF SHARED.NSF*.** If you have never used shared mail before, you can use this command to cause previous messages to be placed in the Object Store file. You can also specify an entire directory by simply leaving off the mail file name (Mail\). See an example of this command in figure 8.64.

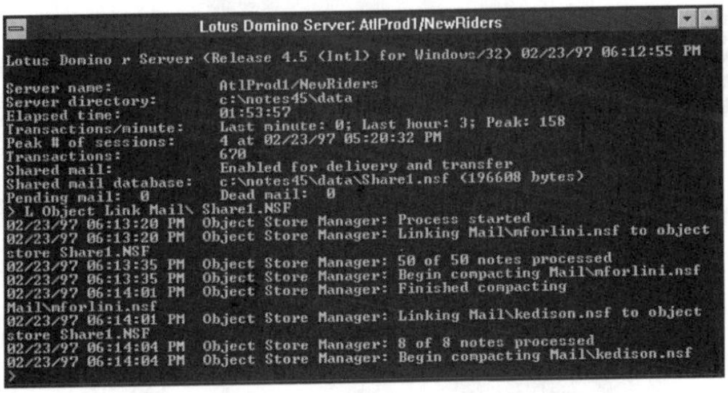

Figure 8.64

*The Load Object
Link command.*

◆ **Load Object LinkRelink *Mail\USERMAIL.NSF SHARED.NSF.*** This
command should be used after moving a mail file to a new server or if you
desire to use a different shared mail database. Relink causes all corresponding
message bodies to be placed in the Object Store regardless of previous linkings.

◆ **Load Object Info *USERMAIL.NSF.*** With this command, you can determine
whether a mail message is using the Object Store database. See figure 8.65 for
an example of this command.

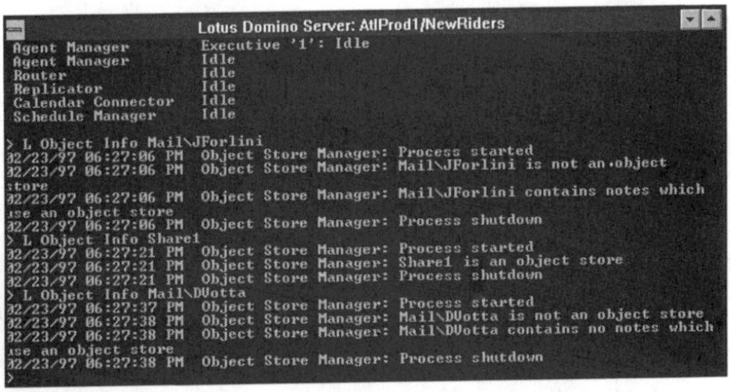

Figure 8.65

*The Load Object
Info command.*

AdminP

AdminP (another advanced administration feature) is used to reregister, change
names, or delete servers or users. The name change could be due to such circumstances as a marriage, a move, or a change in departments. With AdminP, the name
of the user is changed in the person record, groups, all ACLs (where the correct
Administration Server is set), Reader Name, and Author Name fields. Most requests
can be done in the People view of the Public Name & Address Book as shown in
figure 8.66.

Figure 8.66

People view.

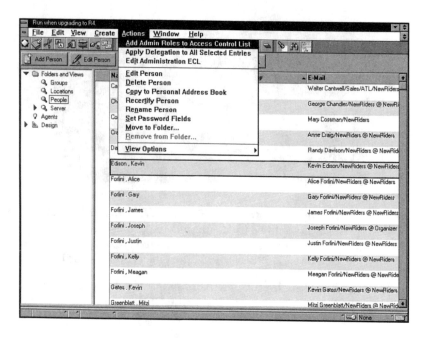

The following is needed for AdminP to work correctly:

◆ An Admin4.NSF file

◆ A CertLog.NSF file

◆ Editor Rights to the Public Name & Address Book, Admin4.NSF, and CertLog.NSF

◆ Membership in the UserModifier or ServerModifier roles in the Public Name & Address Book

◆ Listing of the correct administration server in the ACLs of all databases that should be changed

The following sections will guide you through setting up AdminP. You will see examples and explanations of how the process functions and learn of the needed steps to use the process.

The Admin4.NSF File

The Admin4.NSF file is created automatically the first time you start your Lotus Domino server. All change requests are submitted to this database and then the AdminP process periodically checks to see these requests and carry them out. One of the several views (All Requests by Action) is shown in figure 8.67.

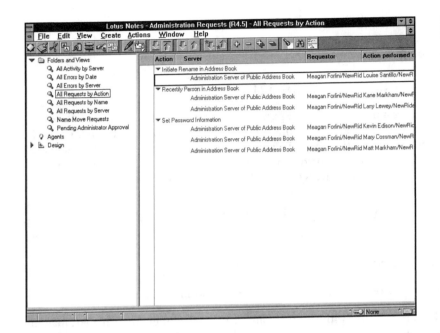

Figure 8.67

All Requests by Action.

The CertLog.nsf File

A CertLog file is not created automatically by the Domino server. You must create this file by hand. Follow these steps:

1. Select File, Database, New.

2. Type **CertLog** in the title menu (this automatically makes the file name CertLog.NSF).

3. Be sure to select the CertLog.ntf file as the template. As shown in figure 8.68, it is called Certification Log. If you do not find it on your local system, use the Template Server button to locate the file on any server.

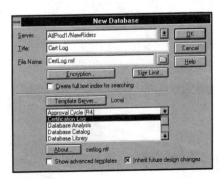

Figure 8.68

New CertLog file.

4. Select OK.

By default, you are made manager of this file unless you created it at your server. If you created the file directly from your server's workspace, you should change the ACL to reflect your name with editor rights.

Editor Rights in the Access Control List

To use AdminP, you need to change the Access Control List (ACL) for the Public Name & Address Book (Names.nsf), the Administration Database (AdminP.nsf), and the Certification Log (CertLog.nsf). To change the Access Control List of a database, select File, Database, Access Control. You can either hand type names or use the Person button to open the address book and select from the list.

Roles in the Public Name & Address Book

The following roles exist in the Public Name & Address Book (see fig. 8.69):

- **GroupCreator.** A user in this role can make new groups.

- **GroupModifier.** This role enables a user to modify existing groups.

- **NetCreator.** A user with this role can create new connection, certifier, mail-in database, setup profile, domain, and configuration documents.

- **NetModifier.** Persons in this role can modify connection, domain, and configuration documents.

- **ServerCreator.** An individual in this role can make new server documents. (This should be done from the registration process.)

- **ServerModifier.** This role enables persons to change server records.

- **UserCreator.** Individuals in this role can register new people.

- **UserModifier.** Users in this role can change Person records.

Figure 8.69

ACL for address book.

To use AdminP, you must be a member of the role UserModifier or ServerModifier (depending on whether you are changing users or servers respectively).

Assigning Administration Server to an ACL

To assign an administration server to the Access Control List of a database, choose File, Database, Access Control. Select the advanced tab (it has a beanie) to view or change the administration server. The first field is for Administration Server. You can either type in the fully distinguished name (such as Hub1/DAL/SingerToys) or select a server from the list. After the server name is entered, you can also select whether to change Reader and Author Name fields. By default, these fields are changed. Reader Name and Author Name fields are used to grant rights to documents. For more information, see Chapter 11.

There are many automated changes to IDs that you can accomplish with AdminP. The following sections will aid you in discovering how the most common changes work. You will see examples and explanations of changing a user ID to hierarchical and recertifying a person with AdminP.

How to Change an ID from Flat to Hierarchical

To change an ID from flat (such as Alice Forlini) to hierarchical (such as Alice Forlini/Sales/NewRiders), you can use two different methods:

◆ Altering a safe ID (a nonfunctional ID used to mail IDs) sent by the user

◆ Using AdminP

Altering a Safe ID Sent by the User

The easiest way for a user to request a change to an ID is to use File, Tools, User ID, Certificates Tab (it looks like a gold certificate), Request Certificate. The user is then presented with a mail dialog box. He or she can then address the message and alter the message that automatically appears:

```
My ID is attached. Please certify it and send it back to me by using the
Actions menu "Certify Attached ID File..." option.
```

After you receive this safe copy from the user, you can follow the instructions just as they are: Actions, Certify Attached ID File. You should then put in the diskette that contains the hierarchical certifier. You can even create a button to accomplish the certificate request:

Create a piece of mail and use Create, Hotspot Button. From the Command options, use @Command([MailSendCertificateRequest]).

Using AdminP to Upgrade to Hierarchical

For initial setup procedures, see the AdminP setup section of this chapter. From the People View, select Actions, Change Name, Upgrade to Hierarchical (see fig. 8.70).

Figure 8.70

Change name menu.

As the user signs on after this change, he or she sees a message that reads "Do you wish to accept the new certificate?" If he or she selects Yes, the new hierarchical name is accepted into the ID. (If the person chooses No, the new name is not placed into the ID). After the new name is selected, AdminP continues the process of renaming the individual. All Groups, Access Control Lists, Reader Name Fields, and Author Name fields are changed (provided that the correct selections have been made for the databases).

The following occurs during this process (see fig. 8.71):

1. The request for the change is made by the administrator in the Public Name & Address Book.

2. A change request is written to the Admin4.NSF database and the event is logged in the CertLog.NSF database.

3. Replication occurs (if needed).

4. AdminP finds the request and it alters the Person record in the Public Name & Address Book.

5. Replication occurs amoung other servers in the organization (if needed).

6. When the user seeks access to any server in the domain, he or she is prompted to accept the change.

7. After selecting Yes, the user.id file is changed. A request for changes in the Public Name & Address Book is made to the Admin4 database.

8. Replication occurs back to the administration server (if needed).

9. AdminP alters all Group, Connection, and Server records that are applicable.

10. A request for changes to ACL and name fields (if applicable) is placed in the Admin4.nsf database.

11. The administration server replicates with other servers in the domain (if needed).

12. AdminP alters all ACLs and author and/or reader names fields that apply.

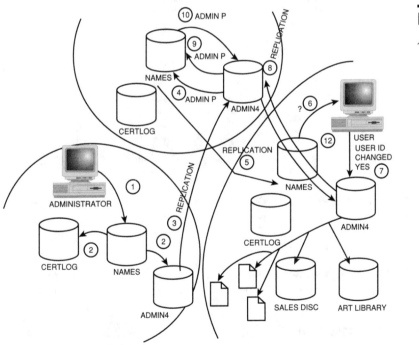

Figure 8.71

AdminP.

The CertLog.nsf is written to (via replication) during this process, but the file is not a key player in this change. The administration server does not have to be your Hub if the file does not replicate. The following fields exist on the server record to further configure AdminP:

◆ **Maximum number of threads.** The default is three. Do not increase this setting unless you are changing many users or servers at once. You may consider decreasing the number of threads if you are having performance problems with the server.

◆ **Interval.** This field can be changed to reflect the desired number of minutes that AdminP searches for requests.

You can change the following options for AdminP with a Configuration document:

◆ **ADMINPINTERVAL.** You can change the frequency (in number of minutes) that AdminP runs on your server. The default is every sixty minutes. See figure 8.72 for an example of this Configuration record.

Figure 8.72

ADMINP-INTERVAL.

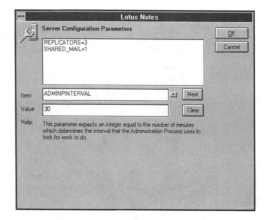

◆ **ADMINPMODIFYPERSONDOCUMENTSAT.** By default, AdminP changes person records at midnight on your administration server. If this is in conflict (with a backup process for instance), you can change it to another time using the 24 hour format (military time).

◆ **NAME_CHANGE_EXPIRATION_DAYS.** You can specify how long the Admin4 database keeps a change request. You can choose from 14 to 60 days.

Recertifying a Person with AdminP

User IDs expire two years from the time they were certified (unless you change the default). When a certificate on an ID is due to expire, you must recertify the ID. You can do this with the AdminP process before the ID expires but not after the date has passed.

After you have the AdminP setup (see the "AdminP Setup" section), you can change user or server names. To recertify a person, select a Person record and then choose Actions, Recertify Person from the People view of the Public Name & Address Book. The following explains the process that occurs on the Domino server:

1. After you specify the user or server ID to recertify, the Lotus Domino server automatically posts a "Recertify Person in Address Book" document in the Administration Requests database. This document is a request to start the process of recertifying the specified ID.

2. The Lotus Domino server posts an entry in the Certification Log (CertLog.nsf) on the same server on which you made the request. This entry appears in the By Certifier Name view of the Certification Log. (If any errors occur, the documents appear in the Updates Status view of the Certification Log.)

3. The Administration Requests database replicates to your Public Address Book's administration server (likely your Hub).

4. The Administration Process on the Public Address Book's administration server verifies the request in the Administration Requests database and updates the appropriate Person document with the new certificate. The updated Public Address Book replicates throughout the domain.

5. When the user (being recertified) uses his or her server, the server verifies the change and then copies the new certificate to the user.id file without need of intervention from the user.

Moving a User to a New Certifier with AdminP

If a user is changing departments or relocating, you may need to move the person to a new certifier. Follow the steps below to perform this function:

1. Select the name you wish to move in the Public Name & Address Book.

2. Use Actions, Rename Person, Request Move To New Certifier.

3. Use the Original Certifier for the person so that you can confirm the change. Type in the name of the certifier.

Note You must spell the new certifier name correctly for this process to work correctly.

4. After your request is made, the Administration Process posts a request to the Name Move Requests view of the Administration Database.

5. You should enter into the Administration Database and select the record in the Name Move Requests view. See figure 8.73 for an example of moving a user to a new certifier.

Figure 8.73

An AdminP move request.

6. Click on Actions, Complete Move Request. When prompted, put in the new Certifier ID and password.

 A certifier document must be present in the Certificates view of the Public Name & Address Book for this action to take place. If one does not exist, you can make one by copying the public key of the file to a new certifier document. For more information, see Chapter 12, "Troubleshooting Notes and Domino 4.5."

7. After you specify the user or server ID to move, the Lotus Domino server automatically posts a "Recertify Person in Address Book" document in the Administration Requests database. This document is a request to start the process of recertifying the specified ID.

8. The Lotus Domino server posts an entry in the Certification Log (CertLog.nsf) on the same server on which you made the request. This entry appears in the By Certifier Name view of the Certification Log. (If any errors occur, the documents appear in the Updates Status view of the Certification Log.)

9. The Administration Requests database replicates to your Public Address Book's administration server (likely your Hub).

10. The Administration Process on the Public Address Book's administration server verifies the request in the Administration Requests database and updates the appropriate Person document with the new certificate. The updated Public Address Book replicates throughout the domain.

11. When the user (being recertified) uses his or her server, the server verifies the change and then copies the new certificate to the user.id file without need of intervention from the user.

Removing a User with AdminP

When an individual leaves your company, you should first deny him or her access and then remove all references to the name. To deny access to a server, you should use a group (often called Terminations) that is specified in the server record of the Public Name & Address Book. For more information about server security, please see Chapter 6. After you have AdminP set up (see the "AdminP Setup" section of this chapter), you can delete user or server names. To remove a user, follow these steps:

1. Select the person to delete in the People view of the Public Name & Address Book.

2. Click on the Delete Person button and then select Yes to confirm the operation.

3. A trash can is placed next to the record. When you exit the database, select Yes to confirm the deletion.

4. After you specify the user or server ID to delete, the Lotus Domino server automatically posts a "Delete Person in Address Book" document in the Administration Requests database.

5. The Lotus Domino server posts an entry in the Certification Log (CertLog.nsf) on the same server on which you made the request. This entry appears in the By Certifier Name view of the Certification Log. (If any errors occur, the documents appear in the Updates Status view of the Certification Log.)

6. The Administration Requests database replicates to your Public Address Book's administration server (likely your Hub).

7. The Administration Process on the Public Address Book's administration server verifies the request in the Administration Requests database and removes entries for the person on Group and Connection records (if applicable). The updated Public Address Book replicates throughout the domain.

8. A post is made in the Administration Database to remove all ACL entries. The Administration Database replicates throughout the organization.

9. The User's name is removed from all ACLs in every database where an administration server is set.

10. The Reader Names and Author Names fields are updated accordingly.

The preceeding sections have given you details for using and configuring AdminP. The next section will focus attention on how to change the Notes.ini file. The Notes.ini file must be changed on occasion to further configure your Domino server and make changes to the functions that run on your Domino server.

Changing the Notes.ini File

You can change the Notes.ini file manually with any text editor. However, for changes to take effect, you must shut down and restart the server. Additionally, it can be very easy to get the syntax incorrect when writing directly in the Notes.ini file. With two other methods, you do not need to shut down the server in most circumstances and typographical errors can be avoided. These methods include:

◆ Creating a Configuration document

◆ Using the Set Config command

The following parameters cannot be changed dynamically without restarting the server:

◆ ServerTasks and ServerTasksAt

◆ NSF_Buffer_Pool_Size

◆ Domain

◆ ModemFileDirectory

◆ ServerKeyFileName

◆ Ports

Configuration Records

Configuration documents are kept in the Public Name & Address Book for the Domino server. With these documents, you can change many Notes.ini parameters without having to down the Domino server. To create a Configuration record, you can open the Public Name & Address Book directly and select the Configurations view or you can use File, Tools, Server Administration, Servers, Configure Servers. As shown in figure 8.74, you can create a new Configuration record by selecting the button Add Configuration.

After you have the document open, you can accept the default asterisk (*) to modify all servers in the domain, or you can specify a server or a group. When the Public Name & Address Book is read for changes, it only recognizes the first configuration record that it encounters and ignores the rest. (The view is sorted alphanumerically.) Additionally, you should not have more than one document with the asterisk (*). The server only reads the first one that it encounters.

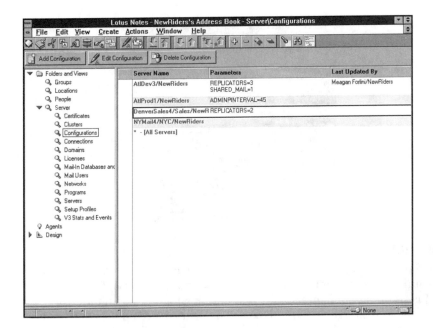

Figure 8.74

Configuration view.

To add or change Notes.ini settings, you can click on the Set/Modify Parameters button. After the dialog box appears (see fig. 8.75), you can use the small arrow button to select the parameters from the list (highly recommended).

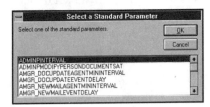

Figure 8.75

Configuration parameters.

After you select the option, a help message appears in the dialog box (shown in fig. 8.76).

Figure 8.76

The Configuration help dialog box.

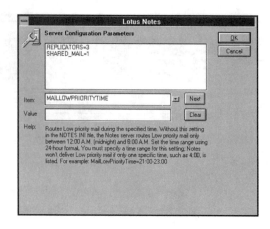

Set Configuration

The Set Configuration command can also be used to change the Notes.ini file. Before using this feature, you can view any current settings with the Show Configuration command. Just as in the Configuration document, you have little room for error because you are not hand typing the commands in a text editor and the command does not accept incorrect switches.

PassThru Server

The PassThru server feature gives users the ability to attach to one server and then access many (see fig. 8.77).

Figure 8.77

Illustration of PassThru.

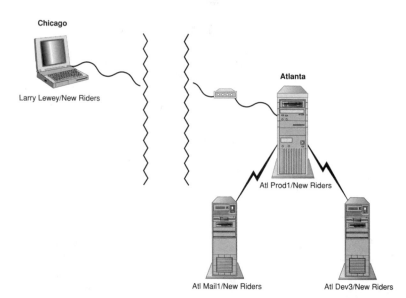

Notice in figure 8.77 that Larry Lewey wants to call the production server to catch up on company news, read mail on the mail server, and replicate design changes to a database on the development server. He first calls the AtlProd1 server. After he is there, the server acts as a connector to the AtlMail1 server and the AtlDev3 server.

Setting Up PassThru on the Server

The Server record must be changed in all three servers in the Larry Lewey example. The AtlProd1 server must have Larry Lewey listed in some manner (group or explicitly) in the PassThru field (of the restrictions section) in the Server record. The AtlDev3 server and the AtlMail1 server must list Larry Lewey in some manner in the Access This Server field of the restrictions section. Notice the example Server record in figure 8.78.

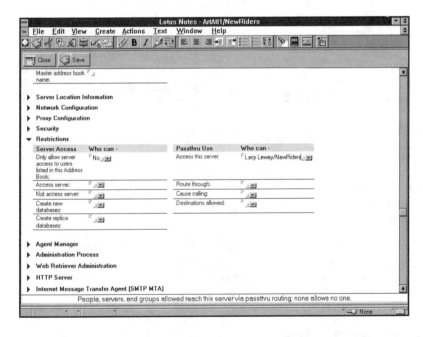

Figure 8.78

Server record.

For more information about security for PassThru, see Chapter 6.

Setting Up PassThru on the Workstation

In the example, Larry Lewey must also set up PassThru on his laptop. In the Location record (Personal Name & Address Book), he must specify the AtlProd1 server in the PassThru Server field. For an example of a Location record, see figure 8.79.

Figure 8.79

Location record.

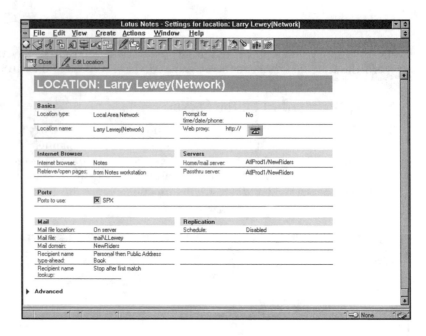

Expiring Password in Person Record

With release 4.5, you can now force password expiration and check passwords to gain access to the server. For these features to work, you must enable the option on both the Server and Person records. Additionally, both the workstation and server must be running with 4.5 and the IDs must be hierarchical. For an example of password features, see figure 8.80.

If you know a copy of an ID has been lost or stolen and you want to prevent the use of the ID, you can accomplish this in the Person record. You can specify a password by changing the Check password field on the Person record (in the administration section). The password must match what is kept in the ID and what is stored in the Public Name & Address Book.

With the Expiration field of the Person record, you can force passwords to be changed. You also have a Grace Period field on the Server record to specify a certain number of days in which you wish the password to expire.

You can also lock an ID out of the server. The Password check field also includes a lock out option. This lock out is similar to placing an individual in the Deny Access field of your Server record.

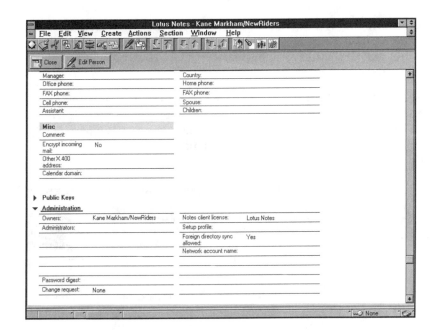

Figure 8.80

Person record.

Advanced Server License

You can obtain three Advanced Server features by purchasing an Advanced Server License:

◆ Billing

◆ Clustering

◆ Partitioning

Billing

Billing can be used to determine the number of users that access your system and what they do after they arrive. You can monitor mail routing, sessions, database usage, replication, and agents with the billing process. For more information about billing, please see Chapter 22.

Clustering

Clustering allows you to fail over from a busy server to another server in the cluster. With this Advanced Server feature, you can specify thresholds that make a server unusable when it has too many active sessions or when the server is generally tied up. In this manner, you can use clustering to better balance the workload of your servers.

The largest factor surrounding clustering is replication. It is imperative that the same databases with the same information are available on all clustered servers. Cluster replication ensures that all changes are immediately passed to other databases or servers in the cluster.

To set up clusters, you must first install the advanced services features and then complete setup in the Public Name & Address Book. For information about installation, please see Chapter 6. After you have installed advanced services, simply open the address book to the Servers, Servers view. As shown in figure 8.81, you can click on the button Add to Cluster while a server is selected.

Figure 8.81

Servers view.

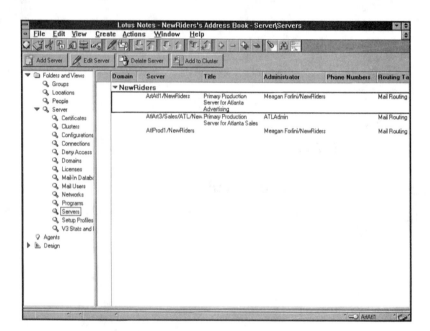

The following items can be changed in the Configuration record for clusters:

- ◆ **MAILCLUSTERFAILOVER.** When set to 1, mail router finds alternative paths to mail files when the server is in a busy state. The user mail files must be replicated to the other clustered servers for the router to be able to find the files.

- ◆ **SERVER_AVAILABILITY_THRESHOLD.** Used with clusters, you can specify thresholds for a busy state. By using this parameter, you can determine how to distribute the workload to servers. You can select any number between 0 and 100. If you set the variable to 0, workload balancing is disabled. The server builds a server's availability index based on server resources and this number is never higher than 100.

◆ **SERVER_MAXUSERS.** Used with clusters, you can specify the total number of users before the server considers itself in a busy state. For an example of this Configuration record, see figure 8.82.

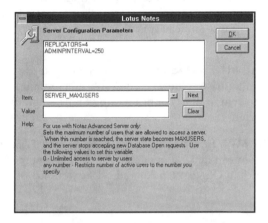

Figure 8.82

*SERVER_
MAXUSERS.*

◆ **SERVER_RESTRICTED.** You can disable (users cannot use databases) a server. A setting of 0 means the server is available. A setting of 1 means that the server is unavailable only until the server is restarted. A setting of 2 means the server is currently unavailable and remains unavailable after restarting.

Partitioning

Partitioning allows you to use one machine to act as multiple servers. This advanced server feature is supported on Unix and Windows NT. By using separate directories, you can install up to eight partitioned servers on one machine. This feature needs about 100 MB additional disk space and an additional 32 MB of RAM.

A Configuration document can be used to invoke the Killprocess command. The Killprocess command cleans up all server tasks prior to an unplanned server shutdown on a partitioned server.

Gateways and MTAs

Many add-on products may be of great interest to you depending on how you use Lotus Notes and what you believe your future endeavors may be. Some of the add-on products that Lotus supplies include the following:

◆ **Fax Server for Notes Release 1.1.** This is actually a Lotus Notes client that sends and receives faxes for Notes and cc:Mail users. Anyone that can get to the same domain can send or receive a fax with this product. Currently this is supported with Windows 3.1 and Windows NT 3.51. However, it is known to work on Windows 95 and Windows NT 4.0.

◆ **Pager Gateway for Notes Release 2.0.** Any user in the same domain can send pages to numeric and alphanumeric pagers. This can also be very beneficial to administrators because you can specify messages to alert you about server problems.

◆ **Lotus Notes cc:Mail MTA Release 1.0.** The cc:Mail Message Transfer Agent can be used so that Lotus Notes and cc:Mail can communicate. This is ideal for organizations that want to continue using or are migrating from cc:Mail with Lotus Notes.

◆ **Lotus Notes SMTP MTA Release 1.1.** The Simple Mail Transfer Protocol Message Transfer Agent can make it possible to send Internet mail. Currently this is designed to work in OS/2 Warp 3.0 and NT Server 3.51 or greater.

Summary

In this chapter you have explored many aspects of administering a Domino 4.5 server. You first read about the many details for using the Admin Panel. You further discovered Remote Console commands that you can use to maintain your Domino server. You then gained knowledge about some advanced server features: Shared Mail, AdminP, Notes.ini changes, Expiring IDs, PassThru Server, and Advanced Server License.

CHAPTER 9

Statistic Tracking and Event Notification for Domino 4.5 Servers

O ne of the most important parts of a Domino administrator's job is monitoring the server or servers for problems and potential problems. Lotus has given the administrator several tools for this monitoring including a statistic collection series of databases and executables for trend tracking and Alarm generation, an Event notification process, and database and log analysis tools.

The interaction between the various components in the Notes reporting tools is fairly complex. This chapter describes how to set up these processes. The breakdown of the components that may be involved in the overall reporting process include the following:

◆ **Statistic collection.** This process is used to collect statistical information for Domino servers on a timed basis. This information can be used for tracking server trends and for report generation or graphing through additional products such as Lotus Approach or Notes Reporter.

◆ **Statistic tracking.** This process tracks individual statistics for comparison against set thresholds. When the threshold is crossed, an Alarm document is generated in the tracking database. A very common statistic to track, for example, is called Diskc.free, which tracks the available disk space for drive C on the server. The threshold is set based on the number of bytes remaining on the specified drive. In the case of drive C, a common threshold setting is 20,000,000, or around 20 MB free. If drive C on the server fell below 20 MB, an Alarm document would be generated that indicates the actual available disk space on that drive.

◆ **Trouble tickets.** Trouble tickets are generated from Alarm documents and are used to track assigned individuals for Alarm resolution and the amount of time taken for the resolution, and anything done by the assigned individual to resolve the problem.

◆ **Event notification.** The event notification process is used to notify based on events occuring. The events are generated by the statistic tracking process or the Notes logger process (that process that writes the log file). The notification techniques include e-mail (usually to an individual or group of administrators), database logging (to the same database used for statistic collection and Alarm documents), and so forth.

Although most of these processes report on errors or warnings at the server level (such as event notification), others are used to either prevent problems (such as Alarms from the Reporter) or prevent problems from escalating.

Additional monitoring covered in this chapter includes mail performance and dead mail, server performance, and memory availability. And finally, the new interface to Windows NT for event tracking through the operating system is addressed.

Terms Used in the Statistic and Event Process

The following is a list of terms used in this chapter:

◆ **Report.** Report is an executable that runs from the Domino server console by issuing the Load Report command. This executable, referred to as Reporter, is used for the statistic collection and Alarm generation processes.

◆ **Collect.** Collect is an executable that runs from the Domino server by issuing the Load Collect command. This executable, referred to as the Collector, is used for statistic collection across multiple servers.

◆ **Alarm.** An Alarm is generated by the reporter process when a set threshold is crossed for a specific statistic. This generation is controlled by Statistic Monitoring documents stored in the Events and Statistics database.

◆ **Statistic.** A statistic is an individual piece of data about the Domino server task. For example, statistics exist that report the number of current users, the amount of free disk space on every available drive, the current Notes revision, and so forth.

◆ **Statistic tracking.** This process generates a Statistic Report document, which is stored in that server's Statistic database (Statrep.nsf). The document is a collection of statistics from that server generated on a timed basis. The setting for each server that collects statistics is served in the Event and Statistic database (Events4).

◆ **Statistic collection database (Statrep.nsf).** This database is used to collect the statistic report and Alarm from the report process, as well as logged events from the event process.

◆ **Statistics and events database (Events4.nsf).** This database is used as a control database for both the report and event processes. Documents in this database indicate what servers to gather statistics from, the statistics to monitor, and the events to notify on.

◆ **Event.** Event is an executable that can be run on a Domino server by issuing the Load Event command. This executable is responsible for tracking events as indicated in the Statistics and Events database and performing notifications based on documents in that same database. The Event process tracks events generated by the report process and the logger process.

◆ **Event.** An event can also be something that occurred on the server, such as sending or receiving mail, users logging on, errors, and so forth. These events can be tracked using Event Notification documents in the Events4 database. This information is used by the Event process to perform notification.

◆ **Logger.** Logger is an executable that runs on every Domino server. The logger process writes the Notes log file (log.nsf). The logger process is a real-time reporting tool for events that occur on the server (as opposed to the reporter process, which runs on a timed basis).

◆ **Alarm generation or statistic monitoring.** The generation of Alarm documents in the Statrep database is called Alarm generation or statistic monitoring (based on the statistic monitoring documents in the Events4 database).

◆ **Severity.** Event severity is one of the two items needed for the Event process to notify based on events occurring. Severity levels have general meaning, although the administrator decides what the severity level will be. The levels are: Fatal, Failure, Warning (High), Warning (Low), and Normal. Severities are found in statistic monitoring documents and event documents in the Events4 database.

The Statistic Collection and Alarm Generation Process

Statistic collection is an important first step when setting up server monitoring. Statistic collection can be accomplished on a given server using a server task called the Collector or the Reporter. The Collector is used as a simple process for collecting statistical information across servers. The Collector task, however, is limited in the type of reports that it can generate. The Reporter is a more powerful process that can collect statistics for a specific server. The Collector can collect statistical documents from multiple servers to a central collection database, although the report process must be run on every server.

Statistics are important in their own right as tools for identifying trends on a Notes server. Recognizing trends is important to determine when the server is going through peak loads, including the number of users, tasks, the memory used, and so forth. Statistic collection can be used to generate Alarms using set thresholds.

Reporting Server Statistics

The types of statistics collected by the Collector or Reporter task include the following:

◆ System, including information about sessions, disk and memory usage, server configuration, and load

◆ Mail, including shared mail

◆ Database and replication, including database utilization

◆ Communications, including COM port usage

◆ Network, including LAN port usage

◆ Cluster statistics

These statistics are compiled into a Statistic document that is kept in a statistic reporting database called Statrep.nsf.

Starting the Collection of Statistics

Setting up the collection of statistics is a simple chore for the administrators. To start the collection, the administrator first decides whether to run Collect.exe or Report.exe. Both of these processes send the statistic information to Statrep.nsf. The Collect process runs on a single server and can potentially collect statistics from multiple servers to a single copy of Statrep.nsf on a single server. The Collector process, however, does not generate statistical analysis reports or file statistic reports. If you need these reports, or if the servers need to collect their own copies of Statrep.nsf, Reporter needs to be used.

To start the Collector process on the server, type the following at the server task:

`Load Collect`

To start the Reporter process on the server, type the following at the server task:

`Load Report`

 Note To make sure the appropriate task is started when the server reboots, add the appropriate task to the ServerTasks= line of the Notes.ini.

When either of the collector processes start, the appropriate pieces to make the statistic collection process work are put into place by the task. The pieces include:

◆ The creation of the Statrep.nsf database for collection. This database is generated from a template called Statrep.ntf. If that template doesn't exist, the process fails.

◆ The creation of the control database for the collection process. If the process is Collector, the database is Collect4.nsf. If the process is Reporter, the database is Events4.nsf.

◆ The addition of a server document to the control database for every server that is collecting statistics.

◆ The creation of the mail-in database document needed to mail statistics to the Statrep.nsf database from the Reporter task.

◆ The move of all statistic- and event-related documents and views from the Name & Address book (if appropriate) for migration from Notes 3.x to 4.5.

Reporting Statistics for Multiple Servers

Lotus recommends using the Collector task to collect statistics for multiple servers. Only the server collecting the statistics has to run the Collector task.

The Collector cannot generate Analysis Reports or File Statistic Reports, however; to generate these for multiple servers, you must run the Reporter task instead. To use the Reporter task to report statistics for multiple servers to a database on one server, you run the Reporter task on each server that reports statistics. In the Statistics and Events database (Events4), you create a Server to Monitor document for each server and in each document you choose to report statistics to the same server and database.

Statistic Monitoring (Alarms)

As statistics are collected by the Reporter process, certain user-defined statistics can be monitored versus a set threshold. For example, if a server has a drive C:, the administrator may want to monitor whether the available disk space falls below a certain point. The administrator can add a Statistic Monitoring document specifying disk space on drive C: to be monitored, and a set threshold, such as 20 MB, generating a formula that says Disk.C.Free < 20,000,000 (measured in bytes).

As the Reporter runs it checks all the Statistic Monitoring documents. If the threshold is crossed for that specific statistic, an Alarm is generated. Keep two important points in mind:

1. The Reporter is a timed process, so it checks the Statistic Monitoring documents every so many minutes (as defined in the Control Database Server document).

2. The Alarm that is generated is not audible, does not leave an e-mail message, and has no flashing lights. It is another document added to the statistic collection database (Statrep.nsf).

Alarms include information about the actual status of the statistic as well as the monitored value. Alarms documents are not added every time the Alarm occurs, but for each cycle of Alarms. The first time recorded, last time recorded, and the number of occurences are kept in one document. If the Alarm is resolved and therefore the Alarm is not generated by Reporter, the Alarm is removed. If the same Alarm occurs later, a new Alarm document is started.

Creating a Statistics Alarm

To create a new Statistic Monitoring document for potential Alarm generation, follow these steps (see the sample Statistic Monitoring document in fig. 9.1):

1. Open Collect4.nsf if the server is running Collect, or Events4.nsf if the server is running Report.

2. Choose Create, Monitors, Statistics Monitor.

3. In the Server Name field use * (the default) to set this Stat. Monitoring for all servers in the domain running Report or Collect, or enter a specific server name, or choose from the keyword list of servers.

4. Choose Statistic in the Statistic Name field.

5. Click on the "Fill In With Defaults" button to automatically retrieve default values for the remaining fields.

6. Choose the Threshold operator (greater than, less than, etc.) or keep the default.

7. Choose the Threshold value or keep the default value.

8. Choose the Event Severity (remember this ties to Event Notification documents for event notification from Alarms).

9. Type a comment that suggests the course of action to take if an Alarm is reported.

10. Save and exit the document. This document is read and used by the Reporter or Collector task the next time that process runs.

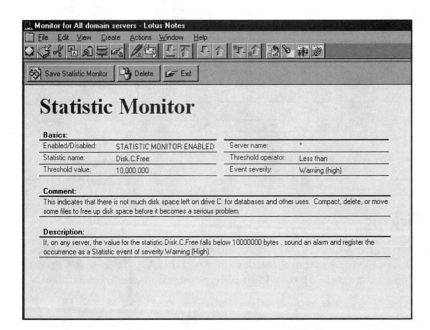

Figure 9.1

A sample Statistic Monitor document.

Modifying a Statistic Document

Although the default settings in the existing Statistic documents are usually adequate, occasionally the administrator may want to change some of the information for site-specific data, such as the suggested response. To modify a Statistic document, perform the following tasks (see fig. 9.2 for a sample document):

1. Open Collect4.nsf if the server is running Collect, or Events4.nsf if the server is running Report.

2. Choose View, Names & Messages, Statistic Names.

3. Chose the appropriate Statistic document.

4. Read and change the fields as needed.

5. Exit and save the document.

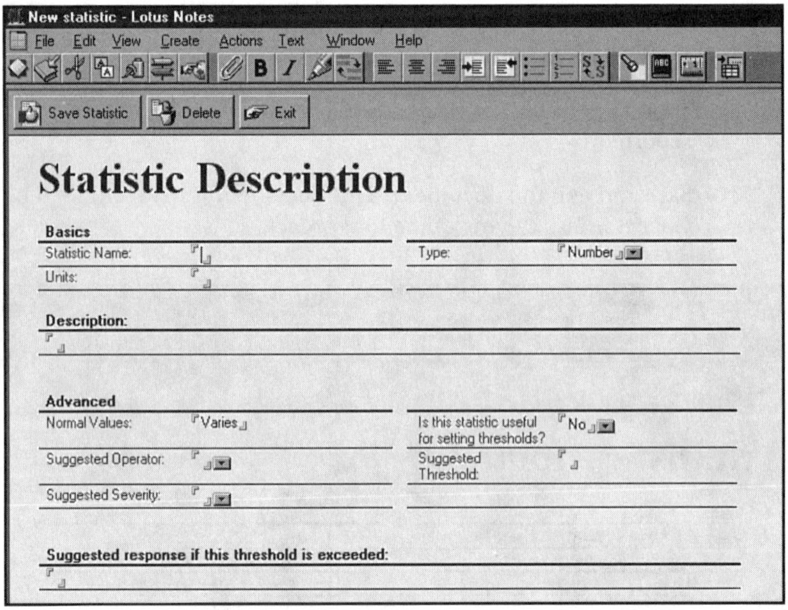

Figure 9.2

A sample Statistic Description document.

Trouble Tickets

As a manual process, the administrator can read though the Alarm documents and decide to create trouble tickets from those documents. Trouble tickets are assigned to an individual, have a start and stop time for problem resolution, and have a unique trouble ticket number. After assignment and setting the resolution start, the trouble ticket can be mailed to the assigned individual or group. The trouble ticket, when saved, goes into the Trouble Ticket view (for Alarms) in the Statrep.nsf.

Creating a trouble ticket is a manual process in which the administrator opens an Alarm document (or event) and follows these steps:

1. Open the Statistics database (Statrep.nsf).

2. Choose View, Alarms.

3. Open the Alarm document for which you want to create a trouble ticket.

4. Click on the Create Trouble Ticket Action.

5. Type the name of the person or group of people responsible for problem resolution.

6. Click on the Mail Trouble Ticket action to mail the trouble ticket to the assigned person(s).

7. Save and exit the trouble ticket (it appears in the Trouble Ticket view).

Although the reporter process is used to collect and monitor statistic on a timed basis, an administrator often needs a real-time monitoring tool for errors or warnings. It would also be nice to be notified via e-mail if those errors occur. Luckily, Domino includes a process called event notification that handles both of the above issues.

Event Notification

The event notification process often runs in conjunction with the Reporter or Collector process, but can run as a stand-alone process. The idea of event notification is that as events occur they can be acted on and some notification process can be used. The events can come from Reporter as Alarms are generated (remember, this is a timed process), from the logger process (this process writes to the log file, this is a real-time process), or from an API program. The event notification process uses Event Notification documents in the Events4 or Collect4 databases to decide what to monitor. When the events occur, one of several notification processes can be used, including sending e-mail to a user or a group.

Event notification is based on the type of event and the severity. Individual errors from logger or statistics from Reporter cannot be monitored.

The following sections explain the concept of event notification in greater detail.

Event Notification Types

Table 9.1 lists the types of event notification that are possible. For each type, an explanation is offered as to what kind of information is reported.

TABLE 9.1
Event Notification Types

Event Type	Information Reported
Comm/Net	Messages related to modem or network communications
Security	Messages related to authentication (this is the type of event for an ACL Database Monitoring document)
Mail	Messages related to mail routing
Replication	Messages related to replication (this is the type of event for a Replication Frequency document)
Resource	Messages related to system resources
Misc	Miscellaneous messages that don't fall into the other categories
Server	Messages related to a particular server (such as problems in the Name & Address book such as Server record Not Found)
Statistic	Messages related to Statistic Alarms
Update	Messages related to indexing on the server

All the event types are generated by logger except for the statistic type, which is tied to Alarms generated by Reporter. Types and severities together often represent a hundred or more different errors, warnings, or other messages. To look at where a specific error message fits as far as type and severity, an administrator can look at the Messages view in the Events4 or Collect4 database.

Event Severities

Event severities are used along with the event name for the event notification process. Severities have a general description, but are subjective in use by the administrator.

◆ Fatal

◆ Failure

◆ Warning (Low)

◆ Warning (High)

◆ Normal

◆ All Severities

Notification Methods and Destinations

The following notification methods are the "where to go" of the event notification process. The notification method selected determines the destination possibilities.

◆ **Mail.** Mail is sent to the user or group in the Notification Destination field.

◆ **Log to a Database.** Logging to a database writes the event to a database on the same server, usually Statrep.nsf.

◆ **Relay to Another Server.** This is the "Passing the Buck" method of notification in which the event is passed to the event process on another server in the same Notes Named Network. The destination is the server name.

◆ **Relay to Another SNMP Trap.** This process sends the event through SNMP to an SNMP monitoring station.

Event Notification from Statistics

To do event notification from Alarms it is necessary to add a Notification document that specifies Statistic as the type and a severity that matches the severity or severities of the Statistic Monitoring documents.

Creating Event Notification Documents

For each type of event (and severity) that needs to be monitored, an Event Notification document must be created correctly. To do so, perform the following steps (see fig. 9.3 for a sample notification document):

1. Open the Statistics & Events database.

2. Choose Create, Monitors, Event Monitor view.

3. Choose the event type.

4. Choose the Event Severity. (All Severities includes all severities except Normal. Typically the Normal severity setting is not monitored.)

5. Choose the Notification method. (Notice that the Notification destination changes to match.)

6. Choose the Notification destination based on the Notification Method (user or group name to receive notification if the event is mail).

7. Choose or type in the server name. Remember that "*" (the default) enables this event notification for all servers running the Reporter task.

8. Refresh the document to pull in additional information (F9).

9. Exit and save the document.

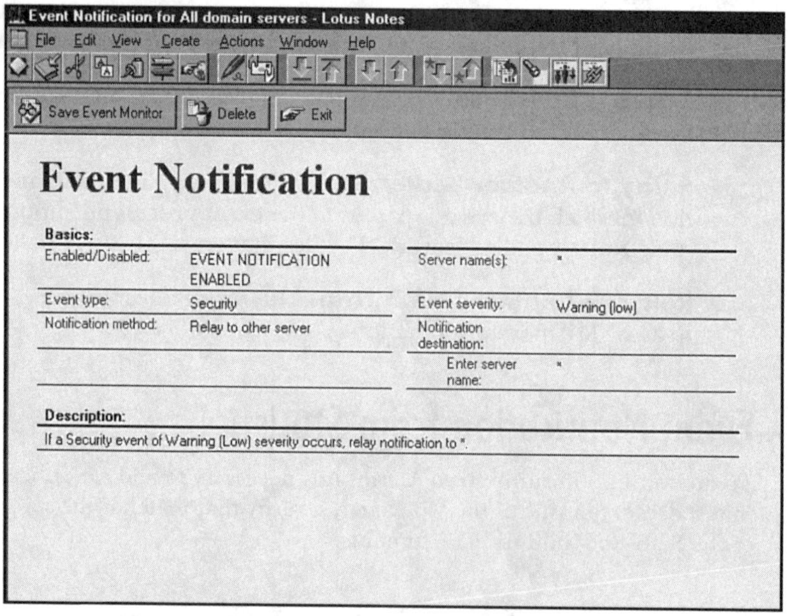

Figure 9.3

A sample Event Notification document.

Database Monitoring Tools

Along with the standard Event Notification documents and standard event notification techniques, there are two specific notification documents.

These specific types of database monitoring documents can be added in the Database Monitoring view in the Events4 or Collect4 databases. The first tool is Access Control List Monitoring for specific databases (see a sample in fig. 9.4). This document sends mail to a user or group when the ACL is changed through the server task.

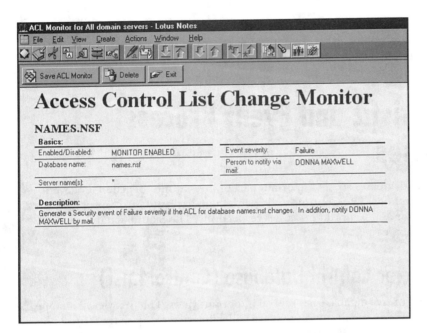

Figure 9.4

An Access Control List Change Monitor document.

The other tool is the replication frequency monitor. This document monitors replication frequency based on a defined time for replication and specific databases (see fig. 9.5).

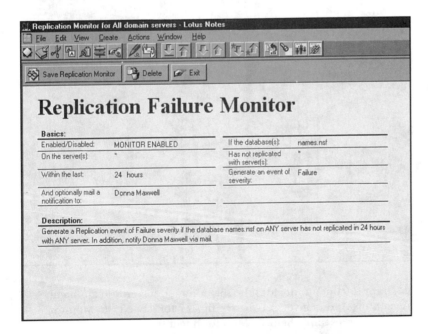

Figure 9.5

Replication Failure Monitor document.

After setting up the Statistic and Event processes, it is necessary for the administrator to understand the databases involved in these processes. The next section covers the Statrep, Events4, and Collect4 databases.

The Statistic and Event Process Databases

The following databases are an important part of the statistic collection and event notification methods. The Control4 and Events4 databases are the control databases for the Collector and Reporter processes respectively. The Statrep database is the collection database.

The Collector Control Database (Control4.nsf)

The collector control database has several important views. The first view that appears contains information about servers that are collecting statistics (see fig. 9.6).

Figure 9.6

The Servers to Monitor view in the Collector database.

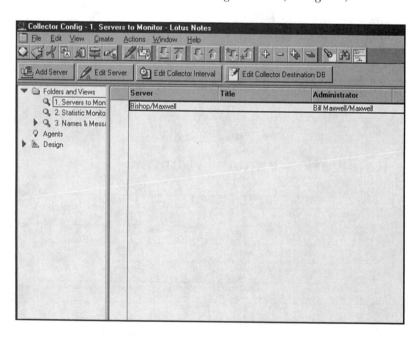

The Servers to Monitor document includes the server name, server domain name, and server administrator(s) for a given server (see fig. 9.7 for a Server to Monitor document, and fig. 9.8 for a sample Statistic Monitor document).

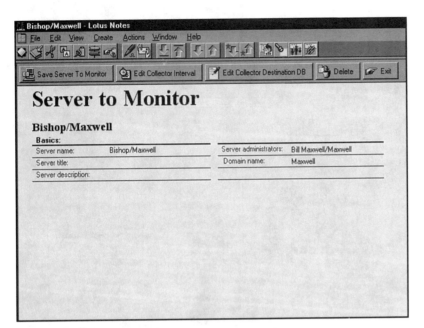

Figure 9.7

A sample Server to Monitor document.

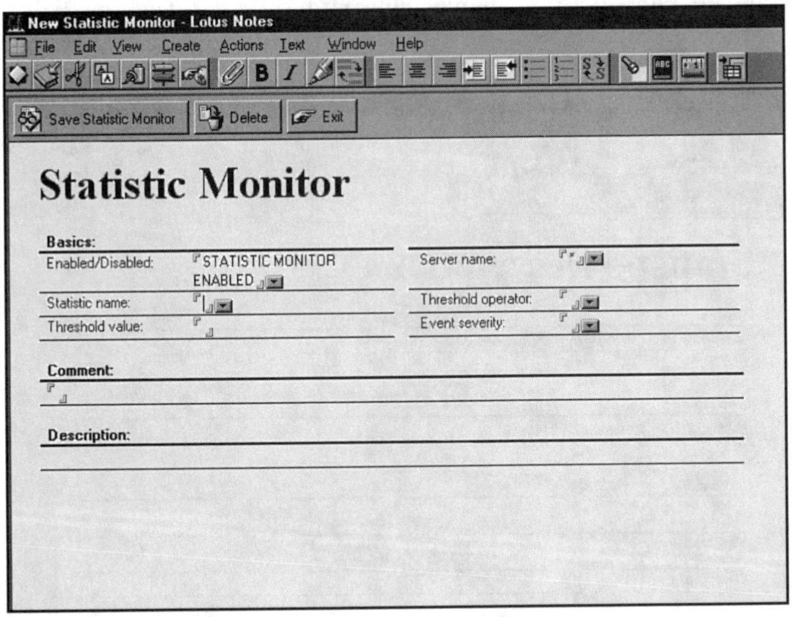

Figure 9.8

A sample Statistic Monitor document.

The Statistic Names view displays information about the statistics that are collected on the server (see fig. 9.9).

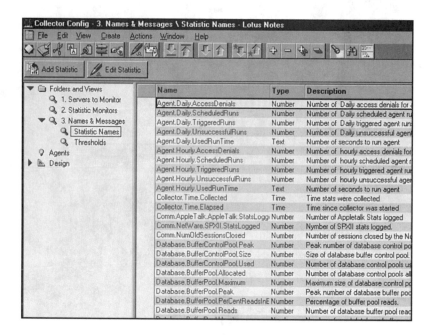

Figure 9.9

Statistic Names view.

The statistic documents contain information including statistic name, type, and field values for setting thresholds (see fig. 9.10).

Figure 9.10

A sample Statistic Description document.

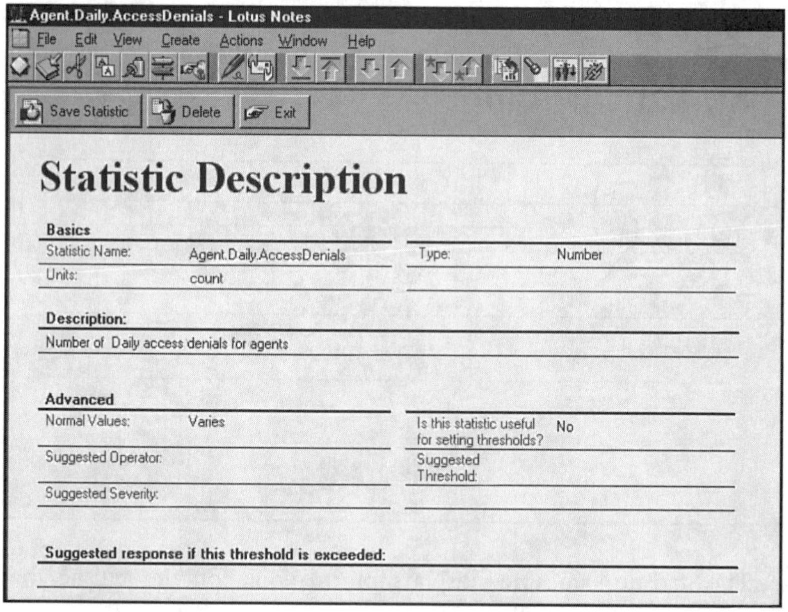

The Thresholds view displays those statistics that can be chosen for Statistic Monitoring documents (see fig. 9.11). The option is turned on and off using the Is this statistic useful for setting thresholds? setting.

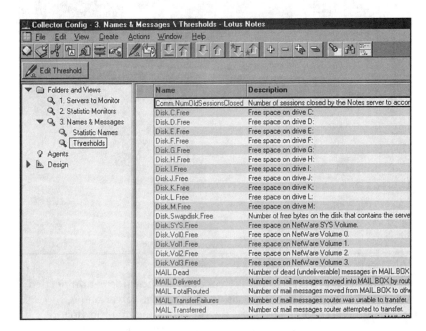

Figure 9.11

Thresholds view.

The Reporter Control Database (Event4.nsf)

The Reporter task uses a database called Event4.nsf. This database is the control database for both the Reporter task for statistic collection and Alarm generation and the event notification process. The database is created on every server independently, but is in fact a replica for every server in the domain. This unusual feat (creating multiple replica copies) is accomplished by using the Public Name & Address book's ID as a way to generate the Replica ID of Events4.

The default view for this database is the Servers to Monitor view (see fig. 9.12), which is a list of all servers in a given domain that are running the report or event tasks.

Figure 9.12

Servers to Monitor view.

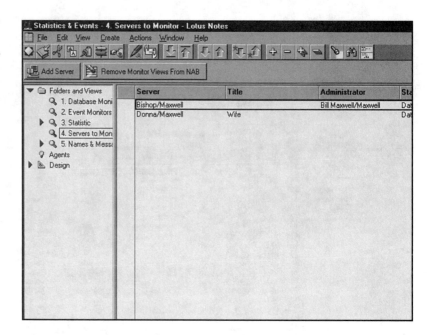

The Server to Monitor document (see fig. 9.13) contains all the information needed for a given server's reporter task. That information includes the server name, administrator(s), the domain name, database title, the reporting method (log to database or mail-in database), the server to log (which by default is the same server for which this record is created), the collection interval (in minutes, minimum is 15 minutes), and information about analysis.

The Database Monitors view (see fig. 9.14) is the list of the available database monitor documents, including ACL and Replication monitors.

The Events Monitor view (see fig. 9.15) is the list of available event monitor documents.

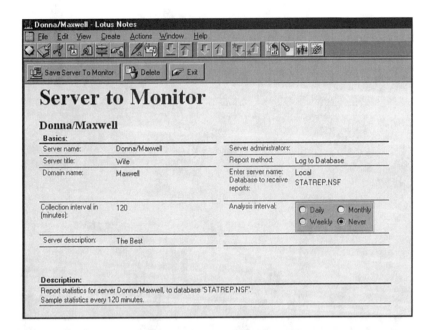

Figure 9.13

A sample Server to Monitor document.

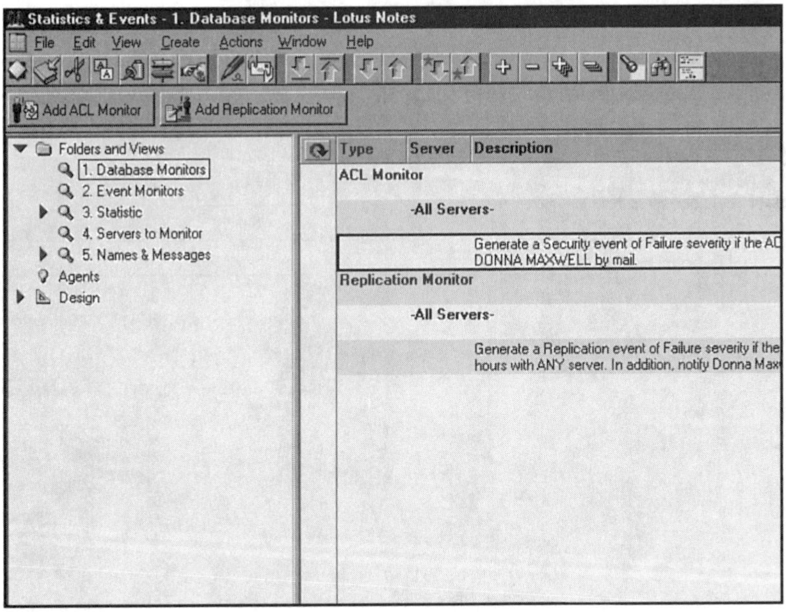

Figure 9.14

Database Monitors view.

Figure 9.15

Event Monitors view.

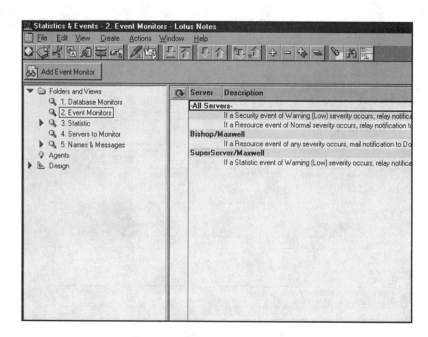

The Statistic Monitors view (see fig. 9.16) shows all the Statistic Monitor documents.

Figure 9.16

Statistic Monitors view.

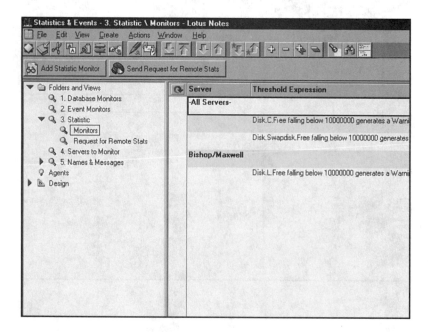

The Messages view (see fig. 9.17) shows the Event notification error messages sorted by type and severity.

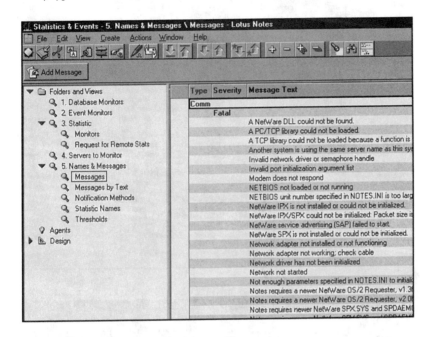

Figure 9.17

Messages view.

The Messages by Text view (see fig. 9.18) shows Event notification error messages by the error message.

The Notification Methods view (see fig. 9.19) is the list of current methods. New methods may be added with additional Notes upgrades. The Event Notification Method document describes the methods currently available (see fig. 9.20).

Figure 9.18

Messages by Text view.

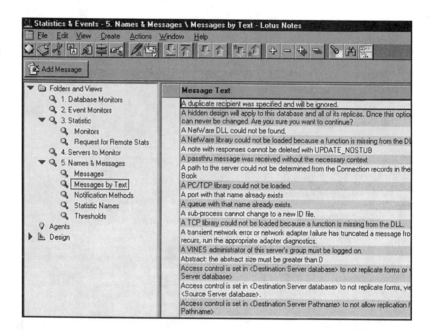

Figure 9.19

Notification Methods view.

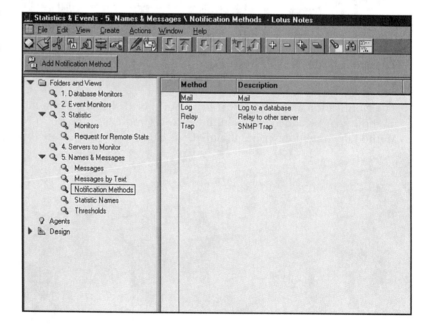

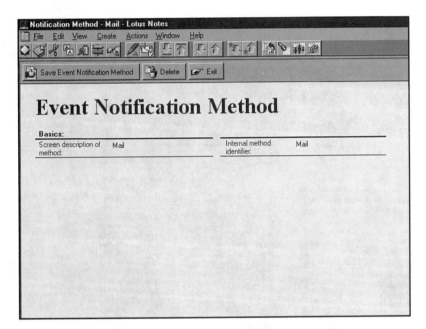

Figure 9.20

A sample Event Notification Method document.

The Statistic Names view (see fig. 9.21) lists the statistic documents used by the reporter process for statistic reports and Alarm generation.

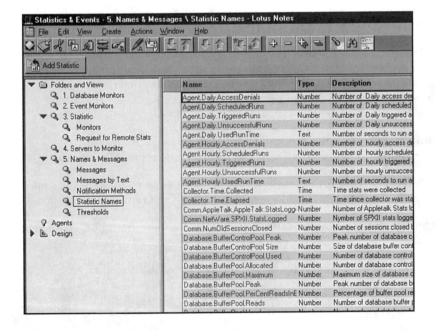

Figure 9.21

Statistic Names view.

The Thresholds view (see fig. 9.22) lists all the Statistic documents available for setting thresholds.

Figure 9.22

Thresholds view.

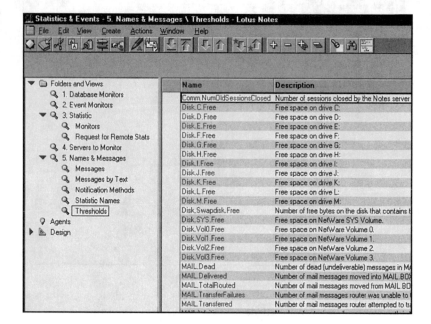

The Statistic Reports Database

After the statistic collection program is running (either Reporter or Collector) on the server, statistic reports are generated and put into a database called the Statistics Database (Statrep.nsf). The Statistics Database has several views that display different parts of the overall statistic document using specific forms. The Statistics Reports views include:

- ◆ **System.** Provides statistics about disk and memory usage, hardware and software configurations, usage levels, and database and replication activity.

- ◆ **Mail & Database.** Provides statistics about mail activity relating to Notes mail and to gateways such as MHS, and provides database and replication statistics.

- ◆ **Communications.** Provides statistics for each communications port enabled on a server.

- ◆ **Network.** Provides statistics for each network port enabled on a server.

- ◆ **Cluster.** Provides statistics for cluster servers.

The following sections discuss each of these views in greater detail.

System Statistic Reports

A system statistic report includes the following types of statistics:

◆ **Session.** The session statistics include current session information.

◆ **Disk.** The disk statistics include the available disk space for all server disks.

◆ **Memory.** Memory statistics indicate the current memory and available memory.

◆ **Server configuration.** Server configuration statistics include configuration information for the Domino server.

◆ **Server load.** Server load statistics inlcude the load information for the specified server.

◆ **Database.** Database statistics include usage statistics for databases on the server.

◆ **Replication.** Replication statistics include information about replication successes and failures.

◆ **Statistics package.** Statistics package statistics include information about the stats process.

The following is an example of a system statistic report:

System Statistics Report

for server:Bishop/Maxwell

Session Information:

Boot ID:	511371
Server started at:	03/03/97 08:25:17 PM
Statistics collected at:	03/03/97 09:01:52 PM
Reporter task running for:	0:33:4 (hr:min:sec)
Server Location:	
Server Administrator:	Bill Maxwell/Maxwell

Disk Statistics (in bytes):

Free space on swapfile disk:	Not Applicable

Volume	Size	Bytes Free	%Free
C:	1,356,070,912	108,658,688	8.01%

Memory Statistics (in bytes):

Free memory:	77,553,664
Memory allocated:	6,288,052
Memory allocated as shared memory:	4,671,828
Memory allocated by server processes:	1,616,224
Memory availability:	Plentiful
Memory quota:	
Memory timeouts:	
Physical RAM memory:	33,058,816
Swap file size:	Not Applicable

Server Configuration Information:

Number of volumes on file server:	1
Server ports:	TCPIP
Operating System version:	Windows 95 4.0
Notes version:	Release 4.5a
Data file path:	c:\notes\data
Swap file path:	Not Applicable
Number of processors:	1
Processor type:	Intel Pentium

Server Load Statistics:

Transactions in last minute:	0
Peak transactions per minute:	0
Time of last peak transactions per minute:	
Total transactions processed:	0
Number of current users:	0
Peak number of users:	0
Time of last peak number of users:	

Number of sessions dropped in mid-transaction:	0
Number of server tasks:	4
Server Tasks:	Database Server: Perform console commands
Database Server:	Listen for connect requests on TCPIP
Database Server:	Perform housekeeping chores
Database Server:	Idle task
Event:	Idle
Reporter:	Idle
Calendar Connector:	Idle
Schedule Manager:	Idle
Admin Process:	Idle
Agent Manager: Executive '1':	Idle
Agent Manager:	Idle
Indexer:	Idle
Router:	Idle
Replicator:	Idle

Replication Statistics:

Number of successful replications:

Number of replication failures:

Number of documents deleted:

Number of documents added:

Number of documents updated:

Database Statistics (in bytes):

Buffer control pool used:	35,646
Buffer control pool peak size:	65,406
Buffer pool maximum:	6,291,456
Buffer pool used:	1,569,642
Buffer pool peak:	1,612,800

Extension manager pool used:

Extension manager pool peak:

NSF pool used: 34,617

NSF pool peak: 130,812

Stats Package Statistics:

Time started: 03/03/97 08:25:10 PM

Agent Statistics:

Hourly agent scheduled runs:

Hourly agent triggered runs:

Hourly agent unsuccessful runs:

Hourly agent used run time:

Hourly agent access denials:

Daily agent scheduled runs:

Daily agent triggered runs:

Daily agent unsuccessful runs:

Daily agent used run time:

Daily agent access denials:

As discussed earlier in this chapter, a system statistic report includes the following types of statistics:

◆ Session

◆ Disk

◆ Memory

◆ Server configuration

◆ Server load

◆ Database

◆ Replication

◆ Statistics package

The following tables discuss each of these in greater detail.

Session

Table 9.2 describes the session statistics.

TABLE 9.2
Session Statistics

Statistic Label	Statistic Name	Description
Boot ID	Server.BootID	Unique number identifying the time the server was booted
Statistics collected at	STATS.Time.Current	The date and time the statistics were collected
Reporter task running for	Reporter.Time.Elapsed	The length of time the Reporter task had been running when the report was generated
Server location	Server.Location	Physical location of a server
Server administrator	Server.Administrator	The server administrator(s) as indicated in the Adminstrators field of the Server document in the Public Address Book

Disk

Table 9.3 describes disk statistics.

TABLE 9.3
Disk Statistics

Statistic Label	Statistic Name	Description
Free space on swap file disk	Disk.SwapDisk.Free	The amount of free space on the Swapdisk (usually drive c:) for OS/2
Volume, Size	Disk.n.Size	Total size in bytes of drive n
	Disk.VolumeName.Size	Total size in bytes of volume named for Novell-based Notes servers

continues

TABLE 9.3, CONTINUED
Disk Statistics

Statistic Label	Statistic Name	Description
Volume, Bytes free	Disk.n.Free	Free disk space in bytes on drive n
Volume, Bytes free	Disk.VolumeName.Free	(NLM) Free space in bytes on the volume named for Novell-based Notes servers
Volume, % free	Disk.n.PercentUsed	Percent of disk space used on drive n

Memory

Table 9.4 describes memory statistics.

TABLE 9.4
Memory Statistics

Statistic label	Statistic Name	Description
Free memory	Mem.Free*	Free RAM and disk space on the swapdisk (for OS/2)
Memory allocated	Mem.Allocated	Currently allocated memory
Memory allocated as shared memory	Mem.Allocated.Shared	Total shared memory allocated
Memory allocated by server processes	Mem.Allocated.Process	Total process-private memory allocated by all currently running processes
Memory availability	Mem.Availability	Assessment of currently available memory: Painful (ouch), Normal, or Plentiful
Swap file size	Mem.SwapFile.Size*	The current size of the Swapfile for OS/2 systems

Server Configuration

Table 9.5 describes server configuration statistics.

TABLE 9.5
Server Configuration Statistics

Statistic Label	Statistic Name	Description
Number of volumes on file server	Disk.Fixed	Number of hard drives available, including network drives
Number of RS-232 ports	Server.Ports.RS232	Number of RS-232 ports on this server
Coprocessor	Server.Coprocessor	Does the server have a coprocessor?
Operating system	Server.Version.NLM Server.Version.OS/2 Server.Version.NT	Version of operating system running on server
Notes version	Server.Version.Notes	Lotus Notes release running on this server
Data file path	Server.Path.Data	Location of the directory that holds the Notes data files
Swap file path	Server.Path.Swap	For OS/2 servers, the path for the Swapfile
Number of processors	Server.CPU.Count	Number of processors on this system
Processor type	Server.CPU.Type	Type of processor on this system

Server Load

Table 9.6 describes server load statistics.

TABLE 9.6
Server Load Statistics

Statistic Label	Statistic Name	Description
Transactions in last minute	Server.Trans.PerMinute	Number of transactions that took place in the last minute. Useful to monitor server use.
Peak transactions per minute	Server.Trans.PerMinute.Peak	Peak number of transactions that took place in any given minute since the server started
Time of last peak transaction per minute	Server.Trans.PerMinute. Peak.Time	Date and time of last peak transaction per minute
Total transactions processed	Server.Trans.Total	Total number of transactions since the server started
Number of current users	Server.Users	Number of users with sessions open on the server
Peak number of users	Server.Users.Peak	The maximum number of concurrent users with open sessions since the server was started
Time of last peak number of users	Server.Users.Peak.Time	Date and time when the maximum number of users were logged on
Number of sessions dropped in mid-transaction	Server.Sessions.Dropped*	Number of users who gave to connect to server
Number of server tasks	Server.Tasks	Number of server tasks currently executing
Server tasks	Server.Task	The name and status of all server tasks currently running

Replication

Table 9.7 describes replication statistics.

TABLE 9.7
Replication Statistics

Statistic Label	Statistic Name	Description
Number of successful replications	Replica.Successful	Number of error-free replication attempts
Number of replication failures	Replica.Failed	Number of attempted replications that generated an error (any replication error adds to the is number)
Number of documents deleted	Replica.Docs.Deleted	Number of documents deleted by replication since the server started
Number of documents added	Replica.Docs.Added	Number of documents added by replication since the server started
Number of documents updated	Replica.Docs.Updated	Number of documents updated by replication since the server started

Stats Package

Table 9.8 describes stats package statistics.

TABLE 9.8
Stats Package Statistics

Statistic Label	Statistic Name	Description
Time started	Stats.Time.Start	Time the Stats package task last started

Mail and Database Report

The following is an example of a Mail and Database report from the Statrep database:

Mail and Database Report

for server: Bishop/Maxwell

Session Information:

Boot ID:	511371
Statistics collected at:	03/03/97 10:01:51 PM
Reporter task running for:	1:33:4 (hr:min:sec)
Server location:	
Server Administrator:	Bill Maxwell/Maxwell

Notes Mail Statistics:

Number of dead mail messages:	0
Total number of mail messages routed:	
Mail waiting to be routed:	0
Total number of mail messages delivered:	
Mail waiting to be delivered:	0
Minimum delivery time per message:	seconds
Average delivery time per message:	seconds
Maximum delivery time per message:	seconds
Minimum size of message delivered:	KB
Average size of message delivered:	KB
Maximum size of message delivered:	KB
Minimum server hops per message:	
Average server hops per message:	
Maximum server hops per message:	
Total number of mail messages transferred:	
Total size of all messages transferred:	
Total number of messages transfer failures:	

Peak number of messages transferred:

Peak message transfer rate:

Time of peak message transfer rate:

Peak number of bytes transferred:

Peak byte transfer rate:

UNIXMAIL Gateway Statistics:

Dead mail:

Total failures:

Total routed:

Outgoing awaiting routing:

X400 Mail Gateway Statistics:

Dead mail:

Total routed to SMTP:

Total routed to Notes:

Total messages received:

Total failures to SMTP:

Total failures to Notes:

Total failures to X400:

Incoming awaiting delivery:

SMTP/MIME MTA Statistics:

Number of dead messages:

Mail waiting:

Total transfer failures:

Total mail transferred:

Total KB transferred:

Total recipients routed:

Number of waiting recipients:

ccMail MTA Statistics:

Number of dead messages:

Mail waiting:

Total transfer failures:

Total mail transferred:

Total KB transferred:

Total recipients routed:

Number of waiting recipients:

X400 MTA Statistics:

Number of dead messages:

Mail waiting:

Total transfer failures:

Total mail transferred:

Total KB transferred:

Total recipients routed:

Number of waiting recipients:

Replication Statistics:

Number of successful replications:

Number of replication failures:

Number of documents deleted:

Number of documents added:

Number of documents updated:

Database Statistics (in bytes):

Buffer control pool used:	37,520
Buffer control pool peak size:	65,406
Buffer pool maximum:	6,291,456
Buffer pool used:	1,897,402
Buffer pool peak:	1,958,400

Extension manager pool used:

Extension manager pool peak:

NSF pool used: 31,434

NSF pool peak: 130,812

Notes Mail

Table 9.9 describes Notes mail statistics.

TABLE 9.9
Notes Mail Statistics

Statistic Label	Statistic Name	Description
Number of dead mail messages	Mail.Dead*	Number of dead mail messages in the server's Mail.Box file
Total number of mail messages routed	Mail.TotalRouted	Number of mail messages routed since the server started
Mail waiting to be routed	Mail.Waiting*	Mail waiting in the Mail.Box file for delivery
Total number of mail messages delivered	Mail.Delivered	Number of messages received by the router
Mail waiting to be processed for either local delivery or transfer	Mail.Waiting-Recipients	Number of recipients awaiting either local delivery or transfer
Minimum delivery time per message**	Mail.Minimum-DeliverTime	Fastest delivery time of messages, in seconds
Average delivery time per message**	Mail.Average-DeliverTime	Average delivery time of messages, in seconds
Maximum delivery time per message**	Mail.Maximum-DeliverTime	Slowest delivery time of messages, in seconds
Minimum size of message delivered	Mail.Minimum-SizeDelivered	Smallest message delivered, in K

continues

TABLE 9.9, CONTINUED
Notes Mail Statistics

Statistic Label	Statistic Name	Description
Average size of message delivered	Mail.Average-SizeDelivered	Average size of messages delivered
Maximum size of message delivered	Mail.Maximum-SizeDelivered	Largest message delivered, in K
Minimum server hops per message	Mail.Minimum-ServerHops	Least number of server hops for a delivered message
Average server hops message	Mail.Average-ServerHops	Average number of server per hops for a delivered message
Maximum server hops per message	Mail.Maximum-ServerHops	Most number of server hops for a delivered message
Total number of mail messages transferred	Mail.Transferred	Number of messages router actually transferred
Total size of all messages transferred	Mail.TotalKB-Transferred	The total sizes of all messages the router actually transferred
Total number of message transfer failures	Mail.TransferFailures*	Number of messages router failed to transfer

MHS Gateway

The statistics in table 9.10 appear if a server is an MHS Gateway server.

TABLE 9.10
MHS Gateway Statistics

Report Label	Statistic Name	Description
Dead mail	MHS.Dead	Amount of dead mail
Outgoing awaiting routing	MHS.Waiting-Recipients	Amount of outgoing mail pending delivery
Incoming awaiting delivery	MHS.Waiting	Amount of incoming mail pending delivery

Unix Gateway

The statistics in table 9.11 appear if a server is a Unix Gateway server.

TABLE 9.11
Unix Gateway Statistics

Report Label	Statistic Name	Description
Dead mail	UNIXMAIL.Dead	Amount of dead mail
Total failures	UNIXMAIL.TotalFailures	Total amount of mail that could not be delivered
Total routed	UNIXMAIL.TotalRouted	Total amount of mail routed
Outgoing awaiting routing	UNIXMAIL.Waiting-Recipients	Amount of outgoing mail pending delivery

X.400 Gateway

The statistics in table 9.12 appear if a server is a X400 Mail Gateway server.

TABLE 9.12
X.400 Gateway Statistics

Report Label	Statistic Name	Description
Dead mail	X400.Dead	Amount of dead mail
Total routed to SMTP	X400.ToSMTP	Total amount of mail routed to the SMTP MTA
Total routed to Notes	X400.ToNotes	Total amount of mail routed to Lotus Notes
Total messages received	X400.ToX400	Total amount of mail received
Total failures to SMTP	X400.ToSMTPFailed	Total amount of mail that could not be delivered to the SMTP gateway

continues

TABLE 9.12, CONTINUED
X.400 Gateway Statistics

Report Label	Statistic Name	Description
Total failures to Notes	X400.ToNotesFailed	Total amount of mail that could not be delivered to Notes
Total failures to X400	X400.ToX400Failed	Total amount of mail that could not be delivered to other X400 users
Incoming awaiting delivery	X400.TotalInTheBox	The amount of incoming mail pending delivery

SMTP MTA

The statistics in table 9.13 appear if a server is a SMTP MTA server.

TABLE 9.13
SMTP MTA Statistics

Report Label	Statistic Name	Description
Dead mail	SMTPMTA.Dead	Amount of dead mail
Total routed	SMTPMTA.TotalRouted	Total amount of mail routed
Total transferred	SMTPMTA.Transfered	Total amount of mail transferred
Total delivered	SMTPMTA.Delivered	Total amount of mail delivered
Mail waiting to be routed	SMTPMTA.Waiting	Amount of mail pending routing
Mail waiting to be delivered	SMTPMTA.Waiting-Recipients	Amount of mail pending delivery
Mail waiting to be converted	SMTPMTA.WaitingConv	Amount of mail pending conversion
Mail waiting to be transmitted	SMTPMTA.WaitingTrans	Amount of mail pending transmission
Total conversion failures	SMTPMTA.ConvFailures	Amount of mail that could not be converted

Report Label	Statistic Name	Description
Total transmission failures	SMTPMTA.TransFailures	Amount of mail that could not be transmitted
Highest number of inbound processes	SMTPMTA.HighInbound	Peak number of simultaneous inbound processes
Highest number of outbound processes	SMTPMTA.HighOutbound	Peak number of simultaneous outbound processes
Total number of bytes (inbound)	SMTPMTA.InboundBytes	Total amount (in bytes) of inbound mail
Total number of bytes (outbound)	SMTPMTA.OutboundBytes	Total amount (in bytes) of outbound mail
Largest message (inbound)	SMTPMTA.InboundSize	Size of largest inbound message
Largest message (outbound)	SMTPMTA.OutboundSize	Size of largest outbound message

About Database and Replication Statistic Reports

A Mail and Database report displays the database and replication statistics shown in table 9.14.

TABLE 9.14
Database and Replication Statistics

Statistic Label	Statistic Name	Description
Bytes Received	Bytes.Received	Number of network bytes received
Bytes Sent	Bytes.Sent	Number of network bytes sent
Sessions Limit	Sessions.Limit	Number of sessions at limit
Sessions Limit Max	Sessions.LimitMax	Number of sessions at maximum limit
Sessions Limit Min	Sessions.LimitMin	Number of sessions at minimum limit

continues

TABLE 9.14, CONTINUED
Database and Replication Statistics

Statistic Label	Statistic Name	Description
Sessions Peak	Sessions.Peak	Peak number of sessions
Sessions Recycled	Sessions.Recycled	Number of sessions that have been recycled
Sessions Recycling	Sessions.Recycling	Number of sessions recycling
Incoming Sessions Established	Sessions.Established.-Incoming	Number of sessions established to the server from clients
Outgoing Sessions Established	Sessions.Established.-Outgoing	Number of sessions established to clients from the server

Database Statistics

Table 9.15 describes the database statistics.

TABLE 9.15
Database Statistics

Statistic Label	Statistic Name	Description
Buffer control pool size	Database.BufferControl-Pool.Size	Largest number of bytes allocated in the buffer control pool. This pool contains information for mapping data on disk to data in the NSF buffer pool
Buffer control pool used	Database.BufferControl-Pool.Used	Number of bytes currently allocated in the buffer control pool
Buffer control pool peak size	Database.BufferControl-Pool.Peak	Peak number of database control pools used
Buffer pool maximum	Database.BufferPool.-Maximum	Maximum size the NSF buffer pool can become. This value is the Notes.ini setting NSF_Buffer_Pool_Size

Statistic Label	Statistic Name	Description
Buffer pool used	Database.BufferPool.Used	Number of bytes currently allocated in the buffer pool
Buffer pool peak	Database.BufferPool.Peak	Peak number of database buffer pools
Extension manager pool used	Database.ExtMgrPool.Used	Number of external manager pools
Extension manager pool peak	Database.ExtMgrPool.Peak	Peak number of external manager pools
NSF pool size	Database.NSFPool.Size	Largest number of bytes allocated in the NSF pool. This pool contains internal Notes data structures
NSF pool used	Database.NSFPool.Used	Number of bytes currently allocated in the NSF pool
NSF pool peak	Database.NSFPool.Peak	Peak number of database NSF pools

Communications Reports

The following is an example of a communications report.

Communications Report

for server: Bishop/Maxwell

Session Information:

Boot ID:	511371
Statistics collected at:	03/03/97 09:01:52 PM
Reporter task running for:	0:33:4 (hr:min:sec)
Server location:	
Server administrator:	Bill Maxwell/Maxwell

Communications Statistics:

COM1:

Active sessions:

Carrier speed:

Port speed:

Status:

Bytes received by user:

Bytes sent by user:

Messages received by user:

Messages sent by user:

CRC errors:

Port errors:

Retransmitted packets:

COM2:

Active sessions:

Carrier speed:

Port speed:

Status:

Bytes received by user:

Bytes sent by user:

Messages received by user:

Messages sent by user:

CRC errors:

Port errors:

Retransmitted packets:

The communications report contains information about all XPC (serial) ports enabled on the server. Table 9.16 describes the session information statistics.

 Each statistic name begins with the prefix XPC.port name but this prefix is omitted in the table.

TABLE 9.16
Session Information

Report Label	Statistic Name	Description
Active sessions	Sessions.Active	Active sessions on this port
Carrier speed	Speed.Carrier	Carrier speed on this port
Port speed	Speed.Port	Port speed
Status	Status	Port status
Bytes received by user	UserBytes.Received	Number of bytes received on this port
Bytes sent by user	UserBytes.Sent	Number of bytes sent from this port
Messages received by user	UserMsgs.Received	Number of transmit requests issued by the sender for one or more packets
Messages sent by user	UserMsgs.Sent	Number of transmit requests issued by the user for one or more packets
CRC errors	Errors.CRC	The number of cyclic redundancy check errors reported on this port
Port errors	Errors.Port	Port errors indicating a port driver buffer overflow or possible parity errors
Retransmitted packets	Errors.Retrans-mittedPackets	Number of retransmissions on this port

Network Reports

The following is an example of a network report:

Network Report

for server: Bishop/Maxwell

Session Information:

Boot ID:	511371
Statistics collected at:	03/03/97 09:01:52 PM
Reporter task running for:	0:33:4 (hr:min:sec)

Server location:

Server administrator: Bill Maxwell/Maxwell

Server ports available: 1 Port

TCPIP:

Bytes received:	0
Bytes sent:	0
Sessions limit:	65,535
Sessions limit Max:	65,535
Sessions limit Min:	10
Sessions peak:	1
Sessions recycled:	0
Sessions recycling:	0
Incoming sessions established:	0
Outgoing sessions established:	0

Network statistic reports display the statistics shown in table 9.17 for each network port enabled on a server.

TABLE 9.17
Network Report

Statistic Label	Statistic Name	Description
Bytes Received	Bytes.Received	Number of network bytes received
Bytes Sent	Bytes.Sent	Number of network bytes sent
Sessions Limit	Sessions.Limit	Number of sessions at limit
Sessions Limit Max	Sessions.LimitMax	Number of sessions at maximum limit
Sessions Limit Min	Sessions.LimitMin	Number of sessions at minimum limit
Sessions Peak	Sessions.Peak	Peak number of sessions
Sessions Recycled	Sessions.Recycled	Number of sessions that have been recycled

Statistic Label	Statistic Name	Description
Sessions Recycling	Sessions.Recycling	Number of sessions recycling
Incoming Sessions Established	Sessions.Established.Incoming	Number of sessions established to the server from clients
Outgoing Sessions Established	Sessions.Established.Outgoing	Number of sessions established to clients from the server

Cluster Report

A cluster statistics report contains server statistics and cluster replication statistics for each server in a cluster.

Cluster Statistics—Server

Each statistic begins with the letters Server.Cluster; for example, Server.Cluster.AvailabilityIndex. This prefix is omitted in table 9.18.

TABLE 9.18
Cluster Statistics

Statistic Label	Statistic Name	Description
Default port name	PortName	Name of the default port that is used for intracluster network traffic. An asterisk indicates that there is no default port and that any available active port can be used.
Server availability index	AvailabilityIndex	Current percentage index of a server's availability. Value range is 0–100. Zero (0) indicates no available resources; a value of 100 indicates server completely available.
Server availability threshold	Availability-Threshold	Current setting of a server's availability threshold. When a server's availability index drops below its availability threshold, the server becomes busy.

continues

TABLE 9.18, CONTINUED
Cluster Statistics

Statistic Label	Statistic Name	Description
Successful redirects	OpenRedirects.-Failover.Successful	Number of times that a server successfully redirects a client to another cluster member after the client fails to open a database by replica ID.
Unsuccessful redirects	OpenRedirects.-Failover.-Unsuccessful	Number of times that a server is not able to redirect a client to another cluster member after the client fails to open a database by replica ID.
Successful redirects by path	OpenRedirects.-FailoverByPath.-Successful	Number of times a server successfully redirects a client to another cluster member after the client fails to open a database by pathname.
Unsuccessful re-directs by path	OpenRedirects.-FailoverByPath.-Unsuccessful	Number of times a server is not able to redirect a client to another cluster member after the client fails to open a database by pathname.
Successful redirects if server busy	OpenRedirects.-LoadBalance.-Successful	Number of times that a server successfully redirects a client to another cluster member after the client tries to open a database by replica ID when the server is busy.
Unsuccessful re-directs if server busy	OpenRedirects.-LoadBalance.-Unsuccessful	Number of times that a server is unable to redirect a client to another cluster member after the client tries to open a database by replica ID when the server is busy.
Successful redirects if server busy	OpenRedirects.LoadBalanceByPath.Unsuccessful	Number by path of times that a server is not able to redirect a client to another cluster member after the client tries to open a database by pathname when the server is busy.
Unsuccessful redirects by path if busy	OpenRedirects.Load.BalanceBy-Path.Successful	Number of times that a server successfully redirects a client to another cluster member after the client tries to open a database by pathname when the server is busy.

Statistic Label	Statistic Name	Description
Database open requests where all servers in cluster are busy	OpenRequest. ClusterBusy	Number of client requests when all servers are busy.
Database open requests where database is marked out of service	OpenRequest. DatabaseOutOf-Service	Number of times a client tries to open a database that is marked as out of service on the server.
Database open requests where this server is busy	OpenRequest. LoadBalanced	Number of times a client tries to open a database on the server when the server is busy.
Number of probes sent to other servers in cluster	ProbeCount	Number of times that a server completes a probe request of the other cluster members.
Number of probe errors	ProbeError	Number of times that a server receives an error when probing another server.

Cluster Statistics—Replication

Each statistic begins with the letters Replica.Cluster, for example, Replica.Cluster.Successful. This prefix is omitted in table 9.19.

TABLE 9.19
Cluster Statistics—Replication

Statistic Label	Statistic Name	Description
Number of servers in replica cluster	Servers	Number of other servers in the cluster that are receiving replications from this server
Number of successful cluster replications	Successful	Number of successful replications since server startup
Number of unsuccessful cluster replications	Failed	Number of failed replications since server startup

continues

TABLE 9.19, CONTINUED
Cluster Statistics—Replication

Statistic Label	Statistic Name	Description
Number of docs added	Docs.Added	Number of documents added by the cluster replicator
Number of docs updated	Docs.Updated	Number of documents updated by the cluster replicator
Number of docs deleted	Docs.Deleted	Number of documents deleted by the cluster replicator
Number of cluster replicas on this server	Files.Local	Number of databases on the current server for which there are replicas on other servers in the cluster
Number of cluster replicas on other servers in this cluster	Files.Remote	Number of databases on other servers to which the cluster replicator pushes changes

Monitoring Mail Performance

Several tools are available to monitor mail performance for a Notes domain. In this section the Mail.Box files (to check for dead and pending mail), statistics, and server tasks are discussed in regard to mail routing problems and resolutions.

Mail.Box

One of the primary databases used in Notes mail routing is the Mail.Box. This database exists on every server participating in Notes mail routing. Looking at the primary view of the Mail.Box two different types of mail documents are displayed: 1) Dead Mail (indicated with a Stop Sign), which are mail documents that cannot be delivered OR have been pending for more then 24 hours, and 2) Pending mail, which is e-mail waiting to be delivered.

Another way to open the Mail.Box file on any server (as opposed to opening the database with File, Database, Open) is to use the Administration screen and the Mail button.

Dead Mail

Administrators need to look at each piece of dead mail. Within the Dead Mail document is the error code that indicates which component of the mail routing system is causing the problem. Most of the time the problem is a connection document that has an incorrect domain name or port address. When the problem has been resolved, the dead mail can be released by using an agent in the Mail.Box file called Release Dead Messages. The router tries to deliver the mail again; if the problem persists the mail becomes dead again.

Pending Mail

The pending mail in the Mail view of the Mail.Box is also a useful view to check for mail problems. If messages exist in the Mail.Box that should have been delivered, then the connections obviously have a problem somewhere.

Server Tasks

The server tasks Show Task and Show Server also display dead mail and pending mail on the server where the command was issued. These commands can be issued at the server or via the remote server console.

Statistic Collection Database

The Statistic Collection database contains mail infomation in the Mail & Database view documents for servers collecting statistics. A Statistic Monitoring document can be added to track the number of dead mail messages, and from there an Event Monitoring document that can notify the administrator or administrators for a given number of dead mail.

Monitoring Memory on a Notes Server

If memory on a server gets low, the server processes slowly and may eventually start to report messages related to buffer pool size allocation problems. The Show Stat server command or the Mem.Availability statistic report on the general amount of free memory on the server (actually the space available in the NSF buffer pool, which is the I/O buffer space between the indexing functions and disk storage). The three possible values for the NSF Buffer Pool are represented in table 9.20:

TABLE 9.20
NSF Buffer Pool

Value	NSF_Buffer_Pool_Size Default Value
Painful	460 KB
Normal	4 MB
Plentiful	From 6 MB to 256 MB

Lotus Notes Events and Using the Windows NT Monitor

In addition to the standard monitoring tools, a Notes administrator can choose to log events to the Windows NT Event viewer. For Notes servers running on Windows NT, simply choose that option as the Notification Method in the Event Monitoring documents. The events are automatically passed to the Event processor for that particular server.

Table 9.21 lists the severity levels that map to the Windows NT Event viewer events:

TABLE 9.21
Notes versus Windows NT Severity Settings

Notes Severity	Windows NT Severity
Fatal or Failure	Error
Warning	Warning
Normal	Informational

Summary

This chapter covers the difficult topic of Domino server monitoring. The tools and components of the various processes, while difficult, are necessary for a fully functional Notes server. The administrator can use the tools for trending, reporting, error tracking and notification, and maintenance based on the reporting.

PART IV

Advanced Adminstration

CHAPTER 10

Migrating to Lotus Notes and Domino 4.5

Migrating to a new release of Lotus Notes and Domino can be a very involved process. As with most servers, interuption of service (something that you have to do when you migrate) can cause severe impact on your company doing business. Therefore, a little planning and getting the right people involved can help you greatly in successfully migrating in little time. In this chapter, you gain knowledge of migrating your Notes servers to Domino 4.5. Depending on the size of your company, these steps may involve selecting a migration team or teams, ordering equipment, creating training material, creating time lines, making a test environment, and tracking questions and solutions. This chapter also takes you beyond just migrating your servers. You may consider adding tasks to your server, changing your operating system, or moving to hierarchical IDs.

This chapter focuses on Notes migration from version 3.x to version 4.5. Migration from 3.x to 4.5 is much more complex than from 4.x to 4.5, so this chapter assumes that you have 3.x. If you have already migrated to 4.x, and consequently need to know how to migrate to 4.5 from this more recent version, see the section found later in this chapter called "Migrating from Previous Versions of Notes 4 to 4.5."

After reading this chapter, you will have in-depth knowledge about the various aspects of migration. Depending on the size of your company, some of these steps you will surely decide to delegate (such as training or support calls). You may want to consider outside assistance if you cannot find in-house solutions to some of the following steps. It is best to involve these outside individuals as early on as possible. However you decide to perform the migration, this chapter should aid you greatly in avoiding common pitfalls.

Migration has become much simpler since Release 4.x of Lotus Notes. You now have new options that make migration a much less painful process:

◆ A conversion utility that causes mail files to use a different template. For more information, please see the "Upgrading Mail Files" section of this chapter.

◆ An Object Link server task to move messages from an individual's mail database to a shared mail database.

◆ The AdminP process to upgrade user and server IDs from flat to hierarchical. You will find more information about upgrading IDs in the "AdminP" section of Chapter 8, "Examining Notes 4.5 Administration Features."

◆ The Release 3 Menu Finder to locate changed menus in Release 4.x. If you are having difficulty finding a menu that used to appear in Release 3.x, you can use this menu to find the menu's new home in 4.x. This finder feature can be found in the Help pull-down menu.

There are many steps involved in migration, but of most importance is the order that you upgrade systems. Whenever receiving a new version of Domino and Notes, you should upgrade your Hub server(s) first, then all spokes, then clients, and then gateways. Only upgrade mail files if you are certain that the user has upgraded the client software as well. The prior version of the mail file can function without difficulty on the server. However, the old client does not function well with the new mail file.

| **Warning** | The order of upgrading machines can be important to the successful migration of Domino and Notes. If clients are upgraded before servers, mail users will receive many script errors and the user could get frustrated. |

| **Note** | If you have a large company, you may want to make your migration a team effort. |

Spend a little extra time determining whether you need to change other things than just the Lotus Notes software. This careful consideration can save you a great deal of time in the long run. See the "Beyond Notes Migration" section of this chapter for some helpful hints about what other factors to consider.

 As you begin your migration, be very careful to pay attention to your typical business cycle. You do not want to be at the peak of a migration at the same time your company has its highest revenue or is doing an inventory or reorganization.

Creating a Migration Checklist

This section includes typical steps for migrating a large-scale Lotus Notes system. Migration for any large mission-critical system requires careful planning; therefore many of the steps required are also typical steps for migrating any mission-critical system to a major new release.

Form Migration Teams

Depending on the size of your company, you may or may not need a migration team. A migration team takes the burden of migrating off the shoulders of just one individual and makes the activity of migrating truly a group effort. The types and numbers of members on various teams may also be affected by the size of your company. You may include team members such as the application developers, advanced end users (to help with testing), application design contractors, database managers, remote site coordinators, Information Services (IS) managers, Chief Information Officer (CIO), network managers, remote site coordinators, and training coordinators.

Communication of issues surrounding your migration can be conveyed quite well in a database. As teams conduct meetings and make decisions, you can track all the information in a database. A simple discussion database can enable all team members to collaborate on the planning of your migration. You may want to separate forms and views for specific topics that pertain to administrators and developers and then one main form and view for an overall discussion of the migration.

You may want to have at least two teams:

◆ Administration team

◆ Application upgrade team

Administration Team

An administration team is primarily concerned with the types of servers in the company and the best way to upgrade them. It is important to determine whether the current servers are adequate for the new software. The team must also have a plan if there are different platforms. The Notes Release 4.5 operating system rollout strategy helps you determine when Lotus Notes will be available on each operating system. If you are using different platforms, this information can be quite valuable in determining whether you are prepared for the migration and which systems must be done first. This information can be found (and is frequently updated) on the Lotus Web site at www.lotus.com.

Application Upgrade Team

The focus of an application upgrade team is to specifically explore and plan for changes to databases. Members of this team plan and control upgrades to applications. Ideally, databases are first copied to a test server so that they can be tested prior to rollout. In general, Lotus has traditionally done a good job providing backward-compatibility for applications. The application team should spend adequate time determining if the old applications will perform as expected on the new release, but this is a much smaller job than the job facing the administration team.

Identify Project Leaders

As with any team effort, some key members should be identified so that parts of this process can be divided into manageable operations. These people are responsible for planning and controlling all aspects of migration. Leaders may be the application developers, database managers, CIO, IS manager, or Notes administrator, depending on the size of your Lotus Notes system.

List the Order of Server Upgrades

Determine which servers should be upgraded first. Compare this list of servers with the Release 4.5 operating system rollout strategy and modify this list if needed. Obviously, you can't upgrade a server platform whose code has not been released yet.

Identify Servers and Workstations That Need Upgrades

Determine whether hardware, operating system software, or network software need to be upgraded. Take into account the additional disk space necessary for additional Release 4.5 features that you want to add to the upgraded databases (such as Calendaring and Scheduling). For more information about hardware suggestions, please see Chapter 6, "Installing Domino 4.5 Server Software."

Order Any Equipment or Software That May Be Needed

Plan well in advance, because the hardware and software must arrive in time for installation (before the servers or workstations are upgraded).

Make a Timeline

Map out the time needed to order software and equipment, distribute software, install the upgrade, modify the database, and so on. After this plan is in place, use your migration planning database to enable everyone to comment on the timeline.

Set Up a Testing Environment

It is vital that you test your new applications to ensure that they work with new features (such as navigators, action buttons, script functions, and the like). Use a separate server to test applications and the migration process. Be sure that this server is in a separate domain and does not replicate with your production servers.

Get the Migration Team Leaders Informed

The migration team and migration project leader should review the Release 4.5 Administration documentation set before beginning the migration. If any information affects either team, documents should be placed into the migration discussion database.

You should also locate a Lotus Authorized Education Center (such as many XLConnect branches) to determine what level of training is appropriate for the team members. The better informed your migration team is about Lotus Notes, the smoother the transition can be. The largest advantage with attending a class is getting the hands-on experience.

Develop a Training Strategy for Your Company

Training is an often overlooked but very important part of the initial rollout of any product or migration. You may not be doing the training yourself so you should involve an instructor. If you do not have one in your company, seek an outside source. Training materials should include a step-by-step guide to the new features included with Notes 4.5. You should test these materials (primarily the exercises) on your testing server just as you are testing your applications. To the best of your ability, you should design your training material so that it addresses all levels of technical experience in your company.

Train the Migration Teams

After you have established team members, it is best to get all parties involved in the needed training. The biggest advantage of formal training is actually performing some of the hands on tasks you will do during a migration. You can schedule this training with your local Lotus Authorized Education Center. Use the testing environment you set up, the documentation that comes with Release 4.5, and the training materials you created to train your teams. Make sure all people performing the actual migration understand the process.

Perform Testing

Document and test mission-critical applications using the testing server you set up. You should document any problems with an older client trying to use script, navigators, buttons, and the like so that support may be prepared for possible phone calls. Make sure you complete testing before the first server upgrade.

Define a Training Strategy

Determine whether you prefer to use an in-house training class or training provided by a Lotus Authorized Education Centers. You should train (or have an instructor train) fellow administrators, Help-desk personnel, and developers before end users.

Communicate During the Migration

Define a support mechanism for those people who are to perform the migration. This can be done in the same database that you are using to comment about the migration planning. Perhaps a separate view or form might be needed. For more information about Lotus Notes database development, see Chapter 13, "Advanced Application Design Issues."

Make Sure the Migration Team Is Ready

Confirm migration plans with the migration team as the final checkpoint before actual migration begins. Adjust any time lines as needed so that you do not have unrealistic deadlines.

Begin the Migration

Inform the appropriate parties (administrators, developers and managers) that servers are about to be be upgraded. Upgrading the server involves installing the software in the same directory as the older software is installed. You should first backup the server to ensure you do not lose any important files. If you are changing operating systems or changing hardware, it can be quite handy to copy all the files in your Notes directory to a file server. You can then copy them to the new system and then install the new software. You can install from CD, file server, shared drive, or diskettes. For more information on installation, see Chapter 6. After upgrading the servers, be sure to monitor them and troubleshoot any problems. As you discover difficulties with your servers, take advantage of the discussion database to see whether anyone else has encountered the same problem. After a solution is discovered put it in the database as well.

Train Managers and End Users

Train managers and end users. Try to upgrade systems during or shortly after they attend the training sessions. This can be a tough thing to coordinate but your users benefit much more if they can practice what they learned in class very soon after the session.

Notify End Users and Upgrade Workstations

Use the workstation upgrade order you specified in the migration schedule to identify end users who are affected by the upgrade. Some users are undoubtedly able to upgrade their stations themselves. For these users, you can use the mail upgrade feature to help them install the workstation. For information on this process, see the next section about Mail Upgrades. If necessary, include instructions on accessing Notes workstation software and installation. Include information on how to report problems to the help desk.

For those users that cannot upgrade their systems on their own, you should have a path for access to the help desk, where they can inform the administrators of difficulty. Following the step-by-step guide your team created, the administrators can upgrade the system for them.

Upgrade All Mail Databases at Once

If you plan to upgrade all mail databases on a server at the same time, be sure to notify all end users before you initiate the command on the server.

Upgrading Mail Files

The biggest change in Domino 4.5 is Calendaring and Scheduling, which resides in user mail files. You can let users upgrade their mail file on their own or you can change all these files at once on the server. Until the file is upgraded (using the new template), users cannot take advantage of the new Calendaring and Scheduling features.

A mail file can be upgraded with Lotus Notes in three ways. These include:

◆ The conversion utility

◆ Users upgrade their own files

The Conversion Utility

The mail conversion utility lets you upgrade multiple mail databases with one server command. The conversion utility has several arguments. The general format is as follows:

```
load convert [-f] [-l] [-r] [-i] [-d] [-n] [drive:\directory]filename
➥[oldtemplate newtemplate]
```

Note The brackets [ ] indicate optional arguments.

As an example, if you wanted to convert all mail files to the Mail45 template, you would use the following command. This command does not check to see which template was previously used:

```
L Convert \mail * mail45
```

If you wanted to only convert those mail databases that are using the standard mail4 template (see fig. 10.1), you would use:

```
L Convert \mail stdr4mail mail45
```

Figure 10.1
Mail upgrade.

Some additional arguments are associated with the convert server command:

◆ **Argument -f.** The conversion utility changes only those databases listed in a text file. If you use this argument, you must specify a text file for *filename.* You can specify -f either before or after the text file name. To use this argument, you must first create the text file with the -l argument.

◆ **Argument -l.** This argument is used to create a text file that contains a list of all mail files on your server. The contents of the text file reflect the database names found in the Mail Users view of the Public Name & Address Book (must be an R4.x Public Name & Address Book). You must specify a text file name where you want to save this information. The extension of the file is not relevant to this operation (the file is still a text file). By default, Notes creates the text file in the Notes data directory (typically C:\Notes\Data). However, you can specify an alternate directory. The mail conversion utility does not override a file with the same name.

◆ **Argument -r.** The -r argument searches the specified directory and all its subdirectories.

◆ **Argument -i.** This argument ignores the maximum folder limit. Without the use of this argument, the mail conversion utility does not upgrade any mail database that has more than 200 categories.

◆ **Argument -d.** This argument does not create folders or subfolders in the new mail file for the users.

◆ **Argument -n.** This option is used to test which databases the mail conversion utility could potentially convert. No databases are actually converted when this argument is used.

The conversion utility is a much more efficient method for upgrading mail files. It requires no user intervention. But, be sure that the user has the Lotus Notes 4.5 client or you will cause many errors for that user.

Users Upgrade Their Own Files

If you plan to have end users upgrade their own mail databases, you can use the notification feature in the Public Name & Address Book. Notice that in figure 10.2 the notification feature is a button found in the Mail Users view of the Public Name & Address Book.

Figure 10.2

Mail upgrade button.

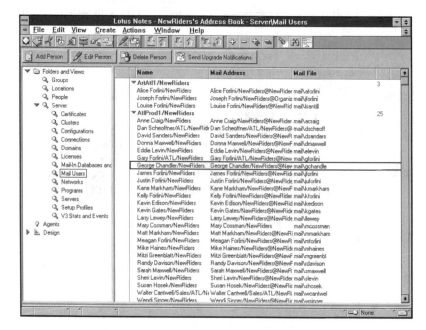

Notice that in figure 10.3 you can fill in the name of the user that receives the upgrade.

The bottom portion of the upgrade message (see fig. 10.4) enables you to configure the template to be used for the mail upgrade. Additionally, you can specify the location of the upgrade software.

An Install Notes button appears as the user receives the upgrade notification *only* if the user has client software of an earlier version than 4.5. See figure 10.5 for an example of the upgrade mail message. The Upgrade Mail File button appears for all versions.

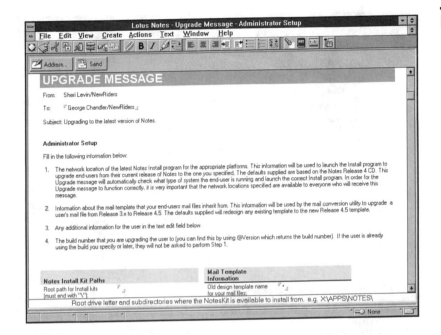

Figure 10.3

Top of upgrade message.

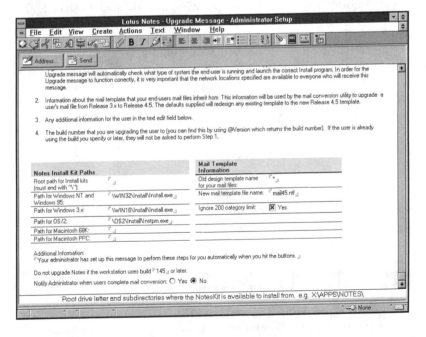

Figure 10.4

Bottom of upgrade form.

Figure 10.5

Upgrade mail notification.

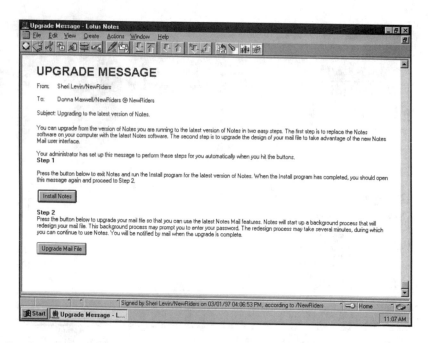

If needed, distribute information manually on upgrading a single mail database and the period of time in which users need to complete the upgrade. A manual upgrade is done by first highlighting the mail file and then selecting File, Database, Replace Design. You can then select the new 4.5 mail template from the menu. If the template is not found, you can use a Domino server to find the template (see fig. 10.6).

Figure 10.6

Replace design.

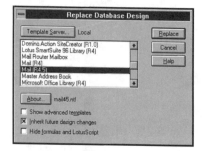

Communicating Problems

As your help desk identifies problems, troubleshoot them and distribute this information to all members of the migration team. The problems may include hardware errors, forgotten APIs, and others. The help desk may also offer suggestions that would make the migration more efficient. You may need to send mail in addition to placing the information in the migration discussion database. The feedback and support calls you get from your first round of migration activities may well alter your plans. Regardless of the level of planning, items or issues are not uncovered until you start your migration.

Handling Application Upgrades

After you complete the migration of users, you can then upgrade your applications as necessary. You should use the list of applications that you created as a guide. The following should be done to upgrade applications:

◆ If you have databases that should not be changed, you can use an .NS3 extension to retain the file format as a Release 3.x database.

◆ Update view and full text indexes of databases on all servers. This prevents substantial startup time on the server.

◆ Determine which features you want to implement (such as navigators, alternating line colors in views, actions, merge replication conflicts, etc). For more information on database design, see Chapter 13.

Implementing New Administration Features

You should use the Public Name & Address Book agents to update roles. These agents enable you to distribute responsibility for the Public Name & Address Book and secure it against any errors. Roles limit who can create or alter records in the Public Name & Address Book. For instance, if you have frequent problems with connection records being altered, you can limit who has the ability to change these records. You must first add the roles to the Public Name & Address Book. As shown in figure 10.7, this is done with an action.

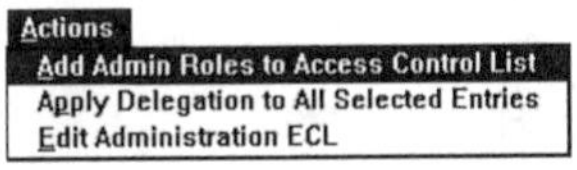

Actions
Add Admin Roles to Access Control List
Apply Delegation to All Selected Entries
Edit Administration ECL

Figure 10.7

The Actions menu.

The different roles in the Public Name & Address Book are:

◆ **Group Creator and Group Modifier.** These roles enable you to delegate group create and modification respectively. If you are a large company with many branches, you could assign this privilege to a group and then place specific members at each branch into the group.

◆ **Server Creator and Server Modifier.** These two different roles grant rights to make and change server records. You should consider significantly reducing this privilege. You may also want to consider a separate Organization Unit just for servers. The advantage with a separate OU is that you can keep this certifier and prevent unauthorized use (such as making a server with the same name). For more information about Organizational Units, see Chapter 6.

◆ **User Creator and User Modifier.** It is often desirable to delegate the creation of new users and the modification of any Person records in the Public Name & Address Book. These two roles give you the ability to grant this access to key people in your organization.

◆ **Net Creator and Net Modifier.** These are "catch all" privileges. These two roles essentially control all the other records in the PUB (such as Domain records, Connection records, Certification records, Configuration records, and so on).

To assign individuals or groups to the role, you can simply use the Access Control List for the Public Name & Address Book. You should be sure to include a server group in the list so that servers have the rights to carry out the changes made.

Implementing New Server Features

You should have determined which features you want to add to your server during the meetings prior to migration. Implementing these new features makes all your migration efforts seem worth it because you will be using the new functionality of the updated code. You may have determined that you wish to use Shared Mail, PassThru Server, Multiple Replicators, or other new server features. Many of these new features are discussed in Chapter 8 in the "Advanced Administration Features" section.

Migrating from Previous Versions of Notes 4 to 4.5

Migrating from 4.<5 to 4.5 is not nearly as monumental as it is from 3.x to 4.<5. Nothing in 4.5 will cause harm to databases. The primary migration issue is that many new classes and methods were added to the LotusScript language in 4.5. If you have developers creating databases for 4.<5 users, you should make sure they are doing this on a 4.<5 client, because the changes will not work on a 4.<5 system. A 4.5 server will, however, support 4.<5 databases and clients perfectly.

If you have custom views or forms that you are using in your Public Name & Address Book (this applies to any prior release of Notes), be sure to make a backup copy of the address book design prior to your upgrade.

Note The 4.5 mail template cannot be used by a prior release of Lotus Notes. Be sure to upgrade the server, then the workstation, and then the mail files. Any other order results in errors.

As you begin your upgrade, you might wish to consider what group or department might need Calendaring and Scheduling the most. You can use these areas as a testing environment for these new features.

The largest change in 4.5 is in a user's mail file. You can upgrade mail files just as you can from 3.x to 4.x (see the "Upgrading Mail Files" section of this chapter). You should use care as you upgrade the files. A 4.5 mail does not function with a 4.<5 client.

Beyond Notes Migration

During migration to new software, spending money and time to make the transformation is inevitable. Some down time is also necessary while servers are changed. If you have to spend time and money, and experience down time, why not make certain you do not need to do it again for reasons you might not have considered? It may prove very beneficial to do an assessment of your environment beyond just the Lotus Notes software. Contacting your help desk to get frequently asked questions and offered suggestions can help you determine what configurations you need to consider changing. Some other things you may need to consider during a migration include:

◆ Changing domains or organizations

◆ Moving to a (or changing an existing) hierarchical naming strategy

◆ Changing to international IDs or international software

◆ Changes in operating systems

◆ Creating specialized servers

◆ Auditing the Public Name & Address Book

The remaining sections in this chapter address each of these options.

Changing Domains or Organizations

If your company is involved in a company merger or changes its name for any reason, you may want to change the domain and the organization names. The domain name is used whenever addressing mail to your end users (such as Randy Davison@NewRiders). The domain name appears in all Person records, Connection records, and server records in the Public Name & Address Book. Additionally, you can find the name in the Notes.ini file. A domain is defined as all the servers that share a common Public Name & Address Book. Therefore, if you change your domain name, it generally means building a new Public Name & Address Book. If you are careful, you can even create parallel domains on an existing server and then switch to the new domain after necessary information has been migrated.

To create a new domain and organization at the same time, you can simply launch a server and select First Server in the Organization. When you select a first server, you make a new Public Name & Address Book and a new Cert.ID. For more information about a First Server, see Chapter 6.

If you determine that only the domain should be changed, you can make a new address book and copy any desired Server, Connection, and Person records into the new address book. You also need to change all the records to reflect the new domain name. If you have many records, you can accomplish this by creating an agent (see Chapter 13 for more information about agents). For Person records, you should change the MailDomain field; for Server records you should change the Domain field. Connection records have both a SourceDomain and a DestinationDomain field. Two domains can exist with relative harmony while you are changing and copying these records. You should see some errors on the server as the router loads (because records refer to different domains), but these are not harmful as much as they are annoying.

You may want to change or add a domain for any one of several reasons:

◆ You have been acquired by another company or your company has changed its name.

◆ The Public Name & Address Book would be too large because all the users in your company are in one database.

◆ You want a test environment for developers.

◆ You want to implement an Internet SMTP MTA server or other Internet server.

◆ You want to cross-certify with other companies but with a separate Public Name & Address Book.

To make it easier on your users, you can set up non-adjacent domain records. These records make is so that a user only has to type one domain rather than two or more (such as Randy Davison@XLCNotes@XLCEXT@Notes Net) to address a piece of mail outside the company. Notice in figure 10.8 that when users send mail to the MaxwellBros Domain, they need only type **@MaxwellBros** rather than include it in the external NewRidersExternal domain name.

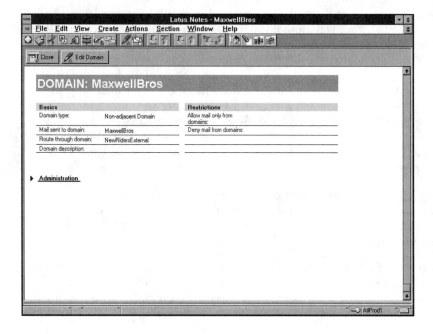

Figure 10.8

Non-Adjacent domain record.

Hierarchical Strategy

If you are changing the name of your company, then you are probably going to change the organization certifier name as well (such as /NewRiders). The organization name appears on all IDs in your company and therefore you should change the name just like you would for door signs or business cards. Creating a new certifier can be accomplished by selecting File, Tools, Server Administration, Certifiers, Register Organization. Notice that in figure 10.9 you then type in the name of the new certifier, the password and the administrator's name (or group). After the ID exists, you can begin making new Organizational Units, Servers, and User IDs.

Figure 10.9

Creation of new certifier.

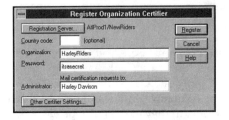

Perhaps your company name has not changed, but you want a more structured certification for your IDs. This is best accomplished by creating Organizational Units. Organizational Units afford you more distinguished names and higher security. For example, Chris Cole/NewRiders is not as qualifying as Chris Cole/Sales/Atl/ NewRiders. This is particularly helpful when you have users that have the same name. You should create Organizational Units based on what changes the least. For instance, you should not create Organizational Units based on departments if your company does a reorganization every six months. You can create new Organizational Units by selecting File, Tools, Server Administration, Certifiers, Register Organizational Unit. You are first asked for your Organizational Certifier (Cert.ID). You then type in the name of the new Organizational Unit, a password, and the name of the administrator (or group).

You can then use the new Organizational Unit certifier to register new servers or new users. If you want to change previous users, you can use the AdminP process on the server. You cannot add an Organizational Unit to a server names with AdminP. For more information about AdminP, see Chapter 8.

If you are one of the few remaining oranizations that have non-hierarchical IDs, you probably have been inundated with information about the need to upgrade. Since version 4.0, upgrading IDs has become much easier with AdminP. For information about AdminP and flat IDs, see Chapter 8.

International IDs

Your company may have become worldwide after your last upgrade and so you must now consider international software and international IDs. Because of the difference in encryption technology, a North American license cannot be taken out of the United States or Canada. You could just supply international software and IDs to those that travel abroad, but this might be much more time-consuming than just changing the entire company to international. Also, a North American ID cannot be cross-certified (and therefore these machines can not communicate) with an International ID, and you cannot use a North American ID with international software. To change your company to international IDs and software, you must make a new certifier and re-register all servers and users. For more information on registering users and server, see Chapter 6.

Changes to Operating Systems

As you assess your current Lotus Notes topology, you may find that the operating system you selected years ago is not ideal for the needs of your company today. Changing your operating system usually involves formatting the hard drives and overriding all the existing data. Before doing so, you should have a known good backup copy.

 You can save yourself some time by copying all the files in your Lotus Domino files and databases to a file server. Prior to upgrading the software, you can copy the files back. Be sure not to forget about any directory links that point to other drives or directories.

Creating Specialized Servers

For various reasons, you may have come to the conclusion that your servers would run more efficiently if they were specialized. For instance, if you design a PassThru server, you can have multiple modems and roll over lines. This server could be dedicated to do nothing but accept calls from fellow workers. Other servers would not need modems because you provide enough call in lines and modems on your PassThru server. Specialized servers may include any of the following:

◆ **Hub.** A Hub server typically does not have any users but rather replicates to other servers in the company.

◆ **Mail Only server.** By placing mail files on one server (or one server per branch), you can better administer mail routing and it is easier to troubleshoot problems.

◆ **PassThru server.** For the remote professional, PassThru has many advantages. You can dial only one Domino server but access many. For more information on PassThru server see Chapter 8.

◆ **Intranet server.** You may want to provide company databases through the Internet for your employees. Take great care not to place any confidential data on servers that can be directly accessed through the Internet.

◆ **MTAs and gateways.** Now that the Internet has become so popular, you may want to get a Lotus Notes SMTP MTA server running so that your fellow workers can send and receive mail over the Internet. You may also want to take advantage of the Lotus Fax Server so that users can easily send and receive faxes without even having to leave their desks.

Auditing the Public Name & Address Book

One of the best times to audit the Public Name & Address Book is during a migration. You should draw diagrams that illustrate replication, mail routing, gateways, and PassThru servers. A call to your support center can also be a terrific aid in determining whether users have had difficulty with any of these servers. You should determine whether your current schemes are logical and efficient.

Next, you should simply scan the database. Look for anything that looks like security violations (cartoon names for instance). Look at the server records and see whether any have security violations (such as anonymous access on servers that should be secure or no termination listing in the Deny Access field). Make sure your group entries have logical names and that there are no duplicates. Also, determine whether you can change any from multi-purpose to mail or security only (this makes your servers more efficient). Look at the certifications view and decide whether any cross certificates should be removed. Scan the miscellaneous events documents view of your log file and watch for routing, replication or security error messages that might indicate a configuration problem.

Summary

In this chapter you have learned about the process of migration. You read about a migration strategy that included making teams, the importance of testing, and upgrading mail files. You also learned of other steps you might do during a migration such as creating specialized servers, changing domains, moving to hierarchical IDs, and much more. With the information and suggestions contained in this chapter, you are now much better prepared to keep your company up to date when new Lotus

Notes software is produced by the Iris Group. Keeping up to date means that you can take advantage of new features that can make your company more efficient in their every day tasks. The following chapter helps you better understand security features included with your Domino servers.

CHAPTER 11

Securing Your Notes and Domino 4.5 System

It is important to have a security policy in place in your company. By having such policies, you will find more consistent control of your confidential data. Often, cultural and social aspects of your company help you derive a security policy. After the policy is in place, it is easier to make decisions about how (or if) you share data with the outside world.

This chapter will help you make decisions on security as well as give you great insight about implementing security measures for your Domino server and Notes clients. You will find details about firewall topology, server access, database access, document access, and more. This chapter will take you a step further so that you not only have information about securing your Notes environment but also gain information about recovering from disasters.

The Notes environment has many different levels of security. Most people that use an application are primarily concerned with maintaining confidential data and screening those that can access that data. However, security is more than screening. Screening is generally defined as denying access to some and allowing others to access data. Security also involves disaster recovery, limiting theft, and many other aspects.

Screening

Lotus Notes offers a very large variety of screening mechanisms. The CIA has used Lotus Notes for many years because it offers so many different levels of security. It has several levels of protection for your systems and the data on these systems. Many of these are outlined as follows (see example in fig. 11.1):

◆ **LAN/WAN** - Access to your overall network

◆ **Physical server access** - Server rooms or keyboard locks

◆ **Authentication** - The process IDs go through to access a server

◆ **Server level access** - Adding databases, server commands, and more

◆ **Directory level access** - Limiting access to specific directories on your server

◆ **Database access** - The Access Control List

◆ **View access** - Granting or denying rights to views

◆ **Form access** - Creation or modification to documents via a form

◆ **Document read access** - Accessing documents

◆ **Document edit access** - The ability to alter documents

◆ **Digital signatures** - Guaranteeing the document is from an origin (person)

◆ **Section access** - Portions of a document

◆ **Field access** - Using keys to limit access to a field

◆ **Encryption** - Using keys to limit access to data

◆ **Workstation security** - Limiting executions of Notes functions at a workstation

The following sections discuss these levels of screening security in detail.

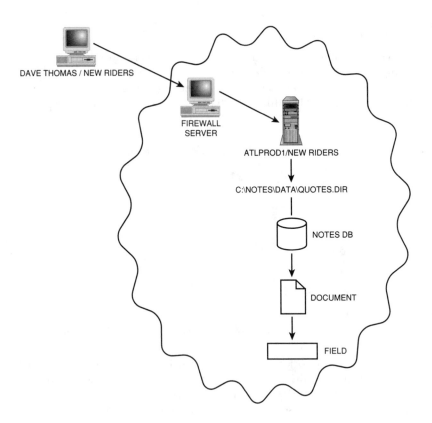

Figure 11.1

Example of security levels.

LAN/WAN

It is important to provide protection for your overall network (LAN/WAN). As your company begins using the Internet, you should be aware that security risks persist, even with the solutions provided below. It is generally not productive to focus your attention on keeping unwanted users off the machines that directly access the Internet. Rather, you should develop a plan to ensure that you can recognize intrusions on vulnerable servers and that you provide no confidential data on those servers. Two methods can aid you with protecting your network:

◆ **Port encryption** - Ports that send packets that only Notes can interpret

◆ **Firewalls** - Servers that generally screen data sent to your network

Encrypting Network Traffic

You can choose to encrypt all data transmitted on a given network port. Encryption involves scrambling the data sent from one server to another. Only a Notes server could interpret the data. This option is available by selecting File, Tools, User Preferences, Ports. As shown in figure 11.2, this menu has a checkbox to enable Encrypt Network Data.

Figure 11.2

Port encryption.

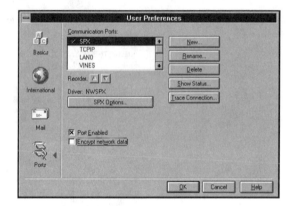

Ports can be encrypted on both workstations and servers. This can be a useful option when the security of the network link cannot be guaranteed, as it often cannot when servers replicate over the Internet. However, encryption slows data transmission. Therefore, most organizations choose not to implement this option for network traffic on their internal networks.

Firewalls

A firewall is designed to limit unwanted and unauthorized access to your servers. Often, your main focus is keeping Internet users from accessing your servers. If your site already has a firewall, you should become familiar with the security policies of your company.

A firewall basically examines the IP packets that attempt to come into your company. You can use a firewall to limit information through an IP address or port in either direction. You can also use firewalls to have you paged, to e-mail you, or even to shut down your server in the event of a violation.

The following are the two primary types of firewalls:

◆ Packet filter

◆ Proxy servers

Packet Filter

A packet filter looks at the address of the packet and the port on which the data travels. A table of addresses controls the traffic. It specifies who is and is not autho- rized to access the network based on the port number of the machine he or she is trying to access, and the source and destination IP addresses (see fig. 11.3). Lotus Notes uses port 1352, so if you want to make sure that the only TCP/IP traffic going into your Notes servers is Notes traffic, you can restrict access to the Notes servers' IP addresses to only this port.

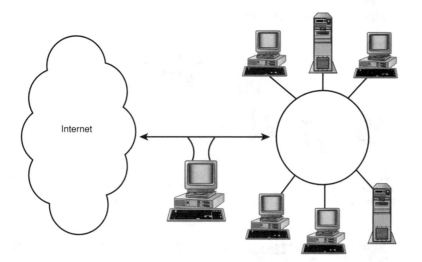

Figure 11.3

Packet filter.

Internet

Protecting your network with a packet filter is implemented at the IP level and is therefore quick, but not very flexible. If you want to use it to ensure that only certain external users have access to your network, then you have to list their IP addresses in the table enabling access. You do run a risk, because someone can impersonate an IP address and therefore be let through the firewall. This security problem arises because IP addresses are unsecured and easily duplicable. To fully secure your Domino server and still use a packet filter, additional security features are included with your Domino software. You can have your users supply an HTTP password in their person records. When they access databases through the Internet, they have to type in their names and passwords to gain access. To be fully secure, you can require your users to always use their Notes clients, which means authenticating via their Notes IDs.

Application Proxy

A proxy server can emulate a client when it needs to use the Internet. For outbound traffic (to an untrusted network), the proxy server rebuilds the packet so that it appears to have originated from the proxy server itself, not the actual client that initiated the traffic. So, from an IP address perspective, all traffic appears to originate from or be destined for the proxy server and that is the only machine in your organization which directly communicates with the Internet is the proxy server. Figure 11.4 gives an illustration.

Figure 11.4

Proxy server.

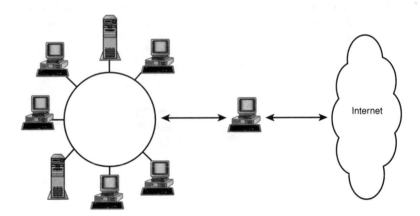

For a Notes Client to use a proxy server, the location record must have the proxy address. As you can see in figure 11.5, the Web proxy field should contain the address of the server.

Figure 11.5

Location record.

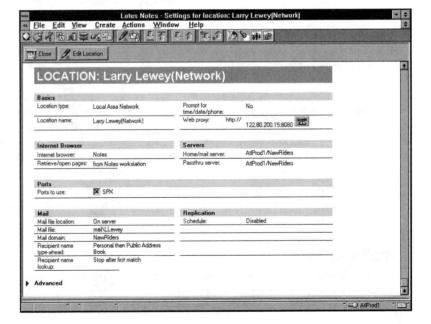

Using the configuration (the beanie) button you can access the Proxy Server Configuration dialog box shown in figure 11.6. Use caution with this menu as you configure your proxy server.

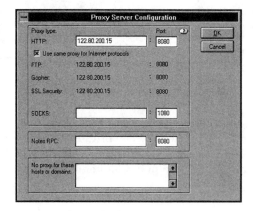

Figure 11.6

The Proxy Server Configuration dialog box.

Physical Server Access

Limiting physical access is essential for your Lotus Domino servers. If users can directly use a Lotus Notes server, they have manager access to databases (assuming Enforce Local ACL is not turned on). They can also delete or copy files, format the hard drive, and other dangerous things. You can use alternative methods such as screen savers or mouse, keyboard, and disk drive locks, but a locked room is far more effective.

Authentication

Authentication is the process that two IDs use to establish communication in Lotus Notes (see fig.11.7). Unless the ID has the correct certification keys, it is not allowed to use the server. This is assuming anonymous access is not used (see Chapter 15, "Domino-Specific Application Development Considerations," for more information). When a user or server presents an ID to a server, the following steps are involved:

1. The workstation for Dan Quinn/NewRiders generates a random number that it encrypts with his private key and sends to AtlProd1/NewRiders server.

2. The server decrypts the number with Dan's public key and sends the number back to the workstation.

3. The server also generates a random number, which it then encrypts (with Dan's public key) and sends to Dan's workstation.

4. The workstation decrypts the number with the private key from Dan's ID. After the number is verified, access is granted.

Figure 11.7

Authentication.

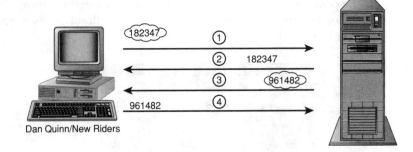

Dan Quinn/New Riders

Public and private keys are created when IDs are created. A public key is stored in the person and server records as well as in each ID. The private key is stored only in the ID for the server or person. For information about creating IDs, see the "Fundamentals of Domino Server Administration" section in Chapter 6, "Installing Domino 4.5 Server Software."

Server-Level Access

You can grant rights to administrators, developers, and users in your company with the server document. You can grant privileges such as creating new databases, using remote console, PassThru access, and other operations. For more information about granting these rights, please see Chapter 6.

Directory-Level Access

Using directory security, you can assign rights to directories and use more than one fixed disk to store files. You can easily manage directories and the security for them with the Server Administration Panel. For more information, please see Chapter 6.

Database Access

The Access Control List (ACL) is the most commonly used security tool in Lotus Notes. Every database has an ACL and you can list servers, individuals, or groups (see fig. 11.8).

Groups are generally regarded as less time-consuming than individual names. With seven different levels of access available, the ACL limits what a person can do in a given database. These levels of access are listed, from highest to lowest, as follows:

◆ Manager

◆ Designer

◆ Editor

◆ Author

◆ Reader

◆ Depositor

◆ No Access

The next few sections discuss each of these levels in greater detail.

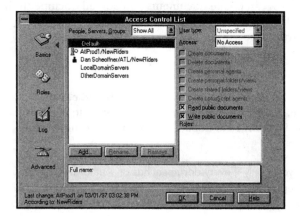

Figure 11.8

*The Access
Control List.*

Manager

A person with Manager access can modify ACL settings (the same settings this section
discusses), encrypt a database for local security, modify replication settings, and
delete a database (tasks permitted by no other access level). Managers can also
perform all tasks allowed by all the lower access levels. Notes requires each database
to have at least one Manager. Especially with 4.x (because of new features such as
enforce local ACL), it is best to assign at least two people (or two groups) Manager
access to each database in case one manager is not available.

Often a manager is also the same person or persons that created the database. You
may also desire to include administrators with Manager access so that the ACL can be
changed if needed.

Designer

A person with Designer access can modify all database design elements (fields, forms,
views, folders, public agents, the database icon, Using This Database document, and
About This Database document), can modify replication formulas, and can create a

full text index. Designers can also perform all functions allowed by lower access levels. You should assign Designer access to the person or persons responsible for updating the design of a database.

Designer access can be a safety net for your designers. If you give all designers Manager access, you make it possible for them to accidentally delete the file. There are exceptions to this suggested policy (such as during testing phases). Often, it is better to give only administrators Manager access.

Editor

Users assigned Editor access can create documents and edit all documents, including those created by others. Editor access is ideal for the monitor of a database (such as the supervisor of a department).

Author

Persons assigned Author access can create new documents and edit these same documents in the future. Assign Author access when you want to allow users to contribute to a database but only read documents created by others.

 Author access works only if every document has an Author field with that user's name (or a group) in the field. Please see Chapter 13, "Constructing Notes Databases," for more information.

When possible, use Author access rather than Editor access. This forces users to take ownership of their documents, which leads to fewer replication or save conflicts. For more information about replication conflicts, please see the replication section of Chapter 6.

Reader

Lotus Notes clients assigned Reader access can only read documents in a database but cannot create or edit documents. Reader access is ideally suited for reference databases such as a company policies or news feeds databases.

Anyone with at least Reader access or higher can also create personal agents in the database. The additional checkbox is called Create personal agents and must be selected for people to use agents. However, users can only run agents that perform tasks allowed by their access levels. In the case of Reader access, an agent is ordinarily used to find data because he or she does not have the rights to alter data.

It often makes more sense to use No Access rather than Reader access, particularly for your default entry. You should make sure that granting Reader access is not going to allow the wrong users access to data. You may find it better to define a group (rather than default) with Reader access so that you are certain to limit which users are accessing your data.

Depositor

Depositor access is used rarely but can be useful for suggestion or ballot databases. Anyone assigned this level can create documents but can't see any documents in the database views (even the documents he or she creates).

No Access

Persons or groups assigned No Access cannot access the database. This does not mean that the database does not show up when doing File, Database, Open. To limit seeing the database with File, Database, Open, you can use File, Database, Properties (see fig. 11.9).

Figure 11.9

Database properties.

 It is very important to keep a Domino server physically secure. People with Depositor or No Access rights to a database may be able to copy the database outside of Notes through the operating system.

More Elements of the Access Control List

Many of the ACL's have additional toggles. For instance, you may have many applications for which Author rights are appropriate, but you do not want documents to be deleted. The following check boxes exist to further configure rights in the ACL:

◆ Create Documents

◆ Delete Documents

◆ Create Personal Agents

- ◆ Create Personal Folders/Views

- ◆ Create Shared Folders/Views

- ◆ Create LotusScript Agents

- ◆ Write Public Documents

- ◆ Read Public Documents

Create Documents

The Create Documents option allows Authors to compose documents. By default, Managers, Designers, Editors, and Depositors are permanently assigned this access level (it is not alterable). As you add people and groups to the ACL, the Create documents option is not selected by default.

Under most circumstances, you select this option for users with Author access; however, you may want to eventually deselect this option for archived data. This prevents Authors from creating new documents but still allows them to read and edit ones they've already created.

Delete Documents

Leaving Delete Documents deselected can be a handy safety net. Even designers and managers prefer leaving this option deselected so that they do not accidentally delete documents. Authors are only able to delete documents they create (assuming they are listed in the Authors field).

Create Personal Agents

With this option checked, Designers, Editors, Authors, or Readers can create personal agents (macros). It is not possible to remove this capability from those that have Manager access.

Personal agents on server databases take up server disk space and processing time, so you may want to deselect this option. For more information on limiting use of agents on your server, please see Chapter 6.

Create Personal Folders/Views

This option can enable Editors, Authors, and Readers to create personal folders and views in a database on a server. All Managers and Designers receive this privilege and it is unalterable.

If this option is not selected, personal folders and views can still be created but they are stored on their local workstations in the desktop.dsk file. Deselect this option if you desire to save disk space on a server. These personal elements are seen only by the creator.

Create Shared Folders/Views

Choosing this option enables Editors to create shared folders and views. Managers and Designers are automatically assigned this access.

Create LotusScript Agents

This option gives Readers, Authors, Editors, and Designers the ability to create LotusScript agents. Managers automatically are assigned this access.

Use care with this privilege. LotusScript agents on server databases have the potential to take up significant server processing time. Ideally, any LotusScript should be tested first on a development server if one is available. For more information on restricting the use of LotusScript on a server, please see Chapter 6.

Read Public Documents

This option exists primarily for calendaring and scheduling. People with this level of access see only documents, folders, and views that have been designated as available for public access in the Form/Folder/View Properties Infobox. Reader access, or an equivalent role, gives a user access to all documents that do not have reader lists (such as in a mail file). The Read Public documents checkbox can only be turned on and off if the people or groups are assigned No Access.

Write Public Documents

As in Read Public documents, this selection is generally intended for calendaring and scheduling. This option enables you to give people create and edit access to specific documents without giving them Author access. The form attributes must be designated as "available for public access viewers" in the properties menu.

View Security

In the properties of a view, you can determine whether all readers or a subset of users can use a view. By limiting what views a user can access, you are limiting what data the user can see. However, this is security by ignorance because anyone that can make a private view can still see and use documents in the database.

You also have a check box that makes the view Available to Public Access users. This feature makes the view usable for databases published on the Internet (see fig. 11.10).

Figure 11.10

View properties.

Form Security

Form Security can limit who can read or create documents with a particular form. The security features for a form include:

◆ Default Read Access

◆ Creation Access

◆ Encryption Keys

◆ Disable reproduction of the document

◆ Available to Public Access users

Default Read Access

The default read access feature defaults to all users. If you desire to limit the users that can read the document, you can select them from the list in the ACL or use the Public Name & Address Book by clicking on the purple person button (shown in fig. 11.11).

When you use this feature, you create a $Readers field. To change read access, you can create an editable field or use an action on the documents. Roles give you more flexibility with read access.

Figure 11.11

Form properties.

Creation Access

You can determine who has the ability to create a document with a particular form. This is accomplished by using the "Who can create documents with this form" feature. You can find more flexibility using a role rather than individual names.

Encryption Keys

The default encryption keys option enables you to determine an encryption key for fields on the form. The key must first be made in the ID menu of the designer. For more information, please see the "Encryption" section of this chapter.

Disable Reproduction of Document

You can disable reproduction of a document by using the feature entitled "Disable printing/forwarding/copying to clipboard." Notice in figure 11.12 that a user gets an error message when attempting to print, copy, or forward the message.

 You should include a message in the form to inform users of the database that this feature has been turned on, or you may cause them think that something is wrong with their system.

This feature is not true security because any screen capture program can copy the contents of the document. The feature is intended only to discourage access or remind users that the data is confidential.

Figure 11.12

Cannot execute the specified command.

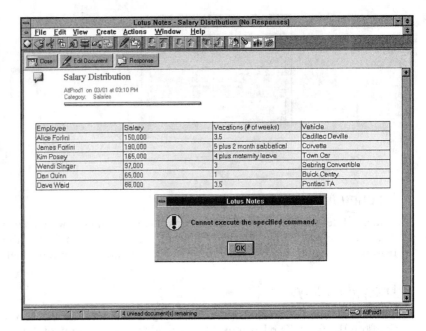

Available to Public Access Users

The Available to Public Access users feature can enable the form for use in databases that are published on the Internet.

Document Read Access

You can limit who has the ability to read a document with three methods:

◆ A document property

◆ A form property

◆ A reader field

As shown in figure 11.13, any user can restrict access to a document.

Simply by selecting a document and then choosing File, Document Properties you can assign users or groups read rights to the document. When this feature is used, a file called $Readers is created. If you intend to still replicate the document between servers, you should be certain to select the LocalDomainServers group when assigning Reader access. Notice you can also use public keys or use a key made from the user's ID.

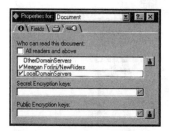

Figure 11.13

Document properties.

By using a form property, you can set a default set of readers each time a new document is created. As shown in figure 11.14, you should be certain to include the LocalDomainServers group if the database is going to replicate.

Figure 11.14

Form properties.

You may also consider using a role to provide flexibility.

You can also use a Reader Names Field on a form to restrict read access to fields (shown in fig. 11.15). The largest advantage of this option is that you can readily see who has the rights to read the document. You should be sure to include LocalDomainServers as a default formula in the field so that the documents can replicate between servers.

Figure 11.15

Reader name field.

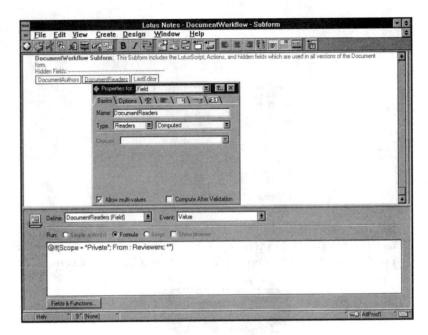

Document Edit Access

Author Name fields grant or deny edit access to documents. All forms should generally have an Author Names Field or you may find that users cannot edit their own documents. You can leave the field open by using the Editable field type. This gives users the ability to grant others (such as an administrative assistant or fellow team member) access to edit their documents. If you use a Computed field type, you can essentially force users to take ownership of their documents.

Digital Signatures

With signatures, you can ascertain which user was the last to use a document. It is more or less the equivalent of receiving a sealed envelope. If the document was altered by someone that did not sign the document, a message appears at the bottom of the workspace informing the user. With the ECL (Execution Control List), you can grant privileges based on whether the document is signed. Please see the "Workstation Security" section of this chapter.

Encryption

You can encrypt databases and fields. For traveling laptops or shared workstations, encryption requires an ID to gain access. To encrypt a database, you can simply select the database and then choose File, Database, Properties. From the Basics tab, you can enable three levels of encryption. As shown in figure 11.16, you can use Strong, Medium or Simple encryption on a local database. The levels of security vary based on the size of the key that is created for the encryption.

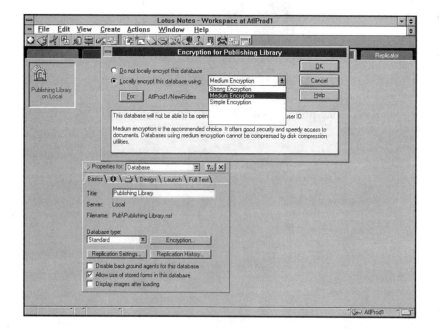

Figure 11.16

Database encryption.

To encrypt a field, the designer must first create an encryption key. This is accomplished in the User ID menu. Select File, Tools, User ID. As you can see in figure 11.17, you can create new keys and distribute them as needed.

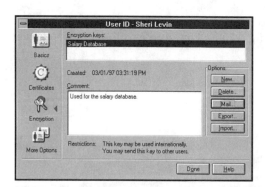

Figure 11.17

Creating an encryption key.

After the key exists, you can simply choose the key name from the Properties of a form. As shown in figure 11.18, select the key tab inside the properties InfoBox and then choose the appropriate key in the Default encryption keys option.

Figure 11.18

Form encryption.

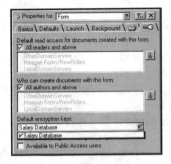

Finally, you should enable encryption on each field that you want to encrypt (see fig. 11.19).

Figure 11.19

Field encryption.

Section Access

You can limit who can edit a portion of a document with section security. You may wish to do this in applications that require fields to be changed only by the manager of a department. You must first create a section on the form by highlighting the area and then selecting Create, Section, Controlled Access (see fig. 11.20).

Then, from the Formula tab, you can create a formula that determines whether the user can edit the section (fig. 11.21). For more information about formulas, see Chapter 14.

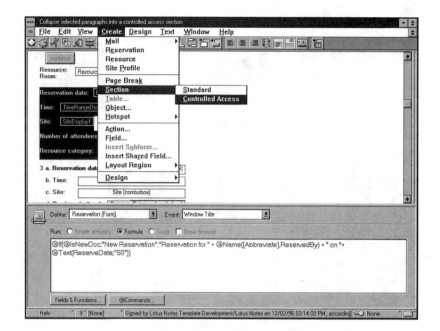

Figure 11.20

The Section menu.

Figure 11.21

The Selection formula.

Workstation Security

The Execution Control List (ECL) limits operations that can be performed on a workstation. When workstations use the Internet, it is possible to encounter mail bombs, viruses, Trojan horses, or unwanted application intrusions. Execution Control Lists can assist you with managing whether such executable files should be enabled to execute, and what level of access the program should be permitted.

As you can see in figure 11.22, ECLs are managed in the File, Tools, User Preference menu.

Figure 11.22

Execution Control List (ECL).

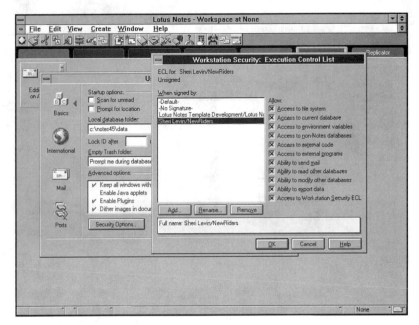

This concludes the discussion of limiting access in your Notes environment with screening devices. The final section guides you through disaster recovery options, storing IDs, and other security devices to better secure your data.

Beyond Screening

Screening those that can access data is not the only security challenge you should be concerned with. Security also involves disaster recovery, storage of IDs, and many other aspects.

Disaster Recovery

You should have a backup solution that keeps you prepared for a potential disk failure or other accidents. A backup solution includes the physical media to which you back up, the backup software you use and the plan of implementation. You can back up your Lotus Domino server to tape, file server, optical drive, CDs, or (if you have a lot of time and no budget) floppy disks. New products are coming on the market that will back up open files (needed with a Lotus Domino server) and that do incremental backups of Lotus Notes databases.

To truly be prepared for a fire or flood, you must have your backup media carried off site. This can be via U.S. mail, courier, or just by having an employee carry the media home or to a safety deposit box. Some companies provide this service for you. You should also select backup software that is compatible with the operating system that you select and with the Lotus software.

An Uninterrupted Power Supply (UPS) provides power to your server when you lose electricity. If the power loss is more than a couple of hours, the UPS eventually downs the operating system. However, very few UPS's also down the Lotus Domino server gracefully. One UPS that downs your Domino server is Power Chute by American Power Conversion.

Storage of IDs

When you register users and servers, you can store their ID files on any drive to which the server has access, or you can store the files in the Public Name & Address Book. The advantage with storing the IDs on some media (diskette, etc.) is that the media can work as a backup for the IDs in the event that a password is forgotten. The advantage with storing IDs in the Public Name & Address Book is that you do not have to get the ID to the person via other means. New to release 4.5 is an Escrow Agent feature that enables you to send all new IDs to a database (including mail files). Following these steps enables the Escrow Agent:

1. When IDs are sent to mail files, they are encrypted. Therefore, each user to whom you send the mail must have a public key in the Public Name & Address Book. If no public key is present, you can reregister the user or use the copy public key option in the User ID menu (from File, Tools, User ID), as shown in figure 11.23.

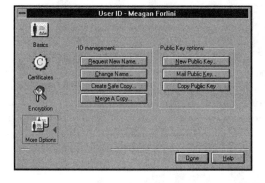

Figure 11.23

The User ID menu.

2. To mail the IDs to one person, you can simply type Escrow Agent in the User name field of the Person document in the Public Address Book (as shown in fig. 11.24). You cannot mail the ID to the same person that registers the user. To mail the IDs to more than one person, you can create a group called Escrow Agent.

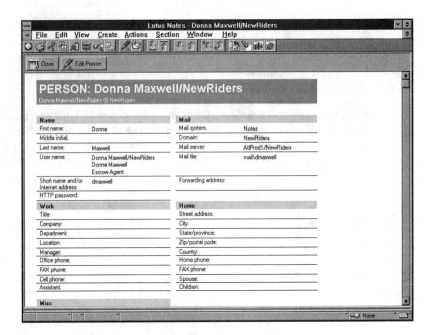

Figure 11.24

Escrow agent.

Use great care with the storage of the Cert.ID that is created by your first server. You do not want this ID to fall into the wrong hands and you do not want to lose it. Storing the ID on a floppy disk and keeping it in a locked drawer until needed is one of the most effective and convenient ways of keeping your Cert.ID. You should also keep one off site with your backup copies of your server so that you might recover from a fire or flood.

Summary

In this chapter you learned of many of the security aspects of Lotus Notes. Security can be a very important part of Administering Domino servers and creating Notes databases. You discovered information about firewalls, physical server security, database security, view security, form security, encryption, and more. You also learned of security issues that are not so apparent such as UPS devices, backup strategies, and storage of IDs.

CHAPTER 12

Troubleshooting Notes and Domino 4.5

T he primary focus of this chapter is common troubleshooting issues with your Domino server. You also can find additional references to troubleshooting in your Domino help files and the Domino 4.5 release notes. This chapter does not focus on flaws in the program but rather on known problems and solutions. In each section, you will find a common problem and the solution to that problem. Hopefully, troubleshooting is a very small part of your daily tasks; this chapter will make it an even smaller part. At the end of the chapter is a section called "Working Smarter," which can assist you in administering your server so you are not just "putting out fires."

Incomplete Replication

The following are common factors that can affect replication:

◆ The Access Control List

◆ Groups not set correctly (LocalDomainServers)

◆ Non-replica copy existing on the destination server

◆ Disk space

◆ Cut-off date in the Replication Settings dialog box

◆ Reader name fields

You can find information about replication in the Replication Events view of the log file (Log.nsf). In the log, you can find information about complete and incomplete replication. You can also see how many documents are read, updated, written, and deleted (see fig. 12.1).

Figure 12.1

The replication view of the Log file.

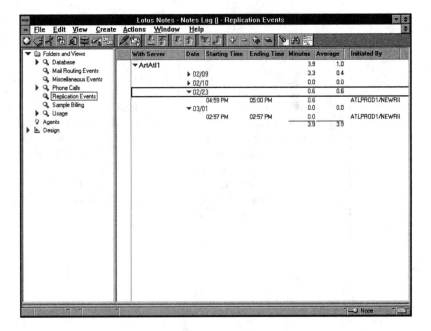

The Access Control List

The Access Control List (ACL) is the most common cause of failed replication. Be sure the server you are trying to replicate with has at least Editor rights. Also be sure that any intermediate servers also have adequate rights to send changes.

 To ensure you are typing a server name correctly, it is recommended that you click on the Add button, then the address list button (blue person button) that takes you to the address book (see fig.12.2).

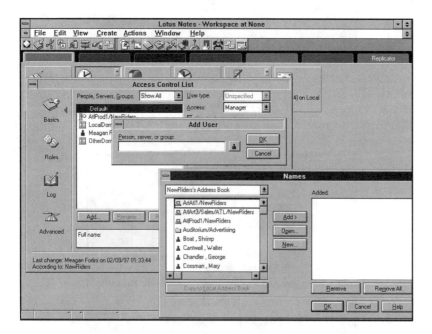

Figure 12.2

Adding servers to the ACL.

It might be necessary for a server to be part of a role. *Roles* are similar to groups in the address book, but they are used inside only one database.

If any LotusScript is present in the database, it is necessary to give the server privileges to Create Lotus Script agents. This is enabled using a check box in the Access Control List dialog box (see fig. 12.3).

Figure 12.3

LotusScript in the ACL.

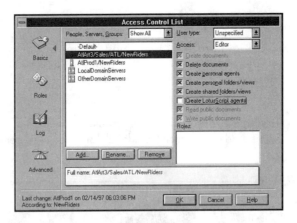

A new feature (in Domino Release 4.x) for the ACL is the capability to enforce local security. This option is located in the Advanced section of the Access Control List dialog box. Notice in figure 12.4 the feature is enabled by marking the check box. Enforce a consistent Access Control List across all replicas of this database.

Figure 12.4

Enforcing a local ACL.

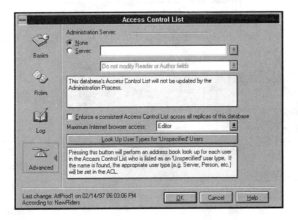

The advantage of this is that laptops with local replica copies will have the same rights as they would if the database was on the server. Prior to Release 4.x, you always had manager rights on all local copies.

You should use a great deal of caution with this option. If you specify only one user with manager rights and that person is not available, you cannot change the ACL. Furthermore, if there is only one entry for manager rights and that entry is specified as a server type, you have essentially locked yourself out of the database's Access Control List, and it cannot be changed without making a new file. One way around this is to create a user new ID with the exact same name as the one in the ACL with manager rights. For more information about registering users, see Chapter 7, "Installing Lotus Notes 4.5 Client Software."

Exceptions to this problem (being locked out with consistent ACL turned on) are all the administration databases (the Public Address Book, Notes Log, Certification Log, and Statistics). Opening these files through the Administration Panel is treated as "server type" access.

Groups Not Set Correctly

Groups are often listed in the ACL of a database because they offer more flexibility and convenience than individual names. The most commonly used group for servers is LocalDomainServers. As you create new servers, an entry is automatically added to your Public Name & Address Book. However, if you are using other group names for servers, then you obviously have to be sure that servers are added to the correct group so the servers can gain the access that is needed.

Non-Replica Copy Existing on the Destination Server

Non-replica copies of a file on a destination server cause no replication to occur. You should not use File, Database, New Copy if you expect to do replication. Always use File, Database, New Replica so that a common replica ID is carried with the new file. Copying a file with the operating system also yields a replica.

Disk Space

Be sure you have enough disk space on the destination server. You get no obvious error when a drive is out of disk space. The documents simply are not sent to the destination server. You can use the Show Disk command to see how much disk space is available on the server you are attempting to replicate with. Remember that it is possible to redirect files to other drives, so you have to specify the drive letter with Show Disk X.

Cut-Off Date in the Replication Settings Dialog Box

The Cut-Off Date in the Properties menu can also effect replication. To view this menu, select the file (highlight the icon) and then choose File, Replication, Settings. If the first line is turned on, double-check that it is set correctly. If you did not intend to remove documents from the database on a periodic basis, you should turn the feature back off.

Reader Name Fields

When a reader name field exists, it limits either servers or clients from viewing a document. This often is the last place an administrator looks for an error with replication. Reader name fields can be puzzling because they can be created by an end user or a developer. An end user can create one by highlighting a document and using File, Document Properties (see fig. 12.5).

Figure 12.5

Changing entries in the Reader name field.

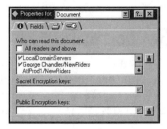

In both cases (whether a designer or user changes the field), you can see the contents of the field by finding $Readers. The easiest way to determine the existence of this field is by using File, Document Properties (you have to use a system that can view the document that is not replicating). See figure 12.6 for an example.

Figure 12.6

The $Readers field.

The most common problem in the $Readers field is the lack of LocalDomainServers. LocalDomainServers is a group of all the servers in a particular domain. Without some entry in the Reader name field that enables the server to read the document, replication does not occur.

Inability to Move Documents to a Folder

Move to Folder (found in the Actions menu) does not function from a view to a folder. Folders contain pointers to documents and views contain the documents. Move is actually defined as a copy and then a delete. If you delete a document in a view, you also are deleting it from the database. This can confuse your end users.

You also cannot use the Delete key on a document in a folder. You should always use Actions, Remove from Folder (see fig. 12.7). Otherwise, you will delete it from the database entirely.

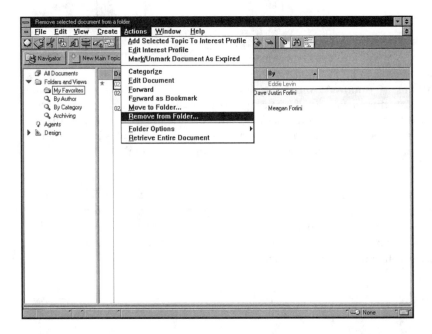

Figure 12.7

Removing a document from a folder.

Documents Reappear after Being Deleted

Documents reappear after being deleted if the purge interval is set too short for the database. When a document is deleted from a database, a *deletion stub* is created so that the next replica copy of the database will also delete the document (and get a deletion stub and then the next replica copy will delete the document, and so on). The *purge interval* specifies when these stubs should be removed (usually in 90 days). A purge interval can be changed in the SpaceSavers section of the database's Replication Settings dialog box. Change the number in the first line, even if the item is not checked (see fig. 12.8).

Figure 12.8

Replication Settings.

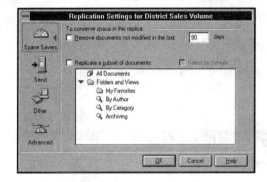

As deletion stubs are removed from a database, and as an end-user or server replicates with the database, the documents might reappear because there are no markers (the deletion stubs) to delete the documents. When this occurs, the database recognizes the documents as new. The solution is to be sure your purge interval is longer than the longest interval for replication (either by server or workstation).

In the Replication Settings dialog box, the first line Remove documents not modified in the last *XX* days is a dual-purpose check box. When the box is checked, documents are removed and the purge interval is one third of the number specified. When the box is not checked, documents are not removed but the purge interval is still one third of the number specified.

NDS Error with SPX

A Novell Directory Services (NDS) error with SPX likely means you do not have an NDS server. Figure 12.9 shows a failure with NDS.

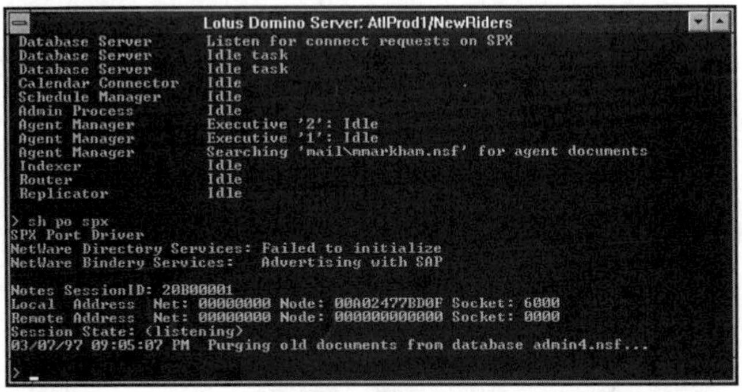

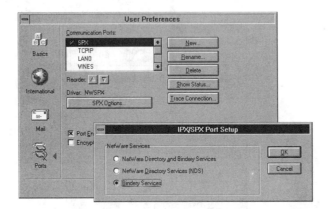

Figure 12.9

SPX failure with NDS.

If you do not have an NDS server, you can disable the NDS option in the IPX/SPX Port Setup dialog box. To disable this setting, down your server using Quit or Exit. Then open your WorkSpace on the server and choose File, Tools, User Preferences, Ports. With SPX selected in the Communication Ports list, click on the SPX Options button. Then select Bindery Services in the IPX/SPX Port Setup dialog box (see fig. 12.10).

Figure 12.10

Changing SPX settings.

Problems with SPX and Microsoft Systems

If you are having difficulty with a Microsoft operating system running SPX, it likely is because you have not loaded necessary files for NetWare. In NT, be sure to load the Gateway Services for NetWare and the SAP Agent (see fig. 12.11). The SAP agent is found in the services dialog box.

Figure 12.11

Changing network settings.

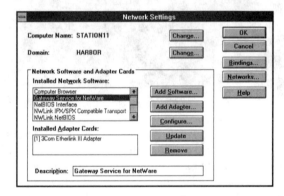

On a Windows system, you should load Client for NetWare Networks (see fig. 12.12).

Figure 12.12

Client for NetWare networks.

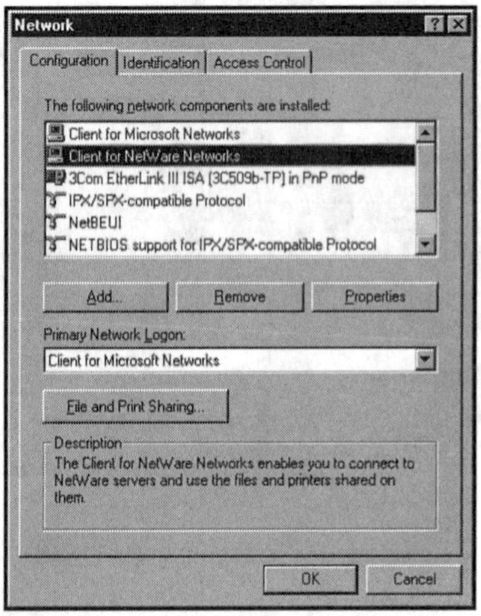

Not a Known TCP/IP Host with a New Client Setup

Notes sends a message that the TCP/IP host is unknown when the server name has been typed incorrectly or you do not have a DNS server. The error message is shown in figure 12.13.

Figure 12.13

Not a known TCP/IP host.

Double-check your server name and make sure you are typing in the fully distinguished server name (such as SFProd1/SF/LawrenceBros).

It is not possible to set up a Notes client with TCP/IP unless you have a DNS server. The server name must be resolved to the TCP/IP address and, without a DNS server, this is not possible. Therefore, you should select another protocol to initially setup your workstations, then change them to TCP/IP after installation. You can even choose no connection to the server, then change to TCP/IP after the workstation is set up. If you elect to use No Connection and then want to use TCP/IP, follow these steps:

1. Go into the user's Personal Address Book.

2. Choose the Add Connection button (see fig. 12.14).

3. Select the Local Area Network connection type in the first field.

4. Enter the fully distinguished server name in the Server name field (such as MiamiDev2/Miami/WadeToys).

5. In the Advanced section, enter the TCP/IP address of the server in the Destination server address field (see fig. 12.15).

6. Add the mail file (File, Database, Open) for the user and any other desired icons.

Figure 12.14

*Adding a
connection.*

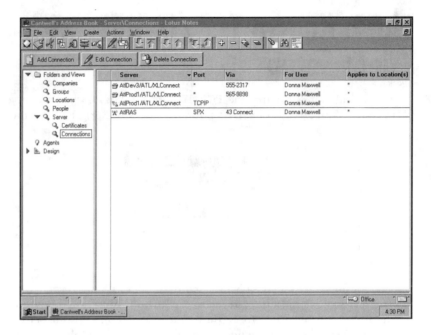

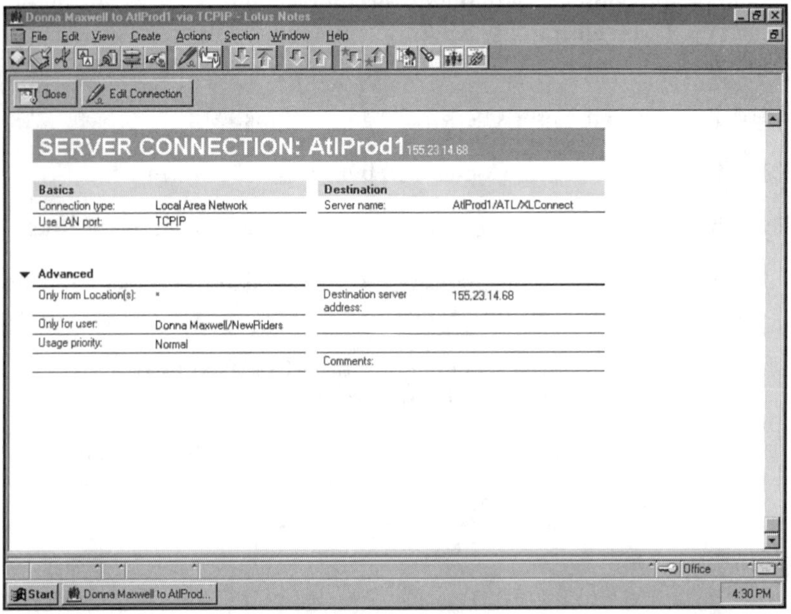

Figure 12.15

*The Server
Connection record.*

Cannot Find Path to Server

If you have set up a new Domino server and you cannot reach it, you can check for several things. You should first check the status of the ports on the server you cannot reach. You can do this using Sh Port [*port name*]. If you find no errors with the port (or even better, you can connect a client on that LAN segment), then you might have a problem through your WAN. If you are using a router, you cannot use NetBios (it requires a bridge). Another good diagnostic tool is to ping (from a DOS Prompt) the TCP/IP address of the server from the client (assuming you are using TCP/IP).

As you diagnose the servers broadcasting on your network at a particular site, you should be aware that the SAP address of a Domino server is 39B. Make sure the server is not going through secondary bridges or routers. Also, NT assigns a random frame number, and this might conflict with what your branch should be using. You should contact your corporate network administrator to find out what frame number your site should be assigned.

Mail Routing Problems

Mail routing involves four different kinds of documents: Person records, Server records, Connection records, and Non-Adjacent Domain records. All these records are found in the Public Name & Address Book. An error in any of these records can cause routing problems. You should begin diagnosing any errors by checking your log. A separate view called Mail Routing Events will aid you in determining the problem (see fig. 12.16).

Often the error can be found in the spelling of a domain name or the fully qualified name of a server on either the Server record, Person record, or Connection record. These records must agree.

If you discover excessive routing hops, you likely have a flaw in Connection records or in a Non-Adjacent domain record. If you have more than one path to a Notes Named Network (discussed in Chapter 6, "Installing Domino 4.5 Server Software"), the mail router cannot resolve this and bounces between servers up to a maximum of 25 times. Messages also bounce if a Non-Adjacent record is used with only two domains. Non-Adjacent records are intended for three domains. See Chapter 6 for more information.

If mail does not recognize new or changed connection documents, you can stop and restart the router so it will recognize the change. This is done using the command T Router Q. You then can restart the router with L Router. For more information about server commands, see Chapter 6. If you find a reference (in your log file) to no access to the mail.box on the destination server, this means either someone changed the ACL (something that should never be done in most cases), the LocalDomainServers group has not replicated, or the group contains incorrect data.

Figure 12.16

The Mail Routing Events view.

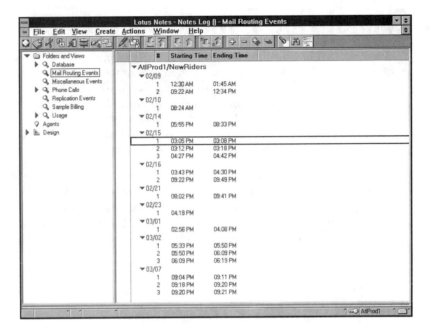

Cannot Remove the Password for the Server

It can be quite convenient to have your server reboot without any intervention from you (for more information, see the section "Working Smarter" later in this chapter). If you want your server to start up without you typing in the password for the ID, you must remove the password. If you find that you cannot remove the password, it likely is because it was registered with the default password length of one character (or digit). You must reregister the server, making sure to set the password length to zero.

Duplicate Templates

If you see an error eluding to duplicate templates on your server, you have two databases that claim to be a template with the same name (just as the warning suggests). This same name is *not* the file name. To discover which databases are claiming to be a template, you should select File, Database, New, then select the appropriate server name. You then can see a list of all the database templates on that server (assuming none of the files are hidden).

After you find the two templates that are in common (be sure to write down both file names), you will likely want to delete or rename the template name of the oldest file. To rename a template, first you open it. Because template names do not show up in File, Database, Open, you need to type the template name at the bottom of the dialog box. You then can use File, Database, Properties to change the name of the template in the Design tab. Figure 12.17 shows the Properties dialog box.

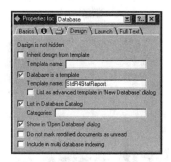

Figure 12.17

The Properties dialog box.

File Is in Use by You or Another User

If you attempt to compact or delete a file still in use on your server, the error in figure 12.18 appears.

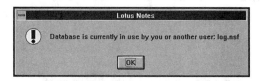

Figure 12.18

The database is in use.

A handful of files are in constant use on a Domino server. These include the server's mail box (Mail.box), shared mail file (such as Share1.nsf), and log file (Log.nsf). The server also frequently uses Notes.ini, Names.nsf, BusyTime.nsf, and others. If you need to do anything with these files, you should down your server first using E (for exit) or Q (for Quit). If you want to delete a file, you can use the operating system after the server has stopped running. If you want to compact your Mail.box, you can use T Router C (for compact). Your log file automatically compacts nightly as shown in the following:

```
01/17/97 04:00:04 AM  Router: Shutdown is in progress
01/17/97 04:00:04 AM  Router: Beginning mailbox file compaction
01/17/97 04:00:05 AM  Router: Completed mailbox file compaction
01/17/97 04:00:47 AM  Starting purge of old documents in log file
01/17/97 04:00:49 AM  Finished purge of log file
```

If you receive an in-use error with your DeskTop.dsk file, it generally means your server did not down gracefully. A graceful server exit means you do not have to force the process to stop by using the operating system. Your DeskTop.dsk file can become corrupt if the server does not down correctly. If you receive a message that Notes cannot open the desktop file (see fig. 12.19), you should reboot your server when it is convenient. It is likely the workstation was stopped with the TaskList rather than closing the program. Deleting the DeskTop.dsk file so that another can automatically be created also works, but you also have to rebuild the desktop (put the icons back).

Figure 12.19

DeskTop unable to open error.

Server Is Already Running in Another Process

You might see the message Server is Already Running in Another Process very quickly when you try to launch your Domino server. You receive this error if the Domino server is already running, but this also occurs if you have not gracefully downed the server with either E (Exit) or Q (Quit). If the latter is the case, you must reboot the machine.

Additional Server Setup Error

If you get a message similar to Mem Admin is not found in the Name and Address Book, it is because the server is also the administrator's workstation. This option can be changed in the Additional Server Setup dialog box (see fig. 12.20) when you are setting up the server.

When registering a server, you can type in the administrator's name in the administrator field of the registration dialog box. Often it makes sense for the entry in this field to be a group rather than an individual. But if you then try to set up the same server with the check box selected, setup tries to find that "user" (the group) in the Public Name & Address Book A group is not a person, therefore setup cannot find an entry for a "him" or a "her" (error shown in fig. 12.21). You can either turn off the check box or reregister the server using a person's name instead of a group name.

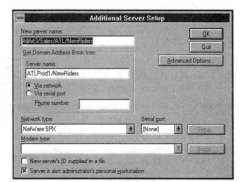

Figure 12.20

The Server setup dialog box.

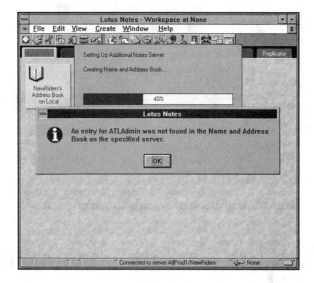

Figure 12.21

Entry not found in the address book.

Replication Conflicts with the Public Name & Address Book

Replication conflicts in the Public Name & Address Book. Using separate group documents to deny access (one per site) helps you avoid conflicts commonly found when using only one group. If conflicts occur on LocalDomainServers, be sure to first look at the conflict record to see what was changed. After you have determined this, you can copy and paste the change, and delete the conflict. For documents other than groups, you might be able to avoid conflicts by using the Merge replication conflicts feature on each form. You should change this setting in the template (PubNames.NTF), then the Public Name & Address Book will be updated by the template overnight. You can access the Merge feature by opening each form in design mode. Then you can click on File, Document Properties. On the Basics tab, you can turn on Merge replication conflicts (see fig. 12.22).

Figure 12.22

Form properties.

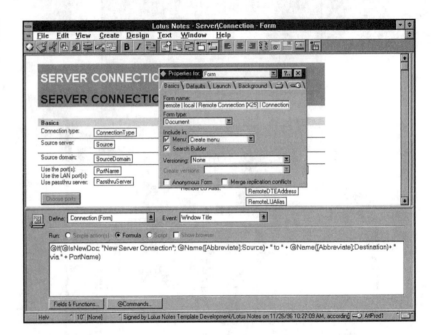

Cannot Add a Database or Use Remote Server Console

If you cannot add a database or use remote console on a server, it likely is because you do not have appropriate rights. The restrictions section of each Server record gives you the capability to add databases to your server. There are separate lines for adding new databases or replica copies (see fig. 12.23). There also is a separate line at the top of the record for administrators. This field grants rights to use remote console.

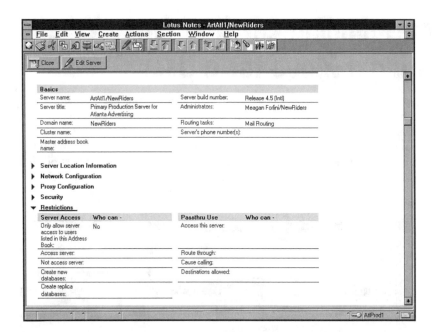

Figure 12.23

The Server record.

Files Not Found When Launching Workstation Software

If you receive the error message Notes.ini file not found, it is usually due to an incorrect path statement. A path is generally set when the server boots. When the software is installed, the path statement is automatically changed. You must reboot for the change to take effect, however, and if you use an old configuration file (such as Autoexec.bat for OS/2 and Microsoft operating systems), you must add the path to your Notes.ini file. For workstations attached to a Novell file server, the system will be remapped with scripts. Be sure to include the Notes.ini path in these scripts.

If modem files or SmartIcons are not found, you should check the SmartIcons path in the Notes.ini file and be sure the files are in the correct subdirectories. The line for SmartIcons is:

```
WinIconPath=C:\NOTES\WIN
```

Modems are found in a separate directory (called modems) in the data subdirectory.

No Corresponding Certifier Entry When Completing a Move for a User

You might receive the error No corresponding entry found in the Public Name & Address Book when trying to move a user to a new certifier. If this occurs, you can create a Certifier record in the Public Name & Address Book. You need the public key of the certifier, and you get it by using the menu Administration, ID File. What is baffling to many is that the Administration menu is not present unless you first bring up the Administration Panel (File, Tools, Server Administration), as shown in figure 12.24.

Figure 12.24

The Administration menu.

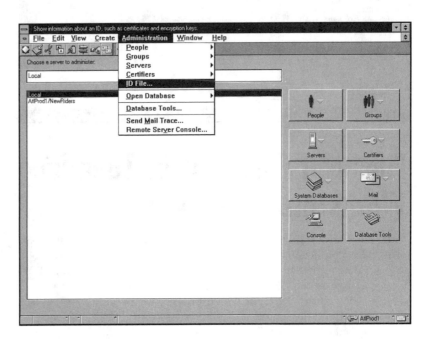

After you open the file, you can choose Certificates, Copy Public Key. Then you can go into your Public Name & Address Book and choose Create, Server, Certifier. After you name the certifier, you then should pass the public key to the record (see fig. 12.25).

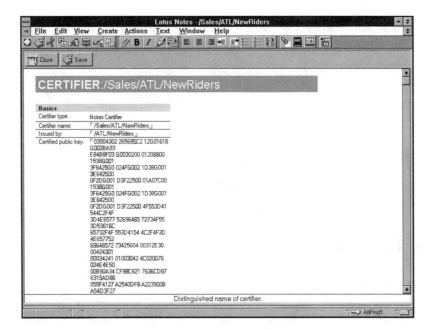

A Server Is Denied Access to Another Server

A server can be denied access to another server if the Server record is incorrect or if a group is inaccurate. The LocalDomainServers group is generally used to grant access to servers. If this group has been deleted or contains inaccurate information, your server is denied access. Or if you turn on the feature Only allow server access to users listed in this Address Book (see fig. 12.26), you deny access to all servers in the company.

This feature quite literally means *users* in the Public Name & Address Book. Therefore, you should not use the feature if you intend to route mail or replicate with another server.

Figure 12.26

Only users listed in the address book can access the server.

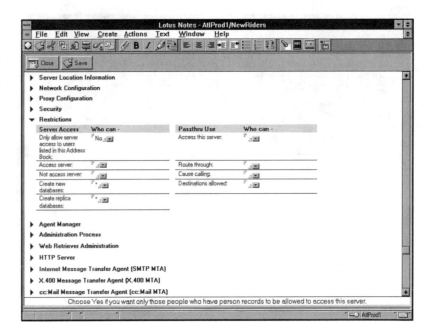

Duplicate Forms or Views During Migration

When duplicate forms or views are found in your Public Name & Address Book or mail files, they are often Conflict records. As servers are upgraded, new templates are added to the server and then replicated throughout your domain. As the templates replicate, duplicate forms, views, and script libraries appear because there is a conflict with the modification date of the records. Duplicate entries in either the Public Name & Address Book template (Names.ntf) or the r4.5 Mail template (Mail45.nft) cause script errors with various documents in your Public Name & Address Book or when using the calendar of the mail file. You should fix this by removing the duplicate entries in the templates. You can open the templates using File, Database Open, then type the name of the file at the bottom of the menu. After the templates have been corrected, design runs at night and corrects the Public Name & Address Book and the mail files. If you want to change all the files immediately, you can use L Design so that each file is updated by the corresponding template.

Tip   If it does not matter whether you replicate the template, you can simply copy the template from any workstation to your server. The load design and the errors will go away.

No Person Record in Public Name & Address Book

You have registered users but sometimes they do not show up in the Public Name & Address Book This might have occurred for a couple of reasons:

◆ When the person was registered, Local was selected as the registration server. You can copy and paste the record to the Public Name & Address Book, but be sure to change the server name field from your name to the server's name. It might be easier for you to just reregister the user.

◆ The Public Name & Address Book has not replicated. You can force replication of the Public Name & Address Book using Rep [*servername*]. For more information about replication, see the "Fundamentals of Domino Administration" section of Chapter 6.

New Directory Does Not Appear

When you add a new directory to a Domino server, it does not immediately appear in File, Database, Open. You can either wait until the next day and the new directory will appear, or you can run the catalog command on your server. The command L Catalog "rebuilds" the directory structure (and includes all databases) on your server. For more information about server commands, see the section "Remote Console" in Chapter 8.

Rooms Still Show Up in Scheduler after Deleting Them

If rooms still exist after you have deleted them, they likely were deleted only in the resources database. When rooms are created, an entry is added to the Public Name & Address Book If you use the deletion agent to remove resources, AdminP removes all corresponding entries. If you do not use the deletion agent, you must delete the records from the Public Name & Address Book manually. You can remove the entries in the Public Name & Address Book from the Mail-In Databases and Resources view. After you have selected the entry, you can use the button Delete Mail-In Database/ Resource (see fig. 12.27).

Figure 12.27

*Deleting resources
in the Mail-In
Databases and
Resources view.*

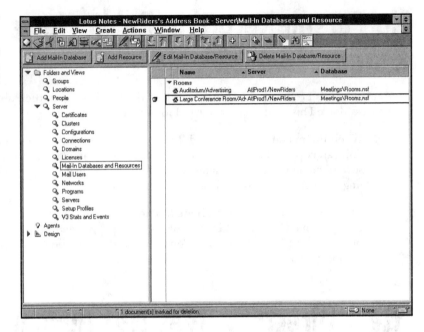

You have seen many common problems and solutions in the preceding sections. In
the rest of the chapter, you will read about how to work smarter with your Domino
servers. With a little preventive maintenance, you can avoid troubleshooting many
problems. Additionally, you can set up policies and procedures that can free up your
time and keep you from forgetting daily requested changes from your end users.

Working Smarter

You can do a number of things to make administration of your Domino servers easier.
This section is designed to help you be more proactive in your approach to administration of your Domino servers. Rather than spending much of the day apologizing
for fogetting to set up new users or running backups, you can set up procedures and
automate many requests. You also can make your server more efficient and your users
happier with many of the tricks mentioned in the following sections.

Hiding Directories and Files

A typical user does not need a number of the files on your Domino server. When
these files appear in File, Database, Open, users must scroll to find the directories
they want. Moving these files to a separate directory, however, can cause problems

with your server or the clients attached. You can hide these files from the Open menu using File, Database, Properties. From the Design tab, you can turn off the Show in 'Database Open' dialog option (see fig. 12.28).

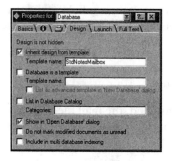

Figure 12.28

Removing files from File, Database, Open.

Not showing these files does not mean they cannot be used; it simply means the file name must be typed rather than selecting it from a list. Files you should consider eliminating from the Open Menu include:

- ◆ **Log.nsf.** The Domino Log file generally is only read by administrators.

- ◆ **Catalog.nsf.** This file is rarely accessed but the server needs the file to "build" directory structures.

- ◆ **Help.nsf.** Many users want to use the Help file, but it does not need to appear in the Open menu. Whenever help is requested at a workstation, the client machine searches and finds the Help file on the server automatically. Also, HelpLite.nsf can be deleted from your Domino server because the larger Help file is present.

- ◆ **Names.nsf.** The Public Name & Address Book is automatically added to every client during an installation. There should be no need to have the file also appear in the Open menu.

- ◆ **CertLog.nsf.** The Certification Log file generally is only accessed by the administrator when troubleshooting errors with certification.

- ◆ **DomGuide.nsf.** The Domino 1.5 User's Guide is most often accessed by administrators when the server is used as an intranet or Internet solution.

- ◆ **SSLAdmin.nsf.** The Domino SSL Administration database generally is only used with remote clients that are using Mail through the Internet.

- ◆ **ReadMe.nsf.** The Lotus Notes 4.5 Release Notes are needed by administrators or your support staff but not by the typical Notes client.

There might also be some directories many people do not need. A directory can be hidden by the operating system. Even though the directory is hidden, it can still be used by the server and end-users.

- ◆ **Doc.** The Doc directory contains many help and documentation files, but these files are typically only needed by administrators or developers.

- ◆ **Domino.** Many configuration files are used by an Internet or intranet server. If your Domino server is not communicating through the Internet, you do not need these files to show up for your users.

- ◆ **Mail.** When a client is installed, the mail file is automatically added to the workspace. By deleting this directory, you can deter users from going into mail files that are not theirs.

- ◆ **Modems.** These files are only used by the server's modem. No workstation needs them.

- ◆ **w32.** This directory contains all the SmartIcons for the server, and client machines cannot use or access the files.

For more information about files and directories, see Chapter 6.

Program Documents

You can automate many external tasks with Program documents in the Public Name & Address Book. These documents can launch virus detection programs, backup software, export utilities, and more. To create a program document, open the Public Name & Address Book and select the Server/Programs view (see fig. 12.29).

Once there, you can select the button Add Program. Notice in figure 12.30 that you can type in the directory and file name of an executable and the times you want the program to run. You might decide to run compact each Sunday so you can free up disk space on your server. For more information about compact, see the "Fundamentals of Domino Administration" section of Chapter 6.

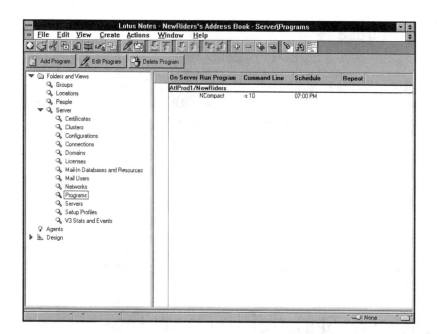

Figure 12.29

Server/Programs view.

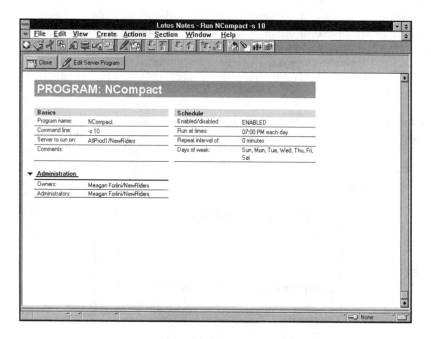

Figure 12.30

A Program document.

Request Database

For checking out software, you can track CDs and books with a request database. This hopefully will keep you from saying "I don't know who last had it" and possibly losing your job. Ideally, you should have the phone number and pager number of the person that last checked out the software. If you have a database that already contains names and phone numbers, you can tie this into the database with @DBColumn, @DBLookup, or @PickList. See Chapter 14, "Advanced Application Design Issues," for more information about development.

Project Database

As requests come in for client installations, new IDs, server upgrades, and the like, it can be quite convenient to house them in a central database. This can alleviate the many requests in "hallway meetings" you have (and never get done because you forget). The project database should list the type of request, and you should be able to send a link to the request via e-mail.

Automatic Server Startup after a Power Loss

You can do a couple of things to make sure your server will start after a power loss without the need for any intervention. First, your server ID should not have a password. On the surface, this might sound like a security risk. If your server is behind locked doors, however, people cannot get to server and therefore cannot use the server's ID. If you have a password on a server, the server waits at the password screen rather than launching the needed files for the server.

If you are running Microsoft NT, you will want the server to run as a service. To install a Domino server as a service, you must select Custom during installation. Be sure to check the box for Notes as a service (see Chapter 6). After the option is installed, you should enter the Control Panel and select Services. You will see that the Domino server is listed as Manual. Change this to Automatic (see fig. 12.31).

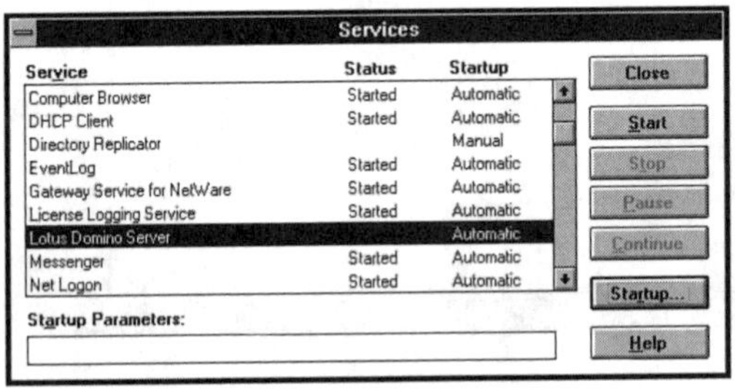

Figure 12.31

Automatic start.

As a secondary advantage, you also can lock the workstation so that an ID and password are needed to use the machine (of course, there are ways around this that an experienced NT user could figure out). When the system is not in use, press Ctrl+Alt+Delete and then select Lock Workstation.

In OS/2, you can make the server launch by adding the Server icon to the Startup group. The Startup group is found in the OS/2 System folder.

Terminations

To keep a current list of employees that leave your company, you should try to obtain at least a quarterly list from your payroll department. You can then add these users to a Terminations group in your Public Name & Address Book. You then should also use the Delete action to delete the Person record in the Public Name & Address Book. This is accessed in the Person view of the Public Name & Address Book. You can select several documents and then use the Delete Person button. This launches AdminP and removes all entries in the Public Name & Address Book, and corresponding ACLs will be updated.

Summary

In this chapter, you have explored some of the many troubleshooting aspects of a Domino server and how you can work smarter in your daily duties. You have discovered how to troubleshoot replication, moving documents to a folder, mail routing, port errors, template errors, and much more. In addition, you learned some tricks to make working with your Domino server easier.

PART V

Notes Application Architecture

CHAPTER 13

Constructing Notes Databases

Most Notes professionals gravitate toward one of two certification paths: administration or development. Administrators and developers alike focus on their particular specialty, but maintain a level of familiarity with the alternative path necessary to address day-to-day issues. With the advent of Domino and Web-enabled development, "cross-training" is more important than ever for the Notes professional, as administrators and developers collaborate to design and implement business solutions through the Internet.

Although other chapters in this book deal specifically with Web-enabled applications issues, this chapter lists and defines all of the available elements for database construction (by providing a thorough graphical tour of these elements). The last section of the chapter goes a step further with detailed instructions for actually creating a database utilizing all the elements of database construction described herein.

The topics covered in this chapter include an overview of programming in Notes and the following database elements:

◆ Databases and design templates

◆ Forms

◆ Fields

◆ Views and folders

◆ Navigators

◆ Agents

◆ Actions and button bars

◆ Subforms

◆ Layout regions

◆ Sections

◆ Tables

◆ Hotspots

Programming in Notes

Notes programming options include simple actions, formulas, LotusScript, and LSXs (LotusScript Extensions). External development tools include the Lotus Notes C API, Lotus Notes C++ API, and Interflox API for REXX (OS/2 only). Simple actions and formulas are best suited for manipulating data in the current document. LotusScript extends programmability to perform data manipulation in sources external to the current document—a collection of documents in the database or in another database. LSXs provide access to external sources—other Relational Database Management System applications, transaction systems, and operating systems. This chapter provides an overview of simple actions and formulas.

Simple Actions

Simple actions are predefined actions that provide quick programming options for users who do not know a programming language. Some simple actions require some customization to choose field names or determine field values or mail destinations. Simple actions are great tools for end users who want to create personal agents, and also for developers who can save coding effort. The available simple actions include the following:

◆ Copy to Database

◆ Copy to Folder

◆ Delete from Database

◆ Mark Document Read

◆ Mark Document Unread

◆ Modify Field

◆ Modify Fields by Form

◆ Move to Folder

◆ Remove from Folder

◆ Reply to Sender

◆ Run Agent

◆ Send Document

◆ Send Mail Message

◆ Send Newsletter Summary

◆ @Function Formula

Formula Language

The Notes formula language provides three formula types for evaluating and manipulating constants and variables, and for performing simple logic or actions: @Functions, keywords, and @Commands. Variables, constants, and operators are used in conjunction with @Functions, keywords, and @Commands to write Notes formulas.

@Functions are predefined Notes formulas that perform specific calculations. Many @Functions require arguments to specify the document, field, variable, or to supply constants. Notes contains more than 300 @Functions to perform a wide variety of operations from manipulating data or prompting users for information, to looking up information in Notes databases and other ODBC-compliant sources or executing DDE statements. If a formula can be written with one or very few statements, @Functions provide better performance than LotusScript. If the formula requires a great number of @Functions, LotusScript may provide a better solution.

Keywords perform special functions in Notes formulas. Notes saves keywords in all uppercase letters. The five keywords function as follows:

◆ **DEFAULT** temporarily associates a value with a field in the event the field value is null. If the current document contains a value, the DEFAULT value is not used.

◆ **ENVIRONMENT** writes a value to the local Notes.ini file. Values stored in the Notes.ini file are called environment variables and are saved as text only (the Notes.ini is a text file). The value remains in the Notes.ini permanently until it is modified or removed through a Notes formula or manually by opening the Notes.ini file and modifying the value. Environment variables in the Notes.ini are preceded by a dollar sign ($).

◆ **FIELD** sets a field value in the current document. If the field does not exist in the current document, it is created. If the field already exists in the current document, it is replaced with the new value.

◆ **REM** statements are not calculated. A REM statement is used by the developer to document the code. REM statements generally serve as subheaders or description.

◆ **SELECT** statements contain formulas that choose which documents are displayed in a view. Every view contains one SELECT statement. Documents are generally chosen according to form names, field values, and relationships (such as parent-child).

@Commands mostly mimic Notes menu commands. @Commands are used in SmartIcons, buttons, hotspots, and actions. @Commands are also utilized in agent formulas that run on the current document. @Commands require careful attention for applications that run in Notes 3.0 and Notes 4.0; the @PostedCommand is required to force @Commands to execute last in the formula, a feature of Notes 3.0 and Notes 4.0.

Note If the NoExternalApps environment variable (in the Notes.ini) is set to 1, @Commands are ignored. When the formula is run, most @Functions and keywords still run and the user does not receive an error message that the @Commands were ignored.

Databases and Design Templates

All the elements that comprise a Notes database are stored in one file called a Notes Storage Facility and saved with the NSF extension (*.nsf). A database is created either from scratch, by copying or replicating another database, or by using a design template. Similar to databases, design templates contain all the database elements in one file called a Notes Template Facility and saved with the NTF extension (*.ntf). Also like databases, design templates are created either from scratch, by copying (not replicating) databases, or by copying other design templates. Templates exist primarily for two purposes: to provide a predesigned source for creating databases and to refresh or replace the design of databases on a scheduled or ad-hoc basis.

Database Properties

The Properties for: Database dialog box contains the following tabbed pages: Basics, Information, Print Options, Design, Launch, and Full Text.

Basics

The title entered here appears on the database icon in the user's workspace. Server and file name information is provided just below the title field. Figure 13.1 shows the Basics tab.

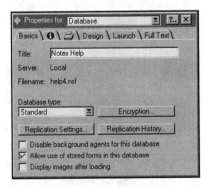

Figure 13.1

The Database Properties dialog box's Basics tab.

The Database type options are Standard, Library (for storing lists of databases), Personal Journal (for use with the Personal Journal, R4 template (JOURNAL4.NTF)), Address Book (to make the database in the Notes Name and Address Book format), and Multi DB Search (for use with the Search Through Multiple Databases template (SRCHSITE.NTF)).

The Encryption options for a local database may be set to None, Simple, Medium, or Strong. Local encryption prevents the database from being opened by unauthorized IDs.

The Replication Settings and Replication History buttons contain options and information with regard to replication. These buttons may be utilized by users with local replicas (usually laptop users) or database managers and designers to control and monitor replication. Some replication features are available on the Replicator page at the Notes workspace.

The Disable background agents for this database option stops all scheduled agents from running. This is useful for designers to stop background agents from acting on documents during testing.

The Allow use of stored forms in this database option permits the use of documents with the form stored. Storing the form with documents adds significant size to each document created using the form.

The Display images after loading option loads text first from Internet pages. Users can "surf" faster if they don't need the graphics. If this option is chosen, users of versions prior to Notes 4.5a cannot view graphics on Internet pages.

Information

The Information tab contains general information on the database size, number of documents, percent used, created and modified dates, user activity, and Replica ID. Most databases on the server are compacted automatically. Local databases require manual compaction. The Compact button compacts a database, which frees unused disk space within the database. Figure 13.2 shows the Information tab.

Figure 13.2

The Database Properties dialog box's Information tab.

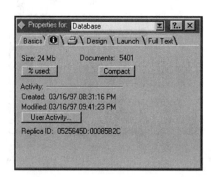

Print Options

The Print Options tab provides settings for headers and footers for documents printed (see fig. 13.3).

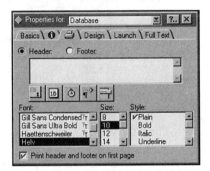

Figure 13.3

The Database Properties dialog box's Print Options tab.

Design

The Design tab displays template information and other miscellaneous design information. Figure 13.4 shows the Design tab.

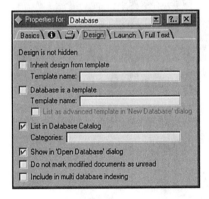

Figure 13.4

The Database Properties dialog box's Design tab.

The Inherit design from template option specifies a design template for the database. The Database is a template option makes the design available as a template for other databases. List as advanced template in 'New Database' dialog makes the template available for creating new databases.

The List in Database Catalog option includes the database in the Database Catalog, a database of database listings. The Categories box entry makes the database appear in categorized views in the Database Catalog.

The Show in 'Open Database' dialog shows the database in a list when users choose File, Database, Open.

The Do not mark modified documents as unread option only enables unread marks for documents that have never been read. If this box is not chosen, modified documents are marked unread.

The Include in multi database indexing option designates the database for inclusion in multi database searches performed through the Search Through Multiple Databases database.

Launch

The Launch tab provides options for how the database opens (see fig. 13.5).

Figure 13.5

The Database Properties dialog box's Launch tab.

On Database Open options include the following:

◆ Restored as last viewed by user

◆ Open "About database" document

◆ Open designated Navigator

◆ Open designated Navigator in its own window

◆ Launch 1st attachment in "About database"

◆ Launch 1st DocLink in "About database"

Choosing a Navigator option enables another field to specify which navigator to open.

Two options for opening the "About database document" are when database is first opened or when the "About database document" is modified.

The Preview Pane Default button controls the location of the document preview pane.

Full Text

The Full Text tab contains buttons to create, update, and delete the index for the database. Database indexes can be set to update automatically on the server at a specified frequency. Index settings information is also provided. Figure 13.6 shows the Full Text tab.

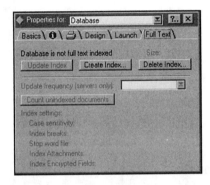

Figure 13.6

The Database Properties dialog box's Full Text tab.

About and Using Documents

Every database should have an About document and a Using document. These documents provide the user with information on the purpose of a database and how it is used. The About document generally provides a description of the database and a contact name for questions or problems. The Using document provides more detailed information on how to use the database, the available forms, views and actions, and any other details such as workflow, security, or use. The About and Using documents are accessible by the user through the Help menu.

 See the last section in this chapter for detailed instructions on how to create a template and a database.

Forms

Forms provide a document-level user interface to information stored in the database in a format that can be viewed on-screen or printed. Users also utilize forms to create and modify documents. This discussion first reviews form properties, and then it examines the elements of which a form is comprised.

Form Properties

The form properties can be viewed and modified through the Form Properties dialog box. The form must be open to view this dialog box. From the menu, choose Design, Form Properties, or press the Design Form Properties SmartIcon to view the Form Properties dialog box. The dialog box contains the following tabs:

◆ Basics

◆ Defaults

◆ Launch

◆ Background

◆ Printing

◆ Security

Basics

The Basics tab of the Form Properties contains fields for basic settings for the form (see fig.13.7).

Figure 13.7

The Form Properties dialog box's Basics tab.

Form Name

The form name is used as a programmatic reference to a form and as a visual reference for the user. The same name can be used for both purposes, or a pipe symbol (l) can be used to separate a name as the user will see it from an alias name for use in Notes formulas. It is strongly recommended that you use an alias for all form names because the name chosen for the user might change before development is completed. The alias will save you from added programming effort in the event of a form name change.

Form Type

Notes databases have three form types: Document, Response, and Response to Response. These form types have the following hierarchical relationships:

◆ **Document.** A database may contain many forms of the Document type. These Documents are not related in any way. The Document type is a parent to a Response type. The Document may also be a parent to a Response to Response type. All documents created by the same Document form are siblings.

◆ **Response.** A Response is a child to a Document type. All Responses that share the same parent document are siblings. Use a Response form when you require only one level of response to a Document.

◆ **Response to Response.** A Response to Response may be a child to a Response type or to a Document type. Documents created with the Response to Response may utilize up to 31 levels in a Notes view. The documents at each level that share the same parent are siblings.

Include In

You may make the creation of your form available through the Create menu (optionally the Create, Other menu) or enable the form to be used for full-text searching.

Versioning

Any versioning chosen besides None forces any subsequent save of a modified document to create a new documents according to the versioning rule chosen. The modified document therefore saves as either a parent, child, or sibling. The original document is not modified.

 Tip Actually, two fields' values change on modified version documents. Notes utilizes two hidden fields, $REF and $Revisions, to track the parent doc ID and revision date/times. You may find these useful in view form formulas if you want to write document locking rules for versioned documents.

Versioning rules are also invoked when documents are modified by agents.

Create Versions

This option may be set to enforce a specific versioning rule, or to give the user the flexibility to choose whether the document is edited or versioned.

Anonymous Form

The Notes field $UpdatedBy contains the names of the author and all editors of a document. Documents created from a form with Anonymous Form option enabled do not contain this field. Instead, they contain a field called $Anonymous with a value of 1, denoting them as anonymous documents.

Merge Replication Conflicts

Choose the Merge replication conflicts option to reduce the number of replication or save conflicts to one conflict document. This makes the job of the editor easier because all the conflicts are consolidated in one place.

Defaults

The Defaults tab contains default settings for the form and for documents created using the form. Figure 13.8 shows the Defaults tab.

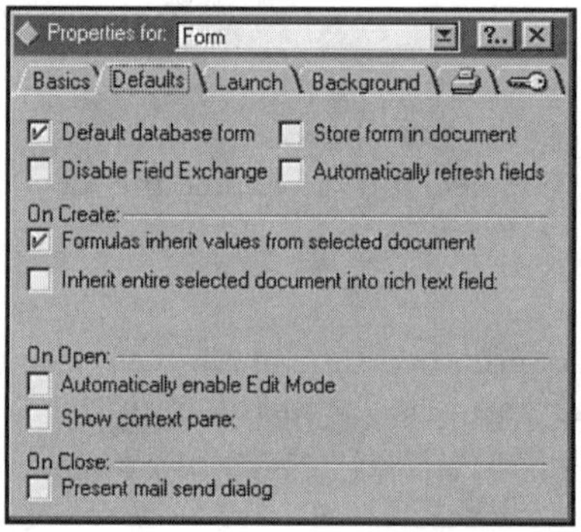

Figure 13.8

The Form Properties dialog box's Defaults tab.

Default Database Form

Each database may contain only one default database form, although one is not required. Setting a default database form is useful for viewing documents for which the form cannot be found. If a document is pasted or mailed into a database that does not contain a form, for example, a user is prompted that the default form is being used to view the document. If no default form is found, the document may not be viewed.

Store Form in Document

Storing the form in the document significantly increases database size but may be appropriate for mail-enabled forms. This enables the form to be viewed if the document is mailed to a database wherein the form is not contained in the design.

Disable Field Exchange

This option disables Notes/FX functionality, even if the form contains Notes/FX fields.

Automatically Refresh Fields

If the Automatically refresh fields option is enabled, the fields automatically refresh when the user exits each field. Depending on the size of the form, this feature may adversely affect performance. For specific fields, consider using the Refresh Field on Keyword Change field property or writing a LotusScript subroutine to handle document recalculation or field updates.

On Create

Through the Formulas inherit values from selected document option, you may create Document type forms that inherit values from the current document, even though there is no parent-child relationship.

The Inherit entire selected document into rich text field option is also useful for clarifying information while creating documents without parent-child relationships. The form must contain a rich text field for the embed. It is recommended that you make the rich text field collapsible to maintain a clean and readable form.

On Open

Check the Automatically enable Edit Mode option if the user typically opens the document to record or modify information.

Check the Show context pane option to automatically enable a view pane of a DocLink or the parent document.

On Close

Check the Present mail send dialog option if the document is going to be mailed on close. The form must contain a SendTo field for this feature to work.

Launch

Check the Launch tab contains options for an automated event on the opening of a document. Figure 13.9 shows the Launch tab.

Figure 13.9

*The Form
Properties dialog
box's Launch tab.*

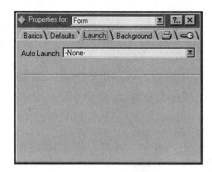

You can choose from the following Launch options:

◆ None

◆ First Attachment

◆ First Document Link

◆ First OLE Object

◆ URL

◆ 1-2-3 Worksheet

◆ Bitmap Image

◆ Image Document

◆ Lotus ScreenCam Movie 2.0

◆ Lotus Word Pro 96 Document

◆ Media Clip

◆ Microsoft Excel Chart

◆ Microsoft Excel Worksheet

◆ Microsoft Project 4.1 Project

◆ Microsoft Word Document

◆ Microsoft Word Picture

◆ Midi Sequence

◆ Netscape Hypertext Document

◆ Package

◆ Paint Shop Pro Image

◆ Paintbrush Picture

◆ TvMap Document

◆ Video Clip

◆ Visio 4 Drawing

◆ Wave Sound

◆ WordPad Document

Options to launch in place, create object in field, when to launch, and when to hide offer a variety of choices dependent on the object type. The option to Present document as modal dialog disables Notes menus. This restricts the user to entering or modifying data, launching the object via a Launch button on the dialog box, or choosing from designer-specified commands in an Action menu at the bottom of the dialog box.

Background

The Background tab provides background options for color and graphics. Figure 13.10 shows the Background tab.

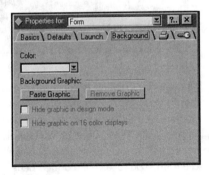

Figure 13.10

The Form Properties dialog box's Background tab.

Print Options

The tab with the picture of a printer provides for header and footer settings. Figure 13.11 shows the Print Options tab.

Figure 13.11

*The Form
Properties dialog
box's Print
Options tab.*

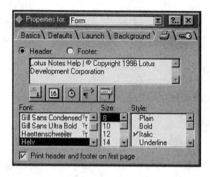

Security

The tab with the picture of a gold key contains options for default reader and author access to be specified at the form level. Figure 13.12 shows the Security tab.

Figure 13.12

*The Form
Properties dialog
box's Security tab.*

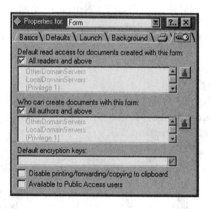

> **Tip** Developers designing templates for creating multiple databases (that is, multiple project tracking databases that use the same template) may not want to exercise form security using this feature. It is likely that access control will vary from one database to the next, thus requiring the creation of new templates for each new database. It is recommended that you create configuration settings forms and views for form security or create roles. You receive the added benefit that these settings can be easily modified by a database manager.

The Default encryption keys field contains options for one or more encryption keys to encrypt all encryptable fields automatically when the new documents are saved. The appropriate encryption keys must be distributed to all users allowed to create documents with this form and those allowed to read the encrypted fields.

Choose the Disable printing/forwarding/copying to clipboard option to prevent sensitive information from being printed or electronically copied or forwarded.

Choose the Available to Public Access users option to make the form available to users who are denied access to the database through the Access Control List.

Form Elements

In addition to the properties previously mentioned, a form may contain the following elements to help the user create, modify, or gain information:

◆ Static text

◆ Fields

◆ Hotspots

◆ Action bars

◆ Subforms

◆ Layout regions

◆ Sections

◆ Tables

Static Text

Examples of static text are field names, the form title, and other textual information typed on to the actual form. Use the Properties dialog box for Text to make modifications to appearance including font type/size/color, justification, lists, margins, spacing, pagination, tabs, and hide-when options. You may also create your own named styles and apply them to highlighted text.

Fields

The fields on a form provide a place for the document-specific information to be created, viewed, and edited. Other fields may be hidden on the form or assigned to the document but not physically a part of the form. Hidden and assigned fields are generally necessary information for processing or sorting documents but not required or intended for the user to view. More detailed information on fields is provided in the next section.

Hotspots

Hotspots may be added to static text or a graphic image on the form. A border around text indicates to the educated user that a hotspot exists at that location on the form. More detailed information on hotspots is provided in the section titled "Hotspots" later in this chapter.

Action Bars

Action bars may be added to Notes forms and views. An action bar contains action buttons that contain a graphic image, a text title, and a programmed action. The programmed action may be defined using a simple action, the Notes formula language, or LotusScript. A user presses an action button with a single-click of the mouse and the code is executed. Commonly, actions are used to modify fields, create new documents, print or mail selected documents, or start an agent. More detailed information on action bars is provided in the section titled "Actions and Button Bars" later in this chapter.

Subforms

Subforms have the same properties as forms. They also contain many of the properties and elements of forms. Subforms are used to standardize specific form design elements for inclusion in multiple forms. The use of subforms for this purpose saves programming effort when these design elements require a change. More detailed information on subforms is provided in the section titled "Subforms" later in this chapter.

Layout Regions

Layout regions provide a visually attractive interface for the user. Layout regions contain static text, fields (except rich text), graphic images, graphic hotspots, or hotspot buttons. More detailed information on layout regions is provided in the section titled "Layout Regions" later in this chapter.

Sections

Notes has two types of sections: standard and access-controlled. *Standard sections* are used to better organize information on a form and may be viewed expanded or by a title collapsed. *Access-controlled sections* are utilized to allow only specified users access to edit the fields in the section. Access-controlled sections are also collapsible. Both standard and access-controlled sections may also be assigned hide-when options. More detailed information on sections is provided in the section titled "Sections" later in this chapter.

Tables

Tables are used to align form elements, usually static text and fields. More detailed information on tables is provided in the section titled "Tables" later in this chapter.

Fields

Notes forms primarily utilize fields as containers for data. Each field on a form may possess unique properties and formulas to control and manipulate data. To review the features of fields, this section examines the tabbed pages of the field properties.

Basics

The Basics tab contains required information for every field, the field name, data type, and field type. The field name should be descriptive of the data for which it is intended. As with forms, you may use the pipe symbol to add an alias form name for formulas. Figure 13.13 shows the Basics tab.

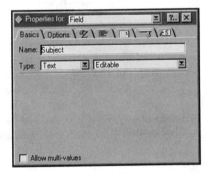

Figure 13.13

The Field Properties dialog box's Basics tab.

A Notes field may be defined to handle one of the following eight types of data:

◆ Text

◆ Time

◆ Number

◆ Keywords

◆ Rich Text

- ◆ Authors

- ◆ Names

- ◆ Readers

A Text field contains string data. The appearance of all data in a Text field is controlled by the designer of the form.

A Time field contains date, time, or a combination of date and time information. The designer determines the format of the data.

A Number field contains general, fixed, scientific, or currency types of numbers. The designer determines the number type and format.

A Keywords field contains a list of alternate values. This list may be a hard-coded list, generated from a formula, address dialog, Access Control List, or view dialog. Keywords lists may either be controlled by the designer or enable the user to enter values not present in the keywords list.

A Rich Text field may contain string data, pictures, graphs, hotspots, attachments, or embedded objects. Users may format their text in a Rich Text field. A Rich Text field may not be used in a layout region.

An Authors field enables users with author access to extend editor access on a document-by-document basis. If an Authors field is Editable, anyone allowed to edit the field may modify the field value, adding or deleting allowable editors of the document. An Authors field affects only users with author access. A user with reader access to the database cannot be promoted to author a document through an author field. Users with editor access to the database are still permitted to edit documents without their names appearing in the author field. Authors fields extend, rather than restrict, access to data.

A Names field displays user names in their abbreviated format. Use a Names field if you want to display a user's name.

A Readers field is used to restrict allowable readers on a document-by-document basis. Replicating servers must be included in this list to enable replication of the document. A Readers field may refine, but not override, the Access Control List. A user with no access to the database may not see the document even if his name appears in the field. Users with editor or higher access, however, can be restricted from viewing documents either through the form, a view, or an agent. Users with editor access or higher can still edit the document if they are listed in the form or document's Read Access list or Readers field, or if the document has no Read Access list restrictions and no Readers field. Readers fields restrict access to data.

The other basic element of a Notes field is its field type. The four types of fields are as follows:

◆ Editable

◆ Computed

◆ Computed for display

◆ Computed when composed

Editable fields may be modified by the user. The value is stored with the document. Editable fields have three formulas associated with them: default value, input translation, and input validation. None of these formulas is required. The default value formula runs only when the document is composed. The input translation formula is used to convert data to conform to a format or adjust the value, and runs when the field is refreshed or saved. The input validation formula is generally an @If statement used to test the field value, and evaluates to an @Success or @Failure result that allows or denies saving the document. The input validation formula runs immediately after the input translation formula.

Computed fields contain only a value formula. This formula runs when the document is created, refreshed or saved. The value is stored with the document.

Computed for display fields contain only a value formula. This formula runs when the document is opened for reading or editing. The value is not stored with the document.

Computed when composed fields contain only a value formula. This formula run only one time, when the document is created. The value is stored with the document.

Keyword Options

The Keyword Options tab is available only to a Keywords field. Optional interfaces are a dialog list, check box, or radio button. The dialog list is a "pop-up" list of values. A user may choose one or multiple values. The check box interface shows all available values in a check box. A user may choose multiple check box values. The radio button interface shows all available values in a radio box. A user may choose only one value from a radio box. Figure 13.14 shows the Keyword Options tab.

Figure 13.14

*The Form
Properties dialog
box's Keyword
Options tab.*

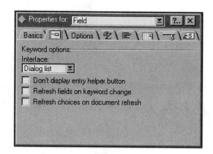

The Don't display entry helper button option applies only to the dialog list interface. A helper button will appear by default to the right of an Editable keywords dialog list field. Choose this option to prevent the display of the entry helper button.

The Refresh fields on keyword change option refreshes all fields in the document when the keyword value is changed.

The Refresh choices on document refresh option refreshes the keywords list each time the document is refreshed.

Options

The Options tab contains help information, multi-value options, and security options. Figure 13.15 shows the Options tab.

Figure 13.15

*The Form
Properties dialog
box's Options tab.*

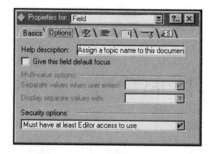

Use the Help description field to supply the user with a description of the information requested in an Editable field. The user will see this help description on the field help bar that appears immediately above the status bar. If a user does not see the field help bar, have him or her choose View, Show, Field Help.

The Give this field default focus option places the cursor in the field when a document is first opened in Edit mode. There can only be one default focus field on a form.

Use the Separate values when user enters option to define delimiters for multiple values entered. The next entry, Display separate values with, controls the delimiter for display.

Security options provide four levels of security: None, Sign if mailed or saved in section, Enable encryption for this field, and Must have at least Editor access to use. Use the Sign if mailed or saved in section option if you require verification that a specific user ID was used to save the data in this field. Use the Enable encryption for this field option if the data might be confidential in nature. Choose the Must have at least Editor access to use option if you want to deny edit rights to users with author access.

Fonts and Colors

The Fonts and Colors tab provides default font and color settings for the field. If the field is rich text, users may modify these settings. Use the Set Permanent Pen font option to provide users a shortcut to a useful setting. Figure 13.16 shows the Fonts and Colors tab.

Figure 13.16

The Form Properties dialog box's Fonts and Colors tab.

Alignment

The Alignment tab provides default settings for justification, a first line setting, list options, left margin, and spacing options. Figure 13.17 shows the Alignment tab.

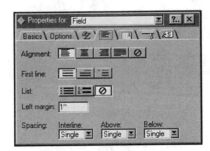

Figure 13.17

The Form Properties dialog box's Alignment tab.

Print Options

Use the Print Options tab to control page break options, set the right margin, and set tabs. The Page break before paragraph option forces the field to appear at the top of a new page. The Keep paragraph on one page option forces the field to appear at the top of a new page if the paragraph will not fit on the current page. The Keep paragraph with next paragraph option forces the field to appear at the top of a new page if the next paragraph will not fit on the current page. Figure 13.18 shows the Print Options tab.

Figure 13.18

The Form Properties dialog box's Print Options tab.

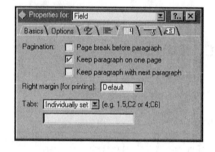

Hide Field Options

The Hide Field Options tab contains default options to hide the field when the document is in the following states:

◆ Previewed for reading

◆ Opened for reading

◆ Printed

◆ Previewed for editing

◆ Open for editing

◆ Copied to the clipboard

You may also specify a formula to control when a field is hidden. Figure 13.19 shows the Hide Field Options tab.

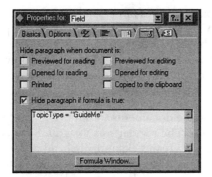

Figure 13.19

The Form Properties dialog box's Field Options tab.

Style

The Style tab provides options to use a predefined style or create new styles and apply them to the field. Styles may be modified through the Redefine Style button or deleted through the Delete Styles button. Figure 13.20 shows the Style tab.

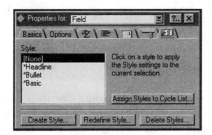

Figure 13.20

The Form Properties dialog box's Style tab.

Note See the last section in this chapter for detailed instructions on how to create forms.

Views and Folders

Notes views and folders provide the user a collection of the documents in the database. The documents in a view share common elements such as form names, hierarchical relationships, or field values, defined by a view selection formula. Folders have a greater propensity for containing unrelated documents because users can arbitrarily choose documents to place in folders.

The navigation of Notes databases involves three panes: the navigator pane, the view pane, and the preview pane. A later section discusses the navigator pane. The view pane contains column headings at the top, a selection bar down the left side of the pane, and a collection (rows) of documents. The preview pane provides a preview of the document without opening the document. All three panes may be viewed simultaneously or individually. Users can resize the panes to their liking.

The view pane contains a list of the documents sorted by either of two sort types: a regular sort or a categorized sort. The regular sort sorts all the documents according to the rules set. A categorized sort creates expandable headers for groups of documents sharing the same field value or property. To review the features of fields, this discussion turns to the View Properties dialog box for the Discussion (Notes 4.0) database By Author view.

 When a view design is first opened, the view selection formula appears in the design pane. The view selection formula defines the rules for choosing documents to appear in the view.

The view properties contain five tabbed pages: Basics, Options, Style, Advanced, and Security.

Basics

The Basics tab provides fields for the view name, alias, comment and style. The options for style are Standard Outline and Calendar. This chapter is a review on the Standard Outline. For information on the Calendar style, see Chapter 3, "Introducing Calendaring and Scheduling," and Chapter 4, " Incorporating Calendaring and Scheduling into Your Applications." Figure 13.21 shows the Basics tab.

Figure 13.21

The View Properties dialog box's Basics tab.

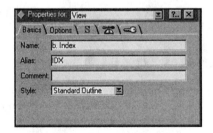

Options

The Options tab contains default settings for the view. Figure 13.22 shows the Options tab.

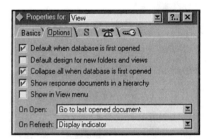

Figure 13.22

The View Properties dialog box's Options tab.

Only one view can be set to default when database is first opened.

Also, only one view can be set to default design for new folders and views.

Choose the Collapse all when database is first opened option if the view is categorized, and you want users to see only the categories when they first open the view.

Choose the Show response documents in a hierarchy option to visually link documents sharing a hierarchical relationship.

Choose the Show in View menu option to include the view in the pull-down View menu.

On Open options include Go to last opened document, Go to top row, and Go to bottom row. Generally, users find it productive to go to the last opened document. The Go to top row and Go to bottom row options are more useful when documents are organized by a time/date value or a creation date.

On Refresh options include Display indicator, Refresh display, Refresh display from top row, and Refresh display from bottom row. Display indicator will show a Refresh icon in the left corner of the view when new documents have been created in the database since the view was opened. Refresh display just refreshes the view. Refresh display from top row and Refresh display from bottom row are useful for reverse chronological or chronological views where the user is looking for information at the top or bottom of the view.

Style

The Style tab provides options for color settings of the view background, column totals, unread rows, and alternating row colors. Figure 13.23 shows the Style tab.

Figure 13.23

The View Properties dialog box's Style tab.

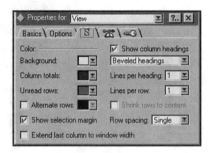

The Show selection margin option may be disabled if users do not need this feature and screen space is needed.

The Extend last column to window width option defaults the view to fit the user's view pane so that multiple line entries can be read without scrolling.

Disable the Show column headings option if column headings are not needed. Headings appearance options are beveled and simple. Lines per heading may be set up to five lines.

The Lines per row option may be set between 1 and 9. Choose Shrink rows to content to minimize vertical space in the view if you set more than 1 line per row. Row spacing options might make your views more readable for some users.

Advanced

The Advanced tab contains settings for indexing, unread marks, a form formula, and unique keys. Figure 13.24 shows the Advanced tab.

Figure 13.24

The View Properties dialog box's Advanced tab.

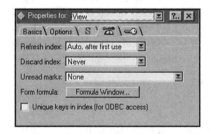

Refresh Index

Refresh index settings options are auto, after first use; automatic; manual; auto at most every *n* hours.

Auto, After First Use

This is the default setting for views. Auto, after first use sets the view to begin indexing automatically after the first use. Performance may be slow the first time the view is opened because the index must be refreshed. Thereafter, the index refreshes incrementally and response times are faster.

Automatic

Automatic indexing provides the best performance for the end user. The view always contains up-to-date information and displays quickly unless it contains a very large volume of documents.

Manual

The user must refresh the view to refresh the index. This view contains up-to-date information only after the user manually refreshes the view. Only choose this option if you have a large database in which users do not require the most recent information. The displays quickly except during a refresh of the index.

Auto, At Most Every *n* Hours

The user is not required to refresh the view, but may not have an up-to-date collection of documents. The view index requires less time to refresh by the user manually compared to a manual setting because the server periodically refreshes the index. Choose this option if you have a large database in which the information changes frequently.

Discard Index

The index may be deleted if the view is seldom used. You have three Discard index options: Never, After each use, If inactive for *n* days. Deleting an index can save significant space with large databases. If the view is discarded, the server does not actually delete the index until the UPDALL task runs (usually scheduled to run at night).

Never

The index is never discarded. Opening views are faster because the index already exists and refreshing an already indexed view does not take long. This is the default setting and appropriate for most views accessed on a regular basis.

After Each Use

The index is discarded after each use. This option is best suited for seldom-used views, particularly hidden (look-up) views accessed infrequently by agents. If a user view is set to this option and the database contains a large volume of documents, the user may have to wait a while before the view displays.

If Inactive for *n* Days

The view's index is discarded only if the view has not been accessed in the number of days specified. This option compromises between never and after each use.

Unread Marks

Unread marks appear as stars in the view selection margin. Additionally, Unread row text colors may be set. If the Show selection margin option is disabled, unread marks do not appear, but the unread color still indicates unread documents. The options for unread marks are standard, unread documents only, and none.

Standard

Standard unread marks show unread marks next to unread documents and the category if the view is collapsed. This way readers can quickly find unread documents in a fully collapsed view.

Unread Documents Only

Unread documents show only the unread marks next to unread documents, but not next to the category in a collapsed view.

None

Unread documents are not marked.

Form Formula

Press the Formula Window button to create a form formula. Form formulas are used to determine the form used to display a document in a view. Alternate forms can be used to format the document information, control Editable fields (perhaps based on a user ID), or to lock documents from further revision through the UI (perhaps based on a field value).

Unique Keys in Index (for ODBC Access)

Unique keys are used when accessing an ODBC database outside of Notes. Choose this option to include unique keys in the view index.

Security

The Security tab provides options to make the view available to All readers and above or specific individuals or groups from the database ACL or a Name and Address book. The Available to Public Access Users option makes the view available to users who have no access to the database. This option works only if the default ACL entry contains the enabled option to allow public readers. Figure 13.25 shows the Security tab.

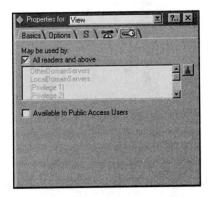

Figure 13.25

The View Properties dialog box's Security tab.

Folders contain an additional security feature that enables the contents of the folder to be updated by All authors and above or specific individuals or groups from the database ACL or a Name and Address book.

View Columns

Columns are the only elements in views. A column defines the information about the document shown to the user in the view, usually field values. Columns can sort documents in ascending or descending order so that users can find documents quickly.

Column Formulas

A column formula can be defined with a simple function, field, or formula. Simple functions include the following:

- ◆ Attachment Lengths

- ◆ Attachment Names

- ◆ Attachments

- ◆ Author(s) (Distinguished Name)

- ◆ Author(s) (Simple Name)

- ◆ Collapse/Expand (+/−)

- ◆ Creation Date

◆ Last Modified

◆ Last Read or Edited

◆ Size (bytes)

◆ # in view (for example, 2.1.2)

◆ # of Responses (1 Level)

◆ # of Responses (All Levels)

The Field option provides a list off all the fields available from forms in the database. Only one field can be chosen.

> **Note**   Be certain that the field chosen is available on documents chosen for the view.

The formula option provides flexibility generating view information. Multiple fields may be combined or the formula may evaluate to a text value or graphic images available for views.

Column Properties

The Column Properties dialog box contains the following tabs: Basics, Sorting, Text Properties, Number Properties, Date/Time Options, Title Properties, and Advanced Options.

Basics

The Basics tab contains basic settings for the column. Information entered in the Title field will appear in the column title bar and is not required. Categorized columns (see the subsequent discussion on sorting) often do not contain a column title. The column width can be set and a multi-value separators option chosen. The Resizable option enables users to resize the column while the view is open to facilitate their needs. Figure 13.26 shows the Basics tab.

Figure 13.26

The Column Properties dialog box's Basics tab.

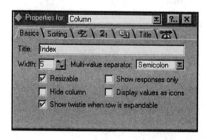

The Hide column option provides the option to hide the column from users. Hidden columns are used to sort the view by using information the user does not require.

The Show twistie when row is expandable option provides a graphical twistie on the left side of the column when a row is expandable due to categorized sorts (see the discussion on sorting) or the existence of child documents in a hierarchical view.

The Show responses only column is used in hierarchical views when you want the information to appear only for response documents or response to response documents. This feature makes views more readable.

The Display values as icons option converts the evaluated column formula to a graphic icon. Notes has more than 100 predefined icons from which to choose.

Sort Properties

Views are sorted by two methods: Standard sort and Categorized sort. A categorized view groups documents with a common field (category) together under a header.

Sorts can be case-sensitive and accent-sensitive. The option to Show multiple values as separate entries causes a document to appear several times in the view if the sort field or "category" field contains multiple values. The document appears alphabetically under each of the multiple values. Figure 13.27 shows the Sorting tab.

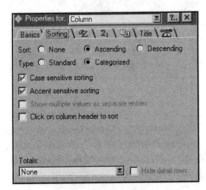

Figure 13.27

The Column Properties dialog box's Sorting tab.

The Click on column header to sort option can minimize the number of required views for the database. The same view can show information sorted in many different ways according to rules set here.

Tip   Another great use of this feature is to open another view when the column header is selected. With this feature, a user can move between categorized views by clicking on column headers—useful if the column headers logically refer to other views, particularly if the navigator pane is collapsed to allow for more data in the view. When using this feature, be sure all views are easily accessible so that users do not get lost looking for a specific view.

Text Properties

The Text Properties tab contains the standard Notes options for choosing, fonts, font size, color, style, and permanent pen. Figure 13.28 shows the Text Properties tab.

Figure 13.28

The Column Properties dialog box's Text Properties tab.

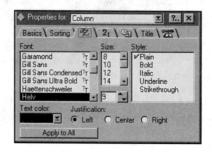

Number Properties

If the column formula evaluates to a number, this tab provides display options for the number. Figure 13.29 shows the Number Properties tab.

Figure 13.29

The Column Properties dialog box's Number Properties tab.

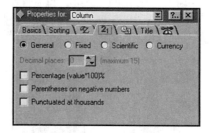

Date/Time Options

If the column formula evaluates to a TimeDate value, this tab provides options to display the date only, time only, or both. This tab also contains options for formatting dates and times and an option to adjust the value for time zone differences. Figure 13.30 shows the Date/Time Options tab.

Figure 13.30

The Column Properties dialog box's Date/Time Options tab.

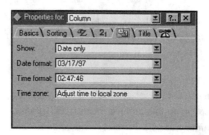

Title

The Title tab provides the standard Notes options for formatting text, including fonts, font size, color, style, justification, and permanent pen. Figure 13.31 shows the Title tab.

Figure 13.31

The Column Properties dialog box's Title tab.

Advanced

The Advanced tab contains a Name field used for programmatic access to the value of the column. This value is associated with the simple function, field, or formula used to evaluate the column value. Figure 13.32 shows the Advanced tab.

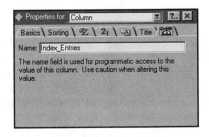

Figure 13.32

The Column Properties dialog box's Advanced tab.

Hidden Views

Hidden views are used to choose documents for use by formulas such as @DbLookup or @DbColumn. The number of hidden views necessary for databases is significantly reduced by the inclusion of LotusScript into Notes. The NotesDocumentCollection class can be used by LotusScript routines to perform the same functionality.

 A large number of views in a database can significantly degrade performance when users open views. View indexing can require several minutes on very large databases with many views, even when refresh index options are optimized for performance. The necessity for a large number of views in a database can be reduced greatly by enabling column sorting and using the NotesDocument Collection class in LotusScript routines.

Navigators

All Notes databases have a navigator pane called Folders. This navigator contains the names of the folders, views, agents, and design elements of the database. The Folders navigator provides end users easy access to folders, views, personal agents, and any public agents they are permitted to use. This navigator also provides developers access to all the design elements of the database.

Developers can design customized navigators for databases. Users find navigators easy to understand and use because they are graphical in nature and provide drill-down functionality much like Internet pages. Navigators may contain two types of objects: graphic objects created using another application and pasted into the navigator and objects created using the navigator drawing tools. The objects on a navigator perform actions when pressed by a mouse click. The navigator object may open another navigator or view, provide drag and drop functionality for folders, or open a database, view or document link, or URL. Navigator objects also may run Notes formulas or LotusScript.

The Navigator Properties dialog box contains two tabbed pages: Basics and Grid.

Basics

The Basics tab contains the name of the navigator and an option for the initial view or folder. The options for the initial view or folder contains the names of all the views and folders in the database and a default option of None. The Auto adjust panes at run time option sizes the navigator to its graphics depending on the end user's resolution. There is also an option for the background color of the navigator. Figure 13.33 shows the Basics tab.

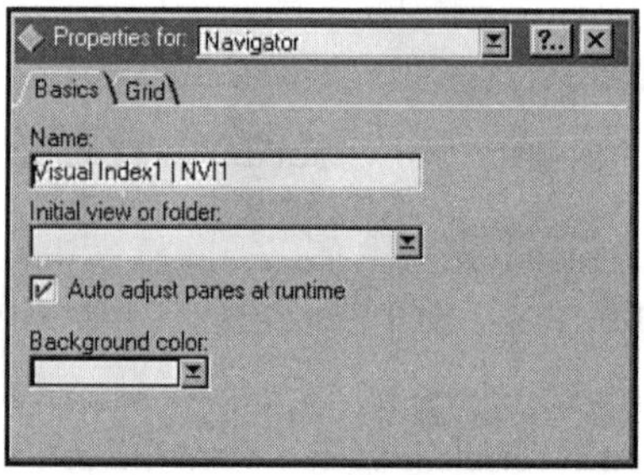

Figure 13.33

The Navigator Properties dialog box's Basics tab.

Grid

The Grid tab provides options for enabling a snap to grid and setting the size (in pixels) to help align objects as you position them. Figure 13.34 shows the Grid tab.

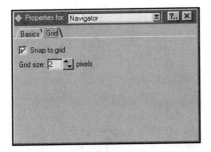

Figure 13.34

The Navigator Properties dialog box's Grid tab.

Agents

Agents are miniature programs (simple actions, formulas, or LotusScript) that run on multiple documents and search for data, modify fields, manage documents, or send mail. Agents may be personal or public. Personal agents are created by end users and cannot be shared with other users. Public agents are written by developers and may be made available to all users or triggered to run at a scheduled time or by a specified event.

 If agents are scheduled to run at the same time, the server executes them in alphabetic order. Start your agents with numbers to sort them in the desired execution order.

Agent Triggers

A trigger is required for an agent to run. The trigger can be a manual start by a user through the Agents menu or an action button or navigator object, a predefined schedule at set times or at intervals between 30 minutes and once a month, or by an event such as documents being pasted or mailed into the database or documents being newly created or modified. The specific options for database triggers are as follows:

◆ Manually from Actions Menu

◆ Manually from Agent List

◆ If New Mail Has Arrived

- ◆ If Documents Have Been Created or Modified

- ◆ If Documents Have Been Pasted

- ◆ On Schedule Hourly

- ◆ On Schedule Daily

- ◆ On Schedule Weekly

- ◆ On Schedule Monthly

- ◆ On Schedule Never

Scheduled agents contain options to specify the time of day, start and end dates, and restricted to run only one specified server or prompt the user to choose the server and database on which the agent is to run. Hourly and daily agents may be scheduled to not run weekends.

Document Selection

Selecting the documents on which the agent runs involves two elements: a SELECT keyword section formula (for agents using Notes formulas) and a selection from the field called Which Document(s) Should it Act On.

The available options for Which Document(s) Should it Act On vary depending on the trigger selection, but include the following options:

- ◆ All documents in the database

- ◆ All new and modified documents since last run

- ◆ All unread documents in view

- ◆ All documents in view

- ◆ Selected documents

- ◆ Run once (@Commands may be used)

Agent Construction Options

An agent is constructed using one of three options: simple actions, formula, or LotusScript. See the previous section entitled "Programming in Notes" for descriptions of these options.

Actions and Button Bars

A button bar can be an element of a form or a view, and is located at the top of the document or view pane, immediately below the SmartIcons row. A button bar contains action buttons pressed by the user to automate tasks, much like macros. Action buttons can run simple actions (predefined but customizable), formulas, or LotusScript.

Access to a list of actions is made available in design mode through the action pane. The action pane can be opened through the View, Action Pane pull-down menu, the view show/hide action pane SmartIcon, or by click-dragging the right margin of the form or view pane.

The Action Properties dialog box contains three tabs: Basics, NotesFlow Publishing, and Hide Action Options.

Basics

The Basics tab contains fields for the title and an icon option. Entries in these two fields appear on the button. Also through the Basics tab, options are provided to include the action in the Action menu and/or in the button bar. Finally, the Position field determines the order of the actions. Figure 13.35 shows the Basics tab.

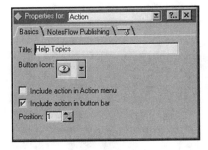

Figure 13.35

The Action Properties dialog box's Basics tab.

NotesFlow Publishing

Applications that support Notes/FX 2.0, such as Lotus Freelance Graphics 96 and Lotus Word Pro 96, enable information sharing to and from Notes and the application. The options here are used only if the Notes application utilizes Notes/FX 2.0. Figure 13.36 shows the NotesFlow Publishing tab.

Figure 13.36

The Action Properties dialog box's NotesFlow Publishing tab.

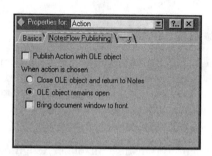

The Publish Action with OLE object option makes the action available in the Actions menu of other Notes/FX 2.0 applications. When the action is chosen, you may choose to close the OLE object and return to Notes or leave the OLE object open. Leave the OLE object to open if the user might utilize multiple actions before returning to Notes. The Bring document window to front option returns focus to the Notes document while leaving the OLE object open so that users can refer to or modify the Notes document.

Hide Action Options

This tab contains rules for hiding the action to prevent users from utilizing the action according to the options set. Standard options hide the action when previewed for reading, opened for reading, previewed for editing, or opened for editing. Additionally, a Notes formula may be written to determine when the action is hidden. Figure 13.37 shows the Hide Action Options tab.

Figure 13.37

The Action Properties dialog box's Hide Action Options tab.

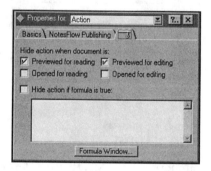

Subforms

Subforms provide a central location for a group of elements that appear formatted the same across multiple forms and stores them as a single element of the form.

The use of subforms saves programming effort when these design elements require a change. Subforms have the same properties as forms and contain many of the same elements.

 Tip Subforms may slow performance when users open or refresh documents. If you experience performance problems due to subforms, you may be able to improve performance by minimizing the number of subforms used or the number of elements in the subform.

The Subform Properties dialog box does contain a few options not available in forms: Include in Insert Subform... dialog, Include in New Form... dialog, and Hide Subform from R3 Users. Choose Include in Insert Subform... dialog or Include in New Form... dialog to make the subform available to developers through the pull-down menus. Choose Hide Subform from R3 Users to hide the contents of the subform if it contains elements unavailable to Notes 3.0 users, such as layout regions. Figure 13.38 shows the Basics tab.

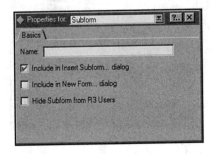

Figure 13.38

The Subform Properties dialog box's Basics tab.

Layout Regions

Layout regions not only provide applications a nice graphical boost, they also offer added functionality. The three-dimensional option makes a layout region appear graphically sharp. Also, the fields in a table can be assigned a tab order so that the developer can better control the order in which users move from field to field by using the tab key.

Layout Region Elements

Layout regions may contain most of the elements available to forms: static text, fields (except rich text), graphic images, graphic hotspots, or hotspot buttons. Layout regions cannot contain tables, sections, subforms, or layout regions. The elements in a layout region can be sized and aligned for better appearance than available by placing fields on a form. The height and width of fields are well-defined on layout regions. No field height and width options are available directly on a form (although tables can help; see the section on tables that follows).

Layout Region Properties

The Layout Region Properties dialog box contains two tabs: Basics and Hide Layout Region Options.

The Basics tab provides options to set the left margin, height, and width of the layout region. The size of the layout region can also be modified by click-dragging the dots that appear around the layout region. This tab also contains options to show a border and to show a three-dimensional texture. Grid options show a grid, use snap-to to align elements, and set a custom size for the grid. Figure 13.39 shows the Basics tab.

Figure 13.39

The Layout Region Properties dialog box's Basics tab.

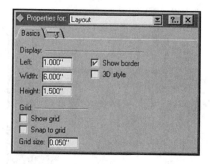

The hide layout regions are as follows:

◆ Previewed for reading

◆ Opened for reading

◆ Printed

◆ Previewed for editing

◆ Opened for editing

◆ Copied to the clipboard

You may also write your own formula by using the Notes formula language to determine when the layout region is hidden. Figure 13.40 shows the Hide Layout Region Options tab.

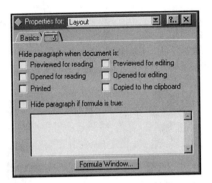

Figure 13.40

The Layout Region Properties dialog box's Hide Layout Region Options tab.

Sections

A section is an area of the form in which all the elements may be viewed or hidden from view by clicking on a twistie. The elements in a section generally relate in some logical way, and an appropriate section header is assigned to accommodate the end user.

Section Types

Notes has two types of sections: Standard and Access-controlled. Standard sections are used to better organize information on a form and may be viewed expanded or, when collapsed, by a section header. Access-controlled sections are utilized to allow only specified users access to edit the fields in the section. Both standard and access-controlled sections may also be assigned hide-when options.

Section Elements

Sections may contain any of the elements available to a form: static text, fields, hotspots, subforms, layout regions, sections, or tables.

 Note It is possible to create sections within sections. This will become confusing to users, however, because a section within a section won't appear indented (or hierarchical).

Section Properties

The Section Properties dialog box contains tabs for the title, expand/collapse options, text properties, and hide section options.

The Title tab contains an optional title, which may be entered as text or a Notes formula. This tab also contains options for border styles and colors for the title. Section titles are not required, but help the user better understand the arrangement of data on the form. Figure 13.41 shows the Title tab.

Figure 13.41

The Section Properties dialog box's Title tab.

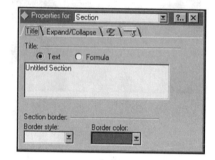

The Expand/Collapse tab contains options to default the section to auto-expand, auto-collapse, or don't auto-expand or collapse when the document is used in the following scenarios:

◆ Previewed

◆ Opened for reading

◆ Opened for editing

◆ Printed

The Hide title when expanded option is most useful if the first field in the section contains a title for the section. The Preview only option applies the section to the preview pane only, and not to the document when opened for reading or editing, or when printing. Figure 13.42 shows the Expand/Collapse tab.

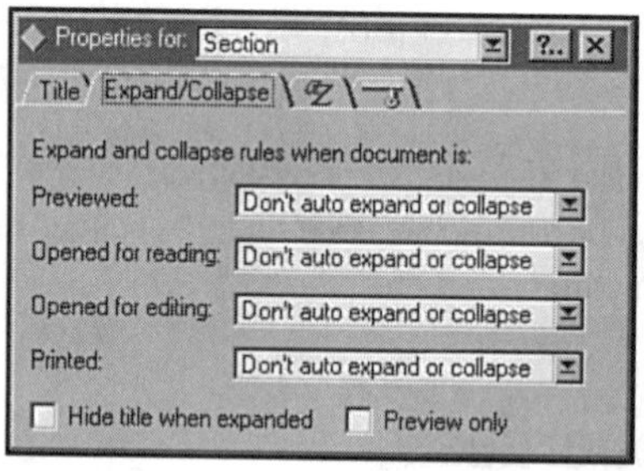

Figure 13.42

The Section Properties dialog box's Expand/ Collapse tab.

A great example of the Preview only option is found in the Notes e-mail database. The SendTo field is contained in a section in which abbreviated names of the recipients appear in a collapsible section title.

Access-controlled sections provide two tabs for expand/collapse options: one for editors and one for readers. Access-controlled sections also contain a Formula tab to control editor access to the section. Formulas written here generally evaluate to group names and/or user names. The formula may be Editable, Computed, Computed for display, or Computed when composed. If this formula is left Editable, any user with rights to edit the document may change this formula as it applies to the document. To better control access, the Computed formula types enables users to view the results of the formula only, but not to modify it. Figure 13.43 shows the Formula tab.

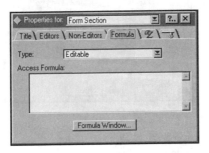

Figure 13.43

The Section Properties dialog box's Formula tab.

The Text Properties tab contains the standard Notes options for choosing fonts, font size, color, style, and permanent pen. Figure 13.44 shows the Text Properties tab.

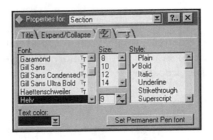

Figure 13.44

The Section Properties dialog box's Text Properties tab.

The Hide Section Options tab contains hide-when options for the section when the document is used in the following ways:

◆ Previewed for reading

◆ Opened for reading

◆ Printed

◆ Previewed for editing

◆ Opened for editing

◆ Copied to the clipboard

A Notes formula may also be written to control when the section is hidden. Figure 13.45 shows the Hide Section Options tab.

Figure 13.45

The Section Properties dialog box's Hide Section Options tab.

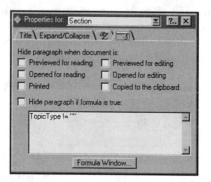

 Note   Options chosen on the Hide Section Options tab take precedence over options chosen on the Expand/Collapse Section Options tab.

Tables

Tables are used to align form elements—usually static text and fields—and help to give areas of the form a neater appearance. An even more effective way to do so may be to use a layout region (see the preceding section).

Table Elements

Tables can contain static text, fields, hotspots, or objects.

Warning   In most environments, users possess a wide variety of computer hardware. The use of tables requires careful consideration for the appearance of elements on the computers of all end users. Allowances must be made for differing resolutions and available fonts. Otherwise, a table will likely make documents more difficult to read.

Table Properties

The Table Properties dialog box contains tabs for borders, layout, and colors.

Borders for cells may be standard, extruded, or embossed, with varying degrees of thickness. Often border thickness is set to zero to keep the form clean. Figure 13.46 shows the Borders tab.

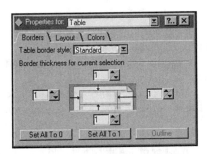

Figure 13.46

The Table Properties dialog box's Borders tab.

The Layout tab provides settings for table sizes. Adjustments may be made to control the margins and distance between cells. The option to Fit table width to window makes allowances for differing user window sizes due to screen size and resolution. Figure 13.47 shows the Layout tab.

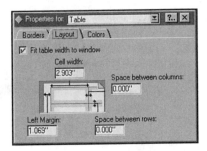

Figure 13.47

The Table Properties dialog box's Layout tab.

The Colors tab provides color options for the background of the table. Figure 13.48 shows the Colors tab.

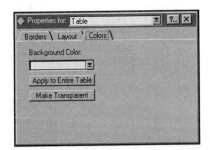

Figure 13.48

The Table Properties dialog box's Colors tab.

Conservative color combinations for the table background and form background accent the information in the table without making it difficult to read.

Hotspots

Hotspots create an area on the form that performs an action when the user chooses the hotspot. The action performed generally provides the user with information in the form of a pop-up box or a link. The action can also run Notes simple actions, formulas, LotusScript, or execute agents. Hotspots may appear on the form as a border around static text or graphic images or as a button. The Hotspot Properties dialog box provides an option to show or not show the border. The appearance of a border helps the user identify the location of hotspots on the form.

 If hotspots are applied to most or all the static text field names (or in some other consistent manner), borders may clutter the form too much, in which case users should be educated as to the location of hotspots that do not have borders.

Hotspot Types

The following six types of hotspots are available to Notes forms:

◆ Text Pop-up

◆ Formula Pop-up

◆ Action Hotspot

◆ Link Hotspot

◆ URL Link

◆ Button

Text Pop-Up

Text pop-ups provide the user with a pop-up box of information, usually contained by a border. When used with static text field titles, this information may be more detailed than the information provided in field help because there is room for more text. Figure 13.49 shows the Formula tab.

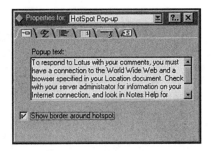

Figure 13.49

The HotSpot Pop-up dialog box's Formula tab.

Formula Pop-Up

Formula pop-ups evaluate to text values, and appear to the user in the same manner as a text pop-up. Formula pop-ups have more flexibility as the text can vary depending on the evaluation of the formula. Formula pop-ups can personalize a pop-up box with a user's name or information specific to the current document.

Action Hotspot

Action hotspots can execute simple actions, Notes formulas, or LotusScript routines. Care should be given to writing action hotspots; some users may not have sufficient access to execute the action.

Link Hotspot

When a link hotspot is chosen, Notes opens a specified database, view, or document. Users must have access to the link or they are denied.

 Do not link provide links to documents on local drives or in e-mail databases; users will not have access to these documents.

Figure 13.50 shows the Formula tab.

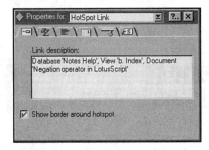

Figure 13.50

The HotSpot Link Properties dialog box's Formula tab.

URL Link

A URL link opens an Internet page. A user must have access to an InterNotes Web database to use this type of hotspot. Figure 13.51 shows the Formula tab.

Figure 13.51

The URL Link Object dialog box's Formula tab.

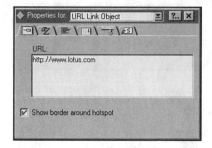

Button

Like an action hotspot, a button can execute simple actions, Notes formulas, or LotusScript routines. The only difference between a button and an action hotspot is their appearance on the form. Figure 13.52 shows the Formula tab.

Figure 13.52

The Button Properties dialog box's Formula tab.

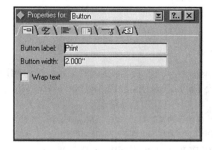

To this point, this chapter has offered detailed discussion on Notes database elements. The following section presents step-by-step instructions for using these database elements to create a Notes database from scratch through a "real-life" scenario.

Creating a Database

ABC Engineering Company has just created an employee organization called ABC People. The employee organization arranges special events for the employees of ABC and their families. ABC People is creating a database to provide a forum for employees to suggest and discuss optional employee events and to provide a schedule of events.

The step-by-step instructions provided in this section assume the reader has already read the preceding sections in this chapter. The details of some settings and related figures not contained in this section are presented in earlier sections of this chapter.

Create the Database File

The database file (*.nsf) is created first. The file can be created from scratch, by copying another database, or by using an existing template. The database in this example is created from scratch. The following steps create a database:

1. From the Notes workspace, select File, Database, New. The New Database dialog box appears (see fig. 13.53).

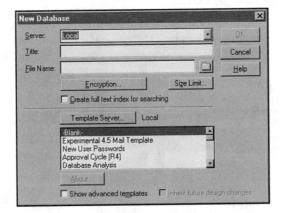

Figure 13.53

The New Data-base dialog box.

2. Select a location (local or select a server) for the database in the Server field. Most initial development is performed locally unless several developers are assigned to work on the database simultaneously. Select Local (the default).

3. In the Title field, type **ABC People Events**. The title will appear on the database icon, so it should be brief and descriptive.

4. The File Name field is automatically populated while typing the title. This file name is defaulted to the notes\data\directory of the location selected. To place the database in a subdirectory, type the subdirectory name in the File Name field or click the Folder icon on the right side of the field to select a subdirectory. Type the name **abcevent.nsf** for the database file name.

5. Enable the Create full text index for searching check box so that employees can perform full-text searches on the database.

6. Select the -Blank- template (the default) to create a database from scratch.

7. Click on OK to create the database file.

On creation of a database, Notes displays the new database navigation pane on the left and an empty view pane on the right. The design of the database is accessed through design elements listed at the bottom of the navigation pane. A new database created from scratch contains a default view (select View in the navigation pane) and three elements under Other: the database icon, the Using Database document, and the About Database document. Generally, the Using Database and About Database documents are written and finalized on completion of the development of a database because design modifications can occur during development.

Create a Form from Scratch

The first document form is a discussion document. A form can be created from scratch or by copying and pasting a form into the current database. The form in this example is created from scratch. The following steps create a form from scratch:

1. Select Create, Design, Form. Notes displays a new form (see fig. 13.54).

Figure 13.54

A new (Untitled) form.

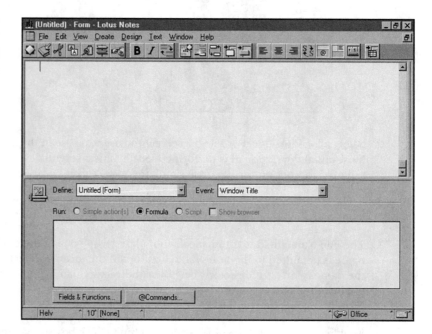

The Form window displays two areas: the design window (above) and the design pane (below). The design window holds and formats the elements of the form (static text, fields, buttons, and so on). The design pane contains calculations for the form written as simple actions, formulas, or LotusScript routines.

2. Select Design, Form Properties to display the Form Properties dialog box.

3. Enter a name for the form. Type **Main Topic | Main Topic** for the form name. The pipe symbol separates the name of the form users see (left) from the name of the form as used in formulas (right). If for some reason the name intended for users requires a change, formulas throughout the database that refer to the form will not also require a change.

4. Note that the default value of Form Type is Document. This value does not require a change for this form.

5. Select the Defaults tab of the Form Properties dialog box and enable Default database form. In the event a user tries to open a document that does not contain a form value or the form value does not match forms available in the database, Notes displays the document by using the default database form.

6. Select the File Save SmartIcon to save the form.

7. Press Esc to close the form.

Note that the form name now appears when you select Forms in the Design section of the navigator pane. The asterisk indicates the form is the default database form. Also note the form name now appears in the Create menu.

Create Static Text

Static text on the form appears the same on all documents created with the form. Good information for static text includes a title at the top of the form and names for the fields. To enter static text, perform the following steps:

1. Double-click on the form to open it in Edit mode.

2. Type **Main Topic** and press Enter.

3. Using the mouse, highlight the text "Main Topic" and select Text - Text Properties. Select a font, size, and color for the text.

 Tip   Take into consideration the fonts available to all potential users at their workstations. For a white background, black or another dark color is easy to read. This example uses Helvetica font, 18-point size, and Black color.

4. Select the second tab of the Text Properties dialog box and select the Second alignment option to center the title on the form.

5. After the title, press Enter a couple of times to allow some space between the title and the first field name.

6. Type **Author:**, and then tab. Press Enter. Repeat this step for each of the following field names: **Date**, **Main Topic**, **Category**, and **Description**.

7. Select the File Save SmartIcon to save your changes.

The form now contains static text.

Create Fields

The Main Topic form contains fields for the author's name, a creation date, the main topic, a category, and a body. Body will be the name of the description field. To create these fields, perform the following steps:

1. Place the cursor at the end of the Author line.

2. Click on the Create Field SmartIcon.

3. Type **Author** for the field name.

4. Select Authors for the field type.

5. Select Computed when composed so that the field only calculates when a document is first composed.

6. Type the formula **@V3UserName** in the design pane. The value returned is the abbreviated name of the user ID in use when the document is created. An abbreviated name contains the values of a hierarchical name (omitting the CN, OU, O, and C identifiers).

7. Repeat steps 1 through 5 for the Date field, using the field name DateComposed and field type Time.

8. Note that the time value is defaulted to show the date and time. Change the value to Date.

9. Type the formula **@Today** in the design pane.

10. Repeat steps 1 through 5 for the Main Topic field, using the field name MainTopic and field type Text.

11. Select the second tab of the Field Properties dialog box.

12. For help description, type **Please type a main topic using one sentence or less**.

13. Select the Input Validation event in the design pane. The Input Validation formula prevents the form from being saved if it evaluates to False.

14. Type the formula **@If(MainTopic = "" ; @Failure("Main Topic is a required field. Please enter a Main Topic.") ; @Success)**. If no value is entered for Main Topic, the user cannot save the document and is prompted to enter a Main Topic.

15. Repeat steps 1 through 5 for the Category field, using the field name Category and the field type Keywords.

16. Note that the Choices section appears on the Field Properties dialog box. Enter **Sports**, **Dining**, and **Entertainment** as the three choices. Click on the Sort button to sort the choices.

17. Enable the Allow values not in list option so that users can suggest events in other categories.

18. Select the Options tab in the Field Properties dialog box.

19. Type **Press ENTER to select a category or to type a new category**.

20. On the line below the field titled Description, repeat steps 2 through 5 for the Body field, using the field name Body and the field type Rich Text.

21. Select the Options tab in the Field Properties dialog box.

22. Type a help description.

23. Select View, Ruler. The ruler is used to modify margins and tab settings.

24. Select Edit, Select All.

25. Click on the 2-inch mark on the ruler. Note that the fields are now aligned and the form has an improved appearance.

26. Select the Author field and click on the Text Bold SmartIcon. Differentiating field data from static text is a part of good form design; the user can more easily read the data on the form. Repeat this step for each of the fields on the form. When this step is completed, the form looks like that shown in figure 13.55.

Figure 13.55

*The completed
"Main Topic"
form.*

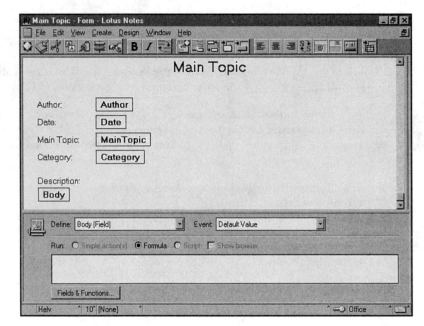

27. Select the File Save SmartIcon.

28. Press Esc to close the form.

The form now contains sufficient static text and fields to make it useful to end users.

Create a Form from Another Form

This database utilizes a Response form so that users can compose Response documents to other users' Main Topics. Because the Response form shares some of the design features of the Main Topics form, development time can be saved by creating a copy of the Main Topic form, then modifying and saving it as the Response form. To create the Response form from the Main Topics form, perform the following steps:

1. Select Forms in the design section of the navigator.

2. Select the Edit Copy SmartIcon.

3. Select the Edit Paste SmartIcon. Note that a new form appears with the name Copy of Main Topic.

4. Double-click on the form Copy of Main Topic to open the form in Edit mode.

5. Change the name of the form. Type **Response | Response** for the form name.

6. Change the value of Form Type to Response to Response. The response to response form can be used to create a response document to a main document or to create a response document to a response document.

7. Select the Defaults tab of the Form Properties dialog box and enable Formulas inherit values from selected document. When a response document is first composed, fields can inherit values from the parent document. Because Notes is not a relational database—a field value is changed in a parent document—response documents created prior to the change do not update the value in the inherited field.

8. Select the Background tab of the Form Properties dialog box. Change the background color to a light color. This example uses light blue. Different colored form backgrounds facilitate ease of use for users.

9. Select the File Save SmartIcon to save the form.

10. Change the static text title at the top of the form from Main Title to Response.

11. Select the Category static text and field. Click on Delete to delete the field; it will not be used with this form. After this step is completed, the form looks like that shown in figure 13.56.

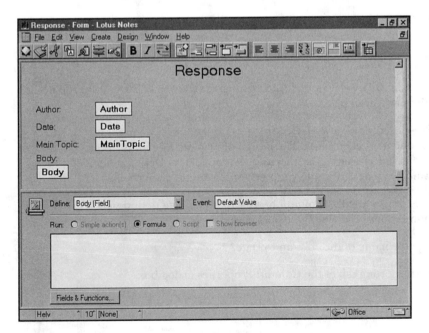

Figure 13.56

The completed "Response" form.

12. Click on the Save File SmartIcon to save the form.

13. Press Esc to close the form.

Create a View from Scratch

Notice that when you select Views from the design section of the navigator a view already exists. A database is required to have one shared view. This default view (named *(untitled)) contains all the documents in the database sorted by document number in the view.

 Tip If a database will not contain a view of all documents, this view may be helpful to keep during development and testing because it provides access to all the documents in the database.

Perform the following steps to create a new view from scratch:

1. Select Create, View. Notes displays a Create View dialog box.

2. Type the name **All Documents** in the View Name field.

3. Enable the Shared option.

4. Click on OK. The new view appears in the Views list.

Modify a View

To open and edit the newly created All Documents view, select Views from the design section of the navigation pane.

1. Double-click on the view All Documents to open the view in Edit mode. Notice that a column already exists. The design of new views defaults to copy the design of the *(untitled) view. Like a form, a view opened in Design mode defaults to two windows, a design window (above) and a design pane (below).

2. Double-click on the first column header (containing a pound sign "#"). A Column Properties dialog box appears.

3. Change the name of the column to **Date**.

4. Select the Sorting tab of the Column Properties dialog box.

5. Select Descending for sort.

6. In the design pane, select Field. A message box appears to confirm your selection. Select Yes.

7. Select the field Date from the list of fields.

8. Double-click on the view header bar to the right of the Date column. A new column appears.

9. Type **Topic** for the column name.

10. Repeat steps 6 through 7, selecting Main Topic as the field.

11. Change to the View Properties dialog box.

12. Select the Options tab.

13. Disable the Show response documents in a hierarchy option. All main topic documents and response documents appear without relation to one another.

14. Select the Styles tab.

15. Enable the Extend last column to window width option. Now the information in the Main Topic can extend the length of the user's view window.

16. Select the File Save SmartIcon to save the view.

17. Press Esc to close the view.

The All Documents view now contains two fields to identify documents in the view, sorted by date in descending order so that new documents appear at the top of the view.

 When developing views, it is helpful to first create test documents that can appear in the view to confirm the appearance and format of data. As development progresses, press the display indicator in the top-left corner of the view design pane to refresh the view.

Figure 13.57 shows the All Documents view displaying a few test documents.

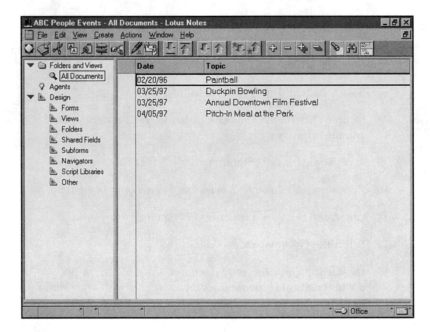

Create a Categorized View

A categorized view groups common documents together under a single category value. An All Documents By Category view is a great place to use categorization.

1. Select Views from the design section of the navigator.

2. Highlight the All Documents view.

3. Select the Edit Copy SmartIcon.

4. Select the Edit Paste SmartIcon. A new view appears named Copy of All Documents.

5. Double-click on the Copy of All Documents view.

6. In the View Properties dialog box, change the name of the view to All Documents By Category.

7. Type **Category** in the Alias field. Formulas use this value to refer to the view.

8. Select the Options tab.

9. Enable the Show response documents in a hierarchy option. This view shows the relationship (or threaded format) of parent and child documents.

10. Select the Date Column.

11. Select Create, Insert New Column to create a column for category values.

12. In the Column Properties dialog box, change the width to 1.

> **Tip** The contents of a categorized view extend beyond the column border, but the title does not. Often, categorized columns do not require a category for the header because the categorization is contained in the view name.

13. Enable the Show twistie when row is expandable option.

14. Select the Sorting tab and sort Ascending and Categorized.

15. Select the Text Properties tab.

16. Set the text to size 12, style Bold, and color Light Blue.

> **Note** Standardize your rules for categorized text properties so that users always know when they are in a categorized view.

17. In the design pane, select the Category field.

18. Select the Topic column.

19. Select the Show twistie when row is expandable option.

20. Select Create, Insert New Column to create a column for response document topics.

> **Tip** The key to building hierarchical views is to create response document columns to the left of corresponding "main" document columns. By enabling the column option Show responses only, Notes automatically indents child documents relative to preceding parent documents.

21. In the Column Properties dialog box, change the width to 1.

22. Enable the option Show responses only.

23. Enable the Show twistie when row is expandable option.

24. In the design pane, select the Main Topic field.

25. Select the File Save SmartIcon to save the view.

26. Press Esc to close the view.

The database now contains two new views. Because the views are shared and display all documents in the database, delete the *(Untitled) view by selecting the view and pressing Delete. A message box prompts for verification. Select Yes. Figure 13.58 shows the new categorized view expanded.

Figure 13.58

The completed "All Documents By Category" view.

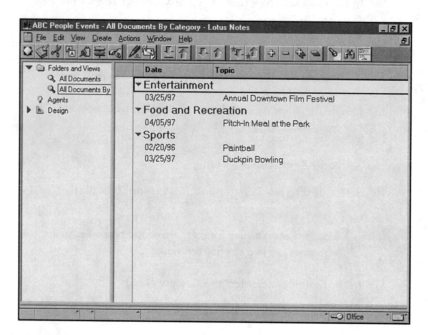

Create a Folder

A folder contains assorted documents placed there manually or programmatically. Users employ personal folders to collect the documents they want to find quickly. To create a Shared - Personal on first use folder, perform the following steps:

1. Select Create, Folder. A Create Folder dialog box appears.

2. Type **Favorite Topics** for the Folder name.

3. Enable the Shared option. All users see the folder as a shared (or public) folder before they select it.

4. Enable the Personal on first use option. The folder converts to a personal folder for the user the first time it is selected or used.

5. Enable the Store in desktop option. The folder is stored in the user's desktop.dsk file on the local hard drive.

6. Click on OK to save.

Modify a Folder

Select Folders in the design section of the navigator pane and highlight the Favorite Topics folder. To modify the folder, perform the following steps:

1. Double-click on the folder name. The folder opens in Edit mode. A folder contains columns just like a view. Because the folder will hold the same information as the views, column design can be copied from a view to a folder.

2. Open the All Documents view in Design mode.

3. Select the Topic column.

4. Click on the Edit Copy SmartIcon.

5. Return to the Folder in Design mode.

6. Delete the First Column (with a pound sign header).

7. Paste the Topic column.

8. Return to the All Documents view in Design mode.

9. Select the Date column and click on the Edit Copy SmartIcon.

10. Return to the Folder in Design mode.

11. Select the Topic column and click on the Edit Paste SmartIcon.

12. Select the File Save SmartIcon.

13. Press Esc to close the folder.

Documents can now be dragged from a view to the folder.

Create an Agent

Agents provide short cuts to performing tasks. This database will contain an agent that moves selected documents to the Favorite Topics folder. To create an agent, perform the following steps:

1. Select Create, Agent. A new agent appears in Design mode (see fig. 13.59).

Figure 13.59

The new "Untitled" agent.

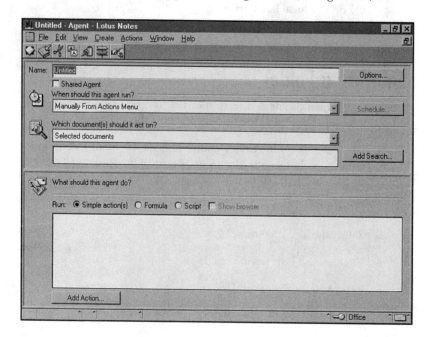

2. Type **Add Selected Documents to Favorite Topics Folder** in the Name field.

3. Note that the agent default settings are to run Manually From Actions Menu and to run on Selected documents. These settings are correct for this agent.

4. Click on the Add Action button at the bottom of the design pane. The Add Action dialog box appears (see fig. 13.60).

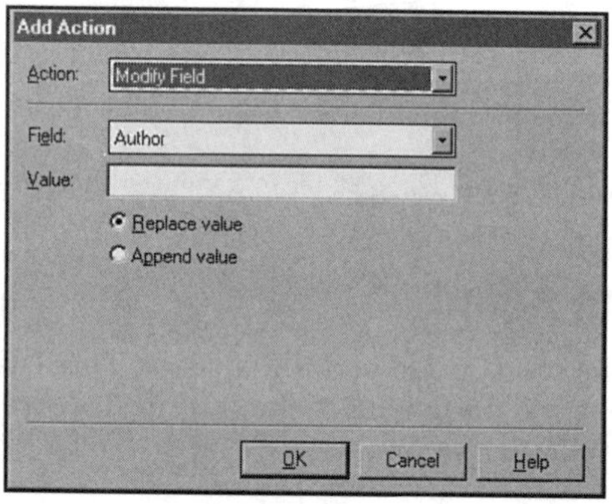

Figure 13.60

The Add Action dialog box.

5. Select Move to Folder in the Action field.

6. Select the Favorite Topics folder in the Folder field.

7. Click on the OK button.

8. Click on the File Save SmartIcon to save the Agent.

9. Press Esc to close the Agent.

Note that the agent now appears on the Actions menu.

Create an Action Button

Users are not required to manually execute an agent through the Action menu. An action button can be provided in the view to run the agent. To create an action button, perform the following steps:

1. Open the All Documents by Category view in Design mode.

2. Select Create, Action. Note that the action pane opens on the right side of the design window and the Action Properties dialog box appears.

3. Type **Move to Favorites** for the action Title.

4. Select an appropriate icon (the blue arrow pointing into a folder is appropriate here).

5. Toggle the position value to 1.

6. In the design pane, select Simple Action.

7. Click on the Add Action button at the bottom of the design pane.

8. Select Run Agent in the Action field. Note that the only agent in the database is selected in the Agent field. If other agents were available, they could be selected here.

9. Click on the OK button.

10. Click on the File Save SmartIcon.

11. Press Esc to close the view.

Select the All Documents by Category view to see the new action button. Now, users can select multiple documents in the view and move them to the Favorite Topics folder with one mouse click.

Create a Navigator

End users may find a customized navigator easier to use than the Folders navigator. Perform the following steps to create and implement a navigator:

1. Select Create, Design, Navigator. A navigator appears in design format, including a design window and a design pane.

2. Type the name **Main Navigator** in the Navigator Properties dialog box.

3. Select All Documents for the initial view or folder.

4. Enable the Auto adjust panes at runtime option.

5. Select a background color for the navigator.

6. Click on the Create Textbox SmartIcon.

7. Click-drag a small text box on the left side of the screen.

8. Type **All Documents** for the name of the text box in the Text Properties dialog box.

9. Type **All Documents** for the caption of the text box.

10. Modify the text appearance and text box background by using the tabs in the Text Properties dialog box.

11. Enable the Highlight when touched option on the HiLite tab.

12. In the design pane, select the simple action Open a View and select the All Documents view.

13. Repeat steps 6 through 12 to create text boxes for the All Documents by Category view, the Favorite Topics folder, and a Close View text box.

14. The Close View text box requires a formula rather than a simple action. Select Formula and click on the @Commands button. Select FileCloseWindow from the list. The Navigator now looks like figure 13.61.

15. Click on the File Save SmartIcon

16. Press Esc to close the Navigator and Esc again to close the database.

17. Open the Database Properties dialog box.

18. Select the Launch tab.

19. Select the Open designated Navigator option in the On Open field.

20. Choose the Main Navigator in the Navigator field.

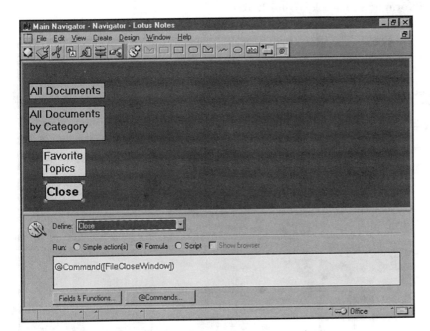

Figure 13.61

The completed "Main" navigator.

With the database open, the Main Navigator now appears in the navigation pane. Documents can be dragged to the Favorite Topics folder in Main Navigator. To return to the default Folder's navigator, select View, Show, Folders.

Create a Subform

Subforms can be used as one design location for common design elements in multiple forms. Common design elements are developed in the subform, and then the subform is inserted into forms. A subform in the current database could replace the author and date fields on the Main Topic and Response forms. To create a subform, perform the following steps:

1. Select Create, Design, Subform. The subform design window and design pane appear.

2. Type **Header Subform** in the Subform Properties dialog box. Note that the Include in Insert Subform ... dialog option is already selected.

3. Open the Main Topic form in Design mode. Highlight the Author and Date static text and fields.

4. Click on the Edit Copy SmartIcon.

5. Return to the Subform in Design mode and click on the Edit Paste SmartIcon. The subform now looks like figure 13.62.

Figure 13.62

The completed "Header" subform.

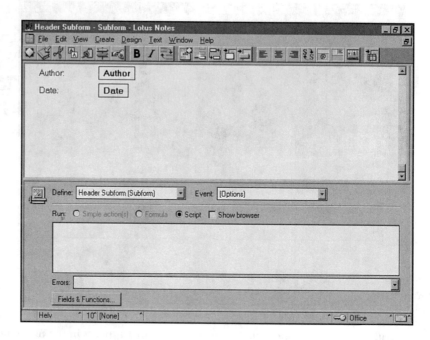

6. Click on the File Save SmartIcon.

7. Press Esc to close the Subform.

The subform now appears in the subforms list and is available in the Create, Insert Subform menu.

Insert a Subform in a Form

To insert the subform into the forms, perform the following steps:

1. Open the Main topic form in Design mode.

2. Highlight and delete the Author and Date static text and fields.

3. Select Create, Insert Subform. The Insert Subform dialog box appears and Header Subform is already selected because it is the only subform.

4. Click on the OK button. The form now looks like figure 13.63.

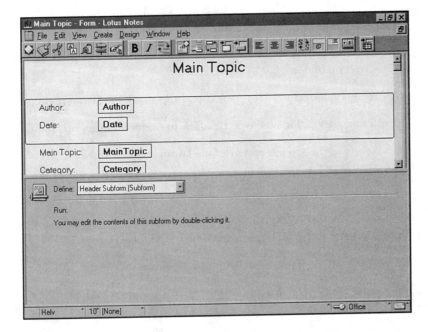

Figure 13.63

The "Main Topic" form with "Header" subform.

5. Click on the File Save SmartIcon.

6. Press Esc to close the form.

7. Repeat steps 1 through 6 for the Response form.

The forms still function the same with the new subform. Now design changes to these elements need to be made only one time in the subform.

 A subform can be placed in Edit mode by double-clicking on the subform appearing in a form.

Create a Layout Region

A layout region might improve the appearance of a form. This application will contain a layout region in the Main Topic form. The layout region will contain three fields and static text. To create a layout region, perform the following steps.

1. Open the Main Topic form in Design mode.

2. Add a new line after the Category field by pressing Enter.

3. Select Create, Layout Region, New Layout Region. An outline for the layout region appears on the subform. In the Layout Properties dialog box, enable the 3D Style option.

4. Enable the Snap to grid option.

5. Click on the Create Textbox SmartIcon. A text box appears in the layout region.

6. In the Control Properties dialog box, type **Deadline to Commit** in the Text field.

7. Position the text box in the top-left corner of the layout region. Adjust the size so that all the text can be seen.

8. Click on the Create Textbox SmartIcon. A second text box appears in the layout region.

9. In the Control Properties dialog box, type **Maximum Attendees/Group Size**.

10. Position the text box on the left margin below the Deadline text box.

11. Click on the Create Textbox SmartIcon. A third text box appears in the layout region.

12. In the Control Properties dialog box, type **Cost** in the Text field.

13. Position the text box on the left margin below the Size text box.

14. Click on the Create Field SmartIcon. A fourth text box appears in the layout region.

15. Type **Deadline** for the field name in the Field Properties dialog box.

16. Choose the second tab and enable the Multiline option.

17. Choose the Options tab and type **When must plans be finalized?** for the help description.

18. Position the Deadline field next to the appropriate static text and modify the size (click-drag the borders) to contain two lines of text. Drag the right margin of the field close to the right margin of the layout region.

19. Click on the Create Field SmartIcon.

20. Type **Size** for the field name in the Field Properties dialog box.

21. Choose the second tab and enable the Multiline option.

22. Choose the Options tab and type **Enter the group size requirements here** for the help description.

23. Position the field similarly to the Deadline field.

24. Click on the Create Field SmartIcon.

25. Type **Cost** for the field name in the Field Properties dialog box.

26. Choose the second tab and enable the Multiline option.

27. Choose the Options tab and type **Enter any required costs for employees or the company** for the help description.

28. Position the field similarly to the other two fields.

29. Click on the File Save SmartIcon.

    A layout region is great for field entry, but can be confusing to users when viewing a document in read mode because the fields appear to be in Edit mode. A good solution is to employ hide-when features and add some Computed for display fields.

30. In the Layout dialog box, select the second tab for hide layout options. Enable Previewed for Reading and Opened for Reading.

31. Insert a couple of new lines after the layout region and type the static text **Deadline:**. Then press Tab.

32. Click on the Create Field SmartIcon.

33. Type **DeadlineDisplay** for the field name in the Field Properties dialog box.

34. Select Computed for display.

35. In the design pane, type **Deadline** for the formula.

36. On the next line of the form, type the static text **Size:**. Then press Tab.

37. Click on the Create Field SmartIcon.

38. Type **SizeDisplay** for the field name in the Field Properties dialog box.

39. Select Computed for display.

40. In the design pane, type **Size** for the formula.

41. On the next line of the form, type the static text **Cost:**. Then press Tab.

42. Click on the Create Field SmartIcon.

43. Type **CostDisplay** for the field name in the Field Properties dialog box.

44. Select Computed for display.

45. In the design pane, type **Cost** for the formula.

46. Using the mouse, highlight all three fields and select the Hide Paragraph tab in the Text Properties dialog box.

47. Enable the options to hide when Previewed for Editing, Opened for Editing, and Copied to the clipboard. The layout region now looks like figure 13.64.

Figure 13.64

Completed layout region.

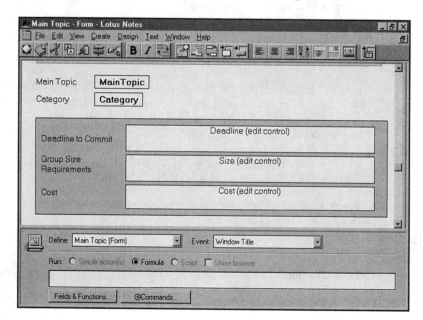

48. Click on the File Save SmartIcon.

49. Press Esc to close the form.

Now the layout region appears only when a document is being edited and the display fields appear only when the document is being read.

Create a Section

To create a section, perform the following steps:

1. Open the Main Topic form in Edit mode.

2. Highlight the DeadlineDisplay, SizeDisplay, and CostDisplay fields and static text by click-dragging the mouse.

3. Select Create, Section, Standard. Note that the fields disappear and the text "Deadline" appears with a twistie and a horizontal line.

4. In the Section Properties dialog box, change the title to **Logistics**.

5. Select the first border style for the title.

6. Select the Auto-collapse section value when the document is Previewed or Opened for reading. Select the Auto-expand section value when the document is Printed. The section now looks like figure 13.65.

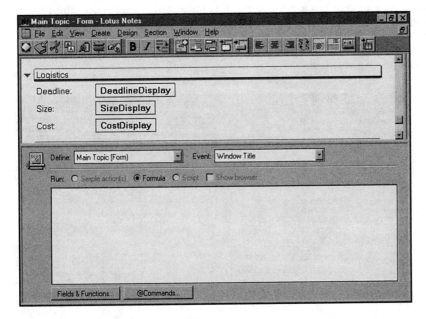

Figure 13.65

The completed section.

7. Click on the File Save SmartIcon.

8. Press Esc to close the form.

The form now contains an expandable section. This becomes more effective when a greater number of elements are contained in the section.

Create a Table

A table can be used to align the fields on a form. To create a table, perform the following steps:

1. Open the Header Subform in Edit mode.

2. Select Create, Table. The Create Table dialog box appears.

3. Enter the dimensions for the table, the default 2×2 is appropriate for these fields. Click on the OK button.

4. Cut and paste the Author static text into the upper-left cell.

5. Cut and paste the Author field into the lower-left cell.

6. Cut and paste the Date static text into the upper-right cell.

7. Cut and paste the Date field into the lower-right cell.

8. Highlight all four cells by click-dragging the mouse, and then click on the Text Align Paragraph Center SmartIcon.

9. In the Table Properties dialog box, select the border type Extruded. The table now looks like figure 13.66.

Figure 13.66

The completed table.

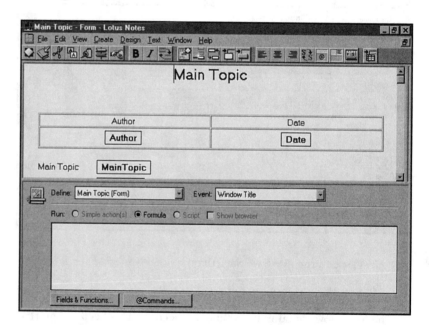

10. Click on the File Save SmartIcon.

11. Press Esc to close the form.

Both forms now contain the Author and Date fields in a table because the subform was modified.

Create a Hotspot

To create a hotspot, perform the following steps:

1. Open the Main Topic form in Edit mode.

2. Highlight the static text Description.

3. Select Create, Hotspot, Text Pop-up. The Hotspot Pop-up dialog box appears.

4. In the Pop-up Text field, type **This Description field is a rich text field. You may format your text, embed files or graphic objects, or attach files applicable to the event being proposed in this document. Call the Lotus Notes help desk at x5555 if you have any questions.** The hotspot now looks like figure 13.67.

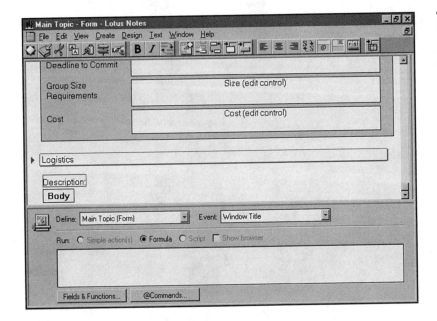

Figure 13.67

The hotspot border around the "Description:" text.

5. Click on the File Save SmartIcon.

6. Press Esc to close the form.

The form now contains a Text Pop-up hotspot to provide the user with more information than could be supplied in the field help description.

Summary

The elements of database construction presented in this chapter provide more than an introduction to application development in Lotus Notes. Understanding the features of these construction elements establishes a sound foundation for developing databases and provides a developer the requisite tools for addressing application design issues.

CHAPTER 14

Advanced Application Design Issues

T his chapter helps shed some light on many major issues in application design, and provides tools and techniques to enhance your Notes applications.

In this chapter, you will add the following to your utility belt of development techniques:

◆ A single, dynamic formula that can be used in lookups, document composition, and other functions. Plus, it behaves identically whether the databases using the formula provided are located on the Win95/3.1 client or on the Domino 4.5 server.

◆ A way to return multiple fields in a single lookup formula.

◆ A technique to export Notes documents to comma-delimited files. Using this method, users and administrators can share Notes information with almost any commercial software package.

◆ Methods to reduce view indexing time.

◆ View construction methods that show end users exactly what they want to see.

◆ An explanation and demonstration of the new Profile document feature and how to implement this powerful function.

Although this chapter focuses on efficiencies of database design and is primarily targeted toward developers, it still is of great benefit for administrators. First, administrators more often than not provide post deployment refinement. Administrators might have to add commonly used groups to the ACL, ensure that replication settings are correct, and so forth. Further, most of the ideas presented in the chapter have positive server side ramifications.

Efficiency in Form and View Design

All of the wonderful user interface enhancements in Notes 4.x provide developers a world of application design possibilities. Developers can become so immersed in making the application look great that they all too often lose track of their real purpose in developing applications: to design applications that automate complex business processes that are fast, error-free, and easy to use. This should be the primary goal of any application development effort. Graphically appealing applications are wonderful, but if a user must wait for tons of lookups to be performed, layout regions to load, and large graphics to load before they can begin doing work, then chances are that users will reject the application. The application life cycle for such an application will be considerably shorter than if the focus of the application design was placed on performance.

So what is meant by efficiency in design? The specific focus of this chapter is on forms and views. Huge performance gains can be achieved by optimizing the way that you perform various tasks in Notes. This chapter endeavors to show you better ways to achieve common programming goals, with the least amount of drag placed on the server, client, end users, and you.

Dynamic Server, Database, Path Information

Many applications require consistent functionality and data integrity between the server- and workstation-based databases. This presents substantial challenges to the Notes developer when multiple databases are involved. A major challenge is ensuring inter-database functionality, regardless of directory structures and operating systems.

In most organizations, Notes users need the ability to replicate server-based information to their local machine, typically laptop computers, so that the same information is available locally without the necessity for a physical connection to the server.

Databases can quickly grow far beyond expected sizes. The result is that most developers learn that it is wise to segment information into many different databases in order to optimize database performance. Applications using multiple databases require more work on the part of the developer. Information often needs to be looked up from one to another database.

Because Notes is not a relational database management system and resembles a flat file architecture, the idea of tables and keys is not truly applicable. Therefore, when developers want to pull information from one Notes database to another, lookups are the typical solution.

A practical example of this would be a database lookup that is being performed within an inventory database. A dbLookup within a form of the inventory database might return a list of all the red colored fruits in the ViewFruitByColor view. The code might look like the following:

```
@dbLookup("Notes":"NoCache";"Chicago01":"fresh\fruit.nsf";"ViewFruitByColor";"Red";2)
```

"Chicago01" is the explicitly listed server name. If both of the databases were replicated to a local machine and the lookup was attempted, it would fail because the proper argument for the server would be a null value or simply double quotes with no space between quotes, as illustrated as follows:

```
@dbLookup("Notes":"NoCache";"";"fresh\fruit.nsf";"ViewFruitByColor";"Red";2)
```

To prevent this, the developer must ensure that the server and database arguments of the dbLookup will work on a local machine or on a server.

The underlying problem is that if users have replicated the databases to any directory other than the Notes data directory, the pathing is not identical to that of the server (provided the database was located in the server's data directory). The result is that most @Functions will fail if the server and database arguments of the @Functions do not account for the possibility of being replicated into a different subdirectory structure.To overcome this dilemma, some developers explicitly list the 32-character replica ID of the database in place of the server and database arguments used in many @Functions. The following is a dbLookup using a replica ID:

```
@dbLookup("Notes":"NoCache";"85256451:006D2F0F";"fresh\fruit.nsf";
➥"ViewFruitByColor";"Red";2)
```

Notes can locate the database this way regardless of its location in the directory structure. This will cause problems in the future, however, if the administrator takes some action that requires the replica ID (UNID) of the database to be changed. The result of which is that if a @Function or @Command uses the replica ID of the target database, each and every function that uses the replica ID must be updated to the new replica ID value.

If you have determined that using a replica ID is the only solution to this problem, a quick way of accessing the UNID is to select the database you want the ID from and then choose File, Database, Design Synopsis. Next, check the replication checkbox. You will be presented with replication information. Here, it is easy to highlight the 32-character replica ID, copy it to the clipboard, and paste it into any formula.

Many different @Functions rely on two common arguments:

◆ The server argumment

◆ The database and file path argument

Path information should always be supplied if the database is located in a directory other than the default data directory created during the server installation.

The following code is designed to return both the server and database attributes of the target database. The two temporary variables, SERVER and DATABASE, can be used with many different @Commands and @Functions. Keep in mind that the following code only works if both the target and referencing databases reside in the same directory.

```
REM "Declare any additional arguments that you might need";
REM "for the particular function here.";
REM "Such as: form, view, title, prompt, navigator, key etc.";

filename :="filename.nsf";
SERVER := @Subset(@DbName;1);
path := @LeftBack(@Subset(@DbName;-1);"\\");
DATABASE :=
 @If(@Elements(@Explode(path;"\\")) < 1;
  filename
 ;
  path+"\\"+filename
 )
;
REM "Insert any of the particular functions shown below."
```

The preceding code is known to work with each of the following @Functions and @Commands on a Windows 3.1 or Windows 95/NT client and certified NT server:

```
@Command([Compose];SERVER:DATABASE;"form")

@Command([FileOpenDatabase];SERVER:DATABASE;"viewName";"key";"newinstance";
"temporary")

@Command([FileOpenDatabase];SERVER:DATABASE;"navigator";"solo";"newinstance";
"temporary")
```

```
@DbLookup("class":"NoCache";SERVER:DATABASE;"view";key;columnNumber)

@DbLookup("class":"NoCache";SERVER:DATABASE;"view";key;fieldName)

@DbColumn("class":"NoCache";SERVER:DATABASE;"view";columnNumber)

@PickList([Custom];SERVER:DATABASE;"view";"title";"prompt";"column")
```

Efficient Lookups

Now that a way to use dynamic formulas has been illustrated, there are a few basic ways to optimize lookup coding that can pay strong performance dividends.

Use Cache When Applicable

Both @DbColumn and @DbLookup provide the capability to cache the values they return. Use the cache keyword if it is not necessary for the very latest information to be returned. If cache is used, the function stores the lookup values in memory as a text list. If used again, these values are returned from memory and less disk access time is required.

Use Column Numbers Rather Than Field Names

The temptation to create lookups that reference the field names rather than the column numbers should be avoided. In the following code example, FruitColor is a field name located in the target database:

```
@DbLookup("Notes":"Cache";SERVER:DATABASE;" ViewFruitByColor ";red;FruitColor)
```

 Tip   You can reference the column number of a hidden column in lookup formulas.

Although this would enable designers to shift columns around in the view design without the need for changing @DbColumn or @DbLookup formulas, developers should avoid this practice. Instead, reference the column number. The reason is that in this case the @Function is actually opening each of the documents and returning the value of the FruitColor field for each of the documents. Using a column number of a view utilizes the view index that has already been constructed.

View designs can change frequently. To avoid changing the column number in lookup, place the lookup column in the first position in the view and change the column attribute to hidden. If you do this, though, do not sort or categorize the hidden column. In this way, lookup @Functions will always reference the correct column number.

Concatenate Fields to Lookup Multiple Field Values

If your application requires that more than one field value be returned from a document, do not place each field in an individual column and perform multiple lookups against multiple columns. Instead, concatenate all the required fields in a single column (see fig. 14.1).

Figure 14.1

Concatenating multiple fields for more efficient lookups.

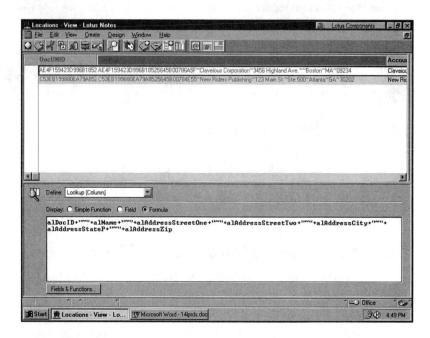

In figure 14.1, you will notice that the first column illustrates this concept. Fields to be returned by a lookup are married together, concatenated in other words, using the tilde key (~). This specific character is used here because it is used very rarely and does not conflict with other Notes keywords or functions.

Use Temporary Variables to Store Lookup Values

Notes developers can gain a performance boost by using temporary variables intelligently. An excellent example of when to use temporary variables is any time you need to make decisions based on lookup return values.

If the number of items returned from a lookup is less than three, for example, the application developer would rather return a single text string: "unavailable." The developer could write the formula in the following way:

```
@If(
@Elements(
@DbLookup("Notes":"Cache";SERVER:DATABASE;" ViewFruitByColor ";red;FruitColor))
➥< 3 ;
"unavailable";
@DbLookup("Notes":"Cache";SERVER:DATABASE;" ViewFruitByColor ";red;FruitColor))
➥< 3 ;
)
```

Notice that two dblookups are actually being performed in the previous example. Developers should avoid this practice and instead use temporary variables.
In the following example, a temporary variable called "Fruits" will store the value
of the lookup that can then be tested to see the number of elements it contains. If
the number returned is less than three, it will return the string "unavailable;" otherwise, it will return the value of the lookup.

```
Fruits := @DbLookup("Notes":"Cache";SERVER:DATABASE;" ViewFruitByColor";
➥red;FruitColor;1);
@IF(
  @Elements(Fruits) < 3;
  "Unavailable";
  Fruits
)
```

Lookups can be taxing on system resources. The previous example, although very
simple, eliminates unnecessary lookups while providing the same functionality.

In some cases, the value being returned from a lookup is an error such as "File Does
Not Exist." If composition of a form relies on a lookup to be performed, the form
may simply present the error and then close the form, never allowing composition of
the document. A common resolution to this issue is to test the lookup for errors, as
follows:

```
Fruits := @DbLookup("Notes":"Cache";SERVER:DATABASE;" ViewFruitByColor ";
➥red;FruitColor;1);
@IF(
  @IsError(Fruits);
  "Lookup error";
  Fruits
)
```

The previous example would return the text string "Lookup error" if an error was
returned, and allow the document to be composed.

Figure 14.2 illustrates error checking of dblookups in a field design.

Figure 14.2

The use of temporary variables for lookup values.

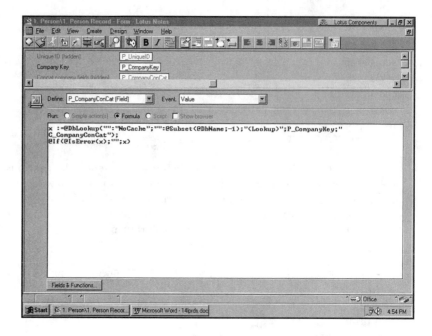

Administrators often need to integrate legacy data with a new Notes installation. Sometimes just a quick export of Notes data to a different file format is required. In the following section, an answer to a common question of many developers and administrators is answered: How can I export my Notes data to ASCII comma-delimited format?

Exporting Notes Data

Although there is not an ASCII comma-delimited export option for Notes files, most developers eventually will need this capability. A little experimentation and creativity quickly gives way to a workable solution. Creating comma-delimited files is easier than it might first appear.

To avoid confusion, an example of comma-delimited text appears in the following code. Note that if number type fields are to be preserved, no quotes should surround those field values (as in the number 1 in the first record). If quotes surround numbers, other applications import routines can recognize numbers surrounded by quote marks as text.

```
"Susan Crisafulli",1,"03/15/97 12:04:38 PM","SmartSuite 97"
"Chuck O'Briant",2,"","Notes"
"Steve Finn",3,"","NotesView 4.1"
"Jeff Brockway",4,"","LNDI"
"James Sanders",5,"","Components"
```

Unfortunately, Notes does not have an ASCII comma-delimited export type. From any view, a user can select File, Export and see that only three available export formats are available.

◆ Lotus 1-2-3 worksheet

◆ Structured text

◆ Tabular text

To work around this limitation, you can construct a new view in your application. The view will contain only one column.

Begin by creating a new view, then create five temporary variables in the first column. (There will be only one column in the view.) The following shows a temporary variable, StartEnd, which is the first and last value in the list. Next is the Text2Text variable that is used to delimit, or separate, text fields. The Text2Number variable is third. This variable enables concatenation between text to number. Text2Number, the fourth variable, enables transition from a text to a number field. The Number2Number field allows for separation between number fields.

```
StartEnd := "\"";
Text2Text := "\",\"";
Text2Number := "\",";
Number2Text := ",\"";
Number2Number := ",";
```

These variables make it easier to read the concatenation formula of the view. Figure 14.3 shows an example of a simple column definition.

The following code is the formula that defines the first and only column of the export view. For example, "StartEnd" will translate to a simple double quote. Then the field mrNameRequestor will be appended to the quote, followed by a quote, a comma, and so on. The value of the temporary variables is that they are much easier to read and debug. If numeric values do not need to be preserved, then only the variables StartEnd and Text2Text are necessary.

```
StartEnd+ mrNameRequestor+Text2Number+ @DocNumber+Number2Text+
➥@Text(mrCheckedOut)+Text2Text+mrMediaName+StartEnd
```

After the view has been saved, the end user can open it and choose File, Export to send the view data data to the ASCII text file (see fig. 14.4).

Figure 14.3

The formula in the first column is a definition of the export view. This single column constructs the entire view to be exported.

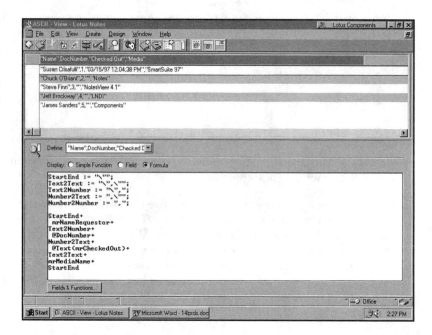

Figure 14.4

The resulting view constructed from the concatenation of temporary variables along with field values.

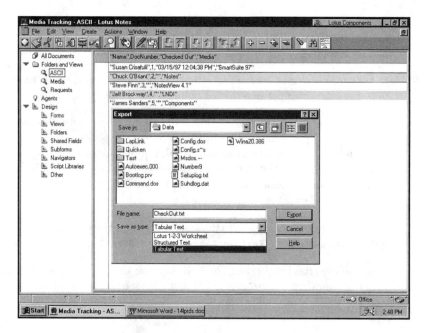

At this point, change the "Save as type:" setting to tabular text. The option to export the row heading is also made available to the end user. Choose the directory in which to place the file. When naming your file in the Win95/3.1 environment, use the standard eight-digit file naming convention along with the .txt file extension. Usually, a file saved with a .txt extension will be recognized by other software packages as an ASCII text file.

Having just covered a valuable yet unconventional use of a view, how might view design in general be improved? The following section answers this question.

View Design Considerations

Of all the design elements available in Notes, view design arguably has the greatest impact on application and server performance. The reasons for this fact are many.

First, a substantial amount of server resources is applied to updating view indexes. Because of the way that view indexes are constructed, they can quickly grow to one half the size of the database itself, placing a strong demand for RAM on the server. Second, under previous versions of Notes, views have served as a reporting tool. This has lead to the building of an enormous number of views. Fortunately version 4.x of Notes provides new facilities that can slash the number of views necessary to slice and dice data efficiently. The improvement in Notes 4.x makes navigation of databases easier for users, development times shorter for developers, and database and server management much easier for administrators.

Applying basic view design fundamentals can benefit application performance significantly. The next few sections detail some of these fundamentals.

Keep the Number of Views to a Minimum

As a rule of thumb, keep the number of views to the absolute minimum. A commonly accepted maximum number is four or possibly five. If this seems extreme, consider the further division of data into additional databases rather than additional views.

In release 4.x of Notes, several features help to reduce the number of views needed. Previously, if users wanted to sort a view by more than one column, the developer had to create a new view. No longer. Now designers can provide users with sorting on demand. Figure 14.5 shows the columns Categories, Media, Status, and Location with a column sort indicator. In the past, using Notes 3.x, a developer might be forced to create four separate views with each one of these fields as a sorted and categorized column. The developer can now construct a single view, and the user can simply click on each one of the four columns to sort the column on demand.

Figure 14.5

A view using sorting on demand.

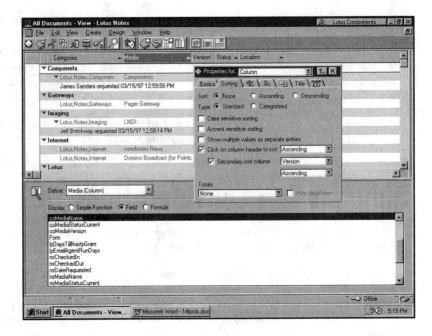

In figure 14.5, the Properties dialog box shows that Click on column header to sort is selected, as is Secondary sort column. The first setting enables end users to click on the column heading and sort the view by the selected column. If the view contains more than one item of the same value in the sorted column, the second setting, "Secondary sort column" will come into effect and will sort duplicate data in the first selected column by the column name selected in the "Secondary sort column" selection of the view design.

Adding this functionality to more than one column adds additional overhead to the view design. It is significantly less, however, than that of an entirely new view design.

Pay Close Attention to View Indexes

Another rule of thumb is to keep view indexing in mind when creating your views. Building view indexes is a server-intensive process.

View indexes are rebuilt under the following circumstances:

◆ When the database designer edits the selection formulas or when column formulas are edited and saved.

◆ When the end user presses Ctrl+Shift+F9.

◆ After replication, view indexes are rebuilt and any full-text indexing is completed if the view index update setting is set to hourly or immediate.

◆ If the view is corrupt, it will be flagged. After all users have logged out of the view, it will be reconstructed the next time a user opens the view or if UPDALL is run.

◆ If agents modify documents in a database, the views that contain the modified records will be updated.

◆ Setting the cutoff date to be earlier than when the view index was last updated, the index is forced to be rebuilt.

◆ Changes to the collation table force complete reindexing of all views. Collation tables are stored in CLS files installed with Notes. Complete reindexing can also occur if a user changes the Collation/Casing settings via User preferences.

Figure 14.6 illustrates the little-used collation table setting. To open this dialog, a user can select File, Tools, User Preferences, International from the menu structure.

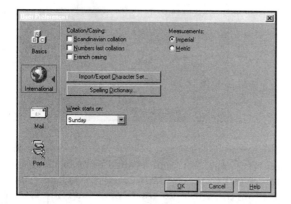

Figure 14.6

Collation/Casing under the International Settings of the User Preferences dialog box.

Create Views for the Individual User

Eventually, the need for user-specific view selection will arise. In other words, users will want to see only their documents. This is a common user request and a danger area for new developers. The intuitive response for new Notes developers is to create a selection formula for the view that relies on @UserName or @Author. Or, using the @Environment function in the view selection formula might come to mind.

None of these work in a shared view. The reason for this is that, on the server, the user and modifier of the view is not the end user but rather the server. For purposes of view selection, the server ID file is the ID file used (not the end user's ID file). As a result, end users do not see what was intended by the developer.

Several different methods enable developers to satisfy the request that users see only their own documents.

To satisfy such a request, the only option is to create a shared, private-on-first-use view. Selecting this option in the Create View dialog box will typically satisfy this need. Unlike the shared view, a view of this kind can use the @UserName function in its selection formula after the view has been opened for the first time. If the database designer wants to change its design, however, and if a user has already opened the shared, private-on-first-use view and then saved it, the user must first delete the now private view. Next, the user must again open the view and save it to see the view design changes.

A major consideration of a shared, private-on-first-use view is where it should be stored. Figure 14.7 illustrates the creation of a view with the option to store the view in the desktop file, desktop.dsk.

Figure 14.7

Creating a shared, private-on-first-use view.

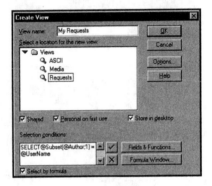

In release 4.x, the Access Control List mandates where the view is stored. The manager of the database can select Create personal folders/views. If this option is disabled, a private view is stored in the users desktop.dsk file, as it had been in release 3.x. In the previous illustration, the option to create personal folders/views was enabled on the server, so placing the view in desktop.dsk file is now an option to the designer of the view.

 If the view is large, users should allocate sufficient drive space for the desktop.dsk. This is accomplished in the Workspace Properties dialog box.

 Copying a shared view to create a shared, private-on-first-use view is prohibited. To work around this, click on the Options button of the Create View dialog box to start with a existing design.

This brings to mind yet another issue—the ID type. If the Notes ID is of the desktop type and not a full designer type, then users are not able to modify the view after it becomes a private view. In order to avoid this limitation, the user license must be upgraded by the server administrator to the ID type of Lotus Notes.

Tip To tell what type license a user has, choose Help, About Notes... In the lower left hand corner, in bold print, will be the current IDs license type. Because the license information is stored in the person's ID file, this may be different among various users. The following are the possible license types:

◆ **Lotus Notes** - Full design capabilities, provided the user has Designer or better rights

◆ **Lotus Notes Desktop** - No design capability

◆ **Lotus Notes Mail** - No design capability

Note A designer should keep in mind that a shared, private-on-first-use view is not a security device. If it is required that users be able to see their own documents and not those of other users, then reader names fields should be used. Reader names are a security device and are arguably the most powerful, aside from local encryption keys.

Avoid Calculations in Views

It is possible to avoid creating formulas within a column's definition by creating the fields on the form that evaluate to the necessary formula. Doing so helps reduce the view index size and enhances view performance. In addition, using totaling for numeric columns has a performance hit; if such a feature is not necessary, it should be avoided.

Eliminate Time Calculations in Views

Sometimes displaying documents based on a time calculation is necessary. Users will see the refresh indicator, however, and will not be able to remove it.

The reason for this is that if the view uses @Now to evaluate a difference in time, the @Now function is constantly being updated. Therefore, the view is never up to date.

Figure 14.8 shows the column definition of the column labeled "Days since last request." Since this column uses the @Now function, the view refresh indicator, shown in the upper left, will always display once the view is saved.

To work around this issue, deselect the option to show the selection margin. Along with the selection margin, the refresh indicator will disappear. This can be done on the Style tab of the Properties dialog box for the view. This does not prevent @Now from evaluating correctly, it just prevents the refresh indicator from displaying.

Figure 14.8

A view column design using the @Now function.

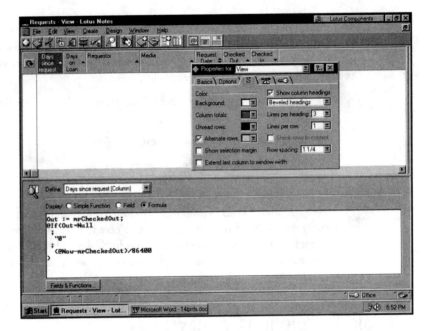

Use Input Translation Formulas

Input translation formulas are the means by which a Notes developer can clean up raw user input. In the following example, the @ReplaceSubstring function is used to strip all ancillary characters from the telephone field. Next, the formula checks to see if the field is blank. If it is, the formula does nothing; otherwise, it continues. If the remaining text string is not at least 10 characters long, the formula provides an error message. This code ensures that the user provides an area code. If the text is exactly 10 characters long, it formats the phone number with two hyphens. If the text is greater than 10 characters long, the formula assumes the remaining characters are an extension, and it separates that portion of the string accordingly.

The temporary variable "sourceList" is located in the telephone number field in the input translation event.

```
sourceList := TelephoneNumberFieldHere;
fromList :=" ":";":":":",":",":"(":")":"[":"]":"{":"}":"<":">":"~":"`":".":"!":
"@":"#":"$":"%":"^":"&":"*":"_":"-":"=":"+":"|":"\\":"?":"/":"\'":"a":"b":"c":"
d":"e":"f":"g":"h":"i":"j":"k":"l":"m":"n":"o":"p":"q":"u":"r":"s":"t":"u":"v":"w":"x":"y":"z":"
A":"B":"C":"E":"D":"E":"F":"G":"H":"I":"J":"K":"L":"O":"P":"Q":"R":"S":"T":"U":"V":"W":"X":"Y":"Z";
```

```
hold:=@ReplaceSubstring(sourceList;fromList;"");
@If(@Trim(hold)="";"":@Return("");"");
@If(@Length(hold)<10;
@Prompt([OK];"Error";"Telephone must be ten numbers or greater .")
➡:@Return(hold);"");
@If(@Length(hold)=10;
@Left(hold;3)+"-"+@Middle(hold;3;3)+"-"+@Middle(hold;6;4);
@Left(hold;3)+"-"+@Middle(hold;3;3)+"-"+@Middle(hold;6;4)+
➡"ext="+@Right(hold;@Length(hold)-10)
)
```

Input translation formulas, like the one shown in figure 14.9, can provide very sophisticated formatting of user input. These translation formulas can get complicated quickly, often due to some reliance on other field values. Therefore, it is a good practice to complete the formulas toward the end of the development process. Figure 14.10 shows the result of the telephone translation formula after it has been evaluated.

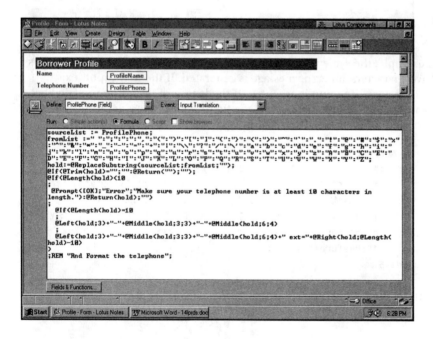

Figure 14.9

The translation formula.

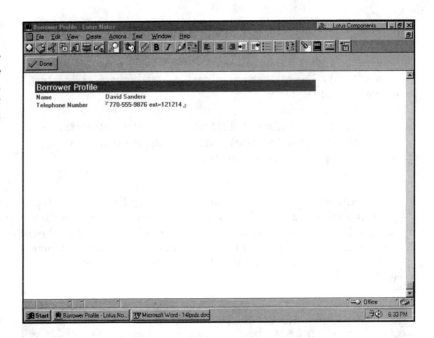

Figure 14.10

The result of the telephone translation formula after it has been evaluated.

In a second example, the same method is used to format zip codes. If the user inputs fewer than five characters, an error message is generated. If the user inputs exactly five or nine characters, the input is accepted. If the length of the string provided by the user is between five or eight characters, the first five characters are returned, a hyphen is added, and four question marks are appended to the five digit zip code.

```
sourceList := acAddressBOneZIP;
fromList :=" ":";":":":",":"(":")":"[":"]":"{":"}":"<":">":"~":"`":".":"|":
"@":"#":"$":"%":"^":"&":"*":"_":"-":"=":"+":"¦":"\\":"?":"/":"\'":"a":"b":"c":"
d":"e":"f":"g":"h":"i":"j":"k":"l":"m":"n":"o":"p":"q":"u":"r":"s":"t":"u":"v":"w":"x":"y":"z":"
A":"B":"C":"E":"D":"E":"F":"G":"H":"I":"J":"K":"L":"O":"P":"Q":"R":"S":"T":"U":"V":"W":"X":"Y":"Z";
hold:=@ReplaceSubstring(sourceList;fromList;"");
@If(@Trim(hold)="";"":@Return("");"");
@If(@Length(hold)<5
;
 @Prompt([OK];"Error";"Make sure your ZIP code is at least 5 characters in
length.")
 :
 @Return(hold)
;
 " "
)
;
```

```
@If(@Length(hold)=5
 ;
 hold
 ;
 @If(@Length(hold)!=9;
  @Return(@Left(hold;5)+"-"+"????")
  ;
  @Left(hold;5)+"-"+@Right(hold;@Length(hold)-5)
  )
)
```

Take Advantage of Subforms

The subform design element was introduced in release 4.0 of Notes. Subforms come in basically two flavors, standard and computed, and should be thought of in the same light as shared fields. In essence, a *subform* is a collection of fields that can be added to a form as a single design element. When a document is composed with a particular subform, the fields on the subform become part of the document. The fields are referenced in @Functions and script just as they would be outside the subform.

During the iterative design process, try not to intentionally place fields within a subform. Instead, add the fields to a single form. When the design of the form is nearly complete, cut the fields and paste them into a new subform design. Then insert the subform into the old form on which you had the fields originally. This can help the designer visualize the integrity of form layout. In addition, try to avoid colored backgrounds on your main form because subforms do not support background color.

Subforms provide the advantage of shared design elements within a database. In addition, if the designer adds an action to the action bar within the subform, the form that uses such a subform will display the subforms actions to the right of the base or host form's actions.

Profile Documents

Profile documents provide a completely new document type that can be used programmatically to hold a single or several unique variables. They can best be thought of as a superior form of environment variable storage.

Profile documents are superior to environment variables because they do not show up in views but are still easily accessible. They are not like a hidden view for DbLookups,

Picklists. However, they can be used for this purpose. Profile documents offer many of the same functions and behaviors as environment variables, with a significant advantage being that they are stored in the Notes database, not in a Notes.ini or preferences file, which is stored on the local machine or Domino server. This means that Profile documents can be replicated.

The following are key attributes of Profile documents that set them apart from standard documents:

- ◆ Profile documents do not show in views.

- ◆ Profile documents are not counted in the document total. The information tab in the Properties dialog box for the database does not reflect Profile documents in the total document count.

- ◆ $NoPurge is an internal Notes field that is added to the document upon creation. The job of $NoPurge is to prevent the document from being removed from the database, no matter the purge interval setting.

- ◆ $Name stores the name of the person with whom the profile is associated.

- ◆ Profile documents are cached in much the same way as environment variables, the result is speedy access.

- ◆ Only one Profile document per person and per type can be created. If no user name is associated with a Profile document, it is assumed the document applies to the entire database. To create a document of this type, the creator must have designer rights to the database.

Begin by creating a form just as you would normally. Create the fields on the form that are to be referenced. On the Basics tab of the Properties dialog box for Form, remove the check marks next Menu and Search builder under Include in.

Creating the Profile Document

Referencing Profile documents can easily be done using the @Function language. The @EditProfile function creates a new Profile document if necessary or enables the editing of an existing one.

The syntax for @EditProfile is as follows:

```
@EditProfile([EditProfile]; formname [;username])
```

The formname argument is the name of the Profile document to be created or edited. The username is an optional argument. @UserName is used if you desire to create a user-specific document. This method is illustrated when creating a document for the telephone number. If the username argument is not used, Notes assumes only one document of type formname exists, and it edits that document.

In LotusScript, the equivalent command is the EditProfile method of the NotesUIWorkspace class.

Reading from the Profile Document

The value of Profile documents is their capability to read information as if Notes were reading a standard environment variable.

The syntax for reading an individual profile field is as follows:

```
@GetProfileField(profileName;fieldName [;UserName])
```

The equivalent in LotusScript would be to call the GetProfileDocument method of the NotesDocument class.

Writing to the Profile Document

To send values to a Notes Profile document, the following syntax is used:

```
@SetProfileField(profileName;fieldName [;UserName])
```

The related function in LotusScript is the EditProfile method of the NotesUIWorkspace class.

Summary

This chapter showed you how to construct dynamic variables that can be used both on the server and in any subdirectory on the local machine. It offered information concerning a better way to return multiple fields using only a single lookup formula. It showed you how to build comma-delimited files and offered methods to reduce view indexing time. The possibilities of view construction for an individual were covered. And finally, this chapter provided a complete overview about the new Profile document feature and how to use its power.

CHAPTER 15

Domino-Specific Application Development Considerations

L otus Domino provides the tools to create high-quality Internet and intranet sites. This chapter demonstrates how to take maximum advantage of these tools.

The skill set required to develop Web sites in Domino is the same as the skill set needed for developing databases in Notes. However, the information presented in this chapter helps you improve your Web site by using Domino-specific design features to significantly enhance the visual quality and functionality of your Web-based applications.

To demonstrate the most basic features of Domino, take any standard Notes database and place it on a Domino server. Then call up the database in a Web browser such as Netscape or Microsoft Internet Explorer. A surprising number of features continue to work over the Web. In fact, if you base your database on one of the standard Notes 4.5 templates, all the features may continue to work. Applications intended only for an intranet often have only one real requirement: functionality. Using Domino, you can move many existing Lotus Notes applications to your intranet with little modification. On the other hand, Internet applications must not only be functional, they must also be visually appealing. To achieve this level of quality, a proper Internet application needs to incorporate many Domino features.

Domino administrators play various roles in the creation, implementation, and maintenance of a Domino-powered Web site. First, the administrator must safeguard the integrity of both the site as a whole and of the individual applications hosted by the site. Security of the site as a whole is discussed in Chapter 24, "Security and Reporting." The current chapter presents an in-depth description of Domino's application-level security features, including the new significance of the default Access Control List setting.

Second, Domino administrators are often responsible for ensuring site continuity. Site continuity is achieved by following a set of guidelines that produce a common look and feel across all of your database. A consistent appearance is implemented through the use of special Domino-related fields and forms that are use to customize the appearance of documents, forms, and views when rendered on the Web.

Finally, although the primary responsibility for the development of databases may reside in theory with application developers, in practice, this may become part of the administrator's role. Previously completed applications, for example, can be selected for inclusion on the Web site. Certain modifications might need to be added by the administrator to ensure the quality of the application is consistent with the standards of the Web site as a whole. It is essential, therefore, that administrators are familiar with basic Notes development as well as with Domino-specific application development considerations.

This chapter provides the required knowledge for using Domino to create Web applications of the highest quality. First, the target audience of an application must be identified. Often both Notes and Internet/intranet clients need to be supported by an application. Second, an understanding of how HTML renders the basic features of a document greatly enhances appearance and functionality. Third, Domino's conversion of core Notes design elements—forms, views, and navigators—requires particular consideration. Fourth, Domino specific features, such as security requirements, Domino-related functions and commands, are addressed. Fifth, special Domino fields and forms are examined. Finally, advanced Internet features can also be included using Domino.

The theoretical information presented here will be augmented by applying it to the creation of a practical Web-based time tracking system in Chapter 16, "Building a Sample Web-Centric Application."

Notes or the Web

Before learning how to create a Web-based application, it is important to understand when a Web-based application should be created. The question of whether to go with a pure Notes or pure Domino solution appears quite simple at first. One might expect that the determining factor is based on the target audience: an external user requires a Domino-based Web application and an internal Notes user should have a standard Notes-based application. This solution seems logical because it is unlikely that you want to make the distribution of Lotus Notes to all your potential clients a requirement of your database implementation. But in regard to the internal user, the situation is not so clear.

Just because your clients have Notes on their desktops does not mean that the application needs to be Notes-based. In today's world, any of your clients who have Notes probably also have Netscape or some other Web browser. The decision concerning the target environment for your database is not based solely on whether the client group is internal or external. Consider these additional factors when deciding which environment your Notes application should target.

The following are reasons to provide access to your Notes databases to clients via their Web browser software instead of their Lotus Notes client software:

◆ Web-based applications normally generate less network traffic than Notes-based applications for a number of reasons. For instance, a properly designed Domino application takes advantage of the cache in the client Web browser to reduce the number of times the same image is downloaded.

◆ Web-based applications require no installation of additional software or drivers at the user's workstation. The server performs all the access to backend data such as Oracle, so only the server needs to have the special software installed.

◆ Notes-based applications require that every user have Lotus Notes installed. Web-based applications run on any Web browser.

◆ Domino supports effective logging of all requests. This allows the generation of detailed usage statistics.

◆ Domino applications move easily from an intranet to the Internet because design elements within both environments are identical.

◆ Users can register themselves for the Domino environment. Only a Notes administrator can register Notes users.

◆ Web-based applications can incorporate animated GIFs, ActiveX, Java, and other formats.

Programming choices in Notes are evaluated by comparing the benefits and trade-offs of the individual approaches. The choice between Web-based and standard Notes-based databases also has trade-offs.

The following are some reasons for creating standard Notes-based databases:

◆ Screen items can refresh in real time based on their dependencies upon other fields on the same form. For instance, a budget system can calculate totals every time a user updates a value.

◆ Applications can be extremely interactive. Buttons, field exits, and many other design features enable Notes to perform actions based on the user's activity. Web-based applications cannot perform any activities except for calling another document or submitting the current document.

◆ Embedded graphics may distort over the Web.

◆ The appearance of the interface on the client desktop matches the development environment in a pure Notes database. Web-based databases usually need some tweaking to maintain their appearance.

◆ Security is better in Notes due to private/public key encryption.

◆ A Web-based navigator must be a single image with hotspots. This is much harder to create than a simple button-based navigator.

◆ Navigation aids such as navigators or action bars become essential for operating the database because Web-based applications have no other menu system.

◆ Notes users can activate embedded objects if they have the correct software. Embedded objects cannot be activated and appear only as images over the Web.

◆ Complex tasks are easier to program in standard Notes applications because LotusScript code can be placed just about anywhere. Over the Web, script code only runs when the document is opened or saved.

Both Domino- and Notes-based applications have strong points. When designing internal applications, a number of factors should be considered when deciding which environment to target. Domino applications are not just for the Internet.

Another decision that needs to be made for every Domino application is whether a standard Notes interface is required in addition to the Web interface. Rather than design for one environment or the other, it is possible to create a Lotus Notes database that works in both the Notes environment and the Web environment. A typical database probably requires no more than a 20 percent increase in development time to make it work in both environments. The example in Chapter 16 demonstrates the creation of a database that operates properly for both the Notes clients and Web clients.

HTML Rendering

With the exception of some rare Java or ActiveX applications, the World Wide Web is entirely based on HyperText Markup Language (HTML). Even complex CGI-based systems that connect to Oracle or other backend data repositories use HTML as the format for interaction with the user. Because HTML is an industry standard markup language, HTML authors are limited to using only the formatting features that are included in the defined standard. If a desired format cannot be achieved using pure HTML, then it is also not achievable using Domino. Domino is merely a Web server task that renders a Notes object as HTML. Understanding this rendering of Notes objects into HTML pages is important for a Domino Web developer. An application developer's creative use of the HTML language is a requirement for producing an artistic Web site. One can become quite an effective Web programmer using only Notes programming techniques and Domino. Yet to be a leading developer, who produces Web sites of the highest quality, a developer should thoroughly understand HTML.

As little as one afternoon of training followed by a week of practical experience can turn a person with little programming experience into a very effective HTML author. This section and its supporting subsections describe how to use HTML and Domino together to create the best Web databases possible.

HTML is an ASCII-based format. If you view a typical Internet document through a plain text editor you see a rather simple set of text surrounded by a number of formatting tags. The following sample code provides an example of an HTML document that contains a table:

```
<HTML>
<BODY BGCOLOR=#C0C0C0>
<H1>Demo Page</H1>
<TABLE BORDER=3>
  <TR><TH COLSPAN=2>This is a table</TH></TR>
  <TR><TD COLSPAN=2>This is the second row</TD></TR>
  <TR><TD>This is a cell</TD>
  <TD><B>This is another cell in the same row</B></TD></TR>
</TABLE>
</HTML>
```

HTML works through the use of pairs of open and close tags. For instance, <B> means start bold text and </B> means stop bold text. Tag pairs can also be nested inside other tag pairs to provide compound text attributes. Tables can even be nested within other tables.

HTML has two peculiarities that you need to take into account. First, Web browsers reduce multiple spaces to a single space, and second, hard returns and tabs are ignored completely. When viewed through a Web browser, the previous code listing produces the document illustrated in figure 15.1.

Figure 15.1

A sample HTML document.

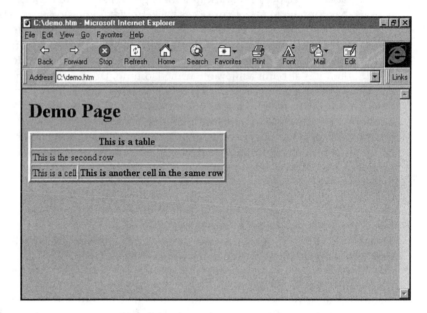

This chapter is not intended to be a manual for HTML coding. Many excellent HTML guides are available in bookstores and over the Internet if you wish to have a complete list of tags. The following sections describe how Domino renders text, tables, and graphic objects into HTML. The descriptions focus on the resulting HTML document's appearance in a Web browser and include detailed discussion of the steps required to refine the quality of this appearance.

Text Rendering

Domino renders all text within a document into HTML when the document is viewed over the Web. The nature of the text, be it part of the static text placed on the form by the designer, text entered by a document author, or text imported from a word processor file, does not matter.

Creating exciting-looking documents is a matter of maximizing the formatting options within the HTML language. Domino makes this quite easy because you need only design the form using normal Notes features; Domino handles the conversion to HTML. If users need to create complex documents on the Web, then as a designer you simply put a rich text field on the form. Domino converts any formatting that the user inserts within the rich text field.

When Domino makes this conversion, it is important to keep in mind that, unlike Notes, HTML supports only a limited number of format options. For instance, HTML only supports only seven font sizes, although Notes supports any font size from 1 to 250 points. Domino handles this limitation by mapping Notes font ranges to specific font sizes in HTML according to table 15.1.

TABLE 15.1
Font Pitch Rendering by Domino

Notes Point Size	Web Font Size
1 to 7	1
8 or 9	2
10 or 11	3
12 or 13	4
14 to 17	5
18 to 23	6
24 to 250	7

The font ranges shown in table 15.1 may be slightly different from those given in the online documentation. As a developer, you may want to try a number of font sizes on your own system to determine whether your font mapping matches table 15.1 or the Notes online documentation. Figures 15.2 and 15.3 demonstrate text pitch rendering by Domino.

Another issue to keep in mind is that the seven font sizes supported by HTML do not necessarily correspond to a specific point count. The point count for each font size is a property of the browser and can normally be reconfigured by the user. Those who have been coding HTML for some time have often made use of a concept of heading levels <h1> through <h6> rather than font sizes. Domino does not make any use of the headings tags. Apart from the font size, Domino properly converts all font attributes within Lotus Notes other than Shadow, Emboss, and Extrude.

One of the strange features of HTML is that the Web browser trims multiple spaces in proportional text down to a single space. This means that any formatting in the data or the form design that is based on spaces does not render properly over the Web.

Figure 15.2

Demonstration of text options inside a Notes memo.

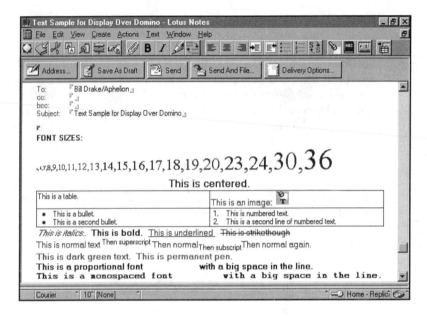

Figure 15.3

Text options as rendered over the Web by Domino.

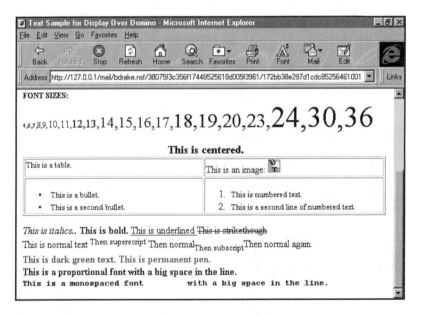

Two methods of maintaining formatting in Web documents are common. The first method is the most common and involves putting formatted data into tables. This method is discussed in the "Alignment" section later in this chapter. The second method is to use a monospaced font such as Courier. HTML does not trim spaces from monospaced text so your formatting is maintained. Domino renders both tables and monospaced fonts properly. An important caveat to keep in mind, however, is that monospaced text does not look as good as proportional text. For this reason, it is very rare to find monospaced text on Web sites.

The other strange property of HTML is that the browsers ignore hard return codes. The break or <BR> tag is used to indicate a line feed rather than the normal ASCII character 010 or character 013 codes. This is not a problem in the Domino environment because Domino renders a line feed character properly as a <BR>. Appearance is a significant aspect of a Web site and a Domino designer can expect to spend a major portion of the development time on the visual aspects of the Notes database. Figure 15.2 demonstrates the most common Notes text options.

The memo form within Notes mail is used to create the document shown in figure 15.2. The Text Options menu is used to perform the text formatting. This same document is then saved and called up in a Web browser via the Domino server. The result is figure 15.3, the Domino-rendered Web version of the same document.

Tables

Tables are even more important over the Web than they are in Notes. In Notes, tables are important for ensuring the proper alignment of multi-row, multi-column data. Over the Web, tables become essential for almost all layout control. Understanding how Domino renders tables is important for the developer. The "Alignment" section of this chapter builds upon this knowledge for controlling the appearance of rendered HTML documents. Keep two important aspects in mind when developing tables:

- ◆ **Column width settings do not apply in HTML.** In fact, HTML tables are normally as wide as the browser window. When a table occurs within a document your Web browser downloads the entire table and then formats the cell width and height so that the column width fits the widest entry. Just as do Notes table cells, HTML table cells support word wrap.

- ◆ **Table borders have many options within HTML.** The Domino rendering only supports two styles: borders off or double border. Domino checks the border setting of the top-left cell of the table within Notes when it is creating the HTML version of the document. Domino creates the HTML table border options for the entire table based on this single cell. If borders of any size are anywhere around the first cell in Notes, then Domino renders the table with double borders; otherwise the borders are off.

Graphics

Probably the most important part of any Web site, graphics generally appear on every page of a Web site. Graphics are not actually stored in HTML files. HTML makes use of graphics by containing references to discrete graphics files. When a Web user retrieves an HTML document, he is actually retrieving not just the HTML document, but also each of the graphic files that are referenced within the HTML document. Notes stores graphics as embedded bitmap files and Domino renders them as Graphics Interchange Format (GIF) or Joint Photographic Experts Group (JPEG) files. From a pure Notes perspective, embedded graphics, in design elements or document content, are stored as two versions: a platform-dependant metafile and a 256-color platform-independent bitmap. Domino uses the platform-independent bitmap. Domino renders the bitmap as either a GIF or JPEG file depending on a setting within the server document.

Understanding the way Domino treats graphics is important for the Domino application developer. Unlike most of the other Notes design features, graphic design features do not always render properly. In fact, the developer must use graphics in very specific ways for them to even work. The following sections contain information on using graphics effectively in Domino. The Notes Color Palette sometimes causes graphics to look different in Notes than they do over the Web. Passthru HTML provides a technique that can be used to guarantee complete control over the graphics files as well as many of the other design features. The "Image Scaling" section alerts developers to the potential problems related to resizing images within Notes. There are several approaches for making background images and colors work properly over Domino. Animated and transparent GIFs are two graphic types that you can use in Web applications. Images in the form of graphic buttons can act as links to other pages. A graphics library is an example of an advanced manner of storing stand-alone image files. The final discussion on repeating images builds upon the graphics library to optimize the performance of the Web site.

Color Palette

When a graphic is imported or pasted into Notes, not only is its format converted, but so is its color palette. The color palette determines how the colors are represented. However, not every application uses the same 256 colors. Notes provides some files (LOTUS.ACT and LOTUS.PAL) that are available on the Lotus Web site that may be used by your graphics program to create images with the proper palette from the very beginning. This type of graphic work is normally performed by a graphic artist or by someone who is an expert with advanced graphic packages such as CorelDRAW! or Adobe Photoshop. However, it normally falls upon the application developer to ensure that the final result has the proper appearance.

It is important to note that the color problems you might experience occur not just in the Web-based environment, but also in the Notes environment. In the Notes environment, you must work around the color problems by changing the original source file. In the Web environment, that choice is still available, but passthru HTML provides an even better option.

Passthru HTML

Domino supports a concept called passthru HTML. Passthru HTML enables the Notes developer or the Notes user to create complex HTML documents by entering their documents directly in HTML format. Passthru HTML eliminates any shortcomings in the Domino rendering by bypassing the conversion step altogether. If Domino does not provide an adequate rendering of a Notes feature, then passthru HTML can be used to create the desired result by entering HTML tags directly in the text of a Notes document.

Passthru HTML is exactly what the name implies: an attribute that tells Domino to pass the HTML text through to the Internet without trying to translate it. You can use passthru HTML not only for graphic references, but also for any other object or formatting code.

You can create passthru HTML in two ways. The first and most common method is to simply include the passthru text within square brackets. The following line of text would refer to an image file called logo.gif using this approach:

```
[<img src="\logo.gif">]
```

The second method is to use a paragraph style called HTML. If this paragraph style is not already available, then it is easily created using the Text, Properties, Create Style option in Notes and then typing HTML as the style name. The text would then appear as:

```
<img src="\logo.gif">
```

Notice that the two lines of text are identical except for the square brackets. Figure 15.4 provides an example of both of the previous methods for creating passthru HTML. The table cell on the left has the graphic embedded. The table cell in the center has no special attributes and will not work. The table cell on the right refers to the graphic using passthru HTML identified by square brackets. The reference below the table uses the HTML paragraph style.

Three points to remember when using passthru HTML are:

◆ The HTML paragraph style cannot be used within tables. Instead include the passthru text within square brackets.

◆ All text formatting is ignored and only the ASCII version of the text is delivered in HTML.

◆ The Internet ignores hard returns, so you must include a <BR> tag wherever you want a hard return to appear.

Reading the preceding items may leave you with the impression that passthru HTML is only for text. This is an accurate impression. The HTML text is extremely versatile, however. HTML can also be used to reference graphics and other objects. Graphics are never actually stored in HTML; they are identified by reference only. The references correspond to stand-alone files that are loaded separately by the browser, which then merges them back into the document. Effectively, passthru HTML need only deal with text, regardless of the data type of the object that is being referenced.

Figure 15.4

Passthru HTML used to reference an image file.

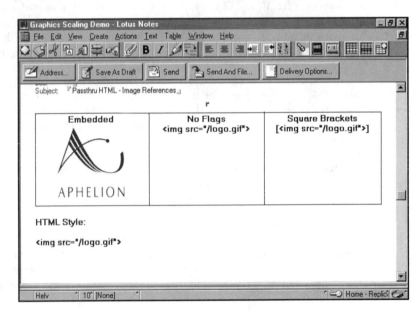

This same document, seen through Microsoft Internet Explorer after it has been rendered by Domino, appears as in figure 15.5.

Look at the results in figure 15.5. As expected, the embedded graphic in the left cell of the table renders properly. The text in the center cell simply renders as plain text despite looking like HTML. The passthru HTML identified by the square brackets in the right-hand cell also renders properly. The passthru HTML below the table also appears to render properly. Notice, however, that the bold attribute on the label and the hard returns above the graphic had no effect. This is expected behavior because Web browsers require a <BR> tag to include a hard return and a <B> tag to produce bold text.

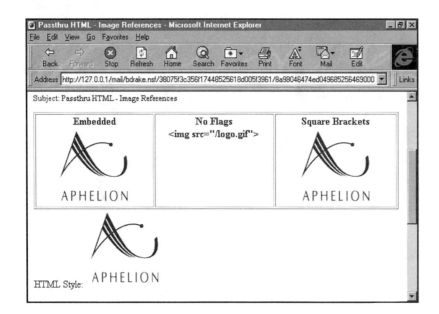

Figure 15.5

Passthru HTML sample as seen in Internet Explorer.

Image Scaling

Domino renders image size and scaling properly when it creates the necessary HTML codes. If the browser supports scaling, the graphic appears as it does in Notes; otherwise the graphic appears in the size in which it was originally created. Inside HTML the scaling code is simply a hard-coded reference to the width and height of the displayed version of the image:

```
<IMG SRC="/logo.gif" WIDTH=159 HEIGHT=156>
```

Just as scaling produces poor results in Notes, it also produces poor results on the Web. Domino renders the scaling properly into the HTML code. The problem occurs when the browser adjusts the size of the graphic to the specified scale. If an image needs to be resized then it should be resized by a graphics package not by a Web browser. To achieve this result, always resize images in the same package that creates them rather than in Notes. Figure 15.6 shows the same image twice, once at the original size and once resized in Notes by about 20 percent.

Notice that the resized image on the right has more jagged edges and that the text is distorted. Only the simplest graphic images scale properly, so scaling is best avoided altogether.

Figure 15.6

*Resized graphic
results.*

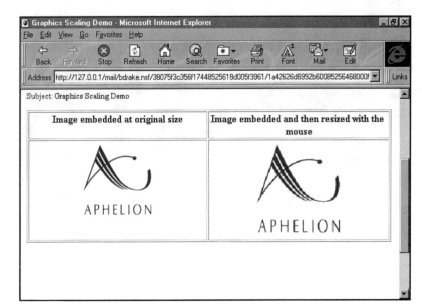

Backgrounds

Background images are commonplace on the Internet. Look at just about any Web
site and you can find graphic backgrounds. Web browsers render background images
in their original size as repeating tiled images. There are three ways to create background images: the background property, the $Background field, or passthru HTML.

In Notes 4.5 and above, set the background property in design mode by using the
Properties dialog box, and clicking on the Paste Graphic button under the Background tab. This method applies the same background to all documents that use this
form.

An alternate option that works in any Notes 4 version is to create a rich text field
called $Background on the form. The graphic must then be pasted into the $Back-
ground field by the user creating each individual document. Do not forget to hide
the $Background field when not in edit mode; otherwise it displays as both a back-
ground and an embedded image when rendered over the Web.

The disadvantage of this approach is that the person composing the form must place
the image into the $Background field in order for it to appear. Alternatively, the
advantage of this approach is that because the users are responsible for inserting the
image, they have the flexibility of choosing a different background image for every
document.

The final approach for creating background images is to set the appropriate HTML code using passthru HTML. The necessary code for referencing an image file called logo.gif using passthru HTML is:

```
[<BODY BACKGROUND="/logo.gif">]
```

The passthru HTML can either be included in the form design or typed in by the user.

When creating background images, keep in mind that the images need to be kept quite simple in order not to detract from the real content of the document.

Solid colored backgrounds are also common on the Web. Normally, Web pages are designed to maintain proper appearance in your own Web browser. Your Web browser may have a different default background than your neighbor's Web browser. Simply coding a background color into the rendered HTML page is much safer than gambling on the different default setting of each user's browser. This way you as designer can take complete control of the appearance.

Background colors can be created in a different ways. The easiest method is again accomplished in design mode, by using the Properties dialog box and selecting a color from the color picklist under the Background tab. This produces the same background color for every page. A more dynamic method is to create a numeric field called $PaperColor and set it to the appropriate value.

Lotus has an excellent sample database available for downloading from www.lotus.com called Color Swatches, which demonstrates this concept. By using a special field, the developer can create a form where the background color of the page changes depending on values stored in other fields on the form. For example, in a Web-based help desk application, urgent requests can be given a red background using a computed formula for $PaperColor similar to:

```
@If(Status="Urgent";2;1)
```

The complete color list is available in the Color Swatches sample database. The colors corresponding to the first 10 values of 0 through 9 for $PaperColor are: black, white, red, green, blue, magenta, yellow, cyan, dark red, and dark green.

Passthru HTML is also an option for determining the background color. To use passthru HTML simply type in a line of text similar to the following:

```
[<BODY BGCOLOR="FFFFFF">]
```

"FFFFFF" is the code corresponding to a white background. Normally backgrounds are either not set or they are set to white or light gray. The color code for light gray is "C0C0C0." Just like graphical backgrounds, dark background colors make it difficult to read the content of the document.

Animated GIFs

Lotus Notes does not support animated GIFs. That means that you cannot embed them in your documents. Nonetheless, they are still quite easy to use in Domino with passthru HTML. The actual graphic is stored in the file storage area; therfore it does not need to be supported within Notes. The passthru code appears within the document as follows:

```
[<img src="/animatedlogo.gif">]
```

Transparent GIFs

Transparent GIFs are supported in Notes 4.5 and above, but only through the Import function and not through Paste. Pasted transparent GIFs lose their transparency. For versions of Notes below 4.5, use passthru HTML to refer to the GIF that is stored in the file storage area.

Positioning Images

Positioning images explicitly is not possible in Notes. It is, however, possible in passthrough HTML. Rather than trying to adjust the position of an image by hard coding it, it is both easier and quicker to position an image by placing it in a table.

Graphic Buttons

Graphic buttons are commonplace on every Web site. An example of a graphic button is an image of a telephone that connects to a corporate directory, or an image of a clock that connects to a time tracking system.

In a normal HTML document on the Web, buttons are just links to other documents. Domino restricts the way that buttons may be used in applications. Refer to the "Forms" section later in this chapter for a detailed description of using standard buttons in Domino.

Graphic objects, on the other hand, are normally either simply present for visual appeal or they can be linked to other Notes objects such as documents or views. You can create graphic buttons in four ways:

◆ Paste the graphic into Notes then select Create, Hotspot, URL Link. Type the URL into the prompt box. The image now works as a link to the URL both in Notes and on the Web.

◆ Paste the graphic into Notes, then select a document or view and select Edit, Copy as Link, View Link or Document Link. Highlight the graphic and select Create, Hotspot, Link Hotspot. The graphic image now works as a link both in Notes and on the Web.

◆ Paste the graphic into Notes, then highlight the image and select Create, Hotspot, Text Popup. Enter the URL as passthru HTML. This link only works over the Web. In the Notes environment, clicking on the image only brings up a text box with the URL written inside it.

◆ Do not paste the image into Notes. Use passthru HTML for the entire code. The text appears as:

```
[<a href = "www.lotus.com"><img src="/lotuslogo.gif"></a>]
```

Graphics Library

You can store graphics for your Web site in any of three ways:

◆ The first and most common method for storing graphics for your Web site is storing graphics in the HTML file area in the root directory or in their own directory. In this case all graphics are referred to using HTML passthru in a format such as: [<IMG SRC = "/logo.gif">] for graphics stored in the root HTML directory, or as: [<IMG SRC = "/graphics/logo.gif">] for graphics stored in the graphics subdirectory below the HTML directory. This is the easiest method that retains all the features of the image. This approach has one major downside, though: someone needs to have access to the Domino server's hard drive to place the files.

◆ The second method involves simply embedding the graphics within the design elements. This is the quickest method. The downside to this approach is the potential rendering problems discussed earlier in this chapter. This is the only method that provides full compatibility in Notes.

◆ The third method is to use a graphics repository in a Notes database to hold the graphic files. This is the best method in terms of ongoing maintenance because the graphics are managed from any Notes client. Make all references to these graphics using passthru HTML.

To create a repository database, create a new database and add a form called Attachments and a view called Files. The Attachments form needs only one rich text field to hold the attachment. The view only needs one sorted column based on the attachment file name using the following formula:

```
@LowerCase(@AttachmentNames)
```

Next, attach graphics by composing a new Attachments document and attaching one image per document. For a repository named graphics.nsf, refer to the graphics as:

```
[<img src="/graphics.nsf/Files/logo.gif/$File/logo.gif?OpenElement">]
```

The ?OpenElement part of this URL is actually optional so the shorter form of the same URL is:

```
[<img src="/graphics.nsf/Files/logo.gif/$File/logo.gif">]
```

Rather than use a central repository, developers can create this graphics storage area within each individual database. The developer can thereby guarantee that all replicas continue to work because the database is entirely self-contained. In other words, since the graphics files are stored in the same database as the documents, that single database file is all that is required in order to ensure the same functionality in all replicas.

Repeating Graphics

Consistent look and feel in a Web site is important to make the site user-friendly. Graphic headers on each page are typical in most sites. Figure 15.7 shows a typical header.

Figure 15.7

A typical Web page header.

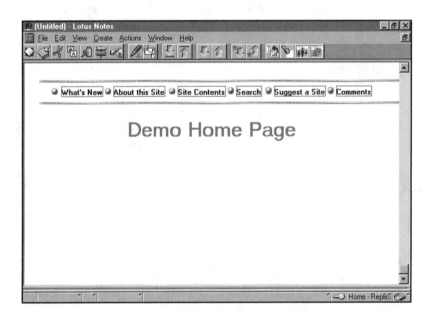

Notice how the bullets in front of each menu option and the bars above and below create a recognizable theme for the Web site. This header appears on every page on the Web site. However, if you open it in Internet Explorer or Netscape, you notice something quite strange. The document loads the bars and the bullets one image at a time. If you open this document over a slow modem, you see each image download separately. This can be annoying to anyone hitting your site. The reason this happens is that Domino has no way of knowing that these are all the same image. After pasted into Notes, the images lose their original identity. As far as Notes is concerned, they are unique images. Again, you can eliminate this problem by using passthru HTML within the header to reference the source image files directly. Use the following line to replace each individual bar:

```
[<img src="/graphics.nsf/Files/yellowbar.gif/$File/yellowbar.gif">]
```

Similarly, replace each of the colored bullets with the next line:

```
[<img src="/graphics.nsf/Files/yellowball.gif/$File/yellowball.gif">]
```

These two small changes result in one download of the colored bars rather than two and one download of the colored bullets rather than six. If the footer is similar to the header, then the benefits continue to get even better. Instead of downloading 16 graphic files, the users only need to download two graphic files. This will have an enormous impact on the response time for your Web site.

This completes the discussion of basic rendering of Notes objects over Domino. HTML can be used to enhance the default rendering of text, tables, and graphics. The knowledge gained in this section will now be applied to the basic Notes design objects in order to understand the complete picture.

Domino Conversion of Notes Core Design Elements

Database users are only aware of the three main design elements that are used in Lotus Notes development: forms, views, and navigators. This section deals with these design elements and their rendering by Domino. These design objects are converted using the same guidelines that were presented in the previous section on HTML rendering. The earlier information provides the groundwork for this discussion.

Domino also provides a few extra conversion options to improve the quality of your Web site further. The Domino rendering of Notes forms and the developer's approach to maximizing the quality of the Internet forms is discussed first. Placing your Notes views on the Internet requires the developer to make some decisions on view numbers and content. The views section helps you make those decisions by describing how Domino renders views over the Web. Finally, this section concludes by describing the Domino aspects of developing Notes navigators for use on the Web.

Forms

Forms are probably the easiest part of your Web-based database to create. As an exercise, design a Notes form without using any buttons in the form design, create a document using this form within the Notes environment, and then call it up in your Web browser. Notice that the form is still completely functional for reading.

This section presents some form-related topics that allow a developer to create Web-based applications with the same quality of appearance as the Notes-based applications. Tables can be used to control formatting. Passthru HTML is helpful in the creation of a reset button that is not supported directly by Domino. Editing a document or creating a new document is not a trivial process on the Internet; these options will also be discussed. Finally, large blocks of HTML can be included using specially formatted editable fields. These discussions provide the information that the developer needs to ensure that there is little or no loss in functionality over the Web.

Alignment

Once more, design a Notes form without using any buttons in the form design, create a document using this form within the Notes environment, and then call it up in your Web browser. The only potential problem that you notice relates to the appearance of the form. These appearance problems arise because HTML ignores spaces and tabs. Now go back to the original form design. If you remove all the extra spaces and tabs, it looks similar to the Web version. The fields are now aligned immediately against the static text labels. If you had several fields on the same line, they are now run together into a single string. Anywhere that you used tabs to create a column in the Notes document the formatting is now gone. The obvious question now becomes, how is appearance maintained without the use of spaces or tabs? The answer is to use tables wherever formatting is required.

You probably do not want the table borders to always appear over the Web. To remove the border from the Web version simply remove the border of the top left cell in Notes. In a typical Web-based database, many of the fields need to be placed in tables to achieve good results.

Another issue to keep in mind is that Web browsers resolve tables by downloading the entire table before rendering it to determine the column widths. This can result in lengthy delays before anything is displayed to the user. To improve performance at the browser side for large documents with many fields, do not put your entire design into a single table; instead, create multiple tables. By using multiple tables, the browser will download and display the tables sequentially. The first table will then be able to display while the second table is still downloading. When you create these tables do not spend too much time adjusting the column widths in Notes. Column widths are ignored by Domino and are resized by the user's Web browser.

Buttons

If you do not already have a Submit button, Domino automatically inserts one at the end of a document when the user is in edit mode over the Web. By inserting your own button you can change the label from Submit to anything you want, and you can also control the position of the button. Remember that this button will perform the submit function regardless of the button's formula. To insert a button, select Create, Hotspot, Button. Domino only uses the first button that appears on the form. No other buttons are rendered by Domino, so they do not appear over the Web. In read-only mode, buttons do not appear at all.

When you are filling in an HTML form over the Web, in any environment except Domino, the form usually has two buttons:

◆ Submit

◆ Reset

Reset is used to clear the contents of the editable fields. Although Domino only supports the Submit button, you can create a reset button with passthru HTML by entering the following line of code:

```
[<INPUT TYPE="Reset" VALUE="Reset">]
```

Normally this button appears near the Submit button.

Edit or Create Over the Web

The concepts of read mode and edit mode do not exist on the Internet. The Internet achieves this same goal with HTML documents for reading and HTML forms for editing. Unlike in Notes, the two objects have no connection. A user cannot simply look at a document and then switch to edit mode on demand. Instead a user can look at a document and then submit a request to the server to see the same document as an HTML form. The Domino server makes it easy to request the same document in such a way that users can have the impression that all they did was switch modes. To make this request the user needs a graphic link to click upon. A graphic link is made by creating a Form Action in Notes. Domino renders certain Form Actions over the Web.

Your first tendency might be to simply take the predefined system action or the simple action for Edit Document and put that on the action bar. However, Domino does not support a number of common Notes design approaches, particularly the following:

◆ System actions

◆ Simple actions

◆ LotusScript in actions

Domino does support actions using @Commands. For the Edit Action example, the formula for the action is:

```
@Command([EditDocument])
```

The designer can include the icon with this action if desired. Similarly, if the designer wants to allow users to create new documents, an action can be created with the following formula:

```
@Command([Compose];"Response")
```

The "@Command" section later in this chapter provides a list of the Domino-supported @Commands.

Formatting Data Entry Fields

You have learned how to create a document that maintains its alignment over the Web. You have also learned how to request the currently displayed document back from the server as an HTML form. If you stop development at this point and call up a document it appears as it does in figure 15.8.

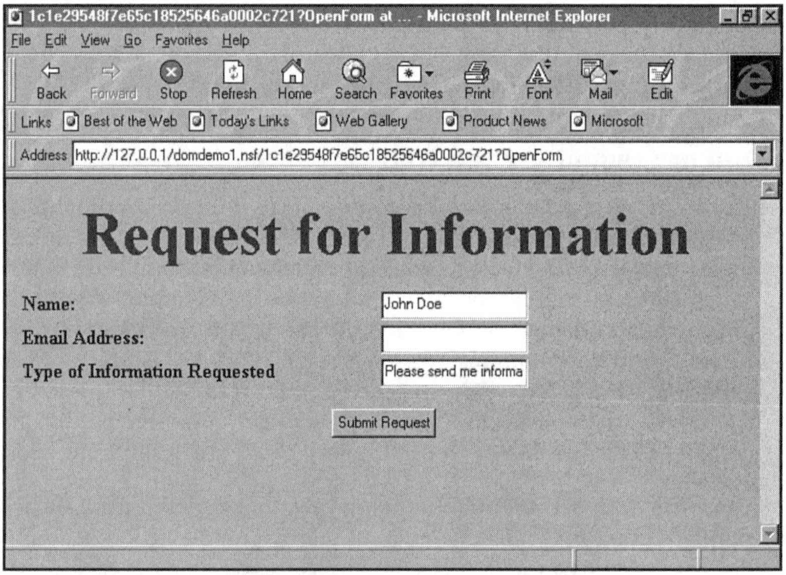

Figure 15.8

Editing a document over the Web.

Notice that the document looks quite good. A table was used so all the fields line up properly. A button was added with a button label of Submit Request so that the label and position are controlled. The data entry fields, however, have a problem. Notice that they are all very short. When a Web user tries to use this form, the text scrolls as he or she types; but the data entry window remains the same size. Users find this extremely difficult to use. To remedy this problem, Domino can be instructed to change the field size that it renders over the Web. To modify a field size, enter passthru HTML in the Help description area under the Options tab within the Field Properties dialog box.

Depending on its data type, fields require different treatment in order to be resized:

◆ For regular text fields a valid entry for the Help description appears as [<SIZE=30 MAXLENGTH=40>]. This creates a data entry box of 30 characters in length that accepts up to 40 characters. Because the default browser font may be proportional, the actual numbers of characters varies a little.

◆ For rich text fields the valid entry is [<rows=3 cols=35>] or [<wrap=virtual>]. The number of rows corresponds to the number of lines. The number of columns corresponds to the width of the data entry. If wrap=virtual then automatic word wrap is enabled.

◆ For keyword fields the valid entry is [<size=5>]. The number in the size statement specifies the maximum number of entries to display before displaying the scrollbar.

Figure 15.9 shows the same form as figure 15.8. The field help descriptions were filled in using [<SIZE=30 MAXLENGTH=40>] for the first two text fields. The third field was converted to rich text and was set to [<rows=3 cols=35>].

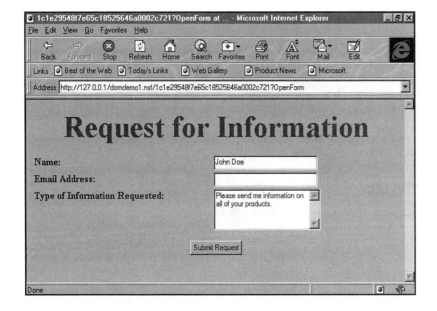

Figure 15.9

Editing a document over the Web with field lengths defined in the Help description.

Figure 15.9 demonstrates the importance of setting the field size for use on the Web. The form displayed in figure 15.9 is much easier for the users to fill in than the form in figure 15.8.

 Note Some browsers ignore the field length settings and fit the fields to size of the window. Developers should test their applications under a few different browsers to ensure a consistent appearance.

HTML Content

You can include HTML content in a couple of different ways. Passthru HTML and the HTML paragraph style have already been discussed. These are approaches for embedding HTML code with the standard Notes data. Some Web sites may want to include more hard-coded HTML, especially if the HTML originates outside of Lotus Notes. In order to support large blocks of HTML, create a field called HTML. In read mode, Domino serves up the contents of the HTML field without any changes. In edit mode, the HTML field is ignored.

This completes the discussion of Domino specific forms design. In the normal course of developing a Notes database, views are usually developed right after the forms are done.

Views

Views are probably the most important tool within Lotus Notes. Views enable you to categorize and sort data. Lotus Notes can work effectively with views containing thousands of documents. Notes users are quite accustomed to opening any view and then typing in a few letters to take them to the appropriate place within the view.

The Internet user, on the other hand, does not have this luxury. The Internet user can only access the portion of the view that is downloaded to him or her as HTML. Quick search is not an option. So how can the requirement of quick access to information for the Web user be satisfied? Using a search button is an obvious and effective option. This enables users to sort through enormous numbers of documents quite quickly. The problem with this solution is that it does not meet the needs of the Internet user who prefers to peruse through your site looking for information.

This typical Internet user may not have a specific keyword in mind; but may instead be hoping to find documents by moving through the conceptual groupings that you have created. You can create these groupings in a number of ways. The first method to consider is the use of collapsed categories. Collapsed categories present the user with all the major information groupings in one page. The user can then drill down through the information collections by simply opening the appropriate sections.

Be aware, however, of some major caveats in this approach. For instance, the use of twisties is not an intuitive process. Twisties may work extremely well for intranet or specialized sites where users have had some training or have built up experience at using the site. Twisties do not work as well over the Internet where a large percentage of daily hits come from first-time users. Users today expect a graphical and intuitive approach to finding information. Domino provides a number of approaches for creating a more impressive Web site. The most common are the following:

◆ **Create a separate view for each category.** Consider this option if the main categories in the database are static. This method eliminates the twisties from the view because the category name is in the design of the view and not in the view data. This method also enables the designer to create an image to represent each category and then to create a page that uses the linked images to bring up the document lists. This method results in a graphical Web site, while still maintaining the benefits of document management within Notes.

◆ **Do not use views at all.** Use hypertext links within documents. Before Domino existed, Web sites were often coded in HTML entirely by hand. Links were maintained by manually updating numerous documents each time a new document was added or an old document was deleted. Notes provides an easier approach through the use of doclinks. The concept behind this approach is that documents are connected together at the document level rather than at the view level. If a document needs to appear within the information collection, a link must be created to it from another document. These links can be text-based or graphical. This approach results in a high-maintenance site because links have to be created and periodically verified. If errors can be avoided, this brute force approach can result in a very high-quality site.

◆ **Do not provide an interface to the documents.** Many large data sets on the Internet have a search screen as their only interface. Unlike Notes servers, most other repositories lack an interface. Searching is often the only way to get information out of these systems. In certain cases, however, nothing is wrong with using a search screen as a primary interface. Domino provides the programming features to enable developers to create very effective custom search pages. This approach works best when dealing with very large numbers of documents. Just because Notes provides an easy method for creating interfaces does not mean that the developer needs to follow this approach.

Before making any changes to the way views appear over the Web, you should have a thorough understanding of how the default view format works. To see the default format, take any non-Web database or create a new database and then open a view. You should see something similar to figure 15.10.

Figure 15.10

The default view format rendered over the Web by Domino.

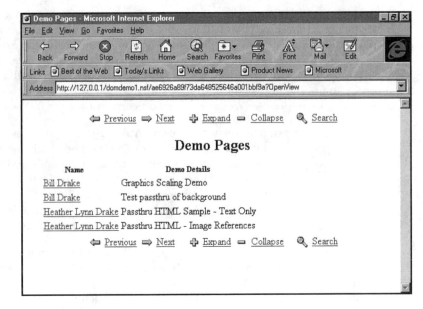

The default view format has a number of properties:

◆ No actions are added, but the view on the Web does include compatible actions that were already in the Notes view.

◆ Previous, Next, Expand, Collapse, and Search buttons are included at the top and bottom of every page.

◆ The view title is placed in the center of the view in a larger font.

◆ Multi-line features are supported.

◆ View column icons are supported.

◆ Categories are supported.

◆ Expand and collapse are supported, but the only options are all categories or one category.

◆ Twisties are present to expand or collapse a single category. If a second twisty is activated while another category is already open, the first category closes when the new category opens.

◆ Resizable columns and "click on column header to sort" are not supported.

While looking at the rendered view, choose "View Source" and take note of the HTML code. Notice that the icons are loaded out of the file storage area and that a table is used to control the view format. This corresponds to some of the information presented earlier in this chapter. One of the annoying aspects of Notes views over the Web is the inclusion of the "previous" and "next" links regardless of whether the document actually has a previous or next page. Notice that the first non-categorized column is used as the link to the document. Consider re-arranging the columns if this column does not make the best link.

So far, only the default view appearance has been discussed. Some options are available while designing views to improve their appearance over the Web. Just like most of the other design elements, passthru HTML can be used to create very fancy columns that improve the appearance of the entire view. View actions can also be added to provide the user with some power beyond the opening of documents contained in the view.

Enhanced View Columns

You can include graphics in view columns in two ways: view column icons or passthru HTML. View column icons are standard Notes design features and will not be discussed here. Passthru HTML is Domino-specific and as in the previous examples can be used by simply enclosing the HTML text within square brackets. In this case, the HTML belongs in the view column formula. This approach allows Domino databases to show dramatic improvements over traditional Notes views. For example, the following column formula can be used in a Web-based help desk application:

```
testvalue:=Priority;
columnvalue:=ProblemDescription;
@If(testvalue="Urgent";
 "[<b><font color=\"FF0000\">"+columnvalue+"</font></b>]";
columnvalue)
```

This changes the font to bold and red for any problem report that has a priority of one. This makes the help desk view much more useful because the high priority requests stand out. To make the high priority tasks stand out even further, the fourth line of the code can be replaced by:

```
"[<img src=\"/graphics/animatedalert.gif\"><b>"+columnvalue+"</b>]";
```

This produces an animated alert GIF running in the column alongside the problem description. Do not try to use any special text attributes on the first non-categorized column. The font attributes may be ignored because the first non-categorized column is the link, which ends up with its own text attributes.

View Actions

Users often need to do more from the view than just open existing documents. Just as forms do, views rendered by Domino support view actions. A typical view action might include the option to return to home page or compose a new document. These buttons must be coded using @Commands to translate properly over the Web. To compose a new document, the view action has the following formula:

```
@Command([Compose];"Main")
```

To return to the homepage the view action has a formula similar to the following formula:

```
@URLOpen("//www.lotus.com")
```

Navigators

Image maps are Web graphics containing clickable regions that activate links. An image map of the United States, for example, might contain a clickable region or hotspot for each state. Notes supports a similar concept through the use of navigators. Domino can translate navigators into image maps only if the navigator uses a single background image containing hotspots. The background image of the navigator becomes the graphic, and the hotspot polygons and rectangles become the image map regions. Pasted images and buttons are ignored when Domino renders the navigator.

Domino supports both server-side and client-side image maps. The hotspots can be simple actions to open views, databases, documents, or navigators. The hotspots can also be based on a formula. For instance, the formula can check whether the client is a Web user or Notes user and then go to a specific view. The following code listing is an example of a possible approach:

```
IsWebClient:=@IsMember("WebClient";@UserRoles);
@If(IsWebClient;
    @Command([OpenView];"WebView");
  @Command([OpenView];"NotesView"))
```

The @UserRoles function is described in the "@Function" section later in this chapter.

Domino-Specific Development Issues and Commands

The preceding sections of this chapter have shown how Domino renders Notes databases for the Web. In the preceding section, brief mention was made of the @UserRoles function in one of the code examples. This section explains how to use the @UserRoles function as well as the other commands and functions that relate to Domino development. The section begins with a discussion of security. Security assumes a new importance in Web-based applications. Web users have anonymous identities until the developer implements certain steps.

Certain @Functions, such as @UserRoles, @URLOpen, @DbCommand, and others take on special significance in Web applications. Other @Functions, such as @Environment, @Prompt, and @DeleteDocument, do not work at all over the Web. A similar discussion will also take place for @Commands. Within the Domino environment, @Commands are limited to operations dealing with opening new pages. The Domino-specific features of certain @Functions and @Commands are examined in detail. This section concludes by introducing a new method of calling up pages by URL that can be used in place of the @Commands.

Security

Domino enables Web browsers to replace Notes desktops. To protect your data, therefore, some sort of security must apply to users accessing data via the Web. Naturally one cannot distribute Notes ID files to every possible user on the Internet. The necessary alternative is for Domino to use standard Internet security. Domino performs basic authentication over the Internet based on user name and password only. This type of authentication precludes public key/private key encryption; in fact, Domino does not normally use encryption of any kind, unless SSL is used. The concept of SSL allows users to connect to the Web site using an enhanced level of authentication and encryption.

The following list presents some of the security differences between Notes and the Web:

◆ The users themselves, through the registration database, perform Web user registration. In a standard Notes environment, the Notes administrator performs registration.

◆ Authentication in the Web environment is a simple name and password system. In the Notes environment, authentication uses certificates held in user ID files.

◆ Encryption over the Web is only available through SSL. Users who access the server without using SSL cannot use encryption. In the standard Notes environment, many levels of encryption are available based on the public key/private key system, or on a shared encryption key system.

◆ Access Control Lists (ACLs) operate in the same manner for Web clients and Notes clients. A Domino-related enhancement to the ACL now enables database managers to specify the maximum level of access over the Internet.

◆ Server access lists, electronic signatures, and ACLs for databases accessed through directory pointers do not work over the Internet.

Basically, the ACL for a Web-based application in Domino is just as important as it is for a Notes application that is not Web-based. To make the ACL work properly, however, the developer or system administrator must provide a method for Web users to register. The designer must also set the default ACL level properly in order to force Web users to identify themselves at the required time. Within the realm of security issues, the developer must also be aware of the restrictions and benefits of SSL, sections, and Readers fields.

Registration System

In a regular Notes environment, you do not need a registration system. All access is based on user ID files, which are controlled by the Notes administrator. Only an administrator who has access to the Name & Address Book and the Certifier ID can properly create new users. Because the authority to create users is limited to a small number of individuals, a registration system is not necessary.

The Internet, however, has a greater number of potential users. It is impractical to control all access through a single person. The typical Internet user is accustomed to immediate access. The registration system is the key to your entire Internet site. In order to develop a registration database, simply download the most recent version from the Lotus Web site and modify it to meet your requirements. This process is relatively straightforward. Instructions are included with the database. In many cases the default registration system will work without modification.

Default Access Control List Settings

In one sense, the use of the ACL is one of the easiest Domino concepts to understand. The traditional method of using the ACL to provide security for your databases continues to work for users who access the database over the Web. Just as in a standard Notes database, users can be limited either specifically by name or as members of a group that is listed in the ACL.

In a Web application, the default ACL setting takes on significant importance. Web users have no real identity until your system forces them to enter their names and passwords. On a traditional Web site, users are normally given open access for certain tasks and are only prompted for a name and password when they try to perform tasks that exceed the base security level.

Domino controls this through the "-Default-" or the "Anonymous" ACL setting. Unauthenticated users enter under the user name Anonymous. If the database manager fails to specify "Anonymous" as a user in the ACL, the default setting applies.

From a performance perspective, using Anonymous has no real advantage over using default. From a maintenance perspective, it is easier to compile security information if the unauthenticated Web users all fall under the "Anonymous" name. "Anonymous" should be included in the ACL for every database even if it simply set to No Access.

Another important item to keep in mind when creating the ACL for your database is that the Internet users normally have non-hierarchical names. This is not a requirement; but keep in mind that Internet users are not necessarily Notes users, and hierarchical names add an unnecessary amount of complexity for users when they sign on.

The ACL setting for the Anonymous user is extremely important because it determines when users are forced to authenticate. For instance, users may be enabled to read anonymously, but they may only edit after they are authenticated. The following scenarios describe the appropriateness of the various ACL levels for the Anonymous user:

◆ **Anonymous has No Access.** Remember that this does not mean that a user cannot access the database. It only means that a user must be authenticated first to fall into one of the other ACL entries. This is the most secure setting. The effect of this setting is to cause the sign on screen to appear the moment the Web user tries to interact in any way with the database. This setting is common for applications that are restricted to only certain people or groups, such as a sales force automation system. It is somewhat annoying for Internet users who are simply browsing your Web site to be prompted for a name and password. Links to databases where Anonymous users have no access normally make it clear that the links connect to a secure area of the Web site. If a database contains Readers fields then denying anonymous users access is strongly advised. If a user was not authenticated before creating documents, the documents have Anonymous as the value in the Readers field. If the same user is forced to authenticate by another part of the Web site, he or she is no longer operating under the Anonymous identity. In this scenario, the user is not even able to read his or her own earlier documents since they are owned by "Anonymous" and the user is now using his or her actual name, which is not included in the Readers field.

◆ **Anonymous has Depositor access.** This setting is for a very specific type of database that allows all Web users to submit but not read documents. This type of database is typically used for a confidential suggestion box, voting system, survey, or job application system. This is a very effective setting because it allows users to participate in confidential aspects of your site without having to register.

◆ **Anonymous has Reader access.** This is the most common setting for any Web database. This default setting allows Web users to read documents, activate hyperlinks and perform searches without signing on. As soon as the user attempts to compose or edit a document, the sign-on prompt appears. As was stated previously, after users authenticate, ACL security operates in the standard way.

◆ **Anonymous has Author access.** This setting only forces users to sign on when they want to edit an existing document. This is normally used for registration databases because users must be able to create documents before they are given a user account name and password. This setting is also appropriate for anonymous discussion areas where users can generally create documents but not edit them.

◆ **Anonymous has Editor or above.** This security setting makes very little sense. This setting enables any Web user to create, edit, or delete any document. The only instance where this might be practical is for a database that serves as a technology demonstration. For instance, if your company sells an Internet-based document management system, you might give open access to the system so that potential clients can try out all the features without registering. Of course, if you force them to register first it is easier for you to follow up with them later.

The ACL in a Web-based application is identical to the ACL in a standard Notes application except for the entry for Anonymous. The Anonymous entry is not normally used to define Web user access; but rather, it is intended to determine the maximum access allowed before authenticating.

Secure Sockets Layer (SSL)

Implementation of a Secure Sockets Layer (SSL) is generally a system administration issue rather than a development issue. Nonetheless, the developer is often the person to identify the need for SSL. SSL is an Internet security protocol that allows for authentication and secure communication using RSA public key/private key encryption. SSL is based on a certificate system normally authenticated by Certificate Authorities such as VeriSign. From a user's perspective, SSL is a very effective feature for ensuring communication security through encryption. From a developer's perspective, SSL is somewhat ineffective for database security because you cannot force users to connect to the database with SSL. The choice of connection method to the Web site is up to the end user.

Sections

Sections work very well over the Web. Sections can be collapsed or expanded just as in standard Notes applications. Section security is also enforced over the Web. The only aspect of sections that does not work is the use of signed sections. Because Web users do not have a certified private key, they cannot sign sections.

An important design issue to keep in mind is that expanding or collapsing a section over the Internet causes the entire document to be downloaded again. This effect causes sections to be impractical while editing because the user has to submit each time the user wants to expand or collapse a section.

For read-only databases, sections can be used quite effectively to format large documents and to prevent information the user does not normally need to see from downloading. For instance, users in a document management system rarely want to look at the document edit history. By keeping it on the form in a collapsed section, you can still provide easy access to the data without wasting the user's time by downloading it every time a document is viewed.

Readers Fields

Readers fields work the same way in Web applications and standard Notes applications. Nonetheless, it is important to keep in mind that the Web user's identity is Anonymous until he or she is forced to authenticate. To make Readers fields effective requires that the developer set up the database security in such a way that users are forced to authenticate before entering the database. This is accomplished by changing the Anonymous ACL setting to No Access.

Having established a proper security model for the database, the time has come to enhance the functionality by taking advantage of some Domino-specific functions and commands.

@Functions

It should be obvious by now that the main difference between application development in the Domino environment and in the standard Notes environment is in the area of user interaction. The thin client environment of the Web does not support things such as dynamic picklists or prompt boxes. Any information that the user needs while working on a document needs to be delivered to the user's browser at the time that the HTML document is created.

Differences in the user interaction options are restrictive, however it should be possible to rework just about any Notes application by avoiding certain functions so that it can still work properly in the Web environment. The rest of this section outlines the areas in which these @Function differences may affect Web development.

@UserRoles

Certain @Functions have been enhanced or added to make Domino programming easier. One of the most useful of these new functions is @UserRoles. The @UserRoles function now adds $$WebClient to the list of user roles for users who are using a Web browser. This makes it extremely useful for determining whether the client is a Web client or a Notes client.

Consider a database developed using the programming approach that was presented in the section of this chapter that discussed repeating graphics for headers and footers. The resulting form only works properly over the Web. If the application is targeted for both Notes users and Web users, then this is not acceptable. The developer must create two versions of the header and footer, one that is optimized for the Web and one that appears properly for Notes users. The developer can then use a computed subform to determine which version should appear. The following computed subform formula is an example of this concept:

```
IsWebClient:=@IsMember("WebClient";@UserRoles);
@If(IsWebClient;"WebHeader";"NotesHeader")
```

@UserRoles is also useful in hide-when formulas for embedding HTML code that should only appear to Web users.

@URLOpen

The @URLOpen is a new function that is very useful for hotspots and action bar formulas. For instance, the following line of code within a view or form action causes the button to open the Lotus Web site:

```
@URLOpen("http://www.lotus.com")
```

@DeleteDocument

The @DeleteDocument function is not supported over the Web. Documents should instead be deleted by a form action with the following formula:

```
@Command([EditClear])
```

They can also be deleted by requesting the proper URL from the Domino server. This concept is covered in the "Domino URL Command" section of the this chapter.

@DbCommand

The @DbCommand function is only appropriate for use with views that are rendered over the Web. This command is only valid in the following two cases:

```
@DbCommand("Domino";"ViewPreviousPage")
@DbCommand("Domino";"ViewNextPage")
```

These commands create links to the previous or next page of a view that was too large for a single page.

@DbLookup

Keyword fields that are based on @DbLookup functions work perfectly over the Web.

@Prompt, @DialogBox, @Picklist

These functions do not work over the Web. The only interactions that a user can have with the backend system are either to submit the current document or to request a new document.

In standard Notes development the developer often removes picklist fields from the form design and replaces them with computed fields that are set by buttons that use @Prompt to resolve the user selection. This approach is taken for two reasons:

◆ The form opens significantly faster because it no longer resolves the picklist before opening.

◆ The picklist portion of the button bases the query on user input and can therefore be much more dynamic than a simple hard coded keyword field.

Because @Prompts are not supported by Domino, buttons cannot be used to replace keyword fields. Effectively what is considered poor design in a standard Notes database is considered proper design in a Web database. Because keyword fields are the only way to present picklists over the Web, they must be used.

@Environment, @SetEnvironment

These functions are not supported. The Internet has no .INI file concept to store these values. The concept of environment does exist over the Web, but it does not mean the same thing as it does in the Notes environment. See the sections at the end of this chapter on CGI variables and Cookies for more information. Cookies are being supported by Domino, and in some cases they can be used to hold environment variables.

@UserName

The @UserName function works the same way in Domino as it does in Notes. Keep in mind when using this function that the user's name is "Anonymous" until after he or she is authenticated. Often Web-based applications have the annoying tendency to repetitively ask users to re-enter the same information. When creating new documents the designer can take advantage of the @UserName function to pre-fill some of the fields.

@Mail Functions

Mail functions such as @MailSend and @MailSavePreference are not supported over the Web. These types of functions cause mail-enabled applications to interact with the client mail system. In the case of the Web users, the mail system on the Web browser is not accessible except through URLs.

@DDE Functions

The @DDE functions are not supported over the Web.

@Commands

The use of @Commands provides a particularly easy method to create action bar items that request other pages such as views, documents, navigators, or About Documents. These commands can be coded using Domino's somewhat cryptic URL syntax, but they work no better than the @Commands.

Another benefit of using @Commands is that the form and view actions also function in the Notes environment. This saves the programmer from having to create a double set of actions that are controlled through hide formulas based on the @UserRoles function. The @Commands described in the following sections have particular significance for Domino development. For clarity, the @Commands have been grouped according to the Notes design element that they interact with:

- ◆ Navigators
- ◆ Views
- ◆ Documents

Navigators

Domino supports two @Command methods for opening navigators using form or view actions. The first only works within the same database that the user currently has open, and it uses the following syntax:

```
@Command([OpenNavigator];"navigator name")
```

The second method can open a navigator in any database on the server. It uses the following syntax:

```
@Command([FileOpenDatabase];"":"database";"navigatorname")
```

Views

Domino supports a number of methods for opening views. The following method only works within the same database as the action:

```
@Command([OpenView];"viewname")
```

This next method works on any database on the server:

```
@Command([FileOpenDatabase];"":"database";"viewname")
```

Documents

Unlike the read-only interaction with navigators and views, interaction with documents can involve a number of activities. Documents can be created, read, edited, or deleted. Normally, read-only documents are opened from a view by using the corresponding hypertext link. Similarly, one normally presents the read-only version of a document to a user before allowing him or her to edit or delete it. Creating new documents can occur from anywhere.

Create documents in the user's current database with the Compose command using the following syntax:

```
@Command([Compose];"formname")
```

Adding more arguments to this same command allows the creation of documents in a different database than the user's current database:

```
@Command([Compose];"":"database";"formname")
```

Existing documents are normally opened from hypertext links. Nonetheless, at times the designer may want to create links to documents using two @Commands. This is done in two steps. The first command locates the proper document:

```
@Command([OpenView];"viewname";"key")
```

After the document is located, the next command brings it up for reading:

```
@Command([OpenDocument])
```

In order to open the document in another database, change the first command to:

```
@Command([FileOpenDatabase];"":"database";"view";"key")
```

After the document is opened, the user may want to go into edit mode. A form action accomplishes this with the following formula:

```
@Command([EditDocument])
```

Rather than edit, the user may want to simply delete the document. A form action accomplishes this with the following formula:

```
@Command([EditClear])
```

Domino URL Commands

It is not always possible to use @Commands to generate your links. For instance, within a hard-coded HTML document, a view column, or between two second domino servers, the @Commands do not work.

To meet the developer's requirement to generate links from these locations, Domino supports a URL syntax that accesses all the possible Domino features. In fact, if you view the source of the Domino-rendered HTML pages you see these same URLs.

Domino URLs follow the following format:

```
http://Host/NotesObject?Action&Arguments
```

The elements within this format are defined as follows:

◆ **Host.** Web server name or IP address.

◆ **NotesObject.** Notes object such as database, view, document, form, navigator, agent, or search. The + sign can be used to represent spaces within the NotesObject name.

◆ **Action.** Desired operation such as ?OpenDatabase, ?OpenView and many others. If the action is omitted then ?Open is assumed.

◆ **Arguments.** Additional information such as CollapseView to return the view in collapsed mode.

Numerous options are available for referring to the NotesObjects. Only the most intuitive approach is demonstrated here. A complete list of these URLs is available in the domguide.nsf database installed with the server software. The majority of the actions and arguments are optional because the default of ?Open for the action and nothing for the arguments works fine in most cases. If two Notes objects have the same name, include the action so that the server knows which object to take.

OpenDatabase

The following URL opens a specific database on the Domino server. This particular URL is also a good URL to pass out to clients who might want to go directly to a specific database on your Web site without going through your home page.

```
http://Host/DatabaseFileName?OpenDatabase
```

No additional arguments are required for this URL; in fact, even the ?OpenDatabase is optional. For instance, the following URL will open the Name & Address Book on www.dominodemo.com:

```
http://www.dominodemo.com/names.nsf
```

OpenView

To open a specific view within a Domino database, use this URL:

```
http://Host/Database/ViewName?OpenView
```

Allowable arguments are Start=n, Count=n, ExpandView, CollapseView, Expand=n and Collapse=n. The ?OpenView is optional. The following example opens the People view of the Name & Address Book on www.dominodemo.com:

```
http://www.dominodemo.com/names.nsf/People
```

OpenAbout

The following URL opens the About document of the specified database:

```
http://Host/Database/$about?OpenAbout
```

This is an important URL because many databases use the About document as their home page. Once more, the ?OpenAbout is optional. The following example opens the About document of the Name & Address book at www.dominodemo.com:

```
http://www.dominodemo.com/names.nsf/$about
```

Login Argument

Append & Login to any URL and Domino forces authentication to occur before the page is brought up regardless of what is in the ACL. For instance, the following example would open the Name & Address Book to the People view after authenticating the user:

```
http://www.dominodemo.com/names.nsf/People&Login
```

OpenForm

The following URL creates a new document:

```
http://Host/Database/FormName?OpenForm
```

When composing documents that use inheritance from other forms, the URL will also accept a Document Universal ID (UNID) as an argument. The UNID will be used by Domino to determine which source document to use for the inheritance formulas. Just like the other URL strings, the ?OpenForm is optional. The following example composes a person document in the Name & Address Book at www.dominodemo.com:

```
http://www.dominodemo.com/names.nsf/Person
```

OpenNavigator

The following URL opens a navigator:

```
http://Host/Database/NavigatorName?OpenNavigator
```

Once again the ?OpenNavigator argument is optional. The following example would open a navigator called OrgChart in the Name & Address Book at www.dominodemo.com:

```
http://www.dominodemo.com/names.nsf/OrgChart
```

OpenDocument

To open an existing document for reading, use this URL:

```
http://Host/Database/View/DocumentKey?OpenDocument
```

This enables a document to be requested by a key, as opposed to by the document's Notes ID or Universal ID. The DocumentKey parameter must contain the contents of the first sorted column in the referenced view. If the document has no view containing unique document keys then the document's Universal ID or Notes ID can be used as follows:

```
http://Host/Database/View/DocumentUniversalID?OpenDocument
```

Notice that the view name is still a part of the query. This enables the developer to take advantage of any form formula that the view might have for displaying the document. The following URL opens Jane Doe's person document by retrieving it from the FullName view of the Name & Address Book on www.dominodemo.com. Assume that this view has the users' full names as its first sorted column:

```
http://www.dominodemo.com/names.nsf/FullName/Jane+Doe
```

The plus sign in the previous example is used to represent a space. URLs cannot include spaces.

EditDocument

The following URL opens an existing document in edit mode:

```
http://Host/Database/View/Document/?EditDocument
```

The document is retrieved as an HTML form, provided the user has the appropriate level of access. Editing the same document that was used in the open document URL example requires the following URL:

```
http://www.dominodemo.com/FullName/Jane+Doe/?EditDocument
```

DeleteDocument

The reference document is deleted by using this URL:

```
http://Host/Database/View/Document/?DeleteDocument
```

The specified document will only be deleted if the user has the appropriate level of access. In order to delete the Jane Doe document from the previous two examples, use the following URL:

```
http://www.dominodemo.com/names.nsf/FullName/Jane+Doe/?DeleteDocument
```

OpenElement

The following URL opens any element that is stored within a document:

```
http://Host/Database/View/Document/$File/Filename?OpenElement
```

This URL provides access to file attachments, OLE objects, and image files. The ?OpenElement portion of the URL is optional. Although this URL is most commonly used for graphics files, it can be used for any attachment. The following URL, for example, once more accesses Jane Doe's person document; but this time the URL extracts Jane's user.id file:

```
http://www.dominodemo.com/names.nsf/FullName/Jane+Doe/$File/user.id
```

SearchSite

The following URL can be used to bring up the search screen or to issue the search command directly:

```
http://Host/Database/$SearchForm?SearchSite&ArgumentList
```

The optional parameters for this URL are $SearchForm and ArgumentList. The inclusion of $SearchForm precludes the use of ArgumentList to refine the search, presenting a search form as the interface for the search. The appearance of this form can be customized by creating a form with $$Search as its alias. The $SearchSite parameter can be replaced with $SearchView to restrict the search to a single view.

```
Argumentlist=Query;SearchOrder;SearchThesaurus;SearchMax;SearchWV
```

If ArgumentList is used, the Query argument represents the search string and is required. The optional SearchOrder argument is used to determine the format for the display of search results: 1=By Relevance, 2=By Date Ascending, or 3=By Date Descending.

This example issues a search for all person documents that contain the name Jane in the Name & Address Book on www.dominodemo.com:

```
http://www.dominodemo.com/names.nsf/People?SearchView&Query=Jane
```

These URLs can be included within the design of the database or can simply be typed into the browser. Using these URLs in the browser provides an easy method for the developer to test each of the design features within the database. Of course, unlike a developer, a user would rather just activate a link to the appropriate Notes object. One of the best locations for these links is inside the $$Form or $$Field design elements, which are described in the next section.

Special Domino-Related Fields and Forms

To provide the developer with a place to put Domino-specific program code, Lotus has enhanced the Notes programming environment by adding a number of special field and form names. By using these Domino-specific $$Fields and $$Forms together, the developer can create a highly customized Web site. First, this section introduces the $$Fields that the developer can place within forms. These $$Fields can be included on specially named $$Forms to be even more useful. Finally, some of the $$Fields can be used to activate LotusScript code when documents are created or saved.

Customizing the Database with $$Fields

Special fields and forms can be included as part of the database design. $$Fields added to forms customize the appearance of documents, views, and navigators. Fields such as $$NavigatorBody, $$ViewBody, $$ViewList, and $$HTMLHead enable the developer to modify the content and appearance of the HTML documents that are rendered by Domino. The $$Return field provides a place for developers to include code to create customized response documents. The $$QueryOpenAgent and $$QuerySaveAgent fields provide a place for developers to specify the name of a Notes agent that should be run when a document is created or saved.

$$NavigatorBody, $$ViewBody, $$ViewList

$$NavigatorBody displays a specific navigator as part of a form. Multiple navigators can be referenced by adding additional fields in the $$NavigatorBody_n format. $$ViewList displays a list of views and folders available in the database. By default the Notes Folders navigator is used for this purpose. $$ViewBody displays a particular view as part of a form. Unlike navigators, only a single view can be associated with a form, so only one $$ViewBody field may be used. Chapter 16 demonstrates how these special fields are used.

$$Return

When a user submits a completed form, he or she receives the standard confirmation page. Figure 15.11 is a screen shot of the standard response.

Figure 15.11

The default response after submitting a form.

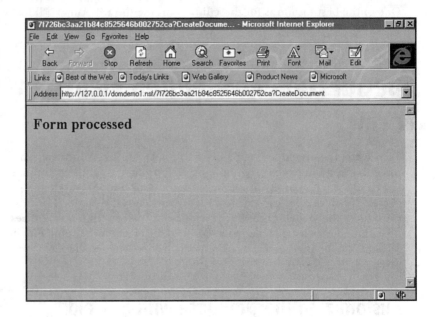

Usually, this default response is inappropriate or inadequate. The confirmation screen can be customized by including a $$Return field. This field can launch a CGI script, return HTML on the fly, or open another URL. For instance, a survey form can have the following $$Return field formula:

```
PersonString:=@If(@UserName="Anonymous";"";@UserName);
ReturnString:="<h1>Submission Received</h1>" +
     "<h2>Thank you, "+PersonString+" for completing the survey</h2>" +
     "<br><a href=\"http://www.surveycorp.com\">" +
     "Return to homepage</a>";
ReturnString
```

This results in a much more effective return message, as shown in figure 15.12.

Notice from the code listing that passthru HTML was not required because the output is understood to be HTML by definition.

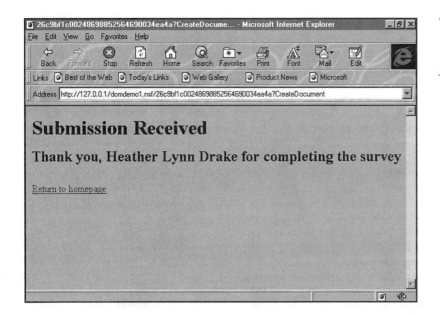

Figure 15.12

The $$Return field generated response.

$$HTMLHead

The $$HTMLHead field is used to pass HTML information within the Head tags of the document. This is commonly used to load CGI code, JavaScript code, or Internet Cookies. An excellent JavaScript example is available in the online help database domguide.nsf.

$$QueryOpenAgent and $$QuerySaveAgent

Often, a functional requirement of a database is that an agent must be run in conjunction with the creation of a document. The $$QueryOpenAgent field is a hidden field that contains the name of an agent that runs when the document is opened. Similarly, the $$QuerySaveAgent field contains the name of an agent that runs prior to saving a submitted document.

Customizing the Database with $$Form

Special forms customize the display of navigators, views, and search results. $$Forms included in the database create associations between forms and either views or navigators. Essentially, the navigator, view, or search result is encapsulated in a form that is designed for that purpose. In this manner, the basic appearance of views, navigators, and search results can be extended to include custom formatting, additional graphics, and text. These special forms are manually created. The form name or alias must be based on the specified $$Form value.

The customization is broken down into two different approaches. If a specific custom form is available for the object, then that custom form is used. If no specific form is available, then the default custom form is used. If the default custom form is also not available, then the system-defined layout is used.

This type of customization is available for navigators, views, search screen, and search results.

Navigators

When a Web user requests a navigator, it is displayed according to the $$NavigatorTemplate forms that are stored within the database. Domino first tries to use the custom navigator template for the requested navigator, if it is available.

To create a custom template, you must establish an association between a navigator and a specific form. This is accomplished by creating a custom $$NavigatorTemplate form. For a navigator called "Main," for example, the developer needs to create a form called "$$NavigatorTemplate for Main." This form needs to include a field called "$$NavigatorBody." The value of $$NavigatorBody field is ignored. Domino is concerned only with the position of the field. The position of the field is used to define the location of the "Main" navigator.

The $$NavigatorTemplateDefault form is the default form associated with any navigator that does not have an association with a specific form such as the one previously described. The special field $$NavigatorBody must again be included on this form. Once more, its value is ignored. The $$NavigatorBody field is again used simply to define the position of the user requested navigator.

If neither the custom template nor the default template are found, Domino uses the navigator without any enhancements. Normally a navigator would not require any customization since navigators are already highly customized by their very nature. Views, on the other hand, all follow the same basic layout. Domino allows developers to customize a view's appearance over the Web by using the $$ViewTemplate form.

Views

The special $$ViewTemplate forms are similar in use to the $$NavigatorTemplate forms. To reiterate this process: when a Web user requests a view, it is displayed according to the $$ViewTemplate forms that are stored within the database. If it is available, Domino first tries to use the custom view template for the requested view. For example, for a view called "People," Domino searches for a form called

"$$ViewTemplate for People." Domino requires that this form include a field called $$ViewBody. The $$ViewBody field positions the area on the form where the "People" view is displayed.

If the custom $$ViewTemplate is unavailable, Domino retrieves the $$ViewTemplateDefault form. This form is the default form associated with any view that does not have an association with a specific view template form. The special field $$ViewBody must again be included on this form to define the position where the user requested view should appear. Once more, its value is ignored.

If neither the custom template nor the default template are found, Domino uses the view by placing it in the system-defined view template. This system-defined layout includes all of the necessary functions such as expand, collapse, previous, and next. The problem with the system-defined template is that its appearance is rather plain and it is also very much directed toward users who are already familiar with Notes. Most databases require that the developer create a $$ViewTemplateDefault form.

Once the views are redesigned using this technique, the developer is likely to want to improve on the remaining system defaults. The appearance of the search system can be redesigned using the $$Search and $$SearchTemplateDefault forms.

Searches

Customizing the Domino search system is a little more complicated than enhancing the appearance of navigators or views. The search system has two customizable interfaces: one to allow the Web user to enter the search criteria and another to return the search results.

The screen for entering the search criteria can be customized by creating a form called $$Search. Converting a form that contains a large number of fields into a properly formatted query is not a trivial task. Lotus has greatly simplified the process by providing two sample forms that can be used as a model: Web Search Simple and Web Search Advanced. They can be found in the Search Site database that was installed along with the Domino server. Simply copy one or both of these forms into your own database and then customize them as required.

The final step of a search is the display of the search results, which are displayed through views. The appearance of these views can be customized by creating a $$SearchTemplateDefault form for all views. Search queries always search the documents displayed in a particular view. Each view, then, can have two customized templates: one for the normal view display and one for the search results. For a specific view such as "People," create a "$$SearchTemplate for People" form. Like the custom view templates described earlier, these forms require a $$ViewBody field in order to properly position the view on the form. Developers should be aware, however, that the customized search results form does not support displaying the total number of matches. This count is found on the system-defined default search results form.

LotusScript

Other sections of this book describe the basics of what LotusScript is and how to use it (see Part VI, "Notes Advanced Development"). This discussion focuses on the aspects of LotusScript relevant to Domino application development.

LotusScript has revolutionized the way applications are created. It has provided programmers with the ability to create applications of just about any level of complexity. The LotusScript extensions (LSX) have also made it easy to connect to other backend systems such as Oracle.

LotusScript works quite differently in a Web-based application than it does in a standard Notes-based application. In a standard Notes-based application, LotusScript runs on the user's desktop. This means that if a Notes user is running a script that queries an Oracle table, then that user must also have the necessary additional Oracle drivers installed and configured on his or her computer. In the case of Oracle access, the user must have SQLNet and the Oracle LSX installed.

Web-based applications do not perform any of the logic at the user desktop. This means that the LotusScript agents are executed by the Domino server. Consequently, Web-based applications do not have additional software requirements for the Web user. All processing occurs on the server. This benefit is of significant appeal to any large organization where application rollout and maintenance are often more significant in terms of cost and time than the entire development project.

The use of LotusScript in Web-based applications has limitations. In a standard Notes application, LotusScript code can occur within almost every design element. In a Web-based application, any LotusScript found in the design of a form, including the action bar, is ignored. Background agents, however, continue to function normally because they are not affected by the users. In order to incorporate some real-time script power for the Web users, Lotus has provided two special $$Fields called $$QueryOpenAgent and $$QuerySaveAgent where the designer stores the desired agent names. The agents are actually separate design elements that are found in the agent list. The agents should be defined as "Shared Agents" that are set to run "Manually From Agent List." These agents run every time a document is opened or submitted.

The agent referred to by the $$QueryOpenAgent field runs before the document is converted to HTML, during the QueryOpen event. An excellent use for this agent is to modify the document prior to its conversion to HTML. For instance, the agent referred to by $$QueryOpenAgent can be used to access an SQL table to retrieve information that is then presented as part of the document. The techniques to access SQL are beyond the scope of this chapter. The concept is being mentioned here to identify one possible use for this design element. Another appropriate use for the agent referred to by $$QueryOpenAgent is to compile statistical information from the user when he or she opens the document. For instance, every time any user creates a new document, the agent referred to by $$QueryOpenAgent can update a summary document, recording the user activity.

The agent referred to by $$QuerySaveAgent runs before the document is saved, during the QuerySave event. This means that the agent referred to by $$QuerySaveAgent can access all the fields on the document and then modify, add, or remove items before the document is saved. In a more complicated database, the agent referred to by $$QuerySaveAgent can be used to capture the information submitted by the user and forward it to a host-based system using the MQSeries LSX. The agent can then pause while it waits for a reply from the host, which is in turn converted to an HTML response for display to the user. One of the more simple agents that can be created to with the $$QuerySaveAgent field is one that sets a sequential document number for every new document. The following listing is an example of this type of code:

```
Sub Initialize
     Dim session As New NotesSession
     Dim doc As NotesDocument
     Set doc = session.DocumentContext

     Dim db As  NotesDatabase
     Set db = doc.Database

     On Error Goto processError

     Dim counterdoc As NotesDocument
     Set counterdoc = db.GetProfileDocument("Counter")
     oldhighcount = counterdoc.GetItemValue("LargestDocNumber")
     highnum = Val(oldhighcount(0))
     highnum=highnum% + 1
     counterdoc.LargestDocNumber = highnum
     Call counterdoc.Save(True,False)

     doc.DocumentNumber = highnum
     Call doc.Save(True,False)
processError:
     Exit Sub
End Sub
```

Developers familiar with LotusScript should take special note of the fourth line of the preceding code listing. The DocumentContext property is used to get a handle on the document object. Within the agent, the print command can be used to send HTML code back to the user. For instance, the previous agent can be improved by adding some print statement to inform the user of his or her document number.

The use of $$Fields, $$Forms, and LotusScript enables the developer to fully customize a Web-based database. The skills presented in this section and the preceding sections provide the developer with the knowledge necessary to create a powerful and unique Web site. In order to create a cutting-edge Web site, however, some additional features are required.

Advanced Internet Features in Domino

Domino supports a number of advanced Internet features. It is beyond the scope of this chapter to cover everything that is possible; this section briefly describes some of the most common Internet features, such as:

◆ Attachments

◆ Frames

◆ ActiveX

◆ JavaScript and Cookies

◆ CGI variables

◆ Calendaring and Scheduling over the Web

Attachments

A developer needs to accommodate two aspects of attachments within a Web-based application:

◆ Web users must be able to access pre-existing attachments in Notes databases.

◆ Web users must be able to create attachments.

Providing the capability to share existing attachments is not a development issue. Lotus has included the concept of serving attachments to Internet users as part of Domino. Users create the attachment by editing a document in Lotus Notes. The user positions the cursor inside a rich text field, then uses the File, Attach menu command to select a file to attach. The attached file is represented in Notes by a small graphic. This document viewed through a Web browser displays the attachment icon in the same place that it appears in Notes.

If the attachment is a recognized MIME type, clicking on the icon plays it through the browser's helper application. If the file is not a recognized MIME type, clicking on the icon brings up the Web browser's File Save dialog box. Domino defines the supported Multimedia Internet Mail Extension (MIME) types in the server's HTTPD.CNF file. The HTTPD.CNF file may need to be modified to support additional MIME types that were not present in the default installation. A properly identified MIME type identifies files so that the browser can play the file rather than simply downloading it. Web users must have the required helper application to play the MIME files.

Providing the facility to enable Web clients to upload files requires preparation of the form by the developer. In order to support attaching files from Web clients, follow these steps to add the necessary design features:

1. Create a rich text field for holding the attachments.

2. Enter static text near the field such as "Attach Files."

3. Highlight the static text and select Create, Hotspot, Text Hotspot.

4. In the hotspot box enter Command([EditInsertFileAttachment]).

The Web users now only need to click on the Attach Files link to bring up their Attach File menu.

Frames

To use the Internet terminology, frames "look cool." Domino supports frames quite effectively through the use of passthru HTML. Frames can be set up just about anywhere. The following frames set resides in an About document. To create frames, the developer creates a layout or frameset and then populates each of the frames with their own documents. The document within the frame can be any valid URL.

```
<frameset cols=25%,75%>
  <frame src="http://www.domino.com/Homepage.nsf/MainNavigator"
 scrolling=auto name="main" target="left">
 <frame src=" http://www.dominodemo.com/products.nsf/products/ProductList"
 name="product">
</frameset>
```

The preceding code generates a screen with two vertical frames at 25 percent and 75 percent of the screen width. Each frame has its own document that was loaded through the URL.

ActiveX

Embedding ActiveX for Web users is identical to embedding the same application for Notes users. Because this is not a Web-oriented development issue, the steps to embedding these applications are not presented here. The Domino server takes care of serving the ActiveX application out to the users. Lotus Components is probably the most common ActiveX application that you can expect to deal with. The ActiveX applications work well in Internet Explorer. Users of other browsers may need to install additional plug-ins.

JavaScript and Cookies

The discussion database on the Lotus Web site domino.lotus.com uses Internet Cookies. Cookies enable developers to store information on the Web user's computer. The most common method of creating the Cookies is to use the $$HTMLHead field that was described in the "$$Field" section earlier in this chapter.

JavaScript code can also be included in the same place. JavaScript is too complex to describe within this chapter; however, JavaScript programmers can find a sample program that demonstrates how to integrate JavaScript with your Notes database in the domguide.nsf help database. Java is also discussed in more detail in Chapter 20.

CGI

CGI variables are easily collected by creating an editable field with the same name as a CGI variable and then hiding the field. If the CGI variable exists, it fills in from the CGI environment. These CGI values can then be used in Computed for Display fields or Hide-When formulas. The form in figure 15.13 gathers the CGI variable called Remote_Addr, which is the Web user's IP address. It also gathers the CGI variable called HTTP_Referer, which is the URL of the page from which the user request originated.

Collecting CGI variables can be very important for statistical purposes. The approach of including the CGI variables within the design of the form allows developers to specifically choose which CGI variables to collect on a database-by-database basis.

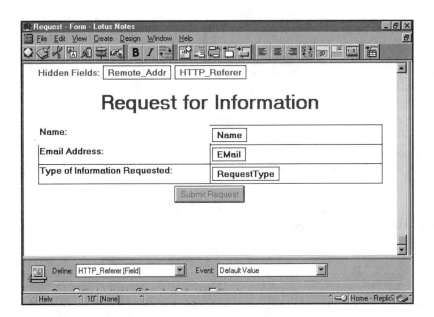

Figure 15.13

Capturing CGI variables.

Calendaring and Scheduling

Calendaring and scheduling applications are still rare on the Internet. They no longer need to be. The best way to work with calendaring and scheduling is to start with the Web-based mail template that is available from the Lotus Domino Web site at domino.lotus.com. The basis of calendaring over the Web is the calendar view. As a developer, you do not program the complex appearance of this view. You simply select Calendar as the style in the Properties box and add the required columns. This results in a calendar-based view that works very well over the Internet. The remaining design issues around a calendaring and scheduling application are the same as they are for non-calendaring applications.

Summary

You now have the knowledge required to create a quality Internet or intranet site using Domino. An important decision prior to beginning any development is whether to provide features that support both Notes clients and Internet/intranet clients. The development of an Internet application is greatly enhanced by knowledge of how HTML renders text, tables, and graphics—the basic features of a document. Any HTML code can be supported by Domino using passthru HTML.

Domino development begins with the creation of the core Notes design elements: forms, views, and navigators. Special consideration must be given to these elements when an application is intended for Domino distribution. Domino-specific development features require particular techniques for the maintainance of Web-based database functionality. Of particular interest is the default ACL security settings required to ensure authentication of users at the appropriate time. Special Notes @Functions, @Commands, and Domino URL commands exist to improve the functionality of Notes over the Web. Special Domino fields and forms are essential to customize fully the appearance and operation of your Web site. Advanced Internet features such as the support of frames, Java, and CGI can further enhance your Domino applications.

The knowledge acquired in this chapter will now be applied to the creation of a Web-based time tracking system in Chapter 16.

Building a Sample Web-Centric Application

The easiest way to learn Domino development is to create a Web-based Notes application. An experienced Notes programmer has skill sets that are adequate to create fully functional Web applications. This chapter leads you through the development of one such database and also shows, by example, how specialized Domino features can be used to enhance an application to give it a polished Internet-quality appearance.

Specifically, this chapter is broken down into the following sections:

◆ Application requirements

◆ Basic design

◆ Advanced design

◆ Application implementation

Application Requirements

The design of any database must begin with an analysis of the requirements that the application must fulfill. Applications are intended to meet a specific business needs and to facilitate certain business processes. Without a proper analysis, it is difficult to achieve the most appropriate result. For the purposes of this chapter, this analysis will be relatively cursory and will be limited to presenting information needed during the development of the database. The analysis will be broken down into three sections:

◆ Business needs analysis

◆ Target environment

◆ Anticipated technical hurdles

The remainder of this chapter uses a fictional consulting company called Key People Consulting Corp. as a model. Key People has many consultants working on client sites across the continent. Key People has experienced enormous growth in business, and their current paper-based systems are causing delays in generating the monthly invoices. They are looking for a solution.

Business Needs Analysis

Although the user requirements may seem straightforward, it is always worthwhile to do a business needs analysis before starting any project. This analysis phase normally involves a series of meetings with the principal people involved in the business process to be addressed by this application. Focus groups are also usually formed during in this phase to ensure that the project goals are properly defined.

The process of undertaking a business needs analysis is outside of the scope of this chapter. This chapter discusses using the results of the analysis. For the purposes of developing the application, assume the business requirements were identified according to the following lists. The lists are broken down into features that are provided within the scope of this chapter and enhancements that are left for future development.

The following features are covered in this chapter:

◆ The application must be operational over the Internet.

◆ The application must also function within the Notes environment.

◆ Time sheets are submitted monthly. Each time sheet records one full month of daily hours.

◆ The business requires one time sheet per consultant per month for each contract.

◆ Consultants must be able to print the time sheet from either Notes or the Internet to deliver it to the client.

◆ Consultants must be able to include a list of deliverables on the time sheet.

◆ Users need views, by Company, by Consultant, by Month, and by Contract Number.

◆ The system should not require user training. Assume the users are already familiar with either Notes or the Internet.

◆ Online help is required even for Internet users.

◆ The system must maintain an audit trail of every edit-level access to a time sheet. The details of the changes are not required.

Future enhancements to this application, outside the scope of this chapter, may include the following features:

◆ Integration with the financial system should not require the re-entry of any of the data. Manually launching the export from the Time Tracking system, followed by the manual launching of the import from the financial system is acceptable, however, the preferred integration should not require manual intervention of any kind.

◆ Management reports such as a comparison of billable hours to non-billable hours should be generated by the Time Tracking system and should not take up any consultant time.

◆ The system should track expected versus actual time sheets, and should send e-mail or fax notices to timekeepers when their time sheets are missing.

◆ After a time sheet has been entered into the financial system, record locking should prevent anyone from changing it.

◆ Some sort of change mechanism must be available to allow changes or at least notations to locked records under certain circumstances.

◆ To protect the client list, externally sub-contracted consultants should only be allowed to see their own time sheets.

Target Environment Analysis

The primary application environment is going to be the Internet. If Key People does not already have its Web server configured, then a number of system administration tasks need to be undertaken while the development is underway so that the application can be implemented after it is finished. The employees at Key People also need to get Internet accounts and software so that they can access the new system.

The configuration of a Domino Web server and the distribution of Internet accounts are primarily system administration issues. The developer's role in the area of target environment analysis is to identify the requirements and perhaps to perform a load analysis study to determine whether the application can run properly with the current or proposed infrastructure. As with all Internet applications, the developer must also create a design that does not require excessively large downloads to operate.

Anticipated Technical Hurdles

Creating an application that runs both in Notes and over the Web is always more difficult than working in just one environment. The example in this chapter makes extensive use of features that work well in both environments. No trade-offs in terms of functionality are expected due to this dual-environment requirement.

When dealing with a Web-based application it is always important to optimize the way that graphics download. On many Domino sites users can expect to download the same graphic over and over. This typical Web site problem is addressed within this sample application. Field validation is much more complicated over the Web, but an effective solution is presented.

Having been provided with the required background information, the developer is now able to proceed with the creation of the basic design elements of the database.

Basic Design

The core design of the system encompasses all of the basic design elements and issues that are required by the system in order to provide the requested functionality. Specifically, the following items will be developed:

◆ Forms

◆ Views

◆ Security model

◆ Navigators

Development of these items will proceed sequentially. At the end of this section, a functional database will be available.

Users interact with the Time Tracking system through a single form, the Time Sheet. The Time Sheet needs to contain some sort of calendar type of data entry area to record the daily hours.

Form Description

Two versions of the Time Sheet form are required so that Web users can have a version that prints properly. The print version is an exact copy of the original except that the form actions are turned off. There are also two subforms for the corporate banner so that a Web version and a non-Web version can be created.

Development of this form begins by creating the subform that is used to store the corporate logo. The completed subform is used as the starting point for the actual Time Sheet, which is somewhat complex due to the monthly calendar that is contained within it. After the time sheet is completed and tested, the developer will further enhance it by adding some field validation to control the required fields.

Corporate Banner Subforms

The first visible item on any time sheet is the company name and address. This is also a good starting point for the form design. Given the graphical nature of modern applications, the company address section should also include the corporate logo. Together the address and logo comprise the corporate banner.

This corporate banner should have a consistent appearance across all Notes applications. This reuse requirement makes the banner an ideal candidate for a subform. The corporate logo that comprises a large part of this banner probably appears in many places on the Web site. If the logo uses an embedded image, then Domino treats it as a new image in each different form on which it appears. This affects the response time of the application over the Internet because these unique graphic files have to be downloaded each time a new one is encountered. To improve performance, refer to the GIF by using a URL that accesses either the graphics library or the file system. Each time a user accesses any page containing the corporate logo the URL references the same physical file. The image then downloads only once per session. Subsequent requests for the image are resolved from the user's own browser cache.

When the image is replaced by a URL, however, you lose the capability to display it properly in the Notes environment. To solve this problem, create two subforms for the banners, one for the Web and one for Notes. Figure 16.1 demonstrates the Notes client subform, and figure 16.2 demonstrates the Web subform.

Figure 16.1

Banner for Notes clients.

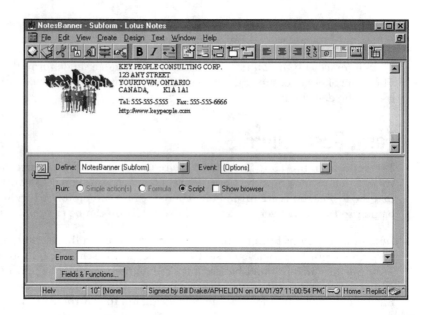

Figure 16.2

Banner for Web clients.

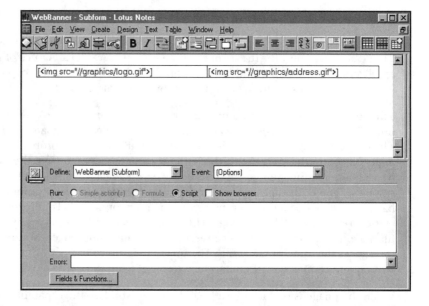

The code in figure 16.2 has a weakness. The URLs referring to the graphic images in the WebBanner subform are calling the graphics from the graphics subdirectory in the HTML file system on the Domino server. This adds unnecessary complexity to application rollout and testing. In many environments, designers do not have physical access to the Notes servers. That means that to configure or modify that part of the database the designer has to involve the system administrator. Because there are alternatives to this approach, the best time to change is now, while the design process is still only beginning. The preferred solution is the creation of a graphics library area within this database. Create the graphics library by following these steps:

1. Create a form called Attachment.

2. Create a text field called FileName to hold the file name.

3. Create a rich text field called Attachment to hold the image.

4. Save the form.

5. Create a view called Files with a selection formula that includes only documents created with the Attachment form.

6. Modify the first column to display the contents of the FileName field. Sort the column.

Complete the graphics library by creating Attachment documents for each of graphics. After this is done, the WebBanner subform needs to be changed to refer to the new graphic storage area.

When this new subform is viewed through a Web browser, it may not appear as intended. Web browsers' default backgrounds are set based on user preferences. In order to guarantee that the document appears as intended, Web developers must control the background color. Because the WebBanner subform is always at the top of the Web document, this is a good place to set the background color using the following line of code:

```
[<BODY BGCOLOR="FFFFFF">]
```

These changes result in the subform in figure 16.3.

The banner portion of the form is now complete. Although the banner subform may only be required once in this application, in other databases the use of this subform on every document helps to create a consistent look and feel.

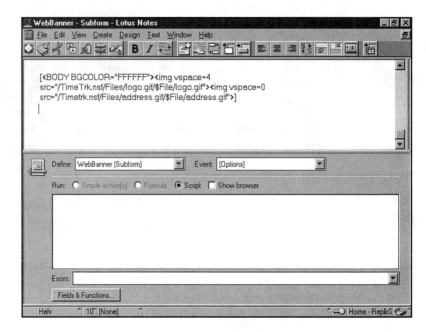

Figure 16.3

Revised banner for Web clients.

Time Sheet Form

The application's main form is the Time Sheet. This form can be broken down into six logical sections:

- ◆ Corporate banner
- ◆ Time sheet details
- ◆ Calendar
- ◆ Comments
- ◆ Buttons
- ◆ Form Actions

The first object to appear on this form is the corporate banner that was previously developed.

Corporate Banner

There are two versions of the banner:

◆ NotesBanner

◆ WebBanner

The @UserRoles function can be used in conjunction with the $$WebClient role to determine the method used to access the database, and hence which of these subforms to display. Begin creating the Time Sheet form by following these steps:

1. Create the Time Sheet form.

2. Choose Create, Insert Subform from the menu.

3. From the subform prompt box, choose Insert Subform based on formula.

4. Enter the following formula:

```
@If(@Contains(@UserRoles;"$$WebClient");"WebBanner";"NotesBanner")
```

Chapter 15, "Domino-Specific Application Development Considerations," describes this formula in more detail.

Detail Area

The next area of the form collects some basic information from the user. The security model, which is described later in this chapter, forces users to authenticate before entering this database. Because the user now has an authenticated identity, the developer can capture this identity in the Consultant field using the @UserName function. The detail section also contains project details such as the client name, contract number and project manager name. The remaining fields that need to be in this section are the month and the year. These fields are good candidates for keyword fields because the option list is quite short. Keyword fields also work well over the Web. Complete this area of the form by creating the fields and static text as displayed in figure 16.4.

Figure 16.4

*Detail area of
Time Sheet.*

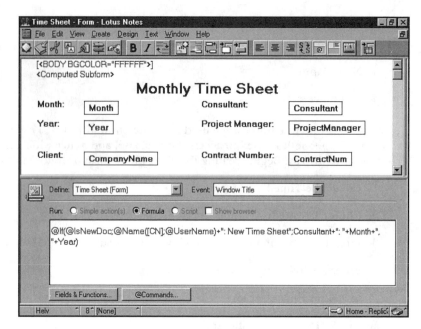

Calendar Area

This time sheet requires some sort of calendar on which the hours can be entered.
One month's worth of daily hours are recorded on each time sheet. Given that this
application so clearly involves calendar-type functions, an obvious question arises.
Why not use a Notes calendar view? The Notes calendaring interface looks good over
the Internet. However, the Notes calendaring system focuses on discrete daily activities rather than ongoing month-long activities. If Notes calendaring functions are
used, the users have to enter a separate time sheet for every day of the month.
Because Notes calendaring tools do not meet the requirements of a monthly or even
a weekly Time Tracking system, the Key People application has to include its own
calendaring system.

A table must be used to maintain the proper appearance of a calendar over the
Internet. The first thing to determine when working with calendars is the number of
rows. A 31 day month can actually be spread across six different weeks. The calendar
needs to have one row for the static description of the weekday (Sunday, Monday,
Tuesday, and so on), and two rows for each of the six weeks: one row for the date and
one row for the users to enter their hours. Key People Consulting requires weekly and
monthly totals of hours as well as the final monthly total expressed in days. The
calendar table therefore needs a total of 15 rows. It also needs seven columns for the
days of the week plus one column for the weekly totals.

To create the calendar area, follow these steps:

1. Create a 15 row by 8 column table on the Time Sheet form.

2. Center the alignment of the first seven columns, and right align the last column.

3. Enter the days of the week at the top of the first seven columns and the heading "Sub-Total" at the top of the last column. Use an eight-point bold font.

4. Create a computed numeric field anywhere on the form called "Day" using the same size font, and copy it into the clipboard.

5. Paste this value sequentially into the first seven cells of the even numbered rows. It pastes as Day 1, Day 2, and so on.

6. Create a numeric field called "Sun" using a 10-point font. Copy it to the clipboard.

7. Paste this field down the Sunday column in the cells below the Day fields. It should appear as Sun 1, Sun 2, and so on.

8. Repeat the preceding two steps for the other days of the week.

Your results should look like figure 16.5.

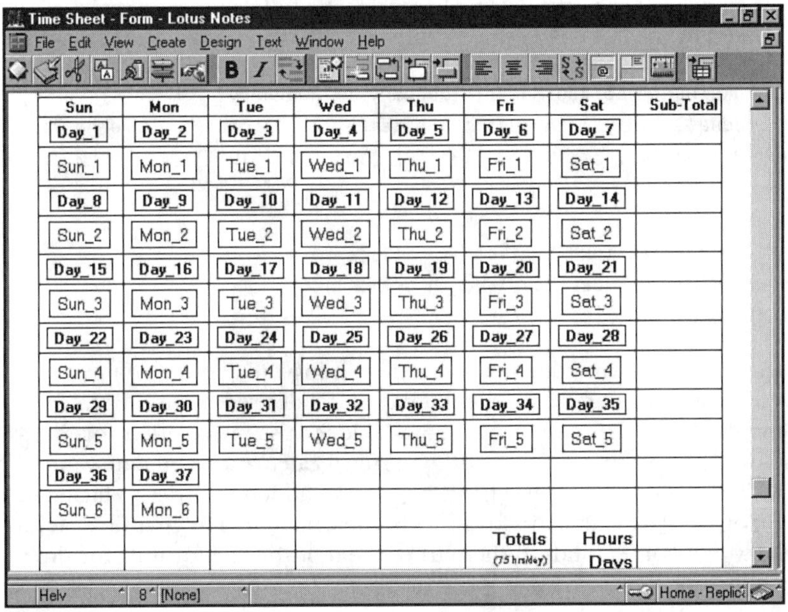

Figure 16.5

Calendar table in design mode.

After all the fields are created, try to save the form. Notes notifies you that the computed field Day_1 is missing a formula. In fact, all the computed fields are missing formulas. The fields need to be populated with formulas that will generate a proper calendar. Looking at a paper-based monthly calendar, you will notice that the month does not always begin on a Sunday. The calendar being developed here is no exception. If the month begins on a Sunday, then "Day_1" is 1; if the month starts on a Monday, then "Day_2" is 1 and Day_1 is blank; and so on. Converting this algorithm to Notes is not trivial because Notes has no function to determine the day of the week for the first day of the month. It does have, however, a function that enables you to generate a date value equal to the first day of the month and another function that tells you the weekday that corresponds to that date. It is possible to compute the date within the formula for each of the fields, but for the sake of performance, the date should be calculated only once. A hidden field above the table is the best method for storing the results. Create a hidden field called MonthStartDate and give it this formula:

```
MonthNum:=@TextToNumber(@Replace(Month; "January": "February": "March":
"April":"May": "June": "July": "August": "September": "October": "November":
"December";"1":"2":"3":"4":"5":"6":"7":"8":"9":"10":"11":"12"));
@Date(@TextToNumber(Year);MonthNum;1)
```

The end of the month has similar problems. There is no simple formula to determine where to stop numbering the calendar dates. To work up a formula, you must first determine how many days are in the selected month. The following code sets the MonthEndDate field to the last day of the month:

```
MonthNum:=@TextToNumber(@Replace(Month; "January": "February": "March":
"April":"May": "June": "July": "August": "September": "October": "November":
"December";"1":"2":"3":"4":"5":"6":"7":"8":"9":"10":"11":"12"));
NextMonth:=
        @If(MonthNum=12;
                @Date(@TextToNumber(Year)+1;1;1);
              @Date(@TextToNumber(Year);MonthNum+1;1));
@Adjust(NextMonth;0;0;-1;0;0;0)
```

The basic algorithm behind this code involves determining the first day of next month and then going back one day to the last day of the desired month. Both the start and the end date for the month are now available for use in the other formulas. For optimal peformance, it is preferable not to perform calculations on date values repetitively. Two more hidden numeric fields need to be added in order to facilitate the optimization of the date calculation process in the calendar. The first field simply holds the weekday that corresponds to the start of the month. The formula for the MonthStartDate then becomes:

```
@Weekday(MonthStartDate)
```

The other number needed is the number of days in the month. The formula for the MonthEndDate then becomes:

```
@Day(MonthEndDate)
```

After these fields are created, they should be hidden. For the purposes of debugging, however, the developer may continue to display these fields until the calendar is working properly.

The next step is to develop the formula for the computed fields within the calendar. Three different formulas are required: one for the first week, one for the last week and one for the remaining weeks. It is possible to create a different formula for every field, but future maintenance becomes more difficult if there are 37 different formulas to verify. For the first week, the following formula determines when the date numbering should start and whether it should be incremented or not:

```
daynum:=1;
@If(daynum>=MonthStartNum;daynum+1-MonthStartNum;"")
```

The formula listed is for the Day_1 field. In order to change it for the Day_2 field, the only change is to assign the value 2 to "daynum." The weeks in the middle of the calendar are the easiest to follow because they need only take the preceding day's value and add one. The formula for the last week needs to determine whether there are any more days in the month before it assigns the field. The following formula takes care of that requirement:

```
daynum:=29;
@If(daynum<(MonthEndNum+MonthStartNum);Day_7+daynum-7;"")
```

This completes the main calendar fields. The form can now be saved and tested. In order to test the form, call it up through your Web browser with the following URL:

```
http://yourdominoserver/timetrk.nsf/time+sheet
```

Any developer using the same physical machine for the Domino server and for development can normally also use the following URL:

```
http://127.0.0.1/timetrk.nsf/time+sheet
```

After the form comes up in the Web browser, you can check how well the design is working. Figure 16.6 shows how the form looks at this point.

Figure 16.6

Calendar area as seen through the Web browser.

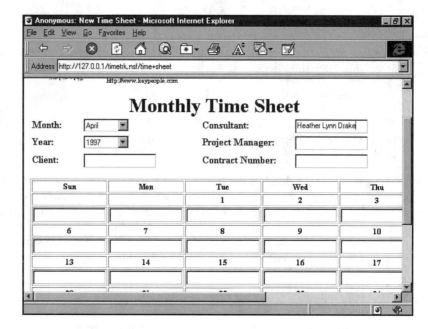

At this point, the document is working well. The detail section is properly pre-filling the user name, and the month and year picklists are very easy to use. The calendar looks like a calendar and is properly assigning the date numbers. However, a number of problems are visible. The calendar stretches past the edge of the screen. Because few things infuriate computer users more than horizontal scrolling, the calendar needs to be adjusted so that it fits the screen. The calendar table is also inappropriately displaying editable fields for days prior to and following the current month. The totals formulas are still missing.

In order to fix the calendar, the problem must first be identified. One of the first places to help locate errors is in the actual HTML code the Domino renders. To view the HTML code, select View Source from the Web browser menu. Developers who are familiar with HTML notice right away that the HTML produced for the calendar table is quite simple. In fact, nothing within the HTML gives any help in this case. The only thing that is wrong with this calendar is the fact that it is simply too large. The size is being affected entirely by the data entry field. In order to reduce the size of the data entry fields the only change required is some passthru HTML. Figure 16.7 shows the additional code that is required for each of the data entry fields.

The next step is to hide the unnecessary fields. The reason for hiding these fields is to remove the extra table cells from the calendar. One might think that simply setting the computed fields equal to NULL is adequate. When Domino renders the NULL fields it does not include any information from the field, which is what one expects. However, Domino includes any formatting information that surrounds the field such as bold or alignment tags. These tags are enough for the Web browser to assume the cell has content and hence display the table cell. Because field values are not adequate for hiding the field, the Hide-When attribute must be used instead. The formula for hiding the cells for calendar day number one is:

```
1<MonthStartNum
```

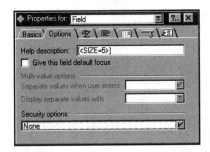

Figure 16.7

The Properties box for calendar field.

This formula should be placed in the Hide-When formula for each of the cells in the first six dates of the calendar. Modify the formula by replacing the number 1 to match the corresponding day number. The cells after day number 28 may also need to be hidden. The formula for the Hide-When attribute for the cells relating to day number 29 is:

```
29>=(MonthEndNum+MonthStartNum)
```

This takes care of all the issues dealing with the data entry portion of the calendar table. The sub-totals and totals fields still need to be created. The important issue surrounding the calculation for the totals fields is that some of the daily data entry fields will not have any value because the consultant may not have worked every day. In Lotus Notes a blank value is not the same as zero. Specifically, blank numeric fields do not necessarily adopt their proper numeric data type. This means that if a developer creates a formula that involves these fields, the end user probably receives a data type mismatch error message. In the case of this database, Notes considers this error severe enough to prevent the application from working. The following formula for the sub-total for the first week circumvents this problem:

```
total:=
@If(@IsNumber(Sun_1);Sun_1;0)+
@If(@IsNumber(Mon_1);Mon_1;0)+
@If(@IsNumber(Tue_1);Tue_1;0)+
@If(@IsNumber(Wed_1);Wed_1;0)+
@If(@IsNumber(Thu_1);Thu_1;0)+
@If(@IsNumber(Fri_1);Fri_1;0)+
@If(@IsNumber(Sat_1);Sat_1;0);
@If(total=0;"";total)
```

Place this formula in the sub-total fields, which total the weekly hours worked for each row of calendar data. The sub-total fields initially appear to be good candidates for Hide-When formulas. One of the design requirements is that a printable version of the time sheet be available to consultants who do not have access to the Internet. If the sub-total cells are hidden, the box surrounding the area where the sub-totals are supposed to be entered also disappears. This is not a desirable effect, so no Hide-When formulas should be entered for the sub-total fields. Now that the sub-totals are available, the monthly totals can also be calculated by adding the sub-total fields. This addition has the same potential problem with NULL values that the preceding subtotal calculation had. This potential problem is easily avoided with the following formula:

```
total:=
@If(@IsNumber(Total_1);Total_1;0)+
@If(@IsNumber(Total_2);Total_2;0)+
@If(@IsNumber(Total_3);Total_3;0)+
@If(@IsNumber(Total_4);Total_4;0)+
@If(@IsNumber(Total_5);Total_5;0)+
@If(@IsNumber(Total_6);Total_6;0);
@If(total=0;"";total)
```

Finally, the monthly number of days worked is a simple calculation. Divide the total number of hours by length of a working day, for Key People Consulting this number is 7.5. The following formula takes care of this field:

```
@If(!@IsNumber(TotalHours);
            "";
       TotalHours>0;
            TotalHours/7.5;
       "")
```

Now that all the fields have been created and defined the calendar area is almost finished. Shading the day number rows of the calendar brings about a noticeable improvement in the appearance. The final version of the calendar area is presented in figure 16.8.

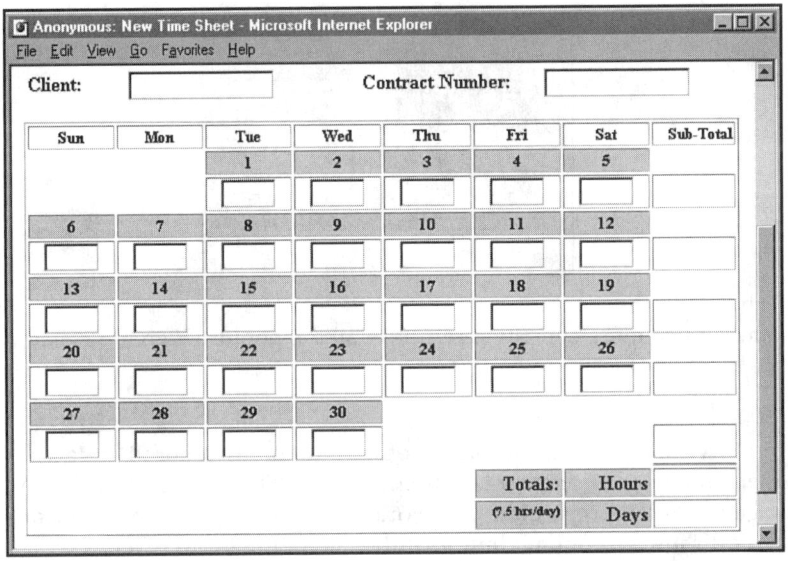

Figure 16.8

Final version of calendar area as seen through the Web browser.

Comments Area

The design specification requires that consultants be able to list deliverables and other comments on the time sheets. In order to create a multi-line data entry area through Domino, a Rich Text field must be used. Create this field called Deliverables at the bottom of the form.

If you were to immediately call this revised form up in your Web browser you would see a data entry box of a strangely small size. The data entry area default size created by Domino is 7 rows by 50 columns. If you were to take this default data entry area and start typing a long line, you would notice something even stranger. Microsoft Internet Explorer automatically uses word wrap whenever you reached the edge of the data entry box. In this same test Netscape Navigator does not use word wrap; instead it continues scrolling to the right until the user hits a hard return. This type of inconsistency can cause major problems during rollout, because users may use browsers that were not checked during the development phase. In order to minimize the potential problems it is a good idea to hard code the preferred settings so that all browsers interpret it the same way. The desired code is listed in figure 16.9.

Figure 16.9

*The Properties box
for Rich Text
field.*

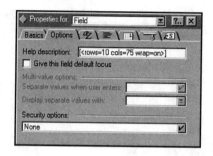

This code produces much more consistent results in all the popular Web browsers.

Buttons

Domino only displays the first Notes button. All other buttons are ignored. In fact, only the placement and label of the first button is retained. The button's actual function is changed to Submit regardless of the original code. If there are no buttons, Domino automatically inserts a Submit button at the end of the form. When the developer creates the button, the developer can control the text label that appears on the button. For this form, create a button labeled "Submit Time Sheet" underneath the calendar. This button now works properly over the Web without any additional code. Because this application must also function in the Notes environment, add the following lines of code:

```
@Command([FileSave])
@Command([FileCloseWindow])
```

This button now works properly in both Notes and the Internet. The only other button that is commonly found on HTML form-based applications is the Reset button. A Reset button can be accommodated on this form by using passthru HTML. Because the passthru HTML needs to be hidden from Notes users, it should be placed on its own line so that the text Hide-When properties can be used. Place the following code immediately underneath the Submit Time Sheet button:

```
[<INPUT TYPE="Reset" VALUE="Clear Time Sheet Entries">]
```

After the text has been entered, highlight the line, choose Text Properties, and insert the following line of code in the formula area:

```
!@Contains(@UserRoles;"$$WebClient")
```

Save the form and call it up in your Web browser again. Try the Clear Time Sheet Entries button. Notice how it only clears items that were entered by the user during this session. This is beneficial because we do not want users to clear the Consultant, Month, or Year fields. Nonetheless, users may have different expectations for this button. Because there is no way to change the button's functionality, the best that the developer can do is either remove the button or describe the behavior fully in the on-line documentation.

Form Actions

Navigation within an Internet-based application is achieved through links. In order to create links that work in both the Notes and Internet environment, form actions need to be used. Several Form Actions need to be considered for inclusion:

◆ Main Menu

◆ Edit

◆ Show Printable Version

◆ Help

Actions can be created so that they are available while reading, editing, or both. Normally a developer does not provide a user with any method for exiting the HTML form except through the submit button. The reason for this is that Web browsers are not good at launching secondary pages and then seamlessly returning to the original page. Users who are filling in a form and then move off to another page may also forget to hit the submit button before closing the Web browser. Unlike Notes users, Internet users are not warned when they try to abandon an HTML form that they were editing.

Taking a "Better safe than sorry" approach to the Time Tracking application means that no actions are available while editing. The order of the actions is also important to the consistent look and feel of a Web site. It is much easier for users to use your Web site if certain buttons are always in the same place. For this database, the Main Menu button is always on the left and the help button is always on the right. Now that the scope and positions of the actions are determined, it is time to start coding them.

The first action opens a navigator called MainNav. The formula for this action is a single @Command:

```
@Command([OpenNavigator];"MainNav")
```

The Edit Document action is equally straightforward:

```
@Command([EditDocument])
```

The Show Printable Version action is a little more complex because it must first locate the proper version. The best document locator in Notes is the DocumentUniqueID, so it is used as the key. Create a hidden view in the database called LookupDocUNIDPrint and give it only one sorted column that is equal to @Text(@DocumentUniqueID). We need to create a printing version of the time sheet later and then add a form formula to this new view. For the time being, the view brings up the current version of the form rather the print version. The code below can now access this new view and open the document. The standard code to perform this task is actually just the first two lines of the code below. The remaining lines are to solve a problem that the pure-Notes user would have encountered. In Notes, the first two lines of this code would have resulted in the view being left open in the background. The repeat of the open view command followed by the close window command is a standard Notes trick to solve this problem.

```
@Command([OpenView];"LookupDocUNIDPrint";@Text(@DocumentUniqueID));
@Command([OpenDocument]);
@Command([OpenView];"LookupDocUNIDPrint");
@Command([FileCloseWindow])
```

The last form action is the Help action. This action is actually a little trickier than the others are, because the code needed for the Notes client is not supported for the Internet client and vice versa. The following code satisfies both types of clients by first testing to see which environment is making the request:

```
@If(@Contains(@UserRoles;"$$WebClient");
                @URLOpen("/timetrk.nsf/$about");
@Command([HelpAboutDatabase]))
```

The form actions appear with the Time Sheet, as displayed in Figure 16.10.

Figure 16.10

Time Sheet with form actions.

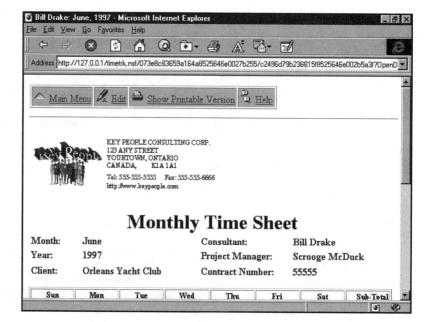

This completes the form actions. Remember to adjust the Hide-When properties to hide all the actions when the user is in edit mode.

Now that the initial layout of the Time Sheet form has been completed, another factor needs to be considered. Data integrity of the information stored in the database can only be guaranteed if a certain minimum number of fields are completed by the users. This data integrity is guaranteed through the use of field validation formulas.

Field Validation

The quality of information entered by end users often needs to be verified. Certain fields may require an entry, or the entry may need to be in a particular format. Typically, in a Notes-based application, validation is accomplished for individual fields by Field Input Validation formulas or by LotusScript formulas in the Field Exit Event. Validation can also apply to multiple fields if a more complex formula is used in the QuerySave event of the form.

Validation for Web-based applications is somewhat limited because Web-based applications cannot perform actions based on the user's activity. Interactions with Web-based applications are limited to calling another document or submitting the current document. How does the developer satisfy the requirements for validation over the Internet? The next two sections offer a couple of ideas.

Single Field Input Validation

The field-level Input Validation formulas that are used in standard Notes applications continue to evaluate properly in a Web-based Notes application. They do not, however, evaluate in exactly the same fashion. In Notes, Input Validation formulas run each time a document is saved or refreshed. Over the Web, there is no concept of refreshing field values. Input Validation formulas run only at the time the document is submitted.

The Time Tracking application might require entries in the ProjectAdmin, Client, and ContractNum fields. The developer has the ability to control the appearance and text of the error message using HTML formatting. A sample formula for the ProjectAdmin field might be:

```
BlankMessage:="<H1>An entry is required in the Project Manager field.
          </H1><hr>"+"<H2>Please return to the Time Sheet to enter a
          Project Manager "+
          "by clicking the BACK button in your browser.<hr> Thank you.
</H2>";
@If(ProjectAdmin!="";@Success;@Failure(BlankMessage))
```

Input Validation formulas first assess the validity of information entered in a field, and then display a message to the user. In the case of this current application the preceding code is actually flawed because it displays its message in HTML, which fails to accommodate the pure Notes user. Input validation formulas have two options in this type of cross-environment application. They can either ignore formatting for the messages to the Web clients or they can carry both environments within the same code block.

In Notes, the messages appear in a dialog box, which immediately returns the user to the document. The user's cursor is positioned on the field in question to facilitate the completion of the required field or the modification of its existing contents. The format of the message is therefore not as important in the Notes environment.

Over the Web, this is not the case. The error message appears as a new document. The user is required to manually return to the form and find the field that is in error on his or her own. The browser displays the error message as in figure 16.11.

Figure 16.11

Result of failed field validation.

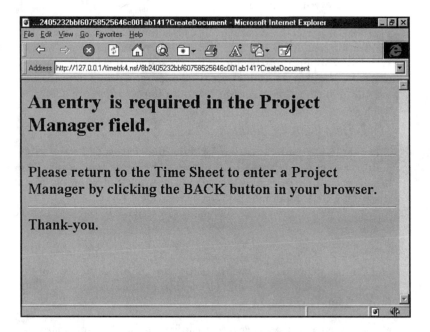

Using the browser's Back button is awkward. Finding the correct field can also be difficult if its location is not described properly in the message. Another potential problem occurs when the application requires the verification of multiple fields.

The user is only notified of the problem in the first field. After returning to the form, locating and fixing the error, and resubmitting the form, he or she may be faced with a second error document. This process needs to be repeated for each field in error. The cumulative effect of repeating this process proves to be annoying and time-consuming, and should be avoided.

Multiple Field Input Validation

A more efficient alternative is to combine the verification of several fields into a single formula. The ProjectAdmin, Client, and ContractNum fields can all be assessed simultaneously using the validation formula of a hidden field. Create the hidden field at the bottom of the Time Sheet form and give it the following formula:

```
ErrorText:= "";
FrontText:= "<center><H1>Missing Information</H1></center>"+
    "<h3>The following fields require entries before the "+
    "time sheet can be submitted:</h3><ol>";
EndText:= "</ol><h3>Hit the BACK button on your browser to "+
    "return to the Time Sheet";

@If(@Contains(@UserRoles;"$$WebClient");

@Do(
@If(ProjectManager="";@Set("ErrorText";ErrorText+"<li>Project Manager
➥Name<p>");"");
@If(CompanyName="";@Set("ErrorText";ErrorText+"<li>Client Name<p>");"");
@If(ContractNum="";@Set("ErrorText";ErrorText+
"<li>Contract Number. <br>"+
"<font size=-1>If you do not have the contract number, and are unable
to "+" obtain it <br> from the Admin Officer at 613-555-5555, enter the
word "+"&quot;Missing&quot; <br> in the contract number field.<font
size=+1><br>");"")
);"");
@If(ErrorText="";@Success;@Failure(FrontText+ErrorText+EndText))
```

When the user submits the form, the Validation field verifies each of the three required fields in turn. If both the Client and ContractNum fields are blank, the browser displays the error message shown in figure 16.12.

Figure 16.12

Result of failed multiple-field validation.

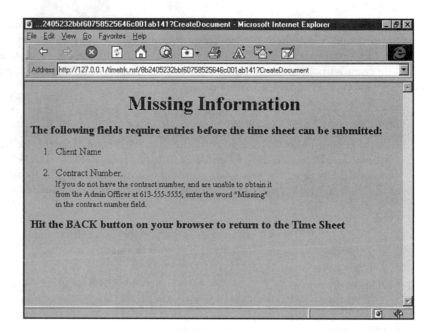

The validation formula not only verifies the field value, but also checks to see whether the user came in from the Web. For standard Notes users the regular field-by-field validation is preferable because it brings the cursor back to the field in error after the error message closes. If a combination of validation approaches is taken, then do not forget to exclude the Web users from the field-by-field validation in the same way that the Notes users were excluded from the multi-field validation. The following is an Input Validation formula for the Project Manager field:

```
@If(@Contains(@UserRoles;"$$WebClient");
     @Success;
   @If(ProjectManager="";
     @Failure("Project Manager Name is Required");
   @Success))
```

View Description

The two administration views, Files and LookupDocUNIDPrint, were already developed as the need for them arose. Focus now on the views that the users need for their interaction with the system. Based on the original design specifications, the users require four views:

◆ By Month

◆ By Company

◆ By Consultant

◆ By Contract Number

At first glance, it seems like a rather trivial process to create the required views. After the By Month view is created and tested, however, there will be an obvious problem with the sorting of the month field. Furthermore, this problem will show up in any of the views that have a sorted month column. To create the By Month view, follow these steps:

1. Select Create, View from the menu.

2. Under View Name call the view: By Month.

3. Select Shared.

4. Under Options select Blank.

5. Under Options click Design Now.

6. Click OK to start editing the view design.

7. Click Add Condition under View Selection.

8. Change Condition to By Form Used.

9. Select only the Time Sheet form.

10. Double-click the first column.

11. Under Basics remove the title.

12. Under Basics change the width to 2.

13. Under Basics select Show Twistie.

14. Under Sorting select Ascending and Categorized.

15. Choose 12-point Bold font.

16. Choose the Month field for the column value.

17. Create the second column.

18. Repeat steps 12–16 for the Consultant field.

19. Create the third column.

20. Choose the CompanyName field.

21. Sort but do not categorize.

If you look at this view after adding some data, you will notice that the first column looks a little strange. The months are alphabetical rather than chronological. This is not totally unexpected because the Month field is a text field. It appears as in figure 16.13.

Figure 16.13

By Month view.

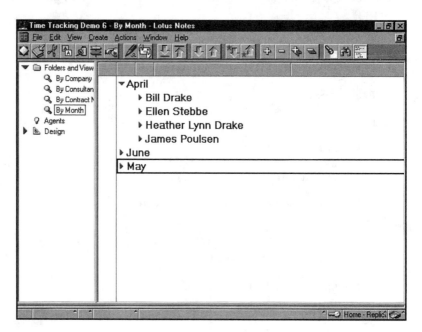

This is a very common problem when working with text versions of dates. We can switch and use a date field, but it is not really necessary. In fact, this problem is resolved when the calendar area is created on the Time Sheet form. Borrowing some of the code from the MonthStartDate field gives the following formula for the new first column that needs to be inserted into the view:

```
@TextToNumber(@Replace(Month; "January": "February": "March": "April":
"May": "June": "July": "August": "September": "October": "November":
"December";"1":"2":"3":"4":"5":"6":"7":"8":"9":"10":"11":"12"))
```

Add the new column by following these steps:

1. Put the view back into design mode.

2. Select the first column.

3. Select Create, Insert New Column from the menu.

4. Enter the preceding code in the formula area.

5. Under Basics set the width to 1.

6. Under Basics select Hide Column.

7. Under Sorting select Ascending.

The view now looks correct. Create the other views in a similar fashion. Whenever a column that requires sorted Month values is encountered, paste in the column that was created above.

Now that the views are finished, the next normal development activity is to create some view actions to perform tasks such as creating a document or switching view. The "Views" section of Chapter 15 describes this technique. View actions do not have the same impact that a graphical interface has, so wait until a graphical interface is generated. The creation of this interface is described in the "Navigators" section of this chapter.

Security Model

This database has a few of security issues to address:

◆ In order to keep the client list confidential, consultants can only read their own Time Sheets.

◆ After finance accepts a time sheet, the users can no longer edit the document.

◆ Anonymous access is not allowed.

◆ Audit trails are required for tracking the edit history.

The first two issues will be addressed by the addition of Readers fields and Authors fields. The anonymous access issue will be addressed by changing the ACL. Audit trails will be enabled by adding an additional field to the Time Sheet form.

Readers Field

The purpose of the restriction on allowing consultants to only read their own time sheet is to prevent someone from walking away with the client list. This protection has to be real. In other words, assume that the person seeking the list is willing to put some effort into the search. Simply hiding a view is not adequate. Anyone with a lot of Notes experience can get around that type of security. Encryption keys are also not an option for a number of reasons. The first reason to exclude encryption keys from the security model is that they do not work over the Internet; user IDs are not even a part of the authentication scheme. The second reason to exclude encryption from the security model is that the person the keys are intended to block is already entitled to the keys because this scenario probably involves a departing employee.

The most secure method for achieving secrecy in this case is a field of the Readers data type. Readers fields have their own problems as well. The designer must be extremely careful to ensure that the servers, Notes administrators, database managers, agents, and corporate management do not get unintentionally locked out. The best way to prevent this problem is to include a number of Readers fields rather than just one. For this application, create the Readers fields on the Time Tracking form with the following values:

Field Name	Value
NotesAdminReaders	NotesAdmin; LocalDomainServers
DatabaseMgrReaders	TimeTrackManager; NotesDevelopers
UserReaders	Consultant field; ProjectManager field

Create all three fields in the hidden section at the bottom of the Time Sheet form. The first two should be "Computed When Composed" because they never change. The last item should be "Computed" with the following formula:

```
@UserReaders:ProjectManager:Consultant
```

The group names vary from organization to organization, but the concept should be clear. With Readers fields you cannot be too safe. If you only have one Readers field and it gets set to the invalid value, due to a change in group names or an error in the formula, you can never get the data back. Normally, it is better to avoid Readers fields altogether. In this case, the developer should ensure that this really is a true business requirement.

Restricted Editor Privileges

In order to give editor privileges in a controlled manner, author ACL rights and Authors fields must be used together. Any user who has author access is able to create new documents and edit existing documents if his or her name is present in an Authors field. For this application the majority of the users are limited to author access. In order to maintain the author access list, create a computed Authors field called AuthorList on the Time Sheet form and set it equal to:

```
@UserName:Consultant:ProjectManager
```

Anonymous Access

Normally, the first component of any Web security system is the Registration database. Users must be registered somehow. In the case of this application, the Registration database is not required because this application is intended for a specific set of people and it is not intended for the general public. The only issue that the developer has to deal with concerning the access from the Web is the issue of authentication. In order to use the Time Tracking system users must authenticate before they enter the database. Chapter 15 includes a lengthy discussion of this issue, but basically all that is required is to create an ACL entry for "Anonymous" and set it to No Access. After this is done users are forced to authenticate as soon as they open the database, unless they have already been authenticated for another database on the same server. After they are authenticated, the regular ACL settings apply. The primary ACL setting should be based on a group that contains all of the consultants. This group should be given Author access to the database.

Audit Trail

Many databases require audit trails. Usually a developer can find an old database and simply copy the code and paste it into the new database. This audit trail is based on text fields because they are easier to work with. The text fields on the form have a limit of 15 kilobytes, so if a lot of activity is expected against these documents a rich text field is required. To enable the audit trail, start by creating a field at the bottom of the form. The field should be computed with the following formula:

```
tMonth := @Select(@Month(@Now); "01"; "02"; "03"; "04"; "05"; "06";
  "07"; "08"; "09"; "10"; @Text(@Month(@Now)));

tDay := @Select(@Day(@Now); "01"; "02"; "03"; "04"; "05"; "06";
  "07"; "08"; "09"; "10"; @Text(@Day(@Now)));

tYear := @Right(@Text(@Year(@Now)); 2);
tTime := @Text(@Now; "T1S1");
tWhen := tYear + "/" + tMonth + "/" + tDay + " " + tTime;

@If(
   @IsDocBeingLoaded & @IsNewDoc;
           tWhen + " created by " + @Name([CN]; @UserName);
   @IsDocBeingSaved & !@IsNewDoc ;
           (tWhen + " edited by " + @Name([CN]; @UserName)):History;
   History)
```

Unless there is a need for users to see this information over the Web, the developer probably wants to hide this field from the Web users. The field should also be hidden when printing. The Hide-When options are set from either the Field Properties or the Text Properties boxes.

Navigators

Navigators provide the ease-of-use features that modern applications require. Navigators over the Internet only work if they are made using a graphic background with hotspots for the links.

In order to create a graphic background you must first get an image loaded into the clipboard. After the image is in the clipboard, select Create, Graphic Background and the image pastes into the navigator. After the image is in the navigator, the navigator hotspots can be created. Use the following formula to create new Time Sheets:

```
@Command([Compose];"Time Sheet")
```

To navigate to a different view, use the simple action Open View.

A sample navigator is displayed in figure 16.14.

Figure 16.14

A sample graphical navigator.

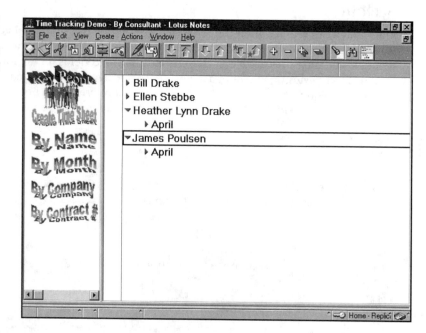

The basic design of the Time Tracking system is now complete. The Time Sheet form has been developed with buttons, form actions, and validation in place. The necessary views and security features have also been included. The database is functional in both the Notes environment and the Web environment. The developer can now advance beyond basic functionality to incorporate some advanced design elements.

Advanced Design

Moving the basic design phase of an application to the advanced design phase is probably the most interesting part of application development. The advanced design phase is the phase of the project where the database is adjusted to include more complex functions, such as approval workflow. For Web-based databases such as this one, visual enhancements should also be made during this phase to give the application a more polished appearance than is provided by the system defaults. Web-based databases also enable developers to collect additional information from the users by including CGI variables in the design.

Approval Workflow

Approval workflow can be quite complex. For this application, approval workflow can involve mail reminders when time sheets are almost due, followed by another series of notifications as the time sheets get later and later. For the notification message to function, some additional tracking is required to know which time sheets are due. That level of detail is beyond the scope of this chapter. The system requires a connection to a contract management system to retrieve the information from the contract details. This additional functionality is based on standard Notes programming techniques and does not require any Domino programming skills.

A more basic level of workflow approval within this application can be implemented here. After a time sheet has been incorporated into the invoice system the original author should no longer be permitted to make changes. This can be accomplished by removing the user's name from the Authors field. The first step is to add a flag to the system identifying the approved time sheets. This flag should only be visible to people who have the authority to set it. A role called "Finance" is used to control this access. Secondly, an agent will be triggered to remove the user's name from the Authors field.

Create a role by opening the ACL and going into the roles section. Click on the Add button and add a role called "Finance." Although you are still in the ACL, add yourself to this new role. Now the Time Sheet itself needs to be changed to include this new flag. The logical place for this flag is just below the totals because that is the area of the document that finance must work with (see fig. 16.15).

Figure 16.15

Finance approval flag.

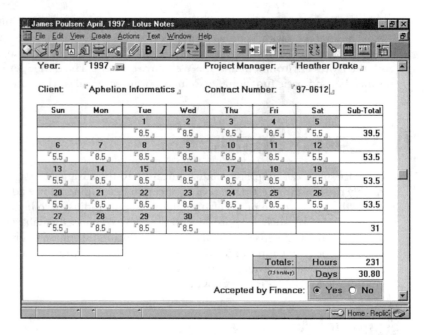

The agent referred to by $$QuerySaveAgent can now be used to test this flag and make any changes to the author fields if necessary.

Use of the agent referred to by the $$QuerySaveAgent field is an essential method for maintaining updates among various databases. For instance, if a company running this system also had its invoice system in Notes then the QuerySaveAgent can easily update the invoice system every time a new time sheet is submitted. In fact, through the use of MQSeries and other tools, the agent referred to by $$QuerySaveAgent can even update a host-based financial system.

No complex environment is in place to which this application can connect. The agent referred to by $$QuerySaveAgent that is used here is much simpler: it only needs to remove author privileges from everyone in the AuthorList field after Finance has accepted the time sheet.

To enable the agent, add a field called $$QuerySaveAgent to the hidden field section at the bottom of the form and give it a default value of "Remove Author."

Now create an agent called "Remove Author" and give it the following formula:

```
Sub Initialize
    Dim session As New NotesSession
    Dim doc As NotesDocument
    Dim ApproveFlag As String
    Set doc = session.DocumentContext
```

```
    ApproveFlag$ = doc.Accepted(0)
    If ApproveFlag$ = "Yes" Then
         Call doc.RemoveItem("AuthorList")
         Call doc.Save (True,True)
    End If

End Sub
```

Ensure that the agent is "Shared," "Run Manually from the Actions menu." The agent should be a "Run Once (@Commands may be used)" type agent.

Visual Enhancements

The Time Tracking application is now fully functional, and can be implemented. By using some additional advanced Domino design features, however, the ease of use and appearance of the application can be dramatically enhanced. The submission message can be customized, and a consistent look and feel can be applied to the application using special fields and forms.

Customizing the Submission Message with $$Return

When the user has submitted a form, Domino displays the default Form processed document, as shown in figure 16.16.

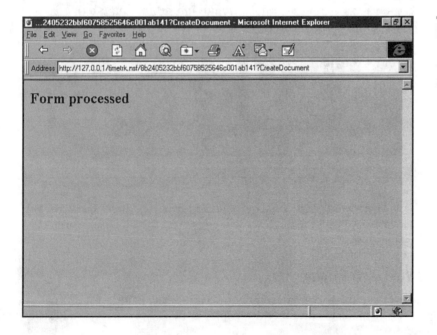

Figure 16.16

The default response to submission.

This document is uninformative and inadequate for the Time Tracking application. The reserved $$Return field may be added to customize the message displayed to the user. To create this field, follow these steps:

1. Create a field labeled $$Return on the Time Sheet form.

2. Add passthru HTML or refer to a URL in the Value event of $$Return. For example:

```
"<H1>Time Sheet Processed</H1><hr>" +
"<H2>Thank-you, " + Consultant +" for submitting your " + Month +
" Time Sheet for the " + CompanyName <hr> "Your total hours are " +
TotalHours+". </H2>"
```

The customized result screen should look like figure 16.17.

Figure 16.17

A customized form processed message.

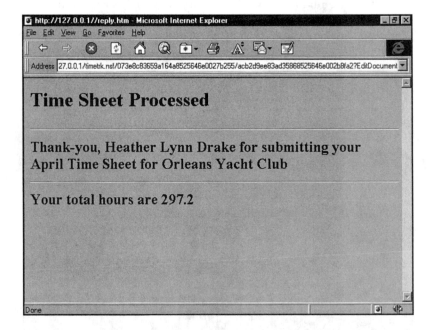

The developer can also include additional graphics and hypertext links if desired. For example, the user may want to have the option to go back to the submitted form, which is ready for printing.

Formatting Views for Display

Although Domino's automatic conversion of Notes views is adequate, several visual enhancements can be made to customize the display of views. Special forms and fields are used to format the Time Tracking views for Domino users. A $$ViewTemplateDefault form and a customized $$ViewTemplate form is added. These forms use the following special fields: $$ViewBody, $$ViewList, $$NavigatorBody.

The default format for views adds action hotspots to perform the following functions: NavigatePrevious, NavigateNext, Expand Collapse, and ShowSearchBar. These actions are inappropriate for a Time Sheet application. They are replaced with the inclusion of action hotspots and the MainNav navigator.

Format the appearance of views by creating a $$ViewTemplateDefault form, using the following steps:

1. Create a new form called "$$ViewTemplateDefault." The form name may be changed, provided the form alias stays the same.

2. Insert a computed subform that displays the corporate banner for Web clients. Use the following formula:

```
If(@Contains(@UserRoles;"$$WebClient";"WebBanner";"")
```

   Notes users do not use this form, so there is no need to include the NotesBanner subform as we did previously on the Time Sheet form.

3. Create a table with two columns. The left-hand column should be 1.5" wide.

4. Create a field called "$$ViewList" in the left column of the table.

5. Create a field called "$$ViewBody" in the right column of the table.

The $$ViewTemplateDefault form is used to format all views that are not associated with a particular $$ViewTemplate form. This form enables the developer to enforce a consistent look and feel for all views in the application.

The $$ViewList field automatically displays a list of all views and folders in the database, without requiring a field formula. Similarly, the $$ViewBody field displays the contents of the chosen view. Before the $$ViewTemplateDefault form was created, the system-defined view template was used for presenting the view. The rendered view featured a prominent display of the view's title. Now that the system-defined layout is no longer used, the view name is conspicuously absent. To correct this omission, add a field to the $$ViewTemplateDefault form, labeled ViewTitle. It has the following formula:

```
"[<H2>"+@DbTitle+" - "+@ViewTitle+"</H2>]"
```

To enhance navigation of the database from this view, the developer may want to include some action hotspots. For example, this view can include the capability to create a new Time Sheet in this manner:

1. Add "**New Time Sheet**" as static text above the $$ViewList field.

2. Import the actn030.gif image from the domino\icons subdirectory, and place this to the left of the static text.

3. Highlight the image and the static text, then choose Create, Hotspot, Action Hotspot. Use the following formula:

```
@Command([Compose];"Time Sheet")
```

For example, the By Month view now looks like figure 16.18.

Figure 16.18

The view through the $$View TemplateDefault form.

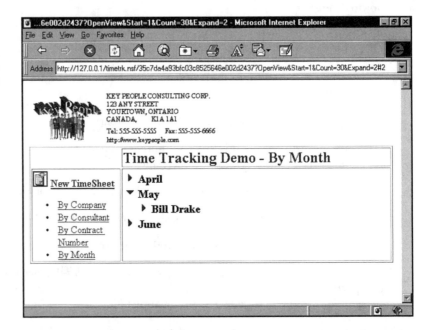

Navigators can be included as part of a view's display on a $$ViewTemplateDefault form. $$ViewList displays a list of all views and folders in the database, using the default Folders navigator. This is impractical in the Time Tracking application, in which only certain views are used. To replace the action hotspot and the $$ViewList with the Main navigator:

1. Delete the hotspot and $$ViewList field.

2. Create a new field called $$NavigatorBody. The value of this field should be the name of the Main navigator.

Formatting Navigators for Display

Developers can enhance the visual appearance of navigators in a couple of ways. Navigators can be included as part of a view's display on a $$ViewTemplate form, as described earlier. Navigators can also be encapsulated in a special form of their own, the $$NavigatorTemplate. The primary Time Tracking application navigator ("MainNav") is enhanced using this latter method.

Navigators are automatically converted by Domino into a functional graphical imagemap. To include a navigator as part of a form, use the $$NavigatorBody field. In this manner, the developer has the flexibility to combine the navigator with additional text and graphics. Several navigators can be displayed simultaneously by adding additional $$NavigatorBody_n fields, in this format: $$NavigatorBody_1, $$NavigatorBody_2, $$NavigatorBody_3, and so on. For example, the Time Tracking application likes to display the corporate banner in addition to the Main navigator. An additional navigator for the Key People site is also used.

1. Create a new form called "$$NavigatorTemplate for MainNav." The form name may be changed, provided the form alias stays the same.

2. Insert a computed subform that displays the corporate banner for Web clients, as above.

3. Create a table with two cells, for the placement of the two Navigators.

4. Create a field called "$$NavigatorBody." Set the value of this field to the name of the navigator ("MainNav").

5. Create a second field called "$$NavigatorBody_1." Set the value of this field to "SiteNav."

Additional enhancements can be made with the inclusion of additional graphics and text. The $$ViewBody field may also be added to allow access to documents from the navigator if required.

CGI

In order to further enhance the audit trail for edit access, which is already being recorded, it is possible to collect even more information. Collecting CGI information is a simple manner of including the CGI field on the form. To collect some CGI variables perform the following steps:

1. Open the Time Sheet Form.

2. Add a hidden field at the bottom of the form called Remote_Addr.

3. Add a second hidden field called Remote_Host.

From now on, any time a form is edited over the Web these two fields automatically fill in by themselves.

Application Implementation

Implementation for Web-based databases is very easy. Generally, just moving the database from the test server to the production server is all that is required. In the case of this application that should hold true as well. User registration is required for the users who do not already have Notes accounts. If the site registration system is in place, users can register themselves. The users then have to be added to one of the corporate groups that has access to the database. Unless this is the driving force behind the organization's Web site, it is likely that these steps have already been taken.

Summary

In this chapter, the theoretical information presented in Chapter 15 was applied to the creation of a practical application for a fictitious client. The application developed in this chapter is a fully functional Web-based Time Tracking system. The initial analysis of the application requirements resulted in a required feature set based on the business needs of Key People Consulting, the target environment and anticipated technical hurdles of the application. The final application takes advantage of a number of specialized Domino features to provide an effective, attractive, and easy to use business tool.

Development began with the creation of the core design elements: forms, views, navigators, and the security model. Consideration was given to both Notes and Internet clients. Emphasis was placed on the visual and functional enhancements made possible by Domino-specific development features. Special Domino fields and forms were used to fully customize the appearance and operation of this application.

Despite its ease of use, Domino enables developers to produce sophisticated mission-critical applications with a minimal investment of time and effort.

PART VI

Notes Advanced Development

CHAPTER 17

Notes Advanced Development

T wo issues of vital importance for applications are data integration and data security. Data integration issues concern the capability to send, retrieve, or modify data from other sources such as another Notes document, another Notes database, or an external data source. Notes applications address data security through ID-based access control at the database, document, and field levels. Notes also utilizes encryption keys to make data available only to people or servers possessing a copy of the encryption key. This chapter addresses data security and data integration through advanced Notes development techniques and presents advanced user interfaces in the following sections:

◆ Notes Internal Data Integration

◆ Notes External Data Integration

◆ Application Security

◆ Data Encryption

◆ Advanced User Interfaces

In addition to the Notes formula methods discussed in this chapter, data integration issues can be addressed by using LotusScript, Java, and other tools such as NotesSQL, Notes C++ API, Notes HiTest C API, MQSeries, and NotesPump. See Chapters 18, 19, and 20 for more information on LotusScript and Java.

Notes Internal Data Integration

Notes applications store, share, and manage information within a single database, across multiple databases, and with external applications (described later in this chapter in the section entitled "Notes External Data Integration"). Fields values are generated based on other fields in the document, fields in other documents, fields in other databases, and other data sources. Additionally, workflow applications move entire documents between databases. This section discusses these two data integration features.

Data Integration Within a Notes Database

Notes active documents acquire data through inheritance (on creation), user input, and computed formulas that change data based on field values or other characteristics of the environment (such as the current date).

Inheritance just requires a formula that evaluates to a field in the selected document when a new document is created and the form option Formulas inherit values from selected document is enabled. Direct user input requires that a field is editable to the user. Computed formulas may be contained in default field formulas, input translation formulas, computed field formulas, computed-when-composed field formulas, action buttons, manual and automated agents, and hotspots.

This section discusses two @Functions used in computed formulas to find data within Notes databases:

- ◆ @DbColumn

- ◆ @DbLookup

@DbColumn and @DbLookup can also be used to access data external to Notes through Open Database Connectivity (ODBC) (see later section in this chapter).

@DbColumn

@DbColumn returns a list of values from a view column. @DbColumn is intended mainly for use as a formula to generate a keyword list. @DbColumn can also be used in field formulas, execute once and background agents (except mail agents), action buttons, SmartIcons, and some hotspots.

Using @DbColumn in lieu of hard-coded entries allows a list of choices to dynamically change as documents in the lookup view are created and deleted. Further, if the @DbColumn formula returns a view column wherein the current field in the current document appears, the Allow values not in list option of the keyword field enables users to enter their own keyword value, which then becomes a member of the keyword list.

The arguments in @DbColumn are as follows:

```
class:"NoCache" ; server:database ; view ; columnNumber.
```

The following list explains each of the arguments:

◆ *Class* specifies the database type, which is either "" or "Notes" for Notes databases.

◆ "NoCache" forces the lookup on each use; "Cache" (or "") caches the lookup result for re-use within the same Notes session.

◆ The *server* value requires the name of the server or "" for current database or local database.

◆ The *database* value is the database path name.

◆ The *view* value is the name of the view containing the column.

◆ The *columnNumber* is the number of the column in the view beginning with 1 for the first column.

> **Tip** Use "" for the *class*:"NoCache" to default to a Notes database and cache. Use "" for the *server:database* to default to the current database. Use the database Replica ID for the *server:database* to specify a database by using its Replica ID. Formulas may be used within @DbColumn to determine argument values, such as @DbName to return the *server:database* or an @If formula to conditionally determine an argument value.

@DbLookup

@DbLookup returns a value from a field in a document or returns multiple values if multiple documents match the lookup key. @DbLookup is intended mainly for use in computed fields. @DbLookup can also be used in keywords formulas, execute once and background agents (except mail agents), action buttons, SmartIcons, and some hotspots. Like @DbColumn, @DbLookup retrieves values from documents in a view. But @DbLookup offers more powerful features through the *key* argument and the option to use a field name in lieu of a column number. @DbLookup can work similarly to @DbColumn by returning values from multiple documents if they share the same *key* value. The value returned by @DbLookup may be from a column in the view or a named field in the document.

> **Tip** Lookups perform faster when the value is retrieved from a column in the view than when retrieved from a named field in the document.

The arguments in @DbLookup are as follows:

```
class:"NoCache" ; server:database ; view ; key ; fieldName or columnNumber.
```

The following list explains each of the arguments:

- ◆ *Class* specifies the database type, which is either "" or "Notes" for Notes databases.

- ◆ "NoCache" forces the lookup on each use; "Cache" (or "") caches the lookup result for re-use within the same Notes session.

- ◆ The *server* value requires the name of the server or "" for current database or local database. The *database* value is the database path name.

- ◆ The *view* value is the name of the view containing the column.

- ◆ The *key* is the value the lookup will match. Each document in the first sorted column of the view that matches the key will return the columnNumber or fieldName value.

- ◆ The *fieldName* is the name of the field containing the value to return.

- ◆ The *columnNumber* is the number of the column in the view beginning with 1 for the first column.

Tip   Use "" for the *class*:"NoCache" to default to a Notes database and cache. Use ""
for the *server*:*database* to default to the current database. Use the database Replica
ID for the *server*:*database* to specify a database by using its Replica ID. Formulas
may be used within @DbColumn to determine argument values, such as @DbName
to return the *server*:*database* or an @If formula to conditionally determine an
argument value.

Tip   Hidden lookup views are often used for @DbColumn and @DbLookup formulas.
Using hidden lookup views for these formulas helps keep view structure clean for the
end user and eliminates the need to modify @DbColumn and @DbLookup code
when views are modified for users. View performance decreases as the number of
views in a database increases. If view performance becomes an issue, some or all
hidden lookup views may be omitted by utilizing the LotusScript NotesDocument
Collection class in lieu of @DbColumn and @DbLookup formulas.

Moving Documents between Notes Databases

Documents can be moved between Notes databases manually through copy and paste
or programmatically through the @MailSend @Function.

Copy and Paste

Developers and users alike can utilize the clipboard to copy and paste information.
Developers can copy and paste forms, fields, views, navigators, subforms, agents,
actions, navigators, formulas, graphics, and so on to reduce development time. Users
can copy and paste documents, text, and other data contained in Notes documents.

    Using copy and paste on shared fields contained within forms creates new fields,
not new shared fields. Notes provides this feature as a method for converting
shared fields to fields.

    To prevent users from pasting documents into a database, create an agent that runs
If documents that have been pasted and select the simple action Delete from
Database.

@MailSend and Mail-In Databases

@MailSend can be used to forward a mail-enabled document or to send a memo. When used with no arguments, @MailSend forwards a mail-enabled document to people, groups, and mail-in databases. When used with arguments, @MailSend creates a new memo and sends it. The use of @MailSend offers developers a greater level of control than copy and paste. @MailSend can be used in an action, field formula, agent, button, or SmartIcon; @MailSend, therefore, can be triggered manually or automatically.

To use @MailSend to forward a document, the form must be mail-enabled by containing a SendTo field. SendTo is a reserved field name in Notes. Notes recognizes reserved field names to perform specific functions. The SendTo field can be editable or computed and the value must be text or a text list. The SendTo field must calculate to a valid person, group, or mail-enabled database to deliver successfully.

Other reserved field names related to mail functions may be added to the form to provide further functionality, including CopyTo, BlindCopyTo, DeliveryPriority, DeliveryReport, and ReturnReceipt. CopyTo and BlindCopyTo can be text or text list values and must calculate to a valid person, group, or mail-enabled database to deliver successfully. If used, DeliveryPriority must be a text value of "L" to route on low priority schedule, "N" to route on medium (normal) priority schedule, or "H" to route on high priority schedule. If used, DeliveryReport must be a text value of "B" (Basic) to create a report if delivery fails only, "C" to confirm successful and failed deliveries, "T" to trace failed deliveries, or "N" to never generate a report. If used, ReturnReceipt must be a text value of "1" to send a receipt when the document is opened by the recipient or "0" to not send a receipt.

 Tip   When providing users DeliveryPriority, DeliveryReport, and ReturnReceipt options, make the fields editable keywords by using text values the user can understand and the required text values as synonyms by using the pipe (vertical bar) symbol.

Use @MailSend with arguments to send a memo. The syntax for @MailSend with arguments is as follows:

```
@MailSend( SendTo ; CopyTo ; BlindCopyTo ; Subject ; Remark ; BodyFields ;
[Sign] : [Encrypt] : [PriorityHigh] : [PriorityNormal] : [PriorityLow] :
[ReturnReceipt] : [DeliveryReportConfirmed] : [IncludeDocLink]).
```

The following list explains each of the arguments:

◆ SendTo, a text or text list value, is the only required argument and must contain a valid person, group, or mail-in database name.

◆ CopyTo, a text or text list value, must contain a valid person, group, or mail-in database name.

◆ BlindCopyTo, a text or text list value, must contain a valid person, group, or mail-in database name.

◆ Subject, a text value, may contain any text and appears in the subject line of the memo.

◆ Remark, a text value, may contain any text and appears at the start of the body field in the memo.

◆ BodyFields, a text value, may contain a field name (in quotation marks) from the selected document to attach the contents of the field to the body of the memo. Multiple fields may be attached by delineating field names with a colon. A temporary variable equal to a field value can be used (without quotations marks) in lieu of a field name.

The flags in brackets are all optional.

◆ [Sign] electronically signs the memo with the sender's ID.

◆ [Encrypt] uses the public key of the recipient to encrypt the document.

◆ [PriorityHigh] immediately sends the memo to the next hop-server if necessary for delivery. PriorityHigh causes the server to initiate an unscheduled phone call, if necessary, to forward the memo. If the recipient is located in the same Notes network or on the same server, this option is no faster than PriorityNormal.

◆ [PriorityNormal] is the default delivery priority if one is not specified. The memo is forwarded to other servers at the predefined schedule set at the server. The memo is delivered immediately if the recipient is in the same Notes network or on the same server.

◆ [PriorityLow] routes the memo overnight if the recipient is not located on the same server or on a server in the same Notes network, in which case the message is delivered immediately.

> **Note** Administrators can control low-priority mail delivery through the environment variable MailLowPriorityTime setting in the notes.ini on the server. The value of the setting is a number between 0 and 23, and determines the hour at which low-priority mail is delivered.

A mail-in database may receive mailed documents. To mail-enable a database, create a mail-in database document by performing the following steps:

1. In the Public Name & Address Book, choose Create, Server, Mail-In Database. The Mail-In Database form appears (see fig. 17.1).

Figure 17.1

The Mail-In Database form.

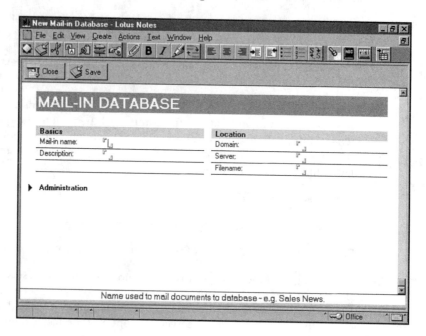

2. Type a name for the database (this name will be used in the SendTo field of a document).

3. Type a description for the database.

4. Type the Domain name where the database is located.

5. Type the Server name where the database is located.

6. Type the file name of the database. The default data directory path is assumed, so the full path name is not required.

7. Click on the File Save SmartIcon to save the document.

8. Press Esc to close the document.

Note After creating or modifying a mail-in database document, replicate the Public Name & Address Book between the server on which the mail-in database resides and any other servers from which mail will be delivered.

Notes External Data Integration

Notes databases can share data with external sources including ODBC-compliant database applications, OLE- and DDE-compliant applications, and popular spreadsheet files, graphics files, word processing files, and text files.

Importing and Exporting Data

Notes allows the following import and export features:

◆ Import files into documents

◆ Import files into views

◆ Export documents to files

◆ Export views to files

Importing a File into a Document

Files can be imported into documents or views. The Notes document must have a rich text field in which to import a file into a document. To perform a file import into a document, perform the following steps:

1. Open the document in edit mode and place the cursor in a rich text field.

2. Choose File, Import. The Import dialog box appears.

3. Type the file name or browse directories to choose the file.

4. Click on the Import button.

5. When importing a 1-2-3 or Symphony file, a prompt box is displayed to choose the entire worksheet or a named range. When importing an ASCII text file, a prompt box is displayed to specify whether to preserve line breaks.

Importing Files into a View

The following files can be imported into Notes at the view level:

◆ Lotus 1-2-3 worksheet

◆ Structured text

◆ Tabular text

File imports require three prerequisites: a file to import, an import view, and a Notes form for the documents created by the import.

To import a Lotus 1-2-3 worksheet, perform the following steps:

1. Open a database to a view where the documents will appear. If the field assignment of data will be view defined, be certain that the view selected has the appropriate view titles in the same order as the data in the worksheet.

2. Select File, Import. The Import dialog box appears (see fig. 17.2).

Figure 17.2

The Import dialog box.

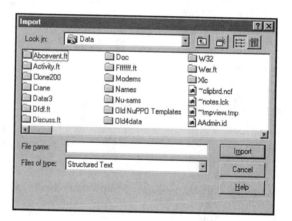

3. Choose the file type Lotus 1-2-3 Worksheet.

4. Type the file name or browse directories to choose the file.

5. Click on the Import button. The Worksheet Import Settings dialog box appears (see fig. 17.3).

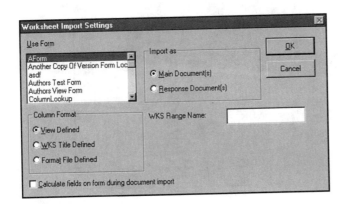

Figure 17.3

The Worksheet Import Settings dialog box.

6. Choose a form to use to import the files. The form chosen is saved as the form value in the document.

7. Choose a column format, view defined, wks title defined, or format file defined. If format file defined, select a *.col file for formatting.

8. Enable the Calculate fields on form during document import option if desired.

9. Choose to import the documents as Main or Response documents.

10. Specify a range if desired. Be certain that the range selected contains the correct data in the correct order if the field assignment is view defined; otherwise, if the field assignment is wks title defined, verify that the range contains labels to identify the field names.

Note   The WKS Title Defined option for assigning fields imports all data into the document, even if columns in the view do not accommodate the data.

11. Click on the Import button. Notes imports the worksheet file.

To import structured text, perform the following steps:

1. Open a database to a view where the documents will appear.

2. Select File, Import. The Import dialog box appears. Note that the default file type is Structured Text.

3. Type the file name (or browse directories and select the file) and then click on the Import button. The Structured Text Import dialog box appears (see fig. 17.4).

Figure 17.4

*The Structured
Text Import
dialog box.*

4. Choose the form to use. The fields in the form must match the fields in the source file. The form chosen is saved as the form value in the document.

5. Choose the inter-document delimiter used in the source file (either a form feed or a special ASCII character code).

6. Choose to import the data as Main or Response documents.

7. Choose to justify or preserve line breaks for body text.

8. Enable the Calculate fields on form during document import option if desired.

9. Click on the OK button to import the data.

To import tabular text, perform the following steps:

1. Open a database to a view where the documents will appear. If the data in the import file will be assigned to fields by using view titles, be certain that the view selected has the appropriate view titles in the same order as the data in the import file.

2. Select File, Import. The Import dialog box appears.

3. Choose the file type Tabular Text.

4. Type the file name (or browse directories and select the file) and then click on the Import button. The Tabular Text Import dialog box appears (see fig. 17.5).

5. Choose the form to use. The form chosen is saved as the form value in the document.

6. Choose to import the data as Main or Response documents.

7. Enable the Calculate fields on form during document import option if desired.

8. Enable and choose a format file if desired.

9. Define the page layout for the source data including header line count, footer line count, and lines per page.

10. Click on the OK button to import the data.

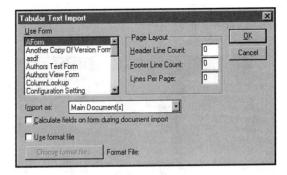

Figure 17.5

The Tabular Text Import dialog box.

Exporting a Document into a File

A Notes document can be exported into a file. All or part of the data from the document can be exported. To export a document into a file, perform the following steps:

1. Open the document to be exported.

2. If exporting only part of the data, select the data by click-dragging the mouse.

3. Choose File, Export. The Export dialog box appears.

4. To create a new file, type the file name. To replace an existing file, type the file name or browse directories to choose the file.

5. Choose a file type.

6. Click on the Export button.

7. If a file is being replaced, a confirmation dialog box appears.

8. If the export is to an ASCII file, a dialog box is displayed to specify a line length.

Exporting a View into a File

View exports require an open view containing at least one document. The most convenient way to export to a spreadsheet file is to export directly into a Lotus 1-2-3 file. If a Microsoft Excel spreadsheet is needed, 1-2-3 can convert files to the Microsoft Excel file format. To export data to a Lotus 1-2-3 file, perform the following steps:

1. Open a database to a view containing the documents to be exported.

2. If all the documents are not going to be exported, select the documents to be exported.

3. Select File, Export. The Export dialog box appears (see fig. 17.6).

Figure 17.6

The Export dialog box.

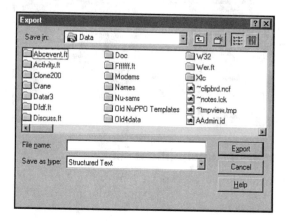

4. Type a file name for the spreadsheet file. Include the extension (*.wk4).

5. Choose the file type Lotus 1-2-3 Worksheet.

6. Click on the Export button. The 123 Worksheet Export dialog box appears (see fig. 17.7).

Figure 17.7

The 123 Worksheet Export dialog box.

7. Choose All documents or Selected documents.

8. Enable the Include View titles option if desired.

9. Click on the OK button to create the export file.

Structured text exports offer the advantage of exporting all the fields in the document and their field names, not just the fields that appear in the view. Structured text exports are also useful for generating documentation. To export data to a structured text file, perform the following steps:

1. Open a database to a view containing the documents to be exported.

2. If all the documents are not going to be exported, select the documents to be exported.

3. Select File, Export. The Export dialog box appears.

4. Type a file name for the structured text file. Include the extension (*.txt).

5. Choose the file type Structured Text.

6. Click on the Export button. The Structured Text Export dialog box appears (see fig. 17.8).

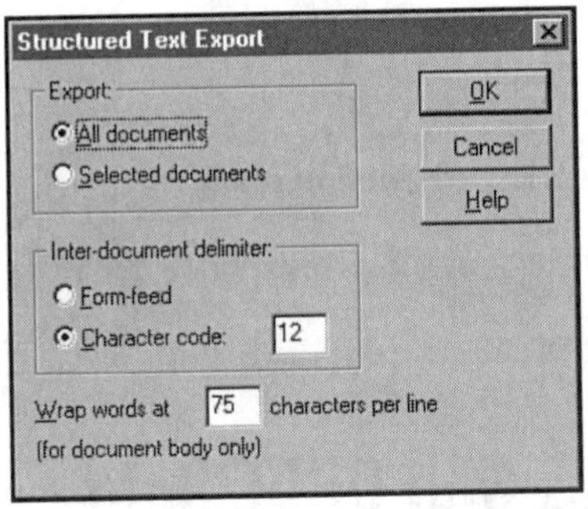

Figure 17.8

The Structured Text Export dialog box.

7. Choose All documents or Selected documents.

8. Choose an inter-document delimiter (form-feed or an ASCII character code).

9. Set a word wrap line length.

10. Click on the OK button to create the export file.

Tabular text exports provide a clean text file with one document per row. The data is stored as it appears in the view and can include the view column titles. Unlike the functionality offered in the import of tabular text files, only fields displayed in the view are accessible for tabular file export. To export data to a tabular text file, perform the following steps.

1. Open a database to a view containing the documents to be exported.

2. If all the documents are not going to be exported, select the documents to be exported.

3. Select File, Export. The Export dialog box appears.

4. Type a file name for the tabular text file. Include the extension (*.txt).

5. Choose the file type Tabular Text.

6. Click on the Export button. The Tabular Text Export dialog box appears (see fig. 17.9).

Figure 17.9

The Tabular Text Export dialog box.

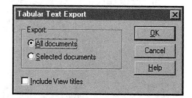

7. Choose All documents or Selected documents.

8. Enable the Include View titles option if desired.

9. Click on the OK button to create the export file.

Using @Db Formulas with ODBC Data

The Notes formula language offers three @Functions to access data from an ODBC data source: @DbColumn, @DbLookup, and @DbCommand. These @Functions present varying degrees of query customization to retrieve data from the external data source. The data source application is not required to be running when these @Functions are used.

Consult the Database Management System (DBMS) application literature for ODBC driver installation instructions, use, and restrictions. To create an ODBC data source, perform the following steps:

1. In Windows 3.1, double-click on the ODBC icon located in the Control Panel icon in the Main Group of the Program Manager window. In Windows NT or Windows 95, double-click on the ODBC icon located in the Control Panel. A dialog box appears containing a list of the available ODBC data sources.

2. Click on the Add button. A dialog box appears containing a list of the available ODBC drivers.

3. Double-click on the appropriate ODBC driver. A data source setup dialog box appears.

4. Type a name for the data source and enter the appropriate setup information. The required information is the data source name and path name.

5. Click on the OK button to create the data source. The data source now appears in the ODBC data source list.

6. Close the ODBC data source dialog box and close the Control Panel window.

The preceding section describes how to create an ODBC data source. Once the data source exists, Notes applications can access the data through three @Functions: @DbColumn, @DbLookup, and @DbCommand.

@DbColumn

@DbColumn returns all the values in a table column. The syntax for @DbColumn is as follows:

```
@DbColumn( ODBC : NoCache ; DataSource ; UserID1 : UserID2 ; Password1 :
Password2 ; Table ; Column : NullHandling ; Distinct : Sort ).
```

All arguments appear in quotation marks unless a variable is used to represent the value. The following list explains each argument:

◆ *ODBC* is a required keyword value and identifies the use of @DbColumn for an external data source rather than a Notes database.

◆ *NoCache* is an optional keyword value and forces the lookup on each use; "Cache" (or "") caches the lookup result for re-use within the same Notes session. A NoCache/Cache value may be omitted from the formula, in which case the formula defaults to cache.

◆ *DataSource* is a required text value and specifies the external data source as it appears in the ODBC data source list (accessed through the ODBC icon in the Control Panel).

◆ *UserID* and *password* values are optional text values (in quotation marks) and can be used to automate access to data if one or two user IDs or passwords are required. If null values are used and a user ID or password is required, the user receives a prompt for that information. If the formula is executed in a scheduled agent and the ODBC data source requires user ID or password arguments, access cannot be gained by using null values.

◆ *Table* is a required text value and identifies the table to access at the ODBC data source.

◆ *Column* is a required text value and identifies the table column from which data is being retrieved.

◆ *NullHandling* is an optional text value and determines the treatment of null values retrieved from the ODBC data source. The value may be "Fail," "Discard," or a replacement value. "Fail" stops the formula and generates an error message. "Discard" removes null values from the column list. A replacement value, such as "****", may be used to indicate a null value; this might be done to bring the null value to the user's attention. If no NullHandling argument is included, null values are discarded.

◆ *Distinct* is an optional keyword value and allows only one occurrence of duplicate values to appear in the retrieved list. More data can be returned from large columns because @DbColumn results are limited to 64 KB. If the distinct keyword is not used, all occurrences of duplicate values appear in the list.

◆ *Sort* is an optional keyword value and determines a sort order of ascending or descending. If a sort order is not specified, list items are returned in arbitrary order.

@DbLookup

@DbLookup returns values from a table column belonging to records whose value in the key column matches the specified key. The syntax for @DbLookup is as follows:

```
@DbLookup( ODBC : NoCache ; DataSource ; UserID1 : UserID2 ; Password1 :
Password2 ; Table ; Column : NullHandling ; KeyColumn ; Key ; Distinct :
Sort ).
```

All arguments appear in quotation marks unless a variable is used to represent the value. The following list explains each argument:

◆ *ODBC* is a required keyword value and identifies the use of @DbLookup for an external data source rather than a Notes database.

◆ *NoCache* is an optional keyword value and forces the lookup on each use; "Cache" (or "") caches the lookup result for re-use within the same Notes session. A NoCache/Cache value may be omitted from the formula, in which case the formula defaults to cache.

◆ *DataSource* is a required text value and specifies the external data source as it appears in the ODBC data source list (accessed through the ODBC icon in the Control Panel).

◆ *UserID* and *Password* values are optional text values (in quotation marks) and can be used to automate access to data if one or two user IDs or passwords are required. If null values are used and a user ID or password is required, the user receives a prompt for that information. If the formula is executed in a scheduled agent and the ODBC data source requires user ID or password arguments, access cannot be gained by using null values.

◆ *Table* is a required text value and identifies the table to access at the ODBC data source.

◆ *Column* is a required text value and identifies the table column from which data is being retrieved.

◆ *NullHandling* is an optional text value and determines the treatment of null values retrieved from the ODBC data source. The value may be "Fail," "Discard," or a replacement value. "Fail" stops the formula and generates an error message. "Discard" removes null values from the column list. A replacement value, such as "****", may be used to indicate a null value; this might be done to bring the null value to the user's attention. If no NullHandling argument is included, null values are discarded.

◆ *KeyColumn* is a required text value equal to the name of the column used for key matching.

◆ *Key* is a required text value used to select records for return values. Multiple key values may be defined in one formula by using a colon (OR operator) to delineate optional values. To define multiple keys with an AND operator, use @DbCommand.

◆ *Distinct* is an optional keyword value and allows only one occurrence of duplicate values to appear in the retrieved list. More data can be returned from large columns because @DbColumn results are limited to 64 KB. If the distinct keyword is not used, all occurrences of duplicate values appear in the list.

◆ *Sort* is an optional keyword value and determines a sort order of ascending or descending. If a sort order is not specified, list items are returned in arbitrary order.

@DbCommand

@DbCommand returns values specified by a command from a table column. The command is executed in the ODBC data source application before the list values are returned. Compared to @DbColumn and @DbLookup, this @Function offers the greatest flexibility for retrieving data from an ODBC data source. Use @DbCommand to select documents by performing nonequivalent or complex queries in the back-end DBMS application. The syntax for @DbCommand is as follows:

```
@DbCommand( ODBC : NoCache ; DataSource ; UserID1 : UserID2 ; Password1 :
Password2 ; CommandString ; NullHandling ).
```

All arguments appear in quotation marks unless a variable is used to represent the value. The following list explains each of the arguments:

◆ *ODBC* is a required keyword value and identifies the use of @DbColumn for an external data source rather than a Notes database.

◆ *NoCache* is an optional keyword value and forces the lookup on each use; "Cache" (or "") caches the lookup result for re-use within the same Notes session. A NoCache/Cache value may be omitted from the formula, in which case the formula defaults to cache.

◆ *DataSource* is a required text value and specifies the external data source as it appears in the ODBC data source list (accessed through the ODBC icon in the Control Panel).

◆ *UserID* and *Password* are optional text values (in quotation marks) and can be used to automate access to data if one or two user IDs or passwords are required. If null values are used and a user ID or password is required, the user receives a prompt for that information. If the formula is executed in a scheduled agent and the ODBC data source requires user ID or password arguments, access cannot be gained by using null values.

◆ *CommandString* is a required text value in the form of an SQL statement, a command statement using the back-end DBMS command language, or the name of a procedure stored in the back-end DBMS. Consult the back-end DBMS application literature to verify which SQL statements are allowable or for syntax in the back-end DBMS application when using the command language. Using a named procedure executes the procedure in the back-end DBMS application before returning a list.

◆ *NullHandling* is an optional text value and determines the treatment of null values retrieved from the ODBC data source. The value may be "Fail," "Discard," or a replacement value. "Fail" stops the formula and generates an error message. "Discard" removes null values from the column list. A replacement value, such as "****", may be used to indicate a null value; this might be done to bring the null value to the user's attention. If no NullHandling argument is included, null values are discarded.

Using DDE

Notes documents can share information with applications that support Dynamic Data Exchange (DDE). DDE applications function as clients and servers. The client initiates the conversation, commands the data manipulation, and terminates the conversation. Notes functions as a DDE client only. Notes utilizes DDE applications to update information or to manipulate data in ways unavailable to Notes, such as using a spreadsheet application to perform complex calculations or create a graph. To return values to the Notes document, use the DDE server application's Edit, Copy command to copy data to the clipboard and use the Notes commands to move focus to the desired field and @Command([EditPaste]) to paste the data into the field.

DDE Requirements

DDE links require both applications to be running and the server application file to be open.

A maximum limit of 10 concurrent DDE conversations may be performed. Be certain to terminate DDE conversations to avoid problems.

 Tip Although you can run up to 10 concurrent DDE conversations, try to close conversations as soon as possible and limit the number of concurrent conversations in order to maintain a high level of performance.

If the user's Notes.ini contains a "NoExternalApps" value of 1, DDE @Functions will not run, and the user will not receive an error message on execution.

DDE @Functions are not supported by Unix or Macintosh.

DDE @Functions

Notes provides four @Functions to automate DDE links:

◆ @DDEInitiate

◆ @DDEPoke

◆ @DDEExecute

◆ @DDETerminate

These @Functions can be used in field formulas, agents, buttons, and SmartIcons.

@DDEInitiate

The syntax for this @Function is as follows:

```
@DDEInitiate( application ; topic )
```

@DDEInitiate initiates a conversation with a DDE server application and returns the conversation ID. The application argument is a text value and identifies the name of the DDE server application. The topic argument is a text value and identifies the file name of the application server file.

When using @DDEInitiate, set a temporary variable equal to store the return value as follows:

```
Conv_ID := @DDEInitiate("ApplicationName";"Filename.XXX");
```

This return value is stored in the temporary variable for use in later @DDE @Functions. After setting the temporary variable, use an @If formula to verify that @DDEInitiate did not return an error as follows:

```
@If(@IsError(Conv_ID) ; @Do(@Prompt([OK] ; "Error" ; "Unable to initiate
conversation") ; @Return("")) ; "")
```

The user receives notification of a conversation failure if @DDEInitiate returns an error.

 Tip For a multiplatform environment, utilize @Platform to return the name of the currently running platform of Notes to determine whether to continue executing @DDE @Functions. Unix and Macintosh do not support @DDE @Functions.

@DDEPoke

The syntax for the @DDEPoke @Function is as follows:

```
@DDEPoke( conversationID ; location ; data )
```

@DDEPoke sends data to the DDE server application at a specified location and returns an acknowledgment value of @True(1) on successful delivery or a negative acknowledgment value of @False(0) if the attempt is unsuccessful. If the *conversationID* is invalid, an error is returned. If no data is specified, the contents of the clipboard are sent. Only the first value in a text list is sent.

@DDEExecute

The syntax for the @DDEExecute @Function is as follows:

```
@DDEExecute( conversationID ; command )
```

@DDEExecute passes a command string (in quotation marks) to the DDE server application and returns @True(1) if the DDE server application successfully executes the command or @False(0) if execution of the command is unsuccessful. The *command* is a text value (in quotation marks), which represents a valid menu command in the DDE server application. This becomes a powerful tool when executing macros written in the DDE server application.

@DDETerminate

The syntax for the @DDETerminate @function is as follows:

```
@DDETerminate( conversationID )
```

@DDETerminate terminates the conversation with the DDE server application and returns an error if the *conversationID* is invalid.

Using OLE

Object Linking and Embedding (OLE) offers some great advantages over DDE; the source application does not need to be running to update data, the source data may be linked or embedded into the Notes document, and OLE extends to Macintosh users. Like DDE, OLE applications function as servers and clients.

 To include OLE objects in full-text indexes, enable the Index attachments option in the Full Text Create Index dialog box. Only databases full-text indexed on a server may utilize this option.

Notes supports OLE 2, the newest release of OLE. OLE 2 provides the following features:

◆ OLE 2 objects can be created in Notes by dragging and dropping the data from the OLE server application to the Notes document.

◆ The OLE 2 server application commands can be used to modify the object in Notes without leaving the Notes window.

◆ Links to Notes documents, views, and databases can be created in Notes documents, other OLE 2 client applications, or on the Windows 95 desktop.

◆ Embedded objects in Notes documents can link to data in other Notes documents or in other OLE 2 client applications.

OLE Form Options

Notes forms contain built-in options for managing OLE objects embedded in the form. An embedded object can be launched when a user creates, reads, or edits a document. A new object can be launched only when a user creates a new document. If the Notes document is in edit mode, changes made while the object is launched can be saved. Forms can manage objects in the following ways:

◆ Launch an object automatically

◆ Launch a new object automatically

◆ Launch an object in-place or out-of-place

◆ Define the conditions under which objects are launched

◆ Have documents created using the form open in a modal dialog box

◆ Hide the Notes document

◆ Hide the original embedded object in documents

Launch an Object Automatically

Notes launches an object automatically if it is the first object in the form, if it is stored in the first Rich Text field, or if it is stored in a specified Rich Text field. To set the form to launch the object automatically, perform the following steps:

1. Open the form in Design mode.

2. Embed the object in the form.

3. Click on the Design Form Properties SmartIcon. The Form Properties dialog box appears.

4. Click on the Launch tab to display launch options. This dialog box has several fields (see fig. 17.10).

5. Select First OLE object in the Auto Launch box.

6. To create the object in a rich text field, select the rich text field name in the Create object in field box.

7. Click on the File Save SmartIcon.

8. Press Esc to close the form.

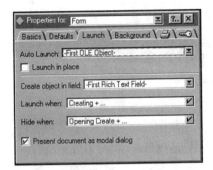

Figure 17.10

The Launch tab.

Launch a New Object Automatically

Notes launches a new object automatically only when a user creates a new document. To set the form to launch a new object automatically, perform the following steps:

1. Open the form in Design mode.

2. Click on the Design Form Properties SmartIcon. The Form Properties dialog box appears.

3. Choose the Launch tab.

4. Select the OLE server application in the Auto Launch box. The list includes registered OLE server applications on the local hard drive.

5. Select the rich text field name in the Create object in field box.

6. Click on the File Save SmartIcon.

7. Press Esc to close the form.

Launch an Object In-Place or Out-of-Place

The option to Launch an object in-place launches the object in the Lotus Notes window pane and displays the menus and tools of the object's server application. This feature works only if the OLE server application supports OLE 2. The option to Launch an object out-of-place launches the object's server application to display the object. Objects are defaulted to launch out-of-place. To set the form to launch an object in place, perform the following steps:

1. Open the form in Design mode.

2. Click on the Design Form Properties SmartIcon. The Form Properties dialog box appears.

3. Choose the Launch tab.

4. Enable the Launch in place option. (Disable the Launch in place option to return to the default Launch Out-Of-Place.)

5. Click on the File Save SmartIcon.

6. Press Esc to close the form.

Define the Conditions Under Which Objects Are Launched

If the form is designed to launch embedded objects (not new objects on document creation), the conditions under which objects are launched can be set to when creating, editing, or reading. Any or all the options may be selected by toggling the option. To modify this setting, perform the following steps:

1. Open the form in Design mode.

2. Click on the Design Form Properties SmartIcon. The Form Properties dialog box appears.

3. Click on the Launch tab.

4. Click on the check box next to the Launch when field. The choices appear in a pull-down menu.

5. Select or deselect the available choices.

6. Click on the File Save SmartIcon.

7. Press Esc to close the form.

Have Documents Created Using the Form Open in a Modal Dialog Box

This option controls the user's available options when editing a document. Launching a document in a modal dialog box deactivates the Notes desktop so that the user can only edit the document, perform actions available through an action button at the bottom of the dialog box, or launch the object by pressing a button on the dialog box. To set a form to launch documents in a modal dialog box, perform the following steps:

1. Open the form in Design mode.

2. Click on the Design Form Properties SmartIcon. The Form Properties dialog box appears.

3. Click on the Launch tab.

4. Enable the Present document as modal dialog option.

5. Click on the File Save SmartIcon.

6. Press Esc to close the form.

Hide the Notes Document

The Notes document can be hidden when the object is launched or when the launched object is closed. This feature provides a user seamless integration from a view to an autolaunched object. To set a form to hide the Notes document, perform the following steps:

1. Open the form in Design mode.

2. Click on the Design Form Properties SmartIcon. The Form Properties dialog box appears.

3. Click on the Launch tab.

4. Click on the check box next to the Hide when field. A drop-down menu displays available options.

5. Select and deselect available options.

6. Click on the File Save SmartIcon.

7. Press Esc to close the form.

Hide the Original Embedded Object in Documents

This option is useful when an object is embedded in a form for autolaunch and the latest representation of the object is displayed in a rich text field. Hide when properties may be applied to the object through the Object Properties dialog box. This feature gives the form a cleaner appearance while still providing object data to users. To hide the original embedded object in documents, perform the following steps:

1. Open the form in Design mode.

2. Click on the object.

3. Click on the Properties SmartIcon. The Object Properties dialog box appears.

4. Select the Hide Options tab.

5. Enable the desired Hide when rules.

6. Click on the File Save SmartIcon.

7. Press Esc to close the form.

Application Security

Security issues discussed in this chapter address ID-based application security applied at the database, document, and form levels.

 Note For details on server-level security, see Chapter 11, "Securing Your Notes and Domino 4.5 System."

Although application security is the responsibility of developers when an application is being developed, this responsibility is shared with Notes administrators and the database managers during application rollout.

Notes security is restrictive at smaller levels; a person or server given low-level access at the database level may not exercise a higher access at a document or field level within the database.

This section discusses security at the following levels:

◆ Access Control Lists and roles

◆ View Access lists

◆ Form Access lists

◆ Readers and Authors fields

◆ Field security

 Tip In addition to the security features presented in this section, Notes offers default and customizable hide options for many database elements. Hidden data is not secure, but hiding data may often suffice when the data is not confidential in nature.

Security through Access Control and Roles

The enforcement of application security in Notes is based on the user ID or server ID in use. A user or server can gain access to a database, view, form, document, or section based on security settings in the design elements or properties of the database. Access to the design elements is assigned by person, person group, server, or server group; or by a role comprised of people, person groups, servers, and server groups. Access lists that contain the names of people, person groups, servers, and server groups in the ACL also contain the names of roles defined in the database.

Database Access

The Database Access Control List (ACL) provides a backbone for application security in the database. People, person groups, servers, and server groups are assigned various levels of access to the database through the ACL. Every database also contains a default access value to assign an access level for all people and servers not specifically listed in the ACL. The seven access levels range from No Access to Manager. Although each access level contains varying options (to control document read access, create access, and so on), the following list of the available access rights provides a general description of the most common options assigned to each:

◆ **No Access.** No Access.

◆ **Depositor.** A depositor may create documents but is not permitted to open the database or modify documents.

◆ **Reader.** A reader may open the database and read documents but is not permitted to create documents.

◆ **Author.** An author may open the database, read documents, create documents, and modify and delete his or her own documents, but may not modify or delete documents written by others.

◆ **Editor.** An editor may open the database, read documents, create documents, and modify and delete any documents in the database.

◆ **Designer.** A designer may open the database, read documents, create documents, modify and delete any documents in the database, and create or modify design elements of the database.

◆ **Manager.** A manager may open the database, read documents, create documents, modify and delete any documents in the database, create or modify design elements of the database, modify the ACL, and delete the database.

To open the ACL, perform the following steps:

1. Select the database icon or open the database.

2. Select File, Database, Access Control. The Access Control List dialog box appears (see fig. 17.11).

Figure 17.11

*The Access
Control List
dialog box.*

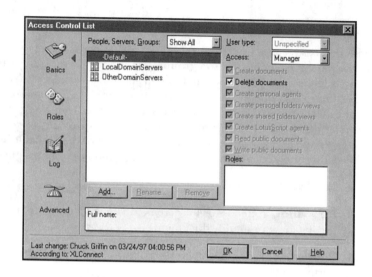

To add a person, server, or group name to the ACL, you must have Manager access to the database and perform the following steps:

1. Click on the Add button. The Add User dialog box appears (see fig. 17.12).

Figure 17.12

*The Add User
dialog box.*

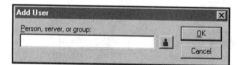

2. Type a name into the field or click on the button on the right side of the field to select a name from an address book.

3. Click on the OK button. The name appears in the ACL.

4. Click on the OK button to save the setting and close the Access Control List dialog box.

To modify an ACL entry, you must have Manager access to the database and perform the following steps:

1. Highlight the name in the ACL.

2. Specify a User type by using the pull-down menu.

The User type "Server" identifies the name as a server, allowing the server to access the database for replication, scheduled agents, and so on. Access to the database is denied through the Notes client software residing on the server, however, even though the server ID is in use. This is a security feature to prevent anyone with access to the server from gaining server-level access to the database. If this security feature is not an issue, set the User type to "Unspecified" to grant access to both the server and client software on the server.

3. Specify an Access by using the pull-down menu.

4. Enable/Disable any of the available options listed below the Access field.

5. Click on the OK button to save the setting and close the Access Control List dialog box.

To remove an ACL entry, you must have Manager access to the database and perform the following steps:

1. Highlight the name in the ACL.

2. Click on the Remove button. The name disappears from the ACL list.

3. Click on the OK button to save and close the Access Control List dialog box.

Using and Managing Roles

A *role* is a customized group defined in the database and comprised of people, person groups, servers, and server groups. A role is created to include a subset of users and servers in a View Access list, Form Readers list, Form Creators list, Author field, Reader field, or Controlled-Access section. Roles are beneficial if a subset of users and servers possess common access to multiple database elements. If the subset of users and servers changes, it is easier and faster to modify the members of the role than to modify each of the elements and all the documents created prior to the change.

To create a role, perform the following steps:

1. Select the database icon or open the database.

2. Select File, Database, Access Control. The Access Control List dialog box appears.

3. Click on the Roles tab. A dialog box like that shown in figure 17.13 appears.

Figure 17.13

The Roles tab.

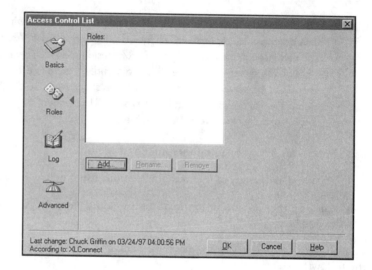

4. Click on the Add button. The Add Role dialog box appears (see fig. 17.14).

Figure 17.14

*The Add Role
dialog box.*

5. Type the name of the role (up to 15 characters).

6. Click on the OK button. The role appears in the Roles list both on the Roles tab and on the Basics tab.

To add members to a role, perform the following steps:

1. Select File, Database, Access Control. The Access Control List dialog box appears.

2. Highlight a person, server, or group name in the Access Control List.

3. Click on a role in the Roles list to make the highlighted name a member of the role. A checkmark appears next to the role.

To remove members from a role, perform the following steps:

1. Select File, Database, Access Control. The Access Control List dialog box appears.

2. Highlight a person, server, or group name in the Access Control List.

3. Click on the role in the Roles list to remove the highlighted name from the role membership. The checkmark next to the role disappears.

To rename a role, perform the following steps:

1. Select File, Database, Access Control. The Access Control List dialog box appears.

2. Click on the Roles tab. The dialog box now displays the Roles tab.

3. Highlight the name of the role in the list.

4. Click on the Rename button. The Rename Role dialog box appears (see fig. 17.15).

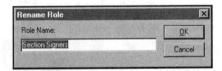

Figure 17.15

The Rename Role dialog box.

5. Type the new name of the role.

6. Click on the OK button. The modified role name now appears in the Roles list.

To remove a role, perform the following steps:

1. Select File, Database, Access Control. The Access Control List dialog box appears.

2. Click on the Roles tab. The dialog box now displays the Roles tab.

3. Highlight the name of the role in the list.

4. Click on the Remove button. The role no longer appears in the roles list.

View Access Lists

The View Access list contains entries from the database ACL. People, groups, servers, and server groups selected from the list are granted access to the view. All other users, including database Managers, do not have access to the view; the view name does not appear in the Folders navigator or in the View menu. The default setting for view access is All readers and above.

Warning | View Access lists do not provide data security. They only hide views from names not selected in the View Access list. Any user with read access may still see the data if it appears in other views, through other means such as keywords list choices, if they have rights to create public or private views, are allowed to perform full-text searches, or are allowed to execute agents on the documents. Data is not secured through View Access lists.

The View Access list default value is All readers and above. To modify a View Access list, perform the following steps:

1. Open the view in Design mode.

2. Open the View Properties dialog box.

3. Click on the Security Options (gold key) tab. The Security Options dialog box appears (see fig. 17.16).

Figure 17.16

The Security Options tab.

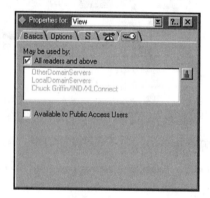

4. Disable the default All readers and above option if it is enabled.

5. Select names from the list to grant view access.

6. Click on the File Save SmartIcon.

7. Press Esc to close the view design.

Form Access Lists

Forms contain two access lists: the document Reader Access list and the document Create Access list.

Document Read Access

The document Reader Access list contains entries from the database ACL. People, groups, servers, and server groups selected from the list are stored in documents created using the form in a hidden field called $Readers. People and servers not included in the $Readers field or a readers field in the document (see the section entitled "Document Security through a Readers Field" later in this chapter) cannot see the document in views and cannot access the data through a query. The document Reader Access list refines the database ACL; people and servers must have at least Reader access to the database to gain Reader access to the document.

Warning | The document Reader Access list value is stored with the document in the $Reader names field when the document is created. This value does not recalculate when the document is edited. So, if the document Reader Access list is modified in the form, the $Readers field in documents created before the design change does not recalculate.

To modify the $Readers field, write an agent or change the value through the Document Properties dialog box. If many documents require a change to the $Readers field, writing an agent to modify the field is a good solution. On a document-by-document basis, the Document Properties dialog box contains a Who can read this document section, on the Security Options (gold key) tab, where any user with Author access to the document may modify the $Readers field by choosing the All readers and above option or by choosing names from the ACL. Note that a user with only Reader access to a document can still modify this setting, but then receives a warning that he or she is not permitted to make the change; the change has not been saved even though the Fields tab reflects a modified $Revisions field. When the view is closed and reopened, the field "regains" its value in the dialog box; no change was made to the document despite the apparent values displayed through the Document Properties dialog box.

Warning | Users not permitted access to a document through the document read access can still see a categorized value of the document if the document appears in a categorized view. This feature could potentially be considered a security risk depending on the data shown in the category. The best practice is to avoid categorizing views by confidential or sensitive data or to only allow database access to users authorized to see the data.

To modify the document Reader Access list for all documents created with the form, perform the following steps:

1. Open the form in Design mode.

2. Open the Form Properties dialog box.

3. Click on the Security Options (gold key) tab. The Security Options dialog box appears.

4. Disable the All readers and above option if it is enabled.

5. Select names from the list to grant Read access.

6. Click on the File Save SmartIcon.

7. Press Esc to close the form design.

To modify the document Reader Access list for an existing document, perform the following steps:

1. Open a view containing the document.

2. Highlight the document.

3. Open the Document Properties dialog box.

4. Click on the Security Options (gold key) tab. The Security Options dialog box appears (see fig. 17.17).

Figure 17.17

The Security Options tab.

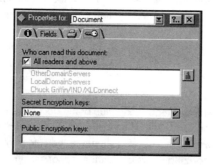

5. Disable the All readers and above option if it is enabled.

6. Select names from the list to grant read access.

Select the Fields tab and highlight the $Revisions and $UpdatedBy fields. Scroll through the values and note that the document's edit history is updated to include changes made through the dialog box.

Document Create Access

The Document Create Access list contains entries from the database ACL. The Document Create Access list refines the database ACL; people and servers selected from the list must have at least Author access to the database to create documents by using the form.

To modify the Document Create Access list for all documents created with the form, perform the following steps:

1. Open the form in Design mode.

2. Open the Form Properties dialog box.

3. Click on the Security Options (gold key) tab.

4. Disable the All authors and above option if it is enabled.

5. Select names from the list to grant read access.

6. Click on the File Save SmartIcon.

7. Press Esc to close the form design.

Readers and Authors Fields

Readers and Authors fields utilize field data type options to define Reader and Author access for documents created with the form. These fields may be calculated or editable so that editors or authors can modify the entries. These fields are often hidden when users do not need to know the values.

Document Security through a Readers Field

A Readers field contains a list of names granted read access to a document. People and servers not contained in a Readers field or $Readers field (see the earlier section on document read access) cannot see the document in views and cannot access the data through a query. A Readers field refines the database ACL; people and servers must have at least Reader access to the database to gain Reader access to the document. A null value restricts no one from reading the document.

To create a Readers field for a form, perform the following steps:

1. Open the form in Design mode.

2. Click on the Create Field SmartIcon. A new field appears on the form.

3. Provide a title for the field; **DocumentReaders** is appropriate.

4. In the Field Properties dialog box, choose the field type Readers.

5. Enable the Allow multi-values option if more than one value is allowed.

6. If the field is editable (so that document editors can modify Reader access), choose the Use Address dialog for choices option or the Use Access Control list for choices option for Choices.

7. If the field is computed, provide a formula in the design pane, entering names in quotation marks as they appear in the ACL.

8. To hide the field (optional), select the Hide Options tab in the Field Properties dialog box and choose the appropriate options.

9. Click on the File Save SmartIcon to save the form.

10. Press Esc to close the form.

Document Security through an Authors Field

An Authors field contains a list of names granted Author access to a document. An Authors field affects only users with Author access to the database. Users with Reader access or lower may not be granted Author access through an Authors field. Users with Editor access or higher are not restricted by Authors fields. An Authors field cannot override the database ACL; people and servers must have at least Author access to a database to create or modify documents.

 Tip | If a user clicks on an Authors field when viewing a document, a prompt box appears displaying the contents of the $UpdatedBy field (not a list of the Authors field values). The $UpdatedBy field stores the names of users who have edited the document in chronological order.

To create an Authors field for a form, perform the following steps:

1. Open the form in Design mode.

2. Click on the Create Field SmartIcon. A new field appears on the form.

3. Provide a title for the field; **DocumentAuthors** is appropriate.

4. In the Field Properties dialog box, choose the field type Authors.

5. Enable the Allow multi-values option if more than one value is allowed.

6. If the field is editable (so that document editors can modify Editor access for other authors), choose the Use Address dialog for choices option or the Use Access Control list for choices option for Choices.

7. If the field is computed, provide a formula in the design pane, entering names in quotation marks as they appear in the ACL.

8. To hide the field (optional), select the Hide Options tab in the Field Properties dialog box and choose the appropriate options.

9. Click on the File Save SmartIcon to save the form.

10. Press Esc to close the form.

Field Security

Notes security at the field level offers three alternatives:

◆ Sign if mailed or saved in section

◆ Enable encryption for this field

◆ Must have at least Editor access to use

These options may be used individually or in combination.

The Sign if mailed or saved in section option creates an electronic signature when the field is contained in an access-controlled section and the document is saved. If the field is not in a section, the signature is applied only when the document is mailed. Multiple signatures may be created but are restricted to one signature per controlled-access section. An electronic signature verifies that the data has not been modified since the document was signed (saved or mailed). This option does not restrict Read access.

The Enable encryption for this field option is discussed in the later section on Data encryption.

The Must have at least Editor access to use option places restrictions on users with Author access when the document is being edited. Users with Author access may modify the field when the document is being created only. This option does not restrict read access.

To set field security for a field, perform the following steps:

1. Open the form in Design mode.

2. Select the field and open the Field Properties dialog box.

3. Click on the Options tab. The Option tab opens (see fig. 17.18).

Figure 17.18

The Options tab.

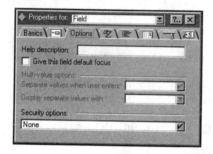

4. Click on the check box next to the Security options field to open the list of options.

5. Select one or a combination of security options.

6. Click on the check box to close the list of options.

7. Click on the File Save SmartIcon.

8. Press Esc to close the form.

Data Encryption

Notes provides data encryption at the database, document, and field levels. Database encryption restricts local database access to users whose IDs have been used to encrypt the database. Document encryption encodes data with a recipient's public key (available to other users) when a document is mailed and the recipient's private key (contained in the recipient's ID). Field encryption utilizes secret encryption keys to encode selected fields in a document; only users possessing copies of secret encryption keys can gain access to the data in encrypted fields.

This section discusses the following data encryption features:

◆ Secret encryption keys

◆ Field encryption

◆ Form encryption

◆ Database encryption

◆ Encryption formulas and reserved fields

Secret Encryption Keys

Secret encryption keys are created by users to encrypt fields in documents. Users can distribute secret encryption keys to grant other users access to encrypted data. A form must contain an encryption-enabled field before a user can apply data encryption to that field. Secret encryption keys are stored in users' IDs. A user whose ID does not contain the appropriate secret encryption key can open a document containing encrypted fields, but cannot view or gain access to encrypted fields.

 One of the full-text index options is Index encrypted fields. If Index encrypted fields is enabled, users can perform full-text searches on encrypted data.

To create a secret encryption key, perform the following steps:

1. Select File, Tools, User ID. The Enter Password dialog box appears.

2. Type the password for the ID and click on the OK button. The User ID dialog box appears.

3. Select the Encryption tab of the User ID dialog box. The encryption keys and options display (see fig. 17.19).

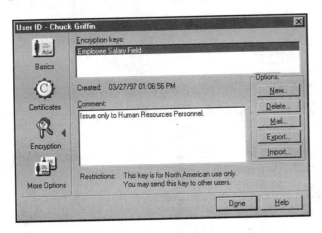

Figure 17.19

The Encryption tab.

4. Click on the New button. The Add Encryption Key dialog box appears (see fig. 17.20).

Figure 17.20

The Add Encryption Key dialog box.

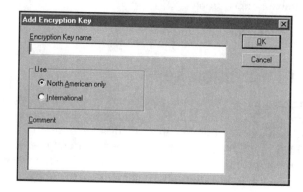

5. Type a name for the encryption key in the Encryption Key name field.

6. Choose North American only or International for the Use field.

7. Enter a comment describing the purpose of the key.

8. Click on the OK button. The new encryption key now appears in the Encryption keys list.

To distribute a secret encryption key to other users, perform the following steps:

1. Select File, Tools, User ID. The Enter Password dialog box appears.

2. Type the password for the ID and click on the OK button. The User ID dialog box appears.

3. Select the Encryption tab of the User ID dialog box. The encryption keys and options display.

4. Highlight the secret encryption key to be mailed.

5. Click on the Mail button. The Mail Address Encryption Key dialog box appears (see fig. 17.21).

6. Type names in the To and CC fields or use the Address button to select names from a Name and Address Book.

7. Modify the default message (optional) if desired.

8. Click on the Send button.

9. A message box appears to confirm Should the recipients be allowed to send this key to other users. Click on Yes or No to send the key. Alternatively, click on Cancel to cancel sending.

10. Click on the Done button to close the User ID dialog box.

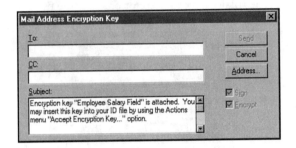

Figure 17.21

The Mail Address Encryption Key dialog box.

To delete a secret encryption key, perform the following steps:

1. Select File, Tools, User ID. The Enter Password dialog box appears.

2. Type the password for the ID and click on the OK button. The User ID dialog box appears.

3. Select the Encryption tab of the User ID dialog box. The encryption keys and options display.

4. Highlight the secret encryption key to be deleted.

5. Click on the Delete button. A message box appears to confirm deletion.

6. Click on the Yes button to delete the secret encryption key.

7. Click on the Done button to close the User ID dialog box.

Field Encryption

Field encryption may only be applied if the field is defined to Enable encryption for this field in the security options for the field in the form design. Documents created with the form encrypt fields for which this option is checked if the user saving the document has a secret encryption key. Users who do not have a copy of the secret encryption key(s) used to encrypt data cannot see or gain access to encrypted data.

To enable encryption for a field, perform the following steps:

1. Open the form in Design mode.

2. Select the field to be encryption-enabled.

3. Open the Field Properties dialog box to the Options tab (see fig. 17.22).

Figure 17.22

The Options tab.

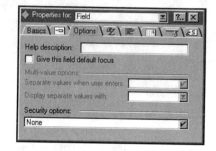

4. Click on the check box next to the Security options field. Three security options appear in a drop-down menu.

5. Select Enable encryption for this field.

6. Click on the File Save SmartIcon to save the form.

7. Press Esc to close the form.

A document may contain multiple encryption-enabled fields. Multiple keys may be used to encrypt a document. Encryption keys cannot be assigned to specific fields. A user must possess only one of multiple secret encryption keys used to view all encrypted data in the document.

Form Encryption

A form can be designed to automatically field-encrypt all documents created with the form. The form must contain encryption-enabled fields. Users creating documents are not required to use the default secret encryption key(s); users can change the keys used for encryption or remove encryption.

  When creating a document, a user can change or remove secret encryption keys before saving by selecting the Security Options (gold key) tab of the Document Properties dialog box and selecting/deselecting secret encryption keys.

To assign default secret encryption keys to a form, perform the following steps:

1. Open the form in Design mode.

2. Open the Form Properties dialog box to the Security Options (gold key) tab (see fig. 17.23).

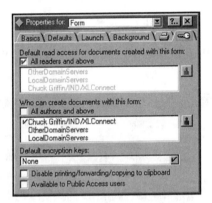

Figure 17.23

The Security Options (gold key) tab.

3. Select the check box next to the Default encryption keys field. A menu appears displaying all available secret encryption keys.

4. Choose the encryption key(s) for the form.

5. Click on the File Save SmartIcon to save the form.

6. Press Esc to close the form.

Database Encryption

Database encryption provides local security for a database by encrypting the database with a designated public key. Only the ID containing the private key can decrypt the database. Database encryption contains three levels of encryption:

◆ Strong

◆ Medium

◆ Light

For tighter security, use strong or medium encryption.

Databases encrypted at strong or medium levels cannot be compressed using disk compression tools.

To locally encrypt a database, perform the following steps:

1. Choose the database icon in the workspace.

2. Open the Database Properties dialog box.

3. Click on the Encryption button. The Encryption Discussion dialog box appears (see fig. 17.24).

Figure 17.24

The Encryption Discussion dialog box.

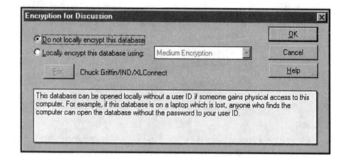

4. Choose the Locally encrypt this database using option and select Strong, Medium, or Light.

5. Click on the For button to choose the IDs to use to encrypt the database.

6. Click on the OK button to locally encrypt the database.

Encryption Formulas and Reserved Fields

This section discusses common programmatic features utilizing encryption, including reserved field names, available functions, and @Commands in the Notes formula language.

SecretEncryptionKeys

SecretEncryptionKeys is a reserved field name predefined to provide a list of frequently used encryption keys. This field is generally used as a Keywords field (although it could be a text field) to provide a user-friendly method of selecting encryption keys on a document-by-document basis.

Encrypt

Encrypt is a reserved field name predefined to determine whether mail-enabled documents are encrypted with the public key of the recipient(s) when mailed. This field is used to override user-selected options when a document is mailed. Use the Encrypt field to force or disable document encryption.

[Encrypt] Flag in @MailSend

@MailSend contains an [Encrypt] flag to determine whether a memo is encrypted when mailed. This flag utilizes the public key of the recipient(s) to encrypt the memo(s) mailed.

User ID Dialog Box @Commands

@Command([MailSendEncryptionKey]) and @Command([UserIDEncryptionKeys]) display the User ID dialog box for a user to mail, create, modify, or delete secret encryption keys. The User ID dialog box requires a user to enter the User ID password each time the dialog box is accessed.

Advanced User Interfaces

This section discusses the features of @Functions used to prompt users for information. Although these @Functions are not directly related to the database integration and security issues discussed in this chapter, they do enhance the interface for end users.

@Prompt

@Prompt is used to generate a prompt box to provide a message to the user or to prompt the user to choose a value (or multiple values). Because the Notes formula language does not contain a debugger, @Prompt can be used to display variable values to a developer—particularly useful when debugging action buttons, formula hotspots, or agents. @Prompt displays text values only, so @Text must be used to convert other data types to be viewed through a message box generated by @Prompt. @DbColumn or @DbLookup can be used in combination with @Prompt to generate lists and return values.

@DialogBox

@DialogBox displays a form in a prompt box with OK and Cancel buttons. Field names in the form matching field names in the original document automatically update both directions. When a dialog box is opened, common fields already containing values display those values. When the OK button in the dialog box is pressed, the field values displayed in the dialog box are applied to the fields in the form. If the form does not contain the field, the field value is added to the form. Any type of field may be used except rich text. Action buttons and hotspot buttons are great places to use @DialogBox.

The great benefit of using a dialog box is a clean user interface. For best results, use @DialogBox to display a form containing a 3D-style layout region and use the [AutoHorzFit] and [AutoVertFit] keywords to seamlessly fit the layout region to the dialog box. For more details on layout regions, see Chapter 13, "Constructing Notes Databases."

To create a dialog box, perform the following steps:

1. Create a form for the dialog box. For best results use a 3D-style layout region in the "dialog" form.

2. Open a form in Design mode.

3. Add an action button or hotspot button to the form. See Chapter 13 for details on creating action buttons and hotspot buttons.

4. Type the **@DialogBox @Function** using the "dialog" form name and use the [AutoHorzFit] and [AutoVertFit] keywords if the form contains a layout region.

5. Click on the File Save SmartIcon.

6. Press Esc to close the form.

@PickList

@PickList displays a view in a prompt box with OK and Cancel buttons. A user can select one or multiple documents from the view. When the user clicks on the OK button, @PickList returns a column value from the selected document(s).

Three keywords are associated with the @PickList @Function: [Custom], [Name], and [Single]. Use [Custom] to display a view in the dialog box. The view displays all documents in the designated view. Use [Name] to display the Address dialog box. The dialog box contains names from the Name & Address Book. Use [Single] to limit the user's choice to one name from the Address dialog box.

@PickList offers many advantages to @DbColumn and @DbLookup. @PickList is not limited to 64 KB of data. @PickList generates view lists faster than @DbColumn and @DbLookup. Users can perform quick searches on a PickList by typing the first few characters. Users can see all the data in the selected view to help them decide which documents to choose.

 The @PickList dialog box provides a view with fully functional column headers. This is a great tool for users if column sorting is built into the column headers. If the Change to View sort option is used, however, users could change views before selecting documents. The PickList would then return undesired results because the return value is based on a column number, not a field name.

Use @DbLookup or @DbColumn to utilize the "Cache" option if the source data is relatively static. @PickList does not offer a "Cache" option and performs a new lookup each time the command is executed.

Summary

The advanced development features presented in this chapter provide optional solutions for critical application needs for data integration and security. Further advanced application development features are discussed in the following chapters on LotusScript and Java.

CHAPTER 18

LotusScript Fundamentals

L otus Notes provides more than 200 @Functions as building blocks for formulas in computed fields, hide-whens, view columns, and agents. However, if you have spent time developing Notes applications with the @Function language, you have probably encountered a situation in which you spent hours weaving webs of forms, fields, and @Functions, only to conclude "I just can't make it do what I want."

LotusScript does not display many of the limitations of the @Function language. With LotusScript, you have the capabilities of iteratively executing your code via a loop, performing complex branching with IFs and GOTOs, and directly manipulating Notes database Access Control Lists (ACLs) with the aid of the Notes Object Model. Although LotusScript is not a panacea, it does greatly enhance the capabilities of the @Function language; it may hold just the cure you are counting on.

The topics covered in this chapter are considered the basic building blocks of LotusScript applications. The next chapter delves more into the advanced parts of LotusScript, and investigates the specifics of using LotusScript within Notes 4.5 itself via the Notes Object Model.

Before you can work with LotusScript, however, you need to know what it is.

Defining and Understanding LotusScript

LotusScript is a BASIC-compatible object-oriented programming language Lotus includes in several products, including Word Pro, Approach, and, of course, Notes. Its interface with each of these products is through a set of pre-defined classes related to that product, and referred to as the Object Model for that product. The topic of the Notes Object Model is reserved for Chapter 19. In order to be adequately prepared to discuss the Object Model, however, you need a good understanding of the basics of LotusScript. This is the goal of this chapter.

Probably somewhere in your past, you have encountered BASIC in some form: perhaps your first computer was a Commodore 64 or an Apple II, which, in comparison to today's machines, illuminate the term "basic" in a different light. Perhaps you are more familiar with LotusScript's first cousin from Washington state, Visual Basic. LotusScript and Visual Basic are related closely enough to be able to speak each other's language, with some minor modifications. Any exposure to a dialect of BASIC, or one of the structured programming languages currently in vogue, will give you a great head start with LotusScript.

From the Notes perspective, LotusScript is a BASIC-compatible, object-oriented programming language used to manipulate database elements such as fields, documents, or the databases themselves. Some areas of these elements require the exclusive use of LotusScript, whereas other areas allow the use of either LotusScript or @Functions. Why use LotusScript? Two reasons are capability and reusability. Many tasks within Lotus Notes simply cannot be accomplished via the @Function language: programming loops, complex branching, manipulating database ACLs, and accessing all the fields of a document without knowing how many there are or what they are named, for example. LotusScript is capable of these tasks, whereas the @Functions are not.

Second, LotusScript offers several methods of reusing code. At the programming level, you can create subroutines or functions to perform frequent tasks within your scripts. LotusScript takes you a step further in Notes 4.5 by enabling you to create Script Libraries within your database to hold routines executed from several locations in that database. Script enables you to go yet another step further by allowing you to include code stored in external text files via the %INCLUDE compiler directive—discussed in more detail later in this chapter. Reusability in the @Formula language is limited to copying existing formulas and duplicating them elsewhere by pasting them into a new location.

To further investigate the capabilities of LotusScript and to begin learning it yourself, you will need a file in which to type some sample LotusScript code. Included on the CD is a Notes database, called lssample.nsf, which can be used for this purpose. The database includes all examples used throughout this chapter; for further experimentation, you can edit the included examples or create new ones by typing directly into the Sample Script field. These scripts can be executed via the Evaluate Script action button at the top of the window.

LotusScript provides a very feature-rich Programming Interface and Debugger as standard issue with Notes. Chapter 19 discusses using these built-in features.

Identifying LotusScript's Basic Language Elements

You may not have consciously realized it, but the predominant language of this book thus far is English. If you remember your early days of English grammar, you may recall that English sentences are comprised of several elements: nouns, verbs, adjectives, adverbs, articles, prepositions, and conjunctions. Putting them all together in a pattern that follows the designated rules of English produces a valid sentence. Similarly in the computer programming arena, computer languages also have rudimentary elements and rudimentary rules. In LotusScript, the three major basic language elements are identifiers, operators, and keywords.

Identifiers are terms a person creates. These include names for subroutines, functions, variables, and user-defined types, as well as any constant or literal values you type. This chapter investigates identifiers used as variables; the other topics are saved for Chapter 19.

In general, *operators* perform a simple function or calculation. You are probably already familiar with most of the arithmetic operators in LotusScript: the symbols +, –, *, and / are operators representing the four basic mathematical operations of addition, subtraction, multiplication, and division, respectively. More insight into LotusScript operators is provided later in this chapter.

Keywords are terms that are predefined to have a special meaning to LotusScript. Keywords can be considered the vocabulary of LotusScript. All the commands built in to LotusScript fall into this category. Details on several specific keywords necessary for rudimentary functioning in the LotusScript world follow later in this chapter.

The upcoming sections discuss each of these language elements—variables, operators, and keywords—in detail.

Variables

Most identifiers you create will be used as *variables*, designed to capture and manipulate data that your script needs to work with. The idea of a variable within LotusScript is similar to the concept of a variable from your high-school algebra class: a symbol or term that stands for or takes the place of actual data. Variables are an important part of any programming language, including LotusScript. Here is a simplistic example of using a variable in LotusScript:

```
Dim AVariable as String
AVariable = "String data stored in a variable"
Messagebox AVariable
```

The first line of this example declares your intent to use a variable named "AVariable" within LotusScript to store string data. The second line assigns a value to that variable; whenever the variable AVariable is subsequently referred to, LotusScript actually operates on the string of data stored within the variable. For this reason, the last line displays the contents of the AVariable variable in a simple dialog box. Each of these concepts is discussed in more detail later in this chapter.

Consider what sort of data these variables may need to work with: information such as names, descriptions, and addresses consist predominantly of text characters. Weights, rates, quantities, and salaries are usually numeric in nature, may need to be used in computations, and may or may not contain decimal elements. If LotusScript is aware up-front of the type of information a variable will be storing, it can work with that data more quickly and efficiently. With this in mind, the next several sections discuss the concepts of declaring and using variables within LotusScript.

Defining Data Types

Each variable in LotusScript has a data type associated with it. This means that the variable generally is set up to hold only one type of data: text characters, integer numbers, or decimal values, for example. Table 18.1 illustrates the simple data types available in LotusScript for variables, and introduces the concept of suffix characters, which will be explained shortly.

TABLE 18.1
Simple Data Types in LotusScript

Data Type	Suffix Character	Allowable Values
String	$	Anything typeable
Integer	%	–32,768 to 32,767
Long	&	–2,147,498,648 to 2,147,498,647
Single	!	–3.402823E+38 to 3.402823E+38

Data Type	Suffix Character	Allowable Values
Double	#	–1.79769331348623158E+308 to 1.79769331348623158E+308
Currency	@	–922,337,203,685,477.5805 to 922,337,203,685,477.5807
Variant	\<none\>	Any data that is not a variable of a user-defined type

Why does LotusScript have data types? First, data types allow more efficient use of memory. LotusScript allocates only the amount of memory necessary to hold that specific type of data. Second, data types help speed up script: once LotusScript knows what type of data is stored in a variable, it knows what sort of operations can be done on that data; there's less trial and error.

 Note The Currency data type does not automatically supply any sort of monetary indicator such as a dollar sign. Rather, it is a numeric data type that provides four decimal places of accuracy, usually sufficient for currency calculations.

Because LotusScript has several different data types, you must indicate which type you need for each variable. In LotusScript, you can accomplish this in two ways: explicitly and implicitly.

Explicit Declaration

In explicit declaration, you tell LotusScript outright that you will be using a variable with a specific name and data type. You accomplish this by using a special reserved keyword designed specifically for this purpose: the DIM statement. For example, to explicitly declare a variable with the name "Index" and the data type of integer, type the following statement:

```
DIM Index AS INTEGER
```

This line instructs Script to set aside enough memory to hold a value between –32,768 and +32,767 that will not contain decimal values. This particular LotusScript will refer to that memory location as Index.

You can use a single DIM statement to create several variables by using commas to separate one declaration from the next. The line

```
DIM Index AS INTEGER, EmpName AS STRING, Balance AS CURRENCY
```

instructs LotusScript to create an integer variable called Index, a string variable called EmpName, and a currency variable called Balance. Using suffix characters with multiple declarations greatly shortens the length of the line. The preceding example becomes

```
DIM Index%, EmpName$, Balance@
```

 Of course, separate DIM statements could have been used in either situation, if preferred.

Implicit Declaration

The other side of the digital coin offers implicit declaration of variables. Implicit declaration is less structured than explicit variable declaration, although the end result is the same. To implicitly declare a variable, simply use the variable somewhere in your script *without* first declaring it via the DIM statement. When LotusScript runs across a term it didn't previously know about, Script figures the term must be a variable that you would like to use, and sets it up as such at that point. An example of code that implicitly declares a variable follows:

```
Index% = 1
```

If LotusScript was previously unaware of a variable named Index% when it encountered this line, it would set aside the necessary memory, make a note to refer to that memory as Index%, and then store the integer value 1 in it. The % symbol at the end is a suffix character used to indicate that Index is an integer value (see the next section for more details).

Allowing the use of implicit declaration can be problematic, however. Consider what happens if you misspell an existing variable: LotusScript views this as a variable you want to define implicitly, and does so without complaint. LotusScript has no way of realizing that this is a misspelled version of an existing variable. Consequently, the calculation or assignment that should have used the real variable now is using a completely different variable. When the time comes later in your program to use the data in the real variable again, it will not have gone through all the computations you expected.

If you want to instruct LotusScript not to allow implicit declaration, enter the option command OPTION DECLARE in the (Options) event for the current module. This causes the compiler to force you to declare each of your variables explicitly via the DIM statement. Declaring variables ahead of time is considered good programming practice as well, and makes your scripts easier for others to follow.

Tracking Data Types via Suffix Characters

You may have noticed that many of the preceding variable examples ended with different symbols. Each of these symbols is a *suffix character* used to visually indicate to you the programmer what data type is assigned to that variable. LotusScript enables you to add one of these characters to the end of each variable, if desired. This can be especially useful in multi-page scripts.

For example, if you inherit a co-worker's script, and notice toward the end that there is a reference to a variable named KeyValue, you may not be able to tell what type of data it contains just by the variable name. Is this an integer value, or perhaps a string? There's no way to be certain without further investigation. By adding a suffix character, however, you can always be certain that KeyValue$ is a string value, regardless of where you run across this variable in script.

Either of the following lines can be used to declare a variable named KeyValue$:

```
DIM KeyValue AS STRING
```

or

```
DIM KeyValue$
```

As the preceding lines imply, you need to use either the AS <datatype> approach or the suffix character approach when explicitly declaring variables. LotusScript does not allow combining the two in a single declaration. *Attempting the following will produce an error:*

```
DIM KeyValue$ AS STRING
```

Regardless of which method you use to declare a variable, you can add the suffix character to the variable name wherever the variable is used in your script. Use of suffix characters is a good programming habit.

> **Note** If using implicit declaration, the only way to specify a particular data type is to use the appropriate suffix character. Otherwise, all variables are assigned the variant data type, because variants have no suffix character. Variables of the variant data type are inherently the least efficient, and should be used sparingly, as the next section details.

The Variant Data Type

By its very name, the variant data type indicates that the information it can contain is allowed to vary. A variable with the variant data type can contain *any* type of data, with one exception. Allowed data includes all the simple data types already mentioned, as well as the upcoming more complex ones such as arrays, lists, and LotusScript objects. A variant cannot, however, contain a user-defined type—a topic that is saved for Chapter 19. Other than that, a variant can hold *any type of information*, and, in fact, must be used under certain circumstances.

Because a variant is capable of holding most types of data, it is the largest basic data type, requiring a minimum of 8 bytes of memory per variant variable. For this reason, it is best to rely on the variant data type only when necessary.

Understanding Conversion Functions

Because LotusScript requires variables to have an associated data type, you may need to use a conversion function when combining data of different types. Consider the following code segment in listing 18.1:

LISTING 18.1   A SAMPLE SCRIPT USING CONVERSION FUNCTIONS

```
DIM aString AS STRING
DIM aSingle AS SINGLE
aString = "12.45"
aSingle = CSNG(aString)
```

This demonstrative yet rather uninteresting script creates a string variable inventively called "aString" as well as a single-precision variable named "aSingle." LotusScript assigns a text value of 12.45 (think of this as the string of characters "one-two-dot-four-five") to aString. Suppose you want to put the numeric equivalent of this string into the aSingle variable. Attempting the simple assignment of

```
aSingle = aString
```

will produce a "Type Mismatch" error, meaning the data types of all the players are not compatible. To successfully accomplish this type of assignment, LotusScript provides a number of conversion functions (see table 18.2). The one used to resolve the preceding problem is the CSNG function, which converts whatever is handed to it into a single precision value. After the conversion has taken place, LotusScript has no problem storing the result, 12.45, in the single-precision variable.

All the conversion functions within LotusScript are similar to CSNG: all are constructed by starting with the letter *C*, and adding a three-letter abbreviation to indicate the data type converted to.

TABLE 18.2
LotusScript Type Conversion Functions

Function Name	Converts To
CSTR	String
CINT	Integer
CLNG	Long
CSNG	Single
CDBL	Double
CCUR	Currency
CDAT	A LotusScript date value

LotusScript does provide a CDAT function for conversion into LotusScript date/time values. Because LotusScript does not have a date/time data type, however, you need to assign date values to a variant.

Understanding LotusScript Date Values

LotusScript stores dates as a decimal number of days since 12/31/1899. This means that the date 1/1/1900 at midnight is represented by the number 1.0. Twelve hours later, on 1/1/1900 at noon, the numeric representation is 1.5; after all, 12 hours is half a day. The number 15317.29 is the numeric representation for 12/7/1941, 7:00 a.m., when Pearl Harbor was attacked. The integer portion of a date/time number tracks the date as the number of days that have passed since 12/30/1899. The decimal portion of the date/time value tracks the time of day as a percentage of time that has passed since midnight of the day in question.

LotusScript's method of tracking date/time values differs from that of the Notes @Function language. The @Function language stores time values as the number of *seconds* since 12/31/1899. Methods of dealing with this difference are discussed in Chapter 19.

Operators

As discussed earlier, operators perform a simple function or calculation. Each operator is usually a symbol used to accomplish a desired function, although many of the operators in LotusScript are terms instead (for example AND, OR, LIKE, IsA).

The next several sections discuss LotusScript operators in more detail.

The Plus Sign versus the Ampersand

Most programmers immediately recognize the plus sign as the addition operator typically used between two numeric values. The plus sign, however, leads a double life, periodically functioning as the string concatenation operator instead. *Concatenation* is the process of gluing smaller items together to create a larger item, usually a string. (In a sense, this is still "addition," adding one string to the end of another, rather than adding one number to another in the usual definition of the term.)

Although the plus sign is available, it is the ampersand, however, that usually performs concatenation. Why use the ampersand instead of the plus sign? The answer lies in the concept of data types. The plus sign requires string values exclusively as its operands; the ampersand can be used to glue together items of different data types. Consider these two lines of LotusScript, both attempting to perform a concatenation:

```
MsgBox 2001 + ": A Space Odyssey"
- - - - - - - - - - - - - - - - - - -
MsgBox 2001 & ": A Space Odyssey"
```

In the first instance, the use of the plus sign results in a Type Mismatch Error because the plus sign holds a different meaning when used with the number 2001 than it does when used with the string value ": A Space Odyssey." LotusScript becomes confused, can't determine which approach it should take, and gives up.

The ampersand indicates to Script that it should glue these items together, converting them to string values first, if necessary. No confusion, no errors. It generates the expected result of "2001: A Space Odyssey."

Other Operators to Look Out For

Although many operators in LotusScript are exactly the same as those in the @Formula language of Lotus Notes, a few exceptions are worth noting.

Equals (=)

First, the equals sign in LotusScript is used for both assignment and comparison; the context of its use determines its function. To store a value in a variable, you use a statement such as:

```
MyVariable = "My Value"
```

The same phrase appearing within an IF statement (detailed later in this chapter), however, is considered a comparison:

```
IF MyVariable = "My Value" THEN MessageBox "Values are equal"
```

The first statement makes a variable equal to a value; the second judges whether a variable is already equal to a value.

Attempting to use the := assignment operator from @Function-land results in the LotusScript compiler generating an error message.

Does Not Equal (<>)

The next caveat deals with the opposite of the "equals" comparison operator: the "does not equal" comparison operator. LotusScript disallows the != and =! versions available in the @Function language of Notes; you must use <> (or ><) instead. The exclamation point, as mentioned in the variables section, is viewed in LotusScript as an indicator of a single-precision variable, and causes confusion when appearing next to an equals sign.

Carat (^)

Mathematical operators in LotusScript also have been expanded in comparison to those in the @Function world. In LotusScript, you can use the carat symbol (^) to denote exponentiation, allowing you to specify functions such as x^2 as x^2. There is no exponentiation operator in the @Functions; rather the @Power() function would have to be used to achieve the same result.

Backslash (\)

In addition to "regular" division via the standard slash (/) character, LotusScript also allows the concept of integer division via the backslash character. Think of integer division as how many times one integer will fit completely within another integer, ignoring any remainder. This means that 5\3 = 1, because 3 fits completely into 5 only 1 time, ignoring the remainder of 2. The expression 7\3 = 2, as would 6\3, because 3 fits completely into both 7 and 6 only 2 times. The remainder of 1 in the 7\3 operation is not considered.

Logical Operators

The LotusScript language has the same logical operator capabilities as the formula language; however, the operators are slightly different. In the formula language, the logical concepts AND, OR, and NOT are represented by the symbols &, |, and !, respectively. In LotusScript, each of these symbols is used elsewhere, so you must use the actual terms "AND," "OR," and "NOT" in logical operations.

Underscore (_)

The underscore character is used in LotusScript as the line continuation operator. Normally, a carriage return at the end of a line of code indicates the end of that statement. Situations do arise, however, in which the code you need to write is so complex that it simply will not fit on a single line. By entering a space followed by an underscore, then hitting the Enter key, you can instruct LotusScript to view several lines of screen code as a single LotusScript statement. The following two example lines are logically equivalent:

```
MessageBox "This is viewed as a single LotusScript statement."
- - - - - - - - - - - - - - - - - - -
MessageBox _
"This is viewed as a single LotusScript statement."
```

The one exception is within a string constant. You cannot use the underscore as a line continuation character in a text string; it is treated as any other part of the text string, and will display exactly as you type it. As a rule of thumb, do not attempt to use the underscore as the line continuation character when typing literal text between quotes.

Pipe Symbol (/) and Braces {}

These characters are not technically operators, but rather delimiters. Either the pipe symbol, generally found on your keyboard in the Shift position of the backslash key, or open and close braces can be used in place of the double quote character (") in relation to string values. The important difference is that carriage returns *are* allowed within strings delimited by pipes and braces, whereas carriage returns *are not* allowed in text strings delimited by quotes. The MessageBox command is covered in more detail later in this chapter. Until then, take a look at the example in code listing 18.2.

LISTING 18.2   A LOTUSSCRIPT USING THE PIPE SYMBOL AS A STRING DELIMITER

```
MessageBox |This is the first line of the MessageBox.
This is the second line.|
```

Keywords

Keywords, or reserved words, are the next area of LotusScript Basic Language Elements. As mentioned earlier, *keywords* are predefined commands within LotusScript. Some that you have seen already include DIM, MESSAGEBOX, VARIANT, and IF. The Notes Help file contains a complete list of all keywords in LotusScript. You can find this list in the Notes Help Database (choose Help, Help Topics), in the Contents: Scripts and formulas section. Look under the "LotusScript Core Language Rules and A–Z" heading to find the "Statements, Built-in Functions, Subs, Data Types, and Directives" section.

 Because keywords have a reserved use in LotusScript, declaring a variable with the same name as an existing keyword is not allowed. Unfortunately, the resulting "Expected Identifier" error message that LotusScript generates does not quickly lead you to a solution. The terms NAME, DATE, and ME are three keywords most commonly attempted to be declared as variables. Watch out for them.

Performing Simple Input and Output

Even the most basic LotusScript program needs the capability to communicate with the outside world if it is going to produce useful results. After all, any work done on your data via a script is useless unless you are aware what the result is. LotusScript provides rudimentary commands both to prompt the user for input your script needs as well as to display information from a script as output to the user. This section investigates the reserved words LotusScript provides to accomplish simple input and output. An alternate Notes-specific approach is reserved for Chapter 19.

Communication via MessageBox

The most commonly used command to display information on-screen is the MessageBox command. Although primarily a vehicle for providing information to the user, it can also be used to request information from the user, if needed. The basic syntax of MessageBox in its simplest output role is as follows:

```
MessageBox "Message"
```

The one parameter listed as "Message" is any combination of literal text, functions, and variables that produce a single string value. The resulting OK dialog box displays this string.

| Note | Because the MessageBox command is so frequently used, LotusScript allows the use of an abbreviated version, MsgBox. |

There are actually two MessageBox commands: one is a LotusScript subroutine, the other is a LotusScript function. The subroutine version only performs a task: it displays information to the user. In contrast, the function version returns information to your script from the user. Both versions of MessageBox allow an integer parameter to indicate what buttons should display (just OK, OK and Cancel, Abort/Retry/Fail, Yes and No, and so on), as well as what icon (Question Mark, Exclamation, Error for example) should appear on the resulting dialog box. However, only the function version of MessageBox enables your script to know which button was pressed—by returning a unique integer value corresponding to the button the user clicked in the dialog box. Consequently, the general syntax of MessageBox's function version appears as follows:

```
ReturnCode% = MessageBox( "Message", Display_Settings, "Title")
```

You can put the integer values needed for the Display_Settings parameter directly into the MessageBox command, but stray numeric values displaying in code quickly lose their significance. In order to make your Lotus scripts more easily understandable, LotusScript included a text file that contains a list of predefined constants corresponding to these integer values making the process more programmer-friendly. This file, called lsconst.lss, is installed by default in each user's Notes directory. Pointing LotusScript to this file via the %INCLUDE compiler directive enables you, the programmer, to use the constants defined within this file, rather than relying on cryptic integer values. The following two code listings in 18.3 display a MessageBox with Yes and No buttons. See which one is easier for you to understand.

LISTING 18.3   INCLUDING THE LSCONST.LSS FILE CAN MAKE MESSAGEBOX() STATEMENTS EASIER TO UNDERSTAND

```
DIM ReturnCode AS INTEGER
ReturnCode%=MessageBox("Would you like to continue?", 36, "Go Again?")
----------
%INCLUDE "LSCONST.LSS"
DIM ReturnCode AS INTEGER
ReturnCode%=MessageBox("Would you like to continue?", MB_YesNo +
➥MB_IconQuestion, "Go Again?")
```

Using the MB_YesNo and MB_IconQuestion constants readily indicate that the resulting dialog box will have Yes and No buttons and a question mark icon; the basic integer value of 36 does not.

Because there are Yes and No buttons on this message box, you need to know which button the user presses. This is the purpose of the ReturnCode% integer parameter in the preceding listing. The MessageBox command returns a unique integer value representing the button the user selected. The lsconst.lss file also provides constants that represent these return codes. If the user clicks on the Yes button, an integer value of 6 is returned, which can also be represented by the IDYes constant. The No button returns a 7, which can be referred to as IDNo.

Print (Output)

An additional, although less frequently used, output function is the PRINT statement. This command displays information in the status bar at the bottom of the Notes window, if the script is running on a Notes workstation; it displays information on the server console (and consequently the server log database) if the script is running on a Notes server. If a Web client is accessing Notes data via Domino, any text PRINT displays will appear in the Web browser.

The command

```
PRINT "Execution Completed Normally"
```

produces displays text on the status bar of a Notes Workstation.

Of course, messages displayed on the Status Bar scroll off as additional messages are displayed. If you want to clean up after yourself, as is only proper, you can clear the status bar by printing a null character; execute the command

```
PRINT ""
```

The InputBox Function

Do you need to ask the user how many widgets he needs to order? If so, you have found a use for the InputBox function. This function presents a prompt to the user, allows the user to respond, then returns that response to a variable in your script to be used as necessary.

The general syntax of the InputBox command is as follows:

```
ReturnValue = InputBox("Message Text", "Title Text", "Default Value")
```

Consider code listing 18.4 for example, combining the three previous commands:

LISTING 18.4   A SAMPLE LOTUSSCRIPT USING THE MESSAGEBOX, PRINT, AND INPUTBOX COMMANDS

```
DIM ReturnValue AS VARIANT
ReturnValue = InputBox("Enter Text to Display on the Status Bar.", "Enter
➥Something")
MsgBox "Press OK to display """ & ReturnValue & """ on the Status Bar"
Print ReturnValue
```

Note that the ReturnValue variable in the first line is a variant. Because the InputBox function returns data as a variant type, this enables you to use the same function in LotusScript to prompt for both numeric as well as string data. Although not absolutely necessary in the preceding example, it is good practice to use variant variables to hold the results of the InputBox function. This prevents possible type mismatch problems caused by attempting to store string data in a numeric variable.

The MsgBox line in the preceding script also contains information worth further comment. To display the quote character (") as part of the concatenated text of a MessageBox or Print command, you must type two consecutive quotes as part of the script command. This means that the script command

```
MessageBox("Print ""this"" with quotes around it.")
```

displays text containing quote marks.

Thus, on either side of the ReturnValue variable in the MsgBox line, you need to put two consecutive quotes to indicate that a quote mark should be displayed, and one more quote to indicate the end of that particular string constant. The result is three quotes in a row appearing in the MsgBox statement.

Decision Making: Branching to a New Path

Consider a typical task in your day: pouring yourself a cup of coffee. If you have a ceramic mug at your desk, you take it to the coffee machine. When did you last wash it? Is it due for a good scrubbing first? If you have no ceramic mug (or if your ceramic mug *really* needs washing), you look for a paper or foam cup somewhere in the break room or near the coffee maker. Is there coffee made? If so, you pour yourself a cup; if not, you decide whether it is worth the effort to make a pot, or simply wait for someone more desperate to come along and make it. If there is coffee, you choose whether you need regular or decaf, and whether or not you need a full cup or a half cup. Next, you decide if you need sugar and/or creamer, and in what quantities.

Finally you evaluate the state you are leaving the coffee pot, and determine whether you should make a new pot. If you should, you further consider whether or not anyone will notice if you choose not to, and whether you think you can avoid it. Conscience and consideration kick in, and convince you that you should. It is easy to see that even a simple, everyday task as this is fraught with decisions to make.

Likewise in the LotusScript world, even the simplest LotusScript will probably need the capability to evaluate conditions and react accordingly: what button did the user just press in your Yes/No MessageBox, and what should your script do in each case? The result of the evaluated condition dictates which path the program should take. In the programming world, this process of making a comparison and then selecting a specific path from several available is called *branching*, and can be accomplished in LotusScript via the keywords discussed in the next few sections.

IF...THEN...ELSE

In the preceding coffee example, the word "If" precedes practically every choice made. Similarly, most branching done in almost any LotusScript program is accomplished through the IF...THEN...ELSE statement. Indeed, many of you are probably familiar with the @Function incarnation of this concept, @IF.

In its general form, the LotusScript IF statement evaluates a true/false condition—usually some type of comparison. If the condition is true, the THEN portion of the statement is executed. Otherwise, the ELSE branch is taken.

The IF statement syntax generally follows that of listing 18.5:

LISTING 18.5   GENERAL IF...THEN...ELSE SYNTAX

```
IF <condition> THEN
     <Statements if condition is true>
ELSE
     <Statements if condition is false>
END IF
```

Some special facts to remember about IF statements:

◆ The THEN or ELSE portions of an IF statement can contain multiple lines of code, if needed.

◆ The THEN keyword must be the last statement on the first line of a multi-line IF.

◆ The END IF (two separate words) on the last line of the preceding example IF statement terminates every multi-line IF statement.

◆ If the IF statement is small enough to fit on a single line in the script editor, you must omit the END IF. This includes long IF statements built by using the underscore line continuation operator.

◆ If no action is needed when the condition is false, you can omit the entire ELSE portion, including the ELSE keyword. The END IF terminator must remain, though, if there are multiple lines in the THEN portion.

Listing 18.6 displays a more concrete example of the IF statement.

LISTING 18.6   EXAMPLE SCRIPT USING AN **IF...THEN...ELSE** STATEMENT

```
DIM Var1 as Integer
Var1 = InputBox("Enter an Integer value to compare to 27", "Enter a
➥number","39")
IF Var1 > 27   THEN
     MessageBox "THEN BRANCH: Var1 is More than 27"
ELSE
     MessageBox "ELSE BRANCH: Var1 is 27 or less."
END IF
```

Furthermore, the IF statement also enables you to use the ELSEIF keyword (one single word) to specify additional conditions you want to check, should the initial condition be found false. Using this keyword to refine the preceding example would yield listing 18.7.

LISTING 18.7   EXAMPLE SCRIPT USING AN **ELSEIF** STATEMENT

```
DIM Var1 as Integer
Var1 = InputBox("Enter an Integer value to compare to 27", "Enter a
➥number","39")
IF Var1 > 27   THEN
     MessageBox "THEN BRANCH: Var1 is More than 27"
ELSEIF Var1 < 27 THEN
     MessageBox "THEN branch of ELSEIF: Var1 is less than 27."
ELSE
     MessageBox "ELSE branch of ELSEIF: Var1 must equal 27."
END IF
```

This script allows for the case that the value the user puts in is exactly 27. A value more than 27 branches to the first THEN statement. All other values branch to the

ELSEIF, where an additional comparison takes place. Is the value of Var1 less than 27? If so, the second THEN is executed. Otherwise, the ELSE branch of the ELSEIF portion executes, because the only value left would be exactly 27.

 Tip It is advisable to construct your IF statements to check for the most likely condition first, then the second most likely, and so on, saving the least likely for the final ELSE portion. This will position the most executed commands toward the beginning of the IF statement, preventing unnecessary executions of less common portions. This helps to optimize the performance of your code by allowing it to run more quickly.

SELECT...CASE

If your program is complex enough to require many levels of IF commands, you may be better served by using the SELECT...CASE statement. This programming tool enables you to perform many comparisons for a single value and to execute one of many possible branches. Code listing 18.8 shows a rudimentary SELECT...CASE statement.

LISTING 18.8 A SIMPLE **SELECT...CASE** STATEMENT IN CAPTIVITY

```
Dim ReturnValue as Variant
ReturnValue = InputBox("Enter 10, 20, 30, or 40...")
SELECT CASE ReturnValue
     CASE 10 :
          MsgBox "The number is 10"
          MsgBox "Multi-line Cases are possible"
     CASE 20 : MsgBox "You entered 20"
     CASE 30 : MsgBox "You typed 30"
     CASE 40 : MsgBox "40 was what you typed"
     CASE ELSE : MsgBox "ELSE condition: You typed something other than 10, 20,
➥30, or 40"
END SELECT
```

The SELECT...CASE statement looks at a specified variable, called ReturnValue in the preceding example, and compares that value to each of the possible cases listed. The first case that evaluates to TRUE gets executed. In this example, the distinct values of 10, 20, 30, and 40 produce specific, distinct results. Any other numeric value causes the ELSE case to be executed. What happens if a string value is entered?

Warning Entering a string value in this situation causes a "Type Mismatch" error when that string value is compared to 10 in the first CASE line. This is because each of the CASEs uses a numeric value for the comparison, which cannot appropriately be compared to a string value. A quick fix would be to use string values in all the discrete comparisons, such as:

```
CASE "10" : <Code to execute if 10 is entered>
CASE "20" : <Code to execute if 20 is entered>
CASE "30" : <Code to execute if 30 is entered>
```

This approach should be used only with discrete values, not ranges of values, such as "10" to "30."

The last case, the CASE ELSE line, catches any cases that have not taken any other branch. This statement is optional, but can be very handy to catch curves your users might throw at you.

Although each CASE line in the preceding example is watching for only a single value, you can instruct a CASE to activate for multiple values. Table 18.3 demonstrates each of these.

TABLE 18.3
Ways to Specify a Range of Values for a CASE Statement

General Syntax	Example	Function Performed
<val1>, <val2>, <val3>,...	10, 20, 30	Discrete values of 10, 20, and 30 branch to this CASE statement
<First Value> TO <Last Value>	10 TO 20	Closed range of any value between 10 and 20, inclusive
IS <condition>	IS >= 10	Open-ended range of values of 10 or more

Although only numeric values are listed in the previous examples, string values could be specified if the application needed them.

GOTO or not GOTO

The GOTO command may be very familiar to those of you who are conversant with earlier forms of BASIC. You can use GOTO to branch control of your program unconditionally to another line, or you can use the command with the IF, ON, or

SELECT statements to implement conditional branching. The use of GOTO is waning in programming circles because it often leads to *spaghetti code—*code with so many branches it is difficult to interpret.

In LotusScript, you can use the GOTO command only in a subroutine or function. This means it must appear in code that is between a SUB and END SUB command (or FUNCTION...END FUNCTION). The details of these commands are discussed in Chapter 19, where the advanced concepts of Subroutines and Functions are investigated further.

To specify a destination to which the GOTO command can branch, you need to create a line label. This is a unique identifier followed by a colon and then a carriage return. Code listing 18.9 shows a GOTO statement and its corresponding line label in captivity.

LISTING 18.9 A LINE LABEL AND **GOTO** STATEMENT IN CAPTIVITY

```
Sub GoToExample
    Dim var1%
    var1% = 1
LoopStart:
    MessageBox "Var1% = " & Var1%
    Var1% = Var1% + 1
    If Var1% <= 10 Then GOTO LoopStart
End Sub
GoToExample
```

With the GOTO command, after program control branches to the new location, execution continues from that point in typical, line-by-line fashion. The program has no idea where it branched from, and consequently provides no way to get back, if such a trip is necessary. The GOTO command has a first cousin, however, that does take note of where the program execution was before branching, and that is capable of returning execution back to that line when instructed to do so. This is the GOSUB...RETURN combination.

Just like the GOTO statement, GOSUB relies on a line label to indicate the location to which it should transfer program execution. As it makes the transition to the new location, though, it leaves a trail of digital bread crumbs behind, so it can find its way back. After all necessary statements have been executed at the new location, the RETURN statement instructs LotusScript to follow the trail back, and pick up with the line subsequent to the GOSUB statement.

Looping: Much Work, Little Effort

Now that you have successfully gotten your coffee with the help of the introduction to the Branching section, it is time for you to perform another common task around your office: making copies.

If you have 10 copies of the same document to make, you have basically two available approaches. You can load up your original document, and press the copy button to make copy number one. When that process is complete, you can then press the copy button again, and wait for copy number two to finish. You can then continue in this fashion until all 10 copies are made. Of course, if you choose this approach, you may still be in need of another cup of coffee.

The approach you are more likely to take is that you will set the counter on the copy machine to 10 and press the copy button. The ultimate outcome is exactly the same—you have 10 copies—but the second approach requires much less effort on your part.

Now, consider the LotusScript analog of this: a loop. *Loops* are control structures that allow portions of your program to be executed repeatedly. The previous code listing for the GOTO statement uses that statement to construct a rudimentary loop. The information between the LoopStart: label and the GOTO command is executed repeatedly. Creating a script that repeats information via a loop is similar to setting the number of copies on the copy machine counter. Otherwise, you would be required to run and re-run the same program repeatedly to accomplish the same goal. LotusScript has several types of structured loops available, as the next few sections describe.

FOR...NEXT

The FOR...NEXT loop executes a series of statements a specified number of times, similar to setting the copy counter on a copy machine. You could rewrite the loop from the earlier GOTO example in listing 18.9 with a FOR...NEXT loop instead, as listing 18.10 displays.

LISTING 18.10   A FOR...NEXT LOOP REPLACES THE GOTO FROM THE PREVIOUS EXAMPLE

```
Dim var1%
FOR var1% = 1 TO 10
     MessageBox "Var1% = " & Var1%
NEXT var1%
```

It should be immediately apparent that the FOR...NEXT approach is shorter. This is because the FOR statement takes care of the tasks of setting Var1% to the original value of 1, and checking to see if Var1% has reached the ultimate value of 10. The NEXT Var1% statement is responsible for incrementing the value of Var1% at the end of each iteration, thus taking the place of the Var1% = Var1% + 1 line.

 Note Including the name of the variable after the NEXT keyword is optional.

As mentioned previously, you must use the GOTO statement in a Sub or Function. This limitation does *not* extend to the FOR...NEXT loop; it is valid anywhere.

You also can give the FOR statement an optional STEP keyword parameter to indicate how much is added to the loop control variable at the end of each iteration. Replacing the FOR line in the previous example with

```
FOR var1% = 10 to 1 Step -1
```

transforms that code into a countdown from 10 to 1.

The FOR...NEXT loop is an excellent loop construct to use if you know how many times you will need to execute a set of instructions. What if you don't know the number of times necessary? Or what if the number differs from one execution to the next?

WHILE...WEND

When a set of instructions needs to be executed an indefinite number of times, you may find yourself using a WHILE...WEND loop, or one of its close relatives.

The WHILE...WEND loop executes its set of statements as long as a user-specified condition is true. As soon as that condition evaluates to false, the WHILE...WEND loop terminates, allowing program flow to continue with the succeeding statements. The script in listing 18.11 demonstrates this.

LISTING 18.11 THE **WHILE...WEND** LOOP
AS AN INDEFINITE LOOP

```
DIM GoAgain as String
DIM Total as Integer
GoAgain$ = "Yes"
Total%=0
WHILE GoAgain$ = "Yes"
    Total% = Total% + 1
    GoAgain$ =InputBox("Inside the While: Do you want to continue?","Enter
➥your response","Yes")
WEND
MessageBox "You looped through the While loop " & Total% & " times!"
```

Note that the WHILE...WEND construct is *entrance-controlled*. This means that the condition occurs first, and determines whether LotusScript executes the statements inside the loop. For this reason, you need to give the loop control variable an initial value that causes the program to enter the WHILE...WEND loop the first time. After that, additional statements within the loop reevaluate and modify the loop control variable so the loop will eventually stop looping. In this example, you accomplish this by assigning the GoAgain$ variable to the result of the InputBox command. If the user enters anything other than "Yes," the WHILE loop will not continue. Failing to re-establish the loop control variable within the loop can result in the longest running loop of all, the infinite loop.

DO WHILE...LOOP

The WHILE...WEND loop has an identical twin in the DO WHILE...LOOP construct. You can transform the previous example into its twin using the DO WHILE...LOOP keywords by adding the word DO in front of the existing WHILE, and changing the term WEND to LOOP. The two constructs are identical, and are strictly a question of personal preference.

Why mention this? The WHILE...WEND version of the loop is strictly entrance-controlled: the condition is the gate-keeper to the loop. This is also the case with the DO WHILE...LOOP twin. However, the DO WHILE...LOOP version can be easily modified into an *exit-controlled* loop (DO...LOOP WHILE), meaning the condition to continue is not evaluated until after the loop instructions have executed once. The condition becomes the prison-guard of the loop, only letting the program execution out after it has done its time. Listing 18.12 has made the transformation from DO WHILE...LOOP to DO...LOOP WHILE.

LISTING 18.12 THE PREVIOUS EXAMPLE REWRITTEN TO USE THE DO...LOOP WHILE LOOP SYNTAX

```
DIM GoAgain as String
DIM Total as Integer
Total%=0
DO
    Total% = Total% + 1
    GoAgain$ = InputBox("Inside the DO...LOOP WHILE: Do you want to
➥continue?","Enter your response","Yes")
LOOP WHILE GoAgain$ = "Yes"
MessageBox "You looped through the While loop " & Total% & " times!"
```

DO...LOOP UNTIL

The DO...LOOP WHILE loop has a close sister, perhaps even a fraternal twin. The DO...LOOP UNTIL loop is also exit-controlled, but allows the specification of the condition that causes the loop to stop (UNTIL), rather than the specification of the condition that causes the loop to continue (WHILE). Listing 18.13 demonstrates what the preceding example looks like using the UNTIL approach.

LISTING 18.13 THE DO...LOOP UNTIL LOOP SYNTAX
IMPLEMENTED IN THE PREVIOUS EXAMPLE

```
DIM GoAgain as String
DIM Total as Integer
Total%=0
DO
     Total% = Total% + 1
     GoAgain$ = InputBox("Inside the DO...LOOP UNTIL: Do you want to
➡continue?","Enter your response","Yes")
LOOP UNTIL GoAgain$ <> "Yes"
MessageBox "You looped through the loop " & Total% & " times!"
```

As this example displays, the only difference between the previous two loops is in the construction of the LOOP UNTIL line. The keyword UNTIL replaces the keyword WHILE, and the exit condition is presented in its complement form: the logical NOT of the condition in the preceding example.

```
LOOP WHILE GoAgain$ = "Yes"       becomes       LOOP UNTIL GoAgain$ <> "Yes"
```

Finally, this family of loops also includes the DO UNTIL...LOOP construct, which is the entrance-controlled version of the DO...LOOP UNTIL loop.

Manipulating Arrays

It is often necessary to store or work with a set of related data: a list of test scores or a group of employee names, for example. In such situations, you may need to store each piece of information so that you can retrieve it or work with it at any point. How can this storage be accomplished? It is not only impractical to create individual variables for each possible entry, but also rare that the total number of values is known while you are creating the script. Thus the idea of an array of values enters from stage-left to save the day.

An *array* can be considered as a set of consecutive memory locations all storing the same type of data—a row of mailboxes, if you will. You can put information into each mailbox, or array *element*, and retrieve it later. To further the analogy, just as each mailbox is referred to by a unique address number, so too in LotusScript is each array element referred to by a unique number called an *index*. The index of an array element is similar to the address of a mailbox. The range of possible values that this index can be assigned is referred to as the *bounds* of the array.

Because arrays are used to store and manipulate data, they are declared in much the same fashion as a regular variable, with a special addition. As discussed earlier, the line

```
DIM AnInteger AS INTEGER
```

sets up a single variable to hold integer information. To create an array of integer data, LotusScript expects a line such as the following:

```
DIM AnIntegerArray(1 TO 5) AS INTEGER
```

The (1 TO 5) after the name of the array indicates how many items that array can hold, and what the bounds of the array index are. This example sets up 5 "mailboxes," indicates that they are addressed using the numbers 1 through 5, and tells LotusScript that they are storing integer data.

You can omit the lower bound for the array index, if you prefer, to change the DIM statement into the following:

```
DIM AnIntegerArray(5) AS INTEGER
```

 When the lower bound is not specifically indicated, LotusScript uses a default lower bound value of 0. In the preceding example this produces an array with 6 elements, referred to via the index values 0 through 5.

To access a single element of the array, use the array name as a normal variable, but follow it with the index of the desired element in parentheses. To store data within that array location, a statement such as

```
AnIntegerArray(1) = 42
```

would do the trick. Likewise, you can use the same syntax to access data stored at that location, as in the following:

```
MessageBox AnIntegerArray(1)
```

This line of LotusScript retrieves whatever is stored in the #1 mailbox in AnIntegerArray, and displays the result, the number 42, by itself in a MessageBox.

Arrays also qualify for the use of suffix characters. The first element of the preceding array can be referred to as AnIntegerArray%(1).

In addition, if the situation demands it, you can implement up to seven more indexes or dimensions in your array, for a maximum of eight. You declare a multi-dimensional array by separating each index range from its predecessors via a comma, in this fashion:

```
DIM MultiArray(1 TO 15, 1 TO 20) AS STRING
```

This array can be used as a teacher's grade book, for example, to track 20 separate grades for each of 15 students.

Because the index of an array is an integer value, getting data in and out of arrays is often accomplished by using a loop. Listing 18.14 shows one approach.

LISTING 18.14   STORING AND DISPLAYING DATA IN AN ARRAY VIA A FOR...NEXT LOOP

```
DIM AnIntegerArray(1 TO 5) AS INTEGER
DIM I AS INTEGER
' Use a loop to populate the array
FOR I% = 1 to 5
    AnIntegerArray%(I%) = InputBox("Type in a number for slot #" & I%)
NEXT
' Now display all the values via a loop
FOR I% = 1 to 5
    MessageBox "Element #" & I% & " = " & AnIntegerArray%(I%)
NEXT
```

This script declares both an array of integer values and a single integer value to serve as the index to that array. By using this single integer value in a loop, the array can be easily and quickly filled with data. Reusing that same integer value in the second loop allows the data to be displayed just as easily. This approach is much preferred over attempting to individually address each array element.

The example array used thus far has a set number of elements—five to be exact. What happens if a sixth piece of information comes along? What if you need only three slots for data? Because the array has been set up for five pieces of information, five is what you have to work with. Attempting to access a sixth will produce a "Subscript out of Range" error message. Using only three slots results in wasting some memory storage. Arrays that have a set number of elements are termed *static* because the number of elements they contain never changes.

The opposite of a static array is a *dynamic* array, in which the number of elements it contains can change during the course of the script. Dynamic arrays are useful if you don't know at the time the script is written how many elements you will ultimately need. Dynamic arrays also allow you to designate only the minimum amount of memory needed to hold your data: no unused empty slots unnecessarily taking up resources.

The script in listing 18.15 shows the proper syntax for implementing a dynamic array in your script.

LISTING 18.15   IMPLEMENTING A DYNAMIC ARRAY IN LOTUSSCRIPT

```
DIM AnIntegerArray() AS INTEGER
DIM I AS INTEGER, NumElements AS INTEGER
' Ask the user how many elements the array will need.
NumElements% = InputBox("How many numbers do you need to input?")
REDIM AnIntegerArray(1 TO NumElements%)

' Use a loop to populate the array
FOR I% = 1 to NumElements%
    AnIntegerArray%(I%) = InputBox("Type in a number for slot #" & I%)
NEXT

' Now display all the values via a loop
FOR I% = 1 to NumElements%
    MessageBox "Element #" & I% & " = " & AnIntegerArray%(I%)
NEXT
```

The first line of this script instructs the LotusScript compiler that an array needs to be set up, but that the number of elements has not yet been determined. The REDIM command is used later to RE-DIMension that array with the desired number of elements. The REDIM command is not limited to a single use; if additional elements need to be added or removed in a dynamic array, the REDIM command can be used again with a different upper bound specified.

Note In a multi-dimensional array, only the bounds of the last dimension listed can be changed via the REDIM command.

It is important to note that when you use the REDIM command, the entire array is recreated by default from scratch with the new specifications. Consequently, data existing in the array is cleared. Typically, this is *not* the desired outcome. To add elements to an array without losing any existing data, you must specify the PRESERVE keyword when issuing the REDIM command:

```
REDIM PRESERVE AnIntegerArray(1 TO NumElements%)
```

Two additional keywords related specifically to arrays bear mentioning at this point. You can use the UBOUND(*arrayname*) and LBOUND(*arrayname*) functions to determine the upper and lower bounds of the array index. These can be handy when looping through any array, especially a dynamic array. A FOR...NEXT statement such as the following,

```
For Index% = LBOUND(AnIntegerArray) TO UBOUND(AnIntegerArray)
```

allows every item within the array named AnIntegerArray to be processed via the loop. Also, at any point, your one-dimensional array has UBOUND(*arrayname*) –LBOUND(*arrayname*)+1 elements in it.

Performing an action on each array element within a loop is so common that LotusScript has developed a loop structure designed specifically for use with every element of aggregate data types, such as an array. This loop is the FORALL...END FORALL loop, and can be used as listing 18.16 indicates.

LISTING 18.16 THE FORALL...END FORALL LOOP AT WORK WITH AN ARRAY

```
DIM AnIntegerArray() AS INTEGER
DIM Total AS INTEGER
NumElements% = InputBox("How many numbers do you need to input?")
REDIM AnIntegerArray(1 TO NumElements%)
FORALL x IN AnIntegerArray      ' Populate the array
     x = InputBox("Please type in a number")
End FORALL
FORALL x IN AnIntegerArray      ' Print all values of the array
     MessageBox "Value = " & x
     Total% = Total% + x        ' Total up all values, too
END FORALL
MessageBox "The sum of all entries equals " & Total%
```

First, notice that each FORALL loop starts with the term FORALL and ends with the END FORALL terminator statement. After the FORALL keyword is a *reference variable* that is used to take on the identity of each item within the array. This reference variable refers to the contents of each mailbox, rather than the mailbox itself; thus no index value is necessary. This is the reason you can use the line

```
x = InputBox("Please type in a number.")
```

within the loop to assign a value to the current element of the array. Like any other variable, you can assign any name to the reference variable. This variable must not be explicitly declared ahead of time, and must be a variant variable; no suffix characters are allowed. So, what happens if you have disabled implicit declaration via the OPTION DECLARE setting? Reference variables in FORALL loops are unaffected; LotusScript still allows them to be declared implicitly.

Introducing Lists

As previously discussed, an array requires a numeric index to access the data within each mailbox. Certain situations, however, lend themselves more toward accessing the mailbox via a unique piece of text: in a phone book, for example, you look up the name, and retrieve the corresponding phone number. In LotusScript the data structure that allows the storage and retrieval of data based on a unique text identifier is know as a *list*. The text identifier is called the *list tag*.

Listing 18.17 shows how to declare and use a list in LotusScript.

LISTING 18.17   DECLARING AND USING A LIST DATA STRUCTURE

```
%Include "LSCONST.LSS"
DIM PhoneList LIST AS STRING
DIM PhoneName$, PhoneNumber$
DIM AddAnother%
DO
     PhoneName$=Inputbox("Enter the person's name...")
     PhoneList(PhoneName$) = Inputbox("...now enter the phone number for " &
     ➡PhoneName$)
     AddAnother% = MessageBox("Add another?", MB_YesNo, "More?")
LOOP WHILE AddAnother% = IDYes
FORALL x IN PhoneList
     MessageBox x & ": " & ListTag(x)
END FORALL
```

This example uses the lsconst.lss file via the %INCLUDE compiler directive to access the predefined constants of MB_YesNo and IDYes. MB_YesNo indicates that the MessageBox command should present Yes and No buttons to the user; if the Yes button is selected, the returned integer value equals IDYes.

The LIST keyword on the DIM PhoneList line instructs LotusScript that the PhoneList variable is a list data structure. The line

```
PhoneName$ = Inputbox("Enter the person's name...")
```

prompts the user for the value of the list tag; the next line then uses that tag to place the phone number into the list via the command

```
PhoneList(PhoneName$) = Inputbox("...now enter the phone number for " &
➥PhoneName$)
```

Note also that the FORALL loop structure works with lists and works well; indeed—unlike with an array—there really is no good second choice when accessing all the entries in a list.

Last, within the FORALL loop, the LISTTAG() keyword is used to return the tag text corresponding to the current entry of the list.

Unlike arrays, LotusScript lists do not have a predefined number of elements; you can easily add to them without concern of running out of room. Also unlike arrays, lists must be only one-dimensional.

 The list data structure in LotusScript is a different concept than a data list in the @Function world of Lotus Notes. Programmatically, the two are unrelated.

Summary

This is the end of the fundamental LotusScript topics. In the next chapter, these concepts will serve as building blocks as you explore more advanced topics within LotusScript, and then ultimately learn to use LotusScript to manipulate data in Notes documents and databases.

CHAPTER 19

Advanced LotusScript

T he preceding chapter equipped you with the knowledge necessary to interact with generic LotusScript. The purpose of this chapter is two-fold. First, the LotusScript weapons issued to you in the preceding chapter will be sharpened further. This portion of the chapter includes such topics as entering and debugging scripts with the Notes Integrated Development Environment, modularizing via subroutines and functions, defining user-defined types, and classifying user-defined classes.

In the second portion of this chapter, these newly honed weapons will be turned specifically toward Lotus Notes, enabling you to learn how to apply your arsenal within that application. The battles you undertake will culminate with examining the Notes Object Model, emphasizing classes and capabilities new to Lotus Notes 4.5. This is the ultimate goal of the LotusScript chapters of this book.

Because the topics in this chapter are more advanced than those in the preceding one, you will benefit from the LotusScript Programming Interface (or Integrated Development Environment (IDE)) and the LotusScript Debugger. To take advantage of these portions of Notes, the programming approach in this chapter differs a bit from that in the last. Although you can use the LotusScript discussed in this chapter anywhere within Notes, this chapter's examples are placed predominantly within buttons. This allows you, the programmer, to use the Notes IDE to enter and debug your scripts, and further, to test your script by clicking the button.

You also can place several buttons on a single form for families of scripts. You may wish to create one or more new forms in the LotusScript Samples database from the previous chapter, and place buttons on them to hold your sample scripts. Test the form by selecting Design, Test Form, and then click your button to execute your script.

Mastering The LotusScript Interface

The LotusScript Integrated Development Environment was developed to make entering LotusScripts within Lotus Notes easier. You can access the environment from within any item that can be programmed via script. If you insert a button, for example, you can choose from the following options: Simple Action, Formula, or Script. Choosing Script allows you to enter your script code via the IDE in the Design pane.

What's New InsIDE

Those of you familiar with the Integrated Development Environment in Notes 4.1 or earlier really need to know only what's been added to the IDE in Notes 4.5:

◆ Each term within LotusScript is color-coded, based on the role the term fulfills. Read on for more details.

◆ The IDE also allows you to use Find and Replace throughout your script. You access the commands by choosing Edit, Find, Replace while in the LotusScript IDE.

◆ You can import and export your script via the menu commands File, Import and File, Export, respectively.

The Find function and the Export function allow you to specify the scope of effect: you can locate or export text either in the current script, in the current object (all events in just this button or field), or across all the objects in this database.

One capability still missing is printing your script. Lotus is aware that many programmers rely on this capability when creating complex scripts, so they assure us that printing will be included in the Notes IDE soon.

For now, the best approach is to export all the objects of your script to a text file, and then print the file with Notepad or your favorite word processor.

A Comment about Comments

Comments in LotusScript (or any programming language) are normal language text entries within your program that provide further information or explanation about the program. These comments are for you, the programmer (or the next person to view your source code), but are not intended for the script compiler. For the program to ignore comments and avoid trying to interpret them as LotusScript commands, you must use one of the following three methods to designate what you are typing as comment:

◆ Use the REM keyword at the beginning of each line of your comment. The carriage return at the end of the line will indicate the end of the comment.

```
REM This is a comment, and will be ignored by the compiler.
```

◆ Use an apostrophe (') to include comments on the same line as executable instructions. The comment must appear after the executable code, and ends with the carriage return at the end of the line. The apostrophe must appear immediately before the comment.

```
MessageBox "Execution Terminated Normally"    ' This is an in-line
comment. It must come last.
```

◆ Use the %REM and %END REM compiler directives to indicate the beginning and ending, respectively, of a block comment. All lines of text between the %REM and %END REM directives are treated as a comment. Thus, this approach allows for multi-line comments, as demonstrated in Listing 19.1.

LISTING 19.1 - A BLOCK COMMENT USING %REM AND %END REM DELIMITERS

```
%REM
This script demonstrates the appearance of a block comment in the middle of
your script by using the REM and END REM compiler directives (% sign omitted).
%END REM
```

Color Coding of Language Elements

The LotusScript development environment has the capability of color coding each term in each line of script. The default color for each element defined in Chapter 18 is listed in table 19.1.

TABLE 19.1
Default Colors of LotusScript Language Elements in the Notes LotusScript IDE

Language Element	Default Color
Identifiers	Black
Keywords and operators	Blue
Comments	Green
Compiler directives	Magenta
Errors	Red

The one color you will see all too often is red, because LotusScript uses it to highlight lines containing errors. Somehow, it seems fitting that errors in LotusScript make you see red. No one wants to see this color, yet everyone will.

If you prefer other colors, or would like to change the typeface or point size of the font that displays in the Design pane, you can do so via the Properties box. Right-click in the Design pane, and choose Design pane Properties to start the process. The screen should look very similar to figure 19.1.

Figure 19.1

The Design Pane properties box.

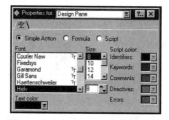

Within the Design pane, several areas of interest are worth discussing.

Define Drop-Down

The Define drop-down list keeps track of all items in your database that can have programmatic elements assigned to them. This list is not limited only to LotusScript, but displays any item in which a Notes Simple Action, @Function formula, or LotusScript can be placed. This is a handy tool for quickly moving from one item to another in Design mode.

Event Drop-Down

Similar to Define, the Event drop-down indicates the portion of the item selected in Define for which you wish to specify code. This includes predefined events for either Notes @Function formulas or LotusScript code, as well as any subroutines or functions that you create.

As with Define, Event is not limited to displaying only LotusScript-specific information. If you choose an editable field in the Define drop-down, the Event drop-down includes the Default Value, Input Translation, and Input Validation events, all of which can contain only an @Function formula (see fig. 19.2).

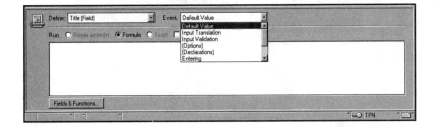

Figure 19.2

The Events drop-down of an editable field.

Additionally, although Script is the default choice for all events starting with and including the (Options) event, many of these can be filled with @Function formulas instead. Similar to a menu entry, Notes will display the word "Formula" in black if an @Function formula is allowed in the currently selected event; otherwise, Notes uses the color gray to display the "Formula" heading.

Furthermore, any subroutines or functions that you create also display in the Events drop-down, allowing you to access them quickly while coding them. How do you create subroutines and functions of your own? This topic is discussed later in this chapter in the "Subroutines and Functions" section.

Browser

How many parameters does the MessageBox command need? Which parameters are required, and what data type does Notes expect for each? Don't remember? Not sure? The Browser may have an answer for you. Thumbnails of LotusScript commands become available when you enable the Show Browser check box; this displays the Browser in the right-hand portion of the Design pane, allowing you to filter through the information listed there. You can browse a range of subjects, from LotusScript Basics to Classes included in the Notes Object Model. Double-clicking an item in the browser inserts it into your script at the current cursor location. If you need more details than the browser provides, pressing the F1 key takes you to the entry in the Notes Help Database corresponding to the selected item in the Browser.

Errors Drop-Down

As mentioned earlier, errors you make while entering your LotusScript display in red in the Design pane. This ensures that you (as well as any co-workers looking over your shoulder) realize that you have made an error. Additionally, Notes lists the name of the defined item, the subroutine or event within that item, and the number of the line containing the error in the Errors area of the Design pane, as figure 19.3 indicates.

Figure 19.3

The Errors drop-down.

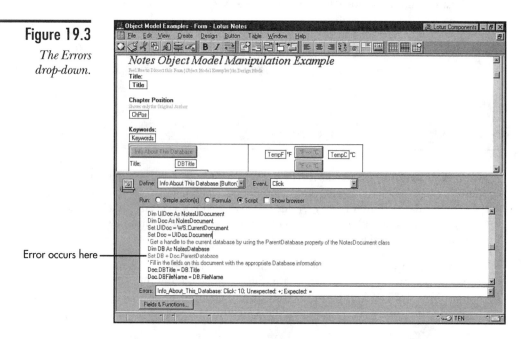

Selecting one of the errors listed here takes you to the offending line and highlights it, making it that much easier for you to correct the error.

Automatic Block Statement Completion

Many of the statements in LotusScript discussed thus far require one keyword to start the statement, and a complementary ending terminator statement to complete it:

FOR is terminated by NEXT, IF...THEN is terminated by END IF, SELECT...CASE is terminated by END SELECT, and so on. To help you remember these terminators, the LotusScript IDE automatically supplies them after you type the appropriate starting phrase and press the Enter key. If you type **%REM** and press Enter, you see that the balancing %END REM is supplied automatically, for example.

Debugger: A Digital Exterminator?

Notes also offers an interactive Debugger to help you ferret out those insidious errors that lie dormant until your script actually executes. To enable its assistance, choose File, Tools, Debug LotusScript. This same sequence of clicks toggles the debug mode off again when done.

 Note Be warned: when you enable Debug mode, the Debugger displays for every LotusScript in *any* database that runs.

In addition, the Debugger itself contains several buttons and tabs designed to help you. Figure 19.4 shows a typical script during execution within the Debugger, and the various parts of the Debugger.

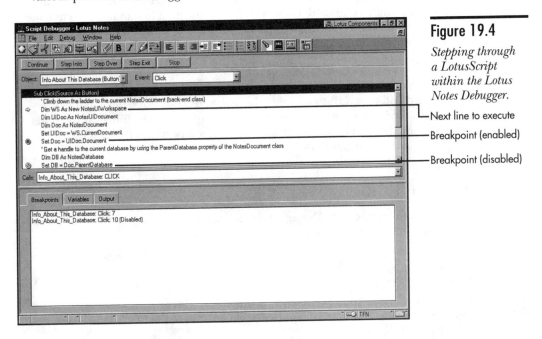

Figure 19.4

Stepping through a LotusScript within the Lotus Notes Debugger.

Continue Button

The Continue button tells the Debugger to execute your LotusScript without interruption from this point forward, until it reaches the next breakpoint, if one exists. The Debugger remains enabled, however, ready for use the next time you execute a script.

Step Over, Step Into, and Step Exit Buttons

When debugging a problem script, it often is helpful to execute one line at a time, watching the results as each command evaluates. This process, often termed *stepping through your script*, is controlled by the Step Over, Step Into, and Step Exit buttons. As you step through your script, the Debugger indicates—with an arrow at the beginning of the line—which line of your script executes next.

Because a LotusScript can contain calls to other subroutines or functions, it helps to understand the difference between Step Over and Step Into. Although Step Into sounds as though you should check your shoes, it really means you want the LotusScript Debugger to show you every line of available code as it executes. You step into subroutines or functions that you have defined, allowing you to watch the execution of each line within them during the process. This differs from Step Over, which does *not* take you into subroutines or functions, but rather executes the entire subroutine as a single command, then moves on to the next line in the current code module. Use Step Into if you suspect a parameter-passing problem or need to see how a subroutine works with a particular global variable; otherwise, you probably need to use only Step Over.

The Step Exit button allows you to execute the rest of the current code module uninterrupted and to return to stepping through your code once this module has finished execution. This button is most useful in a subroutine or function you enter via the Step Into button; otherwise, if used in the main portion of your script, it behaves the same as the Continue button.

The Stop Button

The Stop button instructs the Debugger not to execute your script any further. Your script stops execution completely.

Breakpoints

A *breakpoint* is a line in your LotusScript at which you wish to pause execution. Breakpoints are handy if most of your script works fine, but you have a problem in one area. Rather than stepping through all the working parts to get to the one non-working part, set a breakpoint somewhere near the start of the problem. This allows you to execute your script uninterrupted until it hits that line, invoking the Debugger only when needed. You can step through your remaining lines of code piecemeal until you successfully identify the problem.

How do you specify a breakpoint? After selecting the line on which you want to set a breakpoint, you have a choice of the following three possibilities:

◆ Click the Debug Menu, then choose Set/Clear Breakpoint.

◆ Press the F9 key.

◆ Double-click the line itself within the Debugger.

If your breakpoint has been successfully set, you should see a Stop sign at the beginning of the line.

Double-clicking an enabled breakpoint disables it. This means the breakpoint stays in your script, but does not affect its execution. You can later re-enable a disabled breakpoint via the Debug menu, if needed. Double-clicking a disabled breakpoint clears the breakpoint altogether.

After you have successfully debugged your LotusScript and you no longer need your breakpoints, you can remove them by choosing Debug, Clear All Breakpoints from within the Debugger.

Calls Drop-Down

This drop-down is similar in function to the Window menu in most Windows applications. Just as the Window menu keeps track of every window within an application that you went through on your way to the currently displaying window, so the Calls drop-down tracks each subroutine your script called to get to the line that is currently executing. Furthermore, just as the Window menu enables you to switch to any open window along the way, the Calls drop-down also enables you to quickly switch between the various subroutines along the path to the current line of code.

Breakpoints Tab

After you have set several breakpoints, you may want to refer to the Breakpoints tab in the bottom pane of the Debugger. This tab tracks the Object Name, Event Name, and line number for each breakpoint set within this database. Clicking an entry listed on the Breakpoint tab displays that line of your script in the script pane above.

Variables Tab

The Variables tab is one of the most-used areas of the Debugger. This area displays the name of each variable in your script, its current value, and its data type. This information is listed in a single line for simple data types, such as String, Integer, or Single. For more complex data types, such as arrays or objects, the Debugger displays a twistie next to the name of the variable, as figure 19.5 shows. The Variables tab displays information and a value for each variable in the current script.

Figure 19.5

The Variables tab.

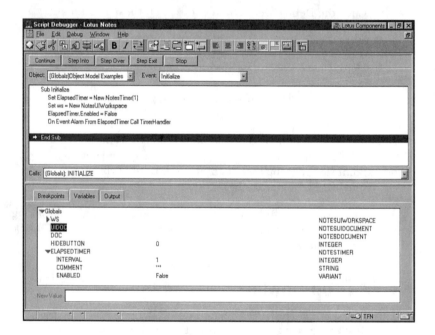

The individual elements of an array or the properties of a Notes object display if the twistie is opened. The information on this tab is very thorough and very helpful.

This tab also has a New Value blank. This implies that you can change the value of any variable while you debug your script. This is basically true. You can specify a new value for the selected variable by changing the value listed in the New Value blank. However, some variables (also known as properties) in parts of the Notes Object Model present their values as read-only; LotusScript does not allow you to change these values. LotusScript does allow you to type a new value in the New Value box, but will not assign your entry as a new value for the selected variable.

Output Tab

This tab tracks the output of any PRINT commands issued in your script. Normally, the PRINT command displays text in the center of your status bar, or in the Notes Log File if your script runs on a server as a scheduled agent. During the debugging process, however, PRINT commands can help track the status of your script or display the interim value of a variable. The output tab allows you to see all the output at a glance.

Subroutines and Functions

Subroutines (subs) and functions within LotusScript give you, the programmer, the ability to modularize your code. You can put tasks that are needed by several portions of your script into a subroutine or function that can be repeatedly called within your script, rather than having to duplicate the code itself in several places throughout your script.

Actually, within Notes, any scripts you create go into a subroutine of some kind. (The term *subroutine* is being used to indicate any portion of separate code that can be executed from another module, and includes both LotusScript subs as well as LotusScript functions.) Notes predefines many of these subroutines and lists them in the Events drop-down. These predefined subs are invoked by occurrences that happen within Notes, and are considered to be events (more details shortly). However, as a programmer, you do have the ability to create your own subroutines and use them in your scripts; subs and functions you create will also be listed in the Events drop-down.

The main distinction between a LotusScript function and a LotusScript sub is that functions perform a task *and* return a value, whereas subs *just* perform a task. There are blurry areas where this characteristic is not absolute, but in general this is true.

Structure of a Subroutine

You may have already noticed the basic structure of a LotusScript sub when looking at the Click event of a button. Listing 19.2 displays just such a Click event.

LISTING 19.2 - THE CLICK EVENT OF A BUTTON IS ACTUALLY A LOTUSSCRIPT SUB

```
Sub Click(Source As Button)
    ReturnCode%=Messagebox("Would you like to execute the DisplayMessage
Sub?", MB_YesNo + MB_IconQuestion, "Go Again?")
    If ReturnCode% = IDYES Then DisplayMessage
End Sub
```

As this example shows, each sub in LotusScript begins with the keyword sub and the name of the sub, and ends with the End sub terminator combination. Lines of executable code occupy the intervening space. You can examine this example in the LotusScript Samples database introduced in Chapter 18. Open the Script in Button form, and examine the Subroutine Example button.

The item in parentheses after the name of the sub (this sub is named "Click") is a list of parameters or values being passed into the subroutine. A subroutine does not *require* parameters, but they often are used to transfer data into or out of the sub. More on parameters will be mentioned shortly in the "Parameter Passing" and "Parameters and Parentheses" sections of this chapter.

You may have noticed the MB_YesNo and MB_IconQuestion constant values from lsconst.lss being used in the MessageBox command. An %Include statement, however, is not visible in this script. Does this work? The answer is yes, because the %INCLUDE "LSCONST.LSS" line has been placed in the (Globals) portion of the Form, in the (Options) event. You can check it by changing the Define drop-down to list "(Globals) Buttons" (where Buttons is the Form alias) and changing the Event drop-down to list "(Options)." There it is, listed in blazing magenta.

Back in the Click event, note the THEN portion of the IF statement. This is an example of calling a LotusScript sub, which in this case is named DisplayMessage. Listing 19.3 contains the code of the DisplayMessage Sub.

LISTING 19.3 - THE DISPLAYMESSAGE USER-CREATED SUBROUTINE

```
Sub DisplayMessage
    Messagebox "In the DisplayMessage Subroutine"
End Sub
```

Clicking the button in which these scripts have been written results in the user being asked, "Would you like to execute the DisplayMessage Sub?" If he answers Yes, the DisplayMessage sub executes, and responds "In the DisplayMessage subroutine." Yes, it's riveting.

Looking in the Events drop-down also reveals that the DisplayMessage subroutine is listed there as an "event." LotusScript lists all subroutines and functions that you enter, making it easier for you to find them. Anytime you type the opening line of a subroutine (the word "SUB" followed by the name of the subroutine), pressing the Enter key automatically places you in a new, empty subroutine, completes the SUB block statement with an END SUB terminator, and adds the name of your sub to the Events drop-down.

Parameter Passing

Consider a brief subroutine whose sole purpose is to accept two values, display them, swap them around, and display them again. The code to such a subroutine, as well as the script necessary to invoke it from within a button, follows in listing 19.4.

LISTING 19.4 - THE SCRIPT OF A CLICK EVENT
CALLING THE SWAP SUBROUTINE

```
Sub Click(Source As Button)
    Dim Number1 As Integer, Number2 As Integer, ReturnCode As Integer
    Do
        Number1% = Inputbox("Enter the first number")
        Number2% = Inputbox("Enter the second number")
        Swap Number1%, Number2%
        ReturnCode%=Messagebox("Swap two more?", MB_IconQuestion + MB_YesNo,
        ➥"Again?")
    Loop Until ReturnCode%=IDNo
End Sub


Sub Swap(Num1 As Integer, Num2 As Integer)
    Dim TempNum As Integer
    REM Nothing up my sleeve...
    Messagebox "Num1% = " & Num1% & |
Num2% = | & Num2%
    REM ...perform the swap...
    TempNum% = Num1%
    Num1% = Num2%
    Num2% = TempNum%
    Print "Swapped"
    REM ...display the result
    Messagebox "Num1% = " & Num1% & |
Num2% = | & Num2%
    Print ""
End Sub
```

This listing displays some interesting information. First, this script is placed in a button, so program execution starts with the Click event. This event asks the user to provide the two initial values, and then stores the values in two variables, invokes the Swap subroutine and passes those variables along to it.

The Swap sub expects to receive two values and intends to call them Num1 and Num2. This is indicated by the (Num1 As Integer, Num2 As Integer) parameter list after the sub name. At points where the Swap sub refers to Num1, the sub manipulates the data set up, stored, and passed in via the Number1 variable in the Click event. The action is the same for Num2 in relation to the Number2 variable.

After receiving those values, Swap displays them via a MessageBox command using the pipe symbol text delimiter, discussed in Chapter 18. This allows the inclusion of a carriage return in the MessageBox, so that each variable's information displays on its own line.

Swap then uses a temporary variable to interchange the values of the two variables. After doing so, the sub displays them again so you can see the result.

When the Swap sub finishes, program execution returns to the Click sub, picking up with the next executable command. In this case, the command asks the user if he wishes to swap two more. The DO...LOOP UNTIL exit condition evaluates next, and the whole process potentially starts over.

An excellent opportunity exists within the Swap sub itself to institute an additional subroutine. The MessageBox statement that displays the Num1 and Num2 values is performed twice, currently with the code duplicated. You can eliminate the two lines of code by creating a subroutine along the lines of listing 19.5.

LISTING 19.5 - THE DISPLAYMESSAGE USER-CREATED SUBROUTINE

```
Sub DisplayVals(FirstNum As Integer, SecondNum As Integer, TitleText As String)
    Messagebox "First Number = " & FirstNum% & |
Second Number = | & SecondNum%, 0, TitleText
End Sub
```

As before, the values this subroutine manipulates are passed in with the aid of two integer parameters, called FirstNum and SecondNum in this situation. A string named TitleText is the third parameter, used to change the title text that appears at the top of the Messagebox.

So now, within the DisplayMessage sub, the lines

```
DisplayVals Num1, Num2, "Before..."
```

and

```
DisplayVals Num1, Num2, "After"
```

replace the duplicated MessageBox commands that were previously there.

Note that when a subroutine is called, the code generally has no parentheses, and the subroutine call appears alone on that line. This usually is the case when invoking LotusScript subs.

Parameters and Parentheses

Does the swapping of the Num1% and Num2% parameter values within the Swap sub have any effect on the values from whence they came—specifically, the Number1% and Number2% variables within the Click sub? The default answer is yes.

To convince yourself, insert the line

```
DisplayVals Number1%, Number2%, "Original variables back in Click"
```

in the Click sub, just after the call to the Swap sub. When this displays the values for the original variables, Number1% and Number2%, you can see that their values are now swapped as well.

Alternatively, turn on the Debugger, step through this script, and keep an eye on Number1% and Number2% on the Variables tab.

This swapping of the original values is a direct result of *passing variables by reference.* When the value of a variable is passed into a subroutine or function the value is *not* a copy of the data within that variable, but rather a *reference* or pointer to the location in memory where that variable has stored its information. Consequently, any changes a subroutine makes to its parameters is made to the exact same memory that is storing the "original" value. This means that changes made within subroutines and functions have a permanent effect.

You may not always want the permanent change. If you do not, you want to *pass variables by value,* which causes subroutines to operate on a *copy* of the original data, rather than the original data. You can accomplish this via two methods:

The first is to enclose the variable in parentheses when the subroutine is called. If this approach is used, the Swap subroutine call in the previously listed Click subroutine would change to the following:

```
Swap (Number1%), (Number2%)
```

The use of parentheses allows the programmer at the time of invoking the subroutine to determine on a variable-by-variable basis whether the subroutine should act on the actual data or a copy of the data. Note that this approach is accomplished during the subroutine call.

The second method is to add the BYVAL keyword to the parameter declaration in the subroutine. The first line of the Swap sub listed previously would change slightly to the following:

```
Sub Swap(Byval Num1 As Integer, Byval Num2 As Integer)
```

This approach changes the definition of the subroutine, so that every time it is invoked, the subroutine works with copies of the original data—effectively insulating the parameters within the subroutine from variables elsewhere. Indeed, there is no way to prevent the sub from working with a copy of the data when using this method.

Investigating a Function

You can apply both methods to LotusScript functions as well as LotusScript subs. As explained earlier in this chapter, you may recall that functions usually return a value. With this in mind, take a look at listing 19.6.

LISTING 19.6 - A LOTUSSCRIPT FUNCTION THAT CONVERTS TEMPERATURES FROM FAHRENHEIT TO CELSIUS

```
Function ToCelsius(F As Single) As Single
    ToCelsius = (F - 32)/1.8
End Function
```

As you can see, the definition of a function is similar to that of a sub: it begins with the word function, and ends with the End function terminator. The name of the function is listed on the first line, and is followed by a parameter list. After this, though, something new occurs. The "As Single" at the end of the function declaration line indicates the type of data the function returns. This function accepts a single precision value as a parameter, performs its magic on it, and returns a single precision value as the result.

Because functions always return a value, the way they are invoked differs a bit from that of a sub. Listing 19.7 demonstrates a common syntax for calling a LotusScript function.

LISTING 19.7 - A DEMONSTRATION OF CALLING A LOTUSSCRIPT FUNCTION

```
Sub Click(Source As Button)
    Dim Fahrenheit As Single, Celsius As Single
    Fahrenheit! = Inputbox("Enter a temperature in degrees Fahrenheit.")
    Celsius! = ToCelsius(Fahrenheit)
    Messagebox Fahrenheit! & "F = " & Celsius! & "C"
End Sub
```

Once again, this code is contained within a button, and is executed when that button is clicked. The line listed as

```
Celsius! = ToCelsius(Fahrenheit)
```

is the line of interest. This line instructs LotusScript to store in the variable named Celsius! (this variable and its exclamation suffix are not celebrating the merits of the metric system, but rather implementing a single-precision floating point variable) the result of having the ToCelsius user-defined function act on the data stored within the Fahrenheit! variable. Because the ToCelsius subprogram is a LotusScript function and thus returns a value, it is usually preferable to have somewhere for that returned value to go: the very purpose in life for the Celsius! variable. Functions within LotusScript are often invoked in the following fashion:

```
AVariable = FunctionCall(ParameterList).
```

Note the different approach to invoking a function. Unlike LotusScript subs, the LotusScript function is generally called in-line with other LotusScript code, and parentheses are used to specify the list of parameters passed to the functions. These are exactly opposite of a sub call, as mentioned previously. To further demonstrate the ability of function calls to appear in-line with other LotusScript code, modify the previous example slightly to produce listing 19.8.

LISTING 19.8 - LOTUSSCRIPT FUNCTIONS CAN BE INVOKED IN-LINE WITH OTHER LOTUSSCRIPT CODE

```
Sub Click(Source As Button)
    Dim Fahrenheit As Single
    Fahrenheit! = Inputbox("Enter a temperature in degrees Fahrenheit.")
    Messagebox Fahrenheit! & "F = " & ToCelsius(Fahrenheit) & "C"
End Sub
```

This listing shows that the ToCelsius function can be invoked in-line with other LotusScript instructions. This would not be possible if a LotusScript sub had been used instead.

Parameters passed into LotusScript functions behave exactly as described for LotusScript subroutines. By default, they are passed by reference, but can be passed by value via either method detailed previously.

For the Record: User-Defined Data Types

Consider an ordinary, everyday Rolodex. Each Rolodex card contains a set of information related to a single person or company. The company name, the contact's first and last name, a mailing address, several telephone numbers, and probably several e-mail addresses would be typical information on each card. The card keeps each person's information together.

Then consider, if you will, how you could implement such a structure programmatically within LotusScript. You could use several string variables for the fields necessary on each card, and an array for the Rolodex, but what would keep related information associated together? What would serve as the index card itself?

Within LotusScript, you have the ability to create a *user-defined type* that serves as just such a function. User-defined types give you, the programmer, the ability to associate several fields of data, possibly of different types, together as a unit. This is very similar to a record of a database. Listing 19.9 demonstrates the code necessary to implement a user-defined type in a simple Rolodex.

LISTING 19.9 - DECLARING AND USING A USER-DEFINED TYPE IN LOTUSSCRIPT

```
Type RolodexCard
     FullName As String
     Address1 As String
     Address2 as String
     CSZ as String
     PhoneNumber as String
     EMailAddress as String
End Type
Dim ARolodexCard as RolodexCard
Dim Rolodex() as RolodexCard          ' A Dynamic Array
Dim Response as Integer, CardNum as Integer
Dim NameEntry as String
DO
```

```
        CardNum = CardNum + 1
        REDIM PRESERVE Rolodex(1 to CardNum)
        NameEntry = InputBox("Enter the Full Name for Entry #" & CardNum)
        Rolodex(CardNum).FullName = NameEntry
        Rolodex(CardNum).Address1 = InputBox("Enter the Address 1 line for entry
        #" & CardNum & ": " & NameEntry)
        Rolodex(CardNum).Address2 = InputBox("Now enter the Address 2 for #" &
        CardNum & ": " & NameEntry)
        Rolodex(CardNum).CSZ = InputBox("What city, state, and zip code for #" &
        CardNum & ": " & NameEntry)
        Rolodex(CardNum).PhoneNumber = InputBox("Now enter a phone number #" &
        CardNum & ": " & NameEntry)
        Rolodex(CardNum).EMailAddress = InputBox("How about an e-mail address for
        Entry #" & CardNum & ": " & NameEntry)
        Response = MessageBox("Enter Another?", MB_IconQuestion + MB_YesNo,
        "Enter more info?")
LOOP Until Response% = IDNo
```

The TYPE...END TYPE keywords designate the definition of the user-defined type. The identifier located immediately after the TYPE keyword on the first line is the name of this type, and is used later in DIM statements to declare variables. The variables between the TYPE and END TYPE keywords store each piece of information this data type should track—similar to the fields on a Notes form. The LotusScript IDE automatically moves the type definition into the (Declarations) event of the current object, regardless of which event or subroutine you were in when you started typing. In the preceding example, all the variables within the user-defined type are the same data type; however, this is not a requirement for user-defined types.

As with any other data type, you need to declare a variable of this type to gain any benefit from it. This is demonstrated in the following lines:

```
Dim ARolodexCard as RolodexCard
Dim Rolodex() as RolodexCard
```

The first line sets up a single variable of RolodexCard type; the second line creates a dynamic array in which each element of the array holds a RolodexCard of information. A static array or a list data structure could be used as well.

After the variables have been declared, you can store and retrieve information from each item within that variable via dot notation. For example, to store a value in the FullName item of the ARolodexCard variable, you need to use something along the lines of the notation

```
ARolodexCard.FullName = InputBox("Please enter the full name.")
```

The period in the ARolodexCard.FullName variable instructs LotusScript to locate the ARolodexCard variable and look within it for the FullName item, then store the result of the InputBox function there.

The syntax with an array is similar, with the additional twist of including the index value. To store an entry within the PhoneNumber item of the third element in the array called Rolodex, the syntax is as follows:

```
Rolodex(3).PhoneNumber = "770-555-1212"
```

Of course, this can be done within a loop if the situation dictates, and the literal 3 can be replaced by a variable.

Because referring to variables of this type is a relatively long process, you do not want to unnecessarily duplicate any reference to one of the values within a variable of a user-defined type. For this reason, keep LotusScript subs and functions in mind for filling in or displaying variables of a user-defined type.

One such subroutine could be used to add an entry to the Rolodex. Another could be designed to display the Rolodex contents.

Listing 19.10 shows two such subroutines.

LISTING 19.10 - LotusScript Subroutines to Add an Entry and Print an Entry Using the User-Defined Type

```
Sub AddEntry(NewRolodexEntry As RolodexCard)
    Dim NameEntry As String
    NameEntry = Inputbox("Enter the Full Name for this new Entry")
    NewRolodexEntry.FullName = NameEntry
    NewRolodexEntry.Address1 = Inputbox("Enter the Address 1 line for entry: "
    & NameEntry)
    NewRolodexEntry.Address2 = Inputbox("Now enter the Address 2 for: " &
    NameEntry)
    NewRolodexEntry.CSZ = Inputbox("What city, state, and zip code for: " &
    NameEntry)
    NewRolodexEntry.PhoneNumber = Inputbox("Now enter a phone number for: " &
    NameEntry)
    NewRolodexEntry.EMailAddress = Inputbox("How about an e-mail address for:
    " & NameEntry)
End Sub


Sub PrintEntry(Cards() As RolodexCard)
    Forall CardItem In Cards
        Msgbox "Name:      " & CardItem.FullName &¦
```

```
Address1:      | & CardItem.Address1 & |
Address2:      | & CardItem.Address2 & |
CSZ:           | & CardItem.CSZ & |
Phone:         | & CardItem.PhoneNumber & |
E-Mail:        | & CardItem.EMailAddress
      End Forall
End Sub
```

Note that each subroutine is being passed parameters involving the RolodexCard user-defined type. These parameters *must* be passed by reference; LotusScript requires any parameter of a user-defined type to be passed in this way. This means that rather than the entire variable being copied into a new memory location and passed into the subroutine, only a special pointer to this variable's existing memory location is passed in. Therefore, changes made to the variable within a subroutine affect the variable outside the subroutine as well. Indeed, the pointer that is passed in still points to the original data.

If these subroutines are taken into account, the main part of this program is adjusted to appear as follows in listing 19.11:

LISTING 19.11 - THE MAIN CODE OF THIS SIMPLE ROLODEX LOTUSSCRIPT

```
Sub Click(Source As Button)
      Dim ARolodexCard As RolodexCard
      Dim Rolodex() As RolodexCard  ' A Dynamic Array
      Dim Response As Integer, CardNum As Integer
      Dim NameEntry As String
      Do
            CardNum = CardNum + 1
            Redim Preserve Rolodex(1 To CardNum)
            AddEntry ARolodexCard
            Rolodex(CardNum) = ARolodexCard
            Response = Messagebox("Enter Another?", MB_IconQuestion + MB_YesNo,
            "Enter more info?")
      Loop Until Response% = IDNo
      If Messagebox("Display All  Entries?", MB_IconQuestion + MB_YesNo, "Wanna
      See 'em?")=IDYes Then
            PrintEntry Cards
End If
End Sub
```

The Click event of this button now refers to the user-defined type, as do the two additional subroutines, AddEntry and PrintEntry. These two subroutines make sense only in conjunction with the user-defined data type RolodexCard, yet they are listed as usual on the Event drop-down. The drop-down is becoming more crowded, as Figure 19.6 indicates.

Figure 19.6

AddEntry and PrintEntry subroutines are listed on the Events drop-down.

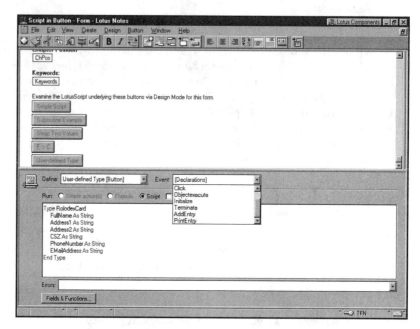

Because PrintEntry and AddEntry make sense only in the context of the Rolodex user-defined type, it would really come in handy if there were some way to associate them with only that data type. Actually, there is. This is one concept behind a *class* data structure, available in object-oriented programming languages such as LotusScript.

Declassifying User-Defined Classes

Think of an everyday typical object, such as a ball. Even though no specific type of ball has been mentioned, you already have the idea of a ball in mind. This ball has characteristics: shape, size, weight, color, and surface texture. It also has actions that it can do, or have done to it: throw, catch, hit, roll, and bounce, to list a few. These are all concepts of the general class of "ball."

The specific instance of the ball class that is known as a tennis ball has been assigned specific values for each of the characteristics listed: shape is spherical, size is a 2½-inch diameter, weight is 3 ounces, color is typically highlighter yellow, and surface texture is fuzzy. Concerning the actions listed previously, the tennis ball can participate in them all: it can be thrown, caught, hit, rolled, and bounced.

The general attributes mentioned in the first paragraph define the *class* "ball:" a member of this class has a shape, size, weight, color, and surface texture, and can be thrown, caught, hit, rolled, and bounced. The possible characteristics of a class are called *properties* of the class, whereas the available actions are known as *methods* of the class. The specific instance of a tennis ball is an *object* of the class "ball:" it has specific values defined for each property, and can perform each method of the class. Consider what values the properties would need to be assigned for a football or bowling ball. Giving different values to each property can drastically change the appearance of the object, but the object will still be able to perform all the methods. (Although, admittedly, the "catch" method of the bowling ball instance would probably be best avoided.)

Now that the concept of a class has been introduced, take a look at listing 19.12 to see the LotusScript code necessary to set up a class called "ball" and *instantiate* (or create an instance of) an object (or *instance*) of that class. Obviously, this is a purely academic example.

Listing 19.12 - LotusScript Code Used to Create a Class of "Ball"

```
Class Ball
      Shape As String
      Size As String
      Weight As Single
      Color As String
      SurfaceTexture As String

      Sub Throw
            REM Steps to throw the ball go here.
      End Sub

      Sub Catch
            REM Steps to catch the ball go here.
      End Sub

      Sub Hit
            REM Steps on hitting a ball go here.
      End Sub
```

continues

LISTING 19.12 - CONTINUED

```
    Sub Roll
          REM Steps on rolling a ball go here.
    End Sub


    Sub Bounce
          REM Steps on bouncing a ball go here.
    End Sub
End Class

Dim TennisBall As Ball
Set TennisBall = NEW Ball
TennisBall.Shape = "Spherical"
TennisBall.Size = "2.5 inch diameter"
TennisBall.Weight = "3 oz"
TennisBall.Color = "Highlighter Yellow"
TennisBall.SurfaceTexture = "Fuzzy"
' A simple game of catch would be something like...
TennisBall.Throw
TennisBall.Catch
TennisBall.Throw
TennisBall.Catch
```

The preceding listing begins to show how a class differs from a user-defined type. Not only does a class contain variables that can be assigned values, but it also contains subs and functions that indicate actions associated with an instance of that class. These properties and methods are all *within* the definition of the class itself. As soon as you create an instance of the "ball" class, the programmer can assign values to the properties of that class, and execute its methods; no additional setup is required.

As with a user-defined type, note the use of dot notation to access both the properties and the methods defined within this class. Any parameters a method needs can be passed using exactly the same fashion as previously discussed in the "Subroutines and Functions" portion of this chapter.

The definition of the class information must appear between the CLASS...END CLASS keywords. An identifier naming the class must follow the CLASS keyword on the initial line of the class definition. This keyword is later used to declare variable containers for this class, as well as the objects those variables contain. More details on these concepts follow shortly.

Now apply the same principles to something more common in the Lotus Notes world: a Notes Database. What identifying characteristics or properties does a Notes Database have? What sort of items does it contain? These questions will lead you to possible properties of the database. "What can a database do or have done to it?" is the question that leads to possible methods of a database.

After you have thought about it for a few minutes, you may have come up with a list similar to table 19.2. This is not an exhaustive list (yet).

TABLE 19.2
Possible Properties and Methods for a Notes Database

Possible Properties	Possible Methods
File name	Open
Title	Create a database
Path	Search
Date created	Replicate
Who has manager access	Create a document
Replica ID	Give access to someone
File size	Compact the database
Server it is on	Create a copy of a database
Documents it contains	Delete the database

Indeed, if you came up with any of the items listed in table 19.2, you successfully identified a property or method of the NotesDatabase class within the Lotus Notes Object Model.

The Lotus Notes Object Model

Everything discussed thus far about LotusScript has been leading up to the Lotus Notes Object Model. The Lotus Notes Object Model is a collection of predefined classes set up by Lotus that mimic and define the behavior of elements within Lotus Notes. The Object Model allows you, the programmer, to manipulate the various parts of Lotus Notes via LotusScript.

The Lotus Notes Object Model provides classes that allow you to work with Notes databases and the various items within them: views, documents, items within a document, and so on. Just about every area of Notes has a corresponding class.

These classes are arranged in two hierarchies: the front-end classes and the back-end classes. The *front-end classes* relate to what a user is working with at that instant: the current Notes workspace, the current database, the current document, and the current view. Each item has to be open on the user's workstation for the front-end classes to access them. The front-end classes rely on and manipulate the user interface of the workstation software. This means that front-end classes cannot be used in scheduled agents, which typically run only on previously-stored data, and only on the server.

The *back-end classes* reach into the data itself and directly manipulate the underlying infrastructure. These classes do not rely on the user interface and can be used anywhere LotusScript is allowed, including scheduled agents.

Table 19.3 lists the various classes contained within the front- and back-ends of Lotus Notes.

TABLE 19.3
Lotus Notes Front-End and Back-End Classes

Front-End Classes	Back-End Classes
NotesUIWorkspace	NotesSession
NotesUIDatabase*	NotesDbDirectory
NotesUIView*	NotesDatabase
NotesUIDocument	NotesDocument
	NotesView
	NotesViewColumn
	NotesForm*
	NotesName*
	NotesItem
	NotesRichTextItem
	NotesAgent
	NotesTimer*
	NotesACL
	NotesACLEntry
	NotesEmbeddedObject

Front-End Classes	Back-End Classes
	NotesInternational*
	NotesDateRange*
	NotesLog
	NotesDateTime*
	NotesNewsletter
	NotesDocumentCollection

* New to Notes 4.5

Note that all the front-end classes begin with "NotesUI."

All the classes are arranged in a hierarchy, so you often need to start at the top of the hierarchy and "walk down the hierarchy ladder" step by step to the part of Notes you need to manipulate. The point of entry usually occurs at one of the top rungs—either the NotesUIWorkspace class, or the NotesSession class, although the NotesDBDirectory class also may serve. Shortly you will also see that, depending on which event your script is in, you may be able to start elsewhere on the ladder as well.

To use these classes to manipulate portions of Notes, you need to declare one or several object reference variables used to point to the objects themselves. The line

```
Dim Session as NotesSession
```

does exactly that. It sets up a variable called Session that points to a NotesSession object. LotusScript does not, however, create the actual object at this point—in fact, the object may not even exist yet. To point a variable to a specific object, use the SET statement. If you need to create a new object, you also use the NEW keyword, ending up with a combination of the two, in the following fashion:

```
Set Session = NEW NotesSession
```

These two statements could be further condensed into a single line, if preferred:

```
Dim Session as NEW NotesSession
```

The NEW keyword in both instances invokes the method named NEW in the specified class—NotesSession in this case. Some classes do not have a NEW method, and so cannot be initialized in this fashion. Other classes require parameters to be passed to the NEW method, similar to the following:

```
Dim DB as NEW NotesDatabase(ServerName, FileName)
```

The NEW method of the NotesDatabase class requires two parameters: the name of the server on which to create the new database, and the file name to use when creating it.

Furthermore, both the one-line and two-line approaches of creating and assigning an object variable may need to be used, depending on circumstances. One-liners are definitely shorter to type and easier to track when you revisit a script six months from now. The two-line approach—the DIM then SET combination—allows you to separate the two statements and place them in different events. The DIM portion usually ends up being placed in the (Declaration) event of the button, form, navigator, and so on, in which you are typing your script. The SET portion can then be used in many subroutines, allowing you to reuse the variable, and consequently the memory, in several places—digitally recycling, if you will.

The last approach to convince an Object Reference Variable to reference the appropriate object also uses the SET statement. However, this time, a new object is not created. Rather, the Object Reference Variable gets its object via the return value from a property or method of another class, which returns an object of the appropriate type. Consider this common example, in listing 19.13, of reaching the back-end document by starting to climb down the ladder at the NotesUIWorkspace class.

LISTING 19.13 - USING THE SET STATEMENT WITH PROPERTIES OR METHODS FROM ANOTHER CLASS

```
Dim WS As New NotesUIWorkspace
Dim UIDoc as NotesUIDocument
' The next line uses the CurrentDocument property of the NotesUIWorkspace class
Set UIDoc = WS.CurrentDocument
Dim Doc as NotesDocument
' Now use the Document property of the NotesUIDocument class
Set Doc = UIDoc.Document
```

Climbing down the hierarchy ladder in this fashion allows you to access information stored in a particular field of a document. More details are just ahead.

The same outcome can be accomplished via the following lines:

```
Dim WS As New NotesUIWorkspace
Dim Doc as NotesDocument
Set Doc = WS.CurrentDocument.Document
```

The two dots in the SET Doc = line can be confusing. (It's starting to resemble a Web address.) In addition, you won't be able to refer easily to any of the properties or methods of the NotesUIDocument class later in the script.

As a general rule, the NEW keyword needs to be used at the top-most level of the hierarchy only, usually with either NotesUIWorkspace or NotesSession. There are situations in which NEW needs to be used with other classes (NotesDatabase, NotesDocument, and NotesItem predominantly), but these are rare.

A word of explanation concerning Object Reference Variables seems in order at this point. Those of you familiar with the concept of a pointer are already familiar with object reference variables, whether you realize it or not. A statement such as

```
Dim DB as NotesDatabase
```

sets up a pointer to a NotesDatabase object. That pointer does not point to a NotesDatabase object until the SET statement is executed. Since these Object Reference Variables are pointers, there are some special behaviors you should be aware of. Listing 19.14 gives an example to consider.

LISTING 19.14 - A SCRIPT DISPLAYING INTERESTING BEHAVIOR IN THE REALM OF OBJECT REFERENCE VARIABLES

```
Dim sess as New NotesSession
Dim db1 as NotesDatabase
Dim db2 as NotesDatabase
Dim OldTitle as String
Set db1 = sess.currentdatabase
msgbox db1.Title,,"DB1"
Set db2 = db1
msgbox db2.Title,,"DB2"
OldTitle$ = db1.Title
db2.Title = "Brand Spanking New Title"
msgbox db1.Title,,"DB1"
db1.Title = OldTitle$
```

This script demonstrates that the line

```
Set db2 = db1
```

does not copy the information from one object into another object; rather, it changes the DB2 Object Reference Variable so that it is pointing to the same object in memory that DB1 is. This is why the line

```
db2.Title = "Brand Spanking New Title"
```

also changes the DB1.Title property, as the ensuing Msgbox DB1.Title line delineates.

Getting Information from a Field

Up to this point in LotusScript, you have been required to rely on the simple input and output function of InputBox and MessageBox, respectively. However, via the Notes Object Model, you can retrieve and store information directly within fields on a Notes document.

This procedure has two plans of attack, and your choice of which to use depends on whether the document you are accessing is the one that is currently displaying onscreen or not. If your document is the currently displaying document, then the NotesUIDocument object is available to you. Remember, this front-end class can be used to manipulate only the currently displaying document. Every document within a database, whether it's currently being displayed or not, can be manipulated via the back-end NotesDocument class.

Being Up-Front About Changes: the Front-End NotesUIDocument Approach

If you wish to access fields in the current document, you may want to use the NotesUIDocument approach. This class is designed solely to manipulate the document onscreen as if you were sitting in front of the workstation manually making the changes yourself. Therefore, it makes sense that this class includes methods to get the contents of a field as well as to set a field value. These methods are appropriately named .FieldGetText and .FieldSetText. In this chapter, the leading dot indicates that they are methods of an object class and must be accessed via dot notation. Listing 19.15 shows their usage. This script also is found in the "Via Front End" button of the Object Model Examples form in the LotusScript Samples database introduced in Chapter 18.

LISTING 19.15 - METHODS OF THE NOTUSUIDOCUMENT CLASS USED TO MANIPULATE FIELD VALUES IN THE CURRENT DOCUMENT

```
Set ws = New NotesUIWorkspace
Set uidoc = ws.CurrentDocument
Dim TempString As String
TempString$ = uidoc.FieldGetText("FieldToGet")
uidoc.FieldSetText "FieldToSet", TempString$
uidoc.FieldClear "FieldToGet"
```

There are no DIM statements in this script because they were performed earlier at the (Declarations) level of the (Globals) portion of the form. The same "ws" and "uidoc" variables can be reused in other scripts elsewhere in this document.

This script uses the .FieldGetText and .FieldSetText methods to their full capabilities. The .FieldGetText method retrieves the contents of the field named "FieldToGet" (now that's inventive), and then the .FieldSetText method stores that information in the field named "FieldToSet." The FieldClear method deletes the contents of the "FieldToGet" field so that it is ready to accept text for the next go-around.

This approach has a few interesting ramifications. The NotesUIDocument class manipulates the document just as a user sitting in front of the machine would. This means that for the .FieldSetText method to do its job, the field must be an editable field and the document must be in edit mode. Just as a user typing in a document cannot enter data in a computed field, so .FieldSetText cannot set values for computed fields. Likewise, a user attempting to edit information in a document in read mode won't get very far. Attempting to use the .FieldSetText in either of these contexts results in an error message.

Furthermore, the .FieldSetText and .FieldGetText methods perform all their work with text values, regardless of which data type has been assigned to the field in question. Performing a .FieldGetText on a field designated as a number or time-date field returns a text value representing how that item is formatted to appear onscreen. For example, a time-date field can be formatted via field properties to display only the date portion onscreen, yet the date element as well as the time element are both stored within the document. Performing a .FieldGetText on such a field would return only the date portion, because the document shows only the date onscreen. The back-end approach, detailed next, returns the date and time portions because it accesses the field stored within the document instead. Because .FieldGetText returns only text values, numbers and dates used in calculations need to be converted first via the appropriate conversion function, mentioned in Chapter 18.

Going in through the Back Door: The Back-End NotesDocument Approach

Every document within a Notes database can be manipulated via the NotesDocument object class. This class offers two approaches to storing and retrieving data in fields within the document. The first, once again, involves methods within the class to accomplish the task. Within the NotesDocument class, these are the .ReplaceItemValue and .GetItemValue methods. Listing 19.16 shows their usage.

LISTING 19.16 - METHODS OF THE NOTUSUIDOCUMENT CLASS USED TO MANIPULATE FIELD VALUES IN THE CURRENT DOCUMENT

```
Set ws = New NotesUIWorkspace
Set uidoc = ws.CurrentDocument
Set doc = uidoc.Document
```

continues

LISTING 19.16 - CONTINUED

```
Dim TempVal As Variant
TempVal = doc.GetItemValue("FieldToGet")
doc.ReplaceItemValue "FieldToSet", TempVal
doc.ReplaceItemValue "FieldToGet", ""
```

This script is similar to the front-end approach. As with that example, the DIM statements for the initial declaration of the ws, uidoc, and doc variables have all been taken care of at a higher level—the (Declarations) event of the (Globals) portion of the form.

You begin climbing down the hierarchy ladder in this approach at the same place as in the previous approach. You go from NotesUIWorkspace to the NotesUIDocument for the current document, and then take advantage of the .Document property of the NotusUIDocument class to return the back-end document object for the document onscreen.

The syntax used for the methods in the back-end approach is also similar to the front-end class example. However, the .GetItemValue method differs from its front-end document counterpart, .FieldGetText, in that .GetItemValue is not limited to returning only a string representation of the data. The .GetItemValue method returns data from text fields as strings and data from number fields as double-precision numeric values. Data from time-date fields also produce double-precision numeric values, because date-time entries are tracked as a number of seconds from 12/31/1899. It is important to realize that the back-end classes return the data that is stored for each field, rather than the data that displays for that field.

The back-end classes also return the data in a unique way. Take note of this or it will surely cause a problem in the future: all field values are returned in an array structure, beginning with an index of 0. This means that if you want to add a MsgBox command to the latest example to display the contents of the TempVal variable, it would look like the following:

```
MsgBox TempVal(0)
```

You need to know that this field contains only a single value in order to rely on this statement alone to display all the information from the field.

Why does LotusScript return an array in this situation? Because fields within Notes can contain a multi-value list. To preserve the separateness of each element from its siblings, the LotusScript designers implemented an array. If the field in question contains a multi-value list, use a FORALL statement from Chapter 18 to work with each value within the returned array.

How will you know if it contains a multi-value list or a single value? Although the FORALL statement works on both a single-element array or a multiple-element array, you can use the UBOUND() statement introduced in Chapter 18 to inform you of the upper bound of the returned array. Your array will have one more element than this number, because the index starts at 0.

The second approach to storing and retrieving information from a back-end document object is called the *extended class syntax* approach. It has been dubbed this because the fields within a document are treated as properties of the NotesDocument class, allowing you to access them via dot notation. Listing 19.17 shows the previous example, transformed to use extended class syntax.

LISTING 19.17 - EXTENDED CLASS SYNTAX CAN BE USED TO ACCESS FIELD VALUES IN THE NOTESDOCUMENT OBJECT

```
Set ws = New NotesUIWorkspace
Set uidoc = ws.CurrentDocument
Set doc = uidoc.Document
Dim TempVal As Variant
TempVal = doc.FieldToGet
doc.FieldToSet = TempVal
doc.FieldToGet = ""
```

As with the previous example, you can add a line that reads

```
MsgBox TempVal(0)
```

if you want to display the retrieved value of the TempVal variable via a MessageBox statement.

Extended class syntax is the approach you will find yourself using most of the time. It seems more straightforward than the previously mentioned method approach, and is generally easier to enter. It is not, however, as clear to a casual observer that you are returning a field value. In dissecting your script, he may think you are accessing an existing property or method of the class, and then become puzzled when he doesn't see it mentioned in the Help database. If your script is going to be inherited or maintained by someone else, the .GetItemValue/.ReplaceItemValue approach can eliminate some confusion.

Notes Events and LotusScript

Where can LotusScript be used within Notes? Generally speaking, LotusScript usually executes in response to something happening; these happenstances that trigger code execution are known as *events*.

All design elements within Notes usually have some sort of event associated with them that can be used to execute a LotusScript. The predominant event used thus far in these LotusScript chapters has been the Click event of a button: script placed in the Click event executes when you click that button with your mouse.

At some point, all scripts within Notes rely on an event subroutine to execute them. The next several pages explain the available events for each element of a Notes database.

Most of the following events begin with the term Query or Post. Those beginning with Query generally occur before something happens, whereas those beginning with Post don't occur until after something happens. The events beginning with Query also have a parameter named "Continue" available for your use. Setting this Boolean parameter to a value of False programmatically stops this event from continuing, thereby preventing a user from opening a document, changing to a view, or deleting a document from the database, for example.

Database Events

Several events are considered to be at the database level. You access these events via the Database script choice under the Other listing within the Design area of the database. Figure 19.7 shows the location.

Figure 19.7

Scriptable database events.

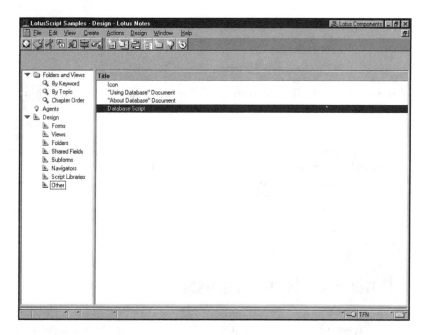

Once in the Database Script area, the Events drop-down allows you access to each of these events (see table 19.4).

TABLE 19.4
Lotus Notes Events at the Database Level

Event Name	When Evaluated
PostDocumentDelete	After the "Do you want to permanently delete..." message, but before the document is deleted
PostOpen	After the database is opened, but before control is given to the user
QueryClose	After the user tells Notes to close the database, but before it closes
QueryDocumentDelete	After the user hits the Delete key to mark a document for deletion, but before Notes marks the document for deletion
QueryDocumentUndelete	After the user hits the Delete key to toggle the delete attribute off, but before Notes removes the mark for deletion

View, Calendar, and Folder Events

The next level of events is related to views and folders. You can access these events from the View Design pane. Make sure the name of the view appears in the Define drop-down, and these events will be listed in the Events drop-down. Some of these events are only available in Notes views using the Calendar interface new to Notes 4.5. See table 19.5.

TABLE 19.5
Lotus Notes Events at the View Level

Event Name	View	When Evaluated
PostDragDrop	Calendar	Just after an item appears in its dropped location, but before control is returned to the user
PostOpen	Standard Outline Calendar Folders	Just after the view is opened, but before control is returned to the user
PostPaste	Standard Outline Calendar Folders	Just after a newly pasted document appears in the view, but before control returns to the user

continues

TABLE 19.5, CONTINUED
Lotus Notes Events at the View Level

Event Name	View	When Evaluated
QueryAddToFolder	Folders	Just after an Add to Folder request via the user, but before the document is added to the folder
QueryClose	Standard Outline Calendar Folders	Just after the user instructs Notes to close the view, but before it closes
QueryDragDrop	Calendar	Just after releasing the mouse button to perform a drag-and-drop in a calendar view, but before the item appears in the dropped location
QueryOpen	Standard Outline Calendar Folders	After the user requests that a particular view be opened, but before that view displays onscreen
QueryOpenDocument	Standard Outline Calendar Folders	Just after the user specifies to Notes to open a document from this view, but before the document displays onscreen
QueryPaste	Standard Outline Calendar Folders	Just after the user instructs Notes to paste documents into this view, but before the documents are pasted
QueryRecalc	Standard Outline Calendar Folders	Just after the user instructs Notes to refresh the view (F9) but before the refresh takes place
RegionDoubleClick	Calendar	Just after the user double-clicks an empty region in a Calendar view (Script here can be used to create the appropriate document for that region)

Form and Document Events

The next set of events is related to Notes documents. You need to enter script for these events in the form that is used to create and display these documents. Access these events from within Form Design mode. Make sure the name of the form appears in the Define drop-down, and the events below will be listed in the Events drop-down. See table 19.6.

TABLE 19.6
Lotus Notes Events at the Document Level

Event Name	When Evaluated
PostModeChange	After the document changes state between Read Mode and Edit Mode, but before control returns to the user
PostOpen	After the document displays onscreen, but before control returns to the user
PostRecalc	After the document has been refreshed, but before control returns to the user
QueryClose	After the user instructs Notes to close the current document, but before the document begins to close
QueryModeChange	After the user instructs Notes to change the document from Read Mode to Edit Mode (or vice versa), but before the mode change occurs
QueryOpen	After the user has instructed Notes to open this document, but before it displays onscreen
QuerySave	After the user instructs Notes to save this document, but before the data is saved

Field Events

The next level of events involves fields. Just like the @Function "events" of Default Value, Input Translation, and Input Validation that are associated with each editable field, the LotusScript events for editable fields are available in the field's Events drop-down when in Design Mode for the form that contains that field.

There are two events available to LotusScript for a particular field. They are

◆ **Entering.** This event executes just after the insertion point enters an editable field.

◆ **Exiting.** The counterpart to the event listed above; this event executes just after the insertion point leaves an editable field.

Because these events occur when entering and exiting an editable field, the field must be capable of being entered and exited, meaning that the document must be in edit mode.

Hotspot and Button Events

The next set of events apply to Notes buttons in their various incarnations: navigator hotspots, action buttons, action hotspots, and everyday buttons on a form. All these items contain the Click event, which is, of course, executed when you click or otherwise activate the button.

With the exception of the navigator hotspot, these items also have an ObjectExecute event. This event is related to Notes Flow Publishing, a process based on Notes FX 2.0 by which Notes actions can appear on the Actions menu of an OLE server application. When you click one of these actions in the OLE server application, the ObjectExecute event within Notes executes. LotusScript within this event would execute at that time.

General Considerations for All Events

All the events listed in the several preceding paragraphs have a parameter named "Source," used to store a reference to the object in which this event resides. Consequently, the data type of Source varies depending on where the event in question is located: the Source parameter for a Click event points to a button, whereas the Source parameter for a QueryModeChange event is a NotesUIDocument instance. In most cases, this Source parameter allows the programmer easy access to other properties about the "parent" of this event, or to start the climb up or down the ladder in search of information elsewhere on the class hierarchy.

Furthermore, all the objects listed above have Initialize and Terminate events. The Initialize event executes when that object is loaded into memory; Terminate executes when that object is closed. Although Agents created with LotusScript must rely on one of these to contain its code (usually Initialize), these events should usually be used only for general housekeeping tasks. Practical experience indicates that code within the Terminate event is not guaranteed to execute.

Script Items New to Notes 4.5

The largest portion of this section is devoted to an investigation of classes new to Notes 4.5. However, two non-class script areas need to be discussed first.

Non-Class Script Additions

The two non-class script items are Script Libraries and Database Scripts.

Script Libraries

Script Libraries are a new element listed under the Design portion of the database. Figure 19.8 shows where this is listed, using the 4.5 Mail Template as an example.

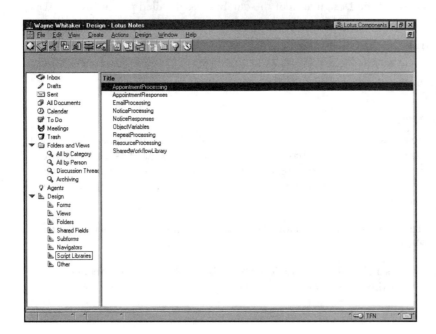

Figure 19.8

Script Libraries.

Script Libraries enable you, the programmer, to store subs and functions in a single location, and use those subs and functions in many places within your database. The advantages of using Script Libraries include:

- ◆ Script Libraries save space because your code doesn't need to be duplicated.

- ◆ Script Libraries are design elements and can be updated via a template.

- ◆ Script Libraries can be copied and pasted from one database to another if the subroutines within them are needed elsewhere.

To inform the LotusScript IDE that you wish to access the contents of a Script Library, enter the following statement:

```
USE "LibraryName"
```

where "LibraryName" represents the name of your Script Library enclosed in quotes. This command can be placed in the (Options) "event" of the object itself, or higher up in the (Options) event of the (Globals) portion of the object.

Database Scripts

The second non-class script-related addition is a Database Script. This script area gives the user access to many scriptable events at the database level. It can be found under the Others section of the Design area of the database, as detailed previously.

Class-Related Script Additions

Many classes have been added to the Notes Object Model in Notes 4.5. Each of these is discussed in the following sections.

NotesUIDatabase

The first of the class-related additions to Notes 4.5 is the NotesUIDatabase class, used to refer to the currently open database. This front-end class is used as the data type for the Source parameter for all the database-level events mentioned earlier, and is only accessible via the Source parameter in one of these events. Within this class, the following properties exist:

◆ .Database allows access to the NotesDatabase back-end object associated with the current database.

◆ .Documents is a NotesDocumentCollection object of the documents being worked on by the currently executing event.

The following method is the only method within this class:

◆ .OpenView can open a view within this database for display onscreen. It accepts one string parameter: the name of the view you want to open.

NotesUIView

Next is the NotesUIView class. This new class is also a front-end class, and is used to represent the current view in the current database. An instance of this class can only be accessed by using the Source parameter within an event at the View level, as discussed previously.

This class has no methods and only the following three properties:

◆ .View allows access to the underlying back-end NotesView object.

◆ .Documents contains the NotesDocumentCollection of the documents the current event is working on.

◆ .CalendarDateTime contains the date and time of the current region of a Calendar view. This is used most in Drag and Drop events.

NotesTimer

The next class addition was long-awaited and greatly welcomed by Notes 4.1 LotusScript programmers. With the addition of the NotesTimer class, the programmer can now repeat actions on a periodic basis.

This class has only the following properties:

◆ .Comment allows the programmer to annotate how the timer is used.

◆ .Enabled is a Boolean value that instructs the timer object whether it should be operating. This value is True by default.

◆ .Interval is a numeric value specifying the number of seconds between occurrences of the Alarm event contained in this class.

This class has only the following method:

◆ New is available in this class, so that you can create a new NotesTimer object via the NEW keyword in either the DIM or SET statement. You must give the New method an .Interval value, and can optionally pass a .Comment string.

This class performs its magic via the use of the following event:

◆ Alarm is the event responsible for doing all the work of this class. This event occurs every .Interval seconds when the NotesTimer object is enabled. Other tasks occurring in Notes can delay this event, possibly affecting the operation of your script.

Because the code is relatively complex to set up, refer to table 19.7 for suggested statements and their placement.

TABLE 19.7
Suggested Statements and Their Event
Placement to Set Up a NotesTimer Object

Suggested Statement	Suggested Placement (Define Drop-Down and Event Drop-Down Values)
Dim ElapsedTimer As NotesTimer	Define: (Globals) Event: (Declarations). Any valid variable name can be used in the place of ElapsedTimer. You can combine this statement with the next statement into the single-line version "Dim ElapsedTimer as New NotesTimer(1)", if applicable.

continues

TABLE 19.7, CONTINUED
Suggested Statements and Their Event Placement to Set Up a NotesTimer Object

Suggested Statement	Suggested Placement (Define Drop-Down and Event Drop-Down Values)
Set ElapsedTimer = New NotesTimer(1)	Define: (Globals) Event: Initialize. This statement creates the NotesTimer object and instructs the Alarm event to occur every second via the parameter 1. Replace the value 1 with whatever value is appropriate for your application.
ElapsedTimer.Enabled = False	Define: (Globals) Event: Initialize. This statement is optional. When a NotesTimer object is created, it is automatically enabled, and consequently starts working right away. If you do not wish the Timer to begin functioning immediately after it is created, set the .Enabled property to False.
On Event Alarm From ElapsedTimer Call TimerHandler	Define: (Globals) Event: Initialize. This statement instructs LotusScript which subroutine should be called whenever the Alarm event occurs. Use your variable name after the From keyword; TimerHandler can be replaced with the name of any valid subroutine that you want to execute when the Alarm event occurs. Note that no parameters are passed to the TimerHandler subroutine.
Sub TimerHandler (Source As NotesTimer)	Define: (Globals) Event: <Sub name>. This is the first line of the subroutine you create to be executed whenever the Alarm event occurs. It must have at least one parameter of NotesTimer data type, or the script IDE complains. Any valid subroutine name works in the place of TimerHandler.
ElapsedTimer.Enabled = True	Placement varies. If the NotesTimer is disabled (.Enabled = FALSE), as listed previously, this statement needs to be executed to start the timer.

As soon as the .Enabled property becomes True, the Alarm event begins occuring every .Interval seconds. The result of each alarm is that the TimerHandler subroutine executes.

NotesForm

The next new class construct in Notes 4.5 is the NotesForm class. This class is used to represent a Lotus Notes form. In doing so, it relies on the following properties:

- ◆ .Aliases contains all the alias names or synonyms for this form.

- ◆ .Fields is an array of the names of all the fields on the form.

- ◆ .FormUsers contains an array of user names allowed to create documents with this form. This property contains the same information as the $FormUsers field.

- ◆ .IsSubForm is a Boolean value indicating whether the current NotesForm object represents a subform within the database.

- ◆ .Name is the name of the form.

- ◆ .ProtectReaders is a Boolean value designating whether the $Readers field can be overwritten during replication.

- ◆ .ProtectUsers is similar to .ProtectReaders, with regard to the $FormUsers field. If this Boolean variable is set to True, the $FormUsers field will not be overwritten during replication.

- ◆ .Readers is an array containing a list of names of who can read documents created with this form. This is the same information stored by the $Readers field.

The NotesForm class also contains only the following method:

- ◆ .Remove can be called to delete the form represented by this NotesForm object from the database.

NotesInternational

The NotesInternational class is the next addition to mention. It is used to track all the information necessary to appropriately format time and numeric values for your part of the world. Notes gets this information from your operating system.

This class contains only properties, which are specified as follows:

- ◆ .AMString holds the text that can be used to display an AM time value.

- ◆ .CurrencyDigits indicates the number of decimal places that currency values should contain.

- ◆ .CurrencySymbol contains the text value that indicates the local currency: "$" in the U.S., for example.

◆ .DateSep stores the character used to separate one part of a date value from the others. An example would be the "/" character, as in 3/6/97.

◆ .DecimalSep holds the character used as the decimal separator. This is the "." symbol in the U.S.

◆ .IsCurrencySpace is a Boolean value that indicates whether a space separates the .CurrencySymbol from a currency value.

◆ .IsCurrencySuffix is a Boolean value as well, which indicates whether the .CurrencySymbol leads or trails a currency value.

◆ .IsCurrencyZero is a Boolean value that determines if decimal numbers have a 0 before the .DecimalSep.

◆ .IsDateDMY is a Boolean value that is True if the date format is Day/Month/ Year.

◆ .IsDateMDY is similar to .IsDateDMY; this Boolean value indicates that the date format is Month/Day/Year.

◆ .IsDateYMD is a third Boolean value that contains a True if the date format is Year/Month/Day.

◆ .IsDST contains a True if the time format takes Daylight Savings Time into consideration.

◆ .IsTime24Hour contains a True if typical time values for this location are in 24-hour format. A False indicates 12-hour format.

◆ .PMString is similar to .AMString. It contains the text string that displays a PM time value. This is usually "PM" in English.

◆ .ThousandsSep contains the character used as the thousands separator for number formats in this portion of the world. This would be the "," character for the U.S.

◆ .TimeSep holds the string used to separate hours from minutes and minutes from seconds in a time value. This is usually the ":" character in the U.S.

◆ .TimeZone contains a numeric indicator for the current time-zone. This number may be positive or negative, and although there are exceptions, often indicates how many hours the current time-zone is from Greenwich Mean Time.

◆ .Today, .Tomorrow, and .Yesterday each contain a text string that can be used in the place of an actual date value for Today's data, Tomorrow's date, or Yesterday's date. The .Today property contains "Today" in English.

NotesDateRange

The NotesDateRange class is a new class in the Notes Object Model. As its name implies, it is used to work with ranges of times or dates, usually when performing calendar functions in a Calendar view.

This class contains no methods; the few properties of this class are detailed as follows:

◆ .StartDateTime is the NotesDateTime value that the range begins with.

◆ .EndDateTime is the NotesDateTime value that the range ends with.

◆ .Text is a representation of the date range in a text format. For example, "7/1/97 - 7/25/97" displays in .Text if the .StartDateTime is 7/1/97 and the .EndDateTime is 7/25/97.

NotesName

The capability to manipulate Notes Canonical names has been added to LotusScript via the NotesName class. A listing of its properties follows:

◆ .Abbreviated displays a canonical name in abbreviated format.

◆ .ADMD stores the Administration Management Domain Name.

◆ .Canonical contains the Notes name in canonical format.

◆ .Common stores only the Common Name portion of the Notes Name.

◆ .Country tracks the country portion of the Notes ID name.

◆ .Generation handles the generation portion of the name, typically Jr. or Sr.

◆ .Given provides access to the given name or first name of the Notes ID.

◆ .Initials displays the middle initial component of the user name.

◆ .IsHierarchical stores a Boolean value of True if the name is a hierarchical name, and False otherwise.

◆ .Keyword returns the various elements of a hierarchical name from the most general to the most specific, separated by backslashes. This is typically used for dynamic categorization on a name.

◆ .Organization tracks the Organization component of the user ID.

◆ .OrgUnit1, OrgUnit2, OrgUnit3, and OrgUnit4 allow for storage of the four organizational units that may be in a Notes ID.

◆ .PRMD is the Private Management Domain of the Notes name.

◆ .Surname stores the surname or last name portion of the Notes ID.

Following is the only method for the NotesName class:

◆ New is the only available method. It can be used as the NEW keyword to create a new NotesName object. It does require one parameter, which is a Text representation of the Name you want to create.

Summary

This chapter has introduced you to many of the advanced concepts of LotusScript. You saw how to use the LotusScript Integrated Development Environment to enter and debug scripts. Then the topic turned to putting repeatable portions of your code into subs and functions. You were also introduced to the concept of a user-defined data type, which offers the capability of grouping different data of different types together.

The idea of user-defined types provided an excellent launching point for the topic of user-defined classes. Data classes that the programmer defines not only group together different data of different types, just as a user-defined type does, but also include subroutines or functions that apply to members of that class. The stored data elements are called the properties of the class; the stored executable subs and functions are called methods.

Lastly, you were introduced to a collection of several predefined classes that Notes provides in order to manipulate databases, views, document, and fields within Notes via LotusScript. This collection of classes is known as the Notes Object Model.

A vast amount of information on LotusScript is still untapped. The Notes Help Database has additional information on many of the topics included here. You can access the information under the Scripts & Formulas portion of the Contents view within the Notes Help Database.

CHAPTER 20

Java: A New Way To Interact with Notes

J ava is the programming environment for the 90's. Java is a programming environment based on the initial C programming language with lots of additions specific to the Interface. Java is a concern for both the system administrator and the Notes developer. For the Notes administrator, Java applets are available for Notes clients from potentially any Web page using the Web navigator native to Notes. Java applets have the power on the local system to do such things as access setup information from Windows and send that data. Obviously, security is a big concern for the Notes administrator. For the Notes developer using the soon to be released interface for Notes from Java, Java can be the primary programming environment for both Web application and Notes application development. This chapter starts with an introduction to Java, covers Java security issues, and finishes with the new Notes Java development environment.

Getting to Know Java

Everyone has heard of Java—it is probably the hottest product currently available for World Wide Web developers. Java is more than just another programming product, however. It is a new evolution in the Web arena.

Java is a programming language based loosely on ideas originally seen in C++. Java is used to create mini-programs called *applets*. Applets are not installed on a user's system (like applications such as Microsoft Word or Excel). Instead they are fully contained in Web pages. When a Java-aware browser encounters a Java applet in an open Web page, it is fully downloaded to that workstation's memory for execution. If the browser is not Java-aware, the applets are ignored (see the next section for more on browsers).

Java applets can do almost anything. They can display interactive graphics, prompt the user for input, or create context-driven menu systems. The applets give Web pages the "live" interactive feel that is not possible with standard, static HTML pages.

Java was created and built by a team of developers, called the Green Team, at Sun Microsystems. The Green Team had the unenviable task of trying to develop software for consumer electronic products such as PDAs and two-way pagers. The software had to be small, self-contained, and able to work easily across platforms. The team came out with a language for this type of code development and called it OAK. Strangely enough, some of the team's first soirees into the consumer market included a Video-On-Demand box that worked with televisions, and 3DO, a full-resolution gaming system. None of these attempts worked out for the team, which was officially disbanded. Luckily for all Web users, several of the team's true believers stayed with Sun and tried to incorporate their ideas into the latest innovation on the Internet—the World Wide Web. In mid-1995, Sun introduced Java to a waiting marketplace (see fig. 20.1).

The next two sections introduce Java in more detail as a development interface and in relation to browser technology.

Java and Browsers

It was not enough for Java to fit the market needs for interactive material on the Web; Java had to be supported by the browsers. Java code is contained in Web pages but has to be run at the workstation level. The browser handles the interpretation and execution of any Java applet. All of the better-selling browsers include this support, including Microsoft Internet Explorer and Netscape.

Figure 20.1

*The Sun Java
Web page.*

The Java Programming Environments

Most Java development is written using the standard Sun Java Development Kit (JDK). The actual Java script is written in text format (like HTML) and can be tested using a Java-savvy browser (see preceding section). Most of the new environments for writing Java code include a graphical front end where objects can be added and tested without the use of a separate browser. Examples of this type of Java development environment include Microsoft's Visual J++, which uses a Microsoft version of a JDK (see fig. 20.2), and the excellent Visual Café from Symantec, which installs and uses the Sun JDK version 1.0.2 (see fig. 20.3).

The following section introduces the idea of Java in the Notes and Domino environment.

Figure 20.2

Microsoft's J++.

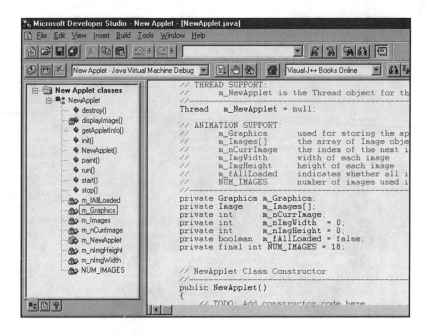

Figure 20.3

Symantec's Visual Café.

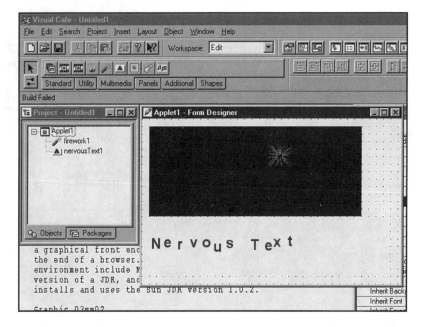

Java in the Notes and Domino 4.5 Environment

Two different combinations of Notes and Java are investigated in this section. The first is the availability of Java in existing Web pages to Lotus Notes Web Navigator users, a feature that did not exist in older revisions of the Notes Web Navigator. The capability to run Java applets can present serious security problems, due to the fact that applets can potentially do anything (within the confines defined by the browser). Security is an important concept when allowing for Java execution in any browser. Because overall system security is the responsibility of the Notes administrator, the administrator must decide if it is appropriate for users to run Java applets, and to what extent Java applets will have access to the user's system.

The second aspect of Notes and Java is the idea of accessing Notes data and objects by using Notes classes in Java. This access gives Java developers standard access to Notes databases, design elements, and documents in a fashion similar to the access capabilities found in LotusScript (see Chapters 18, "LotusScript Fundmentals," and 19, "Advanced LotusScript," for more information). This access enables programmers to develop in standard Java as part of their Web page development (see fig. 20.4).

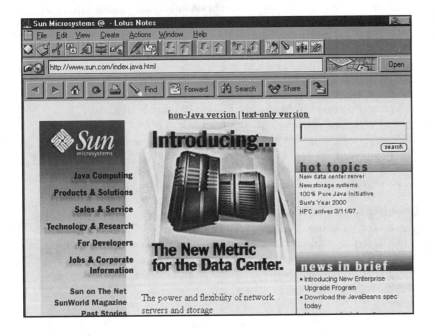

Figure 20.4

Running a Java applet from the Notes browser.

Terminology and the Internet

Working with the Internet requires some understanding of the jargon surrounding it. The following is a list of terms that may be used thoughout this section:

◆ **URL.** Universal Resource Locator (URL) is a string passed to an HTML server to retrieve a specific Web page. To reach the XLConnect Web Server, for example, the user could enter the full URL `http://www.xlconnect.com/index.htm`.

◆ **HTML.** HyperText Markup Language is the standard language used to write Web pages. HTML is a very simplistic language that uses tags to indicate what objects need to be displayed on the Web page. A browser interprets the HTML code and builds the page based on it.

◆ **Java applets.** A Java applet is a mini-program included in HTML pages. The Java applet is indicated by the <APPLET> tag. When Notes reads the tag, the applet's code is copied into memory and executed by the Notes Java interpreter.

◆ **Browser.** Browsers are products that interpret WWW pages into their standard graphical format. The browsers reside on the user's workstation, from which requests are made for Web pages. The most popular browsers are Microsoft's Internet Explorer and Netscape's Explorer (in various makes and models).

◆ **Browser plug-ins.** A browser plug-in adds additional capabilities to existing browsers. Notes supports plug-ins. When the HTML tag <EMBED> is encountered, Notes loads the needed plug-in to execute the object. Plug-ins include audio, video, and environment enhancements such as VRML (virtual reality).

To be able to use plug-ins with Notes, the Enable Plugins option must be selected in the Advanced Options section under File, Tools, User Preferences dialog box. The plug-in must already be installed in the plug-ins folder on the workstation. Notes displays a security alert dialog box each time a plug-in is needed. The user then can choose to activate the plug-in (if installed) or not. The Java code should be installed on a Notes workstation by default.

◆ **ActiveX controls.** Microsoft's ActiveX, like Java, is a component product that allows for executables within Web pages. Unlike Java, ActiveX programs can be written in multiple programing languages (where Java is its own language), usually C++ or VBScript. Also unlike Java, ActiveX programs exist in binary format (compiled), which means the browsers do not need to interpret the code.

Accessing and Using Java Applets in Lotus Notes and Domino 4.5

The Lotus Notes 4.5 client comes with a built-in Web browser called Web Navigator. In older versions of Notes 4, using this browser required using the server as an intermediate to connect to the Web. Domino and Notes 4.5 support both the technique of using a server as a middle-man between the Notes client and the WWW, and the new capability of the Notes 4.5 client to directly reach the Web. The direct access technique requires the workstation to run TCP/IP and to have a direct connection to the Web. This type of connection enables the Notes user to browse the Web without needing to install a separate browser product such as Microsoft Internet Explorer or Netscape. The advantage of server-based Web access is that the workstations do not need a direct connection to the Web via TCP/IP, just access to a Domino server that accesses the Web. Because Java is becoming more and more prevalent on Web pages, the likelihood of running into applets while browsing is very high. To use Java applets, certain settings need to be modified on the workstation. If the settings are not correct, the Java applet will not run (see the section "Troubleshooting Problems Running Java Applets" later in this chapter).

Before the Notes client can run the Java code in Web pages (called applets), several options must be set or changed. Here are the steps required to enable Java applet execution for the Notes Web Navigator clients:

1. From File, Tools, User Preferences, Advanced Options, check the option Enable Java applets (see fig. 20.5). Notes needs to be shut down and restarted for this setting to take effect.

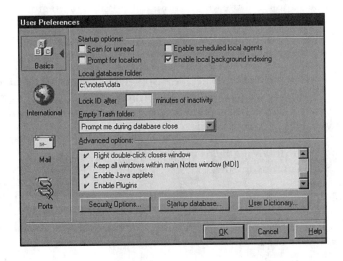

Figure 20.5

Enabling Java applets under File, Tools, User Preferences.

2. Change the Java Applet Security settings in the Location documents in the Personal Name & Address book (see fig. 20.6). This step is optional.

Figure 20.6

The Java Applet section of a Location document.

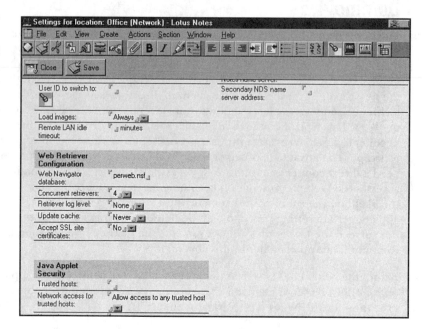

Security Issues

After setting up to run Java applets at the workstation, it is possible to fine-tune the level of access that Java applets have on the workstation on a host-by-host basis. This type of access is useful for companies that want Notes users to have access to intranet Java resources, while restricting Java applet execution from Internet resources.

The default settings in the location document's Java Applet Security section enable all hosts to run Java applets on the local workstation. Regardless of the settings, however, there are limits on the data that can be accessed on the workstation. Resources such as files, environment variables, passwords, and so on cannot be accessed.

To set up greater control, the following fields need to be modified in the Java Applet Security section of the location document:

◆ **Trusted hosts.** In this field, all the trusted hosts are entered by domain name or IP address. Wildcards can be used for the addresses. If the workstation needs access to several Web servers in the same domain, for example, syntax such as `*.XLConnect.Com` can be used.

◆ **Network access for trusted hosts.** This field determines the level of access the trusted hosts have to the workstation (see fig. 20.7). The default is to allow access to any trusted host.

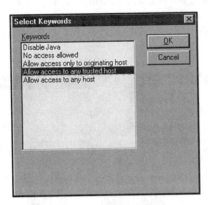

Figure 20.7

The options for trusted hosts.

◆ **Network access for untrusted hosts.** This field determines the level of access the untrusted hosts have to the workstation. The default is allow access only to originating host (see fig. 20.8).

Figure 20.8

The options for untrusted hosts.

◆ **Trust HTTP Proxy.** This field is used if a proxy server has been selected (in the Web proxy field of the location document) to run Java applets for the workstation. The default setting is No. Change the setting to Yes if the proxy server resolves the host names when the workstation can't.

Troubleshooting Problems Running Java Applets

The support of Java is a complex issue—the Notes browser must support the functions written as part of the applet, security must allow the applet to be run, and the workstation Java setting must be correct. One of the tools available for checking the status of Java applets is the *Java Console*. The Java Console lists all of the Java programs that are running, and errors or messages generated by the Java code. To use the Java Console, enable it by going to File, Tools and choosing Show Java Console. The Java Console runs as another window and can be retrieved like any other application (see fig. 20.9) by using the standard Windows navigation techniques such as Alt+Tab.

Figure 20.9

The Java Console.

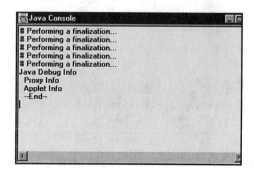

Some things to check when Java applets either do not run or cause strange problems (such as with graphics) include the following:

◆ **File, Tools, User Preferences.** Is Java execution enabled?

◆ **The Location document.** Is security set up for trusted and untrusted hosts in the Java Applet Security section (under Advanced options in the location document)? Are the IP addresses and so on specified correctly?

◆ **The Java support files.** When installing Notes, were the Java support files installed (they are installed by default)?

The following section explores a new concept in the Notes arena: using Java programming tools and a special set of Java add-ins for access to Notes databases for writing applications based on Notes databases.

Using Java to Program Notes Applications

As more and more companies are using the Internet or Internet technologies for data sharing and collection, more and more programmers are turning to Java as a primary development platform. Lotus recognizes that issue and, as a result, has started work on a programmatic way to access Notes databases from Java code. The technique for implementation is a series of Notes classes similar in structure to the LotusScript classes. These classes allow direct access to Notes databases, agents, views, documents, and fields. This section presents the Notes classes that are currently available for Java programmers. This section is not intended to cover the arguments for all of the methods or to be a programmer's guide to using Java or the Notes classes in Java. Because the Notes classes are an "add-in" for the Java programming language, this section is a help for experienced Java developers.

Note This documentation has been written from the alpha release of the Java Notes classes.

Overview

The Java Notes classes provide direct access to Notes databases through Java applets. The classes provided include the Database, or Backend, and the User Interface, or Frontend, classes. Very limited literature or help is available for the Java classes.

The Files

This version of the Java Notes classes was written specifically for Lotus Notes R4.5 Test Build 2 and the Java Development Kit (JDK) 1.0.2 from Sun Microsystems. The JDK is included in software such as Symantec's Café or can be downloaded directly from http://java.sun.com. It is unclear whether this version of the Notes classes will work with later releases of Notes 4.5 or with other products that do not directly support the Sun JDK, such as Microsoft's Visual J++.

The Lotus Notes Java Classes

The idea of classes is a key component in object-oriented programming. A class is similar to a blue print. Whereas the blue print contains information that will be used to construct a building, classes are used to construct objects in memory that represent real Notes elements, such as Notes databases, documents, fields, and so forth. Classes contain properties that describe the components that make up the object (what it is), and methods, which are the functions and subroutines for that class (what it does). For example, one of the classes that will be described in this section is NotesDatabase. NotesDatabase represents a "real" Notes database stored on a disk locally or on a server. Some of the properties for the NotesDatabase class include Created, which is the date the database was created; Size, which is the file size; Server, which is the server that contains the database, and so forth. Methods for the NotesDatabase class include Replicate, to replicate the database; Open, to open the database, and so forth.

Another important concept for the Notes classes is called *containment*. Simply put, objects in Notes are contained in other objects. To access Notes fields using the NotesItem class, for example, the following objects would be used:

- ◆ NotesSession

- ◆ NotesDatabase

- ◆ NotesView

- ◆ NotesDocument

- ◆ NotesItem

All of the available Notes classes for Java developers are summarized next, including all properties, methods, and containment for those classes.

The rest of the sections in this chapter offer information about the Notes classes available for use in Java. This list is very similar to the list of classes for LotusScript in Notes with some subtle changes based on the differences between the Java and LotusScript programming languages. See Chapters 18 and 19 for more information about LotusScript. Many of these changes are due to the limitations of running the applet and its access to the Notes network. The classes overall, however, offer full access to Notes data from Java applets. Notes developers will soon have to decide how to access Notes data, using the Notes front-end or using Java for platform-independent development.

The following sections offer a summarized list of classes, properties, and methods currently (mid 1997) available to Java developers. The format of each section starts with the class name and a brief description of the class itself. In this description, the containment model is referenced to indicate where the class fits in the Notes class hierarchy, and the properties, methods, or statements that are used to access the specific object are indicated. After the class description is a list of all the class properties with a description, and a list of all the methods available for that class. After reading this section, a Java developer should have an idea of the types of data that can be accessed directly from a Java applet in the Notes environment. Finally, a small piece of Java code is included for Java developers as a sample of how Notes classes can be used for Java code.

NotesACL class

The NotesACL class is used to gain access to the Access Control List of any Notes database. This class and the following NotesACLEntry class can be used to add, delete, or change access for users and to grant specific access, such as Private View creation. The NotesACL class is contained within the NotesDatabase class and is created by retrieving the NotesDatabase ACL property.

The NotesACL class is used to grant and revoke ACL rights at the detail level; if basic rights need to be granted or revoked, there are other methods available in the NotesDatabase. The QueryAccess method of NotesDatabase is used to review a given user, server, or a group's current Access Control setting. GrantAccess grants a given user, server, or group a specified rights level; RevokeAccess is a method that revokes ACL access.

Containment

Contained by: NotesDatabase

Contains: NotesACLEntry

Properties

- ◆ **Parent.** Read Only. This property returns the Parent database.

- ◆ **Roles.** Read Only. This property returns a list of roles currently defined in the Access Control List.

- ◆ **UniformAccess.** Read/Write. This property is used to retrieve or change the "Enforce a consistent Access Control List across all replicas of this database" setting for a database.

Methods

- ◆ **AddRole.** This method adds a role to the database ACL with the role name as an argument.

- ◆ **CreateACLEntry.** This method creates a new entry in the ACL using the specified name and access level.

- ◆ **DeleteRole.** This method deletes an existing role when given the role's name.

- ◆ **GetEntry.** Given an entry name, this method returns the current ACL entry for that name.

- ◆ **GetFirstEntry.** This method retrieves the first entry in the ACL.

- ◆ **GetNextEntry.** Using an existing entry as a reference, this method returns the next entry in the ACL.

- ◆ **RenameRole.** This method renames an existing role in the ACL, using the existing role name and new role name as arguments.

- ◆ **Save.** This method saves any ACL changes. If this method is not used, any changes to the ACL will be lost.

NotesACLEntry Class

The NotesACLEntry class is used to represent and manipulate a single entry in the database Access Control List. The CreateACLEntry method of the NotesACL class, as in the preceding, is used to create a new NotesACLEntry. To access an existing entry, one of three methods of the NotesACL class can be used: GetEntry, GetFirstEntry, or GetNextEntry. A save must be issued from the NotesACL object to save changes made to NotesACLEntry objects.

Containment

Contained by: NotesACL

Properties

◆ **CanCreateDocuments.** Read/Write. This property is used to retrieve or change the Create Document flag for an individual ACL entry. It is only used if the ACL entry has Author access to the database. It has no effect for Editor, Designer, or Manager access. For readers and depositors, this property is FALSE.

◆ **CanCreatePersonalAgent.** Read/Write. This property is used to retrieve or change the Create Personal Agent flag for an individual ACL entry.

◆ **CanCreatePersonalFolder.** Read/Write. This property is used to retrieve or change the Create Personal Folder flag for an individual ACL entry.

◆ **CanDeleteDocuments.** Read/Write. This property is used to retrieve or change the Delete Documents property. It has no effect for Editor, Designer, or Manager access. For readers and depositors, this property is FALSE.

◆ **IsPublicReader.** Read/Write. This property is used to retrieve or change an ACL Entry's Public Reader flag.

◆ **IsPublicWriter.** Read/Write. This property is used to retrieve or change an ACL Entry's Public Writer flag.

◆ **Level.** Read/Write. This property retrieves or sets a single ACL entry's ACL level, using the following table:

Constant for Given ACL Level	ACL Setting
ACLLEVEL_NOACCESS	No access
ACLLEVEL_DEPOSITOR	Depositor access
ACLLEVEL_READER	Reader access
ACLLEVEL_AUTHOR	Author access
ACLLEVEL_EDITOR	Editor access
ACLLEVEL_DESIGNER	Designer access
ACLLEVEL_MANAGER	Manager access

- **Name.** Read/Write. This property is used to set the ACL entry's name (User, Server, or Group).

- **Parent.** Read Only. This property returns the parent ACL for this entry.

- **Roles.** Read Only. This property returns the roles associated with this ACL Entry.

Methods

- **DisableRole.** This method disables a role for an ACL entry (removes that role from the list of associated roles for that entry).

- **EnableRole.** This method enables a role for an ACL entry (adds that role to the list associated to that entry).

- **IsRoleEnabled.** This method, given a role name, indicates if the role is active for this entry.

- **Remove.** This method deletes an ACL entry from the database's ACL.

NotesAgent Class

The NotesAgent class is used to represent a Notes 4.x agent or a 3.x macro. The NotesAgent object is created using the CurrentAgent property of the NotesSession class.

Containment

Contained by: NotesSession and NotesDatabase

Properties

- **Comment.** Read Only. This property is the comment describing the agent.

- **CommonOwner.** Read Only. This property is the agent's owner and returns only the common name of the agent's owner.

- **IsEnabled.** Read Only. This property indicates if the agent is able to run at this time.

- **IsPublic.** Read Only. This property indicates if the current agent is personal or publicly available (stored in the database).

- **LastRun.** Read Only. This property retrieves the date when this agent was last run.

◆ **Name.** Read Only. This is the agent's name.

◆ **Owner.** Read Only. This property returns the name of the owner's hierarchical format.

◆ **Parent.** Read Only. This property returns the parent database for this agent.

◆ **Query.** Read Only. This property returns the query used by the agent to select documents.

◆ **ServerName.** Read Only. This property returns the name of the server on which this agent runs for a scheduled agent, as well as the name of the server or user where the database is stored for non-scheduled agents.

Method

◆ **Remove.** This method removes the specified agent from the database.

◆ **Run.** This method runs the agent. This method cannot be used within a given agent to re-run itself.

NotesDatabase Class

The NotesDatabase class is used to represent a Notes database. Several methods and properties can be used to work with existing databases or add new databases. The file name and server name, if known, can be entered while using NEW with Dim or Set, or the OPEN method. The CurrentDatabase property of NotesSession enables access to the current database (open with focus). The NotesSession method GetDatabase is used to retrieve a database object. The NotesDatabase method OpenByReplicaID brings back a Notes Database object with a known replica ID. To create a new database from an existing database, use one of these methods: CreateCopy, CreateFromTemplate, or CreateReplica.

A database must be open before an applet can use any of the database class properties or methods. If you try to use the OpenView method, for example, an error results if the database is not open. Failure to open can result in an incorrect database or server name, lack of rights to open the database, or a lack of capability to reach the database at that moment (with dail-in access, for example). Also, a NotesDatabase object from a NotesDBDirectory or from the AddressBooks property of NotesSession is initially closed; a method such as OPEN must be used to force the database open. Use the IsOpen property to check the status of the current database.

Containment

Contained by: NotesSession and NotesDbDirectory

Can contain: NotesACL, NotesAgent, NotesDocument, NotesDocumentCollection, NotesForm, NotesView

Properties

◆ **ACL.** Read Only. This property is the ACL object for the current database.

◆ **Agents.** Read Only. This property is an array of all agents as NotesAgent objects in the current database.

◆ **AllDocuments.** Read Only. The AllDocuments property is a NotesCollection of all the documents in the current database.

◆ **Categories.** Read/Write. This property is a list of categories used for this database in the Notes Database Library.

◆ **Created.** Read Only. This property is the time/date that the database was created.

◆ **CurrentAccessLevel.** Read Only. This property is the access level of the current user, and by default, the access level of the applet.

◆ **DelayUpdates.** Read/Write. This property determines if updates are batched on the server for improved performance.

◆ **DesignTemplateName.** Read Only. This property is the name of the template database used by the current database.

◆ **FileName.** Read Only. This property is the file name of the current database.

◆ **FilePath.** Read Only. This property is the full path of the current database including file name and extension.

◆ **Forms.** Read Only. This property returns all the forms in a given database.

◆ **IsFTIndexed.** Read Only. This property indicates whether the current database is full-text indexed or not.

◆ **IsMultiDbSearch.** Read Only. This property indicates whether the current database is part of a multi-database index.

◆ **IsOpen.** Read Only. This property indicates whether the database is currently open.

◆ **IsPrivateAddressBook.** Read Only. This property indicates whether the current database is a private address book.

◆ **IsPublicAddressBook.** Read Only. This property indicates whether the current database is a public address book.

◆ **LastFTIndexed.** Read Only. This property is the time/date when the database index was last updated.

◆ **LastModified.** Read Only. This property is the last time/date when the database was modified.

◆ **Managers.** Read Only. This property is a list of users, servers, and groups who are managers of the current database.

◆ **Parent.** Read Only. This property returns the NotesSession that contains the current database.

◆ **PercentUsed.** Read Only. This property is the percent of disk space actually used versus the allocated disk space for the full database.

◆ **ReplicaID.** Read Only. This property returns the replica ID of the current database.

◆ **Server.** Read Only. This property is the name of the server on which the current database resides.

◆ **Size.** Read Only. This property is the current size of the database in bytes.

◆ **SizeQuota.** Read Only. This property is the current quota setting for the current database (in kilobytes).

◆ **TemplateName.** Read Only. This property is the template name if the current database is a template, null if it is not.

◆ **Title.** Read/Write. This property is the database title.

◆ **UnprocessedDocuments.** Read Only. This property returns a NotesDocumentCollection of documents selected by an agent or action.

◆ **Views.** Read Only. This property returns a list of all the views in the current database.

Methods

◆ **Compact.** This method is used to compact a local database.

◆ **Create.** This method creates a new database with the indicated file name and on the server specified. This database is without forms or views.

◆ **CreateCopy.** This method creates a copy of the current database to the specified database and server name.

- **CreateDocument.** This method creates a new document in the current database. The document must be saved or it be lost. Also see the NotesDocument using the New function.

- **CreateFromTemplate.** This method creates a new database using the current database as a template, and using the file and server name specified.

- **CreateReplica.** This method creates a replica copy of the current database. Applets cannot access databases on servers other than the server on which the applet is running.

- **FTSearch.** This method performs a full-text search of the current database using the specified search string.

- **GetAgent.** This method retrieves the named agent.

- **GetDocumentByID.** This method retrieves a document using the given NoteID.

- **X.** This method retrieves a document using the given Universal ID (UNID).

- **GetDocumentByURL.** This method retrieves a Web page as a Notes document object using the specified URL.

- **GetForm.** This method retrieves a form object of the given form name.

- **GetProfileDocument.** This method creates or retrieves a profile document using a specified user name.

- **GetURLHeaderInfo.** This method is used to retrieve HTTP header information for a specified URL.

- **GetView.** This method retrieves a view object of a given name.

- **GrantAccess.** This method is used to grant access to the specified database for a specified user at a specified level.

- **Open.** This method opens a database using the specified file and server names.

- **OpenByReplicaID.** This method opens a database using the specified server and replica ID.

- **OpenIfModified.** This method opens a database if it has been modified after a specified date.

- **OpenMail.** This method opens the mail database for the current user.

◆ **OpenURLDb.** This method opens the default Web navigator database for the current user.

◆ **OpenWithFailover.** This method opens a database using the specified file name and server name. If the database fails to open on the specified server, FailOver attempts to open the same database on other servers, (if they are in the same server cluster as the specified server).

◆ **QueryAccess.** This method returns the access level (from the ACL) using a specified user, server, or group.

◆ **Remove.** This method permanently removes a database.

◆ **Replicate.** This method force replicates the database when given the name of the server to replicate with.

◆ **RevokeAccess.** This method revokes a specified user from the database ACL.

◆ **Search.** The Search method searches a database using a specified query string and a cutoff date. This type of search does not require a full-text index for the database.

◆ **UnprocessedFTSearch.** This method is available for agents. The UnprocessedFTSearch method uses the selected documents (unprocessed documents) and the query string to return documents.

◆ **UnprocessedSearch.** This method is available for agents. The UnprocessedSearch method uses the selected documents (unprocessed documents), the cutoff date, and the query string to return documents.

◆ **UpdateFTIndex.** This method is used to update a full-text index on server-based or local databases, and to create a full-text index for local databases.

NotesDateRange Class

The NotesDateRange class represents a range of times or dates. This range can be created by a static string or the StartDateTime and EndDateTime properties.

Containment

Contained by: NotesSession

Contains: NotesDateTime

Properties

◆ **StartDateTime.** Read/Write. This property is the start date/time for the NotesDateRange.

- **EndDateTime.** Read/Write. This property is the start date/time for the NotesDateRange.

- **Text.** Read/Write. This property represents the text associated with the NotesDateRange.

NotesDateTime Class

This class represents a Notes-formatted NotesDateTime entry.

Containment

Contained by: NotesDateRange, NotesSession

Properties

- **GMTTime.** Read Only. This property is a string representing a date-time converted to Greenwich Mean Time.

- **IsDST.** Read Only. This property returns a Boolean value indicating whether the current system is using Daylight Savings Time.

- **LocalTime.** Read/Write. This property represents the time for running the applet.

- **TimeZone.** Read Only. This property returns an integer representing the time zone for the system running the applet.

- **ZoneTime.** Read Only. This property is a string representing the time from local time adjusted by DST and the TimeZone.

Methods

- **AdjustDay.** This method increments a datetime by the specified number of days.

- **AdjustHour.** This method increments a datetime by the specified number of hours.

- **AdjustMinute.** This method increments a datetime by the specified number of minutes.

- **AdjustMonth.** This method increments a datetime by the specified number of months.

- **AdjustSecond.** This method increments a datetime by the specified number of seconds.

◆ **AdjustYear.** This method increments a datetime by the specified number of years.

◆ **ConvertToZone.** This method is used to change time zone and DST settings.

◆ **SetAnyDate.** This method sets the date component to a wildcard value.

◆ **SetAnyTime.** This method sets the time component to a wildcard value.

◆ **SetNow.** This method sets a timedate to the current time and date (now).

◆ **TimeDifference.** This method finds the difference in seconds between two timedate values.

NotesDBDirectory Class

This class returns a Notes database directory using a specified server. A NotesDBDirectory object is created by the GetDBDirectory method of NotesSession.

Containment

Contained by: NotesSession

Contains: NotesDatabase

Property

◆ **Name.** Read Only. This property returns the name of the server.

Methods

◆ **GetFirstDatabase.** This method retrieves the first database in a NotesDBDirectory.

◆ **GetNextDatabase.** This method retrieves the next database in a NotesDBDirectory, using the specified current database as a starting point.

NotesDocument Class

This class represents a Notes document in memory. This method is part of the Database or Backend classes, as opposed to NotesUIDocument class.

The CreateDocument method creates a new Notes document. Existing documents are accessed using a NotesView object, the GetDocumentByID or GetDocumentByUNID from a NotesDatabase object, or from a NotesDocumentCollection from the AllDocuments or Unprocssed properties of NotesDatabase class, or by using the FTSearch or Search methods.

Containment

Contained by: NotesDatabase, NotesDocumentCollection, NotesNewsletter, NotesView

Contains: NotesEmbeddedObject, NotesItem, NotesRichTextItem

Properties

- ◆ **Authors.** Read Only. This property is a list of users who have modified the current document.

- ◆ **ColumnValues.** Read Only. This property returns an array of values based on the column values for this document in the view from which the document is retrieved. If the document is not retrieved from a view, this property returns null.

- ◆ **Created.** Read Only. This property is the time/date of this document's creation.

- ◆ **EmbeddedObjects.** Read Only. This property represents the OLE-embedded objects in this document.

- ◆ **EncryptionKeys.** Read/Write. This property is an array of encryption keys used for the specific document.

- ◆ **EncryptOnSend.** Read/Write. This property indicates whether the document is to be encrypted when mailed.

- ◆ **FTSearchScore.** Read Only. This property indicates the weighted full-text relevancy score for the given document.

- ◆ **HasEmbedded.** Read Only. This property indicates whether the document has embedded objects.

- ◆ **IsNewNote.** Read Only. This property indicates whether the document is a new document (in compose mode).

- ◆ **IsProfile.** Read Only. This property indicates whether the document is a Profile document.

- ◆ **IsResponse.** Read Only. This property indicates whether the document is a Response document.

- ◆ **IsSigned.** Read Only. This property indicates whether the document is signed (for mailing or when saved within a document).

- ◆ **IsUIDocOpen.** Read Only. This property indicates whether the document was opened using NotesUIDocument.

◆ **Items.** Read Only. This property is an array of all items (fields) on the current document.

◆ **Key.** Read Only. This property returns the user name for a Profile document.

◆ **LastAccessed.** Read Only. This property returns the date/time the document was last accessed.

◆ **LastModified.** Read Only. This property returns the date/time the document was last modified.

◆ **NameOfProfile.** Read Only. This property returns the name of the Profile document.

◆ **NoteID.** Read Only. This property is the Notes ID of the current document.

◆ **ParentDatabase.** Read Only. This property returns the current database.

◆ **ParentDocumentUNID.** Read Only. This property returns the UNID (Unique Document ID) of the parent document if the current document is a response.

◆ **ParentView.** Read Only. This property returns the name of the parent view. If the document was not retrieved using a view object, this property returns null.

◆ **Responses.** Read Only. This property returns a NotesDocumentCollection of all the response documents for the current document (one layer of responses only).

◆ **SaveMessageOnSend.** Read/Write. This property saves a document that is mailed if it has never been saved before.

◆ **SentByAgent.** Read Only. This property indicates whether the current script sent the agent.

◆ **Signer.** Read Only. This property returns the name of the signer for the current document.

◆ **SignOnSend.** Read/Write. This property force signs a document when mailed.

◆ **Size.** Read Only. This property is the size of the document in bytes.

◆ **UniversalID.** Read/Write. This property is the Universal ID of a document.

◆ **Verifier.** Read Only. This property is the name of the certifier used to verify a signed document.

Methods

- **AppendItemValue.** This method is used to create items on a Notes document. The extended notation syntax is also available for creating and accessing items on a documents.

- **ComputeWithForm.** This method validates a document's data by running the translation and validation formulas from the associated form (via the Form item).

- **CopyAllItems.** This method copies all the Notes items from the current document to the specified document.

- **CopyItem.** This method copies a single Notes item to a new Notes document, and optionally specifying a new item name in the new document.

- **CopyToDatabase.** This method copies the current document to a specified database.

- **CreateReplyMessage.** This method creates a reply document to the current document. If this document needs to be mailed, the send method can be used.

- **CreateRichTextItem.** This method creates a rich-text item in the current document.

- **Encrypt.** This method encrypts the current document if the IsEncrypted property is set to true and the EncryptionKeys property contains a key or set of keys.

- **GetAttachment.** This method returns an attachment of a specified name.

- **GetFirstItem.** This method returns the first Notes item (field) of a given name.

- **GetItemValue.** This method returns the value of a named Notes item.

- **HasItem.** This method indicates whether a specified item exists in the current document.

- **MakeResponse.** This method makes the current document a response to a specified parent document.

- **PutInFolder.** This method adds a document to a specified folder. If the folder does not exist, it is created by this method.

- **Remove.** This method removes the specified document from the database.

- **RemoveFromFolder.** This method removes the document from the specified folder.

◆ **RemoveItem.** This method removes a specified item from the current document.

◆ **RenderToRTItem.** This method renders a document to a rich-text field. A rendering is a summary in rich-text format of the data and form structure of a given document. The Notes Mail Forward option uses rendering.

◆ **ReplaceItemValue.** This method replaces a specified item's value with a specified new value.

◆ **Save.** This method saves the current document.

◆ **Send.** This method sends the current document.

◆ **Sign.** This method signs the current document.

NotesDocumentCollection Class

The NotesDocumentCollection class represents a collection of documents (similar to a View structure). A NotesDocumentCollection can be created using the NotesDatabase methods Search or FTSearch, or the properties AllDocuments and UnprocessedDocuments for agents or actions.

Containment

Contained by: NotesDatabase, NotesSession, NotesUIView

Contains: NotesDocument

Properties

◆ **Count.** Read Only. This property returns the number of documents contained in the Notes document collection.

◆ **IsSorted.** Read Only. This property returns a boolean indicating if the collection is sorted. This is only true for a collection built from a full-text search.

◆ **Parent.** Read Only. This property is the database that generates the document collection.

◆ **Query.** Read Only. This property returns the query used for the given document collection.

Methods

◆ **FTSearch.** This method performs a full-text search of a Notes document collection using the specified query.

◆ **GetFirstDocument.** This method returns the first document in the document collection.

◆ **GetLastDocument.** This method returns the last document in the collection.

◆ **GetNextDocument.** This method returns the next document in the collection using the current document as a pointer.

◆ **GetNthDocument.** This method returns a document specified by number in the collection.

◆ **GetPrevDocument.** This method returns the previous document in the collection using the current document as a pointer.

◆ **PutAllInFolder.** This method puts all the documents from the collection into a specified folder.

◆ **RemoveAll method.** This method deletes all documents in the collection from the database.

◆ **RemoveAllFromFolder method.** This method removes all the documents in the collection from the folder.

◆ **StampAll method.** This method replaces the value of a specified name in all documents in the collection.

◆ **UpdateAll method.** This method marks all documents in a collection as processed by an agent or action.

NotesEmbeddedObject Class

The NotesEmbeddedObject class can represent an embedded object, an object link, or a file attachment.

A New embedded object can be created by using the EmbedObject method in NotesRichTextItem. To access existing embedded objects use the GetEmbeddedObject method or the EmbeddedObjects property of the NotesRichTextItem class.

Containment

Contained by: NotesDocument and NotesRichTextItem

Properties

◆ **Class.** Read Only. This property returns the name of the application that created the embedded object.

◆ **FileSize.** Read Only. This property returns the file size (in bytes) for an embedded object.

◆ **Name.** Read Only. This property returns the name of the object or object link. If the embedded object is a file attachment, this property returns null.

◆ **Object.** Read Only. This property returns the OLE handle.

◆ **Parent.** Read Only. This property returns the rich-text item that holds the object.

◆ **Source.** Read Only. This property returns the name used by Notes for objects, or the file name if the object is a file attachment.

◆ **Type.** Read Only. This property returns the type of object as an integer.

◆ **Verbs.** Read Only. This property is the verbs available for an OLE 2 object.

Methods

◆ **Activate.** This method causes an embedded object to be loaded by OLE.

◆ **DoVerb.** This method executes a verb when given the specified verb name.

◆ **ExtractFile.** This method copies a file attachment to a specified disk.

◆ **Remove.** This method removes an object from the document.

NotesForm Class

This NotesForm class is used to represent a Notes form.

Existing forms can be accessed using the GetForm or Forms property of the NotesDatabase class.

Containment

Contained by: NotesDatabase

Properties

◆ **Aliases.** Read Only. This property returns the aliases for a given form.

◆ **Fields.** Read Only. This property returns the names of all the fields on a given form.

◆ **FormUsers.** Read Only. This property returns the name of all the users that can compose documents with this form. The internal field is called $FormUsers and is stored with the form design note.

◆ **IsSubForm.** Read Only. This property indicates if this form is a subform.

◆ **Name.** Read Only. This property returns the name of the form.

◆ **ProtectReaders.** Read/Write. This property protects the $Readers field from being overwritten during replication.

◆ **ProtectUsers.** Read/Write. This property protects the $Authors field from being overwritten during replication.

◆ **Readers.** Read/Write. This property returns the contents of the $Readers field.

Methods

◆ **Remove.** This method deletes a form permanently from the database.

NotesInternational Class

The NotesInternational class represents the international settings in the operating system. In Windows, the international settings are accessed under Regional settings in the Control Panel. The NotesInternational settings are accessed using the International property of the NotesSession class.

Containment

Contained by: NotesSession

Properties

◆ **AMString.** Read Only. This property indicates the string used to designate a.m.

◆ **CurrencyDigits.** Read Only. This property indicates the number of decimal digits.

◆ **CurrencySymbol.** Read Only. This property is the symbol used for currency.

◆ **DateSep.** Read Only. This property is the symbol used to separate day, month, and year in a date.

◆ **DecimalSep.** Read Only. This property is the decimal number separator.

◆ **IsCurrencySpace.** Read Only. This property indicates whether a space is needed between the currency symbol and the number.

◆ **IsCurrencySuffix.** Read Only. This property indicates whether the currency symbol follows the number.

◆ **IsCurrencyZero.** Read Only. This property indicates whether a zero is needed before the decimal point.

◆ **IsDateDMY.** Read Only. This property indicates whether the date format is DMY.

◆ **IsDateMDY.** Read Only. This property indicates whether the date format is MDY.

◆ **IsDateYMD.** Read Only. This property indicates whether the date format is YMD.

◆ **IsDST.** Read Only. This property indicates whether the dates use DST.

◆ **IsTime24Hour.** Read Only. This property indicates whether time is displayed in a 24-hour format.

◆ **PMString.** Read Only. This property indicates the string used to designate p.m.

◆ **ThousandsSep.** Read Only. This property returns the thousands separator.

◆ **TimeSep.** Read Only. This property returns the time separator.

◆ **TimeZone.** Read Only. This property returns an integer representing the time zone as an offset from GMT.

◆ **Today.** Read Only. This property is the string used to indicate "today."

◆ **Tomorrow.** Read Only. This property is the string used to indicate "tomorrow."

◆ **Yesterday.** Read Only. This property is the string used to indicate "yesterday."

NotesItem Class

The NotesItem class is used to represent an item (field) in a document. All field data stored in a document is available regardless of the form used to construct that document.

To create a NotesItem, the methods AppendItemValue or ReplaceItemValue in NotesDocument can be used. To create a new NotesItem object from one that already exists, use CopyItemToDocument, or CopyItem or ReplaceItemValue in NotesDocument.

Containment

Contained by: NotesDocument

Properties

- ◆ **DateTimeValue.** Read/Write. This property is used to retrieve the datetime value in a Notes timedate item.

- ◆ **IsAuthors.** Read/Write. This property is used to change items into Author (editor) control fields.

- ◆ **IsEncrypted.** Read/Write. This property indicates if an item is encrypted.

- ◆ **IsNames.** Read/Write. This property is used to change items into Names items (fields).

- ◆ **IsProtected.** Read/Write. This property indicates whether a user must have Editor or higher rights to modify.

- ◆ **IsReaders.** Read/Write. This property is used to change items into Reader (editor) control fields.

- ◆ **IsSigned.** Read/Write. This property indicates whether the item contains a signature.

- ◆ **IsSummary.** Read/Write. This property indicates whether the item can appear in a view column.

- ◆ **LastModified.** Read Only. This property is the time/date when the item was last modified.

- ◆ **Name.** Read Only. This property is the name of an item.

- ◆ **Parent.** Read Only. This property returns the document that contains the item.

- ◆ **SaveToDisk.** Read/Write. This property indicates whether the item should be saved when the document is saved.

- ◆ **Text.** Read Only. This property is the plain text of an item.

- ◆ **Type.** Read Only. This property is the type of item. The following table indicates the possible types.

Attachment	File Attachment	
DATETIMES	Datetime value or range of datetime values	
EMBEDDEDOBJECT	Embedded object	
ERRORITEM	An error occurred while accessing the type	
FORMULA	Notes formula	
HTML	HTML source text	
ICON	Icon	
NOTELINKS	Link (to a database, view, or document)	
NOTEREFS	Reference to the parent document	
NUMBERS	Number or number list	
OTHEROBJECT	Other object	
RICHTEXT	Rich text	
SIGNATURE	Signature	
TEXT	Text or text list, Names, Authors, or Readers	
UNAVAILABLE	The item type is not available	
UNKNOWN	The item type is not known	
USERDATA	User data	
USERID	User ID name	

◆ **ValueLength.** Read Only. This property is the size of the item in bytes.

◆ **Values.** Read/Write. This property is the value(s) contained in the item.

Methods

◆ **Abstract.** This method abbreviates the contexts of a text item using the abbreviation file Noteabbr.txt and the specified length for the return.

◆ **AppendToTextList.** This method appends a new text value to an existing text list.

◆ **Contains.** This method uses a specified value to check against a list of values in an item. True is returned if value is an exact match for an item in the list.

◆ **CopyItemToDocument.** This method copies an item to a specified document.

◆ **Remove.** This method permanently removes an item.

NotesLog Class

The NotesLog class is used to enable action and error logging to a specified database. The database used to create the logging database is the agent log template. Logging of this type is used to track activity within a database. Database logging is never done by Notes and must be coded into the Java applet to log events and errors.

The CreateLog method in NotesSession is used to create a new log.

Containment

Contained by: NotesSession

Properties

◆ **LogActions.** Read/Write. This property indicates whether action logging is active. If logging is disabled, the log methods have no effect.

◆ **LogErrors.** Read/Write. This property indicates whether error logging is active. If logging is disabled, the log methods have no effect.

◆ **NumActions.** Read Only. This property is the number of actions logged so far.

◆ **NumErrors.** Read Only. This property is the number of errors logged so far.

◆ **OverwriteFile.** Read/Write. This property indicates whether the log file should be overwritten or appended to. This property only affects files, not logs sent to a Notes database.

◆ **ProgramName.** Read/Write. This property is an identifier for the script doing the logging.

Methods

◆ **Close.** This method closes the log.

◆ **LogAction.** This method records an action in the log.

◆ **LogError.** This method records an error in the log.

◆ **LogEvent.** This method sends an event to the server event processor. This method is for script running on the server only. The type of event send can be any of the following:

Event Type:

EV_ALARM

EV_COMM

EV_MAIL

EV_MISC

EV_REPLICA

EV_RESOURCE

EV_SECURITY

EV_SERVER

EV_UNKNOWN

EV_UPDATE

Severity:

SEV_FAILURE

SEV_FATAL

SEV_NORMAL

SEV_WARNING1

SEV_WARNING2

◆ **OpenAgentLog.** This method opens the agent log.

◆ **OpenFileLog.** This method opens a specific file for logging.

◆ **OpenMailLog.** This method opens a Notes mail memo for logging.

◆ **OpenNotesLog.** This method opens a Notes database for logging.

NotesName Class

The NotesName class is used to represent a user or server name. The CreateName method of NotesSession is used to create a new NotesName.

Containment

Contained by: NotesSession

Properties

- ◆ **Abbreviated.** Read Only. This property is the NotesName in abbreviated format.

- ◆ **ADMD.** Read Only. This property is the administration management domain name of the NotesName.

- ◆ **Canonical.** Read Only. This property is the NotesName in the Canonical format.

- ◆ **Common.** Read Only. This property is the common name in the NotesName object.

- ◆ **Country.** Read Only. This property is the country name in the NotesName object.

- ◆ **Generation.** Read Only. This property is the generation part of the name, such as 'Jr.,' 'Sr.,' and so on.

- ◆ **Given.** Read Only. This property is the given part (first) of a name.

- ◆ **Initials.** Read Only. This property is the initials part of a name.

- ◆ **IsHierarchical.** Read Only. This property indicates if a name is hierarchical.

- ◆ **Keyword.** Read Only. This property returns the hierarchical name in reverse order starting with the country code.

- ◆ **Organization.** Read Only. This property returns the organization for the NotesName.

- ◆ **OrgUnit1.** Read Only. This property returns the Organizational Unit level 1 for the NotesName.

- ◆ **OrgUnit2.** Read Only. This property returns the Organizational Unit level 2 for the NotesName.

- ◆ **OrgUnit3.** Read Only. This property returns the Organizational Unit level 3 for the NotesName.

- ◆ **OrgUnit4.** Read Only. This property returns the Organizational Unit level 4 for the NotesName.

- ◆ **PRMD.** Read Only. This property returns the private management domain name.

- ◆ **Surname.** Read Only. This property returns the surname (last) of a NotesName.

NotesNewsletter Class

The NotesNewsletter class is used to generate NotesNewsletters from NotesDocumentCollections. The NotesNewsletter is used to create newsletter documents that normally include doclinks to other documents in a given database.

Containment

Contained by: NotesSession

Contains: NotesDocument

Properties

◆ **DoScore.** Read/Write. This property indicates whether the results of the newsletter should be scored by relevance. This property only applies if the FormatMsgWithDocLinks method is used and the NotesDocumentCollection is sorted (generated from the FTSearch method).

◆ **DoSubject.** Read/Write. This property indicates whether a subject should be displayed when the FormatMsgWithDocLinks method is used.

◆ **SubjectItemName.** Read/Write. This property indicates the field used for the subject of documents displayed with the FormatMsgWithDocLinks method.

Methods

◆ **FormatDocument.** This method generates a rendered summary document (similar to forwarding a document in Notes mail) for each document in the NotesDocumentCollection.

◆ **FormatMsgWithDoclinks.** This method generates a single document with a rich-text field called Body, which contains a doclink back to each document in the NotesDocumentCollection.

NotesRichTextItem Class

The NotesRichTextItem class is used to represent a Notes rich-text item. This class is derived from the NotesItem class and therefore inherits all the properties and methods of that class.

The CreateRichTextItem method of NotesDocument is used to create a new rich-text item. Existing rich-text items can be accessed using the GetFirstItem and GetNextItem methods of NotesDocument.

Given a document, New creates a rich-text item on the document with the name you specify.

Containment

Contained by: NotesDocument

Contains: NotesEmbeddedObject

Property

◆ **EmbeddedObjects.** Read Only. This property is an array of embedded objects in the current NotesRichTextItem.

Methods

◆ **AddNewLine.** This method appends a new line to a rich-text item.

◆ **AddTab.** This method adds a tab to a rich-text item.

◆ **AppendDocLink.** This method adds a doclink to a rich-text item.

◆ **AppendRTFile.** This method appends a rich-text file to a rich-text item.

◆ **AppendRTItem.** This method appends a rich-text item to another rich-text item. This method is commonly used to build summary documents from multiple documents.

◆ **AppendText.** This method adds the specified text to the rich-text item.

◆ **EmbedObject.** This method is used to attach files, embed objects, or update object links.

◆ **GetEmbeddedObject.** This method retrieves a named object.

◆ **GetFormattedText.** This method retrieves the text in a rich-text item.

NotesSession Class

The NotesSession class represents the current Notes session. The NotesSession class is used to get access to environment variables, address books, the current agent, databases, and users. Only one NotesSession is used at a time.

Containment

Contains: NotesAgent, NotesDatabase, NotesDateRange, NotesDateTime, NotesDbDirectory, NotesDocumentCollection, NotesInternational, NotesLog, NotesNewsletter, NotesTimer

Properties

◆ **AddressBooks.** Read Only. This property is a list of available address books.

◆ **CommonUserName.** Read Only. This property is the common-name portion of the current user's name.

◆ **CurrentAgent.** Read Only. This property is the current running agent.

◆ **CurrentDatabase.** Read Only. This property is the current database (open and with focus).

◆ **DocumentContext.** Read Only. This property represents an in-memory document created though the Notes API.

◆ **EffectiveUserName.** Read Only. This property is the name of the current user (a server name on a server).

◆ International. Read Only. This property is the international settings for the system where this script is running.

◆ **IsOnServer.** Read Only. This property indicates whether the script is running on the server.

◆ **LastExitStatus.** Read Only. This property is the exit status code returned by the Agent Manager the last time the current script ran.

◆ **LastRun.** Read Only. This property is the date this script ran last.

◆ **NotesVersion.** Read Only. This property is the version of Notes currently running.

◆ **Platform.** Read Only. This property returns the platform where the script is running. Possible return values include:

"Macintosh"

"MS-DOS"

"NetWare"

"OS/2v1"

"OS/2v2"

"Windows/16"

"Windows/32

"Unix"

◆ **SavedData.** Read Only. This property is a document used to store data between runs for agents only.

◆ **UserName.** Read Only. This property is the current user's name.

Methods

◆ **CreateDateRange.** This method creates a Notes date-range object.

◆ **CreateDateTime.** This method uses a specified string to create a NotesDateTime object.

◆ **CreateLog.** This method creates a NotesLog object.

◆ **CreateName.** This method creates a NotesName object.

◆ **CreateNewsletter.** This method creates a NotesNewsLetter object.

◆ **FreeTimeSearch.** This method performs a free-time search for the specified people or groups.

◆ **GetDatabase.** This method retrieves a database based on the specified server and file name.

◆ **GetDbDirectory.** This method creates a NotesDBDirectory object from the server specified.

◆ **GetEnvironmentString.** This method retrieves a text environment variable from the Notes.ini file.

◆ **GetEnvironmentValue.** This method retrieves a numeric environment variable from the Notes.ini file.

◆ **SetEnvironmentVar.** This method sets an environment variable.

◆ **UpdateProcessedDoc.** This method marks documents as processed for scheduled agents.

NotesView Class

The NotesView class is used to represent a folder or a view and is a very common way to access documents.

You can access a current folder or view by using the GetView method, or the Views property of the NotesDatabase obect.

Containment

Contained by: NotesDatabase, NotesUIView

Contains: NotesDocument, NotesViewColumn

Properties

- ◆ **Aliases.** Read Only. This property returns all the aliases of the current view.

- ◆ **AutoUpdate.** Read/Write. This property indicates whetherthe front-end view should be updated when the back-end object is changed.

- ◆ **Columns.** Read Only. This property returns all the columns of a view.

- ◆ **Created.** Read Only. This property is the date the view was created.

- ◆ **IsCalendar.** Read Only. This property indicates whether the view is a Calendar view.

- ◆ **IsDefaultView.** Read Only. This property indicates whether the view is the default view.

- ◆ **IsFolder.** Read Only. This property indicates whether the object is a folder.

- ◆ **LastModified.** Read Only. This property is the date the view object was last modified.

- ◆ **Name.** Read Only. This property is the name of the view.

- ◆ **Parent.** Read Only. This property is the database that the view object is from.

- ◆ **ProtectReaders.** Read/Write. This property keeps $Readers from being overwritten by replication.

- ◆ **Readers.** Read/Write. This property is the reader security of the view.

- ◆ **UniversalID.** Read Only. This property is the UNID of the view object.

Methods

- ◆ **Clear.** This method clears the search filter from the view.

- ◆ **FTSearch.** This method uses the specified query string to perform a full-text search of the documents in the view. This method returns an integer of the number of found documents and puts a filter onto the view object in memory displaying only the found documents.

- **GetAllDocumentsByKey.** This method retrieves documents with a specified key.

- **GetChild.** This method returns the first child document of the specified document.

- **GetDocumentByKey.** This method retrieves a single document with a specified key.

- **GetFirstDocument.** This method retrieves the first document in the view.

- **GetLastDocument.** This method retrieves the last document in the view.

- **GetNextDocument.** This method retrieves the next document using the specified document as a pointer.

- **GetNextSibling.** This method retrieves the next response document using the specified current sibling as a pointer.

- **GetNthDocument.** This method retrieves a document specified by the number of the document within the view.

- **GetParentDocument.** This method retrieves the parent document for the specified response document.

- **GetPrevDocument.** This method retrieves the previous document using the specified document as a pointer.

- **GetPrevSibling.** This method retrieves the previous document sibling using the specified document as a pointer.

- **Refresh.** This method refreshes the view.

- **Remove.** This method permanently removes a view from a database.

NotesViewColumn Class

The NotesViewColumn class is used to represent a view or folder column. The columns property of the NotesView class can be used to retrieve a NotesViewColumn object.

Containment

Contained by: NotesView

Properties

- **Formula.** Read Only. This property returns the @Function formula for the selected column.

◆ **IsCategory.** Read Only. This property indicates whether the column is a categorized.

◆ **IsHidden.** Read Only. This property indicates whether the column is hidden.

◆ **IsResponse.** Read Only. This property indicates whether the column is a responses-only column.

◆ **IsSorted.** Read Only. This property indicates whether the column is sorted.

◆ **ItemName.** Read Only. This property is the column's name.

◆ **Position.** Read Only. This property is the column's position in the view.

◆ **Title.** Read Only. This property is the title of the column.

The following is sample code from Lotus Development Corporation for Java developers to get an idea of how the Notes classes fit into a Java program. This code is for example only. To obtain the most-recent code, visit Lotus at `www.lotus.com`.

```
/* Copyright 1996, Lotus Development Corporation
    This source code is provided for demonstration purposes
    only. It is not part of any released product by IBM,
    Lotus Development, or Iris Associates. No representations
    are made with respect to correctness or suitability for
    any application whatsoever.
*/
package NotesJava;
import java.io.*;
import java.awt.*;
import java.util.*;
import java.net.*;
public class RegistryBrowse extends java.applet.Applet {
    List namelist;
    TextField hostfield, dbfield, queryfield;
    TextField valuefield;
    NotesSession Session = null;
    NotesDatabase Database = null;
    NotesDocument CurrentDoc = null;

    static final int ST_NOTE_IDS    = 99;
    static final int ST_ITEM_VALS   = 98;
    static final int ST_NOTHING     = 97;

    int displayState = ST_NOTHING;
    String CurrentItemname;
```

```java
// for error output
FileOutputStream fos;
PrintStream ps;


public synchronized void init()
{
try {fos = new FileOutputStream("registry.err");}
catch (IOException e){}
ps = new PrintStream(fos, true);

String host = getParameter("host");
if (host == null) {
    try {
      Object context = System.getSecurityManager().getSecurityContext();
      if (context != null && context instanceof URL) {
          host = "//" + ((URL)context).getHost() + "/";
      } else {
          host = "//" + InetAddress.getLocalHost().getHostName();
          host += "/";
      }
      } catch (Exception ex) {
      showStatus("Default host is unknown.");
      }
}

setLayout(new BorderLayout());

// Create the host label and textfield as panel using the default
➥flowlayout
Panel hostgroup = new Panel();
hostgroup.setLayout(new GridLayout(4, 1, 5, 10));

hostgroup.add(new Label("Notes Class Factory Connection:", Label.RIGHT));
hostfield = new TextField(20);
hostfield.setText(host + "/NotesObjectServer");
hostgroup.add(hostfield);

// Create the Database name input field
 dbfield = new TextField(20);
 dbfield.setText("");
 hostgroup.add(new Label("Notes Database:", Label.RIGHT));
 hostgroup.add(dbfield);
```

```
        // create the query field
        queryfield = new TextField(20);
        queryfield.setText("");
        hostgroup.add(new Label("Query: ", Label.RIGHT));
        hostgroup.add(queryfield);

        // create (hidden) value field
        valuefield = new TextField(20);
        queryfield.setText("");
        hostgroup.add(new Label("Enter new item value: ", Label.RIGHT));
        hostgroup.add(valuefield);
        valuefield.hide();
        valuefield.disable();

        add("North", hostgroup);

        // Create the names group;
        Panel namesgroup = new Panel();
        namesgroup.setLayout(new BorderLayout());
        namesgroup.add("North", new Label("Notes Output:", Label.LEFT));
        namelist = new List();
        namesgroup.add("Center", namelist);
        add("Center", namesgroup);

        try {loadFromURL(hostfield.getText());}
        catch (NotesException e){e.printStackTrace(ps);}

        hostfield.requestFocus();
      }

public void stop()
    {
    // clean up stuff
    showStatus("Shutting down...");
    try {fos.close();}
    catch (IOException e){}
    ps.close();
    }


public boolean action(Event ev, Object obj)
  {
```

```
    if (ev.target == hostfield)
        {
        dbfield.setText("");
        queryfield.setText("");
        namelist.clear();
        displayState = ST_NOTHING;
        valuefield.hide(); valuefield.disable();
        try {loadFromURL(hostfield.getText());}
        catch (NotesException e){e.printStackTrace(ps);}
        dbfield.requestFocus();
        dbfield.selectAll();
        }
    else if (ev.target == dbfield)
        {
        queryfield.setText("");
        namelist.clear();
        displayState = ST_NOTHING;
        valuefield.hide(); valuefield.disable();
        try {processDatabase((String)ev.arg);}
        catch (NotesException e){e.printStackTrace(ps);}
        queryfield.requestFocus();
        queryfield.selectAll();
        }
    else if (ev.target == queryfield)
        {
        namelist.clear();
        displayState = ST_NOTHING;
        valuefield.hide(); valuefield.disable();
        try {processQuery((String)ev.arg);}
        catch (NotesException e){e.printStackTrace(ps);}
        }
    else if (ev.target == namelist)
        {
        // look up document based on id
        if (displayState == ST_NOTE_IDS)
            {
            try {processDoc((String)ev.arg);}
            catch (NotesException e){e.printStackTrace(ps);}
            }
        // get new value for selected item
        else if (displayState == ST_ITEM_VALS)
            {
```

```
                    // enable the value prompt, save current item
                    String text = namelist.getSelectedItem();
                    int index = text.indexOf("=");
                    CurrentItemname = text.substring(0, index-1);
                    CurrentItemname.trim();
                    String oldvalue = text.substring(index+2);
                    valuefield.enable();
                    valuefield.setText(oldvalue);
                    valuefield.show();
                    valuefield.requestFocus();
                    valuefield.selectAll();
                    showStatus("Enter a new value for item " + CurrentItemname);
                    }
            }
        else if (ev.target == valuefield)
            {
            try {processValue((String)ev.arg);}
            catch (NotesException e){e.printStackTrace(ps);}
            }

    return true;
    }


public void loadFromURL(String where)
        throws NotesException     //, java.rmi.RemoteException
{
    URL url = null;
    try
    {
    namelist.clear();
    showStatus("Connection established");
    Session = new NotesSession(1, "Anonymous");
    if (Session == null)
        showStatus("Could not create Notes session");
     else showStatus("Notes session started");
    }
    catch (Exception ex)
            {showStatus("Host unknown in url " + url);}
}

public String getAppletInfo()
{
```

```java
        return "Example applet programming Notes";
}


public String[][] getParameterInfo()
{
    String[][] info = {
        {"host",        "url",               "//Host:port of Registry."}
    };
return info;
}


public void processDatabase(String dbname)
        throws NotesException     //, java.rmi.RemoteException
{
    if (Session == null)
        showStatus("Notes session not started yet");
    else {
        Database = Session.GetDatabase("", dbname);
        if (Database == null)
            showStatus("Could not open database " + dbname);
        else showStatus("Database " + dbname + " opened");
        }
}


public void processQuery(String query)
        throws NotesException     //, java.rmi.RemoteException
{
    showStatus("Processing query, please wait...");
    if (Database == null)
        showStatus("Database not opened yet");
    else {
        NotesDocumentCollection dc;

        // if the string is null, get all documents
        if (query == null)
            dc = Database.GetAllDocuments();
        else dc = Database.FTSearch(query, 0);
        if (dc == null)
            showStatus("No collection returned from query");
        else {
            int i;
            int count = dc.GetCount();
```

```
                    String c = Integer.toString(count);
                    showStatus("Found " + c + " documents");
                    displayState = ST_NOTE_IDS;
                    for (i = 1; i <= count; i++)
                        {
                      NotesDocument doc;
                      String output;
                      doc = dc.GetNthDocument(i);
                      namelist.addItem(doc.GetNoteID());
                      }
                  }
              }
      }


public void processDoc(String id)
          throws NotesException        //, java.rmi.RemoteException
{
     NotesDocument doc;

     showStatus("Searching for document id " + id);
     doc = Database.GetDocumentByID(id);
     if (doc == null)
          showStatus("Can't find document");
     else {
          CurrentDoc = doc;
          java.util.Vector v = doc.GetItems();
          showStatus("Found " + Integer.toString(v.size()) + " items");
          namelist.clear();
          displayState = ST_ITEM_VALS;
          Enumeration e = v.elements();
          while (e.hasMoreElements())
              {
              NotesItem i = (NotesItem)e.nextElement();
              String s = i.GetName() + " = ";

              // don't grab huge items
              if (i instanceof NotesRichTextItem)
                  {
                  NotesRichTextItem r = (NotesRichTextItem)i;
                  s += r.GetFormattedText(true, 30, 20);
                  }
              else s += i.GetText(30);
              namelist.addItem(s);
```

```
            }
          }
}


public void processValue(String newvalue)
         throws NotesException      //, java.rmi.RemoteException
{
     boolean saved = false;

     if (CurrentDoc == null)
          {
          showStatus("No current document");
          return;
          }
     if (CurrentItemname == null)
          {
          showStatus("No current item");
          return;
          }

     showStatus("Replacing value for item " + CurrentItemname);
     try {CurrentDoc.ReplaceItemValue(CurrentItemname, newvalue);}
     catch (NotesException e){e.printStackTrace(ps);}
     showStatus("Saving the document");

     // save might fail due to access control
     try {saved = CurrentDoc.Save(true, false, false);}
     catch (NotesException e)
          {
          showStatus("Error on update: " + e.getMessage());
          }

     if (saved)
          {
          showStatus("Done replacing value");
          queryfield.requestFocus();
          valuefield.hide(); valuefield.disable();

          // refresh the display
          processDoc(CurrentDoc.GetNoteID());
          }
}
}    // end class
```

Summary

This chapter explored Java as an Internet programming environment. The Java issues faced by Notes administrators were addressed in relationship to security issues and usability. For the developer, the new Notes classes for Java were listed as a summary and some sample code was included. Using Java with the Notes classes gives companies the power of the Internet with the storage and security of Notes. The final section is sample Java code using the Notes database classes. For more information on the Notes classes in general or object-oriented programming concepts, see Chapters 18 and 19.

PART VII

Domino and the Web Up Close

CHAPTER 21

Installing and Setting Up Domino

This chapter covers the details of installing Web-based services provided by a Domino 4.5 server. It also briefly discusses the nature of Web clients to provide a better understanding of their function and interaction with the Domino server. As you will also see, previous releases of the Notes 4.0 and 4.1x servers are capable of providing Web services by supporting a limited set of Web protocols.

Experienced Notes administrators may wonder why the addition of Web services to the Domino server should matter in the everyday operation of their server. The fact that Lotus changed the name of the Notes server to Domino server should provide some indication why it matters!

The introduction of Web services imposes an additional set of administrative requirements on the Notes administrator. As a Notes administrator, you will need to understand how the new client type interacts with your server. The only client type previously was the Notes client.

Now you must deal with Web clients. You will need to understand what is required to install this service and support Web clients on your Domino server. Should you accept the defaults of the HTTP service or change them? What about registering and maintaining Web clients versus Notes clients? Why can't Web clients do as much as Notes clients?

As a Notes administrator you have become well-acquainted with the Notes client and understand its idiosyncrasies. The first part of the chapter will help you understand the new Web client and its limitations and differences.

Understanding Web Clients

Before launching directly into the installation and setup of Domino's Web capabilities, it is essential to understand how the Domino HTTP server interacts with Web clients. Interacting with a browser has some limitations; therefore, it is necessary to have a basic understanding of Web clients and the protocol used for communicating with Web clients.

Some industry observers have characterized a Web client as a file transfer protocol on steroids. The capability of a Web client is limited, however, relative to being able to function on a stand-alone basis.

Web clients communicate with information systems through a standards-based protocol known as the *HyperText Transfer Protocol* (HTTP). Because the HTTP protocol is defined in the Internet Engineering Task Force (IETF) standards as a "generic, stateless, object-oriented protocol," it can be used to build relatively simple clients with the capability to communicate with foreign information systems. The HTTP protocol has been the "language" of the World Wide Web since its inception in 1990. Because Web clients communicate through a generic protocol, the client no longer needs to be a special, single-use client written for the host application.

The appeal of the Web is that it enables access to many information systems around the world from a single client interface based on point-and-click navigation. The client is often referred to as a "thin" client because it does not require specialized functionality for a particular host system. Thin clients typically require less disk space than specialized (often referred to as "fat" or "wide-bodied" clients) clients and represent the potential for simplified user interaction with disparate legacy systems through a common, simple point-and-click interface.

Many IT managers see the value of thin clients as providing the capability to deploy a single, point-and-click user interface throughout the organization. This, in turn, represents potential savings in end-user training and support. Hence, the cost of desktop support can be greatly reduced by using a Web browser for many applications.

Along with the benefits of using a thin client, however, comes a disadvantage in the inherent limitation of the client's functionality. When compared to a Notes client, which provides an underlying local object store and off-line processing capability, the Web client provides little capability when disconnected from its network host.

In its relatively simple form, the Web client is limited in its capability to perform complex functions because it is designed to only understand Web protocols and execute a limited function set based on the commands received. The current standards for HTTP enable Web clients to do little more than make requests to the host and act on responses. This request/response architecture, coupled with hypertext language, enables the Web client to request file transfers and render textual or graphical information to the screen based on the contents of the file received— hence, the observation of the Web client being little more than file transfer on steroids.

The file contents might spawn another request from the browser to retrieve additional information and display it in the context of the information just received. After a request is processed by the host and the response is received by the Web client, the contents of the file are displayed on the user's monitor rather than being saved in a file on the local hard drive.

Web Clients Supported by Domino

In 1995, Lotus began to add Web protocol support on top of the Notes object store. Gradually and, more recently, rapidly even more Web client functionality has been added. This section provides an overview of the various types of support provided to Web clients from the Domino server. The information is current as of the date of this publication.

InterNotes Web Publisher

The InterNotes Web Publisher (IWP) allows Web clients indirect access to a Notes database. The IWP converts Notes documents and views into static HTML pages and stores the pages on a separate HTTP server (for example, the IBM Information Server). The static HTML pages can then be updated from the Notes databases on a scheduled basis or "forced" after a change is made to a document or design element in the Notes database. Interaction between the Web client and the Notes database is through a CGI script processor, running on the Notes server, which can convert messages received from the Web client into Notes documents.

Although the IWP provides an indirect mechanism to access the Notes database, the actual HTTP protocol is provided by a separate HTTP server (such as IBM Information Server).

The future of this product is somewhat unclear, and all indications from Lotus are that it will be dropped once Domino provides the same functionality to publish static pages to an HTTP server.

Domino (HTTP)

Notes Release 4.x servers have been able to interact with Web clients since the first commercially available build of Domino (June 1996). In addition to supporting the native Notes client/server protocol (for example, Notes Remote Procedure Call—NRPC), native HTTP protocol support was added so that Web clients could communicate with the Notes server without the need for a separate HTTP server.

The Domino server provides an HTTP service that handles requests from Web clients for access to Notes databases hosted on the Domino server. The HTTP process receives the request and, based on proper authorization, sends the Notes document requested back to the Web client in the form of a static HTML page.

Note   The fact that Domino returns a static HTML page to the Web client is important. It explains why features commonly used in Notes application development (computed field updates, field refresh, form buttons and their associated macros, predefined system action buttons, and so forth) do not function on the Web client. Seasoned Notes application developers may wonder why their use of these design features show up on the Web client and may report that the Domino server is "misbehaving" when, in fact, it is the Web client's inability to understand Notes-specific features that is the cause of the problem.

Prior to the release of Notes/Domino 4.5, the Notes server and client were always released together and were kept at the same revision level. With the release of 4.5, however, the client (Notes 4.5) and server (Domino 4.5) products were separated in order to enable more rapid development in one area without affecting the other.

One other note about the HTTP server function is that it does not necessarily have to serve Notes databases. The HTTP server provided by Domino serves static HTML pages in addition to Notes databases, making it easier to integrate into an existing Web server environment or to migrate existing HTML directory structures onto the Domino server.

Secure Socket Layer (SSL)

Secure Socket Layer (SSL) support provides the Web client with an encrypted communication channel to the host HTTP server. SSL Version 2 is based on public key certificates that enable the server and client to encrypt and decrypt traffic between the two.

SSL can be configured on Release 4.x and greater servers to support an internally generated key. This can be a key certified by a known Certificate Authority (CA) such as VeriSign or keys certified by an internal Certificate Authority.

For intranets, internal certification is sufficient for most uses. For uses on the Internet, however, certification by a known CA is preferred because the CA provides the Web client with a level of certainty about the host with which it communicates sensitive information (such as credit cards, social security numbers, and so on).

The role of the CA is to certify that the key holder is who he claims to be. Any individual, for instance, can register a domain name with InterNIC to setup a Web server and receive data from any Web client connecting to it. The CA, through a formal investigation of domain name holders, helps to ensure that they are trustworthy so the Web client can have some certainty in the identity of the host receiving the sensitive information.

Simple Mail Transfer Protocol (SMTP)

Beginning with Release 4.11a, support for Simple Mail Transfer Protocol (SMTP) is provided in a new Message Transfer Agent (MTA). Prior to this release, the only support for SMTP was through a gateway product that ran under Release 3.x servers.

The MTA enables Notes clients to seamlessly send and receive electronic mail from Internet mail clients through common Internet mail addressing schemes of the form "user@mycorp.com."

Other MTAs (cc:Mail and X.400) are provided by Lotus but are outside the scope of this book.

Post Office Protocol (POP3)

The Domino 4.5 server provides support for Post Office Protocol (POP3) mail clients such as Netscape, Microsoft Internet Explorer, and Eudora Pro. The POP3 protocol enables such mail clients to access a mail file in a detached fashion. A connection is made only during the retrieval process and then the connection is terminated. Mail is stored and processed (read) off-line on the Web client.

Internet Message Access Protocol (IMAP)

The Internet Message Access Protocol (IMAP) enables the Web browser's e-mail interface to manipulate the mailbox while actively connected to the IMAP server. The Domino server also will provide support for the IMAP protocol in a later release, which will enable off-line or online processing of messages.

Lightweight Directory Assistance Protocol (LDAP)

In addition to the preceding protocols, the Domino server will provide support for Lightweight Directory Assistance Protocol (LDAP), which is essentially an extension of the X.500 standards for a global directory. LDAP support will allow directory lookups into foreign directories such as Novell NetWare's NDS or Banyan's StreetTalk.

Now that some Web background has been covered, the following section discusses the specifics of installing the HTTP Web service.

Domino HTTP Services Installation

This section describes in detail the "how to" of installing Domino Web-based services. The installation and configuration of a Domino 4.5 server has been covered fully in other chapters, so this section deals strictly with the services available for the support of Web clients.

Notes Releases 4.0 and 4.1x

It is possible to install Web-based services on releases 4.0 and 4.1x of the Notes server. A reasonable question to ask would be "Why would I want to keep a pre-Domino 4.5 server release around anyway?" There are reasons, however, why one would want to keep a pre-Release 4.5 server available to Notes and Web clients.

Some IT managers supporting a large installed base of Lotus Organizer might not want to introduce Notes Calendaring and Scheduling into the environment to avoid confusing users. (Organizer97 GS with group scheduling features integrates directly with Notes Calendaring and Scheduling.) They might still want to make use of the HTTP services afforded by Domino, however, and this enables them to do so.

For other organizations that have recently completed a large rollout of of Release 3 Notes clients, a move to Release 4.5 might not be in the immediate plans given the recent outlay to install Release 3 clients. Again, the HTTP services provided by Domino will enable them to serve both Release 3 Notes clients and HTTP clients.

 Warning   The level of programmability available to developers using Domino 4.5 servers is not available in these older releases of the Notes server running HTTP services. For example, in order to use @DbLookup and @DbColumn, a Release 4.5 server is required.

When installing Web-based services on a Release 4.0 or 4.1x Notes server, the HTTP server process is installed as a stand-alone set of files. These files are installed in the directory structure of the Notes server executable files and, as with Domino 4.5, are launched separately after the Notes server starts. In addition, these separate releases are known by their release level or build number, which currently tracks the release of the Domino 4.5 server. (As of this writing, the current release of the stand-alone HTTP server process is Domino 1.5a or Build 169.)

Supported operating systems for this release of the stand-alone Domino HTTP server are: Windows NT/Intel, Solaris/SPARC, Solaris/IntelEdition, AIX, and OS/2.

Note Several Notes functions (such as @DbLookup and @DbColumn) are supported only under the Domino 4.5 server. These functions are covered in Chapter 22, "Using Domino to Publish on the Web."

In order to operate the HTTP Web server under Notes 4.0 or 4.1x servers, changes must be made to the person form to add the HTTP password field and to the server document to add an entry for the HTTP Server subform. Fortunately, Lotus has provided these changes in a template database to facilitate making the changes in your address book. The following procedures describe how to install the Domino code on your existing Notes server and use the provided template to make the necessary changes.

Before beginning the procedure to install stand-alone Domino HTTP server code, you need to know in which directory your Notes server files are stored. Most often, they are located in C:\notes, but this can vary from server to server.

Note The procedure to install stand-alone Domino HTTP server code should be performed at the server and not from a client workstation.

To install the stand-alone Domino HTTP server code, follow these steps:

1. Download the Domino install files from `http://domino.lotus.com` to a temporary directory on the server's disk drive (for example, C:\temp).

2. If you are installing on a Windows NT server, use File Manager (or a similar tool if using a different operating system) to locate the temporary directory (C:\temp) containing the Domino.exe file.

3. Launch the Domino.exe file, which is a self-extracting installation utility.

4. Follow the installation procedures displayed on-screen.

The files needed to run the HTTP server are extracted into the appropriate directories, based on the Notes server directory specified in the preceding installation. The changes required in the Public Name & Address Book (HTTP server section and HTTP password field) to run the HTTP server process and authenticate Web clients are included in the files unpacked during the installation procedure and can be found in the file HTTPCNF.NTF.

After the server code is installed, the Public Name & Address Book template needs a few changes in order for the HTTP server task to function correctly. Before making these changes, however, you should add the icons for the Public Name & Address Book template (PUBNAMES.NTF) and HTTPCNF.NTF to your desktop now. To add these templates, follow these steps:

1. Select File, Database, Open.

2. Enter **PUBNAMES.NTF** in the Filename box.

3. Select Add Icon.

4. Repeat steps 2 and 3 using the file name **HTTPCNF.NTF**.

5. Select Done.

After the templates' icons are on your desktop, follow these steps to update the Public Name & Address Book template:

1. Open the HTTPCNF database template by double-clicking on its icon.

2. In the Design view, open the HTTP Password form by double-clicking on the only form listed "HTTP Password Field."

3. Highlight the HTTP Password field (see fig. 21.1) and select Edit, Copy.

4. Open a new window by selecting Window, 1. Workspace.

5. Open the PUBNAMES.NTF database template by double-clicking on its icon.

6. In the Design view, open the Person form by double-clicking on it.

7. Select an area on the form to paste the HTTP Password field that was copied in step 3.

Note When updating the Public Name & Address Book template, it doesn't matter where on the form you place the HTTPPassword field (see step 7); however, somewhere in the vicinity of the user's name properties would be convenient for administrative purposes later on.

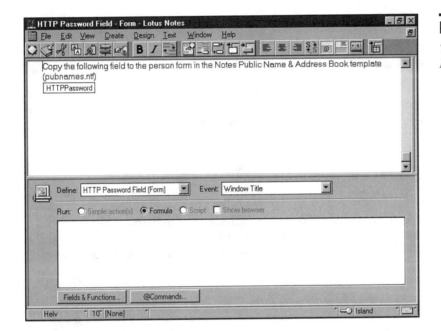

Figure 21.1

*The HTTP
Password field.*

8. Paste the HTTP Password field into the Person form by selecting Edit, Paste.

9. Add a static field label (such as HTTP Password:) to describe the purpose of the field for later when adding Web clients.

10. Save the form by pressing Esc and selecting Yes.

11. Close the currently open databases to avoid confusion before continuing this procedure.

12. Reopen the HTTPCNF.NTF database template.

13. In the Design view, select the $HTTPServerFormSubForm subform by highlighting it.

14. Select Edit, Copy.

15. Close the HTTPCNF.NTF database by pressing Esc.

16. Open the PUBNAMES.NTF template database.

17. In the Design view, select the Subforms design element by clicking on it once.

18. Highlight any subform in the View pane and press Edit, Paste. This places the HTTP Server subform into the design of the template.

19. Highlight the Forms design element by clicking on it once.

20. Select the Server/Server form in the view pane and place it in edit mode by double-clicking on the form.

21. Locate an area of the form (just below the Web retriever section is a good area) to insert the subform. After an area is located, select Create, Insert Subform and select $HTTPServerFormSubForm from the dialog box.

22. Click on OK.

23. Save the server form by pressing Esc and selecting Yes.

> **Note** You don't *have* to use the form and subform included in HTTPCNF.NTF (described in step 21), but it makes life a lot easier. The alternative, if you really like working in the design mode, is to add all the necessary fields to the form and subform yourself.

> **Warning** Be sure you make these changes to the Public Name & Address Book template. If you make them to the Public Name & Address Book itself, your changes will be overwritten when the Designer task runs overnight. If you make the changes directly to the Public Name & Address Book, be sure to turn off the "Inherit design from template" option under the Design tab in the Database Properties infobox.

After the changes are made to the Public Name & Address Book template, you need to refresh the design of the Public Name & Address Book. To refresh the design, do the following:

1. Highlight the Public Name & Address Book database by clicking once on the icon.

2. Select File, Database, Refresh Design.

3. Choose the local server, assuming you are physically working at the server itself. Otherwise, select the server containing the design template you modified in the preceding exercise.

4. Click on OK.

After the changes are made and the design is refreshed, the specifics about the HTTP server process need to be added to the server document, which now contains an HTTP Server section. Refer to the "Server Document Settings for the HTTP Server" section later in this chapter for specifics about setting up the HTTP server.

Domino Server 4.5

The HTTP server process is automatically loaded during the installation of the Domino 4.5 server code. There are no options to select during the installation process in order to add the code. It should be pointed out that the HTTP server shipped on any Domino server CD-ROM could be outdated depending on the length of time between CD-ROM releases. The latest version is always available from the Domino Web site at `http://domino.lotus.com`.

 Note The Domino server administrator should check the Lotus Web site periodically for updates to the HTTP server. As updates appear on the Web, the changes can be downloaded and installed as described in the section "Notes Releases 4.0 and 4.1x."

Installation Directory Structure

After the HTTP server files are installed, either through a full Domino 4.5 installation or the stand-alone installation, a directory structure is created that the HTTP server process expects to find when running.

Server Document Settings for the HTTP Server

Several sections on the server document control how the HTTP services function. The main section is the HTTP Server section. The Security section of the server document contains operational parameters for the HTTP server as well. The security parameters are addressed in Chapter 24, "Security and Reporting."

In any installation case (Release 4.0, 4.1x, or Domino 4.5), the parameters in the following figures apply to configuring the HTTP server process. See figures 21.2 and 21.3 for the appearance of the form in its design mode.

Figures 21.2 and 21.3 show the fields of the HTTP Server section that control the function of the HTTP server process. The function of each field in this section is documented in the Domino documentation database, which installs as a part of both installation procedures mentioned earlier. Most Domino installations can run with the default field values and operate normally. A few of the parameters, however, require a bit more in-depth discussion of their settings, as they can impact other performance areas. For settings that are not discussed in the following sections, refer to the Domino documentation.

Figure 21.2

The HTTP Server section—part one.

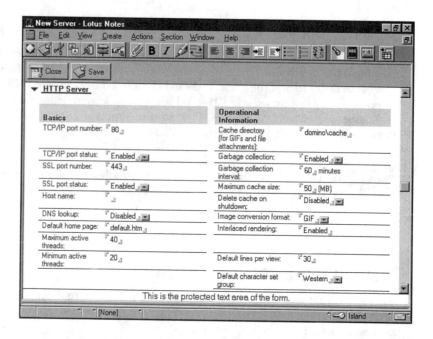

Figure 21.3

The HTTP Server section—part two.

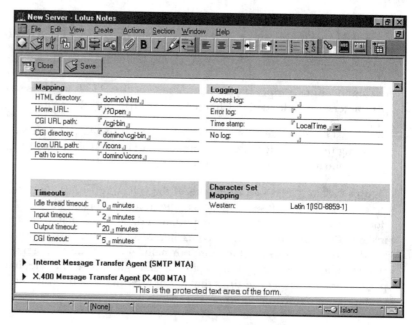

TCP/IP Port Number

It is beyond the scope of this chapter to delve into the details of the TCP/IP protocol. Within the TCP/IP protocol, however, certain ports are defined through which communications between network devices occur. The standard HTTP port is port 80, and this is the default value. Another common port is 1352 for the standard Notes NRPC protocol. SSL communications occur over a different port.

The most important aspect of configuring ports is to ensure that any other network security devices (such as proxies or firewalls) are able to pass traffic on these defined ports. If port 1352 is disabled on a firewall, for example, then Notes cannot carry on replication because it uses the native Notes protocol.

TCP/IP Port Status

The TCP/IP port must be enabled in order to communicate with Web clients. If this port is disabled, only SSL communications will be allowed to occur (assuming that the SSL port is enabled and an SSL has been setup on the server). If both the SSL port and TCP/IP port are disabled, then there is no point in running the HTTP server process.

Host Name and DNS Lookup

The host name should be used only if the machine on which Domino is installed has been assigned a domain name that is defined in a Domain Name Service (DNS). This is the name returned to the Web client after a connection is made.

If a DNS entry (such as mycorp.com) exists for the server, then Web clients are able to access the server by specifying `http://mycorp.com`. If no DNS entry exists for the server, however, enter the TCP/IP address of the machine.

While on the topic of DNS, this is a good time to point out that any communication on the Internet (or an intranet) involves a specific IP address. The convenience provided by DNS is that a Web client does not have to remember a cryptic set of numbers (such as 123.45.67.8) in order to communicate with a specific host. If no DNS is available, Web clients can use a resolution method known as a *local host file*.

The local host file is placed on each Web client and is used by the Web client's browser to resolve domain names into IP addresses. The issues associated with using local host files revolve around keeping them current with the latest host IP addresses. Most often, these files are updated during a network login process. Either method (DNS or local host files) provides clients with domain name resolution, but DNS provides more flexibility for the network administrator.

The HTTP server process logs certain information about each Web client as they access or "hit" the server. The DNS Lookup field, if enabled, forces the HTTP server to "backward-resolve" the incoming Web client connection into a domain name. This information is recorded in the log file and provides a more descriptive entry of who is accessing the Web site. If disabled, only the IP address of the Web client is recorded.

Default Home Page

The default home page, if specified, is the file displayed to Web browsers when they "hit" the site for the first time.

Maximum and Minimum Active Threads

These parameters govern how many threads are available at any given time to service requests from Web clients. There is not a one-to-one correlation between the number of threads and how many concurrent Web clients are allowed to access your site. Instead, threads are processes launched within the server to support a given task or tasks—in this case, the task of processing HTTP requests and sending HTTP responses.

The number of threads is highly processor- and memory-dependent and can only be generally determined here. It is more beneficial to understand the implication as it relates to server performance. If you are designing a highly visible Web site that will potentially serve thousands of hits a day, then you will not only want to increase the number of maximum threads but also the server hardware (memory, hard drive, processor speed or number, for example) on which you run the Domino server.

Domino always keeps the minimum number of threads specified in the Minimum field active and never goes above the value in the Maximum field. If a request comes to the server and no thread is available to handle the request, the new request is held until a thread becomes available.

Cache and Garbage

The cache area holds files the HTTP server has "served" to a Web client previously. This improves performance because the image is stored in the cache. As these images age, the HTTP server collects the older images as "garbage" and disposes of them to conserve disk space. You can specify whether garbage collection is enabled and, if it is, how frequently the cache is cleaned out. Domino starts clearing out the least frequently used files first. Depending on the hard disk size in your Domino server, set the cache size smaller or larger than the default 50 MB. If you prefer, you can have Domino delete the cache when the HTTP service is shutdown to conserve disk space.

The default setting is a good place to start. Once your server is in operation, you can monitor the cache hit rate (see Chapter 24) to determine if you have an adequate cache. If you are only serving a single database to Web clients have have a high cache hit rate, you may be able to reclaim some disk space by lowering the amount of disk used for the cache. If, on the other hand, you are serving several databases to Web clients and see a low (less than 85%) or declining hit rate, you might want to increase the cache size in order to server your Web clients faster.

Warning Care must be exercised in specifying the location of the cache files. If the cache is cleared each time HTTP services are shutdown, all files in the specified directory (folder) are deleted. If the cache directory contains files that should be retained, they also are deleted.

Image Conversion Format

The image "languages" of the Web are GIF and JPEG. The setting of JPEG or GIF in this field specifies the default image conversion format when Domino encounters images (such as bitmaps) in documents. If you select JPEG as the default conversion format, additional options (for example, progressive rendering and image quality) will appear directly underneath the Image Conversion Format field.

Note In order to display the additional options for the JPEG conversion format, you have to press F9 to refresh the document. The fields for these additional options are hidden in edit mode and are not automatically refreshed by changing from GIF to JPEG.

Default Lines Per View

If no URL extensions are given to govern how many lines are displayed in a view, this parameter determines the number of lines.

Note As a general rule of thumb, the more lines displayed, the longer the Web client waits for the screen (in this case a view) to display. This has implications when trying to keep response times at a minimum.

Default Character Set

The Western character set is the default. This field determines which character set is available to Domino to produce HTML pages for Web clients. If you want to set up multilingual support, edit this field and select Multilingual. Otherwise, select the primary language character set (for example, Greek, Cyrillic, Korean, and so forth).

Selecting the Multilingual option in the default character set does not mean that Domino servers translate languages. It only enables Domino to display in the character set that best corresponds to the client's language preference.

HTML, CGI, Icons Directories, and URL Paths

These directories specify where the particular file types can be found. The associated URL paths, when specified in the URL from the Web client either explicitly or through a URL link, will be redirected into the respective directory.

By separating HTML, executable (CGI script files), and image files into different directories, the overall administration of the Domino server is made much easier. This is similar to how you install a word processing software package. Although you could save documents in the same directory as the executable code, common practice has become to separate files into different directories by function. In this same manner, image files all occupy the same directory and are not co-mingled with files of different types.

The "URL path" provides an alternate method of referring to the entire path so that the user or Notes developer does not have to type the entire path to retrieve an image. For instance, instead of generating a URL that reads `www.mycorp.com/domino/icons/mycorp.gif`, the developer can simply use `www.mycorp.com/icons/mycorp.gif`, which Domino will redirect to the full path.

Home URL

If your Domino server has a default HTML home page (Default.htm) it will be presented to Web clients when they first hit your server. If you do not have a Default.htm page, the Domino server presents a view that is equivalent to the information presented when a Notes user selects File, Database, Open and chooses the Domino server. You can, of course, present any HTML file as your default home page by specifying its name here.

Timeouts

Several timeouts can be "tweaked" to tune the performance of the Domino HTTP server. These timeouts are:

◆ **Idle thread.** After a thread completes a task, it goes into an idle mode. Domino enables you to determine how long the thread should remain idle before terminating it altogether.

A short analogy will help you understand the concept of thread timeouts. Think of the idle thread timeout process as being the same as deciding when to turn off your car's engine. Turning the engine off after you stop at each red light on your way to work would not be too efficient (or smart) because, when the light turns green, the entire engine "start" process must happen again, delaying your ability to get underway quickly. In this case, it is better to let the car idle while stopped. Once at your office, however, it becomes much more efficient to turn the engine off instead of letting it idle until you go home at the end of the day. In other words, there are times when it is more advantageous to turn off the engine.

The same scenario applies to an idle server thread. As long as the thread is idle, the server can assign a task to it quickly because it is "ready to go." If the thread is "torn down" (or shut off), the process to restart it takes longer and presents a greater workload on the server.

The idle thread timeout parameter works in conjunction with the minimum and maximum active threads to specify how long an inactive (or idle) thread should be allowed to idle. Domino keeps the minimum number of threads running at all times—even if they are idle—but never goes above the maximum. If the number of threads available is higher than the minimum but less than the maximum, Domino will tear down (shut off) any thread that has been idle for the number of minutes specified in this field.

Warning	As indicated in the Domino documentation, a value of 0 in this field means an idle thread is never terminated. If you specify a fraction of a minute (such as .25 minutes), the field value will be .25 but the HTTP service will still behave as though a 0 was entered. Do not use fractions of a minute.

◆ **Input.** Domino terminates a connection from a Web client if the client establishes the connection but then fails to send a subsequent request. It is possible, however, to make a connection with the Domino server but make no HTTP request. In this case, the server drops the connection after the timeout period.

◆ **Output.** This parameter specifies the number of minutes the Domino HTTP server process has to respond to a request. This is only applicable to Domino's capability to provide local files. It does not apply to an external process such as a CGI script. If Domino cannot respond within the time specified, the connection is dropped.

◆ **CGI.** This parameter specifies the amount of time a CGI task has to return an output to the Domino server. If the CGI process started by the Domino server fails to respond within the specified time, the Domino server terminates the CGI program.

Logging

Domino allows two different logging methods: text file output or Notes database. The fields in the server document specify the text logging parameters for the access log and the error log. Before discussing the text logging, let's look at setting up the Web server database log.

The simplest method for setting up logging is to create a Domino log database. This is done with the following procedure:

1. Select File, Database, New.

2. Type in any title you want, but specify the file name as domlog.nsf (see fig. 21.4).

Figure 21.4

*Domino Web
Server Log
creation.*

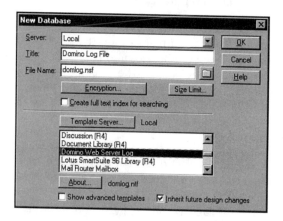

3. Select the Domino Web Server Log from the template window.

 The Web server log is a great tool for generating reports. You can customize views as you want, but if you change the log file, make sure to protect your changes from being removed by the server's design process.

Be sure to place domlog.nsf in the Notes data directory rather than a subdirectory. If it is placed in a subdirectory, no activity will be logged.

4. Click on OK.

Logging is now set up and ready to log user access to your Domino server in a Notes database.

If values are specified for the Access and Error log fields, the following files will be created when the Web server starts. mmmddyy represents the date stamp (such as Feb0197) for each file.

- acclog.mmmddyy

- errlog.mmmddyy

- cgi_error.mmmddyy

- agent_log.mmmddyy

- referer_log.mmmddyy

The names of the files reflect what information is logged to each. Acclog contains an entry for each time the Domino server is accessed. Errlog contains any internal errors generated by the Domino server. Although the access and error logs are the only two files specified in the HTTP section, three other files are generated by Domino automatically. The file cgi_error captures information about any errors generated by a CGI program launched by Domino. Agent_log captures the type of browser accessing the Domino server. Referer_log captures the referring URL that linked to your Domino site.

Here are a few considerations when enabling logging:

- If domlog.nsf exists and text logging parameters are provided in the HTTP server section, both logs will be maintained.

- Text logging is more difficult to use for reporting purposes without an external program to assist in compilation and formatting.

- Notes database logging is somewhat slower than text logging. If site activity is high, database logging can slow the response times of the Domino server.

- Text log files can grow quite large and numerous. At midnight each night, the day's log file is closed and a new one is generated for the new day. These files must be monitored and purged regularly. Domino does not automatically purge these files.

- Notes database logging provides an agent for clearing out documents over than 10 days old. This can be tweaked for optimal performance based on the activity on your site.

Time Stamp and No Log

The Time Stamp field determines how Domino records the time for each log entry. Specify either LocalTime or GMT (Greenwich Mean Time).

The No log field enables the Domino administrator to specify a list of addresses or hosts for which Domino is not required to make a log entry. This applies to either text or database log files or both. In some instances, there is little or no need to record the activity of certain hits on your site (such as company IP addresses, company sub-domains, and so on).

Enter either a template for the IP address range to exclude from logging (such as 123.45.*.*) or the host template (such as *.edu, *.lotus.com). In order to use the host template, DNS lookup must be enabled (see the section "Host Name and DNS Lookup" earlier in this chapter).

You can separate multiple values in this field with a space even though the field design is not set for multi-values.

Character Set Mapping

If you want to enable international users to use a non-Western character set when creating or displaying documents, you must first set the default character set to something other than Western in the Operational Information section. After that is done, press F9 to refresh the display and the other choices will appear. Select whichever language support you need to provide.

Person Document

A Person document is more for controlling security to the Domino server from the Web client's standpoint. Therefore, this document and its impact on the Domino server's interaction with the Web client is covered fully in Chapter 24. For the time being, it is sufficient to indicate the two primary elements of the document which control access: the user's name and his or her HTTP password.

Starting, Stopping, and Checking the Web Server Process

Now that your server is set up and ready to run, the only remaining task is to start the HTTP Web server process. To start the process, either from the server console or remote console type **load http**, as you would when starting any other server process on a Domino 4.5 or pre-Domino 4.5 Notes server.

To stop the HTTP Web server process, type **tell http quit** at the server or remote console. Wait until you see the console report HTTP Web Server shutdown to ensure the process has actually stopped and all clean-up processing is complete.

> **Note** Any configuration parameter of the Web server process can be changed without taking the Domino or Notes server out of service (for example, typing **quit** at the server console). For the Web server configuration changes to take effect, however, you have to stop and restart (a process commonly referred to as *bouncing*) the HTTP Web server process as previously described.

Again, it is not necessary to bounce the entire server for Web server changes to take effect, only the HTTP Web server process.

Advanced Domino Web Features

We have now covered the basics for installing, configuring, and running the HTTP Web server process. This is sufficient for allowing Web clients to access Notes databases hosted on the Domino server. This is entirely sufficient if one desires to host a single, uncomplicated Web site on a single server. However, many organizations hosting Web sites require a single server to support several sites or perform more complex functions.

This section looks at some advanced features provided by the Domino server that enhance the basic set HTTP services. The Domino server supports the following enhanced features:

◆ **Secure Socket Layer (SSL).** For encrypted communication between the Domino server and the Web client.

◆ **POP3 mail clients.** Provides an interface for POP3 clients to use NotesMail.

◆ **Multi-homing and URL redirection.** Allows the Domino server to support more than one Web site (IP address) and redirect URLs to different locations.

Thus far, we have concentrated on the HTTP configuration controls found in the Public Name & Address Book. Some of the advanced features venture outside the Public Name & Address Book and are configured in separate Notes databases. As the Domino server administrator these additional configuration locations will become important in the event that you are required to support one or more of these enhanced features on your server. This section will define not only which files are used to administer these enhanced features but will also cover the details of configuring and using them.

Setting Up Secure Socket Layer (SSL) Communication

SSL communication gives the Web client some measure of assurance that the server is who it claims to be. There are two options for setting up SSL based on either internal (self) or public (third-party) certification. Which one you choose will depend on how you want to set up security for your site.

Before proceeding with the installation, the Domino administrator must decide if SSL will be setup using an internal Certificate Authority or a public Certificate Authority. The difference between the two will potentially affect the confidence the Web client has in sending confidential information to your Domino server.

A public Certificate Authority uses a disinterested third-party to verify the identity of an HTTP server to the Web client while an internal authority does not. Therefore, any Web client using your site would be prudent to send confidential information only to a site which uses a third-party certificate since anyone can generate an internal certificate.

Chapter 24 contains a more detailed discussion of SSL from a security standpoint. If, at this point, you are not sure which certification option you need to set up, you might want to read Chapter 24 and then return to the setup procedure.

To set up SSL, begin by adding the SSL Administration database (ssladmin.nsf) to your workspace (select File, Database, Open). This database is part of the Domino installation and is created in the Notes data directory.

The database has been designed to facilitate the setup process through a "navigator," although it is actually a document that appears when the database is opened.

Note This setup process must be performed on the Domino server itself and cannot be done from the client.

There are three options for how to set up SSL:

1. **Self Certification.** Self certification is the quickest way to set up SSL. Use this option simply to test the SSL capabilities of Domino. This process creates a key ring certified by your own server. Hence, no Web browser recognizes your certificate when connecting to your HTTP server using an https directive.

   To install a self-certified certificate, click on the button labeled Create Self-Certified Key Ring and complete the information in the dialog box, as shown in figure 21.5.

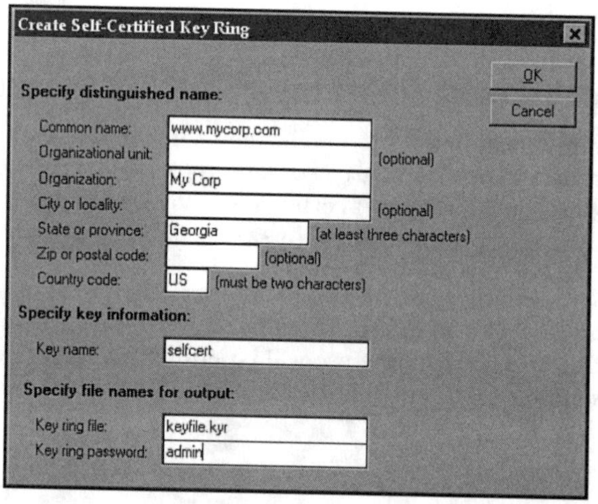

Figure 21.5

The Create Self-Certified Key Ring dialog box.

Be sure to complete all fields not marked optional, and do not forget the password or key name.

This process creates the key ring file (keyfile.kyr) and a second file called keyfile.sth. Both these files are required to support SSL sessions with the Web client and should be backed up and controlled.

When a client connects requesting a secure connection (for example, `https://mycorp.com`), the Web browser enables the user to accept or reject the unrecognized certificate through a process similar to that shown in figure 21.6.

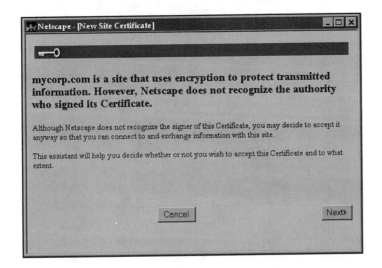

Figure 21.6

Netscape's New Site Certificate dialog box.

In figure 21.6, Netscape advises that it does not recognize the certificate but will add it to the list of certificates if the Web client wants. Netscape continues the process and walks the client through the acceptance process.

After being added to the list of certificates in the browser (see fig. 21.7), SSL connections can be made as necessary.

2. **Commercial Certification.** Commercial certification provides an independent Certificate Authority that vouches for the identity of the server. The commercial Certificate Authority (CA) "certifies" that the server is who it claims to be (through the issuance of a digital ID) and that it can be "trusted."

Whereas self-certification makes a "claim" to an identity, commercial certification acts as independent, third-party verification of the identity "claim." The process involves sending a certificate request to the CA which, in turn, performs a background check into the identity of the server. Typically, a CA checks several independently verifiable factors about the server requesting the certificate. These items can include checking that the domain name claimed is actually registered to the company in the request, that the company is located at the address provided, that the server is at the domain name provided, and so on. After the CA verifies this information, a digital ID is issued to the requester.

Figure 21.7

Netscape security preferences—site certificates.

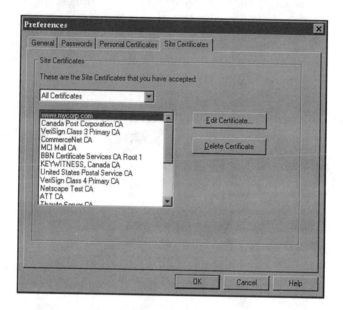

> **Note**   Public certificates are not a panacea for fraud on the Internet, but they do serve as an effective means of deterring fraudulent activities. Ultimately, it is up to the client to be discerning about giving sensitive information to any host on the Internet.

The process to obtain commercial certification of a Domino server involves sending a request to the commercial Certificate Authority and paying a registration fee, which covers the cost of the investigation and issuance of the certificate. In the case of Domino's SSL administration database, VeriSign is the CA and Lotus has provided an automated e-mail process for sending the certificate request to VeriSign. As of this writing, the fee was $290 with an annual renewal fee of $75.

The process is initiated by clicking on the button labeled Create key ring and certificate request in Step 1 of the section Create Key Ring—Commercial Certification. This brings up the dialog box shown in figure 21.8, containing an additional field called Certificate request. After the information is completed, a certificate request file (the default is CertReq.txt) is created in addition to the key ring files (keyfile.sth and keyfile.kyr).

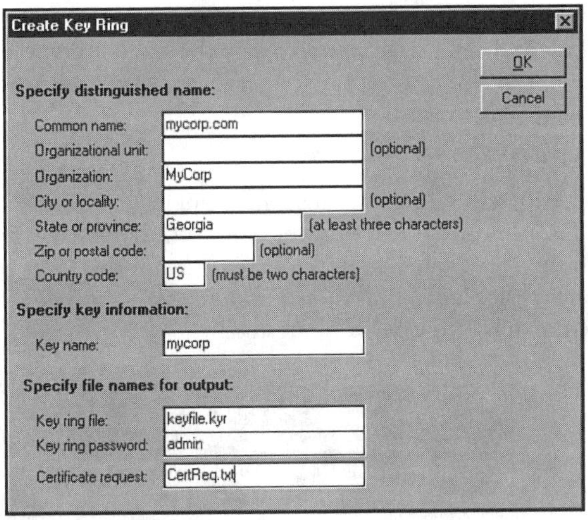

Figure 21.8

The Create Key Ring dialog box with with the Certificate request field.

If your Domino server has the capability to generate e-mail, you can continue the process by clicking on the button in Step 2, Create Mail Message for VeriSign. This addresses an e-mail message with the contents of the CertReq.txt file in the body of the message. The same can be done by creating an e-mail message an attaching CertReq.txt. You are given the option to send the message now or to store the message in the Mail view provided in the SSL administration database for sending later.

Warning If you previously set up an internal certificate to test your SSL installation, save the key ring files (keyfile.kyr and keyfile.sth) before beginning this process. You most likely will need to continue testing before you receive your commercially certified ID, and these files will be overwritten with the commercial key ring files.

For each certificate, you need to maintain separate file sets. It is highly recommended that you create separate directory structures for the internal and public key files.

You can swap back and forth between an internal certificate and public certificate by copying the respective files into the data directory of Domino server. Remember to bounce the HTTP Web server process for the copied key to take effect.

After the CA has completed its investigation, you will receive via e-mail a certificate that can be merged into the key ring. This process is also automated in Step 3, Merge certificate into key ring.

Be sure that the key files (keyfile.kyr and keyring.sth) generated when the commercial certificate request was prepared are in the data directory. If the key files are not the same, you will not be able to merge the certificate into the key ring.

After the certificate is merged, most browsers that hit your Domino server are able to authenticate with your server because most will have a trusted root key with your server. This is because most browsers ship with standard certificates already loaded into the certificate list. In this case, the only dialog between the Web client and server is similar to that shown in figure 21.9, notifying the Web client that a secure document has been requested.

Figure 21.9

Notifying the Web client that a secure document has been requested.

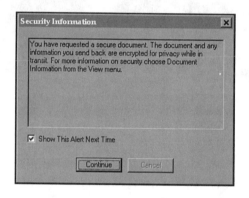

3. **Internal Certification.** The final method for enabling SSL is to set up an internal Certificate Authority. In this case, the process is the same as requesting a commercial certificate except the CA is internal.

In this manner, a company can effectively set up its own internal CA (such as an IT department). This would enable a company to certify any number of Web servers that might be brought into an intranet, for example. The end result would be a series of servers that intranet Web clients would trust as being in the Human Resources department, for example, or in Payroll.

This process begins with creating a Certificate Authority key ring (see fig. 21.10). This key ring is used to certify requests from within the organization.

Notice the differences between figures 21.8 and 21.10. The dialog box now requests a common name to be used to identify the certificate, rather than the name of the server as in figure 21.8. In addition, instead of creating a certificate request file, this process creates a CA certification file to use when certifying requests. After creating the key ring, a message stating that the key ring was created with a self-signed root certificate is displayed.

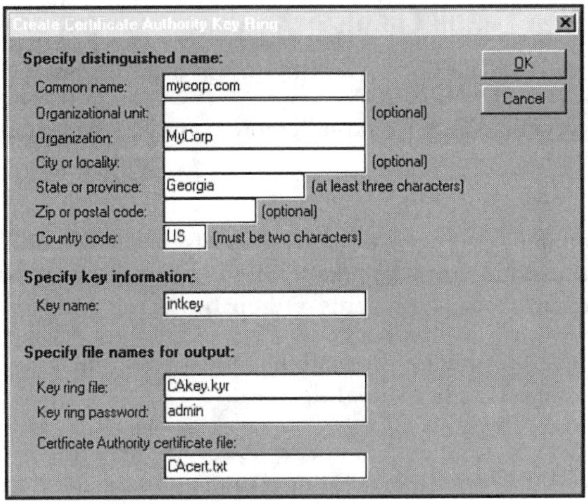

Figure 21.10

The Create Certificate Authority Key Ring dialog box.

The only file created in this process is CAcert.txt.

Now organizations can submit their requests for certificates to you by completing the steps in the section Create Key Ring—Internal Certification.

Again, this process is the same as requesting a certificate from a commercial CA, only the request stays inside the organization.

When the certificate request is received, the internal CA completes the process in the section Certificate Authority—Certify Certificate Request. The Sign Certificate Request dialog box appears. After the request is certified, a new certificate file is created called Cert.txt.

The final step is to merge the certificate into the original key ring. The Web client can now accept the internal certificate offered by the server and secure communications will be established.

There are several points to remember when setting up SSL:

◆ For any dialog box that requires the name of a file or files (such as when merging certificates back into key ring), be sure to specify the entire path for the location of the file. Otherwise, Domino assumes the Notes data path.

◆ After you have created the files for any given task, be sure to make a backup copy that can be secured. This enables you to "roll back" to a previous certificate.

◆ After being commercially certified, inform your Web clients to delete any certificates they accepted from your server previously.

Enabling POP3 for Web E-Mail Clients

To install POP3 support on the Domino server, follow this arduous process:

1. At the Domino server console or from the remote console, type **load pop3**.

You're done!

That's all there is to enabling POP3 service for Web clients on the Domino server. Recall from previous discussion that POP3 enables the Domino server to handle requests from Web clients to send the contents of their Inbox to them.

The more involved process is setting up the mail file, Person document, and Web browser (in that order), but it is rather straightforward.

Each POP3 client requires a NotesMail file in order to receive mail into their Web browser. This process is no different than creating a new Notes database from a template file. For the sake of example, assume the following:

◆ POP3 user name: John Doe

◆ Domino server: Domino1/MyCorp

◆ Company: MyCorp

◆ Internet Domain: mycorp.com

To set up Mr. Doe, do the following:

1. Choose File, Database, New.

2. Select or enter the name of the Domino server that is running the POP3 service.

3. Enter the title of the client's mail file in the title box (for example, John Doe's Mail).

4. Enter the path and file name for the mail file (for example, mail\jdoe.nsf).

5. Select the Domino 4.5 Mail template.

6. Click on OK.

7. Enter **John Doe** in the Access Control List (ACL) and give him at least Editor access with the capability to delete documents. (The delete part will be significant when setting up the Web client later on.)

When setting up NotesMail, you must also add the user's name to the ACL of the mail file just created. The name entered should have at least Editor access with Delete rights and must match the name setup in the next step. Notes ACLs still apply in the Web world.

So that Domino knows whose mail goes into which mail file, the next step is to set up the Person document in the Public Name & Address Book for the user. To accomplish this task, follow these steps:

1. Open the Public Name & Address Book.

2. Select the People view.

3. Click on the Add Person button on the action bar.

4. Complete the fields in the screen the appears.

When entering the password in the password field the value is shown in the "clear." The value will be encoded (not encrypted!) when the document is saved. This is the password that enables authentication when connecting from the POP3 client. The user ID will be the User Name field. This is also the name that must appear in the ACL. The short name is not used for Web client access.

In addition, the mail system does not have to be set to POP3. It can be set to Notes. As long as the mail router function can find the mail file belonging to the user, it will deliver the mail into the file. If the mail user is exclusively a POP3 client, set it to POP3. If the user uses both NotesMail and POP3, set it to Notes. The key question to answer between the two settings is, "Is the user a registered Notes user or simply a POP3 user?"

The final step is to set up the POP3 client's browser to enable it to pass the necessary security information to the Domino server's POP3 service.

Continuing with our example user, the POP3 user name has been set to John Doe and the Incoming Mail (POP3) Server is set to MyCorp's Internet domain name, mycorp.com.

Notice the option "Messages are copied from the server to the local disk, then..." This is when the delete capability comes into play in the ACL for Mr. Doe's mail file. If the option Removed from the server is chosen, all messages will be deleted from the mail file after they are downloaded to the POP3 client.

If your user is both a NotesMail user and POP3 client, it is probably best to select the Left on option when setting up the POP3 client. This way, when the user returns to the office and wants to use NotesMail, the messages are still in the mail file. Otherwise, the user is only able to read those messages previously downloaded to the POP3 client and any unread messages accumulated since the last connection from the POP3 client.

It should also be pointed out that after a NotesMail client reads a message (for example, the document is marked as having been read), that message will not be downloaded to the POP3 client. Only new, unread messages are transferred to POP3 clients.

Also, in order to allow the POP3 client to send an mail message, an SMTP connection must be available. POP3 only supports incoming messages. This can be accomplished using the SMTP MTA on a Domino server.

Multi-Homing, URL Mapping/Redirection

Multi-homing enables a Domino server to respond differently to HTTP requests coming into the server from different IP addresses. This provides the Domino administrator with the capability to host multiple domain names on a single Domino server. Each domain is configured to respond with its own home page when it receives HTTP requests.

URL redirection and mapping enables the Domino Web administrator to:

◆ Hide the actual location of a directory on the disk

◆ Redirect a URL to a different URL

◆ Control read or execute access to a directory's files

◆ Map a collection of URLs to a new URL (useful in maintaining links while moving sites around)

Multi-homing, redirection, and mapping are controlled from the Domino configuration database. This database must be created from the template file domcfg.ntf and must be called domcfg.nsf.

Warning Do not give the Domino configuration file any other name beside domcfg.nsf. If you do, none of these configuration settings will be loaded when the HTTP Web server process executes.

In order to set up multi-homing, multiple IP addresses must first be configured on the operating system. It is beyond the scope of this book to describe the details of setting up multiple IP addresses on the variety of operating systems on which Domino runs. Refer to your operating system's documentation for procedures on setting up multiple IP addresses.

 Do not simply pick an IP address out of the air. This can cause significant impact on your network infrastructure (and it won't be a positive impact). Check with your network administrator for valid IP addresses before proceeding.

With those caveats and warnings out of the way, and assuming you have at least a couple of IP addresses configured and working at the operating system level, let's get the Domino server answering HTTP requests on both IP addresses.

To facilitate the explanation of a couple of these Domino features, an example is in order. Assume that the fictitious company mentioned previously, MyCorp, has determined that its Domino server hardware has plenty of reserve power—far beyond MyCorp's meager Web site needs. The vice president of IT, upon the suggestion of the Domino administrator, has recommended to the president (with other board members present) that it would be a great idea to rent the reserve Domino capacity to MyCorp's subsidiary, YourCorp. "This," he explains, "will result in tremendous costs savings because MyCorp can now drop the ISDN service over at YourCorp's offices and host both Web sites on the T-1 line at MyCorp."

To further complicate matters, YourCorp's Web site is already hosted on a competitor's HTTP server and is written completely in HTML with a registered domain name of yourcorp.com.

First, multi-homing needs to be set up in order to serve requests to both the mycorp.com and yourcorp.com Web sites.

To do this, open the Domino configuration file (domcfg.nsf) created earlier and create a virtual server.

Assume the following conditions exist:

◆ The IP address for mycorp.com is 123.45.67.8.

◆ The IP address for yourcorp.com is 123.45.67.9.

◆ The Domain Name Service (DNS) has been changed to map these domains to the respective IP addresses.

When HTTP requests come into mycorp.com (123.45.67.8), the Domino server responds by opening a Notes database called homepage.nsf in the mycorp directory underneath the Domino root directory.

For each virtual server, the Domino administrator is able to specify a specific directory to map MyCorp's URL paths. This enables MyCorp and YourCorp to maintain separate HTML, executable, and image directories. For example, the administrator has set up a directory for MyCorp's specific HTML (domino\mycorp\html), CGI (domino\mycorp\cgi-bin), and images (domino\mycorp\icons) off the Domino directory under Notes. Now, whenever a URL request comes into 123.45.67.8 specifying \icons, the graphics file will be retrieved from MyCorp's directory of images.

Now you need to set up a virtual server to serve YourCorp's Web site. Recall that the existing Web site for YourCorp is in native HTML files.

 Note   Not only can Domino can handle native Notes databases, it can also handle native HTML files and directory structures. This means that existing Web sites made up of flat HTML files and their directory structures can be hosted by the Domino server.

The Domino administrator only has to copy the directory structure from the existing YourCorp Web site and its associated files into the designated HTML directory.

Note   These settings can be set up, tested, changed, and tested again. Remember to bounce the HTTP Web server process after each change, however, in order for the change to take effect. You do not have to bounce the entire server, just the HTTP Web server (for example, tell http quit followed by load http at the server or remote console).

To redirect an incoming URL to a different URL, use the Redirection URL -> URL form in the Domino configuration database. The example in figure 21.11 shows the URL /opensezme being redirected to domino/mycorp/homepage.nsf?Open. Now, whenever a Web client or link on a page refers to opensezme, the Domino server will actually behave as though the Web client requested that homepage.nsf be opened.

Redirected URLs could point to other servers or databases on the Domino server. It is the only option in the Domino configuration database that enables a redirection to a Domino-specific URL, as in the example in figure 21.11.

An example of a redirected URL's use might be the redirecting of a common company URL to a specific Notes database.

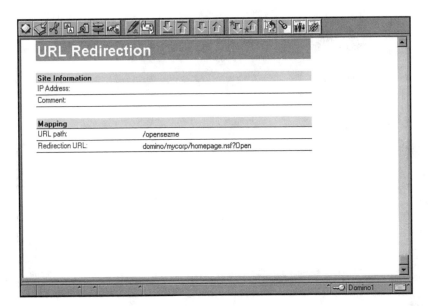

Figure 21.11

Redirecting a URL to another URL.

Suppose MyCorp's Web site uses a form for customers to request help from customer support and accesses it with the URL mycorp.com/support. After converting the support portion of the site to a Notes database, MyCorp can still use existing URL links in the old site by redirecting the old URL to the new URL. For instance, mycorp.com/support could be redirected to the Notes database at the URL domino/mycorp/support.nsf?open, allowing new Notes databases to continue to work with older portions of the Web site where the mycorp.com/support URL still exists.

The next feature of the Domino configuration database concerns mapping of URLs. The first mapping feature maps a URL path to another URL path. This is different than redirection, which responds to the URL request sent to the Domino server by generating an alternate URL. URL mapping involves substituting one URL path (such as domino/mycorp/icons) for another (such as domino/mycorp/images).

Figure 21.12 shows the mapping just mentioned. This mapping enables MyCorp to move all the image files from the icons directory into the images directory and to preserve the links already established in the Notes databases supporting its Web site.

The second mapping feature enables the Domino administrator to move entire files to different locations on the Domino server's drives. In figure 21.13, MyCorp has apparently run out of drive space on its primary C: drive and has added a D: drive to store its image files.

Figure 21.12

URL-to-URL mapping.

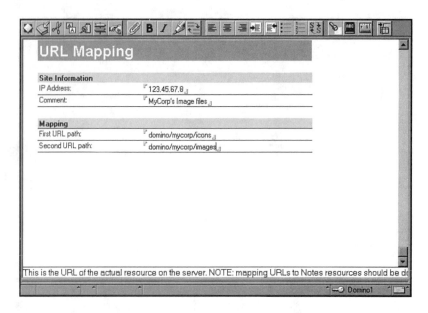

Notice also that with URL-to-directory mapping, an additional attribute is available to give the Web client read or execute access to the directory. In the case of images or HTML files, read access is sufficient. If mapping CGI files, execute access is required.

Summary

If you are just getting started with Domino and do not have the resources to devote to a test server, most of the topics covered in this chapter can be tested on a laptop or desktop system. The following is a suggested configuration, although it is not the final authority on how to set up a test configuration.

The following steps will provide a configuration that will enable you to run the Domino server with the HTTP Web server task, a Notes client, and your browser of choice:

◆ Make a backup copy of your Notes.ini file. You might want to keep everything completely separate (and simple) to avoid confusion when working between my live Notes environment and my test Domino configuration.

◆ If you are working in a completely IPX or NetBIOS environment, you will need an IP address (123.45.67.8, for example). On a Windows 95 machine, this is done by setting up a TCP/IP client in the Control Panel under Networks. You have to reboot after making this change and, for the sake of your network administrator, do not put 123.45.67.8 online. Remove it after you have finished testing.

◆ Install the Domino server into a separate directory on your hard drive, and set up the server as a new server with an O-level certificate, domain and everything.

◆ You now will have two Notes.ini files. I keep a backup copy of each as Notes.srv (test server) and Notes.ws (everyday live workstation). I switch back and forth between these files in my WIN95 directory, but you can keep them separate in your Notes directory.

◆ Bring up the Domino server and kill the tasks that are not necessary (such as router, indexer, and so on), and just run the HTTP Web service. If your laptop is like mine, you'll need all the horsepower you can get.

◆ If you want to use a domain name (such as mycorp.com), you need a HOSTS file in your WIN95 directory. This is just a text file. Edit it with the DOS editor (or whatever text editor you're most familiar with) and add an entry for your IP address, as illustrated in the file HOSTS.SAM (a sample file provided with Windows 95). Add the line **123.45.67.8 mycorp.com**. This enables you to enter mycorp.com in your browser rather than the IP address.

◆ Bring up your browser and begin testing the various features of your Domino Web server.

As a side note, I was on a flight from Atlanta to Anaheim using this configuration when a gentleman sitting behind me saw my Netscape client surfing a Web site. He leaned up and asked, "Isn't it awfully expensive to be surfing the Web from an airplane?" When I explained I had an HTTP server running on my laptop, he just said, "Huh?"

In case you are wondering how powerful your laptop needs to be to do this, I use a 486/75 with 24 MB of RAM and a 500 MB disk drive, which is Drivespaced to 1.2 GB using Windows 95 and the 32-bit Intel version of the Domino server.

CHAPTER 22

Using Domino to Publish on the Web

Depending on who you listen to, a claim often heard about Domino is that "any Notes database can be made available to a Web client." Although the statement is true, the follow-up question that must be asked is, "Would you want to?"

As stated in Chapter 21, "Installing and Setting Up Domino," the Web client supports a "generic, stateless, object-oriented protocol." A Notes client, on the other hand, supports a very specific protocol, the Notes Remote Procedure Call (NRPC) protocol. The Notes client, therefore, has the capability to interact with the Notes object store (that is, databases) in a way that a Web client cannot because the Web client understands only the stateless environment of the Web and not Notes-specific protocols.

Hence the question, "Would you want to publish any Notes database as is?" Many Notes applications are designed around the features that a Notes client supports (for example, lookups, various user interface conventions, button macros, agents, and so on). Just serving up applications that make full use of Notes-specific development conventions to a Web client would not only be "stateless," but meaningless and pretty bland. If a workflow process were implemented through the use of a series of buttons in a Notes form, the functions provided by those buttons would be lost to a Web client.

You may be thinking by now that you should not use Domino to serve Notes applications to Web clients. In the context of the typical Web site with its rich graphics, animated GIFs and other attractions, a plain Notes database would leave the typical Web client looking for something more. When you add some HTML and sprinkle in some graphics, however, Domino takes simple Notes design elements and quickly translates them to the Web environment providing one of the most powerful Web application development capabilities on the market today.

Although the term "publishing" is often used to describe what the Domino HTTP Web server process does, it is "hold-over" terminology from how Web sites have been created in the past. The term "publishing" carries a sense of a resulting static condition after a database is "published." This can be attributed to the InterNotes Web Publisher, because it produced static HTML pages from a Notes database. This is not, however, the case with a Notes database "published" through Domino. As defined in Webster's, publish means to "make generally known" or "to place before the public." (Sounds like the Web.)

This chapter addresses techniques for making Notes databases "generally known to the public" via Domino. The chapter is not intended to provide a "How To" manual on Notes application development. Instead, it provides the background needed for developing Notes applications in a Web context.

The first step required to establish a strong background is to compare traditional Web site publishing with Domino. Next, the Domino Universal Resource Locator (URL) conventions will be addressed, followed by the HTML support provided with Domino. Finally, these concepts will be tied into developing a Web site with Domino.

 It should be recognized that the pace at which new functionality has been added to the Domino Web server is quite fast. It is quite possible that some of the features discussed in this chapter as being "not translated" or "not supported" in the Web environment will some day be supported as Lotus further refines the Domino Web server.

Traditional Web Site Publishing

A bit of background on "straight" HTML is in order to fully appreciate the Domino HTTP Web server.

The language of the Web is the hypertext markup language (HTML). Web browsers are designed to understand and respond to the HTML served up by the HTTP server. Instructions embedded in the text and transferred to the browser instruct the browser how to display the text or request additional information from the server (for example, graphic files).

HTML is stored in "flat" text files in a directory structure. One example of a simple HTML file might look like this:

```
<HTML>
<TITLE>Welcome to MyCorp</TITLE>
<BASEFONT SIZE=2>
<BODY BGCOLOR="#FFFFF2">
<H><IMG SRC="graphics/mycorp.gif" border=0 ALIGN=right></H>
<HR>
<TABLE>
        <TD><A HREF="about.htm"><IMG SRC="graphics/amycorp.gif" BORDER=0></
          ➥A><BR>
          <A HREF="product.htm"><IMG SRC="graphics/bmycorp.gif" BORDER=0></
          ➥A><BR>
          <A HREF="location.htm"><IMG SRC="graphics/dmycorp.gif" BORDER=0></
          ➥A><BR>
          <A HREF="links.htm"><IMG SRC="graphics/cmycorp.gif" BORDER=0></A></
          ➥TD><BR>
        <TD VALIGN=TOP><P><FONT SIZE=4><B>W</B></FONT>elcome to MyCorp!<BR><P>
This site contains information about MyCorp, our products, locations and links.
Click one of links to the left to begin your visit.<BR>
          <P>
          <B>O</B></FONT>our Corporate office is located at:<BR>
          1 MyCorp Blvd.<BR>
          Allpharetta, GA  30202<BR>
          770-555-1040 (Phone)<BR>
          770-555-1041 (Fax)<BR></TD>
    </TR>
</TABLE>
<HR>
<A HREF="http://www.mycorp.com"></A>
<FONT SIZE=1>Send mail to <A HREF="mailto:webmaster@mycorp.com">
➥<B>webmaster@mycorp.com</B></A>
with questions or comments about this web site.<BR>
Copyright © 1996 MyCorp<BR>
```

```
Last modified: January 23, 1997<BR>
<B>Web hosting services provided by MyCorp IT Department.</I><BR></FONT>
</BODY>
</HTML>
```

The preceding HTML code produces a page that looks like that shown in figure 22.1 when viewed with Netscape Navigator. The indentation is for the benefit of the HTML developer...not for the Web client.

Figure 22.1

MyCorp's HTML home page.

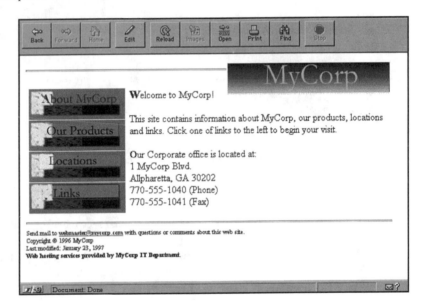

> **Note** Fortunately, this chapter is about Domino and the Web and not creating "catchy" graphics for Web sites. The author, as you can tell by the high-quality graphic examples, is an engineer by training and not a graphic artist.

Several ways enable you to generate HTML files. The simplest way to generate an HTML file is via a text editor (the DOS editor was used to generate the MyCorp home page). This technique would require significant HTML knowledge and a book alongside the HTML developer.

Fortunately, many products on the market today (Microsoft Frontpage, Hotdog, and so on) support HTML generation through graphical interfaces rather than text-based editors. These programs provide helpful tools to HTML developers. Most HTML-generation software, for example, provides for mapping and controlling links and link updates. These products greatly reduce the time and effort required to produce HTML pages.

Once produced, the HTML files are contained in a directory structure—as follows, for example:

```
C:\MyCorp
    HTML
        index.htm
            GRAPHICS
                amycorp.gif
                bmycorp.gif
                cmycorp.gif
                dmycorp.gif
                emycorp.gif
```

When all is said and done, however, the browser "sees" the raw HTML code regardless of how it was generated. The HTML files are static and must be kept within the prescribed directory structure in order to maintain the links. Refreshing the content can be tedious and may result in broken links that can cause the site to be virtually useless to the Web client.

In the old days of the Web, teams of HTML developers were devoted to the single task of keeping Web sites fresh. Adding workflow to a Web site involves an investment of hundreds of thousands of dollars. Adding threaded discussions to a Web site also involves thousands of dollars in development. Domino, however, brings the power to develop and translate these common Notes functions to the Web in hours (not months), using a single part-time developer (not ten or twenty), and at a cost far less than the hundreds of thousands companies used to pay for Web development.

Database Publishing with Domino: An Overview

Domino enables the developer to concentrate on the business process and developing a database that will support the business process. Whether the business process centers around document submission and approval, collaboration on a project, or order entry, Domino generates the HTML when it is needed (commonly referred to as "on the fly") based on relatively intuitive Notes design elements.

> **Note** This should not be misinterpreted to say that designing a Notes database is necessarily easy, but merely that the design elements provided by Notes (for example, doc-links, view links, macro functions, and so forth) translate nicely into the Web framework of linking and performing simple tasks (for example, creating, editing, searching, and so on). These design elements are discussed later in this chapter.

Generating HTML on the fly removes a significant burden from the developer because Domino actually performs the translation from the Notes database content and/or design features into HTML.

Figure 22.2 offers an example as shown previously, but through a Notes database's About document.

Figure 22.2

MyCorp's About document home page.

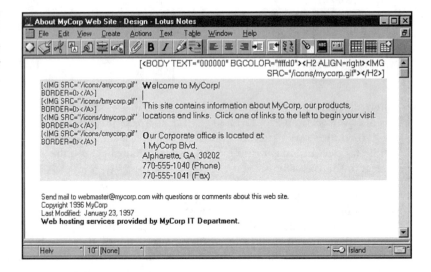

The "look and feel" of the About document in figure 22.2 is completely Notes. Indeed, there is HTML embedded in the About document, but—largely—the textual areas in the table are plain text. This makes the design and content easier to maintain, and thereby provides a more flexible Web development environment.

Figure 22.3 shows the Domino home page for MyCorp through a Netscape Navigator client.

The formatted lines at the bottom of the home page (that is, copyright, e-mail address, and so forth) are completely text with typical formatting. The About document also incorporates hotspots that translate into HTML when requested by the Web client.

Domino translates powerful Notes conventions such as document links into HTML so that links are both easy to create and maintain—not a trivial task. Consider the "flat" HTML example of the home page earlier and compare it with both the About document in figure 22.3 and the following HTML produced "on the fly" by Domino.

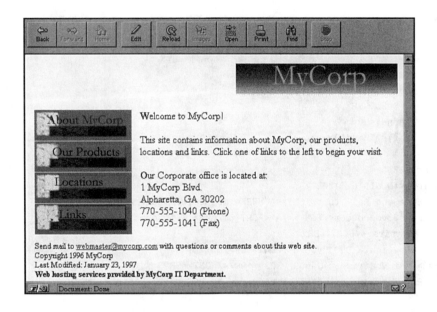

Figure 22.3

MyCorp's About document home page via Netscape.

```
<HTML>
<!-- Lotus Domino Web Server Release 1.5 (RC1, Build 165 on Windows NT/Intel)->
<HEAD>
<TITLE>MyCorp Web Site</TITLE><BODY>
<DIV ALIGN=right>
<P><BODY TEXT="000000" BGCOLOR="ffffd0"><H2 ALIGN=right>
<IMG SRC="/icons/mycorp.gif"></H2></DIV>
<TABLE>
<TR VALIGN=top><TD WIDTH="168" BGCOLOR="f1f1b4">
<P><A HREF="/mycorp.nsf/0fcc97fda94e51e5852563e1003a7483/
5f48f032aac491c4852563dd0024d91a?OpenDocument"><FONT SIZE=2><IMG SRC="/icons/
➥amycorp.gif" BORDER=0></A></FONT></A><BR>
<A HREF="/mycorp.nsf/0fcc97fda94e51e5852563e1003a7483/
c38d0ee7132005b6852563e1003a8bbf?OpenDocument"><FONT SIZE=2><IMG SRC="/icons/
➥bmycorp.gif" BORDER=0></A></FONT></A><BR>
<A HREF="/mycorp.nsf/0fcc97fda94e51e5852563e1003a7483/
0cd8f989980b6fb0852563e1003adbf9?OpenDocument"><FONT SIZE=2><IMG SRC="/icons/
➥cmycorp.gif" BORDER=0></A></FONT></A></TD><TD WIDTH="402" BGCOLOR="f1f1b4">
0cd8f989980b6fb0852563e1003adbf9?OpenDocument"><FONT SIZE=2><IMG SRC="/icons/
➥dmycorp.gif" BORDER=0></A></FONT></A><BR>
<A HREF="/mycorp.nsf/0fcc97fda94e51e5852563e1003a7483/
<P><B>W</B>Welcome to MyCorp! <BR>
<BR>
```

```
This site contains information about MyCorp, our products, locations and links.
Click one of links to the left to begin your visit.<BR>
<BR>
<B>O</B>Our Corporate office is located at:<BR>
1 MyCorp Blvd.<BR>
Alpharetta, GA  30202<BR>
770-555-1040 (Phone)<BR>
770-555-1041 (Fax)</TD></TR>
</TABLE>
<TABLE WIDTH="100%">
<TR VALIGN=top><TD WIDTH="100%">
<P><FONT SIZE=2>Send mail to </FONT><A HREF="mailto:webmaster@mycorp.com"><FONT
SIZE=2>webmaster@mycorp.com</FONT></A><FONT SIZE=2> with questions or comments
➥about this web site.</FONT><BR>
<FONT SIZE=2>Copyright 1996 MyCorp</FONT><BR>
<FONT SIZE=2>Last Modified:  January 23, 1997</FONT><BR>
<B><FONT SIZE=2>Web hosting services provided by MyCorp IT Department.</FONT>
➥</B></TD></TR>
</TABLE>
<P><BR>
```

This HTML was generated based on the contents of the About document. Because the HTML was generated strictly for the Web client, notice that there is no indentation for ease of reading.

Notice also the HTML "HREF" tags generated by Notes. The long number (0fcc97fda94e51e5852563e1003a7483/5f…) generated by Notes is the result of a hotspot link to a document in the database. This number is the document ID (NoteID) of the document to which the hotspot is linked.

The HREF tag in the simple HTML text file "looks" nicer (that is, "About.htm"), but the implication is that the About.htm file must be in the same directory as the file currently displayed by the Web client. Otherwise, the link does not work and the dreaded Internet Error 404 - Not found message is delivered to the Web client.

In the case of the Domino-generated HREF, the document ID is a familiar entity to the Domino server (and Notes developers), and can be located even if the file containing the document is moved into another directory, and this without maintenance of the link. In other words, the Domino administrator can move files (Notes databases) around on the server as needed (to add more disk space, for example) without destroying any referential links that are critical to presenting a coherent Web site.

These topics are covered more fully in the sections to come or other chapters. For now, this background is sufficient to draw some parallels between straight HTML coding and the HTML produced by Domino.

Before diving into the specifics of database "publishing," it is useful to have an understanding of how a Web client interacts with the Domino server through the URL syntax.

Domino URL Convention

A Universal Resource Locator (URL) is defined by the Internet Engineering Task Force (IETF) in RFC 1738 as "the syntax and semantics of formalized information for location and access of resources via the Internet." The URL is generally written as two parts:

```
<scheme>:<scheme-specific-part>
```

The scheme specifies a particular protocol with the particular action or request being contained in the scheme-specific part. Table 22.1 shows the protocols RFC 1738 covers.

TABLE 22.1
URL Schemes

Scheme	Definition
ftp	File Transfer protocol
http	Hypertext Transfer protocol
gopher	Gopher protocol
mailto	Electronic mail address
news	UseNet news
nntp	UseNet news using NNTP access
telnet	Reference to interactive sessions
wais	Wide Area Information Servers
file	Host-specific file names
prospero	Prospero Directory Service

Because Domino produces HTML pages, its URL syntax is that of the http protocol. The HTTP scheme-specific syntax is defined as follows:

```
http://<host>:<port>/<path>?<searchpart>
```

The <host> is the fully qualified domain name of the host or, alternatively, the host's IP address (for example, 123.45.67.8). The <port> portion is relative to the scheme being used and, if left out, defaults to the port used for the particular scheme specified in the URL. The default port for http, for example, is port 80. For ftp, the default port is 22.

The <path> is optional but, if specified, can be used to represent a hierarchical structure (that is, directory paths). This is useful when mapping URLs to different directories or different URLs (see chapter 20).

The URL specification also reserves certain characters that carry special meanings in a specific scheme. These characters are: ";", "/", "?", ":", "@", "=" and "&".

The Domino-specific URL syntax is:

```
http://Host/NotesObject?Action&Arguments
```

The syntax is identical to the generic HTTP syntax previously described up to the "NotesObject" portion. The Domino syntax also uses a "special" character—"$"—in addition to the reserved characters.

The "NotesObject" can be any Notes construct. The construct could be a database or an element of a database (for example, view, document, form, navigator, agent, and so forth).

The "Action" represents the operation to be carried out on the specified object. The action can be any action valid in the context of the object being operated on. An "?OpenView" operation, for example, cannot be used in the context of Notes form object. Valid operations include: ?OpenDatabase, ?OpenView, ?OpenDocument, ?EditDocument, ?OpenForm, and so on.

The "Arguments" provide a qualification on the action to be performed. The qualifier "Start=1" used in conjunction with the ?OpenView action, for example, positions the view to be generated and displayed on the Web client at the top of the view (that is, the first document).

When designing Notes databases to be published to a Web client, the structure of the URL becomes an essential tool in developing links and various "commands" available to the Web client.

Domino HTML Support

The question you may be asking after seeing the earlier figures is, "If Domino generates HTML when it is needed, why use HTML within a Notes database at all?" That is a good question, and the answer may not be readily apparent at first. Assuming that the reader is experienced with the Notes client and application development environment, that same Notes developer must now learn to cope with a thin Web client and its limited understanding of the world around it (after all, it is "stateless").

In some cases, you must resort to giving up some of the robust functionality found in a homogenous Notes environment and "speak" directly to the Web client on its own level. When creating a document with a form, for example, the Notes client saves and closes the document and is returned to the context (view, navigator, document) that existed just prior to creating the document. A Web client, however, deals with each page or screen (that is, HTML file) as a separate entity with no means of relating the current screen to the previous. To a Web client, there is no correlation of a view with a document as there is within Notes.

Hence, when a Web client creates a document in a Notes database, Domino automatically generates a polite but navigationally weak Form Processed message. Recognizing this to be somewhat rude by accepted Web practices, the Lotus development team provided a means to customize the response to the Web client.

This customization must be completely within HTML because Notes does not natively generate an equivalent acknowledgment when a document is saved. In other words, the Form Processed message is just a courtesy to the Web client indicating that an action has completed. If you want to tell the Web client something more, it must be through HTML. This will become clearer as you proceed, but first take a look at how Domino can handle HTML in a couple of specific cases: static HTML, "pass thru" HTML and "directed" HTML.

Static HTML Files

Of course, one can pull an existing HTML directory structure and its HTML files on to a Domino server, and Domino will function the same as any other HTTP server—it serves up HTML pages to the Web client.

In some cases, it may make sense to use existing HTML files in combination with a Notes database. These HTML files do not need to be located on the Domino server. They may reside on a completely different Web host altogether, thereby enabling a Notes application to link to an existing set of HTML files on a different (non-Domino) HTTP server.

In the case of moving existing HTML files on to the Domino server, relocate the directory structure into the HTML directory under the Domino directory. You need to ensure that any subdirectory names (for example, "Graphics") are created as well. Referencing these files can then be done the same as when they were on another HTTP server.

To reference a static HTML file from within a Notes application, the developer may choose to generate the URL through an HTML tag or use the @URLOpen command. Suppose, for example, that the fictitious company from Chapter 20, MyCorp, has a listing of all its locations in a static file that needs to be immediately available under the new Domino Web site until it can be converted into a Notes database.

The About document in figure 22.3 has an image source tag as follows [<IMG SRC="/icons/dmycorp.gif"...>], which is used to display the gif file that contains the "Locations" graphic.

By highlighting the entire "IMG SRC" text line from the "[" to the "]" and selecting Create, Hotspot, Action Hotspot, a Notes formula that generates the URL for the HTML file can be activated whenever the graphic is clicked on by the Web client. The syntax for the function is

```
@URLOpen("/locate.htm")
```

and assumes the locations are contained in a file called locate.htm in the domino\html directory as configured by the server document or virtual server document (refer to Chapter 20 for details on these settings).

In this fashion, Domino enables the Notes developer to mix Notes databases with static HTML files either completely (moving all HTML files on to the Domino server) or on a case-by-case basis (as needed).

Pass-Through HTML

The Domino server's "native language" is the Notes RPC. An HTML "tag" (for example, img src, href, and so on) has no meaning within the context of the NRPC or the "Notes only" environment. Domino is designed to just "pass through" any HTML to the Web client, thereby making the assumption that the Web client knows how to interpret the HTML Domino sends.

Note Pass-through HTML should not be confused with the pass-through function of a Domino server that enables Notes clients to access other Domino servers through a dial-up or other connection to a single Domino server. They are distinctly different processes.

Whenever Domino encounters HTML in any context of Notes (for example, forms, fields, views, and so forth), it passes it along to the Web client without any changes whatsoever, enabling the Notes developer to use HTML as necessary to "speak" directly to the Web client.

This can be seen, again by comparing figures 22.3 and 22.4. Note the main logo for MyCorp is loaded with the "IMG SRC" tag at the top of the About document in figure 22.3. When Domino encounters the "[< ... >]" convention surrounding a text string, it passes the enclosed string through to the Web client. In this case, the tag is for an inline image retrieval that the client then requests from the Domino server.

> **Note** The key point to remember about HTML is that Domino passes it through to the Web client. If you are developing applications for both Web and Notes clients, the HTML is visible to the Notes client (and quite ugly) unless special steps are taken to hide the HTML from Notes clients.

"Directed" HTML

Notes design features provide the underlying mechanism to "direct" HTML to specific Web clients for a given set of circumstances. This direction proves useful when a Notes developer wants to customize a form or response based on any property specific to the Web client or other "run-time" property. Properties of the Web client or the run-time environment can be the client's name or any demographic data (for example, zip code, age, gender, buying preferences, date, time, and so forth).

Consider more closely one of many possibilities: MyCorp typically runs a daily "special" on widgets and wants any Web client to see which items are on special when he or she visits MyCorp's Web site. Figure 22.4 shows a third column added to the About document, serving as the home page for MyCorp; it has entries for each weekday's special. (MyCorp has a pretty unimaginative marketing staff, so the specials are not too varied. They do, however, help to illustrate the point.)

In figure 22.5, the Web client entering the site sees only Monday's specials even though all other specials are actually in the About document.

Notes natively provides a very powerful feature called "hide-when," which can be greatly leveraged when developing Web applications.

Before the Domino server "serves" up the About document, it computes several functions to determine when to hide the paragraph. These functions are @Weekday(@Today). @Today returns today's date and @Weekday converts the date to a day of the week. In this example, "Monday's Special" is displayed whenever the weekday is not equal to "1" or "2" (that is, Sunday or Monday). The same is true for the special item being offered that day (Black Widgets), although it is not displayed.

Figure 22.4

MyCorp's customized daily specials—Notes.

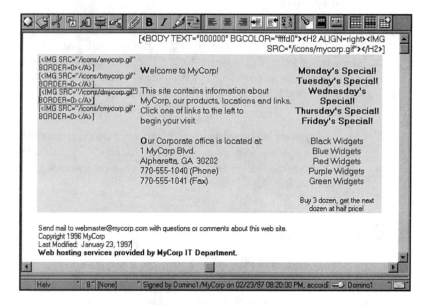

Figure 22.5

MyCorp's customized daily special—Netscape.

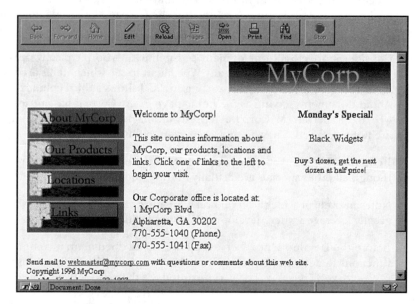

Each paragraph computes its "hide-when" based on its particular day of the week. This appears to the Web client that each day the site is being updated and conveys the "Holy Grail" of the Web—to have "fresh" content. (Try that with straight HTML.)

You may say, "Yeah, but it is just text in a Notes About document and not HTML, so there is really no neat Domino technology involved." Remember that Domino takes the plain text found in the About document and converts it to HTML; hence, the "directed" nature of the HTML.

This is a rather simple example, but Domino forms could customize a page for a customer who prefers green widgets or one whose hobbies from a Guestbook profile include golf, for instance. In more complicated cases, the application could check to see whether the customer's account is delinquent before allowing that customer to complete an order form.

An @DbLookup, for example, could be performed against an account status database based on the user's name to return the value of the account status field showing if the account is in arrears. If the lookup returned such a value, the order portion of the form could be hidden (using hide-when) and a delinquent section made visible (again, using hide-when) to advise the user that their order could not be taken at that time. Again, this is basic Notes application development that translates into a powerful and dynamic Web application.

With the background in place, it is now time to dig a bit deeper into developing a Web site by using the Web-specific features provided in the Notes 4.5 development environment. The rest of the chapter focuses on that very task.

Web Site Development

Up to this point, this chapter has shown how Domino handles HTML. Now it is time to explore how Notes design features translate into the actual development of a Web site. As you go through this section, you will be developing a Web site including more Notes features.

As the Domino administrator, you may be called upon to troubleshoot a Notes application designed by someone who is not familiar with how Domino handles certain Notes design features. The following sections give you a good basis for assisting the application developer while not having to become an expert application developer yourself.

It is assumed that the reader is already somewhat experienced in Notes application development or at least knows where to find the Application Developer's Reference manual. This is not intended to be a primer for beginner application developers. Therefore, there is not a lot of explanation of @Function or @Command syntax included in this chapter.

Formatting Basics

Hopefully, the first few sections have not left you feeling like you need to become an HTML guru. The native text formatting of Notes applications is quite sufficient in most cases to get the message across to the Web client.

Domino supports most formatting features of Notes; certain features, however, either do not fully translate or do not translate at all into the Web context. It is important, therefore, to first establish the basic formatting rules that apply regardless of the Notes design element.

 Since the first beta release of Domino HTTP Web server, great progress has been made to the product in the area of formatting and what is supported. The rules of formatting that follow are accurate as of this writing, but may change in the future. The reader is strongly urged to check the documentation and release notes for supported formatting changes.

Static Text

Wherever static text appears (for example, forms, About documents, views), Domino translates the static text into HTML based on the text properties as shown in table 22.2.

TABLE 22.2
Text Properties

Property	Web Translation	Notes
Size	"Mapped" to HTML font size	Point|HTML Size
		8 | 1
		10 | 2
		12 | 3
		14 | 4
		18 | 5
		24 | 6
		28 | 7

Property	Web Translation	Notes
Alignment	Only left, right, and center	
Tabs	Not supported by Web client	
Indent/Outdent	Not supported by Web client	
Blank spaces	Not supported by Web client	Except when using non-proportional fonts
Line spacing	No inter-line spacing	
Paragraph Properties	Supported where applicable to HTML	Use HTML style to format as pass-through HTML
Font face	Not supported. Fixed fonts convert to Web client's non-proportional font.	
Text styles	All except shadow, emboss, and extrude	

Static text can also be HTML, which will be passed through to the Web client. To indicate the text is HTML, begin the HTML string with "[<" and close it with ">]". The quotation marks are not included.

As an alternative, a paragraph style can be created called "HTML" and used to indicate that the entire paragraph is to be interpreted as HTML. When using the HTML paragraph style, you do not need to enclose the text with "[< >]."

Tables

Tables are the preferred method for formatting blocks of text to present to the Web client. Because tabs and blank spaces (except for spaces using non-proportional fonts—Courier, for example) are not supported by the Web, client tables provide an alternative to aligning fields and static field labels.

Paragraph styles are not supported in tables. It is possible, however, to use bulleted or numbered lists as well as alignment for paragraphs in tables. The example in figure 22.6 shows a table added to MyCorp's home page About document. You may note that a few other changes have been made also. Those are covered in the next section.

Figure 22.6

Tables on the home page.

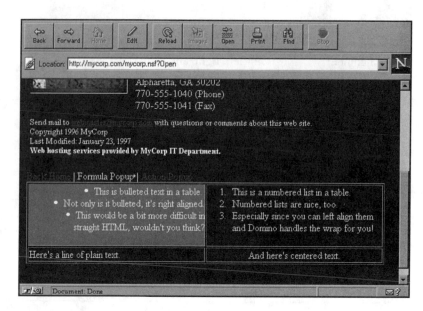

Three properties of tables can be manipulated for Web clients:

- ◆ **Borders.** For bordering, the top left cell of the table determines the border for the entire table. If you want to turn off the lines between cells, it is only necessary to turn off the lines in the top left cell. Neither the variable border widths or special borders (extruded or embossed) are supported.

- ◆ **Layout.** Table layout properties supported are limited to "Fit table to window" and column widths. Because Domino "collapses" empty table cells, however, it is useless to try to control the widths of any columns where there is no text.

- ◆ **Color.** Cell colors can be manipulated collectively or independently. They can be applied to the entire table or, if desired, made transparent to take on the color of the background.

Hotspots

When used in straight Notes application development, a *hotspot* is an area on a form used to:

- ◆ Display pop-up text

- ◆ Switch to a linked destination

- ◆ Perform a Notes action

- ◆ Follow a URL link to a Web page

The hotspot becomes active when the client clicks on the area defined by the developer. The area may surround text or a graphic bitmap. In the context of Web development, Domino supports only the following hotspots:

◆ **Link.** The link hotspot can be used to incorporate a database, view, or document link into the highlighted text or graphic. Of course, the link must be copied to the clipboard before using this type of hotspot.

◆ **URL Link.** This type of hotspot enables the developer to enter a URL by using the syntax as described previously for URLs. This type of link can be applied to highlighted text or a graphic image.

◆ **Action.** The action hotspot enables the developer to enter a Web "context" @Function or @Command. The action must be within the context of actions the Web client can understand and request. @Command([EditDocument]), for example, cannot be used in "context" with a Web client, because there is no method for "pointing" at the document to edit unless the document is already open. @Command([Compose];"Guestbook") would be within the proper Web context when used on a home page or within a view.

The Home Page

This chapter has now covered enough formatting. You can now begin a simple home page for MyCorp. It is a relatively simple design based on the About document. (You will see why the About document was chosen shortly.)

Domino gives the Web developer many options for choosing what to display for the site's home page. These options are configurable based on the parameters of the HTTP section in the server document in the Public Name & Address Book (see previous chapter).

The launch properties of a database are used to control not only what the Notes client sees but also the Web client. Of all the choices for "what" to launch on database open, the option to Launch 1st attachment in "About Database" is not supported.

Of those that remain, a couple behave a bit differently for Web clients. They are:

◆ Open designated Navigator and Open designated Navigator in its own window function the same. They both open a navigator in its own window for a Web client.

◆ Restore as Last Viewed by User displays the equivalent of View, Show, Folders.

This discussion assumes that your site will be made up of Notes databases exclusively. With that in mind, the following two sections look at the two main options for establishing the home page: the About document and a navigator.

The About Document

Figure 22.7 shows the launch properties for the Web site database. The Open "About database" document opens the About document each time the database is entered. Because of this, the About document is a convenient tool for developing the initial home page.

Figure 22.7

MyCorp's database launch properties.

Refer back to figure 22.2 to see the About document used as the home page for MyCorp from Notes. Figure 22.3 shows the About document home page through a Netscape Navigator.

The About document supports the following design elements, which make it handy and quick to use in developing the home page:

◆ Static text (subject to limitations described previously)

◆ Tables (subject to limitations described previously)

◆ Graphic bitmaps (pasted bitmaps or HTML tags for images)

◆ Pass-through HTML

◆ Hotspots

In this home page, MyCorp's graphic images were brought in through the HTML tag "img src." This tag instructs the browser to request the file specified to the right of the "=" sign. For instance,

```
img src="icons/mycorp.gif" border=0
```

instructs the browser to request and display the file called mycorp.gif without a border.

The HTML tags for these images are used extensively throughout this home page. In addition, by highlighting one of the "img src" tags, it can become an action hotspot as described earlier, which is how the "Locations" image becomes a hotspot pointing to an HTML document called locate.htm.

The About document provides good flexibility in creating a home page. It has some drawbacks, however, that should be kept in mind:

◆ **Background colors.** Unlike a Notes form, an About document has no capability for setting a background color or graphic. HTML must be used to set a background color (for example, "[<BODY TEXT="ffffd0" BGCOLOR= "000000">]) or background image ([<BODY TEXT="ffffd0" BACKGROUND= "icons/bkgrnd.gif">], for example).

◆ **Pasted bitmap graphics.** Domino uses 256-color, platform-independent bitmaps that may not covert into either a GIF or JPEG format as neatly as you might expect.

 Use caution with bitmap images and test the look of your pasted bitmap before releasing it on your Web clients.

Bitmaps are slower for the browser because they require translation to GIF format before transmission. It is recommended that they be used sparingly.

One other point about pasted bitmaps—they are static and must be pasted wherever they are needed. If, for instance, the bitmap is a company logo, it must be maintained wherever it is used. If an "IMG SRC" HTML tag is used, however, the graphic can be modified one time and, because it is incorporated by reference, the changes are reflected wherever it is used.

Navigator

The second option for creating your home page and, as you will see later, an option for adding sizzle to an application is a graphic navigator. A graphic navigator creates a clickable image map for the Web client. It is, by nature, more graphical.

Graphical navigators give Domino applications a typical Web graphics appeal. Like it or not, most Web sites are evaluated on their visual as well as their content. A large portion of the Web appears to be evolving into yet another entertainment medium where a site needs to catch users as they surf by. (This can be loosely related to TV channel surfing. The flashy show hooks you for a moment, but after the channel becomes uninteresting, you surf on.) Enter the graphical world of the image map.

Image maps are handled in two ways: server-side and client-side image maps. For server-side image maps, the browser sends the coordinates for the clicked region on the image map to the server. The server, in turn, generates a corresponding URL and sends it back to the Web client. A client-side image map enables the Web client to generate the URL directly based on the clicked region in the image map.

Domino converts the navigator design element into an image map that is both, meaning that all Web clients are supported automatically. Some Web clients support client-side image maps, so Domino will uses those HTML tags. If the browser supports server-side image maps, Domino uses server-side image map HTML tags.

Follow these rules when using navigators for Web applications:

◆ You cannot auto adjust the panes when serving up a navigator to a Web client as you can with a Notes client.

◆ Objects are highlighted when they are touched by the Web client. They may be hot links, but do not "light up" when the Web client moves over it.

◆ Graphic backgrounds must be created using the Create, Graphic Background option. Creating a graphic button does not translate to an image.

Warning Do not use Edit, Paste to create your graphic. It will not translate into an image map.

◆ The only navigator objects supported are hotspot polygons and rectangles. All other objects (for example, text boxes, graphic buttons, polygons, and so forth) are not translated to a Web client. Hence, static text must be included in the graphic. It cannot be added through the Notes navigator designer.

◆ Formulas can be used to compute a view or database to link to in an action behind a given hotspot. A formula could be written to determine whether the user is a Notes client or a Web client, for example, and then direct the user to a Web-based view or a common Notes view.

Because the very nature of a navigator is a graphic interface, navigators are the preferred device for a graphically intense home page.

 Tip It is the author's opinion (based on his own limited graphic talents) that the use of graphical navigators be limited to those with direct access to a graphic artist.

You should keep the following points in mind when evaluating graphic navigators for your home page:

◆ Anything you want on your home page must be included in your graphic.

◆ Making changes to the navigator later to add a URL link or launch the creation of a new form requires a graphics package to edit the graphic file used to create the navigator. In other words, it takes more than just the design pane of a Notes client.

◆ You can only add hotspots to your navigator.

◆ Associating the navigator with an "Initial view or folder" in the navigator's properties does not translate to a Web client.

Domino GIF Files

Because this discussion has now touched on graphics, this is a good spot to point out that Domino comes with a set of GIF files that can be invoked via an HTML "img src" tag. By providing these GIF files, Lotus has attempted to cover three different categories. The set of GIFs that begin with ACTN are larger and suitable for use in forms. The GIFs that begin with VWICN are smaller and better suited for use in views. The third category is the ubiquitous "miscellaneous."

Form Design Considerations

Now that the basics of formatting have been covered, and your site has a home page, now add some substance to your site. You can approach this in numerous ways, but this discussion covers only some basics that will enable you to expand into more complex Domino Web solutions.

Before adding the substance, you will add another basic building block of any Notes database: the form. When designing Web-based applications, the form is one of the main elements used to communicate with the Web client. The following sections discuss how various form elements translate into the Web environment.

Form Properties

The six tabs on the Properties box for a form describe how the form will behave when in use. The following form properties do not translate to the Web client:

◆ **Basics.** Merge replication conflicts, version controls, and Anonymous Form are not supported.

◆ **Defaults - Store form in document.** Supported in read mode only. For documents that will be created or edited by a Web client, do not select this feature.

- ◆ **Defaults - Automatically refresh fields.** Not supported.

- ◆ **Defaults - Disable Field Exchange.** Not applicable to a Web client.

- ◆ **Defaults - On Create: Formulas inherit values from selected document.** Works at the document level, but not in views. Remember, Web clients have no way to "point" to a document within a view.

- ◆ **Defaults - On Create: Inherit entire selected document into rich text field.** Web clients do not support rich text so this is not applicable.

- ◆ **Defaults - On Open: Show context pane.** Not applicable to a Web client.

- ◆ **Launch.** None of the auto-launch options translate to the Web client.

- ◆ **Security - Default encryption keys.** Web clients do not support Notes encryption. (Refer to Chapter 24, "Security and Reporting," for more details on security.)

- ◆ **Security - Disable printing/forwarding/copying to clipboard.** Does not translate to the Web client.

After that list, you are probably wondering what's left. Well, many more form options are still left for the developer to make use of in developing Web applications.

In general, a form supports every design element discussed previously for the About document, but also has unique elements that are discussed next.

Form Elements

In addition to the About document design features, Domino treats the basic form design elements as follows:

- ◆ **Attachments.** Attachments are supported, but are dependent on the Web client supporting file upload. As always, this must be a rich text field. To give a Web client the ability to upload file attachments, create an action hotspot that executes the following action:

```
@Command([EditInsertAttachment])
```

- ◆ **Buttons.** Buttons are not supported. For any series of buttons placed on a form, the first button becomes the Submit button. All others do not translate to the Web client. The Submit button submits the document only. It will not execute any other function or command.

- ◆ **Layout regions.** These do not translate to the Web client. For alignment of field labels and fields, use tables.

◆ **Components, OLE, and OCX objects.** These objects are supported on Windows NT and/or Windows 95. Even though the Web client may edit the object, however, the changes cannot be saved back into the document on the Domino server.

Fields

Fields are, of course, supported on forms but not on About documents or navigators. Fields exhibit the following characteristics in a Web environment:

◆ **Keywords.** Keyword fields are supported, but are limited to the following choice options: Enter Choices and Use Formula for Choices. No other choice types are supported.

To use @DbLookup or @DbColumn to generate choices, you must be running a Domino 4.5 or higher server. This feature is not supported on pre-4.5 servers.

You may allow multi-values, but the Web client must know to hold down the Ctrl key while clicking on the choices.

Although you can use the following keyword options, they will be of no effect for Web clients because they do not translate or only partially translate:

- ◆ Allow values not in list is not supported.

- ◆ Refresh fields on keyword change is not supported.

- ◆ Refresh choices on document refresh is not supported.

- ◆ Framing (3D, None, nor Standard) is not supported.

- ◆ Number of columns is supported, but the columns do not align in the Web client.

- ◆ Helper button is not supported.

- ◆ Help Description is not supported. This field may be used to "pass" HTML commands to the Web client, however, for formatting the appearance of the field.

- ◆ Give this field default focus is not supported for any field type.

- ◆ Sign if mailed and Enable Encryption is not supported. In fact, no type of encryption is supported from the Web client because there is no Notes ID file with the appropriate public/private keys required to support encryption. In addition, field signing is not supported in any situation.

◆ **Name fields.** Name fields are supported but cannot be used in conjunction with the Use Address, Use View, or Use Access Control List dialog box options.

Note A Web user's name is only available after the user is authenticated.

◆ **Rich text fields.** Although you can provide a rich text field to a Web client, the only data capable of being placed into the field is text.

Warning If you take the time to format the contents of a rich text field (with, for example, colors, bold, italics, and so on) that you intend to allow a Web client to edit, don't plan on keeping your nice formatting. Web clients can only supply text values into rich text fields, so all your formatting is for naught after the Web client opens your document in edit mode. The client can "see" the rich text formatting, but cannot return it in edit mode.

◆ **Computed when composed fields.** These are supported.

Note You may be surprised by some of the values displayed when the document is composed. If a document is "refreshed" by the Web client and your field computes @Unique, for example, the value changes each time the document is refreshed without every having been saved. Caution is advised, and it is recommended that you test any formula computed when the document is composed to ensure that you get what you want.

◆ **Notes field exchange.** Supported.

◆ **Default value formulas.** Supported, but cannot be used to refer to a document selected in a view because Web clients do not support view document selection. They work fine when computing values from a document that is open in read mode.

◆ **You cannot compute after validation.** You can validate an input from a Web client and Domino will serve up the failure message via HTML. This leaves the Web clients in a "navigationally neutral" position, however, requiring them to navigate with their browsers. To provide an elegant re-entry into the form, you must use HTML in the failure message.

◆ **Field help.** Not supported. You can, however, use this field to supply HTML formatting instructions to the Web client.

$$Fields

$$Fields are used to request a special behavior by the Domino server. When used on forms, these fields cause Domino to behave differently than normal fields, because they are translated to the Web client.

These fields are:

◆ **$$Return.** When used on a form that the Web client submits, this field preempts the usual Form Processed confirmation "page," and serves up the contents of the $$Return field to the Web client. The field content may be a computed response and may include anything from a personalized message to a link to another page.

◆ **$$ViewBody.** This field causes Domino to display the body of the view name contained in the field. If the view name is static, it must be enclosed in quotation marks. It can, however, be computed. Only one such field is allowed on a form.

◆ **$$ViewList.** This field contains no value, but causes Domino to display a list of the views and folders using the standard Folders navigator. Whichever font style is used on the field is what translates to the Web client.

◆ **$$NavigatorBody.** This field causes Domino to display the navigator contained or computed within the field. Unlike the $$ViewBody, multiple $$NavigatorBody fields may be used on a form. In this case, just append an underscore with a unique character to each additional field (for example, $$NavigatorBody_1, $$NavigatorBody_2, and so on).

◆ **$$HTMLHead.** This field can contain a formula or static text that passes HTML information into the Head tag.

◆ **$$QueryOpenAgent.** This field either contains the name of an agent or computes the name of an agent to run before sending the document to the Web client. If the agent name is static, it must be enclosed in quotation marks.

◆ **$$QuerySaveAgent.** This field functions the same as $$QueryOpenAgent, except the named agent runs before Domino saves the document.

CGI Variables

Domino supports standard Web features for gathering additional information about who your Web clients are. Although there is nothing especially covert about these features, most casual Web users never know how much information is being gathered about them when they visit a site.

CGI variables are collected by the Domino server when a Web client saves a document. Whether you use this information is up to you.

If you choose to collect CGI variable information, create a field with the CGI variable name on the form to be used for input by the Web client. To collect the Web client's IP address, for example, you name the field REMOTE_ADDR.

Although many CGI variables exist, Domino supports the following most useful ones:

◆ **HTTP_Referer.** This records the URL of the page through which the Web client got to your page.

◆ **HTTPS.** This indicates whether SSL mode was enabled for the server. If the document was created with HTTPS, the field will have ON as its value.

◆ **HTTP_User_Agent.** The type of browser the Web client uses will be captured if this field is used.

◆ **Remote_Addr.** This records the IP address of the Web client.

◆ **Remote_Host.** This records the machine name of the Web client.

◆ **Remote_User.** If the user has been authenticated by the Domino server, this variable reflects the authenticated name.

View Design Considerations

Now that you have some understanding of forms in a Web environment, you need to develop a means of presenting the documents in a relevant manner to the Web client. This can be done through Notes views that can be customized for the Web client.

As with the previous discussions, take a look at the design properties of a view that do not survive the translation or do not fully translate into the Web world.

◆ Calendar-style views are supported, but many of the features found on a Notes client are not translated. These include: conflict bars, clock, and creating new appointments and entry scrolling within a day's schedule. The same restrictions on tables apply to calendar views.

◆ Folders are supported, but documents cannot be moved into a folder (remember, the Web client has no means to select a document in a view).

◆ Multi-line column headings are supported, as are multi-line rows. When producing the HTML for the view, Domino uses the value in the first visible column as the link to the column. If this column is long enough to wrap, it will be awkward and too long for a hotlink. If the second or third column wraps, this may not be so bad.

◆ On Open, Go To options are not supported because a document cannot be selected in a view by a Web client.

◆ Refresh options are not supported. Web clients cannot refresh a view.

◆ Show in View menu option is not supported because there is no view menu outside a Notes client. Hide a view if you do not wish the Web client to see it in the Folders and Views navigator.

◆ Row Style Options (that is, unread, alternate row colors, selection margin, and beveled headings) are not supported.

◆ View index options are not supported by the Web client. It is possible, however, to re-index views on the Domino server.

◆ Column heading sorting is not supported.

◆ Category expand and collapse options are supported, but only one category may be expanded at a time when expanding or collapsing from a twistie.

◆ Resizable columns are not supported.

◆ Twisties cannot be hidden from the Web client because they are the only means whereby a Web client can expand a category.

A few other points not concerned with view design options specifically should be made about views. The following considerations can be best discussed with an example of the default view (see fig. 22.12).

◆ Column headers are somewhat foreign to a Web client and can be left off most views. They add little value because they do not stay fixed at the top of the page.

◆ The default navigation icons (such as Previous, Next, Expand, Collapse, and Search) are standard for each view and cannot be changed within the default view without some additional programming (covered in a moment).

◆ Domino uses the first visible column to generate the link to the document. Make certain that the value used in the first column is representative of the document. Using a date as the first view column makes sense to a Notes client, for example, but will not be too intuitive for the Web client. Long values in the first column make rather ugly links.

◆ Although column totals work, there is no "total" line shown between the total and the number being totaled in the last document. This can potentially lead to the Web client not clearly understanding that the last line represents the total.

◆ HTML can be passed to the Web client via the View title. Reference the view through URLs by using an alias if you wish to pass HTML in the View title.

Lotus has provided tools that enable the developer to enhance how a view, navigator, or search screen is displayed to the Web client. These features cannot be used by a Notes client but are extremely useful in enhancing the application for the Web client.

View Templates

As discussed in the preceding section, the default view produced by Domino is rather bland—functional, but bland. Lotus has provided a means whereby the views can be highly customized, however, with better graphical and navigational devices. The view template is used to achieve the view customization.

Although actually a new type of form, the view template comes into play when a Web client requests a view. Domino first looks to see whether a view template can be found that contains the requested view's name. If it cannot find a match, Domino then checks to see whether a default template view exists. If it does, the default view template is used. If neither a specific or default template exists, Domino uses a very basic design to serve up the view. (This design is seen later.)

To use a view template to customize the appearance of a view, follow these steps:

1. Create the view that displays your documents in the manner you want to convey to your customer—products by part number, for example.

2. Create a form to contain the view template and name the form **$$ViewTemplate for Products by Part Number**.

3. The best way to format the form is through a table, so add a table to hold graphics, logos, or whatever else you wish to appear in the view.

4. In one cell of the table, add field titled $$Viewbody. The default value of this field will be "Products by Part Number"(see fig. 22.8).

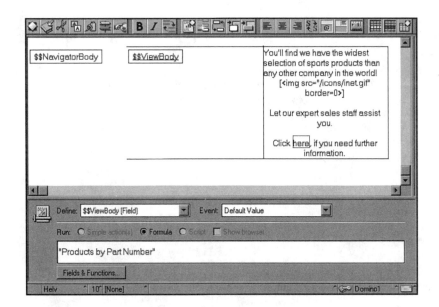

Figure 22.8

View template form for Products by Part Number.

If the view template just created were to be used for all views within the database, the same process would have been followed except the view title would have been $$ViewTemplateDefault rather than for a specific view.

Navigator Templates

Navigator templates work in a manner similar to view templates, except they relate a form to a navigator. The naming convention is the same as view templates.

Search Templates

Search templates enable the Notes developer to customize the form presented to the Web client when displaying or collecting the search criteria. If a search form is not used, Domino serves up a basic search form.

The basic search form in itself is a powerful feature based on the Notes full-text search engine. It is limited, however, in its capability to provide—again—a suitable Web form (that is, graphical intensity).

To customize what a user sees when prompted for their search criteria, use a form with the alias of $$Search or $$Search as its form name.

To customize the display for the results of the search, use either the default template (that is, $$SearchTemplateDefault). To specify a view, use $$SearchTemplate for Viewname where Viewname is the name of the view to use.

Adding Substance to the Home Page: Putting It All Together

Now that you have some context within which forms and views can be used in the Web environment, the next step is to add some functionality behind your home page.

Web sites generally provide three basic forms of "substance." The type of site you design depends on the business need you are addressing. The three types are addressed in order of complexity:

- ◆ Content

- ◆ Collaboration

- ◆ Commerce

Content-based Web sites are designed to provide information about a company's or organization's products or services, reference materials, or other relatively static information.

Some have called such sites "brochureware," because they are largely targeted at providing a Web presence for companies to distribute marketing material by an alternative channel. Whereas printed marketing material ages and must be reprinted, a Web site's "agility" to remain chronologically relevant is remarkable. (Of course, this does not mean that the site can get by with no maintenance.)

The biggest challenge to most Notes application developers beginning to develop Web applications is to develop in both "languages" (Notes and HTML). "Bilingual" development enables the Web client to "see" what is pertinent to its world, and the Notes client to "see" what is relevant to its world.

The fictitious company, MyCorp, wants to establish some depth to its new home page. The intent is to enable the company to use Notes to keep its Web "literature" current. A form is needed to capture its product information.

In addition to capturing product information, you also use this form to capture all other pertinent information about MyCorp (for example, locations, links to other sites, and so on).

Figure 22.9 shows the basic form called "Web Form."

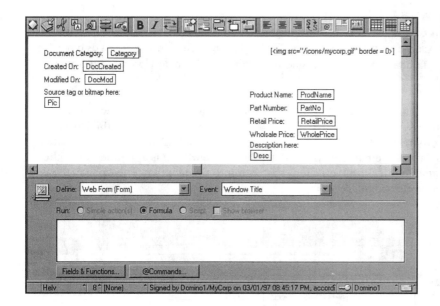

Figure 22.9

*Web form from
MyCorp's home
page.*

The pertinent features of the form are as follows:

◆ **Category.** This field is a keyword field designed to make the form usable for
several different parts of the Web site. Its values are: product, locations, distribu-
tors, links, and about.

◆ **MyCorp logo.** The HTML tag in the upper-right corner pulls in the GIF file
logo. If changes to the logo are made, the Web client sees the changes without
having to redesign the form.

◆ **DocCreated and DocMod fields.** These fields capture the date the document was created and the date of any modifications.

◆ **Pic Field.** The Pic field is a rich text field that can contain an "IMG SRC"
HTML tag for a graphic image or a bitmap. It is intended to provide a place for
relevant graphic images (product pictures, location pictures, and so on).

◆ **ProdName, PartNo, RetailPrice, WholePrice, Desc.** These fields
provide the relevant information for the product "catalog." Using "hide-when"
formulas, Notes can hide these fields when the Category field is something
other than "Product."

A copy of the MyCorp home page database (and all referenced GIF files) is included on the accompanying CD for reference. This file also serves as a point to get started testing and working with some of the Web development features of Domino.

A simple view has been built that will show the catalog. The view is shown through a Netscape browser in figure 22.10. It is rather simple and makes use of the DocCreated field to compute whether the product is over five days old. If the DocCreated date is within five days of the current system date, then a "New!" tag is appended onto the product name to draw the Web client's attention to the fact that a new product has been added to the catalog.

Figure 22.10

Basic view of MyCorp's catalog.

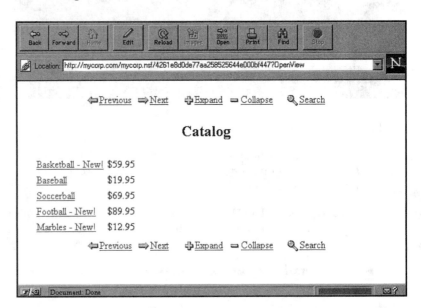

The Our Products link on the home page was created using a simple view link to the Catalog view. Although the view in figure 22.10 is functional, it is not in keeping with the overall "theme" of MyCorp's home page.

Using the view template shown earlier, the view looks much nicer.

One of the most important design considerations for developing Notes Web applications is the provision for navigation queues. Because you navigate the Web environment through URLs (and some of those are not very friendly), most applications are designed to anticipate where the Web client may want to go or return to next. Most applications provide this help through hotspots or other URL-generating aids. In addition, provisions need to be made to help the Web client return to a previous spot in your site.

In the case of MyCorp's home page, the initial navigation takes the Web client to the pertinent locations within the site (About, Products, Locations, and Links). It also aids the Web client in sending e-mail to MyCorp's Webmaster. After the Web client enters the product catalog, however, most of the navigation depends on the Web client's ability to use his Web browser's navigation features. This causes the client to have to leave the actual "page" and use menu bar buttons. This is addressed in a bit more detail later.

Figure 22.11 shows the document that provides the Web product page for baseballs. Notice that the Notes client is able to see the HTML. This can potentially be confusing for the Notes client. To avoid the confusion, follow this advice:

◆ Use "Hide-When" to mask all HTML code from the Notes client.

◆ Create a "Notes Form" that does not display the HTML, and select the form for display by using a Form formula in the view.

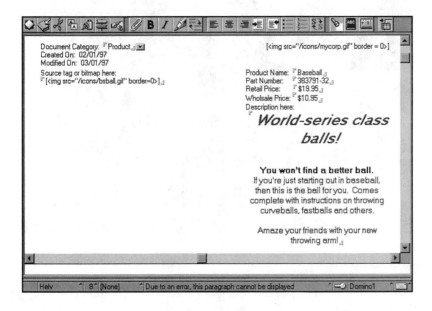

Figure 22.11

Baseball document from MyCorp's home page.

Either method works equally well. Some developers have been known to mask HTML by making the text color the same as the form color. Though it is not a great idea, it does work.

Of course, now that MyCorp has its products on the Web, the next logical step could either be to take orders over the Web or to provide customer service. This would enter into the collaborative phase of Web site evolution.

Suppose, for example, that MyCorp asks its customers to register in their Web Guestbook. (This is a fairly common practice on the Web.) Within the Guestbook form, MyCorp asks several questions that help establish a customers' profile. Based on the Web client's responses, MyCorp could then tailor an area of its Web site for registered customers only. Then, each time the customer visits the "registered access only" site, the page could be tailored toward that client's specific interests.

In this case, you just add the capability for a Web client to sign a "guestbook" type of registration with MyCorp.

Figure 22.12 shows the Guestbook form that MyCorp will use in its effort to register Web clients.

Figure 22.12

MyCorp's Guestbook form.

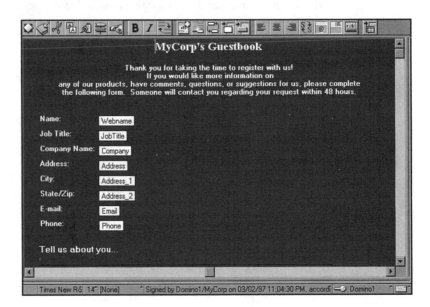

The next step in MyCorp's Web evolution might be to take orders directly over the Web. This, of course, adds additional complexities such as security of financial transactions (credit card data, for example), integration with order fulfillment, and other issues. No attempt has been made, however, to develop an order entry aspect for this sample database.

Additional Sources of Information

In designing Notes applications for Web use, many new aspects of application development enter the picture in dealing with the Web client interface. Several HTML "best practices" guides are available from different sources on the Web. It is highly recommended that these and other HTML references be used when designing Notes applications that will be used by Web clients.

Here are a few Web sites that provide Web design techniques and considerations (they are offered as suggestions for your consideration, not recommendations.) Some are even quite humorous:

◆ Web Page Design for Designers—`http://ds.dial.pipex.com/pixelp/wpdesign/wpdintro.htm`

◆ Sun Microsystems Guide to Web Style—`http://www.sun.com/styleguide`

◆ The Pawluk Pages—`http://www.pawluk.com/pages/webdes.htm`

◆ Web Pages that Suck—`http://www.webpagesthatsuck.com`

◆ Yale C/AIM Web Style Guide—`http://info.med.yale.edu/caim/manual/`

Summary

Lotus has taken most of the pain out of development with two template-type products that enable one to develop a Web site. These products are: Domino.Action and Domino.Merchant. Both provide a step-by-step process for building a Web site with the end result being the databases necessary to support various types of Web site requirements.

Domino.Action ships with Domino 4.5 servers. It is the author's opinion that a basic understanding of the concepts involved in Notes application development in a Web context is beneficial in the use of these products. I liken it to grade school students being required to learn the principles of mathematics (addition, subtraction, multiplication, associative properties, and so on) before they are allowed to use calculators. Calculators make it easier, but are of little value if there is not first an understanding of the basic concepts of mathematics.

What should be apparent by now is that whether you build your own Domino Web site or use the tools provided by Lotus, the site should be well planned and staged. Domino provides excellent support for developing a site bit-by-bit.

One recommended approach for developing your Web site follows here:

◆ Gather your requirements first. What is it you want to accomplish? Find the business requirement needing to be satisfied by putting up a Web site. If you don't know this, there will be little opportunity for measuring the success of the site.

◆ Plan your site in phases. Start simple (with content, for example), and then add complexity (collaboration and commerce) after (and only after) it has been thoroughly tested. It does not all have to be online the first hour of the first day—even though Domino provides rapid application development capability.

◆ Assign the requirements' logical boundaries. These boundaries help determine how many databases are appropriate to form your Domino Web site.

◆ Avoid trying to put all your requirements into one database. Domino has the capability through database, view, and document linking to "tie" many Notes databases into a seamless Web site. This helps to develop in phases and add databases to the site as they are ready.

◆ With hide-when capability and ACL security, it is possible to add functionality to a site and test it without exposing it to the Web community at large—extremely beneficial if you do not have the resources for a test environment.

CHAPTER 23

Building Web Applications with Domino.Action

Lotus Development has a long history of providing proof of its products' usefulness. From 1-2-3, the spreadsheet, to Word Pro, its word processor, to Lotus Notes, Lotus has traditionally provided examples, templates, or sample applications that, at the very least, provide good examples of how the application can be effectively applied in a business setting. Lotus has continued this long-standing tradition by creating the Domino. (pronounced "domino dot") family of applications. The first member of the family is Domino.Action, which was developed to illustrate the effective combined use of Lotus Notes as a development platform and the Lotus Domino server as a Web server platform. This chapter takes a close look at Domino.Action and offers a quick overview of the other members of the Domino. family.

But first, why should you care about Domino.Action and the other members of the family? It's simple. It doesn't matter whether you are a small organization with little or no technical talent available or a large multi-national company with a huge IS department. If you want to create intranet- or Internet-ready business applications that are professional, robust, secure, and flexible, you can't do it faster with any other tool on the market than with Domino.Action, Domino.Merchant, Domino.Broadcast, or Domino.Doc. This is a bold statement, but the remainder of this chapter should convince you of its truth.

Domino.Action is a process designed to help anyone define, design, and create a Web site with absolutely no HTML coding. Domino.Action guides the Webmaster through all the steps necessary to create an attractive, robust business Web site complete with varying levels of security and user registration.

Creating such a business Web site is quite a task, and Lotus has done a masterful job in making it easy. However, there is still a lot to learn. Even someone who is very familiar with both Lotus Notes and traditional Web site development must take great care in reading and following directions and the extensive help text. Few users are completely satisfied with their first efforts. But because it's so easy to start over, you won't hesitate to throw out your first effort and, learning as you go, try again.

This chapter covers the major pieces of the Domino.Action Site builder, the major tasks required to complete the definition of a site, and the task of generating your site. The following topics are covered in detail:

◆ The components of the Domino.Action Site Builder

◆ The structure of a Domino.Action Web site

◆ Getting started with Domino.Action

◆ Configuring your Web site in the Domino.Action Site Builder

◆ Designing your Web site in the Domino.Action Site Builder

◆ Generating your Web site from your design in Domino.Action Site Builder

◆ Completing your site's content via a Web browser

◆ A brief look at the rest of the Domino. family

The Components of Domino.Action

Domino.Action is actually made up of three components that are used in combination with a full Notes client. You cannot use Domino.Action with a Desktop or Mail client because those clients don't give you the capability to design a Notes database. The three components are the Domino.Action Site Creator database, the Domino.Action Library, and the Application Assembler (AppAssmn.exe).

The Application Assembler is an executable created with NotesVIP. It is executed from within the Site Creator and is essentially hidden from the end user, except when it is executing. The Application Assembler takes the definitions from the Site Creator and the appropriate components from the Library and combines them to create the various Notes databases that are used to make up your Web site.

The Domino.Action Library is just what it says: a library of components, (fields, forms, views, subforms, agents, and so forth) that are used to build each of the databases that make up your Web site. If you want to alter the standard look of your applications, you should alter this database before you generate your Web site. If you change the appropriate subform in the Library, the changes are then propagated across the entire site when it is generated.

 In one of the first sites I created with Domino.Action, I wanted to add two small graphics to each main page in each area database. As I added the graphics manually, I realized that I was changing the same subform in each database. So, I started over, changed the subform once in the library and recreated the site. Voilá, the graphics were on each page!

The Domino.Action Site Creator is an elaborate but very user-friendly Lotus Notes database that guides you through every step necessary to build a robust business Web site. This chapter focuses on the site creator and the things you need to know to be successful.

The Structure of a Domino.Action Web Site

Previewing the structure of a Domino.Action Web site, before exploring operational specifics, is very helpful. Each Domino.Action site can consist of one to eleven areas, ranging from a Home Page area to an About the Company area to a user or visitor Registration area. Later sections of this chapter describe the areas in detail.

After you complete all the configuration and design steps, the site generator creates a separate Notes database for each site area you configure and design. The site areas have navigation features such as buttons and links that connect the areas. Also, each area behaves almost like a mini-site in that each area has a main page and at least one other page that can either publish information on a static page or gather information on a dynamic form.

It is certainly possible to create a robust Web site that resides in a single Notes database. However, a multi-database approach provides a tremendous level of flexibility that is not possible if the site resides entirely in a single database. Figure 23.1 shows all of the Notes databases that are generated by the Domino.Action Site Builder.

Figure 23.1

The full compliment of databases generated for the site.

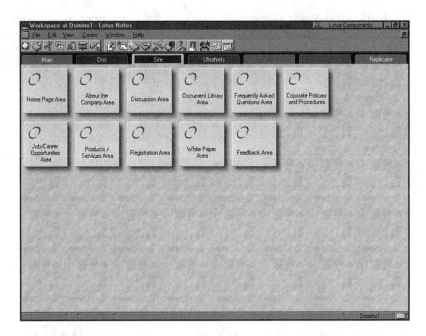

A unique aspect of the structure of a Domino.Action Web site is that the completed site is designed to be managed via a browser, not via a Lotus Notes client. You can perform some management functions with a Notes client, but the site is not optimized for a Notes client. An important fact is that after you configure, design, and generate your site, you still have to perform several administrative steps via a browser to complete your site. Lotus states that a future version of Domino.Action will make sites just as easy to manage from a Notes client as from a browser.

Getting Started with Domino.Action

To start, the SiteCreator and Library must be created from templates that are installed with the Lotus Domino 4.5 Server. Using your full Notes 4.5 client, choose File, Database, New. In the ensuing dialog box, scroll the template list until you see Domino.Action Library R1.0c (see fig. 23.2). If your release number is only R1.0, you can download the latest and greatest version of Domino.Action from http://www.net.lotus.com/action4/homepage.nsf?OpenDatabase.

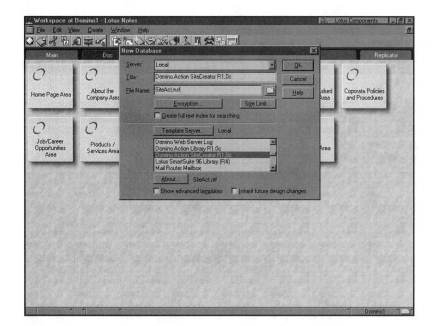

Figure 23.2

File, Database, New showing the two templates.

In either case, create the database from the template in your data directory. You can create the database in your local data directory or, if you have Create rights on the Domino server, create it in the Data directory on the server. Make sure you make the file name LibAct.NSF. The database does not have to be in your Data directory but that's where the application expects to find it, so it works best to put it there.

 I strongly recommend that you deselect the Inherit future design changes check box. Leaving it selected can get you into real trouble if your server administrator runs Design as a server task and any customizations you may have made are deleted. I've always advised clients to deselect this check box unless there is an overriding reason for keeping it selected.

Next, create your SiteCreator database. Again choose File, Database, New, and this time choose Domino.Action SiteCreator R1.0c. You can name the file name anything you like and you can create the database anywhere in or off of your Data directory.

Now that you have the two databases created you can look at the SiteCreator database on a fairly detailed basis.

When you open the database you are presented with the splat screen shown in figure 23.4.

Figure 23.3

The two databases created from the templates.

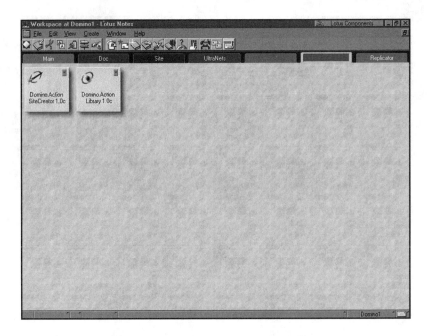

Figure 23.4

The Domino SiteCreator splat acreen.

When you dismiss the splat screen you see the main view of the database (see fig. 23.5). The developers of the SiteCreator have heavily customized this application. It is not recommended that you try to develop a database like this on your own.

The main view presents you with the SiteCreator Overview. This is a good point at which to emphasize the importance of reading the documentation and help text. The developers of the SiteCreator did an excellent job with both instructional text and context sensitive help text. There is a good reason for this application to be so well documented—the simple parts are very easy. To really put in the power, however, you need to read and understand the instructions. As you can see at the top of the navigator pane there are four main sections:

◆ Configure Your Site

◆ Design Your Site

◆ Generate Your Site

◆ Finish Your Site

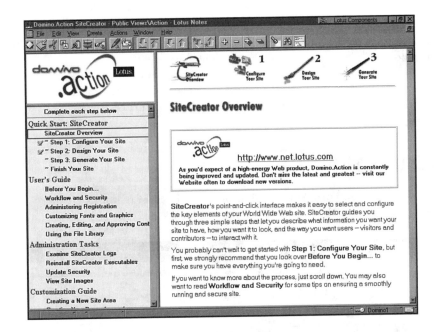

Figure 23.5

The main view of the Site Creator database.

That may look simple, and in many ways it is, but there's even more to do after the site is generated.

Below the four main steps are sections for all the documentation, the User's Guide, Administration Tasks, and the Release Notes. Reading through all this is very valuable, but first consider some possible options.

If you create the SiteCreator and Library databases on your local PC, you can create a site locally. Or if you install the Win95 version of the Domino Server, you can create a totally local implementation of Notes, the Domino Server, your Web site, and a browser. In the case of a totally local implementation you can simulate the operation of your site on your local PC, as it will behave on your intranet or the Internet without being connected to any network at all.

On the other hand, if you create the SiteCreator and Library database on your Domino server and generate your site on the server, you should be able to access your new site immediately, over your intranet or even the Internet, given that the server is configured correctly by the server administrator. Many different local configurations are possible, so it is beyond the scope of this chapter to attempt to guide you through the complexities of setting up a totally local implementation. Instead, the remainder of the chapter is written as if this site is the first site on your existing Domino server and it is accessed via your company's intranet.

 Be aware that you must have Create Database rights on the Domino server before you generate your site. This process actually creates databases on the server and the process fails if you don't have sufficient rights.

Now that the ground work has been laid and the basic elements of the SiteCreator have been introduced, it is time to start the actual site building process.

Configure Your Site

When you click on the Configure Your Site button from the SiteCreator Overview view, you are presented with the view shown in figure 23.6.

Figure 23.6

The Configure Your Site initial view.

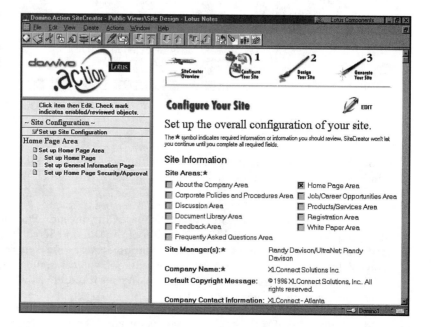

Notice on the left, in the navigator pane, that the SiteCreator assumes that you intend to create a Home Page area. You must specifically choose the other areas in the configuration document on the right. Click the pencil at the top right of the document to place the document in edit mode, and choose the areas you want to include in your Web site. This is one of the first places where it becomes evident how well designed the SiteCreator is. If you have visited many business-oriented Web sites, you have probably noticed some or possibly all the areas available to you here. Here are a few unique features of some of the areas:

◆ The Discussion Area supports threaded, multi-topic, real-time discussions. In real-time discussions, topics and responses are available immediately after they are submitted from the browser. If you attempt to participate in or track a discussion thread in real time you have to hit the Reload button on your browser to refresh the view of the documents; otherwise you don't see new documents until the next time you visit the site.

◆ The Document Library supports both uploading and downloading of files. This is accomplished by attaching files to or detaching files from documents presented to you as Web pages. As of this writing, Netscape is the only browser that supports this feature.

◆ The Feedback area enables you to create a custom questionnaire. Not only can your site users and visitors give you feedback on the site or its content, you can ask them up to five custom questions in either multiple choice or short answer format.

◆ The Product/Services area, just as you would expect, provides you with a place for product marketing information. Additionally, you can create two different kinds of supporting documents, the Product Review and the Product Specs documents. Because these are subordinate documents, they can only be created from a Product Information document. Try that with CGI or Perl.

◆ Finally, the Registration area has several very useful, helpful, and unique features that are available specifically because they are built on the Lotus Notes platform. The Registration area appears later in this chapter in an example, and the unique aspects of this area are covered then.

All other areas of the site are primarily publishing areas that make information available to users, organized in various interest areas and grouped in numerous categories.

Below the Site Areas section of the configuration document are several pieces of information that require input. The requirements for most of these items are self-explanatory.

In the area of the configuration document where you enter the Company Name, Address, etc., make sure you format the information exactly as it appears in the example, placing hard returns in exactly the same places. If any part of your address is longer than the example text, simply continue to type and let the text wrap. Do not add or delete any hard returns from this field. If you do, part of your address may not display on your pages.

Finally, the last items in the configuration section are the Site Images item and the Attach Image button, which are shown in figure 23.7.

Figure 23.7

The bottom half of the site configuration document.

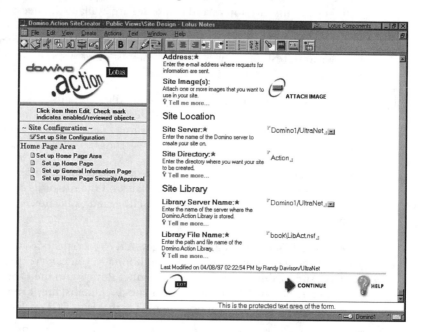

The Attach Image button enables you to add your own graphics to the graphics library in the SiteCreator. Unlike traditional Web sites, where GIF graphics are stored in a subdirectory and are referred to in the HTML code, the Domino.Action Web site stores the graphics as attachments to documents in the Notes database. The graphics are still referenced, but the references are taken care of for you by the SiteCreator. Among other options, Domino.Action enables you to select top-of-page banner graphics for each page. These can be canned graphics supplied with the SiteCreator, or they can be your unique graphics. To add your graphics to the SiteCreator library you need to gather your graphics and then click the Attach Image button and complete a library document for each graphic. You must do this before you generate your site so that the graphics are propagated to every area. If you wait until your site is generated you must add your graphics to each area in which you intend to use them. It's much easier to add each of them here, now.

At the bottom of the library page there is an Attach/Import Image button. This button performs two functions. First, it presents a standard file open dialog box so that you can locate the GIF (or JPEG) file you want to attach. After it performs the attachment, it presents the same file dialog so it can import the same image and display it in the face of the library document. This was confusing to me the first time I did this (without reading the help text) and I skipped the import function thinking the application had a bug in it and simply presented the attach dialog twice. I should have known better. I had to go back and do the import function again so the images were available in the library.

When you complete the Configuration document, click the blue Continue button at the bottom of the document and the SiteCreator automatically moves you to the beginning of the Design section. If you pay attention to the steps, read the instructions in the form, and access the help text under the little light bulbs, it's hard to go wrong.

Design Your Site

The Design Your Site section of the SiteCreator enables you to customize many aspects of each section of your Web site. As noted above, many of the areas have unique capabilities and options while others are fairly simple information publishing areas.

Here you have two primary options: Quick Design and Custom Design.

Quick Design

If you want to get a site up quickly, the SiteCreator provides a Quick Design option that enters the SiteCreator's default settings in each area for you. To create your site, go through the Configure Your Site section normally and choose Quick Design in the Design Your Site section. Even when you choose Quick Design you should still review the Security/Approval documents and the documents marked in the navigator with a star. This may be the best way to start if you have time to experiment. After you generate the site you can compare the site with the configuration settings to more completely understand the relationship between the SiteCreator's settings and the resulting site. Most users prefer to specify the design themselves, however.

Custom Design

Custom Design takes you step by step through each aspect of each area in your site. The example in this chapter has every area in the configuration section selected.

Although it does not detail every aspect of every area, this chapter addresses the features that are common across all areas, and many of the features that are unique to particular areas.

Each area has a Set Up The Area document (see fig. 23.8). For the most part this document simply gives you the option of changing your mind and not creating the area, even thought you specified the area's creation in the configuration process. The nice part of this feature is that you can specify the entire site in configuration and then defer, temporarily or permanently, the creation of specific sections during design. If you change your mind later, you can always generate only the areas you deferred earlier.

Figure 23.8

The first Design Your Site view and Registration Setup.

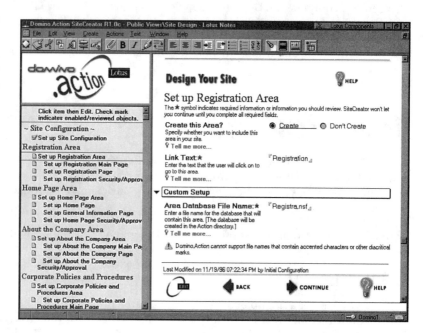

As you can see in figure 23.8, the only real option you have is to create this area or not. You can change the link text but you should not do so, at least not before you create at least one site using the defaults. The Custom Setup section only enables you to override the database file name. As with the link text above, you should accept the default until you have created at least one site using the defaults.

The Registration Section (An Example)

This section does two things. First, it introduces the design aspects that are common across all the areas of your site. Second, it focuses on some specifics of the Registration section because the Registration section has a number of unique aspects.

Each area of your site has at least three things for which you must specify design parameters: the area's Main Page, the area's *Page* (this is explained in a moment), and the area's Security. This structure is consistent for each area except the Discussion area and the Products/Services area. The Discussion area replaces the *Page* with a Main Topic form and adds a Response. The Products/Services area adds a Product Review form and a Product Specs form.

The Registration Area's Main Page

Each area has, at the very least, a Main Page. Figure 23.9 shows the Registration area's Main Page.

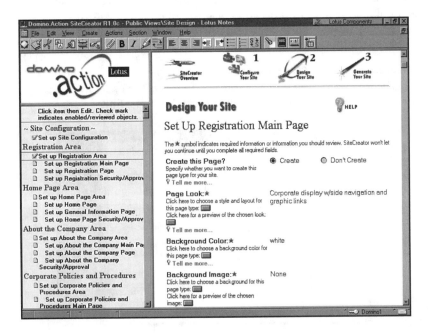

Figure 23.9

The Registration area's Main Page setup document.

The Registration area's Main Page setup document is typical of most area setup documents. You can choose to create the Main Page or not. If you create the Main Page, the Registration link on the Home Page takes you to this page. Navigation to other parts of this area (views, documents, forms) is normally from the Main Page. If you do not create the Main Page, the Registration link on the Home Page takes you to the default view of the area's database and navigation to other parts of this area is from that default view. It is a very good idea to create the Main Page in every area.

Author Note   In every case, when you finish with a page, click the blue Continue arrow at the bottom of the document to save and move to the next step. If you want to stop and continue later, click the blue Continue arrow and then press ESC when the next form opens. This way you are sure your work has been saved.

The Registration Area's Page

Each area has at least one *Page* in addition to the Main Page. Except in the Discussion area and the Product/Services area, it is the *Page* that holds all the formal content for an area. The *Page* actually defines a form that can be used to enter the content in many different categories. For example, the White Papers section *Page* is used to store all white papers, as separate documents. You are given the ability to define multiple categories under which the white papers can be organized.

The Registration Page is the page users and/or visitors use to register on your site. You are, in essence, designing a Notes form. The values you choose affect the appearance and the operation of this form. The setup options for the Registration Page include a Page Look, Background Color, and Background Image. If you choose a background image and a background color, the background color only appears just before the browser loads the background image.

A very unique feature of the SiteCreator is the preview buttons that show you an example of the style that you have chosen. Figure 23.10 shows the example of the Page Look style "Corporate display w/side navigation and graphic links."

Figure 23.10

An example of a Page Look style preview.

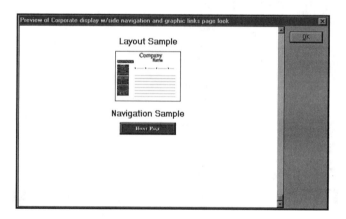

For the purposes of this exercise, choose one of the Background Images for your Main Pages in each area.

 Be careful about selecting a Background Image for content pages in most areas. I'd hate to call it a bug, but the Corporate Side background image, for example, puts a broad black stripe down the left side of the page. In the Discussion area, the black field label text also runs down the left side of the page and is consequently invisible.

Registration Area Specifics

Some of the settings in the Registration area affect the entire site. Figure 23.11 shows the middle section of the Registration Page setup document.

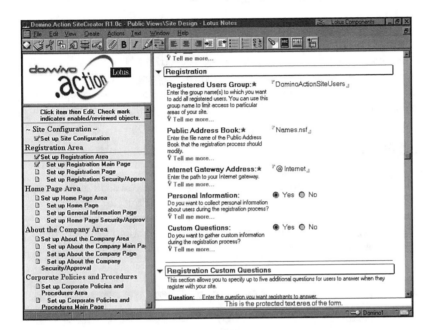

Figure 23.11

The middle section of the Registration Page setup document.

The key part of this section of the Registration Page setup document is the first item, Registered Users Group. This is the group list, in the Public Name & Address Book, to which each registered user is added. You can use this group to limit access to any or virtually all of your sites. If, for example, you add this group to the ACL of each area database except the Home Page and Registration areas, anonymous users can read your home page and access your registration page, but nothing else. Only after they register can they access the remainder of the site. The registration capability provides you with an opportunity to either capture information on each visitor/user and to restrict access to a select group of registered users.

 Several other areas give you the ability to refer to the Registered Users Group, or to create a group that is unique to that area. This gives you additional flexibility in defining access to the various areas of your site.

The Registration area, like several other areas, enables you to build up to five custom questions that are captured at registration time.

In the Custom Question section of the form you can state your question, on the left side, and either create a list of choices for the answer or allow the user free input. To create a list of choices select No for the Allow Other question on this form. Then put a list of choices in the Answers #: field.

> **Warning** Make sure you separate your choices with semicolons. If you separate your choices with commas it is virtually *impossible* to correct. You may not believe this, but in my opinion, it's easier to trash the whole site and the SiteCreator database and start over than it is to correct this mistake. This semicolon requirement holds true in every area that allows you to build choice lists. Be careful.

The Registration Area's Security Setup

In most cases you should allow all users to access your Registration area so they can register and make themselves known to you. Depending on how you structure security in the other areas, registering may give them access to the remainder of the site or just specific areas. This section assumes that you want the Registration area open to the public. Any other areas that you want to have public access should be configured as the Registration area. Figure 23.12 illustrates the Security document of the Registration area.

Figure 23.12

The Registration area's Security document.

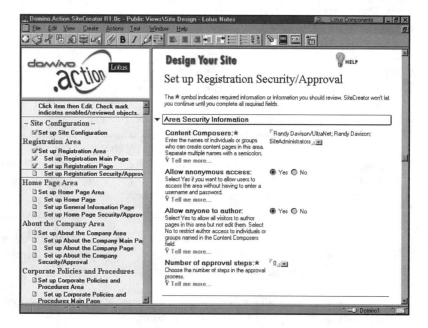

Security is discussed later in this chapter as a separate issue. For now, set up your Registration Security as it is in figure 23.12. This setup does several things. First, it extends the ability to manage the Registration area to the group of people named in the SiteAdministrators group. It also allows anyone to create a Registration document, but restricts read access to the Webmaster and the people named in the SiteAdministrators group. The Yes answers to the Allow anonymous and Allow anyone parameters sets the security to allow anyone to create a registration document. These parameters aren't the only controlling factors. The Registration documents have a readers field that limits access to the submitted registration documents, and the ACL of the Registration area database has a role that limits those who can access the views where the documents are stored.

Finally, the Number of approval steps option enables you to specify that the registration documents must go through a workflow approval process before being approved. If you leave the setting at zero, no workflow is enabled and users are registered in an approved state and can immediately access any parts of the site that are restricted to registered users. If you set this option to one or more, there are two distinct implications. First, users are registered in an unapproved state and do not have access to restricted areas of the site until their registration documents are approved. Second, the registration documents must be reviewed and approved by people in specific roles. After the site is generated, you specify these people as an administrative activity via a browser.

Designing the Remainder of the Site

If you follow the same basic approach in each area as you do in the Registration area, you should do well defining the remainder of your site. There are a few areas that should be mentioned specifically.

Several of the areas have provisions for creating and presenting content, often organized by multiple categories. A simple example is the Home Page area. Figure 23.13 shows the Home Page Security setup document where you can specify Content Composers.

Figure 23.13 shows a new setup option, Content Composers. People named here can create formal content in the Home Page area using the General Information Page that has already been designed. You can see the check mark by the General Information Page in the navigator on the left side of the screen.

As with the Registration page, you can specify approval workflow by putting in a number of approval steps. Use this if you must have one or more individuals approve formal General Information Pages before the pages are made public. Again, you define who the approvers are via a browser after the site is generated. Choosing composers is a common design setting that occurs in every area that holds formal content.

Figure 23.13

The Home Page Security setup document.

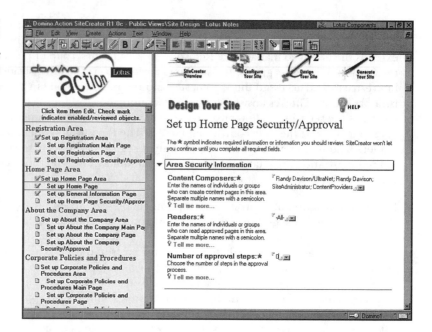

As has been stated before, several of the areas enable you to categorize formal content by multiple categories. The About the Company area is a good example of this feature. Figure 23.14 shows the About the Company design document where you can specify multiple categories.

Figure 23.14

The Content Index section of the About the Company design document.

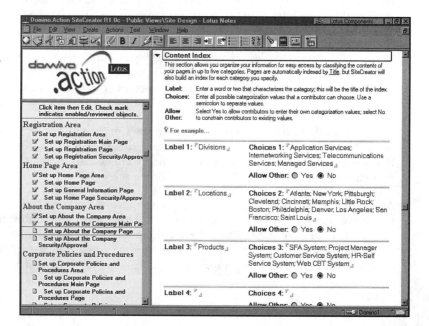

Figure 23.14 shows a portion of the Content Index for the About the Company area of the site. This document illustrates how documents are categorized into three of five possible categories: Divisions, Locations, and Products. By specifying the choices you create a formal limited value list that a content provider uses to further classify documents under the category. The implication is that you have at least one document that describes each Division, Location, and Product. This is equivalent in Notes to a categorized view sorted by choice within category. This is another design feature that is repeated in other areas and that gives you a flexible way to organize formal content.

The Discussion area is quite unique in that it supports multi-topic threaded discussions. The design setup is subtly different than that of most other areas. The Discussion area needs to support a user's ability to create both Main Topic documents and Response documents. Users should also be able to edit and even delete documents they submit to the site. Because the information in the Discussion area is not formal content but informal user-generated content, it should be organized in a simplified categorization structure. Figure 23.15 shows the Discussion area's Content Index section. Keep this simple and don't specify the choices, let your users determine the value for the categories.

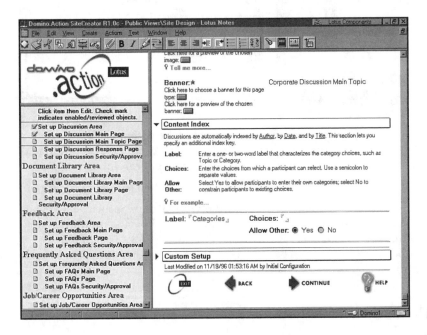

Figure 23.15

The Content Index section of the Main Topic design document.

As you can see in figure 23.15, this section has only one choice for Label and you should not specify a limited set of values. Instead, this area of the site is intended to support whatever topics the users create. Also, the security here should be set a little differently than in any other area. Figure 23.16 illustrates a security setting that allows only registered users to access the Discussion area, but allows all registered users to participate in discussions. Take a close look at the help text, found under the little light bulb at the top of this page. The help text describes six different scenarios for security in the Discussion area.

Figure 23.16

The Security document of the Discussion area.

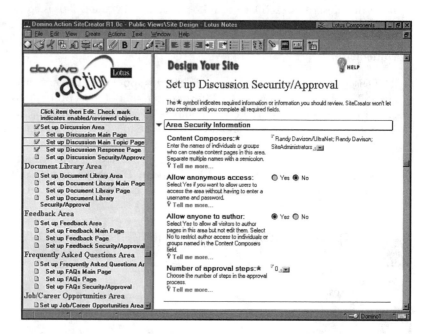

So far, this chapter has presented every unique aspect of the design process in the SiteCreator. You need to use the information above in various places, as appropriate, as you complete the design of your site. Once again, please pay careful attention to the instructions and help text.

As you finish the last setup document (probably the White Papers Security document) and click the blue Continue arrow, the application responds in a non-intuitive manner by putting up a dialog box instructing you to click the #3 – Generate Your Site button at the top of the form. When you click this button you move on to actually generate your site.

Generate Your Site

After you click the Generate Your Site button the application refreshes a large number of documents. This takes five to ten minutes, and then you are presented with the AppAssembler document. At this point you can run the AppAssembler, the task that actually creates the eleven databases of your site, or you can view the process logs or return to the Main Menu so you can review or revise the work you have done so far. So, if you're ready, click the Run button. The process can take as much as an hour, but luckily it does not completely tie up your PC. However, if you are hesitant to challenge your machine with too many concurrent tasks for fear that it will lock up and force you to start over, prepare for a break.

Finish Your Site

After the site generation process ends, you have to "Finish Your Site." The documentation describes this process as one that ensures links are correctly configured, among other things. The operation of this process is transparent to the end user but, unfortunately, ties up your PC for a fairly long time, as much as twenty minutes.

When the "Finish Your Site" process ends, your site is completely generated. Before you try to access your site with a Web browser, however, open the Server document for the server that hosts your site and expand the HTTP section. Figure 23.17 illustrates the HTTP section of the server document.

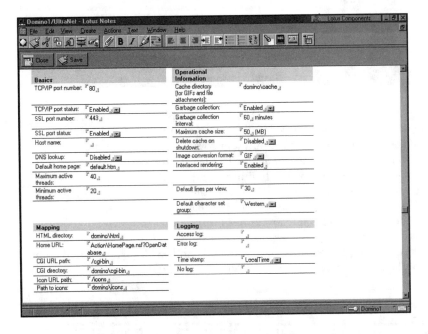

Figure 23.17

The HTTP section of the Server document from the Name & Address Book.

Most of the various settings in this document have been covered elsewhere in the book. Be aware, however, that you need to update the Home URL: field with the correct path and database name that point to your Home Page database. This example generated the site in a subdirectory called Action, and the path is shown in figure 23.17. If your Domino server has both a static IP address and an entry in a

Domain Name Server (DNS), you should be able to access your site by a fairly common URL. Figure 23.18 is the home page in Netscape (note the URL).

Figure 23.18

The home page in Netscape.

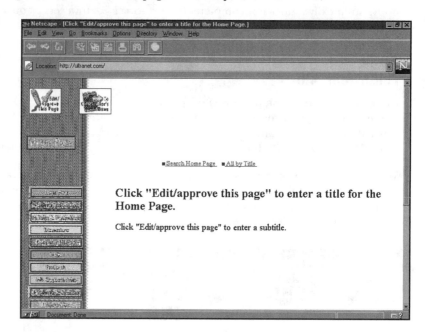

As you can see in figure 23.18, the URL to access this site is http://ultranet.com/ (this URL opens the HomePage database). Figures 23.17 and 23.18 hold everything necessary to make this happen as long as ultranet.com is a valid DNS entry or the workstation has an appropriate entry in a HOSTS file with the correct IP address. It is outside the scope of this section to go into more detail on IP addresses and DNS Names. Because this site is still under construction, the user must log in to access the Home Page. He or she is asked for a user name and password. These values are stored in the Person document in the Name & Address book and should be set up before a user attempts to generate a site. As Webmaster, you should create a person document or make sure you are a registered user in the Name & Address Book. Also, make sure you have an HTTP Password defined in your Person document.

Completing the Configuration via Your Browser

Figure 23.19 shows the home page. It doesn't look very finished, however. Follow directions and click Edit/Approve in the top left to complete this page.

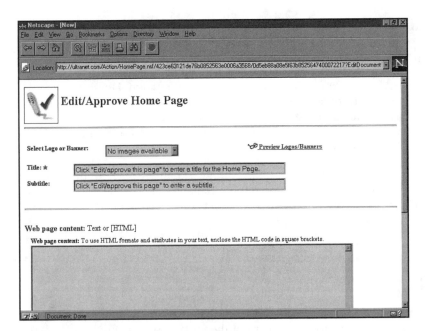

Figure 23.19

*The Home Page
in edit mode via
the browser.*

The resulting home page certainly looks different. Here the user is being asked to provide formal content for the home page and to optionally pick a graphic for a page banner. A page banner cannot be added at this time because no custom banner graphics were added during configuration. There is another way, however.

To add some content, ignore the Logo or Banner choice for now and see what the page looks like when you're done. You can't see it in figure 23.19, but at the bottom of the page there is a radio button toggle to Process or Hold and a Submit button. You can make changes and have them held until you are ready to make them public or process the change right away.

The good news is that you're almost done. The bad news is that you have to perform the Edit/Approve function for every Main Page in each area. Then comes the task of creating the formal content and refining security via the ACL of the various databases if necessary.

Domino.Merchant, Domino.Broadcast, and Domino.Doc

The Domino Dot family has a few other members. Domino.Merchant is a Web-based commerce application built on Domino.Action with the additional features of a shopping basket metaphor and integration with a secure credit card processing service. If you want to sell on the Web and you want to get up and running quickly, Domino.Merchant is your ticket.

Domino.Broadcast is another application built on Domino.Action. However, the Domino.Broadcast applications work in conjunction with the PointCast broadcast server. You configure the PointCast server to dedicate a channel to your Domino.Broadcast application and you can push information to users on your intranet via the PointCast client.

Last but not least is the newest member of the family, Domino.Doc. As of the date of publication for this book, no information was yet available. Try the following URL for "Domino Dot" product information: `http://www.net.lotus.com/action4/homepage?OpenDatabase`.

Summary

The main purpose of this chapter is to demonstrate the power of Domino.Action. The chapter covered all the basics and many of the special aspects of the Domino.Action site creation process. The best thing you can do now is to experiment. If you do not have the latest version of Domino.Action, get it from the URL in the "Getting Started with Domino.Action" section. Build site after site. Try all the different options. Test the security. Really kick the tires and give Domino.Action a good test drive. You will be suitably impressed.

CHAPTER 24

Security and Reporting

Security is one of the topics at the forefront of discussion regarding the Web today. Most Web clients at one time or another wonder whether they can trust that their confidential information will remain confidential and out of the hands of nefarious individuals. Security is a critical issue that must be dealt with head-on. It is not, however, the sole subject of this chapter. In fact, as of this writing, relatively few measures ensure Internet traffic safety enroute to the server.

This chapter mentions the steps to ensure safe enroute passage, but focuses specifically on general considerations for securing any server resource and, specifically, a Domino Web site. For Domino server, this chapter addresses the several steps necessary to assure your Web clients that their information is safe when in your Notes object store.

Reporting is discussed relative to the security and performance of the Domino Web server. Under Notes, reporting is done through the use of views. This is true in the case of reporting Domino statistics with a couple of exceptions: textual reports and console reporting. These two topics are discussed later in this chapter. This discussion explains how to determine who is accessing your server, what they do while on your server, and notification techniques.

Security requirements can largely be determined by the answer to one question, "How paranoid are you about your data?" The answer will help determine the degree of security measures taken to protect your server and the data stored on it and the budget required to implement and maintain the measures.

This chapter approaches security from a "macro" to "micro" level, which is the generally accepted method for determining the appropriate security measures required for any system. Domino administration is no different in this respect. Stated another way, the chapter begins at the 50,000 foot level and works down to ground level in the following areas:

◆ **Threat assessment** - what a threat is and considerations for identifying threats to your Domino installation

◆ **Physical security** - who can "touch" your Domino server and how difficult is it to gain access to the server

◆ **Administrative security** - who takes care of the day-to-day Domino system administration and how safe is your system from them

◆ **Server access** - who is connected to the other end of your wire and how do you protect your Domino server against unauthorized access

◆ **Data access** - once access is gained to the Domino server, how is data access protected

◆ **Reporting** - displaying who is accessing your Domino server and how the server reports its configuration and operating statistics

When all is said and done, your Domino server is like any other "box" on your network that deserves protecting. The following discussion serves as a guide to help you with setting security requirements not only for your Domino server but for any server. Any Domino administrator can set up a server and give Web clients access. In fact, most can give Web clients access to too much of the server. In order to plan an effective and secure Domino server, the topics in this chapter are essential to planning that secure installation.

Threat Assessment

At the risk of sounding too militaristic, a "threat" to data security can be defined as any situation or entity that represents the potential to place at risk the continued operation or integrity of your server or its contents. To understand and prepare to address (that is, counter) a threat, one must analyze the threat and its capacity for inflicting damage. This is the heart of threat assessment.

Threat assessment is the first critical step in planning for data security. Without a firm grasp of the threat, resources may be applied in the wrong area, leaving a system wide open in other areas. Alternatively (and just as dangerous), the threat will not be taken seriously by some, and the consequence will be the same.

Most system architects focus on threats from outside their organization, and neglect to consider very real internal threats. This oversight can lead to significant gaps in security. Internal threats often pose a greater risk than external threats, because most internal threats have far more privileges and capabilities than external ones.

Before deciding the requirements for system security, conduct a threat assessment. By first determining who or what the threat is, you can validate requirements for the necessary resources to address the threat. Avoid just implementing a solution that you may have seen at another company or on another job. The solution may not be appropriate for the threat you currently face.

When identifying threats, consider the following:

◆ **What are the threats to my system?** Internal threats, for example, may come from disgruntled employees, terminated employees, custodial staff (unplugging a server), administrative staff, unwitting (or untrained) system administrators, and so on. External threats may originate with competitors or, simply, "hackers." Although not specifically security threats, sources such as fire, theft, and hardware failure (disk crashes) must also be considered.

◆ **What is the potential damage the threat and its realization could cause in terms of either money, time, or both (in general terms— cost)?** What is the cost to recover an entire system (and its data), for example, if it is stolen? What about the recovery cost from malicious data corruption, deletion, theft, and so on. Or, worse yet, what is the potential cost of losing your corporate data to an unscrupulous competitor.

◆ **What is the probability that the threat either currently exists or could exist?** If you are an employer, for example, you already have most of the previously mentioned threats. If you are a service provider, the threat that an external entity may attempt to gain unauthorized access to your system should be considered.

◆ **What type of data requires protection?** Are you making proprietary and/or business confidential information available over the Web? If so, the threat may be a competitor. Are you gathering sensitive client information (for example, social security numbers, credit card numbers, and so forth)? If so, your company's integrity is at risk if a breach occurs. Your company's integrity is well worth protecting, isn't it?

◆ **Does a generally accepted method for countering the threat exist?**
If so, is the cost of implementing the countermeasure justified based on the cost of the potential damage as previously determined. You must measure the cost of implementing the countermeasure in both cost of acquisition and recurring costs (administration, upgrades, and so on).

The assessment should produce a prioritized list of each threat based on the source, estimated recovery costs, probability the threat will be encountered, value of the data, and the cost to implement countermeasures. In this manner, one can determine the most appropriate area in which to concentrate resources to counter the threat.

In some cases, a countermeasure may be nothing more than a formalized set of policies and procedures that govern your day-to-day operations. Do you have procedures in place, for example, that call for human resources to provide the names of employees who resign or are terminated to the network or Domino administrator? If not, you have the potential for a real threat. Who in your organization establishes the level of access an employee is granted? Who approves that level? These examples point out that most organizations need to first look within to find the high-probability threats and, quite possibly, the lowest-cost countermeasures.

Take, for example, the case where an employee resigns or, worse, is fired. Typically, the employee's manager and the human resources manager are the only two who know of the situation. With a lot of organizations, the last person to know of the employee's departure is the network or, in this case, the Domino administrator. For the period of time between the employee leaving and his or her server access being terminated, a potential security threat exists, especially if the employee leaves on less than amicable terms. This threat is easily countered with policies and procedures to be followed when an employee is terminated. The countermeasure (a P&P document) does not cost a lot but can potentially save the cost of restoring your system to service if the employee takes action against it before his/her access is terminated.

In some cases, the countermeasure may involve the purchase of specialized hardware (a firewall, for example) or physical security to protect your network servers. In the case of a Domino Web server, this will help protect against users who can remain largely anonymous.

Physical Security

The most overlooked but common threat to any data installation is the area of physical security. Obviously, the essence of physical security is to determine "who" is allowed physical access to the server. This should not be too hard to understand, but—amazingly—I have been in companies where Domino servers are placed in the most accessible areas in the office (under the system administrator's desk, for example), with no access controls whatsoever. The most basic level of providing a secure Domino server environment is limiting "who" has access to the server.

Many offices have servers installed in cubicles with "wide open" access to anyone walking past. Theft (of the entire system or just its components) is the most probable risk of poor physical security, but malicious physical access presents other potential risks as well (virus attacks, disk reformatting, vandalism, and so on). Unauthorized users could stop by after hours and upload Notes databases that are not approved onto the Domino server.

Do not overlook this common threat when planning your Domino server environment. Because Domino runs on a multitude of operating systems, some of which are "desktop" operating systems, resist the temptation to place production servers in the general employee population.

 For some installations, finding a lockable closet to limit access to servers is the quickest solution to physical security. Of course, a locked closet does not always prove to be the best solution; environmental conditions (such as air conditioning, humidity, power, and so forth) in the secure area may not be adequate to support server "life!"

Administrative Security

Perhaps the second most overlooked security threat resides in the administrative access to the server. You should limit administrative access to those few "need to know" individuals. Not to say that administrators should not be trusted, but...

Most administrative security breaches occur because of two common mistakes: providing administrative passwords to a large number of individuals, or using common administrative passwords (admin, password, and so forth).

If administrative passwords are distributed to a large number of people, the task of preserving administrative standards becomes increasingly difficult. New users or unauthorized users could potentially be added to the system when control is spread across many users.

Common passwords are easily guessed and represent another potential area of compromise.

Most administrative passwords have privileges with wide-ranging authority. That authority can be exercised over users, can be used to access data, and (in some cases) can enable the administrator to masquerade as other users. In other words, too much power can potentially reside in the hands of a single individual. Potentially, the Domino administrator could grant himself access to individual's mail files or Notes databases with sensitive information, or maliciously restrict access to databases.

Most people have either read books or seen movies that portray the launch of nuclear weapons and the safeguards and authentication procedures required before a launch. The scenario is always the same: The weapon cannot be launched unless both launch control officers enter and turn their respective keys at the same time. And, as usual, the key switches are far enough apart on the console to prevent a single person from obtaining both keys (usually by force) and turning them simultaneously, and thereby effecting the unauthorized launch of a nuclear warhead.

Although not as fatalistic as nuclear weapons, Lotus has designed Notes/Domino to provide a similar capability if you are at all concerned about too much power residing in the hands of a single administrator. Notes administrative access can be controlled by implementing a "two person rule" similar to that used by the military. This method provides a means whereby administrative access can be controlled by requiring multiple passwords on all administrative ID files. The multiple passwords are not known to a single individual, but are distributed to several with administrator access. This way, no single administrator can make unauthorized system changes without at least one other administrator knowingly giving access.

Author Note   All of this can, of course, give way to Notes administrator conspiracy theories and other paranoid schizophrenic symptoms. Since the author is not skilled in the area of psychology, it is probably best not to get too deep into this! As the first part of this chapter explained, the real question is, "How paranoid are you?"

Actually, any Notes ID file can be required to have multiple passwords entered to gain access. Practically speaking, however, they are intended for administrative access. In case you want to consider this as a means of countering an administrative threat, you must set up the ID file for multiple passwords. To do this, follow these steps:

1. Enter the Administration panel by choosing File, Tools, Server Administration.

2. Select the Certifiers button.

3. Select Edit, Multiple Passwords.

4. Select the ID file on which you wish to require multiple passwords. A prompt requests the password of the ID file you select.

5. Select how many passwords are required to access the ID file. Although you may list up to five users, you may require as few as two to provide passwords.

6. Enter the users' name(s) and their password(s) to add to the ID file. You must confirm the password before adding the user to the list.

Remember, these passwords are defined and contained in the ID file that you selected in step 4. They are not the passwords from the users' ID files. Do not forget them!

After this is complete, whenever an attempt is made to access a database (for example, the Public Name & Address Book) to perform administrative functions, a prompt box similar to that shown in figure 24.1 appears.

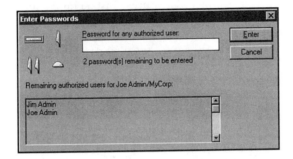

Figure 24.1

Multiple passwords dialog box.

Administrative access in a Notes environment is a critical element when considering the threat against your system. Do not leave the door "wide open."

Server Access

The next area of concern receives the most consideration: access to the server. Accessing any server is, inherently, physical in nature in that a network connection must somehow be made available to the threat. Whether this connection is made through an Internet Service Provider (ISP) to a router to another ISP and then, finally, the router on the network that the Domino server is attached to, or through a network connection at a desktop, a physical connection path must be established.

Several means enable you to prevent unauthorized access to your physical network. If you want to have a presence on the Web, however, none are really practical because the Web, by nature, is "open." You must, therefore, consider some of the drawbacks to implementing server access restrictions.

First, you can certainly ensure that no external access into your network exists by not allowing dial-up or other routed connections (Internet access via ISDN or T1, for example). If you have remote users, this is probably not a good solution and will not work. In today's work environment, remote users are almost a given. In addition, some sort of connection must be made to the Internet if you are hosting a Web site.

If you do provide dial-up access, you face the risk of having your authorized remote users hand out their passwords to relatives or friends. If a remote user loses his remote workstation or laptop through theft or other means, your system incurs risk because his password and the phone number of your system is on the hard drive. If his wallet or briefcase is stolen with phone numbers and passwords, your system faces the risk of unauthorized access.

Because access to the network where the Domino server resides must inevitably be provided in support of a Web environment, measures must be implemented in order to exclude or control access. The following are the four most common methods for controlling access to Domino servers in a Web environment:

◆ Firewalls and proxies

◆ Authentication

◆ Secure Socket Layer (SSL) transmissions

◆ Directory browsing

Firewalls and Proxies

A firewall acts as a "filter" between the Domino server and the Internet. Firewalls are used to establish what is often referred to as a "demilitarized zone" (DMZ) between the internal network and the Internet. Figure 24.2 shows a typical setup.

Figure 24.2

Common firewall configuration.

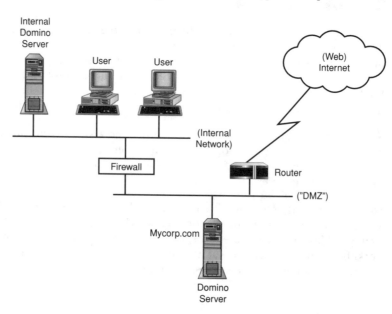

The DMZ is usually a separate LAN segment that contains any traffic received from the Web within its segment. The firewall prevents any Web traffic from entering the internal network.

A firewall may also provide proxy services that enable internal Web clients to access the Web without directly connecting to it. The proxy service retrieves the requested URL and provides the returned pages back to the internal client.

In a typical Domino server setup, the firewall configuration allows Notes traffic (NRPC) between the internal Domino server and the server in the DMZ. The content of the mycorp.com Web site, for example, may be authored on the internal Domino server and replicated out to the DMZ Domino server for Web access.

If a proxy is set up in addition to the firewall, both must be configured to allow Domino to "talk" on the designated IP port 1352. This port is used by Notes-specific traffic, which includes replication. Hence to replicate between an external Domino server and its internal content "source," the firewall must allow traffic on this port. To further tighten security, most firewalls can be configured to allow point-to-point traffic only. The specific IP address of the internal Domino server, therefore, is the only address allowed to "speak" through the firewall to the IP address of the external Domino server.

If internal Notes clients are to be allowed access to the external server, additional ports must be enabled on the firewall, because the Domino server uses port 1024 and higher for Notes client traffic.

In lieu of investing in firewalls and additional network hardware, some companies may implement a "poor man's" firewall. Such a configuration allows the company to set up a completely separate segment for incoming Internet traffic by using modems for communication between the two Domino servers. Figure 24.3 shows this configuration.

Firewalls and proxies provide a buffer level between the Web client and your server. Because the end goal is to allow access to your server, however, one must assume that the Domino server providing Web pages is where this access stops. Consider using a firewall/proxy combination in the following circumstances:

◆ Internal network resources need to be protected.

◆ Server access needs to be controlled.

◆ Internal client access to outside world needs to be controlled.

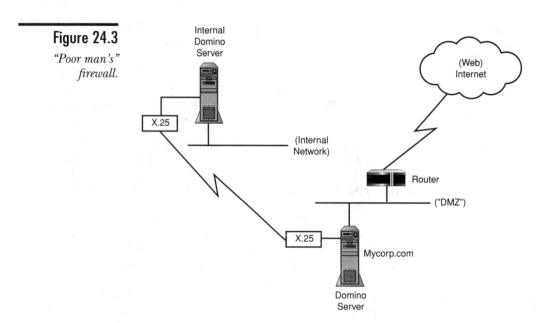

Figure 24.3

*"Poor man's"
firewall.*

Authentication

After physical access to the server is established, the objective becomes to allow only authorized Web users access to the resources on the server. Determining who is allowed or disallowed access is accomplished via authentication.

Authentication of Web clients is a relatively simple process that involves asking the user to provide certain information known to both the client and server. If the information provided by the client can be verified by the server, access is granted. (Hopefully, the information is *only* known to the client and server; otherwise, you have the threat of unknown persons masquerading as authorized users.)

Domino authentication works by prompting the Web client for a user ID and password. Once provided, Domino checks the information against the user's Person document to see whether the name matches the contents of the Full User Name field and the HTTP Password field.

Remember that Domino does *not* check passwords against those in the user's Notes ID file. Domino Web authentication is not nearly as sophisticated as true Notes authentication, but it is no less secure than that provided by any other HTTP server.

It is recommended that Web clients and Notes clients be kept in separate address books. This separation provides a cleaner administrative interface for the Domino administrator. MyCorp's Notes clients are all contained in the standard public address book called names.nsf, for example, but all Web clients who are registered users are contained in a separate address book called webnames.nsf. The address books are cascaded in the Notes.ini file.

Under this dual address book setup, any group names used in ACLs are kept in the Public Name & Address Book (names.nsf). Member names contained within the group can be in either address book. If you are providing an automated registration process for your Web clients, this allows them to access their "person" information in a separate database altogether, providing yet another level of protection.

The traditional methods for denying access provided in the Server document (Access server field, Not access server, and so on) apply only to Notes clients, and are based on the fact that full authentication takes place with the Notes client. Attempting to use these settings for Web client access will have no effect. You must, therefore, use the fields specific to Web clients in the Server document (Allow Anonymous HTTP connections, and so forth) for restrictions on Web clients.

SSL

Once authenticated with the server, the user may desire to pass information in a secure manner. Traffic between a Notes client and Domino server may be encrypted over the wire by specifying that all network traffic be encrypted. In a Web environment, however, a Secure Socket Layer (SSL) transmission must be established.

To establish an SSL session, the Web client must indicate that he desires to set up the SSL session by sending the URL with an HTTPS directive. HTTPS sets up an encrypted communication session through the use of public or private keys.

If a server uses private keys, the Web client must accept the key from the server to encrypt the transmission to be sent to the server. If the server uses public keys from a commercial Certificate Authority (CA), and the Web client has requested a certificate from the CA, the two share a common certificate and can establish secure communications.

Presently, SSL represents the height of Internet traffic security. With the advent of more advanced technology (such as SSL Version 3 and IBM's Cryptolope technology), authentication and communications will become more secure on the Web. It is interesting to note, however, that the direction of increasing security on the Web is ground covered years ago by Notes and Domino.

Directory Browsing

After a Web client is authenticated, the Domino server, by default, serves up an HTML page that contains the equivalent of "File, Database, Open." Figure 24.4 shows this screen.

Figure 24.4

Default Domino "Open" screen.

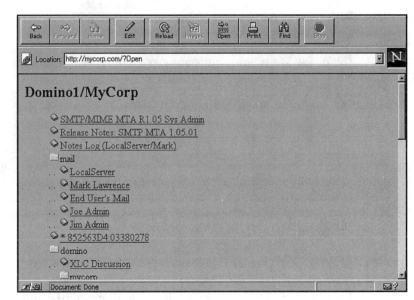

Figure 24.4

Default Domino "Open" screen.

This is not exactly what Web clients are used to unless they hit ftp sites very often.

Recall from Chapter 21, "Installing and Setting Up Domino," that Domino controls what Web clients see when they "hit" the site by the HTTP server section in the Server document from the Public Name & Address Book. In figure 24.4, the "Home URL" field states "?Open," indicating that the Domino server should open with a list of all the databases it contains whose property "Show in 'Open Database' dialog" is enabled.

Even if a value (mycorp.nsf?Open, for example) is entered in the Home URL field, a Web client can still cause the entire list of databases to appear by typing **?Open** with no database specified (for example, `http://mycorp.com?Open`).

To guard against a Web client being able to generate a list of all databases contained on your Domino server, the Security section of the Server document comes into the picture. Within this section, the Domino administrator can disallow any Web client from browsing databases. Figure 24.5 shows this setting in the Security section.

With the Allow HTTP clients to browse databases option set to Yes, Web clients can generate the ?Open URL and at least "see" all databases contained on the Domino server. With this set to No, the Web client receives an error message (`Error 403 HTTP Web Server: Database Browsing Not Allowed`) and cannot browse the list of databases contained on the Domino server.

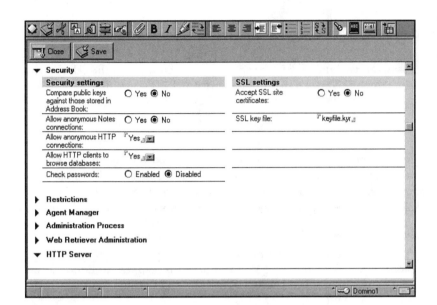

Figure 24.5

Security section of Server document.

| **Note** | This does not mean that they can gain access to the database. It just means they can see the databases on the server. If you host Notes databases for several clients, you probably will not want your competition seeing with whom you are doing business. Hence, this setting becomes important when determining what Web clients see about your server. |

The Allow anonymous HTTP connections setting provides the Domino administrator the ability to globally turn off anonymous access. Whenever any Web clients "hit" your site, they are initially anonymous until challenged for an ID and password, as discussed in the "Data Access" section later in the chapter.

Other settings in the Security section do not apply to Web clients and have no effect on the Domino HTTP Server (for example, Check passwords, Accept SSL site certificates, Compare public keys, and Anonymous Notes connections).

| **Note** | Remember, if you change any of the settings in the Server document governing the behavior of the HTTP server, you must "bounce" the HTTP Web server process but not the entire Domino server. |

Once the user has gained access to the server and been authorized access, the next decision to be made by the Domino administrator is what data on the server should be available to the user. The next section deals with data access and controlling where the Web client can go on your Domino server (that is, what databases are available to them and what data within the database is visible).

Data Access

After authentication and a database are chosen or presented through the "Home URL" setting, the standard Notes Access Control List (ACL) takes control. The ACL determines who can access the database and what they can do within a particular database.

 So that there are no misgivings about ACLs, it must be pointed out that they are not invincible in the fight against security threats. ACLs, for instance, do not protect against someone with physical access. They cannot provide protection against "administrators gone bad" and they do not protect against "sniffing" on the wire.

The specific relation of the ACL to the Web client is through the lower access levels of the ACL up to editor. Because there is no URL syntax for providing access to design features or the ACL, Designer and Manager access is "capped" at Editor access for a Web client. The two most critical access rights affecting the Domino Web client's access to databases are default and anonymous.

Default Access

Default access is the most basic access level for any database. Any client (Notes or Web) receives whatever access level is specified as the Default access level. If a Web client "hits" a database where default access is read-only, that is all he will be able to do. Read-only is the typical setting for a site that provides material for browsing but solicits no responses from the Web client.

The standard access rules apply to the Default category. If Default access is set to Author, for example, a Web client may create documents but cannot edit them unless his name is included in an author name field. In this case, the name Anonymous would have to appear in the Author name field.

If, on the other hand, default access were set to Editor, all editor rights would be assigned to any Web client "hitting" the database.

The following key points should be remembered when considering security on data access:

◆ Default access sets the access level for all users unless modified by the special ACL entry of Anonymous.

◆ Any new databases created on the Domino server are created with Default access set to Designer. This setting could be dangerous if you are hosting a Web site with Domino and do not wish the database to be immediately available to Web clients. You must remember to change this in the ACL.

◆ Even though database browsing may be turned off, a Web client can make "stabs" at NSF file names in an attempt to open a database in which you may not want him. Hence, because any database can be accessed by a "Notes savvy" Web client, you must take proactive measures to ensure that *all* databases on your server are there for a purpose and have the appropriate access levels set in the ACL.

Anonymous Access

Anonymous access is a refinement of Default access and, when entered as a name in the ACL, allows any Web client access to the database at the level specified for Anonymous. Think of Anonymous as a user's name in the ACL, except that Anonymous is not defined through a person document in any NAB—instead, it is a special ACL entity.

If Default access is set to reader, for example, but an entry appears in the ACL for Anonymous and is set to No Access, any Web client will be challenged before even read access is allowed. This setting proves useful if you want to force the Web client to authenticate with the server to just read a database.

Other methods enable you to force logging of the user ID. The most common method is to force the user to log on by generating a URL with the argument "&Login" appended at the end of the URL. This forces the user ID and password dialog box.

Consideration of each of the foregoing topics is essential in establishing a secure Domino Web server site. A sound security strategy can help ensure the smooth operation and availability of your site. Once a Domino site has been installed based on a sound security strategy developed from the "top down," however, it is important to keep track of who is accessing your Domino server and the server "health." This is done through the reporting mechanisms provided in the Domino server.

Reporting

Reporting Web client activity is rather straightforward and, to a degree, limited. The reporting is straightforward because the Domino server provides straight text reports or a Notes database report. And, because these are the only two options for reporting, it is somewhat limited in the regard that there are no graphical reports or tools available natively for statistical reporting.

The tool provided to report on Domino server activity is through the server console. Again, this is somewhat limiting because the console interface is strictly textual in nature.

Even with the limitation of these reporting tools, it is essential that the Domino administrator use them regularly to see who is entering his Web site, what they are doing (or attempting to do), and the condition (health) of the server. The Domino server console helps in determining the condition of the Web server process. The Domino log files help to capture who is accessing the server and what they are doing.

Domino Server Console

The server console can be used to show specific aspects of how the Domino server is performing. Although this is somewhat limiting, if you know the parameter you are interested in, the server console is about the only way of pulling it from the HTTP Web server process.

The Domino server console command "show status domino" generates a listing of all the parameters tracked by the Domino HTTP Web server process and their associated statistics. The more pertinent statistics display how many times a particular URL command has been received (such as CreateDocument, OpenAbout, and so on).

In addition, the current operating configuration of the HTTP Web server process displays. These options include the maximum and minimum active threads, cache settings (for example, delete, directory, maximum size), CGI/HTML/Icons directory settings, DNSLookup, and so forth.

To show a specific statistic or configuration option, the specific options can be entered at the server console as follows:

```
show status domino.<option list>
```

The full option list is shown in Appendix B, "Domino HTTP Web Server Console Options."

Domino Log File

Chapter 21 discussed how to set up the Domino log file (domcfg.nsf). Figure 24.6 shows the main view of the log file, and figure 24.7 shows an individual document.

This view can be modified or additional views added to sort and report on any parameter captured in the document. If you enable DNS lookups, for example, a useful view might be sorted and categorized by the user address to show the domains of any clients hitting your site.

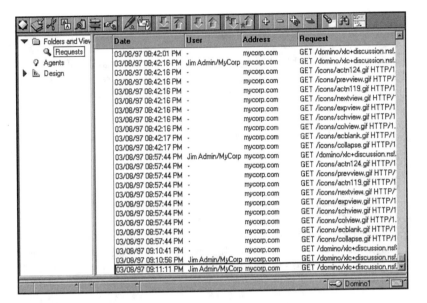

Figure 24.6

Domino log file view.

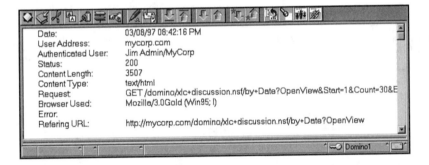

Figure 24.7

Domino log file document.

Keep in mind a couple items when looking at the contents of the log file:

◆ If DNS lookups are turned off in the server document, the IP address of the Web client is recorded rather than the domain name as shown in the preceding figures.

◆ A single document should not be counted as a traditional "hit" in the true sense of the term. As a Web client requests a document, an individual request is logged for each inline image that may be contained within the requested document, view, navigator, or About document. Hence, this is not a true representation of how many "hits" your server is handling. It is an accurate representation of how many URL requests are being handled.

◆ If the user has been authenticated, his name will appear; otherwise, the field will be blank.

◆ The same information available through the Domino log file is available through text logging as well. Text logging is slightly faster, but reporting is more difficult because the logs span several files. Additionally, separate log files are generated for each day, making roll-up reports even more difficult.

Summary

One of the Domino Web server commercials produced by Lotus for use in advertising the Domino server shows Jack Webb (no pun), the Dragnet detective talking with Dennis Leary. Jack and Dennis point out that there are a lot of "bad" people out there on the Web. Although the majority of Web clients are not "bad" people, there are sufficient numbers of them that security must be an integral part of planning and supporting a Domino Web site.

The topics covered in this chapter will help the Domino administrator form the basis of a sound security strategy from the "top" (threat assessment) to "bottom" (data access). It is advisable that a strategy be in place before embarking on the installation of your Domino server for use as a Web server. Once your site is established, the reporting tools offered within the Domino server can keep the administrator "up" on the activity being seen by the Web server and its general health.

PART VIII

Appendixes

Comparing Domino to Other Intranet Technologies

With the introduction of Lotus Notes 4.5, the Notes server product enters a new market: the Internet server market. And although there are not hundreds of competitors, the competitors that have Web server products are the major players on the market—Microsoft and Netscape. Another competitor making a name for itself in the Web market is Novell. This appendix will attempt to list the products that make up the Internet server offering from Lotus, Microsoft, and Netscape. For comparison, the criteria used by Lotus for its Internet server comparisons will be the building block for this appendix. Companies considering implementing Web technologies (and also currently using Notes) must ask themselves an obviously important question: How does the Domino product "stack up" against the competitors?

From a marketing standpoint, the Domino product has a pre-existing market base—current Notes customers. Any server upgraded to Domino 4.5 has the Web server capabilities built in and easily enabled. For those companies also considering using Internet technologies, Domino is an obvious choice.

The Microsoft Internet Information Server (IIS) also has a pre-existing market base—Windows NT Server clients. Because of Microsoft's behemoth marketing machine, IIS looms as the major competitor of Domino 4.5.

The Netscape product is holding its ground against IIS primarily because of the respect in the market for the Netscape product set and company. Depending on whose literature is read, either IIS or the Netscape Web Server is the leading Web server on the market.

This chapter compares the latest release of the Domino HTTP server to both IIS from Microsoft and the Netscape server. One important point to remember is that the Domino server is much more than a simple HTTP server. It introduces the concept that is *the* future of the computer market: Internet technologies (Web servers, browsers, and so forth) for groupware processing. *None* of the other products currently on the market support this groupware concept. Whereas both Microsoft and Netscape are attempting to "shoehorn" groupware capabilities into their Web servers, the Notes product is mature (with years of refinements behind it) and has a large customer base—a big difference, and a major advantage when comparing Domino to IIS or the Netscape server.

The Domino Server

Domino's history can be traced back to its Web Publisher product. That product was used to publish existing Notes databases onto the World Wide Web for Web (browser-based) clients. The product consisted of the following two executables:

- **WebPub.** Converted the databases defined in the Web Publisher Configuration database into HTML files

- **Inotes.** (an option) Handled interaction with Notes databases (such as composing documents) from the Web clients

The Web Publisher product worked well, but needed a separate Web server product to actually post the HTML files to the Web. Because of that, a lot of companies had to implement and learn a separate product such as Microsoft's IIS.

The Domino 1.0 release (and many, many beta releases) replaced the Web Publisher with a product that handled all the services of Web Publisher with an added HTTP server. The Notes databases were no longer converted to HTML format. The Domino product translates Notes elements (documents, forms, views, and so on) directly as they are requested by the Web client. The Domino product also handled all interaction with the Web client, including security based on the ACL and other security levels. This product was an "add-on" for the existing Notes 4.1 server. Domino server 4.5 includes the HTTP executable (release 1.5) and all Web-related enhancements, including the needed changes in the Public Address Book.

The Microsoft Internet Information Server

The Microsoft Internet Information Server version 3 is the current release of the IIS product. IIS includes a Web server, application development environment, full-text search capabilities (using the additional Index Server), multimedia streaming (using the NetShow product), and site management extensions.

The IIS server is combined with Microsoft's Exchange Server version 5 to incorporate some of the groupware concept. Exchange, an upgrade for the Microsoft Mail product, is Microsoft's attempt to pick up some of the groupware market owned by Lotus. Version 5 is much closer to introducing true groupware from Microsoft.

The next two sections describe products that are commonly used as a part of the available Microsoft Internet product set. The inclusion of Microsoft Exchange is used to bring the product set more inline with the Lotus Domino product by offering some programmability and e-mail.

Microsoft Exchange

Microsoft Exchange supports most of the current Internet standards, including SMTP, POP3, NNTP, HTTP, HTML, and SSL. Exchange also supports messaging standards such as MAPI, X.400, and X.500. When one considers the existing Microsoft Mail market and the companies using Windows NT servers to implement e-mail, it is safe to say that Exchange is used in a growing market. Exchange is used for the following purposes:

◆ To communicate with users nationwide or worldwide who are using Exchange mail, Microsoft Mail, Internet mail, or faxes

◆ To collaborate with groups created via the Exchange security for discussion-type interaction or bulletin boards

◆ To work with users on other systems by using the built-in functionality of the Exchange gateways, including the Internet gateway, the X.400 gateway, and others

◆ To participate with Internet news groups using Exchange as an interface, Microsoft Outlook, a Web browser, or an Internet news reader

◆ To use a variety of client software, including Outlook, standard Web browsers, Internet Mail (POP3) or News readers (NNTP), and LDAP clients

OutLook 97

Outlook 97 is a personal information manager. Outlook 97 is a product that can be integrated with Microsoft Exchange to include calendaring and scheduling capabilities.

Microsoft's Outlook 97 is a new Microsoft Office application that includes Microsoft Mail, Microsoft Exchange, and the Microsoft Schedule+ products in a common interface. Outlook 97, interacting with Exchange, can be used to send and receive e-mail, work with Web pages, and interact with other users for group discussions and information sharing.

The Netscape Enterprise Server 2.0

Netscape Enterprise Server is Netscape's high-end HTTP server product. Enterprise Server emphasizes security and support of standard Internet protocols, applications, and interfaces. It is an open platform for developing interactive Web applications based on Java and the JavaScript programming languages. This server also includes full-text and database search capabilities, management and control features, and tools for maintaining rich data.

SuiteSpot 3.0

SuiteSpot from Netscape is an integrated client/server set of products with electronic mail, groupware interactions, and document publishing capabilities. The SuiteSpot is being marketed for the blossoming intranet market. SuiteSpot is an integrated suite of ten products, including the following:

- ◆ Netscape Messaging Server 3.0

- ◆ Netscape Collabra Server 3.0

- ◆ Netscape Enterprise Server 3.0

- ◆ Netscape Proxy Server 2.5

- ◆ Netscape Calendar Server 1.0

- ◆ Netscape Media Server 1.0

- ◆ Netscape Directory Server 1.0

◆ Netscape Certificate Server 1.0

◆ Netscape Catalog Server 1.0

◆ LiveWire Pro 1.0

For the users interacting with SuiteSpot, Netscape has introduced the Netscape Communicator Professional Edition. This suite is a set of client software, including the following:

◆ Netscape Navigator 4.0

◆ Netscape Calendar

◆ Netscape Composer

◆ Netscape Messenger

◆ Netscape Collabra

◆ Netscape Conference

◆ Netscape AutoAdmin

◆ Netscape IBM Host-On-Demand

The General Comparison

When comparing products from Microsoft and Netscape to Domino, all three product suites appear to have similar attributes, including e-mail, intranet tools, and security and data sharing capabilities. It should also be clear that Domino is a single server product, however, that handles all the different aspects of groupware on the Internet. Microsoft is proud of the fact that Exchange is easier to manage than Notes for adding and maintaining e-mail clients. To use Exchange to add a powerful groupware, scheduling, and Web server system, however, requires the addition of several other products (including IIS and Schedule+ or Outlook). The Netscape SuiteSpot product set includes a strong Web server with a discussion product (developed by another vendor), and several other applications to "pull-off" the groupware concept (10 products in all). That is not to say that the Microsoft or Netscape products are poor—far from it—but if a company wants to implement in-house or customer support by using Internet technologies and needs groupware functionality, Domino is this author's recommendation.

The Features Breakdown

In this section, various features are used to compare the different product suites. The information about how the different products implement those features is from the product developers, and is subject to change.

When reading this section, keep in mind that Domino is a product that includes an Internet server, e-mail, and a programmable object store (simply put, databases that can be "coded"). To try and even the playing field in this appendix, other products have been included from Microsoft and Netscape that offer the same or similar functionality. This appendix is in no way a full list of all of the possible comparisons between the various products. For a product developer spin on this type of comparison, check out the Microsoft and Netscape Web sites for their latest reports.

Programmable Content Store

Domino is built on a content store, which is the standard Notes database. The programmable components of the Notes database include agents, form-level fields, actions, events, and so forth.

The following is a list of three products and function implementation:

◆ **Domino.** Domino has a built-in content store with the Notes databases. This includes the capability to store and manipulate data though fields, and to supply multiple indexes to the data via Notes View indexes.

◆ **Microsoft.** Using IIS and Exchange, Microsoft offers data interchange, using the Notes Exchange (e-mail) data store by default for data storage.

◆ **Netscape.** Using Enterprise Server and LiveWire from SuiteSpot, Netscape offers form and data interchange support.

Collaboration Services

Collaboration is the ability of sharing data between users on a Web server.

The following is a list of three products and function implementation:

◆ **Domino.** Domino offers the group-base databases of Notes, enabling threaded discussion in free-form or hard-defined databases. Also, Domino supports document-level authoring control, customizable views, and support for expanding and collapsing with the documents and the view structure.

◆ **Microsoft.** Using Exchange and IIS, Microsoft offers threaded discussions as a part of the mail system, using the Exchange server for authoring control.

◆ **Netscape.** Using Enterprise Server and Collabra products, Netscape offers threaded discussions to Web clients.

Server Executed Agents

Agents allow data to be processed and/or changed on the server itself. The request to run the agent comes from the Web client.

The following is a list of three products and function implementation:

◆ **Domino.** Domino uses the powerful Notes design element Agents to control background or repetitive processes on the server. These agents can be triggered via an Event initiated by the Server or the Web client, or via a predefined schedule that exists as part of each agent. These agents can execute programs on the server, or work with data stored in one or many Notes databases.

◆ **Microsoft.** Microsoft offers mail-based triggers to control how mail is distributed via the Exchange and IIS server(s) only.

◆ **Netscape.** Netscape offers a small amount of agents, using a combination of products including the Enterprise server, LiveWire Pro, and others as needed.

Directory Services

Directory Services are an important part of an Internet server product. Directory Services include user management at the server level.

The following is a list of three products and function implementation:

◆ **Domino.** Domino offers several levels of Directory Services natively, including user and group management and server configuration (Domino, of course, uses the centralized Notes Directory database, the Public Name & Address Book).

◆ **Microsoft.** Microsoft offers standard directory services, using IIS and the Microsoft Directory Server (a new product installed with the Microsoft Windows NT 4 Server).

◆ **Netscape.** Netscape offers directory services, using two of the products included in the SuiteSpot: the Enterprise Server and the Directory Server 1.0.

Application Development Services

Application development services is the ability to add complete Web-based applications to a Web server.

The following is a list of three products and function implementation:

◆ **Domino.** Domino offers the development environment inherent to the Notes product, including a graphical form designer, programmable content store, and programming tools for standard users through advanced Notes developers. These tools include Private views and agents, simple actions for agents, actions, fields, columns, and so forth, and the Notes formula language and LotusScript (an ANSI Basic scripting language). In addition, by mid-'97, Lotus should ship a set of Java-compatible classes that enable direct object access in Notes databases from a Java applet, and APIs for other programming environments including Visual Basic and C.

Messaging is also a part of every Notes server, integrating the application support previously mentioned with electronic mail from applications and workflow support.

The Notes system also includes native support of ODBC for access to RDBMSs, including Oracle, Sybase, Informix, and so forth, drivers for MQSeries from IBM, and dozens of gateways from Lotus and third-party vendors.

The propagation of Notes throughout the computing world means that thousands of Notes databases exist, including several sample Web-centric applications from Lotus.

◆ **Microsoft.** Microsoft has several programmer tools and builder products that enable application development for Web applications. One of those tools is FrontPage, a graphical builder and mini-Web server used to design and implement Web sites. By itself, FrontPage does not offer any content store by default, although other products can be introduced for this purpose, such as Microsoft Access.

A more powerful development tool, expected to ship shortly, is Internet Studio. Internet Studio is the integrated development tool for building active server Web applications based on open Internet standards. Internet Studio enables developers to take full advantage of server-side processing by using Active Server Pages and Active Data Objects—new features of Microsoft Internet Information Server (IIS) version 3. In addition, Internet Studio enables developers to incorporate Active Desktop features such as advanced HTML, ActiveX, Java, and scripting in the Visual Basic programming system, Scripting Edition, or JScript.

- **Netscape.** Netscape's development product for Web application development is called LiveWire Pro.

  Netscape LiveWire Pro includes runtime and developer versions of the INFORMIX On-line Work Group Database and its Database Connectivity Library, accessible via JavaScript. Using JavaScript APIs, developers can easily access corporate data residing in all ODBC-compliant databases. LiveWire Pro also comes with Crystal Reports Professional Version 4.5, an OLE-enabled reporting tool.

Replication Services

Replication is the ability to exchange data between various servers.

The following is a list of three products and function implementation:

- **Domino.** Domino incorporates a redefined secure replication technique. Replication in Domino includes synchronous assured accuracy, conflict resolution, field-level efficiency, and field-level replication.

- **Microsoft.** Microsoft, through IIS and Exchange, offers basic replication at the document level without the ensured replication (such as Domino). Microsoft also does not include selective replication.

- **Netscape.** Netscape's product suite currently does not include true replication techniques, although document-level replication should be available soon (with plans for field-level replication probably in the next year).

Management Services

Management services are used on a server to manage users, and to track statistics and problems.

The following is a list of three products and function implementation:

- **Domino.** Domino offers centralized user/server access control management, SNMP support, event and alarm tracking, notification, topology mapping, and integration with network management tools.

- **Microsoft.** Microsoft has access and user control within the Exchange server and separate management for the IIS server.

- **Netscape.** Netscape has user/server access management and control for the Enterprise Server, and additional access control for different products in Netscape's SuiteSpot with products such as Collabra.

Security Services

Security is obviously an important consideration for all Web servers.

The following is a list of three products and function implementation:

◆ **Domino.** Domino offers several security options such as the Access Control List integrated in every database separately, and other database-level control issues including form and view level access and document level access for read, edit, and author control. It also offers the security options of roles, using users and groups and the workflow model, and the SSL Web Encryption security.

◆ **Microsoft.** Microsoft has implemented SSL at the IIS level, and the Access Control List for documents.

◆ **Netscape.** Netscape offers SSL support for the Enterprise server, and ACL control for SuiteSpot.

Messaging Services

Messaging is more then e-mail, it is also the way that e-mail can be used as a part of an application.

The following is a list of three products and function implementation:

◆ **Domino.** Domino offers the integrated messaging capabilities of Domino servers and Notes mail databases. One of the important unique offerings of Domino as a Web server is server-side mailboxes. These mailboxes are available for both the standard Notes client and Web clients using browsers. Notes also supports the single copy object store, mail processing agents (see previous discussion of agents), SSL and Web authentication protection, MAPI support, POP3, and IMAP support.

◆ **Microsoft.** Microsoft offers POP3 and IMAP support with the Exchange server, but no access to mail files from the Web side.

◆ **Netscape.** Netscape offers POP3 support, but no server-side mailboxes, no single copy object store, and no mail agents.

Domino HTTP Web Server Console Options

The Domino server console can be used to report the current status of a number of statistics and configuration parameters related to the performance of the HTTP Web server process. To display all parameters at a single time, enter the following command:

```
show status domino
```

If you are quick enough to pause and restart the display, you can scroll through the report. However, if you are interested in a single statistic or configuration parameter and do not want the information to scroll off the screen, the specific parameter can be reported using the name of the parameter you want to view, as follows:

```
show status domino.<option>
```

in which <option> is the name of one of the reporting parameters listed below.

The HTTP Web server reporting options can be divided into the following categories:

◆ Version/revision information

◆ Cache statistics

◆ Commands received

◆ HTTP Web server configuration

◆ HTTP request statistics

◆ Server thread statistics

By periodically showing the status of the Domino HTTP Web server process, the Domino administrator can keep track of how the server is performing and look for indications that a configuration change may be needed. The first category reports the build number, operating system, and version of the HTTP Web server. The specific option name to supply to the "show status domino.<option>" console command is:

◆ BuildNumber

◆ BuildPlatform

◆ BuildVersion

The next category reports on cache statistics. During its operation, the HTTP Web server caches certain information in order to reduce the time required to service requests for the information. The cache statistics reported are the displacement rate (rate at which items in the cache are moved out) and hit rate (percentage of requests found in the cache). These statistics are reported for both command cache rates and database cache rates. In either case, if the displace rate is high and the hit rate is low, you might try increasing the size of the cache in order to gain some efficiency. If the hit rate is high and the displace rate is low, you might consider reducing the size of the cache if disk space is at a premium to give back some of the unused space.

To report on a specific cache option, use the following commands in place of <option> in the show status domino.<option> command line:

◆ Cache.Command.DisplaceRate

◆ Cache.Command.HitRate

◆ Cache.Database.DisplaceRate

◆ Cache.Database.HitRate

The next category is used to track the number of times a particular URL command is received. These parameters track a running total of commands received and are informational in nature. In other words, there is not much you can do to control the number of a particular command received by the HTTP Web server. To report on a specific command total, use one of the following commands as the <option>:

- ◆ Command.CreateDocument
- ◆ Command.DeleteDocument
- ◆ Command.EditDocument
- ◆ Command.Login
- ◆ Command.Navigate
- ◆ Command.OpenAbout
- ◆ Command.OpenAgent
- ◆ Command.OpenDatabase
- ◆ Command.OpenDocument
- ◆ Command.OpenElement
- ◆ Command.OpenForm
- ◆ Command.OpenHelp
- ◆ Command.OpenIcon
- ◆ Command.OpenNavigator
- ◆ Command.OpenServer
- ◆ Command.OpenView
- ◆ Command.ReadForm
- ◆ Command.SaveDocument
- ◆ Command.SearchSite
- ◆ Command.SearchView
- ◆ Command.Total
- ◆ Command.Unknown

To verify the current operational configuration of the HTTP Web server process, you can request the particular parameter by using one of the following commands as the command <option>. Any changes made to the server document will be reflected in this category of options. For details of configuration parameters and their use, see Chapter 21.

- ◆ Config.ActiveThreads.Max
- ◆ Config.ActiveThreads.Min
- ◆ Config.AllowDirectoryLinks
- ◆ Config.Cache.Delete
- ◆ Config.Cache.Directory
- ◆ Config.Cache.Size.Max
- ◆ Config.Directory.CGI
- ◆ Config.Directory.HTML
- ◆ Config.Directory.Icons
- ◆ Config.DNSLookup
- ◆ Config.GarbageCollection.Interval
- ◆ Config.GarbageCollection.Status
- ◆ Config.HomeURL
- ◆ Config.HostName
- ◆ Config.Image.Format
- ◆ Config.Image.Interlaced
- ◆ Config.Log.Access
- ◆ Config.Log.Error
- ◆ Config.Log.Filter
- ◆ Config.Log.TimeStamp
- ◆ Config.PortNumber
- ◆ Config.PortStatus

- ◆ Config.SSL.Keyfile

- ◆ Config.SSL.PortNumber

- ◆ Config.SSL.Status

- ◆ Config.Timeout.CGI

- ◆ Config.Timeout.IdleThread

- ◆ Config.Timeout.Input

- ◆ Config.Timeout.Output

- ◆ Config.URLPath.CGI

- ◆ Config.URLPath.Icons

- ◆ Config.View.Lines

- ◆ Config.WelcomePage

The HTTP Web server provides statistics on the number of HTTP requests it receives over a variety of time periods (day, hour, and minute). The reports show the peak number of requests for the period, the time the peak occurred, and the total number of requests. To report on any one of these specific parameters, use one of the following commands in place of <option>:

- ◆ Requests.Per1Day.Peak

- ◆ Requests.Per1Day.PeakTime

- ◆ Requests.Per1Day.Total

- ◆ Requests.Per1Hour.Peak

- ◆ Requests.Per1Hour.PeakTime

- ◆ Requests.Per1Hour.Total

- ◆ Requests.Per1Minute.Peak

- ◆ Requests.Per1Minute.PeakTime

- ◆ Requests.Per1Minute.Total

- ◆ Requests.Per5Minute.Peak

- ◆ Requests.Per5Minute.PeakTime

◆ Requests.Per5Minute.Total

◆ Requests.Total

To view the last time the HTTP Web server was started, use the following:

◆ StartTime

Threads are set in the HTTP server section of the Server document in the Public Name & Address Book (see Chapter 21). To report on the peak number of active threads, the time when the peak occurred, the peak total, and total threads, use one of the following in place of the <option> in the command line. These statistics can help the you decide whether the number of threads for which the HTTP Web server is configured is sufficient, needs to be raised, or whether it can be lowered to reserve some processing power for other tasks. If the peak hits the maximum number of threads for which the server is configured on a routine basis, then raise the number of active threads.

◆ Threads.Active.Peak

◆ Threads.Peak.Time

◆ Threads.Peak.Total

◆ Threads.Total

APPENDIX C

SMTP MTA Gateway

This appendix focuses on the Lotus Notes SMTP MTA gateway. The Lotus Notes SMTP MTA gains more popularity every day because it is very flexible and makes it possible for your company to communicate with anyone else in the world that can send Internet Mail. With the information in this appendix, you will be able to install and configure the SMTP MTA and gain additional knowledge on how to maintain it. It begins with a solid definition, moves on to installation and configuration issues surrounding SMTP MTA, and finishes with information on how to maintain the gateway.

The Lotus Notes SMTP MTA

The Lotus Notes Simple Mail Transfer Protocol (SMTP) Message Transfer Agent (MTA) is used to send and receive mail from a Notes system to and from the Internet. The capability to communicate with anyone else on the Internet is a very powerful and greatly desired feature. You would probably not be surprised that this book was largely created using the SMTP MTA as the communication vehicle.

Contacting your ISP

At some point, you must notify your Internet Service Provider that you intend to use a certain TCP/IP address to act as a mail router. You will want to give your ISP the TCP/IP address and provide a domain name that makes sense for your company. You should keep in mind that this address will likely end up on business cards and a lot of literature, so don't use your pet's name.

Installing the Gateway

The SMTP MTA works in both OS/2 and NT.

What has confused many is that the Lotus documentation says that the SMTP MTA is included with the purchase of a Domino server. What this really means is that the purchase of a Domino server includes a *license* for the SMTP MTA. (Hopefully, in the future you will just receive the files on the same CD as your Domino server.) You can install from a CD or you can obtain the files off the Internet at www.Lotus.com. Many prefer to obtain the files off the Web site because it provides the most recent production of the code.

The SMTP MTA requires a Domino server running on Microsoft NT (or OS/2). See Chapter 6, "Installing Domino 4.5 Server Software," for information on the installation of the Domino server. After you have your Domino server operational and you have the SMTP MTA software, you can install it on your server. You should be certain to down your server prior to installation. This can be done by typing **Q(uit)** or **E(xit)** at the server console. You should also close the Notes Workspace if it is running.

> **Note**   If this is an upgrade of your SMTP MTA from a version prior to 1.05 and you have changed your mtatbls.nsf file, be certain to temporarily copy this file to another directory.

A Welcome screen appears, reminding you to stop all running programs (see fig. C.1).

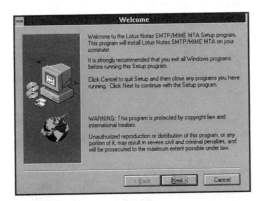

Figure C.1

The Welcome screen.

The next screen enables you to choose between Typical and Custom (see fig. C.2).

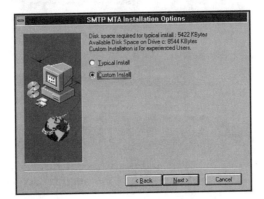

Figure C.2

Installation options.

Although you can select Custom, there are only two options and you need both check boxes selected anyway (see fig. C.3).

As you install the SMTP MTA, a warning message appears. This message reminds you to back up your mtatbls.nsf file prior to installing the software (see fig. C.4). This message applies only to Domino servers that have previously had the SMTP MTA installed on the same machine. If you have never installed the SMTP MTA on the machine, you need not concern yourself with this message.

Figure C.3

*Custom
installation of
SMTP MTA.*

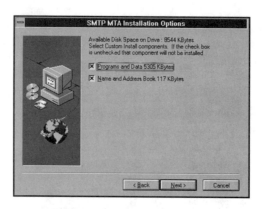

Figure C.4

*Warning message
for mtatbls.nsf.*

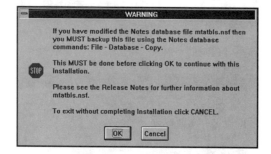

Configuring Your SMTP MTA

After you have installed the SMTP MTA, it is necessary to configure the agent for messsaging. This is done by adding or changing the following four documents:

◆ The Global Domain document

◆ A Foreign Domain document

◆ The Server's document

◆ An SMTP Connection document

The Global Domain Document

The *Global Domain document* is used to configure your SMTP MTA for outbound and inbound messaging. To create the Global Domain document, open your Public Name & Address Book and select the Domains view. You can then select the Add Domain button (see fig. C.5).

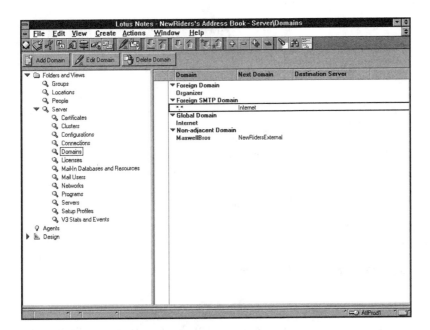

Figure C.5
Domains view.

When creating your new Domain record, you should change the first field to Global Domain. This dramatically changes the document's look. Only the left side of this document is related to the SMTP MTA (see fig. C.6).

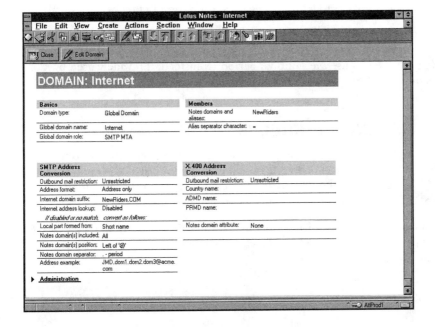

Figure C.6
A Global Domain document.

You must change many of the fields on this document, including the following SMTP MTA fields:

◆ **Global domain name**. This is blank and you should add the word **Internet** to this field.

◆ **Global domain role**. This field has only two choices: SMTP MTA and X.400 MTA. Select SMTP MTA.

◆ **Outbound mail restriction**. You have the option to limit e-mail addressing from only those in the same domain or you can select unrestricted. If you have multiple domains in your company, you should use unrestricted (or answer the many phone calls from those that can't send Internet mail).

◆ **Internet domain suffix**. In this field, enter the domain name that you gave to your ISP.

◆ **Internet address lookup**. You can enable or disable Internet address lookup.

◆ **Local part formed from**. This is mostly a matter of preference. If you want the "outside world" to use your entire name, you can use Common name. If you want to limit the name to eight characters, you can use the Short name option.

◆ **Notes domain(s) included**. You can change the look of the return address by adding Notes domains in addition to the Internet address. You may find it is less taxing on the users to leave this field as None (other choices are 1 or All).

◆ **Notes domain separator**. The default here is the percent sign (%). This means that everyone would type addresses such as Jim Forlini@NewRiders%com. You might prefer to use the optional period (.) instead; it is widely used by most companies.

The Foreign Domain Document

The Foreign Domain document is used to transfer mail from your domain to the SMTP mailbox. You can create a Foreign Domain document just as you created the preceding Global Domain document. The difference is that you change the first field to Foreign SMTP Domain. Figure C.7 shows an example of this record.

Only two fields need changing for this document. You can add ***.*** (a wild card) to the Internet Domain field and **Internet** (to match the Global Domain record) to the Domain name field.

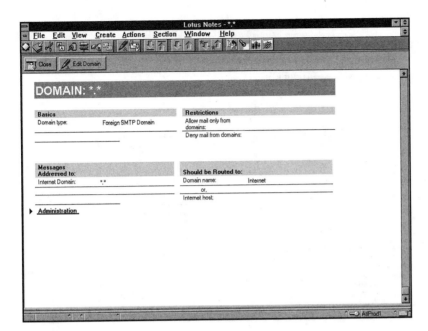

Figure B.7

*A Foreign
Domain
document.*

The Server Document

You do not need to add a Server document. Instead, you just need to change the one that you made when you created the server. You will find an Internet Message Transfer Agent section on the record (see fig. C.8).

You need only change the first two fields in this section. You should enter the Global domain name as **Internet** and the Fully qualified Internet host name should be changed to whatever you gave to your ISP.

An SMTP Connection Document

The SMTP Connection document is used during transfer of mail from your SMTP mailbox to the Internet. An SMTP Connection document should be made in your Public Name & Address Book as well. You can create the document by opening the Address Book and then clicking on the Add Connection button (see fig. C.9).

Figure C.8

A Server record.

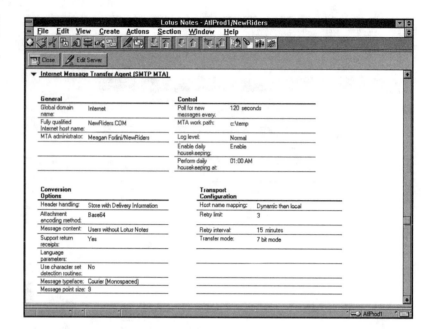

Figure C.9

The Connections view.

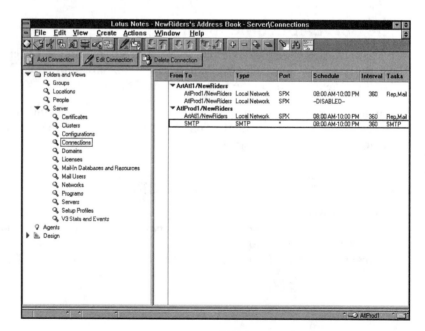

You need to change the first field (Connection Type) to SMTP (see fig. C.10).

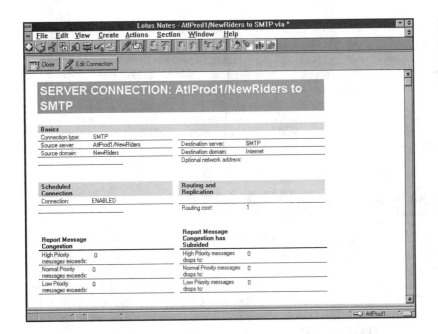

Figure C.10

The SMTP Connection record.

The Source server defaults to the server you are working on. You can change this (if needed) to the server where the SMTP MTA is installed. You should then place the Domain name for the same server in the Source Domain field. The Destination server should be SMTP and the Destination domain should be Internet (to match the Global Domain and Server records). The remaining fields should retain the defaults.

Starting and Stopping the SMTP MTA

You can start and stop the SMTP MTA with server commands or have the process automatically launch by adding a task to your Notes.ini file. To start the SMTP MTA with a server command, you can use L SMTPMTA (see fig. C.11).

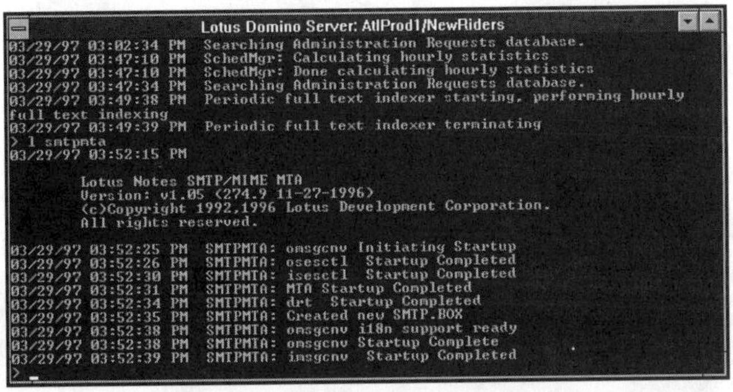

Figure C.11

Loading the SMTP MTA.

If you desire the SMTP MTA to automatically launch and run when your server is started, you should add the SMTP task to your Notes.ini file. This file is typically found in your Notes directory (such as C:\NOTES). Be certain to down your Domino server (type **Exit** and press Enter) and close the Lotus Notes workstation before changing the file. You can use any text editor (such as WordPad) to change the file.

After you have opened the file, locate the ServerTasks= line. You should not add another ServerTasks= line. Instead, add the SMTP task to the line. After adding the task to this line, you can close and save the file.

Compacting the SMTP MTA

On occasion you may need to compact the SMTP MTA. After about every 10,000 messages, you should compact the files (the associated databases) of the SMTP MTA so that they continue to run efficiently and without fail. You can compact these files by using the console command T SMTPMTA Compact. This command automatically stops the SMTP MTA process, cleans up the databases, and relaunches the SMTP MTA. For more information on issuing server commands, see the "Remote Console" section of Chapter 8, "Examining Domino 4.5 Administration Features."

INDEX

I

RAS

1800 546 2571